South Asian Devotional Literature

Studies
in
South Asian Devotional Literature

Research Papers, 1988-1991 presented at the Fifth Conference on Devotional Literature in New Indo-Aryan Languages, held at Paris - École Française d'Extrême-Orient, 9-12 July 1991

edited by
Alan W. Entwistle
and
Françoise Mallison

Manohar
New Delhi

École Française d'Extrême-Orient
Paris
1994

ISBN 81 7304 095 8
First published in 1994

Published by Ajay Kumar Jain for
Manohar Publishers and Distributors
and printed by Rajkamal Electric Press,
G.T. Karnal Road, Delhi 110033

In memory of
Günther-Dietz Sontheimer
(1933-1992)

Contents

Cult and Ideology

The Indo-Islamic Expression of *Bhakti*

Textual Transmission (Manuscripts and Anthologies)

General Information

Preface

The Fifth Conference on Devotional Literature in New Indo-Aryan Languages was convened under the auspices of the École Française d'Extrême-Orient, Paris, from July 9th-12th, 1991. The conference brought together some seventy participants, mostly from Europe, but also from India, the United States, and Japan. Several of them had the pleasure of meeting each other for the fifth time, having attended the previous conferences at Leuven/Louvain (1979), Bonn (1982), Leiden (1985), and Cambridge (1988).

This volume contains all but four of the thirty-six papers and reports that were presented at the Paris conference. The field of research they represent, namely pre-modern literary expressions of "devotion" (i.e., *bhakti*), is vast and varied. Topics dealt with include the classical sources of medieval *bhakti*, the relationship between politics and devotionalism, popular *bhakti* traditions, Islam and *bhakti*, hagiography, iconography, and such aspects of textual study as the stylistic and metrical analysis of devotional lyrics and their transmission through manuscripts and other means. Among the sectarian traditions, most attention is paid to the Krishna cult and Sant movements (especially in Maharashtra). One paper is exceptional in being the first in this series of conferences to concern itself with Jainism and the only contribution that deals with sources in a Dravidian language (viz., Kannada).

When the series began in Leuven twelve years ago, the aim was basically to establish a forum for reports on current research or primary sources relating to *bhakti*. By the time the conference appeared in its Parisian incarnation, the scope had broadened considerably, both in terms of the time-span and the types of source material considered. This confirms the impression gained at the fourth conference at Cambridge that the study of devotional literature has expanded and diversified. From a chronological point of view, the papers deal with *bhakti* from its beginnings in classical Sanskrit and in Apabhraṃśa sources up to its expression through the medium of the cinema. As far as the classification of different types of *bhakti* is concerned, it will be noted that this has been refined either by examining the relationship between *bhakti* and popular and localized forms of Hinduism, or by reappraising and revising the conventional and arbitrary labels given to various aspects of *bhakti*. The field of literary criticism has been enhanced by original papers on neglected genres, unusual metres, and metaphorical forms of expression. In several papers, recourse to narrative and hagiographical sources, combined with a study of archival documents, reveals *bhakti* to have been one of the underlying factors in socio-political history from the fifteenth to the nineteenth centuries.

The conference brought attention to the vigour and importance of research into *bhakti* in Maharashtra, which is represented by seven papers ranging from the early Mahānubhāva precursors to the links between *bhakti* and popular Sufism. The papers also reveal a growing interest in Islamic manifestations of *bhakti*, which became apparent at the previous conference. There are now six papers in this field which cover not only Indian Sufism but also the Ismā'īlī traditions, and which, perhaps intentionally, revive a field of Indian scholarship that was more or less abandoned at Independence. Finally, the conference allowed several young researchers to present papers for the first time and also welcomed its first participant from Eastern Europe who, in addition to his paper, gave a survey of Russian studies in premodern devotional literature. This updates an earlier account that was submitted at Leuven by the late Professor

Zograph and was included among the published proceedings of that conference.

Although they deal with different regional phenomena (ranging from Sind to Bengal - even to Bengali culture in Myanmar, and from northern Bihar to southern Deccan), and comment on sources in several languages (Bengali, Hindi and its literary dialects, Sindhi, Urdu, Gujarati, Marathi, Dakanī, Kannada, Sanskrit, Apabhraṃśa, and Persian), the various contributions, differentiated by their style, format, and perspective, all share the common purpose of analyzing and elucidating some aspect of *bhakti* and its literature. It did not therefore seem appropriate to group the papers according to region or language, but rather to arrange them in terms of their topical, historical, and ideological content. The authors have been given the freedom to choose whether to quote textual passages in Devanagari script or transliteration and also (within limits) to employ their preferred method of transcribing Indian names and terms, provided that the system adopted is applied consistently within any one article.

The Paris conference afforded an opportunity for many French and foreign scholars to pay homage to Professor Charlotte Vaudeville and acknowledge her inspiration and enthusiasm. This volume of papers is dedicated to the memory of Professor Günther-Dietz Sontheimer, whose sudden and untimely death occurred in June, 1992. Unfortunately, he was unable to revise his paper "On the Relationship between Possession and *Bhakti*" for this volume. For many of his colleagues, the last memory of him will be not just his presentation of that brilliant paper but also the showing of his moving film "Vārī: An Indian Pilgrimage". Indology has lost a scholar, and Maharashtra a friend.

A. E. and F. M.

Acknowledgements

Our thanks are due to the École Française d'Extrême-Orient for having hosted the conference and subsidizing the publication of the papers. We are grateful to the École Normale Supérieure de Fontenay/Saint Cloud and the staff of its hostel for their hospitality, as well as to Myriam Ghalmi and Thérèse-Charlotte Mallison for their assistance. We would also thank Françoise Delvoye and Sanjay Subrahmanyam for facilitating our communication with the publishers.

Bhakti in Historical Perspective

Creative Corruption: Some Comments on Apabhraṃśa Literature, Particularly Yogîndu

Friedhelm Hardy

It is no exaggeration to state that the study of Apabhraṃśa literature has been at the very margin of indology. There is obviously, first, a historical reason for this: during the heydays of classical indology, very little actual Apabhraṃśa literature was available. Secondly, the primary concern was then — as is still now in certain quarters — philological. But quite imperceptibly to many indianists, the published corpus has steadily increased over the last hundred years, thanks almost exclusively to the labours of a few Indian (and German) scholars. By a very rough calculation I would venture to suggest that the number of printed pages is rapidly approaching the figure ten thousand, and many more manuscripts are known to exist. At least the absence of literary, textual sources cannot now be used as an argument against the study of Apabhraṃśa literature. But, thirdly, attention can be drawn to ideological reasons for the neglect of this literature. By the yard-stick of classical Sanskrit, Apabhraṃśa represents, as its very name indicates, 'corruption, vulgarity, decadence'. Obviously even the Prakrits have suffered the same image problem. Who is supposed to have spoken Apabhraṃśa, according to the Sanskrit dramas and the grammarians? A king who in his temporary mental derangement talks to trees (I am obviously referring to king Purūravas in Kālidāsa's play *Vikramôrvasī* with its highly disputed Apabhraṃśa passage in Act 4)[1], and tribal people like the rough 'cowherds', viz. the Ābhiras.[2] Moreover, superficially it seems that the actual Apabhraṃśa material available is all Jaina and thus of no interest to the majority of indianists. Thus the purpose of the present paper[3] is a very straightforward one. It wants to convey some impressions of the literature itself that is available now (along with what are hoped to be useful bibliographical references.)[4] In addition, it wants to draw attention to some interesting implications for a wider assessment of Indian cultural history. A brief glance at Yogîndu, whose poetry has so far remained untranslated, will link the paper with a theme of the Conference, *nirguṇa-bhakti.* But let me begin by commenting on the language itself.

The chronological boundaries of (literary) Apabhraṃśa are rather blurred; to suggest AD 800-1300 is relatively safe, but it is much more difficult to speculate on earlier or later extensions.[5] It is clear that it is contemporary with (literary) Dravidian languages and at least in its later phase, with some of the New Indo-Aryan languages.

Older indological literature has introduced a great many problems concerning the very nature of the Apabhraṃśa language — problems caused particularly by the (not infrequently naive) study of the ancient grammarians[6] and not of the texts themselves. Are we dealing with one language, or a whole group, or many dialects.[7] What is the relationship between Apabhraṃśa and the New Indo-Aryan languages? Where did 'Apabhraṃśa' originate?

It is not the purpose of the present paper to discuss in detail once again all these conventional questions. Instead, I shall simply state the position adopted here. One can now reject the once popular theory that 'Apabhraṃśa' is no more than an umbrella term for a more or less variegated group of individual languages, each one representing an earlier stage in the development of an individual Indo-Aryan language.[8]

From exploring the available corpus it is possible to gain the impression that we are dealing here with a basically homogenous single language, at the most slightly differentiated into two or three closely related varieties.[9] But what language are we dealing with? When we plot the available information about Apabhraṃśa texts and their authors on a map of India, we discover an extraordinary spread: from the borders of Tamil Nadu in the south up to the Panjab in the north, and from Sindh westwards to Bengal. [10] What all this means is simply that we seem to be dealing here with a *lingua franca* of medieval India,[11] during a few centuries on either side of the turn of the first millennium, a language of literature used also in areas that have little or no linguistic affinity with it. Such a conclusion finds corroboration when we look closer at the authors. Indeed, as it happens, the bulk of our materials is Jaina (partly for the simple reason that it is predominantly Jaina monasteries which have preserved the manuscripts). But we also find works of a purely secular nature, works by Buddhists, by a Muslim, and Apabhraṃśa material is found in a number of Tantras. There is enough material here to force us to abolish the idea of an exclusive Jaina character of Apabhraṃśa literature and acknowledge it as a truly pan-Indian cultural phenomenon. This also means that we ought to regard the literary activities of various modern vernaculars (whatever their philological relationship with Apabhraṃśa may be) as frequently reacting, or operating parallel, to it.

There is obviously a large amount of linguistic and philological material to be found in this literature which concerns the details of Indo-Aryan linguistics (vocabulary, morphology, etc). But this is not a topic I want to develop further here. Instead, in the grandiose manner of a *vidyādhara* — who, after all, is a ubiquitous character in the literature under discussion here — I shall venture now a brief aerial view of the Apabhraṃśa works known to me, focusing time and again on aspects that might be of a more direct and immediate interest in the context of the present conference.

On the formal side—and what in fact appears to be the most frequently consulted aspect of Apabhraṃśa literature —we find various treatises on metre.[12] While Prakrit metres look backwards, as it were, to the classical past, with Apabhraṃśa a very major metrical revolution has occurred. New forms are proliferating which show sometimes dazzling complexity (and which the theoreticians are hardly able to contain in established technical terminology). But both from the point of view of actual metrical practice and of the content, two works deserve to be mentioned here which have as yet not enjoyed the popularity they deserve, even among 'metre-hunters'. The first is Hemacandra's famous grammar where we find a large corpus of poetic quotations from many different sources. Translated into German as early as 1880, and studied thoroughly by Alsdorf (1937), this poetic material is in itself a miniature anthology of Apabhraṃśa lyrics. The second work has so far remained untranslated. It is Abdul Rahmān's *Sandeśarāsaka.* There is a slight plot here (a *virahiṇī* laments to a traveller, for reasons not necessarily as innocuous as it might appear at first glance, but he consoles her — merely — with poetry). But the way this travelling poet presents his verses makes it clear that the whole work is intended as a poetic, metrical compendium.

But Apabhraṃśa metrics developed far beyond the individual lyrical stanza. For epic narrative, the whole work is initially divided into *sandhis* which in turn consist of *kaḍavakas*. These are sections of normally ten to twenty double lines with complex rhyming patterns, introduced by say a *duvaī* and concluded by e.g. a *ghattā.* A definite musical quality and great variety is introduced here where in Sanskrit we would have nothing but thousands of *ślokas*.

Such complex metrical forms were developed for lengthy epics, frequently called *cariü.* Given the all-important role of the Jainas in the transmission of Apabhraṃśa texts, we need not be surprised to find a good deal of specifically and exclusively Jaina themes treated in this manner. Thus we have long epics dealing with the lives of the Tīrthaṅkaras

Pārśva and Ariṣṭanemi (in the *Pāsanāhacariü* and *Nemināhacariü* respectively), apart from the enormous *Mahāpurāṇa* that treats the whole list of twenty four (besides many other figures of Jaina legend). Of greater interest to the general indianist is the figure of Yaśodhara (written about by Puṣpadanta in his *Jasaharacariü*). It is the story of a king who yielded to his mother's request to perform — no more than a symbolic — animal sacrifice and who, after a number of animal rebirths filled with violence and hair-raising brutality, gets reborn as a prince and is dragged before the goddess Kālī to be sacrificed to her.[13]

But besides such works of an integrally Jaina nature, we find a large store of story material which is merely moulded by Jaina authors to convey their ideas. Here now (in works like the *Kahakosu* or the *Bhavisayatta-kaha*) a fascinating world is opened up for us: a multifaceted vista of medieval India and its people. Popular customs like wedding ceremonies (see *Bhavissaya.* and *Paümasiri.*) are described in loving, not to say folkloristic, detail. Adventure tales tell us about journeys to far-away continents *(Bhavissaya.*, Cārudatta) and about the dangers enterprising merchants had to face. We hear about all kinds of religious customs, beliefs, and professionals. Human relationships are anlaysed, and subjected to a uniquely Jaina psychological theory. Particularly interesting in this context is for instance the story of Śrīpadmā (in the *Paümasiricariü*) who sowed the seed of disharmony among her brothers and their wives, in order to make them continue the support they were providing for her otherwise perfectly legitimate Jaina religious devotions — only to be punished in subsequent lives for this misguided piety. Another long work, the *Jāmbūsāmicariü*, contains within itself a miniature *kathākośa* at the critical narrative juncture. Jāmbūsāmi has agreed to get married, but on condition that after the wedding night he is allowed to pursue his real ambition: to become a Jaina ascetic. The wedding night is spent with the exchange of stories, pro and contra married love, between his young brides and the firm ascetic-to-be, and a robber who is accidentally discovered breaking into the house and turns out to be a great expert on prostitutes. Or we may find stories here in a Jaina garb for which we have parallels in another literature. For instance, Svayambhū narrates[14] a story about Añjanā and Pavanañjaya which resembles the *Vīsaḷadevarāsa*, written by Nālha in some form of old Mārvāṛī.[15] Both wives, by praising some other king, offend their new husbands and make them depart for a fixed number of years. But the Apabhraṃśa version is much richer in that Pavanañjaya secretly visits his Añjanā, makes her pregnant and thereby causes a lot of problems for her, and eventually for himself, before the final happy reunion.

The colours used by these stories and epics in painting such scenes from medieval life are sometimes quite garish; but what better way to preach *ahiṃsā* and *brahmacarya* than by spelling out at great length their opposites and to demonstrate the eventual disaster that must result from them? Thus much of Apabhraṃśa literature deals with battle scenes, heads being chopped off and all that. But quite extraordinary is the *Mayaṇa-parājaya-cariü*, which uses precisely this conventional battle imagery to show how king Mahāvīra fought with the armies of king Madana over the prize coveted by both: the beautiful princess Siddhi — spiritual perfection.

But besides such exclusively or merely remoulded Jaina material, in a number of ways the Jainas used Apabhraṃśa literature to explore pan-Indian themes. As it happens (and I cannot comment on the possible reasons for it) the figure of Karakaṇḍu — the *pratyekabuddha* with the 'scab on his hand', known also to Buddhist legend—is dealt with rather lavishly. Not only do we have a whole work narrating his life story (the *Karakaṇḍa-cariü* by Kanakāmara), but also Śrīcandra (in his *Kahak osu*) treats the theme over a number of *sandhis* (which makes it the longest story by far in his collection). But while Śrīcandra's version follows on the whole the traditional mould of the legend, Kanakāmara is highly innovative. Here the *pratyekabuddha* rather surprisingly marries a number of women before turning to spiritual matters. But there is no need for us to guess as to the possible source of inspiration for Kanakāmara. At some point he introduces Naravāhanadatta, the well-known central hero of the *Bṛhatkathā*, and makes him narrate his life-story. This may be very brief and selective, but together with the thematic changes introduced into the story of Karakaṇḍu itself, it adds a further source — to my knowledge ignored so far by scholars — to our collection of material with the help of which the 'lost' *Bṛhatkathā* may be reconstructed.

Our corpus offers much more material on the *Bṛhatkathā*, this extraordinary tale of the manly pursuit of spiritual perfection accompanied by the acquisition of many a beautiful and passionate woman. The obvious place is in the *Mahāpurāṇa* of Puspadanta, where we find it in the form of Vasudeva's life-story. This version has been discussed by Alsdorf in great detail and thus need not detain us here. But one of the very lengthy secondary narratives, well-known to all of us at least indirectly from the tales of Sindbad the Sailor, viz. the travellogue of Cārudatta, is also treated by Śrīcandra in his *Kahak osu.*[16] Again, this is a version as yet unstudied in the context of *Bṛhatkathā* studies. Finally, we can see a further aspect of the enormous influence of this ancient tale in the specifically Jaina development of the lives of the Kāmadevas. Vasudeva himself is classified as one of them; in Puṣpadanta's *Nāgakumāracariü* we have a polished Apabhraṃśa version about another Kāmadeva, prince Nāgakumāra, who obtained his superhuman attraction to women from being brought up by the *nāgas*

The theme of the *Bṛhatkathā* has led us to the centre stage of classical Indian literature. Logically we may ask what our Apabhraṃśa has to offer on the other, even more famous heroes, Kṛṣṇa and Rāma. As it happens, the former has so far enjoyed less popularity among editors of Apabhraṃśa works than the latter.[17] While the published Kṛṣṇa material is more or less restricted to the section of the *Mahāpurāṇa* entitled *Harivaṃśa-purāṇa* (and has been dealt with by Alsdorf), the student of the literary ramifications of the Rāma theme will find ample material in our corpus.[18] Besides the untranslated Digambara version of the *Rāmāyaṇa* found in the *Mahāpurāṇa*, we have also a very lengthy, equally untranslated, Śvetāmbara version, the *Paümacariü* by Svayambhū. In both works we find a great deal of unusual themes and narrative details at least some of which may be mentioned here. In Svayambhū, Sītā's fire-ordeal makes her so disgusted with the world that she becomes a Jaina nun who, due to her *tapas*, is reborn as Sītendra. When also Rāma, due to Laksmaṇa's death, becomes an ascetic, Sītendra (once again in the form of Sītā) tries to seduce him, but without success. In the Digambara version, Sītā is actually Rāvaṇa's daughter whom he had buried alive—to be saved by a farmer — because of a prophesy. Both versions obviously explore in great detail the past lives of the various figures and the karmic rationale of their actions. It appears to be still fashionable in certain quarters to regard such Jaina versions of the Indian classics merely as 'sectarian distortions'. But we may then discover in unexpected quarters corroborative evidence for the assumption that the Jainas preserved popular features which were weeded out of the better-known 'classical' accounts. I am thinking here for instance of the vernacular eastern Indian[19] or the Thai *Rāmāyaṇa*[20] which like its Digambara parallels knows of Sītā as Rāvaṇa's lost daughter.

Without leaving the grand pan-Indian scene, we can once again turn to the small poetic form. But very much in line with most of the Jaina material we have been looking at, we turn from the matters of the heart and love to asceticism and spirituality. Formally this means a closer look at the *dohā* literature in Apabhraṃśa. One text, the *Sāvayadhammadohā*, which gives advice to the Jaina layman on daily rituals and practices, need not detain us here. Nor for that matter the two Buddhist collections of *dohā*s attributed to Saraha and Kaṇhā, since they are well known. A fourth work, the

Pāhuḍadohākosa, has been translated into French and studied by Caillat. Two further works, as yet untranslated and unstudied, remain for us to discuss here briefly. Both the *Paramappapayāsu* (*Paramātmaprakāśa*) and the *Yogasāra* are attributed to Yogîndu (this apparently is the correct Sanskrit rendering of his name, and not Yogîndra). He is a rather nebulous figure and is said by Upādhye to belong to the 6th cent. A.D. which to me seems rather too early.[21] However, the fact that many stanzas[22] in these two works are also found in the *Pāhuḍadohākosa*, and at least three[23] also among Hemacandra's quotations, can offer us some initial approach to this author. Philosophically, we require the thought of the unduly neglected (Digambara) Jaina teacher Kundakunda[24], in the light of which at least certain of Yogîndu's pronouncements become less sensational than might appear at first sight. But there is much left here which even in terms of Kundakunda's innovative approach to Jaina doctrine and terminology remains revolutionary. It is this aspect of his *dohās* I would like to concentrate on here, because it leads us straight into the realm of well-known antinomian *sants* like Kabīr and Gurū Nānak (as Caillat has pointed out for the *Pāhuḍadohākosa* material.)

Here are some stanzas[25] to illustrate the flavour of Yogîndu's *dohās*.

> One studies the scriptures or performs *tapas*,
> but one does not come to know [thereby] the highest truth. As long as this highest truth is not realized,
> one does not achieve liberation. (*Para.* II, 82)

bujjahĩ satthaĩ taü caraï para paramatthu ṇa veï |
tāva ṇa muṃcaï jāma ṇavi ihu paramatthu muṇeï ||

> Just as the crystal is pure by nature, so is the nature [of the *ātman*]; do not, oh soul! regard it as impure in your delusion, when you look at its body that is impure. (*Para.* II, 177)

jema sahāvī ṇimmalaü phalihaü tema sahāü ।
bhaṃtië maïlu ma maṇṇi jiya maï laü dĕkkhavi kāü ।।

> You fool! The divine is not in a temple nor in a stone, not in a mural nor in a painting: the divine, the *Jina*, is in the temple that is the body. Know this with unbiased mind! (*Yogasāra* 44)

mūḍhā devali deü ṇavi ṇavi sili lippaï citti ।
dehā-devali deü jiṇu so bujjhahi samacitti ।।

> Vows, austerities, self-control and morality, oh soul! — all these are but the relative truth. Regard as your sole cause of liberation [the *ātman*] which is the essence of the three worlds. (*Yogasāra* 33)

vaü taü saṃjamu sīla jiyā iü savvaī vavahāru ।
mŏkkhahā kāraṇu ĕkku muṇi jo taïloyahā sāru ।।

> If you regard as liberated that which is bound, you will certainly become bound. But if you delight in your innate nature (*sahaja*), you will reach the peace of *śivam*. (*Yogasāra* 87)

jaï baddhaü mukkaü muṇahi to baṃdhiyahi ṇibhaṃtu ।
sahaja-sarūvaï jaï ramahi to pāvahi siva-santu ।।

> 'I am a fine brahmin', 'I, a *vaiśya*'; 'I am a *kṣatriya*', 'I belong to the other [class, viz. *śūdra*]'; 'I am a man', 'I, a woman', 'I am a eunuch' — a fool regards these as his characteristics. [For] the *ātman* is not brahmin or *vaiśya*, not *kṣatriya* nor the rest; it is not male, female or neuter. All this the wise person knows. (*Para.* I,81; 87)

haũ varu baṃbhaṇu vaïsu haũ haũ khattiü haũ sesu ।
purisu ṇaüṃsaü itthi haũ maṇṇaï mūḍhu visesu ।।*81*।।[26]
appā baṃbhaṇu vaïsu ṇa vi ṇa vi khattiü na vi sesu ।
purisu ṇaüṃsaü itthi ṇa vi ṇāṇiü muṇaï asesu ।।*87*।।

These are some samples of material that is generally familiar. External religion with its rituals, pilgrimages, bookish learning, physical acts of piety and reliance on external distinctions, is attacked for its lack of inner life, and the cultivation of internal 'knowledge' is encouraged. But how far is Yogîndu prepared to go in this attack, given his Jaina position? Here are a few more *dohās* that make this point quite clear.

> Neither by recitations nor from piles of books, not by entering a monastery nor from pulling out one's hair is *dharma* [realized]. (*Yogasāra* 47)

dhammu ṇa paḍhiyaī hoï dhammu ṇa pŏtthā-picchiyaī |
dhammu ṇa maḍhiya-paësī dhammu ṇa matthā-luṃciyaī | |

> He who is the Jina is the *ātman*. Regard this as the essence of the [Jaina] teaching! (*Yogasāra* 21 a)

jo jiṇu so appā muṇahu ihu siddhantahā sāru |

> He may be a householder or a homeless mendicant: as long as he dwells in the *ātman*, he will easily obtain the bliss of perfection. Thus says the best among Jinas. (*Yogasāra* 65)

sāgāru vi ṇāgāru ku vi jo appāṇi vaseï |
so lahu pāvaï siddhi-suhu jiṇa-varu ema bhaṇeï | |

> Young and old, handsome and brave, learned and divine, a Digambara, Buddhist, or a Śvetāmbara— only the fool bothers about all this. (*Para.* I, 82)

taruṇaü būḍhaü rūyaḍaü sūraü paṃḍiü divvu |
khavaṇaü vaṃdaü sevaḍaü mūḍhaü maṇṇaï savvu | |[27]

This now shakes the very foundations of Jainism with its distinction of Digambara and Śvetāmbara, its stress on monastic life and *tapas*, and its belief in the uniqueness of the Jinas and their teaching. Religion is totally internalized and the soul, the *ātman*, becomes its single locality. The impression we gain here is that thought typical of the *Upaniṣads* and Advaita is employed in the service of this radical internalization of Jaina religion. But we have to be cautious here. A careful look at the, no doubt intentional, usage of terms like *ātman*, *paramâtman*, and even *brahman* reveals that behind it a basically Jaina metaphysic remains intact. The following verse may keep us in doubt:

> When you observe old age and death of the body, do not get scared, oh soul! Regard as your real self that highest *brahman* that knows no old age or death. (*Para*. I, 71)

dehahā pĕkkhivi jara-maraṇu mā bhaü jīva karehi |
jo ajarâmaru baṃbhu paru so appāṇu muṇehi ||[28]

But the following verse brings out in all clarity what is implied in the previous one: the plurality of *brahmans*: this means that the word '*brahman*' is simply used here to denote the liberated individual soul:

> Those who make no distinction of the *brahmans* abiding in the world, oh *yogī*! possess pure knowledge and are preachers of the highest *ātman*. (*Para*. II, 99)

bambhahā bhuvaṇi vasaṃtāhā je ṇavi bheü karaṃti |
te paramappa-payāsayara joïya vimalu muṇaṃti ||

On the one hand, Yogîndu thus maintains typically Jaina ideas about the individuality of the soul even in the state of liberation; but on the other hand, he can be placed alongside typically antinomian popular teachers like Saraha, etc. within the Apabhraṃśa corpus, and Kabīr, etc. in later literatures. Thereby we can regard him as a paradigm of the creative freedom that I have been endeavouring to demonstrate for a variety of aspects of Apabhraṃśa literature, not just its metres or etymologies. The 'corrupt decadence' has revealed itself to be most creative, in a forward direction towards the New Indo-Aryan cultures. It is this cultural relationship, not the problematic philological one, that has been emphasized here.

NOTES

1 See e.g. Tagare p. 17 and H.L. Jain (1955), p. 215.

2 This association goes back to the *Nāṭyaśāstra* (see Tagare, p. 1); compare Gune (pp. 59f in the edition of the *Bhavisayatta Kahā, Gaekwad's Oriental Series*, 1967).

3 The present paper is the by-product of an anthology of c. fifty stories translated from Apabhraṃśa which I have been working on and which I hope to be able to publish some time in the future.

4 The Appendix will list all the published works in Apabhraṃśa consulted by me, together with some additional information that is hoped will be useful to newcomers to the field. I have had no access to further works said to be in Apabhraṃśa which are apparently published: *Sudaṃsaṇacariya* of Nayanandin, [ed. H.L. Jain, 1970]; *Kīrtilatā* of Vidyāpati, and *Sugandhadaśamī-kathā* [Varanasi, 1966]. Svayambhū's *Harivaṃśa-purāṇa* appears to be in the process of being published. Known to exist in manuscript form are Śrīcandra's *Daṃsaṇa-kaha-rayaṇa-karaṃḍaya*, Hariṣeṇa's *Dhamma-parikkha*, Siddha/Siṃha's *Pajjuṇṇakaha*, Śrīdhara's *Sukumālacariü*, Lakṣmaṇadeva's *Neminâhacariü*, and Amarakīrtigaṇi's *Chakkammôvaesu*. Many of the published or known Apabhraṃśa works are listed or discussed in English in the following publications. P.D. Gune (pp. 36-69 in the *Gaekwad's Oriental Series* edition of the *Bhavisayatta-kahā*) surveys the Apabhraṃśa literature known by 1923. Two years later H.L. Jain wrote an article on 'Apabhraṃśa Literature'. Tagare (1948, pp. 16-20) discusses the works used by him. H.L. Jain and M.A. Mehendale survey the situation as pertaining to 1955/1957 (in vols. IV and V of *History and culture of the Indian people*). In Hindī we have the works by H.L. Jain, Kochaṛa (1956) and Tomar (1964). It is unfortunate that I have been unable so far to consult H.C. Bhayani, *Apabhraṃśa Language and Literature—A short introduction*, Delhi: B.L. Institute of Indology, 1989.

5 It will be noted below that Upadhye suggests a date as early as the 6th century for Yogîndu, and H.L. Jain at least appears to suggest that the Apabhraṃśa stanzas in Kālidāsa's

Vikramôrvaśī are genuine (thus 5th century). But the evidence for all this is extremely weak. As far as I can tell, solid dates for compositions emerge only from the second half of the 10th century. But given that these are highly complex and polished works, it seems safe to assume at least a century or so for a period of preparation. The latest works appear to be Lakkhaṇa's *Aṇuvaya-rayaṇa-paīu* of AD 1256 (Mehendale, vol. V, pp. 350) and *Vidyāpati's Kīrtilatā* of the 14th century (H.L. Jain, vol. IV, p. 218).

6 A very detailed account by Gune of the references to Apabhraṃśa in early Indian works can be found in *Gaekwad's Oriental Series*, 1967, pp. 47-67.

7 It is clear that a term like '*apabhraṃśa*', or the related '*apabhraṣṭa*' or '*vibhraṣṭa*', is not originally used with any precise linguistic connotations. Furthermore, it is clear, one could argue, that much or most of the information found in the grammarians on languages other than Sanskrit and the main Prakrits in ancient and medieval India is non-empirical, viz. not based on any kind of reliable and sustained linguistic fieldwork. The categories of modern socio-linguistics are beyond the horizon of the ancient grammarians. Thus it seems doubtful that we shall ever be able to obtain answers to important questions like whether the terms used by the grammarians refer to 'languages' or (regional or social) 'dialects' or 'creoles' or 'pidgins', whether they are referring to philologically continuous earlier forms of any of the established New Indo-Aryan languages or discontinuous speeches that were superseded by later New Indo-Aryan. — Such a critique has obviously nothing to do with the brilliant achievement of Hemacandra's empirically based grammatical analysis of Apabhraṃśa literary works.

8 Thus already Tagare (p. 16) writes: 'We do not subscribe to Grierson's theory of postulating one Ap[abhraṃśa] per every New Indo-Aryan language. This hypothesis is unsupported by the evidence discovered so far.'

9 Tagare suggests such a simple division, viz. into Western, Southern and Eastern. But even this schema raises questions. It could be argued that all the morphological material so meticulously tabulated by Tagare hardly amounts to three different languages and suggests more of a dialect continuum. Such an impression is arguably borne out by reading the works themselves. Furthermore, Tagare's sources for Southern Apabhraṃśa are Puṣpadanta and Kanakāmara — both are poets who wrote in an environment surrounded by Dravidian

languages and both are Digambara. Thus instead of introducing a geographical distinction, Tagare could have simply talked of 'Digambara Apabhraṃśa' (as Alsdorf does with reference to Puṣpadanta).

10 Mehendale, although acknowledging the wide currency of the language, confuses the issue. 'Already during the preceding period (A.D. 750-1000) Western or Śaurasenī Apabhraṃśa came into use as a pan-Indo-Aryan literary speech *binding together the spoken provincial dialects*. It continued right down to the end of the period under review [1000-1300] and established itself as a literary language, *nearest to the vernaculars*, from Bengal to Western Punjab and Sindh, and from Kāshmir and Nepāl to Mahārāshṭra.' (p. 351, my italics) But the emphasized phrases beg the question: for instance, in what sense can Puṣpadanta be said to be near, or bind together, the Dravidian languages spoken in Mānyakheṭa?

11 I shall not speculate here on what region could have been the linguistic home of this language , though there are resonances here e.g. of later Hindi. But I cannot agree with H.L. Jain who claims that the Himalaya-Sindhu region was the 'original home of the Apabhraṃśas' because, according to Bharata, in the speech of that region 'the *u* sound was predominant' (vol. IV, pp. 212f).

12 Besides the well-known *Prākṛtapaiṅgala* and *Chando'nuśāsana*, we have the treatises by Virahaṅka and Svayambhū, both edited by Velankar.

13 Two Sanskrit versions of this story are now available in English translation: Vādirāja's *Yaśodharacarita* was translated by K. Krishnamoorthy (Dharwar, 1963) and I have translated Hariṣeṇa's *kathā* found in his *Bṛhatkathākośa* (pp. 118-39 in *The Clever Adulteress and other stories: A treasury of Jain literature*, ed. P. Granoff, Oakville, 1990.)

14 In *sandhis* 18 and 19 of the *Paümacariü*.

15 John D. Smith, The *Visaḷadevarāsa: A restoration of the text.* Cambridge: Cambridge University Press. 1976.

16 35, 9-36, 14.

17 The proportions will obviously change with the publication of Svayambhū's lengthy *Harivaṃśa-purāṇa* which is said to consist of 112 *sandhis* and c.2000 *kaḍavakas*.

18 Kāmil Bulke (Fr. Camille Bulcke), *Rām-kathā: utpatti aur vikās* (Prayāg, 1950^1, 1962^2, 1971^3) does not appear to be discussing the two Apabhraṃśa versions of the Rāma story.

19 W.L. Smith, *Rāmāyaṇa Traditions in Eastern India (Assam, Bengal, Orissa)*, Stockholm Studies in Indian Languages and

Culture, No. 2. Stockholm. 1988, pp. 14; 72f.

20 *Der Kampf der Götter und Dämonen—Aus dem thailändischen Ramakien übertragen* von C. Velder. Schweinfurt : Verlag Neues Forum. 1962. This is *not* actually a translation of the very lengthy Thai original, but merely a summary, which was then translated from the German into English by R.A. Olsson: *A prose translation of the Thai Ramayaṇa.* Bangkok. 1968. On Sītā see p. 61 (Velder), p. 68 (Olsson).

21 Upadhye discusses Yogîndu's date pp. 63-7, but his arguments abound in *non-sequiturs*. Upadhye acknowledges the indebtedness of Yogîndu to Kundakunda (see also note 24 below), but assigns as his date 'the beginning of the Christian era' (p. 67) which is probably far to early. From all the material discussed by Upadhye, the only reasonable inference that can be made is that Yogîndu's two works are known to and (explicitly) quoted by Jayasena, who 'belonged c. to the second half of the 12th century AD' (p. 64) Thus AD 1150 may be assumed to be the *terminus ante quem* for Yogîndu.

22 H. Jain (*Pāhuḍa-dohā*) p. 20, lists over fifty stanzas in the *Pāhuḍa-dohā* which are either similar to ones found in the *Paramappapayāsu* (abr., *Paramappa* or *Para.*) and *Yogasāra*, or contain at least similar phrases.

23 Alsdorf (1937) discusses three stanzas from the *Paramappa*, which he has found in *Apabhraṃśa-kāvya-trayī, Gaekwad's Oriental Series* 37, pp. 102-6. (He appears unaware of the two editions of *Paramappa* listed in Jain's edition of the *Pāhuḍadohā*, a work used by him, when he says, p. 59, note 2, that the *Paramappa* is still unpublished.) The three stanzas are (in Upadhye's numbering): I, 85 (Pischel's *Materialien No.* 1), II, 139 (*Materialien* No. 389) and II, 140 (*Materialien No.* 427), discussed pp. 59f, 63ff, and 53 respectively. For both verses II, 139 and 140, Alsdorf concludes that Yogîndu's version represents a secondary reworking of a popular stanza ('Umdichtung einer volkstümlichen Strophe', p. 60, note 2; cp. pp. 53; 64). But since i) Hemacandra's examples may be very much earlier and ii) II, 139 and 140 are missing in one important recension (viz. the 'shorter' one, the mss. TKM) of the *Paramappa*, no chronological conclusions can be derived from this. Upadhye, on the other hand, uncritically assumes that Hemacandra is actually quoting from Yogîndu (pp. 45ff; 64) and goes so far as to claim that Hemacandra's versions are 'intelligent improvements' (p. 46) on Yogîndu. The *Yogasāra* was known to Alsdorf. He states his impression that its language is rather late ('Y[ogindradeva]'s Sprache macht

einen recht späten Eindruck, doch bedarf dies noch genauerer Prüfung.' p 60 note 1) and suggests that we are dealing here with original stanzas, not reworkings (p. 60, note 2).

24 See the forthcoming publication of Will Johnson, *The Problem of Bondage in Selected Early Jaina Texts* (D.Phil. thesis, Oxford, 1990) which deals mainly with Kundakunda's *Samayasāra* and *Pravacanasāra*.

25 The text is quoted from Upadhye's edition; the variant readings listed by him (pp. 353....361) contain nothing of major interest. But it may be noted that *Para.* I, 81 and II, 99 are not found in one group of manuscripts (TKM, called 'shorter' or 'Kannaḍa' recension by Upādhye, pp. 83ff). While the content of I, 81 is duplicated by I, 87, II, 99 is indeed idiosyncratic

26 A similar stanza is found, as No. 31, in the *Pāhuḍadohā*. But the construction is different: *haüṃ varu baṃbhaṇu ṇa vi....ehaü jāṇi visesu*, "I am not a fine brahmin..." Realize this [absence of external marks] as your definition!' The reading of *Paramappa.* appears preferable.

27 This stanza is also found, as No. 32, in the *Pāhuḍadohā*, with two *variants: bālu haüṃ* ('I am a child') for *rūyaḍaü*, and *ehaü ciṃti ma* ('don't think of any of such things!') for *mūḍhaü maṇṇaï*. Again, *Paramappa.* seems to have the better readings. *Vandaka* is a Buddhist mendicant (Jain's tentative suggestion of *mandira-mārgi*, 'a follower of the religion of temple [worship]', is obscure to me.)

28 This verse is found also in the *Pāhuḍadohā*, as No. 33; the variants are purely orthographic.

APPENDIX: SOME PUBLISHED WORKS IN APABHRAṂŚA

Apabhraṃśa-kāvya-trayī by Jinadata-sūri: 1) *Carcarī*, 2) *Upadeśa-rasāyana-rāsa*, 3) *Kāla-svarūpa-kulakam*, edited by Lalchandra Bhagawandas Gandhi, *Gaekwad's Oriental Series* No. 37, Oriental Institute, Baroda, 1927 (reprinted 1967). [edited with Sanskrit *chāyā* and commentary, lengthy Sanskrit introduction]

Karakaṇḍa-cariü by Muṇi Kanakāmara: edited by Hiralal Jain; 1) *Ambādāsa Cavare Digambara Jaina Granthamālā* (Karanja Jaina Series) No. 4, Karanja VS 1990 (AD 1934);
2) new enlarged edition *Jñānpīṭh Mūrtidevī Jain granth-mālā, Apabhraṃś granthâṅk* 4, Bhāratīya Jñānpīṭh Prakāśan, [Vārānasi], VS 2021 (AD 1964). [critically edited, Hindi introduction, Hindi and English translations]

Kahakosu by Śrīcandra: edited by Hiralal Jain, *Prakrit Text Society Series* No. 13, Ahmedabad, 1969. [edited from one manuscript, with a Hindi summary of the stories]
(This work should be read in conjunction with Hariṣena's *Bṛhatkathākośa*, ed. A.N. Upādhye, *Singhi Jaina Granthamālā* vol. 17, Bombay, 1943.)

Ludwig Alsdorf, Der *Kumārapālapratibodha* — ein Beitrag zur Kenntnis des Apabhraṃśa und der Erzählungsliteratur der Jainas, *Alt-und Neu-Indische Studien* No. 2, Hamburg, 1928). [Edition and German translation of Apabhraṃśa portions found in the work]

Chando' nuśāsana by Hemacandra: ed. by H.D. Velankar, *Singhi Jaina Granthamālā* vol. 49, Bombay, 1961.

Jasahara-cariü by Puṣpadanta: edited by P.L. Vaidya, *Ambādāsa Cavare Digambara Jaina Granthamālā* (Karanja Jaina Series) No. 1, Karanja Jain Publication Society, Karanja, Berar, VS 1987 (AD 1931). [critically edited, with brief introduction and notes]

Jāmbūsāmi-cariü by Vīra: edited by Vimalprakāś Jain, *Jñānpīṭh Mūrtidevī Jain granth-mālā, Apabhraṃś granthâṅk* 7, Bhāratīya Jñānpīṭh Prakāśan, [Vārāṇasī], VS 2025 (AD 1968). [critically edited from various mss, with Hindi introduction and translation]

Ṇāyakumāra-cariü by Puṣpadanta: edited by Hiralal Jain, *Devendrakīrti Jain Series* No. 1, Balatkara Gana Jain Publication Society, Karanja, Berar, VS 1989 (AD 1933). [critically edited from various mss, introduction]

Dohā-kośa: by Saraha: 1) ed. M. Shahidullah, *Les chants mystiques de Kaṇhā et de Saraha*, Paris, 1928. 2) ed. P.C. Bagchi, *Dohākośa, Calcutta Sanskrit Series* No. 25c, 1938. 3) English translation by D. Snellgrove (Saraha's *Treasury of Songs*, pp. 224-239 in: *Buddhist Texts through the Ages*, edited by Edward Conze, Bruno Cassirer, Oxford, 1954; reprinted Harper & Row, (Harper Torchbooks), New York, 1964).

Paümacariü by Svayambhū: ed. in three volumes by H.V.C. Bhayani, *Singhi Jaina Granthamālā*, Nos. 34-36, Bombay, vol. I, 1953; vol. II, 1953; vol. III, 1960. [text only]

Paümasiri-cariü by ('Divya-dṛṣṭi-kavi') Dhālila: ed. Madhusūdan Ci. Modī and Harivallabh Cu. Bhayāṇī, *Singhi Jaina Granthamālā* No. 24, Bhāratīya Vidyā Bhavan, Bombay, VS 2005 (AD 1948). [text edited from one ms. with many emendations, copious notes in Gujarati, glossary with Sanskrit equivalents]

Paramappapayāsu (Paramâtma-prakāśa) by Yogîndu-deva: 1) earliest edition traced: by Babu Suryabhanu Vakil, Devabanda/ Saharanapura(?) with Hindi translation, 1909 (see *Pāhuḍadohā* p. 19, note and Upādhye, p. 2); 2) *Rāyacandra Śāstramālā*, Bombay, 1916 (see ibidem), which was 3) re-edited by Ādināth Neminath Upadhye, with the Sanskrit *vṛtti* of Brahmadeva and the *ṭīkā* by Paṇḍita Daulātarām in Hindi, Śrī *Rāyacandra Jaina Śāstra-mālā* No. 10, Śrī Parama-śruta-prabhāvaka-maṇḍala, Bombay VS 1993 (AD 1937). [with lengthy introduction in English and variant readings, pp. 353-362] 4) The Apabhraṃśa text alone, as found in the previous edition, was also separately published by R.D. Vadekar, Poona (Pune), in 1941. 5) A free English paraphrase of the work by R.D. Jain was published in Arrah, 1915.

Pāsanāha-cariü by Ācārya Padmakīrti: edited by Praphull Kumār Modī, *Prakrit Text Society Series* No. 8, Vārāṇasī, VS 2021 (AD 1965). [critically edited, commentary and translation in Hindi]

Pāhuḍa-doha by Rāmasiṃha: edited by Hiralal Jain, *Ambādāsa Cavare Digambara Jaina Granthamālā* (Karanja Jaina Series) No. 3, Karanja, VS 1990 (AD 1933). [edited with Hindi translation, notes in Hindi] 2) translated into French by C. Caillat, 'L' offrande de distiques', *Journal Asiatique*, 264, Paris, 1976, pp. 63-95.

Prākṛta-paiṅgalam: A text on Prākṛta and Apabhraṃśa metres: ed. by Bholāśaṃkara Vyāsa (Bhola Shanker Vyas), *Prakrit Text Society Series* Nos. 2 and 4 (parts I and II), Varanasi, 1959 and 1962.

Bhavissatta (or Bhavisayatta)-kaha by Dhaṇavāla: 1) edited by H. Jacobi, Abhandlungen der Königlichen Bayerischen Akademie der Wissenschaften, philosophisch-philologische und historische Klasse, XXIX, 4, Munich, 1918; 2) edited by C.D. Dalal and Pandurang Damodar Gune, *Gaekwad's Oriental Series* No. 20, Oriental Institute, Baroda, 1923 (reprinted 1967).

Mayaṇaparājayacariü by Harideva: edited by Hiralal Jain, *Jñānpīṭh Mūrtidevī Jain granth-mālā, Apabhraṃśa granthāṅka* 5, Bhāratīya Jñānapīṭha, Kāśī, 1962 [with Hindi translation].

Mahāpurāṇa by Puṣpadanta: 1) edited by P.L. Vaidya, *Manikchand Digambara Jaina Granthamālā*, 3 vols., Nos. 37, 41 and 42, Bombay, 1937, 1940 and 1941. [text only] 2) *Harivaṃś-apurāṇa — Ein Abschnitt aus der Apabhraṃśa - Welthistorie 'Mahāpurāṇa Tisaṭṭhimahāpurisaguṇālaṃkāra' von Puṣpadanta*, herausgegeben von Ludwig Alsdorf, *Alt-und*

Neu-Indische Studien No. 5, Hamburg, 1936 [critical edition of *sandhis* 81-92, and German translation]. See also R.N. Shriyan, *A Critical Study of Mahāpurāṇa of Puṣpadanta*, Ahmedabad, 1969.

Yogasāra by Yogîndudeva: 1) edited *Māṇikacandra grantha-mālā*, No. 21, Bombay, 1922 (see *Pāhuḍadohā*, p. 19 note). 2) edited, with Sanskrit *chāyā* and the Hindi paraphrase by Paṇḍita Jagadīśacandra, by A.N. Upadhye (included as pp. 371-394 in his edition of *Paramappapayāsu* mentioned above).

Vṛttajātisamuccaya by Virahaṅka: ed. H.D. Velankar, *Journal of the Royal Asiatic Society*, Bombay Branch, 5, 1929, pp. 34-94.

Sañjamamañjari by Maheśvara-sūri: edited pp. 37ff in the *Gaekwad's Oriental Series* edition of the *Bhavisayatta-kahā*.

Sanatkumāra-caritam by Haribhadra (part of his *Nemināthacaritam*): edited by H. Jacobi [and translated into German], Abhandlungen der Königlichen Bayerischen Akademie der Wissenschaften, philosophisch-philologische und historische Klasse, XXXI, 2, Munich, 1921.

Sandeśa-rāsaka by Abdul Rahmān: edited by Śrī Jinavijaya-muni and Harivallabh Bhāyāṇī, *Singhi Jaina Granthamālā* No. 22, Bhāratīya Vidyā Bhavan, Bombay, VS 2001 (AD 1945). [critically edited, with Sanskrit notes, commentaries and English summary]

Sāvayadhamma-dohā (anonymous): edited by Hiralal Jain, *Ambādāsa Cavare Digambara Jaina Grantha-mālā* (Karanja Jaina Series) No. 2, Karanja Jaina Publication Society, Karanja, Berar, VS 1989 (AD 1932). [critically edited, notes and translation in Hindi]

Siddha-hemacandram by Hemacandra, chapter 8, *Prākṛtavyākaraṇam:* 1) edited by R. Pischel in two volumes, with German notes and glossary, Halle, 1877 and 1880; 2) edited by S.P. Pandit (appendix to his edition of the *Kumārapālacarita*), Bombay Sanskrit Series, Bombay 1900 3) edited by P.L. Vaidya, with notes and word-index, Poona (Pune), 1928. 4) The poetic quotations in Hemacandra's grammar have been analysed by Alsdorf in his *Apabhraṃśa-Studien*, 1937.

Svayambhūchandas by Svayambhū, ed H.D. Velankar, *Journal* of the *University* of Bombay 5, 1936, part III, p. 41-93.

BIBLIOGRAPHY

L. Alsdorf, *Apabhraṃśa-Studien*, Abhandlungen für die Kunde des Morgenlandes, XXII, 2, Leipzig, 1937.

C. Caillat, 'L' offrande de distiques', *Journal Asiatique*, 264, Paris, 1976, pp. 63-95.

H. L. Jain, *Apabhraṃśa bhāṣā aur sāhitya*, Nāgarī Pracāriṇī Patrikā, Benares, 50, pp. 1-8; 100-121.

H.L. Jain, 'Apabhraṃśa Literature', in: *Allahabad University Studies*, I, 157-185, Allahabad, 1925.

H.L. Jain, 'Some recent finds of Apabhraṃśa literature', in: *Nagpur University Journal*, 8, Dec. 1942, pp. 81-92.

H.L. Jain, 'Apabhraṃśa language and literature', pp. 212-18 in: *History and Culture of the Indian People*, general editor R.C. Majumdar, vol. IV: *The Age of Imperial Kanauj*, Bombay: Bharatiya Vidya Bhavan, 1955.

Harivaṃsa Kochaṛa, *Apabhraṃśa sāhitya*, Delhi, VS 2013 (1956/1957).

M.A. Mehendale (with additions by A.D. Pusalker), 'Apabhraṃśa', pp. 348-51 in: *History and Culture of the Indian People*, general editor R.C. Majumdar, vol. V: *The Struggle for Empire*, Bombay: Bharatiya Vidya Bhavan 1957, 2nd ed. 1966.

R. Pischel, *Materialien zur Kenntnis des Apabhraṃśa*, Abhandlungen der Königlichen Gesellschaft der Wissenschaften zu Göttingen, Phil.-Hist. Klasse, Neue Folge, Vol. V, No. 4, Berlin, 1902.

G.V. Tagare, *Historical Grammar of Apabhraṃśa*, Poona, 1948 (Deccan College Dissertation Series vol. 5.)

Rāmasiṃha Tomar, *Prākṛta aur Apabhraṃśa sāhitya*, Hindi Pariṣad, Allahabad, 1964.

The Early *Bhakti* Milieu as Mirrored in the Poetry of Harirām Vyās*

Heidi Pauwels

Scholarly books on the history of *bhakti* usually contain separate chapters on *nirguṇ* and *saguṇ bhakti*. The latter will often have a section on Braj, in which the Kṛṣṇa-*bhakta*s are classified according to their sectarian affiliation. These classifications are didactically useful, but it becomes increasingly evident that they should not be regarded as absolute (Schomer 1987, 3, 7). An interesting case in point is as famous a *bhakta* as Sūrdās. He has been classified traditionally as belonging to a *saguṇ bhakti* sect, namely the Vallabh Sampradāy. However, in recent research the claim that he belonged to a specific sect has been refuted (Hawley 1984, 25-28) and the 'Sant' aspect of his poetry has been highlighted (Hawley 1984, 121-60 and 1987). Is Sūr an exception or do we need to modify our rigid categories for other *bhakta*s as well? To answer this question, we need to investigate what these *bhakta*s themselves have to say on the topic.

This paper presents the case of another sixteenth-century Kṛṣṇa *bhakta*, Harirām Vyās.[1] Traditionally, he is classified in the standard chapter on *saguṇ bhakti* as a *rasik kavi*, a poet who specialized in the aesthetic vision of the divine love-play of Rādhā and Kṛṣṇa. In most histories of Hindi literature[2] he is placed in the same category as Hit

Harivaṁś (AD 1502-52; see Mc Gregor 1984, 88) and Svāmī Haridās (from the beginning of the sixteenth century till AD 1575-1595; *ibid.*, 92). The three of them are referred to collectively as the *Hari-trayī* (Kṛṣṇa-triumvirate), a pun on the common part of their names; alternatively, they are called *rasik-trayī* because the majority of their poetry deals with the divine love-play. Unlike his two companions, Vyās has also left us hymns about predecessors and contemporary *bhaktas*. In fact, for many of these *bhaktas* he is the earliest hagiographical source (Dube 1968, 31).

Harirām Vyās's 'hagiographical' songs are interesting for our purpose because they give us clues about what the early *bhakti* milieu looked like from within. Since poems similar to his have been created by other *bhaktas*, he may be regarded as a representative of the early *bhakti* milieu. In the first section of this paper we try to determine how Vyās situated himself in relation to other *bhaktas* and what his attitudes were towards so-called *nirguṇīs* and *saguṇīs* respectively. The division is merely a technical one, because, as we will see, it is not made by Vyās himself. For him, there is no distinction: *nirguṇīs* and *saguṇīs* basically belong to the same "clan".

If Vyās did not think of *nirguṇ bhaktas* as his antagonists, then whom did he consider to be the 'others'? In the second section of this paper, we will look for an answer in his sermons. As it turns out, Vyās is concerned not so much with Muslims as with hypocritical *bhaktas* and *śāktas*. To identify whom exactly he means, we need to place the poems within their historical context.

Once it has been established that for Vyās *saguṇīs* and *nirguṇīs* were alike, we need to determine when they came to be differentiated. Obviously, later generations of Kṛṣṇa *bhaktas* were interested in distancing themselves from the *nirguṇīs*. This is apparent from the way the later hagiographers interpret some of Vyās's poems, as is explained in the third section of this paper.

The world-view of Vyās corresponds in many ways with

that of Sūrdās, yet there are differences. In the last section of this paper some divergences of the perspectives of Vyās and Sūrdās will be pointed out.

The basis for this study is the *Vāṇī* of Vyās, which is a relatively well-defined corpus. The standard edition by Vāsudev Gosvāmī (1952), which agrees in many respects with the oldest manuscript material, is quoted and referred to throughout. I have also made use of the oldest manuscript of the complete *Vāṇī* yet discovered, which is dated 1737 (VS 1794). Because of its provenance, it is referred to as the 'Jhansi Manuscript' (Jh.Ms.).[3] If available, reference to the folio and *pad*-number in this manuscript is added between brackets.[4]

1. VYĀS AND THE CLAN

1.1. The *nirguṇīs*

1.1.a. *The early Sants.* A set of six early Sants is praised repeatedly in Vyās's hagiographical songs, namely Nāmdev, Kabīr, Raidās, Sen, Dhanā and (except for one occasion) Pīpā.[5] Vyās is not the only one to mention this group of early *bhaktas* in one breath; other more or less contemporary sources do the same. The early Sants themselves cross-refer to each other, e.g., Dhanā (*Gurū granth*, 487) mentions Nāmdev (the *chīprā*), Kabīr (the *jolāharā*), Raidās, and Sen (the *nāī*). Nāmdev, Kabīr and Raidās enjoyed a wide popularity in Dādūpanthī circles at the beginning of the seventeenth century, as is indicated by the inclusion of their poems in the *Pañc-vāṇī* anthologies.[6] The same can be noted for the early Sikh milieu: poems by the Bhagats Kabīr, Nāmdev, Raidās, Dhanā, Sen, and Pīpā are included in the *Gurū-granth.* Kabīr, Raidās, and Nāmdev are also said to have been held in high esteem by other *bhaktas*, such as Sūr, Parśurām, and, in Maharashtra, Eknāth.[7] It is quite clear that early *bhakti* milieu people of all (later established) denominations admit inspiration from the early Sants.

This is also the case in Rāmānandī circles, but not without

sectarian bias.[8] The relationship of some of the Sants with Rāmānand is stressed by the famous hagiographer Nābhādās in his *Bhakta-māl* (*chappāī* 36). Another Rāmānandī hagiographer, Anantdās, wrote his *Paricaīs* mainly about the aforementioned *bhaktas*. His stories too betray sectarian bias, e.g., Kabīr is represented as a disciple of Rāmānand.[9]

A significant *pad* by Vyās that mentions these Sants is the following:

1. Of these my whole family consists:
2. Sen, Dhanā, and Nāmdev; Pīpā and Kabīr, [and] Raidās, the cobbler.
3. Of Rūp and Sanātan, [I am] a servant, Gaṅgal Bhaṭṭ melted [my heart].[10]
4. I have reflected on the *bhakti* of Sūrdās, Parmānand, Mehā[11] and Mīrā.
5. Brahmins, Rajputs of noble family, they too take pride in caste.
6. (But) Rādhāvallabh is the all of *bhaktas* from the beginning to the end (of time).
7. Āsū's Haridās[12] [and] the *rasik*, Harivaṁś, do not forget me.
8. Walking on this path of Śyām and Śyāmā, through devotion, help the drowning Vyās to get across (the ocean of existence).

(*pad* 21, f. 8 r., no. 21)

A first observation to be made on the basis of this song, is that the Sants are not thought to be any different from the Kṛṣṇa *bhaktas*. There is no question of sectarian lineages, but rather of a horizontal affiliation of spiritual kin, or the 'extended family' of *bhaktas*. An appropriate sociological term is "clan", which stands for "consciousness of kinship through broad, historically untraceable generic relationships" (Gold 1987, 18). This term has been applied to the religio-historical phenomenon of the Sants (*ibid.*, 18-20), and seems to be of relevance for the early *bhakti* milieu, including the first generation of Kṛṣṇa-*bhaktas* in Braj. A second observation to be made on the basis of Vyās's poem is the way the legitimacy of this clan is established. There is no reference to a historical guru, but to a pedigree of mythological *bhaktas* of "the beginning to the end" (1.6). By substantiating the connection of the historical *bhaktas* with those of mythology, the timelessness of the *bhakta* as a category is emphasized. Parallels can be found elsewhere: Nābhādās is inspired to begin his *Bhakta-māl* with *bhaktas* from previous *yugas*. Vyās himself in his *Vāṇī* begins the chapter "*Sādhu-stuti*" with praise of Nārada and Śukadeva.[13]

A third conclusion to be drawn from the *pad* quoted is that for Vyās biological descent is even less relevant than sectarian lineage when it comes to spiritual matters. The six Sants he praises so lavishly have in common a low-caste birth. This is no arbitrary matter, since there are occasions where Vyās characterizes them by occupation only: the barber (Sain), the farmer (Dhanā), the weaver (Kabīr), and the cotton carder (Nāmdev).[14] The point is that divine grace is extended to the most humble, and that the clan is open for *bhaktas* of all castes. But this works both ways: *bhakti* is not acquired by birth:

1. A *bhakta* is not born the son of a *bhakta*.
2. *Bhaktas* may be [sons] of *śāktas*, like the sons Śrutidev [and] Sudāmā.[15]
3. Ugrasen had Kaṁsa [as son], Bali the demon Bāṇā; Yam was sonless.
4. Bhīṣma had Rukman, and in Vibhīṣaṇ's home a bad son was born.
5. Sen, Dhanā and Raidās were born (*bhaktas*, though from low caste father).
Jaydev [and] Kabīr were without equal (predecessor or descendant).[16]
6. Kabīr's lineage was blotted when his son Kamālā was born.
7. *Śāktas*, if born from *bhaktas*, must be considered someone else's piss.

8. Brahma had Nārad, Vyās[17] had Vidur, and Śuk was an *avadhūt*.

(*pad* 284, f. 61, no. 157)

The message is clear: access to the clan is not limited to people of good birth. The devout son of a sinner is admitted rather than the bad son of a *bhakta*, the point being illustrated with mythological and historical figures. Interestingly, Vyās voices his disapproval of Kabīr's son, Kamālā. Only one century later, Kamālā was held in high esteem, as is shown by a miniature from the court of Dārā Shikoh which depicts a group of Sants with Kamālā seated right next to Kabīr.[18]

We can conclude that in the early *bhakti* milieu, as represented by Vyās, the main concern was not with sectarian lineage, but rather with the clan of like-minded devotees. Soon however matters of descent (biological and spiritual) were to gain priority.

1.1.b. A specific case: Kabīr. With the broad lines of Vyās's world established, we can now consider some specific matters. An interesting problem is the much discussed relationship between Rāmānand and Kabīr. It has been stated that Vyās has testified that the former was the guru of the latter.[19] However, in the light of Vyās's concept of the clan of *bhaktas*, the matter looks quite different. The *pad* in question deserves to be quoted in full:

1. A true *sādhu* was Rāmānand,
2. Who knew how to love the Lord, having realized that all else is sorrow and duality,
3. Whose servant (*sevak*), Kabīr, was excessively steadfast; Sur Surānand[20] was profound.
4. Then Raidās was Hari's devotee, the hero was Parmānand.[21]
5. Before them [came] Tilocan and Nām (Nāmdev), absolvers from pain, sources of bliss.

6. Khem and Sanātan, and the personification of the essence of the ocean of devotion, Rāghavānand.
7. On the bee, Harivaṁś, shone pollen from Rādhikā's lotus-feet.
8. Kṛṣṇadās and Haridās served the Moon of Vrindaban.
9. Without them, I became a living corpse, suffering the snare of distress.
10. Without them, how can the thorn in my heart be removed? Vyās lives on, completely senseless.

(*pad* 23, f. 8v., no. 23: *sā̃ce sādhu ju rāmānaṃda*)

At first glance, this poem seems rather convincing evidence for Rāmānand's guru-hood because it fits the picture drawn in Rāmānandī hagiographies. All redactions of the *Paricaī* by Anantdās confirm the affiliation of Kabīr to Rāmānand. The list of twelve disciples of Rāmānand in Nābhādās's *Bhakta-māl* (*chappāī* 36) includes three of the names mentioned by Vyās in the first four lines of the poem (i.e., before the "flash-back" to the past with Nāmdev and Tilocan). Nābhādās's list contains Kabīr[22] as well as Sur Surānand and Raidās, but not Parmānand. The testimony of Anantdās and Nābhādās is rather conspicuous because both belong to the lineage of Rāmānand,[23] but Vyās's, as that of a "neutral" party, would add more weight to the case.

Vyās's testimony, however, has to be considered prudently. In the first place, the earliest manuscript source (found so far) for this *pad* is the Jhansi manuscript, which is as late as the first half of the eighteenth century. Interpolation, although not likely, is always a possibility. Secondly, that Rāmānand is mentioned in the refrain (*ṭek*) does not necessarily imply that the whole song is in praise of the lineage of his disciples. From line six onwards *bhaktas* such as Sanātan Gosvāmī and Hit Harivaṁś are mentioned, who definitely have no special relationship with Rāmānand. The real theme of the song, as is poignantly expressed in the final line, is the pain of separation from fellow *bhaktas*. It is about the importance of *satsaṅg* in general, rather than about the disciples of Rāmānand, as the *ṭek* might lead us to believe.

Thirdly, the term *sevak* in line three could be interpreted as 'disciple', but it has also a more general basic meaning.[24] It may simply stand for 'devotee' in general, and here it may relate to God ('Hari' in the previous line) instead of to Rāmānand (who is mentioned in the *ṭek*). Fourthly, Raidās is mentioned together with Parmānand, who cannot be included among the disciples of Rāmānand. Hence, even if the third line does refer to Rāmānand's disciples, the fourth line in which Raidās is mentioned is a different matter. Finally, we have to consider the song in the context of Vyās's work. Since we have established that Vyās considered all *bhaktas* to belong to one clan, it is rather unlikely that he would in this song revert to a lineage-type of connection.

1.2. The *saguṇīs*

Notwithstanding the prominence Vyās gives to the Sants, most references in his poems are to *saguṇ bhaktas*. Among these, he clearly felt most intimately connected to Harivaṁś (16 references in the chapter "Siddhānt pad" of the Jh.Ms.) and Haridās (11 references), whom he often mentions together (9 examples).[25] In this respect, the classification of these two poets together with Vyās, usually under the term *rasik-trayī*, seems justified.

According to Vyās, Harivaṁś and Haridās are so important because they are *rasiks*, that is, they came to 'taste' the essence of reality and to testify to this experience in word (their *pads*) and deed (their *sevā*). They fulfil a soteriological role because they are teachers as well as examples for aspiring *bhaktas*.[26] However, there is an additional dimension to Vyās's portrait of his fellow-devotees: they are depicted in the role that they play in the world of their own songs, namely that of *sakhīs* witnessing the supernal love-play of Rādhā and Kṛṣṇa. This is illustrated by Vyās's use of the feminine suffix *-ī* after the names Harivaṁś and Haridās.[27] In *pad* 256 (f. 28 r., no. 73) he calls them explicitly *sakhī* and *sahelī*, and in *pad* 258 (f. 34-35, no. 92) 1. 3, he seems to refer to Haridās as 'Lalitādāsī'.[28] In the chapter "Samay ke pad," *pad* 597 (f. 239-42, no. 280), Vyās depicts Harivaṁśī and Haridāsī dancing and singing with the Gopīs.[29] Harivaṁś and Haridās are depicted as *sakhīs* in the *virah pads* composed after their deaths, but also elsewhere. It seems that the *parlaukik* or supernal role of the two devotees as Rādhā's *sakhīs* was accepted by their contemporary already during their life-time.

Harivaṁś and Haridās serve Rādhā as *sakhīs* in the supernal world, and as such are subjects of devotion, but they are at the same time objects of devotion for the *bhaktas* who still dwell in this one.[30] Since Harivaṁś and Haridās act in the supernal as well as mundane world, they are perceived as intermediating between the two. Accordingly, Vyās denotes his contemporaries as *rasik* or *dāsī*, while his perspective shifts from this world to the supernal, and back.

Harivaṁś's and Haridās's double role as subject and object of devotion is philosophically sound; the main tenet of *bhakti* is that devotion is simultaneously the way and the goal, and that in the highest kind of devotion subject and object are undifferentiated. Vyās expresses this elsewhere, in his chapter "Rās ke pad," by emphasizing the superiority of Rādhā in order to indicate that the subject has become the object of devotion. Vyās also conceives of the relation between the *bhakta* and God in the same way. Serving the *bhakta* (not only Harivaṁś and Haridās, but also the rest of the clan), is equivalent to serving God; hence by serving the servant, by being dedicated to the devotee, the ultimate goal is reached. This sentiment is expressed several times, e.g.:

> *vyāsa upāsaka sadā upāsī rādhā carana anūpa*
> Vyās is the servant of those who serve Rādhā's incomparable feet.
>
> (*pad* 15, f. 5, no. 13, l. 8)

haribaṃsī haridāsī sevata vyāsa tahā̃ bana pāvai
By serving Harivaṁśī and Haridāsī, Vyās reaches the forest (i.e., heavenly Vrindaban) beyond.[31]
(*pad* 160, f. 2, no. 4 or f. 50-50, no. 123, l. 8)

pahile bhaktana ke mana nirmala...
tinakau nāma leta guna gāvata rati bāḍhai sada seyai carana tala
The heart of *bhaktas* of yore is stainless....If you pronounce their names and sing their praise, love will grow, and you will eternally serve [His] feet.[32]
(*pad* 158, f. 1-2, no. 3, l 4-5)

The reason why Vyās devoted so many songs to *bhaktas* is precisely this belief that acts of devotion to God can be transferred to the devotee. To paraphrase the main point of one *pad*: "the beloved of my beloved (Rādhā and Kṛṣṇa) are my dearest", and one step further: "those who love these beloved ones of my beloved, are my true family" (see *pad* 221 [f. 90-91, no. 209] l. 1-2).[33] At the end of his *Rās-pañcādhyāyī*, Vyās goes as far as to reverse the roles completely: he implores Rādhā to mediate and bring him near the *sakhīs* Harivaṁś and Haridās. The ripples of devotion can be expanded in ever broader circles.

2. VYĀS AND THE 'OTHERS'

Vyās's poems are not only concerned with those belonging to the clan. In fact, the very concept of the clan implies a demarcation against an opposite, a definition that excludes certain other groups. The formation of new group identities in sixteenth-century Vrindaban was, judging by Vyās's testimony, not in opposition to Islam. Vyās is hardly concerned with Islamic authorities, such as *qāzīs* or Shai<u>kh</u>s, whom he only mentions in passing.[34] He regards Muslims as outsiders, yet is not specially troubled by them. In fact, in *pad* 147 (f. 95 v., no. 156), he mentions the *qāzī* and Hindu 'holy men' in the same breath: "Afflicted pandits, shaven monks and *qāzīs* make their tour, roaming from house to house."[35]

Vyās is no exception. Even in regions where Muslims figure more prominently, such as Bengal, they are not really considered to be the foes. Even stronger, in Gauḍīya hagiographies of the period, the Muslim leader's duty is said to be protection of the Vaiṣṇavas against 'subversive Hindus', referred to as *pākhaṇḍīs* (O'Connell 1970, 119).

Vyās's diatribes are mainly directed against the enemy within Hinduism. The 'fifth column' is formed by hypocrites who are *bhaktas* only in name. Vyās includes in this category false devotees as well as false gurus. He often styles them *vimukh* (28 occurrences of this term in the relevant chapters of the Vāsudev Gosvāmī edition). An example where Vyās expresses his disgust for sham *bhaktas* is worth quoting here in full:

1. For (or: within) two days he had people call him "one-pointed (*ananya*) [devotee]".
2. For the sake of money he donned the robe of the dancer, then he entered the [world of] five [distinctions] again.[36]
3. All was spoilt by accepting countless gurus and eating the left-overs of all.
4. No business here (in this world), and no higher goal there, life wasted in between.
5. He dug a granary, [though] sowing in the desert. Taking a useless buffalo,[37] he reckoned on (milk) pails.[38]
6. The prostitute's son offered *piṇḍa* for his father, which name did he recite?[39]
7. Like showing a dance to a blind man, or singing a song to a deaf one.
8. Embarked on a boat of paper, tell me, no one has managed to cross the river.
9. There is no love without [total] faith, *saṃsār* makes all dance.

> 10. Vyās says: If one desires without [cherishing] spontaneous *bhakti*, one invites looting in one's own house.
>
> (*pad* 139, f. 78-79, no. 183)

Religious specialists are not spared in Vyās's criticism. Those who pose as gurus, yet actually cherish worldly aspirations and fall a prey to greed and lust are a favourite object of abuse:

> 1. He sells Guru Govind in the market. (Or: The guru sells Govind in the market.)
> 2. One does not become a *bhakta* by begging like the Ḍoms, the acrobats or the Bhāṭs.
> 3. Cowardly, cruel, crooked and insulting, one can never become pure.[40]
> 4. When in contact with greed and luxury, all is spoilt, like a vessel of sandy clay.[41]
> 5. One wastes one's body by looking at faces of alluring ladies, and feels the weal of Kām.
> 6. No mental balance is reached, crores of frustrations well up.
> 7. When they went to another's house, the Pāṇḍavs were insulted by Virāṭ.
> 8. Drūpad's daughter smashed even Kīcak, a bloody forehead for Dharma's son.[42]
> 9. The lady, whose body he looked at with pleasure, slammed the door on him, not [sharing his] desire.
> 10. Vyās says: one who serves the Lord, and [still] cherishes desire, is waylaid.
>
> (*pad* 128, f. 78-79, no. 186)

The poems quoted may be less representative of the early *bhakti* milieu as they are of the long established cliché in Indian literature of the 'fallen saint'. Also, the *pads* could be interpreted as an internal monologue in which Vyās reproaches himself. Still, there are a few cases where Vyās seems to refer to actual historical circumstances. In one *pad* he chides people who quit Vrindaban and travel to Gujarat and Bengal. It seems obvious that he speaks about followers of Vallabha on their promotional tours in Gujarat, and Gauḍiyas on their way to Bengal.

> 1. They roam and ramble in Bengal and Gujarat.
> 2. Leaving the treasure house of bliss, Mathura and Vrindaban, they are restlessly [seeking] for money.[43]
> 3. That place, where the very dust is the essence of life, they are not ashamed to abandon.
> 4. [Their] accumulation of *mukti* cannot equal one leaf of a bower.
> 5. Its [Mathura's and Vrindaban's] buttermilk is hard to obtain for Indra, yet does not satisfy them.
> 6. Vyās [says]: without discernment, one does not get satisfied, even by plundering *saṃsār*.
>
> (*pad* 133, f. 66 r., no. 157)

It is worthwhile to consider this song in its historical context. After the death of the early charismatic personalities, sects arose in their name and became institutionalized under their descendants. Vyās's *virah pads* about contemporary *bhaktas* suggest that he outlived the first generation of settlers in Braj, and he must have witnessed the early phase of organization into sectarian lineages. He seems to have felt discouraged by the dilution of original sentiments. The poems in which he contrasts the clan with the biological family (see 1.1.a) may well reflect his aversion for the new developments. Even so, he never mentioned anyone by name in his rebukes.

Some of Vyās's condemnations are directed against so-called *śāktas*, a rather vague term that needs to be understood in context. *Śāktas* also figure prominently in Kabīr's expressions of antipathy, and Vyās's tirades are highly reminiscent of Kabīr's.[44] However, Vyās's poems are more than a continuation of a certain poetic genre, they have a fresh and sincere tone and do not strike one as being derivative. Rather than being archaisms, they seem to reflect the ongoing debates in mid-sixteenth-century Vrindaban.

Śāktism was apparently the subject of much controversy. Around 1540 "Bengali goddess worshippers," who had been charged with the service of the image of Śrīnāthjī, were expelled from the temple by the infamous Vallabhan *adhikārī* Kṛṣṇadās (Entwistle 1987, 153-154). The Vallabhan hagiography *Caurāsī vaiṣṇavan kī vārtā* (?1640, see Entwistle 1987, 262) does not hide the economic motives of this 'temple coup', but justifies the expulsion of the Bengalis by focusing on the question of their goddess worship. Also the Bengalis themselves were concerned about Śāktism. In Gauḍīya hagiographies the differences with "*śākta* brahmins" were more prominent than those with Muslims (O'Connell 1970, 119). The relationship of 'orthodox' Gauḍīya Vaiṣṇavism with the Sahajiyā movement and Śāktism is a topic of particular interest in itself. The orthodox Vaiṣṇavas' concern to distinguish themselves from the Sahajiyās is probably late, dating from around the beginning of the eighteenth century (discussed by O'Connell 1970, 254 ff.). However, early hagiographies reflect debates about the relevance of caste and women for the *bhaktas* (Dimock 1966, 68-102), the same crucial points around which Vyās's 'polemical' utterances are centred.

In one of his songs, Vyās condemns what seems to be *śākta* left-hand practice:

1. Senseless *bairāgī*s perform spiritual training in Bengal.[45]
2. By the power of mineral, alchemy and herbs, [their] desire (the bodiless god of love) is inflamed night and day.
3. [They] are not affected by the passionate bliss of Śuk's words, no element of doubt is dispersed.
4. Perversions [and] values of the ephemeral world catch on; in pursuit of wealth, everybody's concen-

tration is broken.
5. Living in the woods they grasp the heavy and high breasts of alluring ladies and serve them.
6. Considering every woman to be a *sādhu*,[46] they leave the holy men and abandon Hari's lap.
7. Words of desire, like arrows in every limb, [and still] the quiver bundling [more arrows] shines brightly.
8. Vyās [says]: [Even with] the firm noose of desire on his neck, he [still] likes desire and passion.

(*pad* 138, f. 77-78, no. 181)

In this song Vyās criticizes *bairāgī*s by an extended metaphor based on the opposition between what is healthy and unhealthy. What is healthy for the *bhakta*, namely the *Bhāgavatapurāṇa* (Śuk's words in 1. 3) with the story of Kṛṣṇa's love-play, becomes destructive when adopted literally for training by the *bairāgī*s. In the words of the metaphor: they abuse medicines and turn them into intoxicants.

This song seems to be a condemnation of *śākta* left-hand practices, especially the *pūjā* of women (1.5-6, although the latter is ambiguous). The *ṭek* can be construed to contain either a direct or punning reference to such practices in Bengal.[47] Even if the reference is not to practices of a Sahajiyā Vaiṣṇava type in Bengal proper, this *pad* allows us a glimpse of the spectrum of religious practices prevalent in the mid-sixteenth century.

3. AN ILLUSTRATION OF THE PROCESS OF SECTARIAN APPROPRIATION: TWO RĀDHĀVALLABHĪYA INTERPRETATIONS

As we have seen, Vyās did not differentiate between *saguṇī*s and *nirguṇī*s, but considered them all members of the *bhakti* clan. However, later generations of Kṛṣṇa-*bhakta*s were obviously interested in distancing themselves from the *nirguṇī*s. This is apparent from the way the later hagiographers interpret some of Vyās's poems in praise of *nirguṇī*s. We will discuss two sources from the Rādhāvallabh Sampradāy that betray some uneasiness with the songs in question, and offer two different interpretations.

The first hagiography is *Rasik-ananya-māl* (RAM), a controversial work usually ascribed to Bhagavat Mudit.[48] Whoever the author was, he clearly wrote from a Rādhāvallabh Sampradāy polemical point of view and makes the claim that Vyās himself belonged to this sect.[49] The author of RAM felt the need to justify Vyās's songs in praise of *nirguṇīs*, for they were irreconcilable with the adoration Vyās was supposed to feel for Harivaṁś. The perceived tension is solved by ascribing the songs to the period before Vyās's initiation into the sect. The RAM's description of Vyās's intellectual search for a guru contains a prospectus of candidates in which, incidentally, all the names of the *bhaktas* praised in Vyās's songs are dropped.

> Only a highly capable man, he (Vyās) considered, could be his guru:
> "I will choose someone who helps me cross (the ocean of existence)."
> Sometimes he felt attracted by Raidās,
> Sometimes by Kabīr's philosophy,
> Sometimes he set his heart on Pīpā,
> Sometimes he spoke of Jaydev,
> Sometimes Nāmdev filled his mind,
> Sometimes he sang of Raṅkā-Baṅkā,[50]
> Sometimes Rāmānand Gosvāmī, who had gone to heaven, came into his mind.
> Other times, he sang about the qualities of Vrindaban, and was longing for the *rasik bhaktas*.
> He acted thus, but was not settled, until he passed the age of forty-two.
>
> RAM II, 5-11

According to this source, Vyās was not satisfied until he met Harivaṁś and chose to be initiated by the founder-father of the Rādhāvallabh Sampradāy. The division of a saint's life into 'before' and 'after' stages is a common hagiographical device that has been used to explain inappropriate *pads* from a sectarian point of view, for example with respect to Sūrdās in the Vallabhan hagiography *Caurāsī vaiṣṇavan kī vārtā.*

A second later hagiography is Uttamcand's *Rasik-māl* (dating from around 1685, see Dube 1968, 119-21).[51] This work is clearly inspired by RAM, yet offers a different explanation for the problematic songs. The story goes that Vyās, shortly after his initiation by Harivaṁś, heard some Sants sing *pads* by Kabīr and Nāmdev. This displeased him because they concerned only *jñān* and *vairāgya,* not *prem bhakti.* His irritation disturbed his concentration, and for the next three days he failed to visualize Rādhā and Kṛṣṇa. Vyās then sought the advice of his guru, and Harivaṁś ascribed this interruption in his *dhyān* to an insult against a *mahant.* Vyās is reminded of his disrespectful musings about the visiting Sants and Harivaṁś taught him that all Sants, no matter of what sect, should be venerated. Vyās had committed an offence against *prem bhakti* itself, because true divine love shuns sectarian prejudices.

This explanation is more ingenious than that of RAM. Vyās's *nirguṇī* songs do not need to be assigned to a preconversion phase. The hagiographer insists that they are consistent with Vyās's Rādhāvallabh Sampradāy affiliation by attributing their inspiration to Harivaṁś himself. Paradoxically, it is exactly in the zeal of sectarianism that the sectarian perspective is broadened.

4. VYĀS AND SŪRDAS: THE DIFFERENCES.

We have tried to highlight the non-sectarian aspect of Vyās's poetry, which parallels the case of Sūrdās as it appears from recent scholarship. There are however a few significant differences between the 'Sant' aspect in Vyās's poetry and that in the early Sūr corpus.[52]

In the first place, many of Sūr's songs are full of complaint and self-accusation (Hawley 1987, 201), whereas Vyās's seldom reflect an internal monologue or self-mortification before God. The rare songs in 'Sūr style' that occur in the Vāsudev Gosvāmī edition (*pad* 279 and 281) are not attested in the Jh.Ms.[53] In contrast, Vyās takes a rather Kabīrian approach, lashing out at his contemporaries. His tone is not one of distress, but of confidence in the path that he has chosen. In contrast to Sūr, Vyās's preferred mode is polemics and sermons rather than *vinay-pads* or prayers.

In the second place, Vyās genuinely seems to believe in the possibility of a worthwhile life in this world, notwithstanding his tirades against hypocrites and *śāktas*. The *conditio sine qua non* is interaction with other *bhaktas*, hence the importance Vyās gives to praising them in his songs. Sometimes he seems to rank them even higher than God himself. In contrast, Sūr recognizes only Hari as his sole refuge; if he mentions the Sants at all, it is only by way of sketching the "religious landscape" (Hawley 1987, 202-03).

Both these differences may be connected with a third one, namely the fact that the main focus of their poetical output differs substantially. In describing the divine love-play the "the early Sūr" is preoccupied with separation or *virah*, exemplified by his fascination with the *bhramar-gīt* theme. Vyās, one the other hand, concentrates on the union of the lovers. He shows a special fondness for the *rās-līlā* theme, and in his *Rās-pañcādhyāyī* even explicitly omits the *virah* episode. So far no *bhramar-gīt* songs are attested in his oeuvre, and the name Uddhav does not even occur once. If a tone of *virah* prevails in some poems, it is not the pain of separation from Kṛṣṇa felt by the women of Braj or the devotee, as described by Sūr. The pain Vyās experienced and expressed in his songs is the *virah* resulting from the death of contemporary fellow-*bhaktas*.

5. CONCLUSION

Vyās's poems seem to mirror a religious environment where *bhaktas* of *nirguṇī* as well as *saguṇī* persuasion were considered to be fellow-members of one clan. The outsiders were hypocrites and *śāktas*. The latter stood for 'sinners' in general, but in one poem a case could be made for a more specific reference to a Sahajiyā-type of worship, perhaps in Bengal. A few generations later than Vyās the process of organizing according to lineage was in full swing and *saguṇīs*, such as the Rādhāvallabhan hagiographers, interpreted the meaning of his poems in that sense. This growing sectarian interpretation of an originally non-sectarian poet is similar to that of Sūrdās. However, there are differences. In contrast to Sūr's, Vyās's tone is more optimistic, in his *pads* about the love-play of Rādhā and Kṛṣṇa as well as elsewhere.

Future research has to determine whether Vyās is representative of the general climate of the early *bhakti* milieu. So far, in the scholarly literature, there are many controversies about the *bhaktas* of the first generation who settled in Braj in the beginning of the sixteenth century. From the point of view of the devotee, such disputes are irrelevant because the men under discussion are all fellow *rasik bhaktas*. It may well turn out that for the historian too, these disputes are misplaced, because they are projections of later concerns onto the past.

REFERENCES

1. Primary sources

1.1. Editions of Vyās's *Vāṇī*

Akhila Bhāratavarṣīya Śrī Hita Rādhāvallabhīya Vaiṣṇava Mahāsabhā, ed. 1934 (VS 1991). *Śrī Vyās-vāṇī*. Vrindaban: Śrī Vrajendra Machine Press.

Gosvāmī, Ācārya Śrī Rādhākiśor, ed. 1937 (VS 1994). *Śrī Vyās-vāṇī*. Vrindaban: Agravāl Press.

Gosvāmī, Vāsudev. 1952 (VS 2009). *Bhakta-kavi Vyāsjī*. Vrindaban: Agravāl Press.

1.2. Editions of Hagiographies.

Bhakta-māl:

Garga, Rāmkṛṣṇadev (Śāstrī). 1960. *Nābhājī kṛt Śrī Bhakta-māl, Bhakti-ras-bodhinī ṭīkā evaṁ Rasāyanī vyākhyā sahit.* Vrindaban: Nimbārkācārya Pīṭh.

Jhā, Narendra. 1978. *Bhakta-māl: pāṭhānuśīlan evam vivecan.* Patna: Anupam Prakāśaṇ.

Rūpkalā, Sītārāmśaraṇ Bhagavānprasād. 1969. *Bhakta-māl.* 5th edn, Lucknow: Tejkumār Book Depot.

Rasik-ananya-māl:

Purohit, Lalitāprasād. 1986. *Rasik-ananya-māl.* 2nd ed. Vrindaban: Veṇu Prakāśaṇ.

Dādūpanthī Bhakta-māl:

Nāhaṭā, Agarcand, ed. 1965. *Rāghavdās kṛt Bhakta-māl.* Jodhpur: Rājasthān Purātan Granthmālā.

Nārāyaṇdās, Svāmī, ed. 1969. *Śrī Svāmī Rāghavdāsjī viracit Bhakta-māl.* Pushkar: Dādūdayālū Mahāsabhā.

1.3. Varia:

Kṛṣṇadās, Gaṅgāviṣṇu, ed. 1986. *Do sau bāvan vaiṣṇav kī vārtā.* Reprint. Bombay: Laksmī Venkaṭeśvar Steam Press.

Śrī Gurūdvārā Śiromani Prabandhak Committee, ed. 1983. *Srī Gurū-granth Sāhibjī.* Amritsar: Śrī Gurūdvārā Śiromani Prabandhak Committee.

2. Secondary Sources

2. 1. Dictionaries

Gupta, Dīndayālu, and Ṭaṇḍan, Premnārāyaṇ. 1974 (VS 2031). *Braj-bhāṣā Sūr-koś.* 2nd ed. 2 vols. Lucknow: Viśvavidyālay Hindī Prakāśaṇ.

Lāḷas, Sītārām. 1962-79. *Rājasthānī sabad-kos.* 9 vols. Jodhpur: Caupāsanī Śikṣā Samiti

Suman, Ambāprasād. 1960-61. *Kṛṣak-jīvan sambandhī Braj-bhāṣā śabdāvalī.* 2 vols. Allāhābād: Hindustānī Academy.

Sundardās, Śyām, ed. 1965-75. *Hindī śabd-sāgar.* 2nd ed. 11 vols. Benares: Nāgarī Pracāriṇī Sabhā.

Tivārī, Bholānāth. 1988. *Hindī muhāvarā-koś.* 2nd ed. New Delhi: Hindī Book Centre.

Turner, R.L. 1973. *A Comparative Dictionary of the Indo-Aryan Languages.* London: Oxford University Press.

Idem. 1985. *A Comparative Dictionary of the Indo-Aryan Languages. Addenda and Corrigenda.* London: School of Oriental and African Studies.

2.2. General

Bryant, Kenneth. 1978. *Poems to the Child God: Structures and Strategies in the Poetry of Sūrdās.* Berkeley: University of California Press.

Burghart, Richard. 1978. 'The Founding of the Rāmānandī Sect.' *Ethnohistory* 25, pt. 2: 121-39.

Caturvedī, Parśurām. 1974 (VS 2021). *Uttarī Bhārat kī Sant-paramparā.* Bhārat Darpaṇ Granthmālā, 6. 2nd ed. Allahabad: Bhāratī Bhaṇḍār.

Dimock, Edward C., Jr. 1966. *The Place of the Hidden Moon: Erotic Mysticism in the Vaiṣṇava Sahajiyā Cult of Bengal.* Chicago: The University of Chicago Press.

Dube, Lālatāprasād. 1968. *Hindī bhakta-vārtā sāhitya.* Dehrā Dun: Sāhitya Sadan.

Entwistle, A.W. 1987. *Braj: Centre of Krishna Pilgrimage.* Groningen: Egbert Forsten.

Gadon, Elinor W. 1987. 'Note on the Frontispiece.' In *The Sants: Studies in a Devotional Tradition of India,* eds. Karine Schomer and W.H. McLeod, 415-21. Delhi: Motilal Banarsidass.

Gold, Daniel. 1987. *The Lord as Guru.* New York: Oxford University Press.

Hawley, John Stratton. 1982. 'A Vernacular Portrait: Rādhā in the *Sūr Sāgar.*' In *The Divine Consort. Rādhā and the Goddesses of India,* ed. J.S. Hawley and D.M. Wulff, 42-56. Berkeley: Graduate Theologian Union.

Idem. 1984. *Sūr Dās: Poet, Singer, Saint.* Seattle: University of Washington Press.

Idem. 1987. 'The Sant in Sūr Dās.' In *The Sants: Studies in a Devotional Tradition of India,* eds. Karine Schomer and W.H. McLeod, 191-211. Delhi: Motilal Banarsidass.

Lorenzen, David N. 1991. *Kabir Legends and Ananta-das's* Kabir Parachai. Albany: State University of New York Press.

McGregor, Ronald Stuart. 1984. *Hindī Literature from its Beginnings to the Nineteenth Century.* Wiesbaden: Harrassowitz.

Mītal, Prabhudayāl. 1968. *Braj ke dharma-sampradāyõ kā itihās.* Delhi: National Publishing House.

O'Connell, Joseph T. 1970. Social Implications of the Gauḍīya Vaiṣṇava Movement. Ph.D. diss., Harvard University, Cambridge.

Schomer, Karine. 1987. 'Introduction: The Sant Tradition in Perspective.' In *The Sants: Studies in a Devotional Tradition of India,* eds. Karine Schomer and W.H. McLeod, 1- 17. Delhi:

Motilal Banarsidass.

Śukla, Rāmcandra. 1958. *Hindī sāhitya kā itihās.* 12th ed. Benares: Nāgarī Pracāriṇī Sabhā.

Thiel-Horstmann, Monika. 1987. 'Baumwollbearbeitung und Weben als religiose Symbole in der Hindī-Bhakti.' *Studien zur Indologie und Iranistik* 13-14: 259-88.

Varmā, Dhirendra, *et al.*, eds. 1986. *Hindī sāhitya-koś.* 2nd ed. vol. 2. Benares: Jñānmaṇḍal.

Vaudeville, Charlotte. 1974. *Kabīr.* Oxford: Clarendon Press.

NOTES

* I owe many thanks to Prof. M. Horstmann, Prof. A. Entwistle, Dr. R. Snell, and Dr. W. Callewaert for sharing their insightful understanding of the subject matter, as well as their patient help with the translation of the poems quoted in this article.

1 His date of birth lies between AD 1488 and 1510. A *floruit* around the middle of the sixteenth century is affirmed by internal as well as external evidence.

2 See Mītal 1968, 374-76; Śukla 1958, 174; Varmā 1986, 585-86.

3 This manuscript is preserved by Ghanśyām and Lalit Prasād Gosvāmī, Mohanlālji kā Mandir, Jhansi (Manik Cauk). I would like to express my gratitude to the two brothers for kindly allowing me to photograph the *Vāṇī* in their possession.

4 The references are to the "serial number" — an assigned number based on uninterrupted numbering — rather than the actual "scribal number".

5 See *pad* 21 (f. 7-8, no. 21), 166 (f. 46 r., no. 112). In *pad* 112 (f. 51, no. 124), Pīpā is not mentioned, and in *pad* 243 (f. 87 r., no. 201), only Raidās and Pīpā are mentioned by name, the others by occupation.

6 Interestingly, Vyās himself is also quoted in these anthologies on several occasions.

7 However, until critical editions of their poetry are available, no definitive statements can be made.

8 The history of the 'lineage' of Rāmānand is problematic in itself. See Burghart 1978, 127-36.

9 In the different recensions and individual mss. of the *Paricaīs* ascribed to Anantdās, different *bhaktas* are described. For a description of some mss., see Lorenzen 1991, 83-90.

10 The line reads: *rūpa sanātana kau sevaka gaṃgala bhaṭṭa*

suḍhārau. One could also translate this as: "Gaṅgal Bhaṭṭ was the servant of Rūp and Sanātan", yet this does not make sense. The only person of the name Gaṅgal Bhaṭṭ remembered today is a Nimbārkīya *ācārya*, who lived in the twelfth century, according to the Nimbārkas. It has been argued that the person described here must have been a contemporary of Vyās (Mītal 1968, 191). However, there does not need to be any historical connection between Vyās and the poet he eulogizes, as with the example of the Sants. Interestingly, Gaṅgal is the only Nimbārkīya poet Vyās mentions. This is surprising, because Srībhaṭṭ and Harivyās Devācārya would have been much more likely candidates for quotation, as both wrote in Brajbhāṣā about Rādhā, just like Vyās.

11 Perhaps this is the *bhakta* Mehā Dhīmar, portrayed in the 154th story of the hagiography *Do sau bāvan vaiṣṇav kī vārtā* (Kṛṣṇadās 1986, 326-30) as a fisherman from Gopālpur near Rāval, and as a pupil of Viṭṭhalnāth.

12 Āsū, is most likely Āsūdhīr, who is claimed by different parties to be the guru or father of Haridās. Vyās's reference is ambiguous and does not settle the question.

13 The Jh.Ms. shows already a redaction of the *Vāṇī* in chapters. The *pads* numbered 5-22 (f. 2 v.-8 r) are grouped as "Sādhani kī astuti ke pad." Other examples are praise of, e.g., Śuk, the Sanakādis, Nārad, etc. (examples in 243 [f. 87 r., no. 201], 1.5; *pad* 76 [f. 97-98, no. 226], 1.3 and 5; *pad* 595 [f. 236-39, no. 278] 1.3-4). Most likely Vyās himself was not responsible for this organization of his work under different headings, since in different manuscripts *pads* are randomly classified under different headings.

14 See *pad* 243 (f. 87 r., no. 209). For the meaning of the weaver and the cotton carder in *bhakti* symbolics, see Thiel-Horstmann 1987.

15 There does not seem to be any blood relationship between Śrutidev and Sudāmā; the former was a devout brahmin from Mithila, visited by Kṛṣṇa and the sages (*Bhāgavatapurāṇa*, X 86), the latter probably Kṛṣṇa's poor *guru-bhāī* (*ibid.* X 80).

16 In the Jh. Ms the reference to Kabīr in this line is missing, but the text is metrically not correct: *sēna dhanā raidāsa bhayo jayadeva abhūta*, as opposed to *sena dhanā raidāsa bhayau jayadeva kabīra abhūta*

17 Pun on the name of the legendary Sanskrit author and the poet's signature or *chāpa*.

18 See E. Gadon's comments on the frontispiece of Schomer and McLeod (1987, 420). For remarks by Kabīr himself about his

son in the *Gurū-granth*, see Vaudeville (1974, 42).

19 E.g., Caturvedī (1974, 865 n. 1) quotes this song by Vyās as the earliest evidence for the affiliation of Kabīr to the Rāmānand Sampradāy.

20 A *bhakta* of that name, also alleged to be a pupil of Rāmānand in *Bhakta-māl* ch. 64-65 (Jhā 1978, 2: 24). Priyādās however does not comment on these *chappāīs*.

21 Presumably Vyās refers to the *saguṇi* poet of the *Aṣṭa-chāp* praised by him on other occasions, e.g., *pad* 26 (f. 9-10, no. 26), 1.7. The reference might also be to the Sant Parmānand of the *Gurū-granth* (McGregor 1984, 54). Caturvedī (1974) gives no contemporary *nirgūṇī bhakta* of that name. Another possibility is to read the second half-verse as: "Sūr (Dās) was the highest bliss."

22 Interestingly, this is the case in *chappāī* 36, which is on Rāmānand, but this information is not repeated in *chappāī* 60, which is about Kabīr proper.

23 Anantdās testifies himself that he is a Rāmānandī in the *Pīpā Paricaī*, chapter 35, verse 27-29. I am grateful to W.M. Callewaert for kindly allowing me to consult the *Paricaī* manuscript material on computer (edition forthcoming). See also Lorenzen 1991, 9-10.

24 In a previously quoted song (21) the word *sevak* is likewise problematic. On could interpret the line where it occurs as: "Gaṅgāl Bhaṭṭ is a *sevak* of Rūp and Sanātan Goswāmī". However, this would make no sense, as he was initiated into the Nimbark Sampradāya, not the Gauḍīya. Probably, the meaning of the word is more general and has no reference to a *guru-śiṣya* relationship.

25 They are mentioned together in the chapter "Siddhānt pad" (in the Jh.Ms.): *pads* 14 (f.5 v., no. 14), 13 (f. 5, no. 13), 19 (f. 7, no. 20), 21 (f. 7-8, no. 21), 23 (f. 8 v., no. 23), 26 (f. 9-10, no. 26), 43 (f. 16 r., no. 41), 256,(f. 28 r., no. 73), 160 (f. 2, no. 4 or f. 50-51, no. 123), and indirectly also in 258 (f. 34-35, no. 92). They are also mentioned together at the end of the *Rās-pañcādhyāyī*.

26 In *pad* 11 (f. 7 r., no. 19), Vyās says that Harivaṁś taught him the basis of his religion. The importance of Harivaṁś as teacher of Vyās is also apparent in *pads* 25 (f. 10 r., no. 27) and 14 (f. 5 v., no. 14), where Haridās is mentioned too. Vyās quotes Harivaṁś's theories in connection with the superiority of *bhakti* in comparison to the Purāṇas, as in *pad* 208 (f. 69-70, no. 163). He puts Harivaṁś and Jaydev on the same level because they are both *rasiks* emphasizing the predominance

of Rādhā, see *pad* 595 (f. 235-39, no. 278). In *pad* 24 he refers to Harivaṁś's *pads* and *sevā*, and in 12 (f. 4-5, no. 12) to that of Haridās. Most of these songs, and also *pad* 26 (f. 9-10, no. 26) are *virah pads*, where the death or Harivaṁś and Haridās is lamented.

27 Examples can be found in *pads* 43 (f.16 r., no. 41), 160 (f. 2, no. 4 or f. 50-51, no. 123) and in the *Rās-pañcadhyāyī* (30).

28 For the identification of *bhaktas* with *sakhīs*, see Entwistle (1987, 105)

29 *gāvata gopī mili nā̃cata haribaṃsī haridāsī jū.* A similar scene is described in *pad* 618 (f. 249-50, no. 294): *haribaṃsī haridāsī gāvati sughara pravīna rabāba bajāvati.* In *pad* 691 (f. 287-88, no. 395) Harivaṁś and Haridās are explicitly described as *samukh* or "facing" Rādhā and Kṛṣṇa: *haribaṃsī haridāsī sanamukha kāna lagai kachu bolata baina.*

30 For a comparable development of the goddess Rādhā from subject to object of devotion in the course of the compilation of *Sūr-sāgar*, see Hawley 1982 and 1984, 65-91.

31 Vāsudev Gosvāmī's edition (and one undated ms.) has this reading with *sevata*. However, the Jh.Ms. substitutes *sā̃tata*: "where Harivaṁśī and Haridāsī [are dwelling] eternally, there Vyās obtains a bower." However, the point to be made is also illustrated elsewhere, e.g., *pad* 43 (f. 15-16, no. 41) where Vyās prays them to call him soon to Vrindaban (where they dwell).

32 Another interesting example is in a *pad* about Nāmdev (17 [f. 6, no. 16] 1.8): *tākī mahimā vyāsa kaha kahai jākẽ subasa kanhāī*, "How can Vyās speak out about the glory of the one in whose power Kanhāī abides?"

33 Line 2 reads: *soī ghara gharanī soī suta guru hita jinakaī rasika naĩnani ke tārẽ.* See also *pad* 160 (f. 2, no. 4 or f. 50-51, no. 123) about Harivaṁś and Haridās quoted supra.

34 In *pad* 3 (f. 44, no. 108), while complaining about bad disciples, Vyās makes Muslim authorities the object of comparison: *jaisī rīti seṣa sophina kī aisī rīti calāvata*, "They start a way of behaviour like that of Shay<u>kh</u>s and Sufis".

35 *pīḍita ghara ghara bhaṭakata ḍolata paṃḍita muṃḍita kājī.* The term '*qāzī*' seems to refer to Muslim religious functionaries in general.

36 The 'five' may refer to the 5 *tattvas*, the 5 senses, the 5 deceits (*kām*, *krodh*, etc.), or even the 5 *devatās*.

37 Suman (1960), 1: 131 no. 252), defines *coḍ* as a buffalo that does not give milk properly or produce enough *ghī* in it.

38 Actually I have translated the reading of the Jh.Ms.: *māda*

instead of *sā̃ḍha*. Vāsudev Gosvāmī gives *mā̃ṭa* as one of the variants in his edition. For the meaning, see Suman 1960, 1: 111 no. 237.

39 Or: "did she make him take".

40 *Nirāṭa* is attested as meaning *ati sūkṣma* in Lālaṣ, II.2: 2148.

41 *bigāryau jyõ rainī kau mā̃ṭa*. See Suman 1960, 1: 66 no 194: *renī* refers to a sandy soil, it is a *deśi* word, although it might be connected with the hypothetical root **rayaṇa* (flowing), *cf.* Prakrit *reṇi*, 'mud' (Turner 1973, no. 10639). The idiom *māṭ bigaḍ-* means "change substance"(Tivārī 1988, 359).

42 The implication is that even Dharma's son himself, if lecherous, will come to a terrible end.

43 The word translated as 'money' *dāma*, usually means 'price', but can also have the meaning of 'coin' or 'rupee' (Gupta and Ṭaṇḍan 1974, 1: 840).

44 The best examples can be found in Vyās's *sākhīs*.

45 *sādhata bairāgī jaḍa baṃga*. The last word of the *ṭek*, *baṃga*, can mean 'Bengal', but also 'dull' (from *vaṅka*, see Turner 1985, no. 11101). It could perhaps stand for *bā̃g*, synonymous with 'stoned', though usually it is the word in the *ṭek* which determines the rhyme and not *vice versa*. The meaning of the whole line would be: "Stoned and dull-minded, *bairāgī*s perform their spiritual training." Another possibility is to read *baṃga* as synonym of *bhā̃ga* (see Sundardās 1970, 7: 3327). The translation of the whole line would be: "*Bairāgī*s perform spiritual training with roots and cannabis." The latter two options do not exclude an intended meaning 'Bengal' as a pun.

46 In the manuscripts there is some (scribal) confusion. The reading given here for the first two words of the line (*dhani dhani sādhu māni samtani taji hari kau chā̃ḍi uchaṃga*) is also the reading of the Jh.Ms. However, alternative readings, according to the Vāsudev Gosvāmī edition are: *dhana dhana* or *dhika dhika*. The confusion shows that later scribes, writing in a different situation, substituted the specific meaning for a more general one. The matter is further complicated because *dhani dhani* can also be translated as 'wealthy people', if one presumes a shortening of the last syllable of *dhanī* for the sake of the metre.

47 This would be one of the earliest 'orthodox' Vrindaban reactions and, in any case, shows a keen awareness of what was happening in Bengal at the time. As far as the Gauḍīya reactions are concerned, O'Connell (1970, 272 ff.) seems to conclude that the Sahajiyās adapted the Rādhā-Kṛṣṇa

symbolism only later, or that the Gauḍīya concern with them came later.

48 Bhagavat Mudit was actually initiated into the Caitanya Sampradāy, which is cited by the Rādhāvallabh Sampradāya spokesmen to stress the neutrality of the work. He is mentioned in *chappāī* 198 of Nābhādās's *Bhakta-māl*. According to Garga (1960, 898) however, this is an interpolation. Priyādās in his commentory (*kavitta* 626-29) and the Dādūpanthī authors Rāghavdās (in *chappāī* 737) and Caturdās (in 642-45) agree that he was a disciple of a *pūjārī* of the Govinddev temple, and as such a Caitanyite.

49 In RAM, Harivaṁś is praised at the beginning of every chapter in an introductory *dohā*. Only in the benedictory verse (*maṅgalācaraṇ*) and, significantly, in the introduction to the chapter about Vyās is Caitanya mentioned. This casts doubt on the authorship of Mudit. The oldest manuscript available to me, dated 1778 (VS 1835) and preserved in the VRI collection (no. 4389), was obviously written in Rādhāvallabh Sampradāy circles; the opening verses are: "*śrī rādhāvallabhojayati. śrī vyās nandano jayatī*". An older manuscript (VS 1799) is preserved in the Caitanya Pustakālay in Patna (reference from Dr. N.C. Bansal). For details about the claim about Vyās, see Gosvāmī 1952, 24-27; 54-57.

50 Interestingly, in the corpus of Vyās's *Vāṇī*, in as far as it is available to us now, no poem on Raṅkā-Baṅkā is found.

51 No edition of this work is extant. The chapter "Śrī Vyās jū kau prasaṅg" is found on f. 17-20 of the manuscript dated 1778 (VS 1835), preserved in the Vrindaban Research Institute (no. 4398).

52 Admittedly, this comparison is somewhat anachronistic, since the earliest material available for Vyās (Jh. Ms., dated VS 1794) is later than 'the early Sūr' (up till AD 1700).

53 The *pad* about his bad son (*pad* 284 in the Vāsudev Gosvāmī edition) quoted earlier, is strictly speaking not one of self-reproach.

Early Kṛṣṇa *Bhakti* in Gujarat: The Evidence of Old Gujarati Texts Recently Brought to Light

Francoise Mallison

Vallabhācārya (1478-1530) first visited Gujarat around the year 1500.[1] During his third and last visit in 1528, he installed the *svarūpa* (idol) of Jagadīśa-Raṇachoḍarāya in the first Vallabhan *havelī* in Gujarat at Beyt-Dwarka. His second son and successor Viṭṭhalanātha (1515-1564) consolidated his work by means of several successful visits that resulted in achieving numerous conversions, the details of which are told in the hagiographic tales contained in the *vārtā* of the 252 devotees.[2] The Vallabhan mission had conspicuous and rapid success among certain well defined social groups: the merchant castes and the wealthy farmers (Bhāṭiā, Luhāṇā, Baniā, Māravāḍī, Kaṇabī-Paṭela), who were generally followers of Devī and sometimes Jaina. They were attracted to the way of life which Vallabhācārya taught them, namely that of the householders who remain embedded in *saṃsāra* while devoting their lives and belongings entirely to Kṛṣṇa, yet still enjoying them. Their means enable them to finance the refined luxury of the *sevā;* they appreciate the notion of "*puṣṭi*" where Kṛṣṇa assuming the attributes of Devī, gratifies them with material goods. Besides, these castes occupy a high rank in a Gujarat where there are comparatively few Brahmins. The ascension of the Kaṇabī-Paṭela is often due to their 'vallabhization', with the prestige of its vegetarianism and stricter purity rules, which represents a certain form of brahmanization that offered an attractive pattern of life.

This proselytizing zeal decreased during the seventeenth century, but in spite of the misuse by certain *ācāryas* of the sacred character attached to their person, the number of *havelīs* increased. At the end of the eighteenth century the success was such that the puritan reform movement of the Svāmī-Nārāyaṇī imitated the sectarian organization and liturgy of the Vallabhans.

Viṭṭhalanātha, the second *ācārya*, introduced the worship of Svāminījī as a consort of Kṛṣṇa, and, in the sectarian literature, intentionally exalted the deeds of Kṛṣṇa as the lover of the Gopīs, in addition to those of the enchanting child, young herdsman and slayer of demons which had been the exclusive concern of Vallabha. This exercised an important influence, so it seems, on the Krishnaite Gujarati literature. Dayārāma (1777-1852), the most important poet of what is called *"premalakṣaṇabhakti"* undoubtedly belonged to this sect, but the enthusiasm fostered by this kind of *bhakti* in the mind of the poet Rāje Bhagat, a Molesalām Muslim, attests the extent of its success.

As far as his religious attitudes, his favourite forms of divine service or the tenets of his devotion are concerned, the Gujarati Vaiṣṇava behaves like a Vallabhan regardless of whether he belongs to the Puṣṭimārga or has been initiated by a Mahārāja. For instance, the *dhoḷa* sung during the public *bhajana* are usually accompanied by a visit to the nearest *havelī* by all of the female participants whether they belong to the Sampradāya or not. One may also cite the example of Divāna Raṇachoḍajī Amarajī (1768-1851), minister of the Bābī dynasty of Junagadh, who tried to install the cult of a new *liṅgam*, Buḍheśvara,[3] after he was refused the right to have *darśana* of Raṇachoḍarāya at the local temple of the caste of Nāgara brahmins, of which he was a member, because he had arrived a trifle late just before leaving for an important battle. He installed for this miniature *liṅgam* the same complicated and abundant *sevā* as was performed for the *mūrtis* of the child Kṛṣṇa in the *havelīs*. The small *liṅgam* is fed, clothed, put to sleep and entertained according to all the rules of devotional esthetics.

Was there any Kṛṣṇa bhakti *already existing in Gujarat before Vallabhācārya arrived there for his highly successful mission?*

The recent iconographic study by Haripriya Rangarajan *(Spread of Vaiṣṇavism in Gujarat upto 1600 A.D.)*,[4] testifies to the large number of Vaiṣṇava idols and Viṣṇu temples in old times. It would therefore be erroneous to assume, as in the case of the Braj country for instance, that the Kṛṣṇa cult directly superimposed itself on the cults of Śiva and the Devī, although this might have happened at certain famous places of Gujarat in the case of Raṇachoḍarāya at Dakor and of Sudāmā at Porbandar.[5] Indeed the cult of the *avatāra* of Viṣṇu had spread over Gujarat and preceded Krishnaite devotion, as it appears at Dwarka for instance.[6] The earliest stone images of Viṣṇu date back to the Kṣatrapa period (AD 78-AD 400),[7] but during the time of the Gupta rulers (AD 415-AD 470), who patronized a cult of Viṣṇu, the first mention of a Vaiṣṇava temple occurs in the third and last of the Girnar rock inscriptions (dated AD 457). In it Cakrapālita, the son of Parṇadatta, governor of Girnar during the reign of Skanda Gupta, erected the temple of Viṣṇu-Cakrabhṛta, apparently on the site of the actual Dāmodara temple at the foot of Mount Girnar, which would bear testimony to the transition of a cult of Viṣṇu to that of Kṛṣṇa.[8]

If only two temples, i.e. Kaḍvār (Kaḍavāra) on the Southern coast of Saurashtra, and Roḍā in North Gujarat, are known under the reign of the Maitrakas (470-788), their number increases in the heyday of the Hindu kingdom, under the Solaṃkī (Caulukya) dynasty (942-1304), who were themselves Śaiva and protectors of Jainism. It is striking that the majority of the Vaiṣṇava idols installed in the temples of the Solaṃkī are of the Trivikrama form, which is one of the twenty four possible combinations of the four attributes in the four hands of Viṣṇu, with the lotus in the lower right hand, the mace in the upper right hand, the disk in the upper left hand and the conch in the lower left hand.[9] The iconographic form called Trivikrama has no link with the *avatāra* Trivikrama-Vāmana[10] and may also be given other names such as Dāmodara, Śrīdhara and, most frequently Raṇachoḍa, which also designates Kṛṣṇa (like Dāmodara) and which seems to have legitimated the present Krishnaite cult of these idols. The passage from Vaiṣṇava cult to a Krishnaite one wherever it is likely to have occurred did not leave any dateable traces. Maybe, after becoming established, Krishnaite cults were instrumental in a renaissance and transformation of an older Vaiṣṇava ritual, such as the one of Dāmodara at Junagadh or of Raṇachoḍa at Dwarka, even at a comparatively late date. In that case one has to look for the sources of Gujarati Krishnaism elsewhere and turn to written witnesses.

According to Professor Bhayani, if the origins of the *bhakti* movement between the eighth century and the fifteenth century are still unclear, [11] there remains nevertheless an uninterrupted series of texts on the life of Kṛṣṇa. Well before the eleventh century, and preceding the compilation of the anthologies of Sanskrit *kāvya* quotations, such as the *Kṛṣṇakarṇāmṛta* and the *Bālagopālastuti* of Līlāśuka Bilvamaṅgala, Jaina texts in Prakrit and Apabhraṃśa relate the deeds of Kṛṣṇa.[12] The Prakrit texts include the *Setubandha* (fifth century) of Pravarasena (the killing of Ariṣṭa, the robbing of Pārijāta), and *Kutūhala's Līlāvaīkahā* (*ca* AD 800), the transmission of which is admittedly quite fragmentary.

Among the works in Apabhraṃśa, the *Riṭṭhaṇemicariya* of Svayambhū, composed, according to H.C. Bhayani,[13] during the last quarter of the ninth century, deals, in its cantos 4 to

8, with the life of Kṛṣṇa, the cousin of Neminātha, from his birth until the foundation of Dwarka. One of the sources of Svayambhū is the Sanskrit *Harivaṃśapurāṇa* (AD 748) of Jinasena, and Svayambhū himself provided inspiration to Puṣpadanta who, in cantos 85 to 89 of his Apabhraṃśa *Mahāpurāṇa*, tells the life of Kṛṣṇa[14] in AD 972.

It is interesting to note two points concerning the Jaina texts in Apabhraṃśa: first of all, the incorporation of probably folklore motives not encountered in the Sanskrit Hindu tradition, such as the piercing of the nose of the serpent Kāliya through which a rope is introduced so that Kṛṣṇa can swing him around. [15] In another recent article, H.C. Bhayani[16] insists on the fact that the features found in texts belonging to folklore and identical with (or similar to) those found in Apabhraṃśa texts do not prove that folk literature was inspired by learned texts, but rather that the latter borrowed from pre-existing folklore.[17] This is confirmed, according to H.C. Bhayani, by compositions from Someśvara, in the sixteenth chapter of the fourth *viṃśati* (that is the seventysixth chapter of the whole) of the *Mānasollāsa*. There Someśvara gives samples of metric poems in regional post-Apabhraṃśa languages, all dealing more or less with the deeds of Kṛṣṇa, which tends to prove that he had available to him Krishnaite poems written in the vernaculars as early as the beginning of the twelfth century.[18]

The second remark concerns the Jaina literature : Kṛṣṇa is presented as a royal hero and not as a divine incarnation. This might have been connected with a type of *bhakti* devoted not to the *gopā* and to the divine lover but to the heroic Kṛṣṇa, a type of *bhakti* which is said to have been particular to Rajasthan, and even to Gujarat, according to R.A. Williams.[19] It is equally quite present in Maharashtra where Viṭṭhala appears mainly as the spouse of Rukmiṇī and the lord of the Yādavas. In his recent work, *Gadyarāja*, Ian Raeside stresses the noticeable lack of interest in Maharashtrian *bhakti*, for the exploits of Gopāla as a lover as well as for love symbolism as an element of *bhakti*.[20]

However, H.C. Bhayani worked equally on the earliest mentions of Rādhā and her companions contained in the Prakrit, Apabhraṃśa, and even Jaina literatures.[21] Considering that poets habitually quote each other, especially when dealing with the art of metrics, one comes to know about works dealing, partly or entirely, with the life of Kṛṣṇa, exclusively by means of quotations. Thus the poet Govinda (*ca* AD 800) is quoted in the *Svayambhūchanda*, as the author of a long poem in Apabhraṃśa on the life of Kṛṣṇa. Rādhā and the Gopīs are also quoted. Many references may also be found in the Prakrit anthologies (Hāla's *Saptaśataka*, second-fifth century; *Vajjālaggaṃ*, *ca* tenth century; Jineśvara Sūri's *Gāhārayaṇakosa*, *ca.* 1195 and quoting anterior texts). It therefore seems that Kṛṣṇa, the lover of the Gopīs, had not remained unknown.[22]

The early diffusion in Gujarat of the anthologies of Bilvamaṅgala and of the *Gītagovinda* (twelfth century) in fact points to a predilection for this aspect of the divine hero. As early as in 1291 an inscription (found in 1904 near Pāṭāṇa in the village of Anāvāḍā, the ancient Solaṃkī capital in North Gujarat) quotes the last line of the first canto of the *Gītagovinda* in praise of the ten *avatāra* of Viṣṇu,[23] and the oldest illustrated manuscript of the *Gītagovinda* is probably of Gujarati origin, according M.R. Majmudar[24] (first half of the fifteenth century). Also a series of illustrated manuscripts of the *Bālagopālastuti* was copied in Gujarat from 1425 onwards, according to the study of E. Gadon,[25] which proves the renown of this text. In another article ("Saint Viṣṇu Purī and his *Bhakti-ratnāvalī*"),[26] M.R. Majmudar underlines the fact that the important texts of Krishnaite *bhakti* owe their diffusion to the pilgrimages where people met, at Dwarka, for instance, saints and *bhaktas* from all parts of India.

Thus, from the fifteenth century onwards, the Gujarati authors had at their disposal not only the classical Sanskrit sources such as the *Harivaṃśa*, the *Viṣṇupurāṇa*, the *Bhāgavatapurāṇa* (mainly its *Daśamaskandha*), but also the

Jaina Prakrit and Apabhraṃśa tradition and the medieval Sanskrit texts of Jayadeva, Bilvamaṅgala or Bopadeva. On the basis of these texts certain poets, predecessors or contemporaries of the first Gujarati *bhaktakavi*, Narasimha Mahetā, wrote on the deeds of Kṛṣṇa in Old Gujarati, using quotations drawn from the *Kṛṣṇakarṇāmṛta* or from the *Viṣṇupurāṇa*, for instance. Some of these authors have been brought to light thanks to the recent editions by Professor Bhayani.[27] Others who are known for their adaptations of the *Bhāgavatapurāṇa* or of its *Daśamaskandha*, like Bhīma, Keśavadāsa or Bhālaṇa, are worthy of re-examination in the light of these editions.

The *Kṛṣṇakrīḍita* of Rāül Kānha, written in 108 verses in the syllabic *Śārdūlavikrīḍita* metre, dates from the fifteenth century. The first 34 verses describe the separation and reunion of Kṛṣṇa and Candrāvali, of Kṛṣṇa and Rādhā and finally of all the three. The *rāsa* dance occupies verses 35 to 71, including the episode of the *vastraharaṇa;* three verses extol Yaśodā's maternal love (72-75); the rest of the poem is in praise of Kṛṣṇa and his *bhakti*, the last eight verses being in Sanskrit. The style echoes the *Gītagovinda*.

The *Kṛṣṇakrīḍita*, first published by H.C. Bhayani[28] in 1988 on the basis of three manuscripts kept at the L.D. Institute of Indology and at the Gujarāta Vidyāsabhā (Ahmedabad), is followed in his book *Rāsalīlā* by the reedition of an anonymous *phāgu*, the sixteenth-century *Harivilāsa*, the only manuscript of which is kept at the Bhāratīya Vidyā Bhavana (Bombay).[29] The first 31 verses of the *Harivilāsa* deal with the deeds of the child Kṛṣṇa and his victories over demons haunting the forest of Braj (Pūtanā, Keśī, Pralamba, Vṛṣāsura etc.). The taming of the serpent Kāliya, the uplifting of Mount Govardhana as well as the cosmic vision offered to Yaśodā, are also mentioned. Verses 24 to 31 describe the *dāṇalīlā*, and verses 32 to 132 describes the *rāsalīlā*, the beauty of autumn, of Kṛṣṇa, his flute, of the Gopīs, their pain at being separated from Kṛṣṇa, their reunion with him and the season of spring, the *bhramaragīta* episode, the *rāsa* dance, the beauty of the Gopīs. It seems that the text is incomplete, but it must be mentioned as a specimen of non-Jaina *phāgu*. Surprisingly, the *Harivilāsa* is based on a passage taken from *Viṣṇupurāṇa* (book V, *adhyāya* 3-16), of which twenty *śloka* are quoted in the text, as well as a *śloka* from the *Kṛṣṇakarṇāmṛta* and another from the *Bālagopālastuti*,[30] the influence of which on this work is noticeable, according to H.C. Bhayani.

The collection intitled *Harivilāsa* contains two more unpublished works by Vāsaṇadāsa: the *Rāghavarāsa* and the *Haricuākharā*, written probably between 1500 and 1550.[31] The manuscript is at the Gujarat Vidyā Sabhā at Ahmedabad. 25 of the 135 *śloka* of the *Rāghavarāsa* are missing, the remaining 110 describe the complaints of the Gopīs, their dialogues, the passion of Rādhā, the dance of Kṛṣṇa, and the *līlā* of his childhood, whereas the 103 verses of the *Haricuākharā* treat of the spring amusements during Holī of Kṛṣṇa and the Gopīs on the bank of the Yamunā.

In addition to these four texts edited or re-edited by him, H.C. Bhayani republishes two more texts, one prepared by M.R. Majmudar, the *Amratakacolāṃ* or *Rādhākrasṇakrīḍāgīta* of Rāma,[32] and above all the *Rāsakrīḍāvarṇana* taken from the *Kṛṣṇakrīḍā* of Keśavadāsa who had composed, in 1536, an adaptation in fourty *sarga* of the *Daśamaskandha* of the *Bhāgavatapurāṇa* of which the *Rāsakrīḍāvarṇana* is the thirteenth *sarga*. Indeed, this passage (the edition is by A. Jani)[33] is the only one of this work not written in quantitative metre *(mātrā-vṛtta)* but in the syllabic metre familiar to the Sanksrit classics, i.e. in *śārdūlavikrīḍita*, the very metre used by Rāül Kānha in the *Kṛṣṇakrīḍita* from which Keśavadāsa takes his inspiration. A similar spirit of stylistic research seems to engross the minds of both these authors, who both belonged to the same literary family. Indeed the Bhīma, Keśavadāsa and Bhālaṇa quoted above are well known for their adaptations in the vernacular of the *Bhāgavatapurāṇa*, especially of its *Daśamaskandha*, which constitute the main vehicles of the spread of the Kṛṣṇa cult before or parallel to the sectarian proselytizing.[34] They were learned authors, as were other authors brought to light by Bhayani. In addition to his ability to use *śārdūlavikrīḍita*, Keśavadāsa gives three quotations from the *Kṛṣṇakarṇāmṛta*. Bhīma adapted for the vernacular the entire *Bhāgavatapurāṇa* in sixteen parts or *kalā*. The *Harilīlāṣoḍaśakalā* is modelled on the Sanskrit *Harilīlāviveka* of Bopadeva (178 *śloka*, thirteenth century), which he quotes. His work is dated from 1485 and includes Sanskrit *śloka* composed by the author himself.

Bhālaṇa, who again adapts the *Daśamaskandha*, but in *pada* form, in the first half of the sixteenth century, using a more recent form of the language (i.e., the form in which the text has come down to us, which seems more recent than Bhīma's or Keśavadāsa's) had not come under the influence of Vallabhism. Thus Śrīdhara's commentary on the *Bhāgavatapurāṇa*, tinged with *advaita*, was chosen by Bhālaṇa as well as by Keśavadāsa or Narasiṃha Mahetā, and not the *Subodhinī* of Vallabhācārya.

By publishing these texts, H.C. Bhayani intended to draw attention to the existence at the end of the fifteenth and in the first half of the sixteenth century of a devotion to Kṛṣṇa of a learned and refined character. Rāül Kānha and the author of the *Harivilāsa*, like Bhīma, Keśavadāsa, Bhālaṇa or Narasiṃha Maheṭā, are scholars and connoisseurs of Sanskrit, able to compose in sophisticated metres. They borrow from Jayadeva and Bilvamaṅgala as freely as from the *purāṇas*. Maybe this learned Krishnaite culture owes something to the scholarly atmosphere of Jainism, in which case there is reason to suspect that these authors were not devoted specifically to Kṛṣṇa, but simply chose to use his deeds as a literary pretext. However the last verses of Rāül Kānha's *Kṛṣṇakrīḍita* overflow with fervour to an extent that makes it impossible to question his sincerity. Neither Bhīma nor Bhālaṇa affirm any exclusive choice concerning the divine person of Kṛṣṇa, yet when they write about him, they always do it in terms of devotion.

If the Krishnaite culture of Gujarat reached such a level as early as the fifteenth century, it becomes useless to question the dates and the sources commonly given for the poems of Narasiṃha Mahetā. In view of the abundance of his *śṛṅgāra* poems, some critics were in favour of considering him to be under the influence of the Braja type of Krishnaism. However internal evidence alone would have been enough to invalidate this claim. Although some beautiful poems of *śṛṅgāra* inspiration carry his mark,[35] the majority of the poems attributed to him are poor forgeries bearing his name only. But this counter-argument does not justify the opposite conclusion, namely to envisage Narasiṃha Mahetā under the exclusive influence of Maharashtrian Santism and of the *Bhāgavatapurāṇa*. Narasiṃha wrote some beautiful *padas* on the love of the Gopīs and Kṛṣṇa, and in doing so, was simply following an already well established tradition in Gujarat.

The question raised at the beginning: *'Was there any Kṛṣṇa* bhakti *already existing in Gujarat before Vallabhācārya arrived there for his highly successful mission, and isn't his success due to the fact that he had to offer something new to the Vaiṣṇavas?'* must be put in a completely new manner. When Vallabhācārya arrived, the country was already imbued with a refined Krishnaite culture. His task was, not to convince, but to evaluate competently the esthetic demands and the propensities for supporting the splendour of the *sevā*. In this he succeeded fully. Moreover, one often attributes the origins of the innovations concerning Kṛṣṇa's consort and the concept of *premalakṣaṇabhakti*, brought into the Puṣṭimārga by Viṭṭhala to his contacts with Puri and Caitanya. But Viṭṭhalanātha visited Gujarat several times as it had become the main stronghold of the Vallabha Sampradāya; and the Kṛṣṇa bhakti he found there is likely to have inspired his innovations. Vallabha and Viṭṭhala did not simply win Gujarat over to their faith; it would be more correct to say that the Kṛṣṇa *bhakti* of Gujarat absorbed and inspired it.

NOTES

1. Parekh, Manilal C., *Sri Vallabhacharya: Life, Teachings, and Movement*, Rajkot: Sri Bhagavata Dharma Mission, 1943, pp. 76-77.
2. Sharma, N., ed., *Dosau bāvana vaiṣṇavana kī vārtā*, Mathura: Śrī Govardhana granthamālā karyālaya, VS 2022 (1965). Harirāya (1590-1715), nephew of Gokulanātha (1552-1641), fourth son of Viṭṭhalanātha, is said to have written down the stories of the 252 Saints handed down to him by his uncle who had heard them from his father. Several influent personalities who were instrumental in spreading the Vallabhan message in Gujarat appear in the 252 *vārtā*, such as Nāgajī Bhaṭṭa of Godhra (n°1) or Bhāīlā Kothārī (n°10), Gopāḷadāsa, son-in-law of Bhāīlā and author of the Gujarati *Vallabhākhyāna* (n° 11) or Jīvā Parekha of Cambay (n°136) etc...
3. *cf.* Desai, Shambhuprasad H., *Itihāsa darśana*, Junagadh: Prabhāsa Prakāśana, 1979, vol. 1, p. 94.
4. Rangarajan, Haripriya, *Spread of Vaiṣṇavism in Gujarat up to 1600 A.D. (A Study with Special Reference to the Iconic Forms of Viṣṇu)*, Bombay: Somaiya Publications, 1990.
5. *cf.* Mallison, Françoise, "Lorsque Raṇachoḍarāya quitte Dwarka pour Dakor ou comment Dvārakānātha prit la succession de Ḍaṅkanātha", in Eck, Diana L., and Françoise Mallison, eds., *Devotion Divine: Bhakti Traditions from the Regions of India*, Groningen: Egbert Forsten and Paris: École Française d' Extrême-Orient, 1991, pp. 197-208, and "The Cult of Sudāmā in Porbandar-Sudāmāpurī", *Journal of the Oriental Institute*, 29 (Baroda, 1980), pp. 216-223.
6. *cf.* Mallison, Françoise, "Development of Early Krishnaism in Gujarat: Viṣṇu-Raṇchoḍ-Kṛṣṇa", in Thiel-Horstmann, Monika, ed., *Bhakti in Current Research, 1979-1982*, Berlin: Dietrich Reimer Verlag, 1983, pp. 245-255, specially pp. 247-8.
7. Rangarajan, *op. cit.* n. 4, p. 3; Shah, Umakant P., *Sculptures from Śāmalājī and Roḍā (North Gujarat) in the Baroda Museum*, Baroda: Museum and Picture Gallery. Repr. from the *Bulletin of the Baroda Museum and Picture Gallery*, n.d. [1960], pp. 73ff.; Majmudar, Manjulal R., "Studies in Varieties of Viṣṇu Images from Gujarāt", *Journal of the Gujarati Research Society*, 1-4 (1939-Dr. Bhagwanlal Indraji Commemoration Volume), pp. 39-60; Dave, Kanaiyalal Bh., *Gujarātanuṃ mūrtividhāna*, Ahmedabad: Gujarāta Vidyāsabhā, 1963, p.

169-242; Shastri, Durgaram K., *Vaiṣṇava dharmano saṃkṣipta itihāsa*, Bombay: Forbes Gujarātī Sabhā, 1939, pp. 348-363.

8. It is interesting to note that old Gujarati Jaina *rāsa* mention the Dāmodara temple, such as the *Revantagirirāsu* (*ca.* AD 1232), or the *Pethaḍarāsa* (*ca.* AD 1302); *Cf.* Bhayani, Harivallabh C., "Kṛṣṇabhakti ane Kṛṣṇacaritra, eka kālānukramika sūci", in *Kāvyaprapaṃca*, Bombay: S.N.D.T. Women's University, 1989, p. 55, and in *Rāsalīlā*, Ahmedabad: Raṃgadvāra Prakāśana, 1988, p. 12.
9. *Cf.* Mallison, F., *op. cit.* n. 6, p. 246 ff.
10. With a few exceptions, see *ibidem*, p. 247.
11. Bhayani, H.C., "Pandaramī-soḷāmī śatābdīnā gujarātanī Kṛṣṇabhakti mūḷastrota", in *Kṛṣṇa-Kāvya*, Ahmedabad: Raṃgadvāra Prakāśana, 1986, pp. 32-41.
12. Bhayani, H.C., "The Childhood Exploits of Kṛṣṇa According to Pre-eleventh Century Prakrit and Apabhraṃśa Texts", in *Indological Studies: Literary and Performing Art, Prakrit and Apabhraṃśa Studies*, Ahmedabad: Parshva Prakashan, 1993, pp. 209-222 (first published in *Sambodhi*, 11 (1982-83), pp. 121-132, and in Parimoo, Ratan, ed., *Vaiṣṇavism in Indian Art and Culture*, 1986, pp. 58-64); "Apabhraṃśa sāhityamāṃ Kṛṣṇakāvya", in *Anusandhana (saṃśodhanātmaka lekhono saṃgraha)*, Ahmedabad: Sarasvatī Pustaka Bhaṇḍāra, 1972, pp. 100-137 (Hindi translation in Mishra, B., ed., *Bhāratīya Bhāṣāonmeṃ Kṛṣṇakāvya*, 1979, part I, pp. 139-151, and in *Sambodhi*, 10 (1981-82), pp. 46-71; repr. in *Kṛṣṇa-kāvya, op. cit.* n. 11, pp. 1-27).
13. Bhayani, H.C. "The Childhood Exploits of Kṛṣṇa ...", *op. cit.* n. 12, p. 211. A first edition of Svayambhū's *Riṭṭhanemicarya* known also as *Harivaṃśapurāṇa* is under way by R. Tomar, with the Prakrit Text Society. Another, of the first *kāṇḍa*, appeared in 1985, prepared by Devendrakumar Jain, with a Hindi translation, published by the Bharatiya Jñānapītha.
14. Among the numerous Apabhraṃśa authors on the life of Kṛṣṇa, after Puṣpadanta, two are important : Haribhadra (*Nemināhacariu*, 1160) and Dhavala (*Harivaṃśapurāna*, 12th century), See Bhayani, H.C., *op. cit.* n. 8, and "Apabhraṃśa sāhityamām ...", *op. cit.* n. 12. For a discussion of the Kṛṣṇa story in the Jaina tradition, see Alsdorf, L., *Harivaṃśapurāna*, Hamburg, 1936, pp. 52 ff.
15. The *Kāliyadamana* episode was very often rendered in Old and Medieval Gujarati, the story ending either with the piercing of the nose of the *nāga* or with Kṛṣṇa dancing on his

hoods. For the early treatment of this theme, see Bhayani, H.C." 'Jaḷakamaḷa' prabhātiyānī prācīnatā ane kartṛtva" in *Kṛṣṇakāvya, op. cit.* n. 11, pp. 84-93.

16. *Cf.* Bhayani, H.C., "Ananya Rādhā-anuragānā saṃketa", in *Parab*, 38-1 (1990, Ahmedabad), pp. 28 ff.

17. The story of Sudāmā, the poor Brahmin friend of Kṛṣṇa, seems to have evolved along the same pattern: profusely attested in the vernacular, especially Gujarati, literature it is treated in a rather sober style at the end of the tenth book of the *Bhāgavatapurāṇa* (chapters 80-81). See Mallison, Françoise, "Saint Sudāmā of Gujarāt: Should the Holy be Wealthy?", *Journal of the Oriental Institute*, 29 (Baroda, 1979), pp. 90-99.

18. *Cf.* Bhayani, H.C., "The Prakrit and Deśa-bhāṣā Passages in Someśvara Mānasollāsa", in *Indological Studies ..., op. cit.* n. 12, pp. 297-309.

19. *Cf.* Williams, R.A., "Research in Rājasthānī Literature", in Callewaert, Winand M., ed., *Early Hindi Devotional Literature in Current Research*, Leuven: Department Oriëntalistiek Katholieke Universiteit Leuven, 1980, pp. 203 ff., on the Jaina influence on Kṛṣṇa *bhakti* and on the *bhakti* for the heroic form of Kṛṣṇa in Rajasthan. It is not unlikely that the Vallabhan *bhakti* mode of worship was structured and inspired by the feudal model of Rajput princes of Rajasthan where several *svarūpa* took refuge (letter of Prof. H.C. Bhayani, 25th January 1992). On the aristocratic romantic 'pastoralization' of the Kṛṣṇa *bhakti*, see also Entwistle, Alan W., "The Cult of Krishna as a Version of Pastoral", in Eck, Diana L., *op. cit.* n. 5, pp. 73-90.

20. Raeside, Ian, *Gadyarāja: A fourtheenth century Marathi version of the Kṛṣṇa Legend*, Bombay: Popular Prakashan, and London: School of Oriental and African Studies, University of London, 1989, pp. XVII-XIX.

21. Bhayani, H.C., "Pālī, Dhanyā and Cārukeśī: Three of the Earliest Mentioned Kṛṣṇa's Sweethearts", in *Indological Studies ..., op. cit.* n. 12, pp. 223-229.

22. *Cf.* Bhayani, H.C., "The Childhood Exploits of Kṛṣṇa ...", *op.cit.* n.12, pp. 211-214.

23. It should be noted that a multilingual reference in praise of the ten *avatāras* of Viṣṇu, dated as early as 1113, was found in South India. *Cf.* Mallison, Françoise, *Au point du jour: les* Prabhātiyāṃ *de Narasiṃha Mahetā*, Paris: École Française d'Extrême-Orient, 1986, p. 25 n. 68.

24. Majmudar, Manjulal R., "A 15th Century Gītagovinda Manu-

script with Gujarati Paintings", in *Journal of the University of Bombay*, 7 (1938), pp. 123-137.

25. *Idem*, "Illustrated Manuscripts of Bilvamaṃgala's Bāla-Gopāla Stuti", *ibidem*, 16 (1947-1948), pp. 33-61, and Gadon, Elinor W., *The* Bālgopālstuti *Manuscripts and Early Kṛṣṇabhakti in Gujarat*, Ph. D. Thesis submitted to the University of Chicago, III. (Faculty of the Division of the Humanities, Department of Philosophy) in September 1983.
26. *Journal of the University of Bombay*, 8 (1939), p. 145.
27. This study could not take into account the recent edition of Prof. H.C. Bhayani (together with Niranjan Vora): *Kīku Vasahīkṛta Kṛṣṇa-bālacaritra* (Bombay: Forbes Gujarātī Sabhā) released in 1993.
28. "Rāül Kānhakṛta Kṛṣṇakrīḍita", ed. H.C. Bhayani in *Rāsalīlā: Kṛṣṇanī praṇayalīla ane anya bālacaritra viṣayaka 15mā-16mā śatakanāṃ virala kāvya*, Ahmedabad: Raṃgadvara Prakāśana, 1988, pp. (19)- (23) and 1-40.
29. The first edition by H.C. Bhayani is: "Harivilāsa-eka madhyakālīna jainetara phāga-kāvya", in *Svadhyāya*, 2-3 (VS 2021, Baroda), pp. 286-304, the second is in *Rāsalīlā ...., op. cit. supra*, pp. 41-69.
30. For the identification of the quotations, see H.C. Bhayani, Introduction to the second edition of the *Harivilāsa* in *Rāsalīlā, op. cit.* n. 28, p. 41, and notes 1, 2, 3. This introduction is reprinted in *kāvyaprapaṃca, op. cit.* n. 8, pp. 69-75.
31. In Bhayani, H.C., *Rāsalīlā, op. cit.* n. 28, the *Rāghavarāsa* is edited pp. 81-119, and the *Haricuākharā* pp. 113-122. On Vāsaṇadāsa, see Bhayani, "Kṛṣṇakavi Vāsaṇadāsa", in *Kāvyaprapaṃca, op. cit.* n. 8, pp. 76 ff.
32. In Bhayani, H.C., *Rāsalīlā, op. cit.* n. 28, pp. 123-128.
33. Jani, Ambalal B., ed., *Kāyasthakavi Keśavarāmakṛta Śrīkṛṣṇa-līlākāvya athwā Daśama-nirodha-līlā*, Bombay: Forbes Gujarātī Sabhā, 1933, pp. 93-103, repr. in Bhayani, H.C., *Rāsalīlā, op. cit.* n. 28, pp. 71-80.
34. For an evaluation of the literary merit of these three authors, see Shastri, Keshavram K., "Prabhāsa Pāṭaṇa, Also a Holy Home of Gujarati Poetry", *Journal of the Oriental Institute*, 38 (Baroda, 1988), pp. 117-121.
35. For instance the *pada* "Prāta havo prāṇapati, indu gayo āthamī" (Desai, Iccharām S., ed., *bṛhat Kāvyadohana*, vol. 2, Bombay: Gujarati Printing Press, 2nd ed. 1903, p. 28, *pada n°* 31).

The Nayanā-Yogin Songs in the Devotional Literature of Mithilā

Catherine Champion

In the Bhojpurī and Maithilī speaking areas, most of the local cults seem to have been preserved in their original form, while a few of the religious and literary traditions bear the stamp of the Sufi trends introduced by the prevalent Islamic orders of the medieval period. The aim of this paper is to initiate a discussion on the following question : what are, in the matter of Hindu devotion, the limits of the influence of medieval islamization? In other words, are there fields which the Sufi trends were not liable to pervade? To illustrate this point, we shall endeavour to bring out the role played by the Nayanā-yogin songs in Maithilī devotional literature. These songs are linked with two different rituals: the Gaṇināth cult and the wedding celebration.[1]

In Mithilā (or Tirhut) the Gaṇināth (also spelt Ganināth or Ganīnāth) cult is mostly popular among the commercial class, the Vaiśyas, especially among those who are concerned with confectionery, called "Halwāī". More precisely, the local sub-castes (or bāni) of the Halwāis are the Kanaujiyās (Kānyakubj or Kandu: who take their origin from Kanauj) and the Madheśiyās (residents of the middle land, Madhya deśa) (Crooke 1974: 482). These terms, which connote their geographic origin, also indicate that they do not belong to the higher rank of their caste. Most of the

Halwāī devotees of Gaṇināth live in Bihar and Uttar Pradesh, in the Nepali Terai and in the Darjeeling region. Two important temples of Gaṇināth are located in Patna, one in Rajendra Nagar and the other at Mahendra Ghat. But the *mūlasthān* is at Palvaiya, near Mahnar, in the Vaishali District, where the fieldwork was conducted. Gaṇināth is the *kuldevtā (gosāunī)* of the Bihari Vaiśyas. According to the devotees, his cult has been established in the medieval period, as a reaction to the Muslim invasion. As the iconography suggests, the similarity of Gaṇināth with Gorakhnāth is obvious. The Siddha is represented in the posture of *abhayamudrā*. He wears the bun of ascetics and carries the *kamaṇḍalu* (alms-bowl) and *cimṭā* (sacred tongs). His ears are pierced with ear-rings as those of the *Kānphaṭa* Yogīs.

Two different versions co-exist in the hagiography of this great Siddha. In the first one, he was a *puruṣāvatār*, sent to earth by Śiva to preach among the people and to show them the right way of living and being saved in this perverted Kali age. When he asked Śiva under what form should he be sent, the god answered: "under the shape of the first man you will meet". The first one he met was a Madheśiyā Vaiśya. He appeared in his present form at Palvaiya, where he became a learned man, well versed in the Vedas, Upaniṣads and Vedānta, and a master of Yoga. In the second version, Gaṇināth was a Tirhuti brahman who had accepted to be married to a lower caste Vaiśya wife, Khemāsatī. His wife gave him three sons. Today, as a token of gratefulness, the Madheśiyā Halwāīs of Bihar still worship him. For the rest of the legend, the two versions concord. Gaṇināth became a saint of great renown, who saved many poor and downtrodden people. Though Gaṇināth himself was married, his disciple, Govind, was a strict celibate.

The Gaṇināth devotees claim to be connected with the Nāth cult. Judging from the religious literature of Mithilā, the Nāth cult is indeed widespread in the area. The links with the Bengali shrines in the East, and the Gorakhpur and

Chunar shrines in the West are attested by many different sources. On their way between India and Nepal, the wandering Nāth ascetics stop at the Śiva Nepali Temple of Hajipur, very near Palvaiya. The Gorakhnāth cycle of legends is represented by the Maithilī versions of the Gopīcand story (*Gopīcand kathā*) and the Sorṭhī story (under the name of *Brajabhanakāgītā).* The *Gorakṣavijaya* composed by Vidyāpati in Sanskrit and Maithilī in the 15th century is another important indication. We can also mention the drama *Bhartṛharinivedam* written by Harihara Upādhyāya as a didactic glorification of the Haṭha-yoga system of Gorakhnāth. Besides Gaṇināth, Niranjan Nāth, Triloki Nāth and Sokhā Śambhunāth are considered as important figures of the Nāthpanth of North Bihar. In spite of his local popularity, Gaṇināth is not mentioned in the lists of the numerous Siddhas of the Nāth branches whose names appeared between the 8th and 12th century, not can he be mistaken for Gahinināth (also spelt Gaininīth) who played a role in the Maharashtrian branch. He was designated by Dñyāndev as the guru of his brother Nivṛtti and he came in third position in the Yoga Sampradāya Viskṛti, after Matsyendra and Jālandhara. His mission was very similar to that of the Bihari Gaṇināth: seeing the ferocity of this Kali age, he gave to Nivṛtti the task of protecting the universe by transmitting to him the teaching of the Ādiguru Śaṅkara (Briggs 1982: 242 and Vaudeville 1969: 9). In a popular booklet entitled *Gorakhnāth carita* one of the miraculous deeds *(camatkār)* of Gorakhnāth is to transform a clay toy made by children into a Siddha named Gahinināth.

What is of greater interest is the reference available in W. Crooke's work on the tribes and castes of Northern India, where he mentions the presence of the "Guninīth" cult in Uttar Pradesh among the Vaiśyas of Ballia. Their subcastes are also Madheśiyā and Kanaujiyā (Kandu): "The Kandus of Ballia regard themselves as the descendants of a saint named Gunīnāth, and all fines for breaches of caste discipline are realised in his name. These Vaiśyas are also known as Gunināthi". (Crooke 1974: 132). Radhakrishna Chaudhary refers to a certain Gaṇanāth who is believed to have written on Tantric philosophy at the time of Vidyāpati (1976a: 315). Besides the question of the identification of Gaṇināth, there are also many differences between the personality and cult of this Siddha and Nāth tradition of Northern India. As an ascetic, Gaṇināth is not such a strict celibate as the Nāths of the Gorakhpur monastery. He is a *gṛhastha.* The form of Yoga he preaches is not Haṭha-yoga, as practised by the Nāths, but Karma-yoga (union through disinterested service).[2] The eight Vaiśya *pujāris* of the temple are householders and do not have the same way of life as the Nāth ascetics. In return, as their devotional literature testifies, they developed, through a combined worship of Gaṇināth and Nayanā, a local form of Tantric Nāth cult, quite specific to Mithilā.

The songs devoted to Gaṇināth were composed in the *bajjikā* (or *vajjikā*) language of Mithilā. The word *bajjikā,* which derives from the Bajji dynasty ruling in the area of Vaishali, refers to the North-Western dialect of Mithilā. Apart from the miraculous birth of the saint, the main topic of these songs deal with his struggle against his enemy and rival, the powerful Yoginī Nayanā (also spelt Nainā). As a magician, she uses her tricks to wean him and his disciple from following their path. She tried to prevent Gaṇināth from getting married by changing herself into an alluring courtesan. During an episode of their fight, Govind managed to bind her to a tree with a rope.[3] When each of her attempts failed, the Yoginī admitted she was overpowered by Gaṇināth, and became the devotee of the Siddha. The songs are sung, inside the temple, by a group of four women, under the name of *gosāunī kā gīt,* on two occasions: at the regular *pūjā* once a week, and during the annual festival which takes place every Saturday following Kṛṣṇāṣṭamī, in the month of Bhādra (August-September), which lasts three days. People also come from Northern India and Nepal in the hope of having their prayers answered. For this purpose, they hang crowns of dry leaves and flowers in the temple. Gaṇināth is supposed to accept only white flowers. On their arrival at the sanctuary, the devotees worship the nine mounds of clay which symbolise the *samādhis* of the Siddha, his disciples and the members of his family. In the first of the *gosāunī kā gīt*, the boons granted by the Siddha, are enumerated:

> O powerful and beloved *jogī*
> You look so beautiful, with your necklace and earrings
> Who wants money and gold? Who wants a son?
> Who wants a healthy body? Who wants beauty?
> The poor man wants money and gold. The prince wants beauty. The leper wants a healthy body. The barren woman wants a son.
>
> *(Bhairo lāl jogiyā, kān mē kuṇḍal śobhai, gale motihār.* Lal 1962: 303)

After this the proper Nayanā-yogin songs begin. At the end of the performance, the Paṇḍās show to the public a set of paintings on glass kept in a small house near the temple, on which the whole story is painted and written.

Far from being confined to the temple and to the repertoire of the Vaiśya singer, these ritual songs are widely performed in the Mithilā region. As a matter of fact, they also happen to be included in the wedding songs.

During two of the numerous rituals of marriage performed at the bride's house, the Nayanā-yogin songs are sung by four young married women. These rituals, which are also celebrated by the Tirhuti Brahmans, are referred to as "Nayanā-yogin". In this context, the songs do not bear the name of *gosāunī kā gīt* but are considered as *jog (jādū ṭonā)*, magic formulae or charms. As the name suggests, and as the images they use show, they rely on Yogic practices such as the closing of the senses, the rising of the *kuṇḍalinī* and the union of the sun and the moon.

The name of Nayanā-yogin is not mentioned in the list of the sixty-four Yoginīs which are given in the *Agni-purāṇa*, the *Gorakṣa-saṃhitā* or the *Māyā-pradīpikā*. Her name does not immediately emphasize the awful personality of the Yoginī. But it reveals as always in the case of a Hindu female deity, her ambivalent nature. This term carries a double meaning. Etymologically, it can derive from the Sanskrit root *nī* (to guide) as well as from *nāyana* (the look, the eye). Though the narration describes the victory of the Siddha over the Yoginī, she is also "the one who leads, the one who guides", and people seek to acquire the protection she can offer. At the same time, she represents a threat, reminding the Tāntrika that her eyes are constantly fixed upon him. The name is also a way of laying stress on the importance given to the eye in the process of Tantric ritual. Considered by most people as coming from Kāmrūp (Assam) and incarnating the Assamese influence of Tantricism in Mithilā society[4], Nayanā belongs to the eastern category of Yoginīs.

The Nayanā songs are first sung during the ritual called *maṇḍap ghumāne*. They reproduce the theme of the fight of Gaṇināth and Govind against Nayanā. The bridegroom is a particular prey for Nayanā, who is said to come specially on that day to bewitch him. These two exchange sharp repartees:

> The well is narrow, the water lies at the very bottom.
> The Yoginī came walking, she drew some water.
> The young (groom's name) arrives, black with dust.
> He stops his horse near the curb of the well.
> — O young man, the heat and dust of Jaiṭh and Vaisākh drive everybody mad.
> Will you take the water drawn by the Yoginī?
> — O no Yoginī I won't take the water you have drawn.
> I'll rather chew my own betel leaf.
> — If you refuse to drink the water I have drawn, I'll take you with me and break your head.

— Then I won't stay, Yoginī, I have to observe my *dharma*, Yoginī.
O beautiful and immortal women,
Why should I not keep my *dharma* pure?
— I'll take you to a forest and kill you, young man.
— If you take me to a forest and kill me Yoginī, I will set fire to this forest.
You, you represent the teachings of Assam,
But I have the blessings of Gaṇināth.
Wherever you go, Yoginī, I'll go.
I will cut your nose and *jhõṭ*.

(*Sakarī kuiyā patāl base paniyā, ghumi ghumi he joginiyā bhare paniyā̃.* Lal 1962: 306)

The act of cutting the *jhõṭ* (sacred bun of the ascetics) is a mean of depriving the Yoginī of her occult powers. On the painting on glass, the picture of the mastering of Nayanā by Govind shows her pulling a wry face and wearing her hair loose.

After the *maṇḍap ghumāne*, the Nayanā-Yogin songs are performed again in a much more important ceremony. This time, homage is paid to her by the newly married couple inside the *kohbar* (or *kobar*), the nuptial room of the first four nights. It is witnessed by four women posted at each corner of the room, reminding one of the four singers of the temple as well as the four directions. The Śaiva feature of the ritual is given by the presence of two painted *kalaśa*s representing Śiva (the *purahar*) and Pārvatī (the *pātil*). The *jog*s of Nayanā are expressed here as *mantra*s. As many Bhojpurī *nirgun*s are attributed to Kabīr, so many Maithilī *jog*s are said to be written by Vidyāpati. Such as:

I want to glorify my parent's house
And to call aloud their great qualities.
Thanks to this *jog* my in-laws will be under my power.
Thanks to this *jog* my husband will never forsake

the pleasures of our marriage-bed.
At night, using my mirror, I will apply collyrium to my eyes.
For you, I will apply collyrium to my eyes, the spell will bewitch you.
Under the watchful eyes of Nayanā (or eyes in the eyes) you will fall in love with me,
You will stay with me and I'll keep you on my heart.
Says Vidyāpati, with that song, the spell has bewitched you.
The bridegroom and his parents are under the power of the bride.

(*Hamrā ke jāo tejab, gun hākab.* Lal 1962:78)

Some *jog*s are attributed to a less known Maithilī poet, Bhān Nāth:

I know all the tricks of magic, whom did you bring?
The people of the city are under my power, they have all surrendered.
If you have fallen out with me, you will fall in love again.
Māyā is a clever sister, she holds us under her power.
Where the sun and moon rise, rush in to rise as well.
Where there is a spider's web, go for a walk.
The poet Bhān Nāth has sung, the spell has worked out
(and the *jog* has been favourable).
(Bride's name) has obtained a good husband, they have all surrendered

(*Jog jugati ham jānal, kīni ānal.* Lal 1962:295)

Most of the *jog*s are anonymous and do not bear any *bhaṇitā*.

1. Nepali temple at Hajipur
Photo C. Champion

2. Gaṇināth
Photo C. Champion

In these songs, the *jog* is also described as the root of a magic plant, the *sāmānya viśākhmūl*. The juice which is obtained from grinding it is given to the bridegroom and is supposed to act as a love-philtre.

Besides binding the bride and bridegroom by these incantations, another kind of *jog* is meant to protect the new couple from evil spirits. In this case it belongs to the *jantarmantar* category. While it is being sung, the bride and the bridegroom have to worship the diagram which has been specially painted for this purpose on the wall of the *kohbar*. It is called *aripana* (or *aipana*) and must represent a lotus and a bamboo tree. The lotus is the image of perfection to be attained by the adepts of Yoga through the mastering of their sexual powers. The bamboo is a symbol of fertility and longevity. Very often, other elements are added, such as four birds or four women called Nayanā-yogin carrying various articles on their heads at each corner, a pair of swans or a human couple in the middle, and a flying parrot (symbol of Kāma). Sometimes, it is even more decorated and less abstract, and includes a sparrow chewing grain, a calf suckling milk, a milkmaid selling curd, a brahman with a book in his hand, a marriage band, a begging renouncer-king, and one or several fishes. The leaf pattern is the commonest form used for social festivities like marriage. The edges are painted with beli-flowers, betel leaf vines, plus clusters of tamarinds and mango trees. Nayanā is expected to descend to take her seat on this diagram. One has to look at the *aripana* while uttering the following formula. The intense mental effort of the Tāntrika to fix his senses on the *aripana* also helps to visualise the *kuṇḍalinī*:

> Wake up, wake up, O mother Yoginī,
> I give my salutation to the Satguru.
> There is a four-sided tank
> Whose *ghāṭ* is made of bricks,
> Where the Devī is sitting, taking her bath.
> I am calling to the guru for help.
> The elegant Devī is wearing a sari.
> (*Jāg jāg joginī māc*. Tivari 1980: 123)

Before her departure to her husband's house, the bride applies vermilion on the bamboo drawn on the wall of the *kohbar*.

Besides the Gaṇināth cult and the wedding celebration, Nayanā is also often invocated in many kinds of *mantras* against snake-bite, toothache, headache, etc., which include the sentence *jāg jāg joginī māe* "wake up, O mother joginī," and end with these words :

> I am calling to the god Mahādev and to Gaurī-Pārvatī,
> To Kāmarakṣā from Assam, and to the ability of Nayanā.
>
> *Dohāi issar Mahādev Gaurā Pārabatī,*
> *Kāmru Kamaracha, Nainā jogit ke dohāi.*

Though Nayanā-yogin is not listed in the principal texts of Hindu Tantric literature, and is very rarely identified in Assam as belonging to the circle of the famous Kāmarakṣā, her worship is an example of the prevalence of the *śakti* cult in Mithilā. It provides also a precise attempt to master the evil forces incarnated by the net of female Yogin *(Yoginī-jāl)* which spreads over the universe. It evokes the Tripurasundarī cult of the Śrīvidyā tradition. The Nayanā *aripana* is elaborated in the spirit of the *Yoginī-tantra*, considered as a probably late work which states that a diagram having the shape of a lotus is essential to the extraction of the *mantra*. It cannot he traced on the ground but requires a support such as the bark of a birch-tree (Padoux 1978 : 72 and 1990 : 91).

We can see how Gaṇināth and Nayanā share different functions and roles. Gaṇināth is supposed to show the path of salvation to his devotees, and to give them children and health, while Nayanā is supposed to look after the amorous and erotic part of their life and to protect them from evil spirits. But a few questions arise concerning the way Nāth (or so-called Nāth) and Tantric pratices are associated. Tracing back the origin of the Gaṇināth cult would most probably help to provide a clue. Unfortunately, it is difficult to establish it precisely. On the one hand, the Nayanā-yogin songs, which are, so far, the only available documents to mention the Siddha's life and deeds, having been orally transmitted, are difficult to date. Moreover, the paintings on glass on which the story is written are obviously quite recent. On the other hand, the archaic nature of the representation of the nine clay mounds in the temple is patent.

Though the devotees agree to link the foundation of the temple with the Islamic invasion, they diverge as to the exact date of the event. According to some Paṇḍās, the cult started in the 14th century along with the first attempts at subjugating North Bihar by Shamsuddīn Ḥāji Ilyas Shāh (1342-1357), but according to the founding legend of the temple, it was instigated by the intolerance of Aurangzeb. After the beheading of the Nandī statue of the village by his soldiers Gaṇināth stepped in to prevent them from destroying the Śiva temple. Four attempts by the Muslim soldiers were foiled by the miraculous intervenings of the Siddha. This account would place the beginning of this cult in the 17th century.

In the face of these contradictory data, we tend to place it during the reign of Akbar. Firstly, there is a widespread tendency to attribute to Aurangzeb many of the aggressions committed by Akbar, and to see in Akbar the champion of tolerance (Gaborieau 1992 : 140). Secondly, in the history of Bihar, the conquests of Akbar during his fight against the Afghan Dā'ūd, in 1574, were far more spectacular than any others. Besides, his intervention marks a step in the history of the country. From then on, the city of Hajipur became the center of Muslim authority in North Bihar. In contrast, Aurangzeb's policy in Bihar was not so decisive: the battle between his army and that of Shujā[c], the governor of Bengal, took place far from Palvaiya, in the Bhagalpur area. After his success, Aurangzeb endeavoured mainly to subdue the tribal Cheros without interfering with the local traditions. Whatever credit we can give to the exactitude of such a legendary narration, it allows us to perceive the importance given to the Islamic dimension. After the expansion of the Firdausīs and the Suhrawardīs in the 14th, century, the renown of the Islamic mystic orders of North Bihar reached its zenith in the 16th century. Hajipur, Lalganj, Muzaffarpur and Vaishali became active Muslim centres.

In the performance of the Nayanā-yogin songs, two different patterns show up clearly. Inside the *mandir*, and under the *maṇḍap*, which are public places, Gaṇināth alone is worshipped. The Yoginī is the secondary deity of the cult. On the contrary, inside the *kohbar*, which is a private space, the personality of Gaṇināth is consigned to a secondary position. It is the Yoginī who is worshipped for her occult powers. The songs do not allude any more to her defeat at the hands of Gaṇināth or of the bridegroom.

This use of inverting power is quite common in Hinduism and enables to focus on a particular point while keeping the usual hierarchy of values (Reiniche 1988 : 373). But whereas the *kohbar* rites can be easily identified with a local form of Tantricism, some aspects of the Gaṇināth cult deserve a few comments. The association of the ritual with the cult of the dead is obvious. The festival takes place in the month of Bhādra. People take ashes from a bowl and apply them to their forehead as a reminder of the brevity of life. The white flowers evoke the colour of mourning. Nevertheless, two elements strike us. One is the complete lack of decoration or of anthropomorphic representation of the deity, which is quite rare in the context of a Hindu temple. The single and very austere room contains only the nine mounds of clay we have mentioned. The pictures of Gaṇināth and the paintings on glass of Gaṇināth and Nayanā are kept in a small house outside the temple. Another phenomenon is the practice of touching the *samādhi* of the saint instead of observing the usual *darśan* custom.

Regarding the plot of the legend of Gaṇināth, some questions also arise: the quest of the Siddha to obtain his wife in spite of the obstacles laid by the courtesan, and also the importance given to the integration of a love-story in the saint's cult, evoke much more the plot of the medieval Sufi *premākhyān* than the traditional king-renouncer *gāthā* of the Nāths. This love symbolism is nearer to Sufi mysticism than to the erotic form of Tantricism or Vaiṣṇava *bhakti*. One knows that in many a North-Indian village, an obscure Nāth is also worshipped as a Pīr. But, *a priori*, these forms of devotion are not expected to develop in the strong Tantric context of Mithilā.

One has to remain very cautious, for it is considered more acceptable to speak about the influence of Hinduism on Indian Islam than the contrary. But the example drawn from the Palvaiya field shows that some aspects of Muslim mysticism are observable in this local form of Nāth-panth and Tantric Yoga. According to Prafulla Kumar Singh "Maun", the historian of the popular cults of Mithilā: "the *gāthā* of Gaṇināth combines the influences of Sahajiyā Siddhas, Nāth-panthī Yogīs and Sufi saints" (1989: 40). In our attempt to find an answer to the questions which have arisen in the course of our research, we wish to mention among other things, in this rather sketchy survey, the possible influence of the prevalent Sufi orders, such as the Firdausīs and the Shaṭṭārīs of Bihār, in the oral traditions linked with the devotional trends of Mithilā.

NOTES

1. I wish to thank Raj Ballava Sah, Mrs. Prafulla Kumar Singh and Kathleen Haddon for their kind help in the course of this study.
2. In the *Gorakhnāth caritra* of C.L. Gautham, Gorakhnāth is sometimes represented as helping people without expecting

any reward or conversion to the sect.

3. A symbol much used in the Nāth literature (*cf.* the story of Sorthī or Mullā Dāūd's *Cāndāyān).*
4. People of Bihar consider as very prestigious the Assamese origin of Nayanā, whereas in Assam the devotees of Kāmarakṣā insist very much on the link of their Devī with the Braj country.

BIBLIOGRAPHY

Bhattacharya, Chakreswar. 1970. *Saktādarśanam.* Gauhati: Bharatsarvakārārthanukūlayen.

Briggs, G.W. 1938. *Gorakhnāth and the Kanphāṭa Yogīs.* Reprint 1982, Delhi : Motilal Banarsidass.

Chaudhary, Radhakrishna. 1970. *History of the Muslim Rule in Tirhut.* Varanasi: The Chowkhamba Sanskrit Series Office. The Chowkhamba Sanskrit Studies Vol LXXII.

—. 1976.a. *Mithila in the Age of Vidyāpati.* Varanasi : Chaukhambha Orientalia. Chaukhambha Oriental Research Studies No. 1.

—. 1976.b. *A Survey of Maithili Literature.* Deoghar: Shanti Devi.

Crooke, W. 1896. *The Trbes and Castes of the North-Western India.* Reprint 1974, Delhi : Cosmo Publications. Vol. II.

Dehejiya, V. 1986. *Yoginī, Cult and Temples.* Delhi : National Museum Janpath.

Diserens, Hélène. 1991. "Les *Yoginī* de la haute vallée du Kulu (Himachal Pradesh)" *Bulletin d' Études indiennes*, IX, pp. 61-73.

Gaborieau, Marc. 1992. " Le legs de la civilisation musulmane aux formations étatiques du sous-continent indien." In J.-F. Bayart (ed.). *Trajectoires du politique en Afrique et en Asie.* Paris : Presses de la Fondation Nationale des Sciences Politiques, pp. 130-150.

Gauth, Caman Lal. s.d. *Śrī Gorakhnāth caritra.* Bareli: Sanskrit Sansthan.

Lal, Tej Narayan. 1962. *Maithilī lokgītō kā adhyayan.* Agra: Vinod Pustak Mandir.

Mishra, Jayakanta. 1976. *History of Maithilī Literature.* New Delhi: Sahitya Akademi.

Mishra, Navina Chandra and Thakur, Sivakant. 1985. *Maithilī bhāṣa vigyān.* Darbhanga: Maithilī Pustak Kendra.

Mishra, Tarakant. 1985. *Maithilī lok-sāhitya kā adhyayan*: Patna: Janaki Prakashan.

Padoux, Andre. 1978 "Contributions ă l'étude du Mantra Śāstra"

Bulletin de 1'Ecole Française d'Extrême-Orient, LXV, pp. 65-85.

—. 1990. "Image mentale, méditation et culte dans la *Śrīvidyā* (quelques exemples tirés du Yoginīhṛdaya)." In A. Padoux (ed.) *L'image divine, culte et méditation dans 1'hindouisme*. Paris: Editions du CNRS, pp. 89-98.

Prasad, Tarkesvar. 1969-1970. "Nayanā Jogin" *Anjor*, X, 3-4, pp. 35-37.

Reiniche, Marie-Louise. 1988. "Un nom, une forme, un lieu. L'invention hindoue de l'autre et du même" *Revue de 1'Histoire des Religions*, CLV-4, pp.376-384.

Singh, Chandramani. 1979. *Marriage Songs from Bhojpurī Region*. Jaipur : Kitab Mahal.

Singh, Prafulla Kumar "Maun". 1988. "Mahnār kī sānskṛtik pṛṣṭhabhūmi" *Viśālā*, Mahnār, pp.1-8.

—. 1989. "Vaiśālī ke lokdevī-devtā" *Vaiśālī Mahotsava 1989*. Vaiśālī: The District Magistrate, pp.37-42.

Thakur, Upendra. 1956. *History of Mithila*. Darbhanga : Mithila Institute.

Tivari, Hira Lal. 1980. *Gaṅgā ghāṭi ke gīt*. Varanasi : Viśvavidyālaya Prakāśan.

Upadhyaya, Krishnadev. 1957. *Bhojpurī lok-gīt*. Prayag: Hindī Sāhitya Sammelan. Vol. II.

Vaudeville, Charlotte. 1969. *L'invocation. Le Haripāṭh de Dñyāndev*. Paris : Ecole Française d'Extrême-Orient. Publications de 1'Ecole Française d'Extrême-Orient, Vol. LXXIII.

Vequaud, Yves. 1976. *L'art du Mithila*. Paris : Les Presses de la connaissance.

Govinddevjī of Vrindaban and Jaipur and its Kachvāhā Patrons from the Mid-Seventeenth to the Mid-Eighteenth Century

Monika Horstmann

The Govindadeva Temple of Vrindaban, built and completed in 1590 by the Rajput prince Mān Singh of Amber of the Kachvāhā dynasty, originally housed three images. These were the images of Govinddevjī (GD) himself, that of his consort, the *ṭhakurānī*, and that of Vṛndādevī. The images of GD and his consort were eventually given a new house in Jaipur, while Vṛndādevī was separated from them. Her image is reported to have stayed behind in the GD temple at Kāmā̃, where there is to be found, indeed, an image whose identity with the original deity seems to be uncontested (Entwistle 1987: 185).

The relationship between the Amber dynasty and GD was close not only because the temple had been built by a member of that princely house. It was also a symbol of the valour of the Kachvāhās, for Mān Singh was at the height of his power and influence at Akbar's court when that great monument was erected. The relationship became even more intimate when, in 1633 (July 24), Shāh Jahān issued a *farmān* in favour of the Amber family by which he transferred the right to issue grants to GD to the Mahārāja of Amber, Jai Singh I (Mukherjee and Habib 1989: 290, 295). At that time the grant of land in favour of GD, which had been carried over from the time of Akbar and covered 135 *bīghās*, was made an *in'ām* of Mirzā Rājā Jai Singh.

The reason why the deities of the GD temple left Vrindaban is seen to lie in the iconoclasm encouraged by Aurangzeb from April 1669 (Sharma 1940: 131-38). This made the transfer of the images to safer regions necessary.

This paper will, after a brief review of the itinerary of the images,[1] attempt to explain the role played by GD in connection with the religious and political attitudes of the Kachvāhā prince Jai Singh II, who ruled from 1700 to 1743.

The three original images stayed together in Vrindaban until they were removed to Kāmā̃ on Bhādõ, ś. 12, VS 1727, (August 1670).[2] Kāmā̃ was, within the limitations of Mughal suzerainty, under Kachvāhā rule. We have no information when exactly GD and his consort on the one hand and Vṛndādevī on the other were installed in separate shrines. In the available documents of the time they are last mentioned together on 3 February 1670.[3] In 1707 we find GD — and, presumably, his consort — in Govindpur (also Govindpurā) alias Raihphoṛā. This place is identical with the modern Govindpurā alias Rohpāṛā (also Rūpheṛā) in the Sanganer Tahsil of Jaipur District (India 1983: 167, 169, code no. 161). The date of the arrival of the images there remains unknown. The former, obviously large, temple of GD at Govindpurā is now dilapidated. Govindpurā, then in *tappā* Khoh of *pargana* Amber, had already in the time of Jai Singh I been assigned to GD.[4]

Both places that gave asylum to GD, namely, Kāmā̃ and Govindpurā, had sustained for some time financial commitment to the deity. In the case of Kāmā̃ this is evidenced by a document dating back to 1660, issued by Kīrat Singh, the governor of Kāmā̃, and reinforced in February 1670 when an order in favour of GD was given to the administrators of the *pargana*. In the case of Govindpurā this is evidenced by a document dated 1667 (Horstmann, forthcoming). That is to say that the move to Rajasthan happened in such a way that extant economic ties between a place and GD were taken well into account.

In 1713 GD and his consort were transferred to the newly constructed Vrindaban (Bahura 1979: Ātmārām, st. 53). This new Vrindaban lies on the outskirts of Jaipur on the Amber Road and its temple was recently restored. In 1716 GD is reported to sojourn in the Jainivās Garden.[5] We do not know how long and under what exact conditions of residence the images of GD and his consort stayed there, and the exact relationship or partial identity with what was referred to later on as Kanak-Vrindaban remains unclear.[6] Jainivās was perhaps a vaster area than the location within it that came to be known specifically as Kanak-Vrindaban. Nowadays Kanak-Vrindaban designates a GD temple and its garden enclosure.

In VS 1796 (Bhatnagar 1974, chart following p. 102) the two images were eventually installed in the GD temple which lies behind the City Palace of Jaipur and within its precincts. Here they have remained to this day.

While the new GD temple became an economically potent institution, the cult was also resumed in the old GD temple at Vrindaban — maybe after some longer or shorter interruption of its functioning — as is shown by documents from 1721 onwards.[7] The custodians of both temples, from the third custodial generation onwards, were interrelated Bengali Cakravartī brahmins.[8]

It is, I think, evident from the foregoing that the very fact that GD travelled to Amber and later on to Jaipur was to some extent caused by political events and constraints. These were, to summarize them, (1) the regulations issued by Shāh Jahān according to which, in 1633, the right to issue grants in favour of the GD temple was transferred to the Kachvāhās, and (2) the inimical political stance taken against the Hindu shrines from the late sixties of the seventeenth century, which called for protective measures on the part of the Kachvāhās. All this prepared the ground for the carefully designed rapprochement of the Kachvāhā court and the Vaiṣṇava deities. This careful preparation is reflected by the decision to relocate GD in the village of Govindpur, which had long provided revenue grants for the GD deity while it was in Vrindaban. GD was not a unique case, for four more Vaiṣṇava images originally belonging to Vrindaban were shifted to Jaipur (Roy 1978: 27). Amongst these, at least one, the image of Gopīnāth, was taken to Jaipur at the time of Jai Singh (Roy 1978: 28).

It is evident that GD, much like other Vaiṣṇava deities from Vrindaban which had been under the tutelage of the Kachvāhās, was close to the heart of this dynasty. The magnificence of the temples and the generosity in giving charities that the Kachvāhās showed speak for themselves. It seems only natural that, when Jaipur was built by Jai Singh II as his new capital, the Vrindaban deities should come to reside there. Yet, beyond his fondness for Kṛṣṇa and his avowed attachment to Gauḍīya theology, Jai Singh's treatment of GD seems to me to reflect his statesmanship rather than merely personal fondness and piety.

Jai Singh was undoubtedly a devout worshipper of Kṛṣṇa as Govindadeva. His biographer Ātmārām gives a lengthy description of the new Vrindaban created by the prince in 1770. The image was installed there (Bahura 1979; Ātmārām, st. 447-53), and the place served Jai Singh as a princely retreat which was considered even more enjoyable than the original Vrindaban (st. 452-53):

utahi karīra kuñja lapiṭi latāni guñja
itahi rasāla baulisirī beli anatāĩ /
utahi phirata rahāĩ kā̃mari valita kā̃ku
āpu hī akele sadā naṃda gāi gana tāĩ /

itahi savāī jayasiṃgha thāyai thira hvai
guviṃdadeva vasana virājata ratna māĩ /
dharama ke pana tāĩ pragaṭi hāũsamana tāĩ su
kinhāũ vṛndāvana tāĩ sarasa vaṃdāvana tāĩ //

There there were the bowers of *karīl* which were
covered by creepers,
here there were the lush *maulisirī* creepers,
There there roamed, his body wrapped in a blanket,
solitary by himself the Ever-blissful with the
cattle.

Here there was Jai Singh, transfixed in attention,
while Govindadeva's garments shone forth with
jewels,
Because of his determinedness in *dharma* which
became manifest through his intelligence
he had created, thanks to his lavish worship, a
Vrindaban which was more enjoyable than
Vrindaban.

Later on, Jai Singh established an especially firm link with GD when he incorporated the deity into the City Palace. Indeed, one author of the time of Rām Singh (Bahura 1979:80 and anon, *ibid.*, st. 60) called the GD temple simply one of the *mahals* of the City Palace.

This suggests that Jai Singh's great consideration for GD should also be seen in the light of the claim of a Hindu prince to supreme rule sanctified by religion. In other words, the temple and the bowers of the new Vrindaban became a religio-politically charged symbol. The emphasis given to them is evident from their subsequent transfer to the politically nodal point of the new capital of Jaipur, namely the precincts of the palace. They are not even separated from the palace but appear much as the extension of the residence quarters, an open pavilion in its garden and facing the palace.

There exists further evidence, beyond that which has already been produced elsewhere, for the political, and certainly the economical, dimension of Jai Singh's Vaiṣṇavism. Soon after GD had been installed in its final abode in the precincts of the City Palace (AD 1739/VS 1796), in the month of Māgh of the year VS 1797,[9] an order addressed to the *mutaṣaddīs* was issued by Jai Singh. It said that in addition to each thousand rupees of all rural and non-rural taxes collected by the *jāgīrdārs* and the *ijāradārs*, of all *peśkaś* and of all revenue from *khāliṣa* land, one rupee had to be given to the deity GD and four annas to Rāmśaraṇ, its custodian. An estimate, based on the calculations given by S.P. Gupta for 1740 (Gupta 1986: 69, 150, 152, 155), yields the result that the charity realized for GD and his custodian from only a single one out of some 90 *parganas* under Jai Singh would have amounted to a sum of fifty-five rupees. Thus the total sum, in which the variable factor of *peśkaś* fees does not even figure, should have been well above four thousand rupees per year.

Jai Singh's religious and ritual attention was, as is well known, not limited to his Vaiṣṇava pursuits. For example, in the same year that he built his new Vrindaban, he also arranged for his brahmins to carry out the Puṇḍarīka sacrifice, by which he ritually acquired the right to call himself a *samrāṭ* (Bahura 1979, note 84 on Ātmārām's text). As we also know, in 1734 and 1741 he celebrated an *aśvamedha* and thus established his claim to an overlordship solemnized by the Vedic tradition.

It is, in fact, incorrect to depict Jai Singh as a ruler obsessed with an exclusive *bhakti* for GD. This view may perhaps be justified for the brief period before his death when he had virtually, and eventually ritually, entrusted Īśvar Singh with the rule of the state (1743) and gradually withdrawn to his worship of GD and to the circle of his *paṇḍit* confidants. The court-poet Kṛṣṇabhaṭṭa Kalānidhi, who was a contemporary of Jai Singh and his successor Īśvar Singh, says (Kṛṣṇabhaṭṭa 1958: ch. 10.2-10):

> Continuously he contemplated full of love Kṛṣṇa's face,
> He had turned a bee that rejoices profoundly in drinking the nectar of the sweetness of bliss. (10.2)

In contact with pious people the like of him, he
listened to the excellences of Govinda; he was a
cakora bird whose gaze was totally abandoned to
Him,
He uttered His name, inhaled the fragrance of His
tulsī-foot and remained absorbed in unity with
Him. (10.3)

He performed the works taught by the Veda and was
in possession of a knowledge for which the valid
proofs were provided by the Upaniṣads,
He worshipped Kṛṣṇa according to the ninefold
mode of *bhakti* and due to its perfection he
attained love (*preman*). (10.4)

When his son, named Īśvar Singh, was able to carry
the burden of rule he put it on him,
Thirsting for all-encompassing enjoyment, he with-
drew gradually and bore himself the load of the
non-dual love of Kṛṣṇa. (10.5).

He had performed his duties which were conducive
to righteous acts and in awareness of the true
being of the Supreme Self,
At the foot-lotus of Govinda he abandoned himself
alone and totally to the love of Him. (10.6)

(Verses 7 to 9 contain a description of Jai Singh's brahmin companions.)

In the early morning of the 14th bright day of Āśvin
of VS 1800
Govinda was led into the lotus of his heart; the ruler
who had become like God expired and was
absorbed in God. (10.10)

While still ruling, Jai Singh's Vaiṣṇava commitment was

broader than that of a Kṛṣṇa *bhakta*, and in this broader dimension it was linked again with his function as a ruler. Kṛṣṇabhaṭṭa indulges in a description of over seventy verses of Jai Singh's relationship to the Kalkī temple which he had built himself (Roy 1978: 23). Here it is obvious how Jai Singh is considered instrumental in the manifestation of Kalkī and the rise of the new age, which will be a Hindu age, liberated from the barbarians. Three illustrative examples will be sufficient to document this.

> Thus made to shine in marvellous beauty and
> accompanied by his two main wives, Padmā and
> Ramā,
> God Kalkī was displayed in the Kali Age by the ruler
> who formed the crest of society. (6.30)
>
> Adorned by the *cakravartī*, God Kalkī, who is the
> sole beloved of the whole earth,
> Will found his own era at the end of the Kali Age and
> kill the hosts of barbarian kings. (6.36)
>
> ...Kalkī, benign, was installed on earth by the
> ruler Jai Singh and his excellences shone forth as
> had been praised by the Veda.[10] (6.46 cd)

A comprehensive and, as it would seem, balanced picture of the politico-religious attitude of Jai Singh is given by the same author (Kṛṣṇabhaṭṭa 1958: ch. 7.31-42):

> In the Kali Age he again and again arranged for many
> rites such as the horse-sacrifice,
> And this ruler thus in many ways became a unique
> repository of great qualities that were conducive
> to well-being. (7.31)
>
> With a firm heart he was grounded in the Vedānta
> doctrine

because he had reflected on the *Brahmasūtras*
and the Upaniṣads.
He had passed beyond the lower *brahman* and,
because his heart was purified, reached the
highest *brahman* which is called *śabda*. (7.32)

He was attached to the path of knowledge which
was combined with the rituals, he worshipped
Viṣṇu according to the ninefold mode of *bhakti*,
Living for the benefit of the world, would there be
likely to exist any wonderful ritual that this ruler
of the world would not perform? (7.33)

He studied the Vedas that are apt to dispel distress,
he always offered sacrifices to the gods, in this
he put his predecessors to shame; he respected
his own relatives and theirs,
He subdued the six cardinal vices, he enjoyed the
dharma that is conducive to welfare and had
been observed by his righteous forefathers; so
that he might ascend to heaven he built a ladder
which consisted of a series of sacrifices. (7.34)

By his ardent might he liberated Būndī from its
thorns,
He made it subject to Dalel Singh and in so doing
he displayed formidable valour.[11] (7.35)

Because he feared his enemies the son of Gopāl
Singh took refuge with him,
He (Jai Singh) invested him to rule after conquering
his usurping enemies.[12] (7.36)

Because he was continuously immersed in the
floods of the stream of Kṛṣṇa's play which flows
from the ocean of nectar called the *Bhāgavata*,
He did not know of the inextricable pain that

incessantly and in many ways is born from the ocean of existence. (7.37)
He spent his time with the contemplative speeches of Vālmīki and Vyāsa and with many Itihāsas such as the *Bhārata*,
With the Vedāṅgas and the Purāṇas, as a given situation would call for. (7.38)

He observed righteous deeds and the Mīmāṃsā-*dharma*, he had realized the non-duality of the Supreme Self and that the Upaniṣads constituted valid proof.
He was uniquely knowledgeable in Kṛṣṇa *bhakti* and, learned as he was, he would not waste his time even for a single moment. (7.39)

He adorned the system of rituals which has been propounded in the *Pūrvakāṇḍa*[13] with a knowledge that followed the path of pure non-duality (*śuddhādvaita*),[14]
And with the Kṛṣṇa *bhakti* which permeated him and which, too, he adorned, because he was without desire. (7.40)

Continuously and in many ways he surrounded himself with Vedic scholars, who were knowledgeable in the rituals, and learned men who were well-versed in the abundant meanings of the *śāstras*,
As well as *bhaktas* who were great Bhāgavatas. (7.41)

He was victorious in difficult battles, renowned for his ability to capture the forts of his enemies; he was deft in appeasing the blazing poverty of learned men,
He built a staircase of a hundred sacrifices so that he might reach quickly the abode of consciousness and bliss, and he was boundlessly victorious. (7.42)

We have here before us a religiously charged attitude to rule. In a time when the fading Mughal rule gives way to flourishing successor-states, a Vaiṣṇava-oriented stance is here reinforced by an emphasis on Vedic rituals which sanctify the cosmic and political status of a Hindu prince as universal ruler. In connection with Jai Singh's Vaiṣṇavism, GD's role is, in fact, prominent within the wider spectre of the Vaiṣṇava cults of Jaipur but it is not exclusive, or at least not so until the last phase of Jai Singh's life.

REFERENCES

Bahura, Gopal Narayan (ed.). 1979. *Savāī Jayasiṃha carita* by Kavi Ātmārām. Jaipur: Maharaja Sawai Man Singh II Museum, City Palace.

Bhatnagar, V.S. 1974. *Life and Times of Sawai Jai Singh, 1688-1743*, Delhi: Impex India.

Entwistle, Alan W. 1987. *Braj: Centre of Krishna Pilgrimage*, Groningen: Egbert Forsten.

Gupta, Satya Prakash. 1986. *The Agrarian System of Eastern Rajasthan (c.1650 - c.1750)*, Delhi: Manohar.

Habib, Irfan. 1991. "The Chaitanya Gosains at Vrindavan in the sixteenth and seventeenth centuries — a documentary history". Unpubl. paper pres. at the conference "Govindadeva Temple: History and Artistic Dimensions", Vrindavan, 4-7 April 1991.

Horstmann, Monika (forthcoming). "Govinddev and his custodians from 1643 through the time of Jai Singh II (1700-1743)". Paper pres. at the conference "Govinda Temple: History and Artistic Dimensions", Vrindavan, 4-7 April 1991.

India. 1983. *Census of India 1981. Ser. 18. Rajasthan. Pts. XII-A&B. District Census Handbook. Jaipur District.* Jaipur: General Administration Dept., Govt. of Rajasthan.

Kṛṣṇabhaṭṭa. 1958. *Īśvaravilāsamahākāvya*, ed., Devarṣibhaṭṭa Śrimathurānāth Śāstrī. Jodhpur: Rajasthan Oriental Research Institute.

Mukherjee, Tarapada and Irfan Habib. 1989. "The Mughal administration and the temples of Vrindavan during the reigns of Jahangir and Shahjahan". *PIHC*, 49th session, Dharwad: 287-300.

Roy, Asim Kumar. 1978. *History of the Jaipur City*. Delhi: Manohar.

Id., 1985. *Vṛndāvana theke Jayapura*, Calcutta: Jijñāsā.

Sarkar, Jadunath. 1984. A *History of Jaipur, c.1503-1938*, Rev. and ed. by Raghubir Singh. Hyderabad: Orient Longman.

Sharma, Sri Ram. 1940. *The Religious Policy of Mughal Emperors*. London: Humphrey Milford, Oxford University Press.

NOTES

1. The next four paragraphs of this paper, which deal with the itinerary of the deities, are, in a slightly abridged version, taken from Horstmann (forthcoming).
2. Inscription in the possession of the Vrindaban Research Institute, exhibited in facsimile at the Conference on Govindadeva Temple in Vrindaban, 1991.
3. Document 1670 (Horstmann, forthcoming).
4. Document 1667 (Horstmann, forthcoming).
5. Document 1716b (Horstmann, forthcoming).
6. For documentation see Horstmann (forthcoming).
7. Horstmann (forthcoming).
8. There seems, however, to be no document telling us how the custodians from the fourth to the sixth generation (father, son and grandson) were exactly related to the custodians of the third generation on the one hand and the seventh generation onwards on the other. Otherwise see Horstmann (forthcoming) for the exact relationship of the custodians amongst each other.
9. Document GD, Jai Singh, fifth dark day of Māgh, VS 1797.
10. The compound *nigamagaṇagītoditaguṇaḥ* can, as already pointed out by the editor of the text and author of its Sanskrit paraphrase, Devarṣibhaṭṭa Mathurānāth Śāstrī, also be translated by "excellences propounded by the *Nigamagaṇagītā*".
11. For details of this event of May 1730 see Bhatnagar 1974: 215-17.
12. Rao Gopāl Singh was the ruler of Rāmpurā who was dispossessed by his son Ratan Singh (Islām Khān), for which see Sarkar 1984: 189-90.
13. Either a text in its own right or just the foregoing chapter(s) of Kṛṣṇabhaṭṭa's own work.
14. It would be astonishing, indeed, if this term indicated the doctrine of Vallabha and if Jai Singh would thus be declared a Vallabhite.

The Establishment of the Sixth *Gaddī* of the Vallabha Sampradāy: Narrative Structure and the Use of Authority in a *Vārtā* of the Nineteenth Century

Vasudha Dalmia

In his book *Benares. The Sacred City of the Hindus: An Account of Benares in Ancient and Modern Times*, published in the year 1868, M. A. Sherring of the London Missionary Society, was to record with a mixture of pride and indignation:

"Since the country has come into our hands, a great impetus has been given to the erection of temples, and to the manufacture of idols, in Northern India. In Benares, temples have multiplied at a prodigious rate; and this rate at the present moment, is, I believe, rather increasing than diminishing. Judged merely by its external appearances, Hinduism was never so flourishing as it is now. With general prosperity and universal peace, and with a Government based on neutral principles, and largely tolerant of the national religious systems, Hinduism, under the leadership of men of the old school—princes, pandits, banyas (tradespeople), and priests—is making extraordinary efforts to maintain its position against the new doctrines of European civilization and religion, which they now begin to recognize as formidable opponents."[1]

Though it is doubtful, whether the increased temple building activity had only to do with recognizing European civilization and religion as formidable opponents, Sherring was certainly an acute observer of the contemporary scene.

The burgeoning of Hindu politico-religious activity can be traced back to a period well before the actual establishment of British political and military power on the sub-continent. The declining Mughal empire saw the rise of the Marathas who operated under a Hindu banner. Renewed activity in the Rajput states testified as well to a nascent consciousness of the historical and pan-Indian dimensions of Hinduism. Jai Singh II of Jaipur (1688-1748) made deliberate efforts to unify the different Vaiṣṇava *sampradāy*s under common doctrinaire principles and to cause them to establish links with Vedic ritual as well as with the Vedānta philosophy of Śaṅkara and Rāmanuja; this was accompanied by a renewed awareness of the *varṇa* system as the organising principle of Hindu society. These characteristics, albeit with shifts of emphasis, were to remain constitutive of those movements in nineteenth-century British India, which came to represent what in retrospect has been designated collectively as neo-Hinduism.

As far as Banaras was concerned, the process Sherring describes had similarly been set in motion during the late Mughal period, largely under the Marathas, who intensified their activities with the further expansion of their own power. They were concerned with rescuing the three holy places of the Hindus, *(tristhalī)* Prayāg, Gayā and Kāśī. In the second half of the eighteenth century they built the ghats which are considered so characteristic a part of the Banaras river front today. Not all their enterprises were to be so successful, for they vainly planned the rebuilding of temples on ancient sites where, in the meanwhile, mosques stood. Yet the building of ghats and temples was not at the initiative of rulers and princes alone. Merchants and landowners, who had come to power and money under the aegis of the British, also participated substantially in the process. Thus, if on the one hand the tendencies to reclaim and occupy symbolically significant holy sites go back to pre-colonial times, they are set forth and prosper under the newer power constellations in the British period as well.

By the end of the eighteenth century, Banaras had established its position as one of the most important trading and banking centres in Northern India.[2] The city's commercial aristocracy consisted of the Naupaṭṭī Mahājans, bankers who rose to prominence in the troubled period before the final collapse of the Awadh *navābī* and the formal takeover of the province by the East India Company.[3] They were called Naupaṭṭī, since they settled in a newly cleared tract of land, which was to become the centre of the city's commercial life. They had much political influence since they had been instrumental in the installation of a Hindu Raja instead of the Muslim military commander Mir Rustam Ali, who had been appointed by the Nawab of Awadh and had served also as the revenue and administrative head of the region. The interests of the Naupaṭṭī Mahājans were closely linked with, though not always identical with those of the Raja and the Company.

I

In the following section of the paper I consider the genesis of the Gopāl Mandir in the city of Banaras, which was duly to be recognised as the sixth seat or *gaddī* of the Vallabha Sampradāy and which grew and prospered in the period Sherring speaks of. The history of its rise to power and status is documented in the hagiographical Brajbhāṣā tract *Mukundrāyjī kī vārtā*, (first published in book form in 1923),[4] which apart from supplying much information on the devotional ritual in Nāthdvārā, the elaborate attention paid to maintain aesthetic harmony in the celebration of divine love, also clearly records the influence of the newer configurations of power and their linkage with older traditional structures, besides providing clear indications of the patterns that were to become characteristic of Hinduism in the nineteenth century.

The Gopāl Mandir, a complex, which was to assume grand proportions later, had been established by the rebel Raja Chait Singh in 1777, who though an illegitimate claimant to the throne, had initially the support of the British and was a popular ruler, to judge by all accounts. He indulged in a fair amount of temple-building activity. But the temple only came into prominence through the services of the charismatic Girdharjī Mahārāj, who traced his genealogy back through six generations to Yadunāth, the youngest of the six sons of Viṭṭhal, that is, nine generations removed from Vallabha himself. The names of this illustrious lineage have been preserved for posterity.[5] Girdharjī was born in 1791 in Banaras and was educated there. He was known in Banaras for his high learning and piety. He had studied the Vedas and Vedāṅgas, so that apart from the knowledge of the *sevā paddhati*, the rituals of his own *sampradāy*, he had the additional advantage of being well versed in traditional schools of philosophy and ritual. This was to help him to establish linkages between the rituals of his own *sampradāy* and what was commonly accepted as Vedic ritual. He has left behind several learned works and commentaries, in Sanskrit as well as in Brajbhāṣā. The two best known, both composed in Sanskrit, are *Śuddhādvaitamārkaṇḍeya*, an exposition of the philosophical-theological tenets of the *sampradāy*, and *Śrutirahasya*, a work which grapples with the thematic complex concerned with Vallabha's manifestation in human incarnation (*mānava vigraha*).

Girdharjī served Gopāllālji in Banaras, the deity worshipped by his family, but he was fascinated and attracted by the much greater ritual wealth and grandeur of Nāthdvārā and spent long periods there. On the strength of his high learning he persuaded Dāmodarjī Mahārāj of Nāthdvārā to part with a *svarūpa* of Śrīnāthjī. The image, Mukundrāyjī, though not one of the *saptasvarūpa*, was reputed to have been one of the two additional images originally in the possession of Vallabhācārya himself. Girdharjī paid a handsome sum in exchange for the image. He further negotiated and paid a large amount, as the *Vārtā* testifies, in order to buy the *havelī* of one Jairāmdās in the Chaukhambā area of the city, in the midst of the residential quarters of the Naupaṭṭī Mahājans, in order to enlarge the temple site of the Gopāl Mandir, as befitted the status of the hallowed image. In 1827 Mukundrāyjī travelled with much pomp from Nāthdvārā to Banaras, in a great train of attendants and *bhaktas*, accompanied for protection on the way by *caprāsī* provided kindly by the British resident in Udaipur. Near Banaras on the outskirts of the city, Mukundrāyjī was received by Harakhcand Agravāl, of a leading Naupaṭṭī family, who then not only saw to the immediate arrangements for the deity, but also contributed substantially to the funding and maintenance of the temple complex, which was ready two years later, in 1829.

The temple took up all the splendid ritual and festivity of Nāthdvārā, supported by the devotion and participation of the great commercial families of the area. The *padas* of the *aṣṭachāp* poets were sung in the temple, the Braj countryside was transported to Kāśī. Harakhcand's grandson, the famous poet Hariścandra, was to commemorate the occasion in verse some decades later : "Kāśī meṁ gokul kari dīnho" and "Brindāvan ko anubhav kāśī pragati dikhāyo"[6] .

The revival of the Puṣṭimārg in the Braj area itself had taken place only in the late eighteenth century, largely at the initiative of one Puruṣottam (b. 1748). The movement was to receive further impetus in the course of the nineteenth century since some of the deities who had fled the Braj country in the reign of Aurangzeb and settled in Rajasthan and Gujarat came back once again to occupy their more traditional seats in Braj.[7] Yet even amidst the general movement, Girdharjī's removal of a deity from Nāthdvārā, the stronghold of the *sampradāy*, to an entirely new scenario in Banaras was a novel venture. Though Vallabhācārya himself had lived in Banaras, as also Viṭṭhal for certain periods, the intervening period had seen little *sampradāy* activity. It was due entirely to the efforts and energy of Girdharjī that the Puṣṭimārg once again gained prestige in the area. It is reported that during his lifetime, the merchants of the surrounding bazars agreed to pay to the temple five and a quarter annas out of every hundred rupees of their business transactions, and though this practice was not so stringent after Girdharjī's death, some continued to do so at least up to the beginning of this century.[8] It is further recorded that the most cordial mutual relations were obtained with the Viśvanāth temple, the central institute of the city, and that on the festive occasions of that temple, in deference to the majesty of the deity, Girdharjī sent offerings made by Mukundrāyjī, who then also donned the costume appropriate to the occasion.[9]

Girdharjī's activities were not confined to Banaras alone, but were extended also to the other cities of the East and even as far away as Hyderabad.[10]

It was by no means 'the men of the old school alone', as Sherring claimed, who were behind the resurgence of pious activity, but an interlinkage of newer structures of power with the old, however fervently they chose to invoke tradition.

II

In this second section of the paper, I shall briefly recount and analyse the narrative structure of the Brajbhāṣā tract known as *Mukundrāyjī kī vārtā* in order to consider the machinations which made possible the establishment of the sixth *gaddī* of the *sampradāy*. The date of the composition of the *Vārtā* has not been recorded. To judge by the style, and the detailed, precise and intimate knowledge of Girdharjī's actions and reactions that the narrator betrays, it seems likely that it was put to paper during Girdharjī's own life-time, and that in fact large stretches of it were dictated by him. It is possible that during the course of the nineteenth century, hand-written copies, as is customary among pious Vaiṣṇavas, were in circulation, for the *Vārtā* is mentioned by writers at the turn of the nineteenth century.[11] It was published in Banaras in 1923, only to become unavailable shortly afterwards and it was as late as 1984, at the time of a grand celebration of the *chappanbhog* in the Gopāl Mandir, that it was reprinted again.

The chief protagonists of the narrative are Dāmodārjī II of Nāthdvārā, known more familiarly as Dāūjī Mahārāj, who lived from 1797 to 1826, and Girdharjī Mahārāj of Kāśī, who lived from 1791 to 1840.

Dāūjī reigned during a period of political peace and financial prosperity, so that it was possible to indulge in much building activity, cultivate the arts, and celebrate each festival with due fantasy and enthusiasm. He is reported to have spent the year 1821 performing a *duherā manorath*, i.e., commemorating each festival twice, so that the year consisted of uninterrupted revelry.[12] It was during his time, that the festival of the seven *svarūpas* was first celebrated with much pomp. James Tod, of *The Annals and Antiquities of Rajasthan* fame, has left a description of Dāūjī's person, which in fact complements the account of the *Vārtā* : "The present pontiff is about thirty years of age. He is of a benign aspect, with much dignity of demeanour: courteous, yet exacting the homage due to his high calling: meek as becomes the priest of Govinda, but with the finished manners of one accustomed to the first society. His features are finely moulded, and his complexion good. He is about the middle size, though as he rises to no mortal, I could not exactly judge his height... In times of danger, like some of his prototypes in the dark ages of Europe, he poised the lance, and found it more effective than spiritual anathemas, against those who would first adore the god and then plunder him... He rode the finest mares in the country; laid aside his pontificals for the quilted *dagla*, and was summoned to matins by the kettle-drum instead of the bell and cymbal."[13] It is this regal gesture and authority but innocence regarding matters of ritual symbol and theology which we meet again in the *Vārtā*. And it is this regal posture which is preserved in the many fine paintings of the time, influenced by the courtly style of Kotah.[14]

After Dāūjī's early death, his widow Lakṣmībahūjī, who was a sister of Girdharjī's own spouse, assumed the powers traditionally due to the dowager and became thereby the object of much attention and cajoling.

Girdharjī Mahārāj of Kāśī (Kāśīvāre, as he was known in Nāthdvārā) was by all accounts an aesthete of powerful presence. His tasteful *śṛṅgāras*, adornment of the deity, created models which were remembered and preserved for posterity in the paintings of the period.[15] In Nāthdvārā, it is reported that he often dressed as Yaśodā, the mother of Kṛṣṇa, draping his shawl like a sari over his head, as an expression of his devotion to the child-god. "It is said, that to identify better with Yaśoda, he allowed his hair to grow long like an Indian woman. One day, however, he failed to attend the *sevā* in time, having taken too long to wash and comb his long hair. This pained him, and to atone for this, he had his long hair shaved."[16]

Mukundrāyjī kī vārtā is divided into thirteen *vārtās*, or *prasaṅgas*, of unequal length. The narrative begins in Nāthdvārā with Girdharjī's ascension into prominence and it ends, as is fitting, in Kāśī. Though conceived of as a pious tract, it is much more in the nature of a confidential state document, since it moves almost entirely within the inner circles, the *bhītariyās* of the temple and records their dealings. The power configurations I mentioned in the first section—the prince, the merchants and the British—are present at strategic points in the narrative, though their mention in the *Vārtā* is often brief.

The narrative is structured as follows:

1-3 the establishment of Girdharjī's authority in Nāthdvārā
4 Girdharjī asks for the *svarūpa*.
5 Interlude, journeys, negotiations, death of Dāūjī
6-7 Girdharjī cajoles Bahūjī into fulfilling his wish

8 establishment of the temple for his own *svarūpa* in Nāthdvārā
9-10 departure preparations and negotiations
11 the journey to Kāśī
12-13 the installation of the *svarūpa* in Kāśī

In recapitulating the sequence of events as narrated in the *Vārtā*, I should like, at the outset, to emphasize those aspects, which make it so strikingly demonstrate the trends characteristic of developments in the period. Firstly, it is noteworthy that, in order to display his learning, Girdharjī chooses to emphasize the correspondence of Puṣṭimārg *sevā* to Vedic sacrificial ritual. He does this by the time-honoured convention of establishing a linkage which serves at once to enhance authority, while at the same time maintaining the adequacy, if not superiority, of the practice of his own *sampradāy* (*vārtā* 1-2).

Secondly, it is important to note that establishing linkages of this kind becomes in fact the source of Girdharjī's own authority, the means by which he is able to manipulate his way through the intricate power structures operating within the temple. The description of the scenes where he finally pushes his way forward is remarkable for its clear appraisal of the situation and its minute registration of detail (*vārtā* 4).

Finally, it is only towards the tail end of the *Vārtā*, when it is not of much consequence and no more crucial for the establishment of authority (though certainly for its perpetuation), that there is some direct experience of the deity, an experience so characteristic of the older *vārtās*, when the *alaukika*, miraculous workings of the deity become apprehensible to a wider circle of *bhaktas* (*vārtā 11*).

1-3. The establishment of Girdharjī's authority in Nāthdvārā.

1. In 1822 Girdharjī witnesses the festival of the seven

svarūpas celebrated by Dāūjī. He is morose, he thinks : "My ancestor has no name in the house of Śrīnāthjī." He begins to display his monumental knowledge of the practices of the *sampradāy*, correcting minute details of Śrīnāthjī's dress, pointing out the significance of the ritual objects in his vicinity. So much so that the narrator protests his inability to record all these discussions, some of which he considers to be of a nature too esoteric to be thus disclosed.

2. The second *prasaṅga* is a continuation of just this kind of exposition, the symbolic significance of rituals and observances, explicated at times on the basis of personal associations, but moving always within a familiar theological system, so that those around him obviously have no problem in respecting his explanations. The narrator, as the invisible presence at the side of Girdharjī, speaks almost with his voice. The usual narrational device consists of Dāūjī first putting a question, thereby giving Girdharjī the opportunity to elaborate. Typical, for instance, is the following discourse:

"Annakūṭa is the *yajña* of the Puṣṭimārg. This has been revealed at great length by Śrīgosaiṁjī. (A reference to Viṭṭhalnāth, the founder of *sevā* in the *sampradāy*) This is the reason why, in the compilation *Nāmaratna*, Śrīgosaiṁjī has the name *govardhanārdrimakhakṛta*, 'made by the sacrifice of the Govardhana mountain'. Hence he is called *yajña makha*, for he revealed the *yajña* of Govardhana. The following are the items required for (Vedic) *yajña*. A *yajña vedī* or sacrificial ground, the installation of fire, *yūpa*, stakes, *maṇḍapa*, a pavillion, *godān*, the presentation of a cow, *balidān*, a gift to the deity, the invocation of all the gods, the recitation of the Vedas, the devotion of the god usually worshipped, the cleansing ablution, the feeding of Brahmans, and others such are the items needed in a *yajña*. The following is the *yajña* of the Puṣṭimārg. It differs from *maryādāmārg*, or the customary way. Just as in *yajña* there is the *vedī*, so here there is the *navcaukīya*, the *siṃhāsan*, or the lion-throne. Just as there are lines engirdling all four sides of the *vedī*, here there are the three steps on all four sides of the *siṃhāsan*, which are for the *bhāvas satva, rajas* and *tamas*. Then a fire receptacle is required on the *vedī*, so here Ṭhākurjī, the lord himself is enthroned. And what of the fire? Why that is the mouth of Bhagvān. *Mukhato jāyate vahni*. Fire emanates from the mouth. From this pronouncement it holds that where Bhagvān himself thrones, what need of fire? And in *yajña* stakes are installed. Call the pillars stakes, by way of which *svarga* is obtained. Here there are the four pillars of the *candovā*, canopy. These are the four posts. For Puṣṭimārg awards all four, *dharma, artha, kāma, mokṣa*. And just as in *yajña* there is the pavilion, so here above the throne there is the canopy. In the canopy there are nine colours, so here if one views them separately, there are the nine varieties of *bhaktas* and it is their *bhāvas* which bear blossom. Just as in the canopy there are nine colours, so there are separate altars for the three kinds of *yajña* fire, *āhavānīya, gārhapatya* and *dakṣaṇīya*, so here the lord himself resides and thus the separate altars have no function. And if there is the presentation of cows, here there is the play of cows. On the day of *haṭaḍī*, or the divine market stall, the ears (of the cows) are awakened (they are made aware) so that on the day of Govardhan-worship they can be made to play. To give is subject to the will of the masters, here the *bhaktas* have hidden wishes. And the hidden *rasa* is attained when it is caused to be revealed, hence there is the play of cows here, both when the ears are awakened and when there is Govardhan-worship. And in *yajña* there is the cleansing ablution, so here Govardhan is washed. Why? Because here there is no difference between the worshipper and the worshipped. You are the worshipped in the form of Govardhan, and as Puruṣottam, you are the worshipper." (7)[17]

A mixture of Vedic *yajña* and later *pūjā* ritual is contrasted and equated with the great festivals of the *sampradāy*, Govardhan Pūjā and Annakūṭa. Girdharjī has displayed all the scholastic splendour of his learning with great dexterity.

3. There is a *śāstrārtha*, dispute, with an Anantācārya, a

follower of Rāmānuja, who has humiliated the learned in the court of Udaipur, and has come to Nāthdvārā with similar intentions. He cannot outwit Girdharjī, who caps his discourse by a volley of quotations from the *śāstras* on the significance of the *tulsīmālā*, which Anantācārya has upto now disdained to wear. From now on Girdharjī is established as an authority in Nāthdvārā, and if Dāūjī has doubts, he turns to Girdharjī.

4. *Girdharjī asks for the* svarūpa

4. He has finally acquired the position to risk the venture and ask for a *svarūpa*. Apart from providing a fascinating glimpse of the kind of internal operations behind the benign *jhāṃkī* of Śrīnāthjī the *vārtā* also gives us an impression of the battle of wills that now ensues regarding the question of authority and subversion of authority within the temple community. The following is a description typical for its minute observation of emotional action and reaction :

"In this manner, after he had examined him in all kinds of ways, it entered the mind of Śrī Dāūjī Mahārāj, that it was from him alone (Girdharjī) that he would receive the *gopālamantra*. He resolved this in his mind. Then one day he said, what I ask of you now, tell me instantly, without first consulting books and compilations. Then Girdharjī Mahārāj said, I have the blessings of the feet of my guru, Śrī Dvārikānāthjī Mahārāj. He had asked me something one day, and I replied instantly, so he had been most delighted, and had blessed me, saying that if anyone queries you regarding the *śāstras*, then you will respond with a thousand answers. When he heard this, Śrī Dāūjī Mahārāj was most delighted. After this, on the tenth day of the bright half of Māgha, *saṃvat* 1879, on the day of the lunar eclipse, acclaiming it as a solemn occasion, he thought of receiving the *gopālamantra* from him. Upon this some near relative said to Śrī Dāūjī Mahārāj, it is not proper to take the *gopālamantra* from him. If you have to take the *gopāla-*

mantra, then it has been the tradition to take it from one's own self. Besides you have your own blood relatives, take it from them. But he did not agree to this. So the near relative went to Śrī Dādījī Mahārāj, (the revered grandmother) and said that it is not proper to take the *gopālamantra* from him. So Śrīdādījī Mahārāj, Śrī Kamalābahūjī sent for Śrī Dāūjī Mahārāj and said this. She explained it to him in many different ways. But it would refuse to enter his mind. Then in the name of twenty-one of the Vallabha family, a missive was placed before Śrīnāthjī. And the reply authorized Śrī Girdharjī Mahārāj. Then he received the *gopālamantra* on the day of the eclipse. Then Śrī Dāūjī Mahārāj asked, what should I give you as *gurūdakṣiṇā*. Upon this Śrī Dvārikeśjī Mahārāj observed, he will only take something *alaukika* (otherworldly) as *dakṣiṇā*, he won't take *laukika* (worldly substance). When they heard this, all the near relatives became very silent. After some time had passed, he inquired again, what is this *alaukika* substance. Then Śrī Girdharjī Mahārāj said, if I were to ask for it, you would not be able to part with it. Then Śrī Dāūjī Mahārāj said, ask and I will give. Then he said, my ancestor had no name in the house of Śrīnāthjī. For my ancestor did not claim a *ṭhākurjī*. So let me have a single *svarūpa* of the *ṭhākurjī*s who reside by the side of Śrīnāthjī." (15-16)

Dāūjī offers some resistance and puts forward theological arguments as to the impossibility of granting this wish. He is easily outwitted. Then Dāūjī asks him to keep the matter quiet; he will do the needful sometime when Dādījī is away. For he knows, and he says this with some anger, that Girdharjī will not let go of him until this is done. So Girdharjī decides to observe silence for a while.

Dādījī does leave town and Dāūjī is forced, for the present, to part with a *veṇu*, a flute of Śrīnāthjī, in order to represent his presence in Kāśī, and to provide protective company for the *svarūpa* which will follow one day, and for which he is pressed into signing a document. Girdharjī offers an unspecified amount of gold, which Dāūjī does not refuse.

He leaves the city and spends some time with the army of Mahārāj Daulat Rāo Sindhiā. It is probable that he gets financial and political support from the Maratha chief, though there is no explicit mention of this. However, once in Kāśī, he is able to buy the *havelī* of Jairamdās Pansārī for twice its value.

5. Interlude, journeys, death of Dāūjī

5. The fifth *prasaṅga* is a brief account of various journeys. There is much movement. Dāūjī goes to Calcutta, he stops on the way in Banaras, but Girdharjī is himself on the move. Dāūjī expires in the Braj country. Shortly afterwards, his widow, Lakṣmībahūjī, summons Girdharjī to Nāthdvārā. On the way Girdharjī stops at several key places, meets various personages of royal blood, allays their doubts and performs *sevā*.

6-7. Cajoling Bahūjī into fulfilling his wish

6. Bahūjī is pleased with him in several ways, and is similarly pressed into signing a document. Like her late husband, she further allows him the right to perform several kinds of *sevā*. In return, though she is a mere woman, she receives the *gopālamantra* from him.

7. Girdharjī manages to secure a temple in the precincts of the Śrīnāthjī complex for his own *svarūpa*. There is much festivity, but that night, there is a pitched battle between his people and mixed Hindu-Muslim troops led by a Bhaṭṭ, who is not further identified. Girdharjī has the vision of Śrīnāthjī himself with a *cakra* coming to his rescue. It is as if seeing him the inimical troops flee. After some further negotiations, and the offer of further gifts, he finally manages to carry off both the tiny *svarūpas* in triumph to the new temple. The *Vārtā* records his immense gratification at being able to

celebrate the ceremony of *rājbhog* with his own *svarūpa*.

8. Establishment of the temple for his own svarūpa

8. The eighth *prasaṅga* is an account of a riotous celebration of Annakūṭa and Govardhan Pūjā, with detailed descriptions of ritual, costume and the delicacies prepared for the delectation of Śrīnāthjī. Mukundrāyjī has come into his own.

9-10. Departure preparations and negotiations

9. Girdharjī, after having spent a year thus in Nāthdvārā, prepares to depart. He asks for the traditional regalia (*prācīn ābharaṇ*) of his own *svarūpa*. Further Mukundrāyjī now possesses the hereditary retainers that a *svarūpa* requires, all twenty two of them (their names and their duties are inventoried). Girdharjī meanwhile performs the most prestigious *sevās* in the temple. He is also gaining in stature as a prospective *tilakāyat*. For the first time, a dream, important in the repertoire of the religiously empowered, is reported. Navnītapriyājī, the second most important image in the temple, chooses to communicate with him thus.

10. Once the question of departure comes up, and the problem of safety on the way, it is inevitable that the British come into play. The Adhikārī of the temple asks the British resident in Udaipur for protection, and he graciously provides him with a single *caprāsī*, (peon), and a *farmān*, (letter of authorisation). As regards finances, a banker is applied to, who only parts with cash, after a *huṇḍī*, (promissory note) is put forward. It is from Lālā Rādhākṛṣṇadās of Kāśī, whose reliability as a pious Vaiṣṇava is further confirmed by the Adhikārī.

There is some commotion, once it is to be decided who will accompany the procession to Kāśī. The retainers, one and all, refuse, for they are afraid that there will be violence (*upadrav*) when Mukundrāyjī actually leaves the temple premises.

11. The journey to Kāśī

11. Bahūjī Mahārāj comes to the rescue and issues firm orders that all the necessary personnel assemble. She threatens that if due respect is not shown to Girdharjī, then the offender will not be allowed to re-enter the village of Nāthdvārā. The train now consists of 600 armed soldiers, Hindus and Mlecchas, 23 wagons, big and small, 54 *motī kā bel* (?), 2 carpenters, 1 washerman, and 1 tailor. The journey commences each day after *rājbhog*. It is like a bridal party. Musical instruments are procured on the way. They fear attack from a party of Bhīl marauders, but by the grace of Mukundrāyjī the attack is warded off and a real bridal party is looted instead. In one of the overnight camps, the British Resident and the Rāṇā of Kheḍā come to pay their respects. Several wonders, small and big, are recorded: Mukundrāyjī is flowering into a full-fledged deity, with his own choice taste and caprices. Thus for instance :

"There was a tank on the way, where there was a huge tree. We rested the palanquin there in the shade of the afternoon. Suddenly a *naṭ* (acrobat) appeared, in order to perform a *tamāśā* (show). He sent word to the Mahārāj. But Mahārāj said it would cause delay. Give him something and send him off. So we gave him something and sent him away. Meanwhile, we prepared to leave. As the palanquin was lifted, it became heavy. Mukundrāyjī was pouting, just as a child who insists upon seeing a *tamāśā*. The palanquin would not be lifted. So Śrīmahārājjī asked, what is going on. He thought: he wants to see the *naṭ* perform. So the *naṭ* was summoned straight away and was made to perform. So there was quite a *tamāśā*, and afterwards he was well rewarded. Only after the *naṭ* departed could the palanquin be lifted. He performed many such *bālalīlās* on the way. How far can one write it down ?" (33)

Thus an incident typical of Vaiṣṇava *vārtās*, the personal experience of the deity, occurs towards the end of the narrative. Once they reach the vicinity of Kāśī, the city's fabulously wealthy banker Harakhcand is summoned and told to make preparations for the reception in the city.

12-13. The Installation of the svarūpa *in Kāśī*

12. There is a brief account of the arrival in Kāśī, with Harakhcand heading the reception, the colourful procession through town, the elephants, the guns, the soldiers, and the gaily attired *vaiṣṇava jan*, the singing women, the shower of rupees, the rituals, till finally Mukundrāyjī arrives in the house of Girdharjī.

13. Finally all three, Śrīnāthjī's *veṇu*, Mukundrāyjī and the older image Gopāllāljī receive *rājbhog* together. A dream incident has already warned Girdharjī's mother into taking care that a *dhvajā* (banner) is installed over the sanctum (*nij mandir*). Asked by a banker *bhakta* as to what kind of *bhakti*, devotional attitude, he would prescribe, Girdharjī lays down that Gopāllāl is to be served with *pitṛ bhāva* (paternal devotion) and Mukundrāyjī with *pati bhāva* (marital devotion). The elaborate devotional ritual in the temple is carried out faithfully and the deity thus fully installed.

Thus, of the thirteen *vārtās*, three are concerned with Girdharjī demonstrating his prowess in Nāthdvārā, the fourth involves a testing of his lately gained power, the fifth is a bare account of strategic manoeuvres and, with the death of Dāūjī, a temporary power vacuum. The sixth and seventh *vārtās* are further exercises of power, this time with Lakṣmībahūjī, the eighth records the final triumph over opposing forces in Nāthdvārā, and the establishment of his own temple. The ninth and tenth show the process of extraction of the deity from the intricate weave of the temple complex. Only in the eleventh is there some record of the impact of the deity Mukundrāyjī, whose *vārtā* it ostensibly is. The last two *vārtās*, the twelfth and the thirteenth, repeat the festive ritual of Nāthdvārā in Kāśī, coming full circle as it were.

III

I will now attempt a preliminary comparison between this nineteenth century *Vārtā* and the main stream *vārtā* literature of the Vallabha Sampradāy, in that I consider the perspective and the ambient of the *vārtās* as well as their overall direction. Inevitably, the generalizations involve some simplification.

Apart from the *vārtās*, contained in the well-known collections *Caurāsī vaiṣṇavan kī vārtā* and *Do sau bāvan vaiṣṇavan kī vārtā*, which focus on the exemplary lives of single *bhaktas*, and concern themselves with some aspects either of their original moment of conviction by Acāryajī or Gosāīṁjī, or other edifying incidents in their lives, there are *vārtās* which are in the nature of more general accounts. These are narrations of the evolution and consolidation of the faith along with the history of the Vallabha clan, which are centrally connected with this development. As a prototype of this last variety, I take the *Śrīnāthjī prākaṭya kī vārtā*, which chronicles and elucidates the history of the *sampradāy* from its very inception—the manifestation of Śrīnāthjī, the flight from the persecution by Aurangzeb—to the settlement, under the protection of the Rāṇā of Udaipur, in the village in the Vindhya hills known henceforth as Nāthdvārā.[18] Here as in our *Vārtā*, there are negotiations and journeys, yet the whole consists of short episodes, and the perspective changes constantly. The listener moves from person to person and from landscape to landscape, but most important of all, the deity can communicate directly with the people of Braj and primarily through the medium of dreams, ask that his own needs and caprices be attended to, which he can reward generously and in very concrete ways. He can also intervene directly in their lives and perform miracles. It is simple in language and is directed primarily towards the faithful. Though the Gosvāmīs, as patriarchs, have dealings with the highest political personages, the tone remains colloquial, didactic, and edifying. Hariharnāth Ṭaṇḍan, in his study of the *vārtā* literature has noted as typical characteristics of the older *vārtās*:

"There is as much variety in the subject matter of the *vārtā* as there is in the various portrayals (*caritra*). No difference has been made with regard to caste and rank, male-female, high-low, rich-poor, and if one were to count, then people of ordinary rank will be found in larger numbers. From this point of view, the *vārtā* literature is a thing of ordinary folk, and is connected to the literature of the people."[19]

In contrast, our *vārtā* moves almost entirely in the world of the Gosvāmīs, within their orbit of power; they have no need of dealing with the lowly, and there is no mention of them, apart from their function as retainers. Śrīnāthjī, in so far as there is any need to consult him, communicates directly with the Gosvāmīs. His presence is confined to *nij mandir*, (the inner sanctum); the Braj countryside is symbolically represented by the temple complex itself. The negotiations are confined to figures of power, and the language is correspondingly measured and none came up for explicit criticism. Even the Bhaṭṭjī, who leads the armed attack, is neither located for us in the temple hierarchy nor further mentioned. In fact, people are only mentioned when they react to Girdharjī's moves. Similarly, the machinations of the others are registered and recorded only if they affect Girdharjī. The perspective is thus almost entirely confined to that of Girdharjī himself. The camera moves along with him, so to speak, viewing the surroundings almost entirely from his angle of vision, in terms of his particular need of the moment, and focusing on the persons he has dealings with.

The need of political and financial protection involves delicate negotiations with the Marathas, and with the princes of the adjoining Rajput states ruling under the aegis of the British. And all important is the patronage of the merchants, who make the maintenance of the establishment in Banaras possible. Their interests in the linkage are apparent—apart from the prestige attached, and the opportunity to gain public approval for their largesse and piety, there is the solidarity which is generated within their own community, and which is commemorated with each festivity in the temple. It is no coincidence that Girdharjī buys a *havelī* and establishes himself in the midst of the residential and commercial area of the Naupaṭṭī Mahājans, Lālā Rādhākṛṣṇadās's support is available at a decisive juncture, which makes the move out of Nāthdvārā possible, Harakhcand finances the festivities to welcome the deity in Banaras and organizes the further maintenance of the temple complex. These classes of people are present in the older *vārtās*, but as so many *bhaktas* amongst the *bhaktas*, and they tend to speak and are spoken of in the same familiar idiom as the people. If they do not comply with the wishes of the deity, they are often shown as humbled for some didactic end. In *Mukundrāyjī kī vārtā* they are present as part of a power constellation, which provides the givens of the situation, apart from offering their power and wealth as part of their devotion, they are not themselves affected by the deity in any noticeable way.

The means of establishing authority, as Girdharjī so ably demonstrates, is the knowledge of the most minute details of ritual and ornamentation, a science that has become so rarified and at times so pedantic, that the practitioners themselves display perplexity when asked to explain the significance of a precise sequence. When this knowledge is blessed with the appropriate genealogical connections, for Girdharjī is a descendant of Yadunāth, it is still possible to influence and extend the prevailing hierarchies. The hagiography here becomes an account of sacral power and the authority this bestows. This is in sharp contrast to the source of authority in the older *vārtās*, where it is also possible to wield power and receive due acknowledgement from the community, if there has been direct experience of the deity, whether in person or in a dream.

The only concession that is made to the general *vārtā* style is towards the end, in the eleventh *vārtā*, when Mukundrāyjī assumes the characteristics of the whimsical child god who would buy certain items and reject others. This does indeed establish a link, however tenuous, to the vast corpus of Vaiṣṇava *vārtā* literature, well known to the pious.

Mukundrāyjī ki vārtā is essentially a document of the nineteenth century, which, amongst other notable features, in the attempt to establish the elaborate series of equations with Vedic sacrifice, testifies to the awareness of the need to establish links with an authoritative canon. This points to the developments later in the century, when Hinduism consolidated itself increasingly by various integrative devices, one of the most effective being that of providing the overall umbrage of the Vedas, in order to absorb traditions and *sampradāys*, which both differed and overlapped. On the whole, with *Mukundrāyjī kī vārtā* we have moved a long way from the pious tracts that comprise the early *vārtās*. Our *Vārtā* has all the restraint and the diplomacy of a confidential state document, a recitation of the machinations and manoeuvres of Girdharjī Mahārāj, who caters for and reflects the concerns of newer constellations of power, namely the 'princes, pandits, banyas and priests' invoked in Sherring's book—some of a vintage newer than they would care to acknowledge—operating in linkage with older institutions of power.

NOTES

1. Sherring 1868:38.
2. *Cf.* Motīcandra 1985: Chap. 8 *Banāras ke mahājan*, 313-330; Bayly 1978: 181-182.
3. There are various stories associated with the rise and formation of this group of banker-merchants. Motīcandra 1985: 410-412 provides a list of their names as available in a contemporary document.
4. The full title of the work is *Śrīmukundrāyjī kī vārtā tathā śrīgopāllāljī kī vārtā.* I am grateful to Dr. Kalyan Krishna of the Banaras Hindu University for drawing my attention to the *Vārtā* and to Professor Anand Krishna for elucidating many aspects, which would otherwise have remained closed to me.

5. See Ṭaṇḍan 1960: 395 for an account of the distribution of the *svarūpas* amongst the sons of Viṭṭhal. For Girdharjī's genealogy see the article by Mādhav Śarmā in *Gosvāmī Śrīgiridharjī mahārāj dviśatābdī mahotsav smārikā.* 1990:11.
6. "Śrīgirdharjī kī badhāī", "Uttar ārdhabhaktmāl", *Bhāratendu samagra*, p. 146, p. 70.
7. Entwistle 1987: 221-224.
8. Rādhākṛṣṇadās 1904:18.
9. Rāykṛṣṇadās 1976: 10 notes that the *prasādī mālā*, flower garland of Mukundrāyjī was sent everyday to Viśvanāth, who showed his regard to the deity by wearing it. On *vaikuṇṭha caturdaśī* he even donned a *tulasī mālā*. On *śiva rātri* Mukundrāyjī in his turn wore a *bāghambarī chiṁt kā bānā*, an attire which resembled a tiger skin.

   In Kāśī there is no getting past Viśvanāth. The *Caurāsī vaiṣṇavan kī vārtā* narrates the deeds of Seṭh Puroṣottamdās of Kāśī, who was so staunch a Vaiṣṇava that he offered no obeisance elsewhere. Biśesvar (Viśvanāth) appeared to him in a dream and asked him, since he did not bother to maintain neighbourly ties (*gāṁv ko nāto*), to at least let him partake to the *mahāprasād* that the Seṭh offered to his deity. One consequence of his resulting gratification at being so honoured, was that Biśesvar attended henceforth to the safety of the pious Seṭh and appointed Kāl Bhairav himself as his personal watchman (62-63).
10. *Cf.* Mādhav Śarmā in *Gosvāmī Śrīgiridharjī mahārāj dviśatābdī mahotsav smārikā* 1990:13.
11. Rādhākṛṣṇadās 1904:18.
12. *Cf.* Ambalal 1987:64-68.
13. Tod 1920: 642-643.
14. *Ibid.* pp. 66-67.
15. Ambalal includes the painting depicting *Candramā kā Śṛṅgār* in his selection (p. 111). I quote from his description of the *śṛṅgār*: "The Moon and moonlight provide the inspiration for this *shringara*. Śrināthjī wears a shimmering *gherdar vagha* of silver brocade. Over his *pagha*, a *dohra katra*, double plume, is ornamented with a single pearl at each of its two ends. The *pichvai* is deep blue and has a tiny crescent-shaped new moon of silver suspended at its top centre." (p. 154).
16. *Ibid.* p. 154.
17. Vallabhācārya recognized the Vedas as the highest authority. However, the equating of Vedic sacrifice with *puṣṭimārg sevā*, which had developed independently of it, serves to

underline the hightened significance of the Vedic ritual as legitimising ritual practice at this juncture.
I am grateful to Catharina Kiehnle for helping me to elucidate the passage translated.

18. See Ṭaṇḍan 1960 for detailed information on the first two mentioned *vārtās* and Barz 1976 for his useful introduction. Vaudeville's analysis 1980 of *Śrināthjī prākaṭya kī vārtā* remains exemplary.
19. Ṭaṇḍan 1960:53.

REFERENCES

Ambalal, Amit. 1987. *Krishna as Shrinathji. Rajasthani Paintings from Nathdvara.* Ahmedabad: Mapin Publishing.

Barz, Richard. 1976. *The Bhakti Sect of Vallabhācārya.* Faridabad: Thomson Press.

Bayly, C. A. 1978. "Indian Merchants in a 'Traditional' Setting, Benares 1780-1830." *The Imperial Impact : Studies in the Economic History of Africa and India.* Ed. Clive Dewey and A.G. Hopkins. London: Institute of Commonwealth Studies.

—. 1981. "From Ritual to Ceremony : Death Ritual and Society in Hindu North India since 1600", *Mirrors of Mortality: Studies in the Social History of Death.* Ed. Joachim Whaley. London: Europa Publications. pp. 154-86.

Caurāsi vaiṣṇavan kī vārtā. Ed. Dvārikādās Pārikh. Mathura: Śrī govardhan granthmālā kāryālay. *Saṃvat* 2027.

Entwistle, A. W. 1987. *Braj. Centre of Krishna Pilgrimage.* Groningen: Egbert Forsten.

Glasenapp, Helmuth von. 1934. "Die Lehre Vallabhācāryas". *Zeitschrift für Indologie und Iranistik.* 9, 3.pp. 268-30.

Gosvāmī Śrīgiridharjī mahārāj dviśatābdī mahotsav smārikā. 1990. Ed. Lakṣmī Śaṅkār Vyās. Vārāṇasī Bharatnārāyaṇ Gupt Śudhādvaita japa-yajña samiti.

Hariścandra. 1987. *Bhāratendu samagra.* Ed. Hemant Śarmā. Vārāṇasī: Hindī pracārak saṁsthān.

Motīcandra. 1962. *Kāśī kā itihās.* 2nd ed. Vārāṇasī: Viśvavidyālay Prakāśan.

Rādhākṛṣṇadās. 1904. *Bhāratendu bābu hariścandra kā jīvan carit.* Repr. Lucknow: Hindī Samiti, Uttar Pradeś śāsan, 1976.

Rāykṛṣṇadās. 1976. "Bhāratendu saṃsmaraṇ 1." *Dharmayug*, 29. Aug., pp. 10-12.

Sherring, M. A. 1868. *Benares. The Sacred City of the Hindus: An Account of Benares in Ancient and Modern Times.* Repr. Delhi: B. R. Publ. Corp., 1975.

Śrīmukundrāyjī kī vārtā tathā Śrīgopāllāljī kī vārtā. (first pub. *saṃvat* 1980). Ed. Pandit Rāmnāthjī Śāstrī. Vārāṇasī: Rāmdās Agravāl, *saṃvat* 2041.

Ṭaṇḍan, Hariharnāth. 1960. *Vārtā sāhitya, ek vṛhat adhyāyan.* Aligarh: Bhārat Prakāśan Mandir.

Thiel Horstmann, Monika. 1990. "Jai Singh II (1688-1745) Hinduherrscher in einer Wendezeit." Antrittsvorlesung, Universität Bamberg. 19. February 1990.

Tod, James. 1920. *Annals and Antiquities of Rajasthan Or the Central and Western Rajput States of India.* 3 vols. Ed. with an Introduction by William Crooke. Repr. Delhi: Motilal Banarasidass, 1971.

Vaudeville, Charlotte. 1980. "The Govardhan Myth in Northern India". *Indo-Iranian Journal.* 22. pp. 1-45.

[illegible] 1980. [illegible] Varanasi, [illegible] 2041.

[illegible] 1960. [illegible]

[illegible] 1991. [illegible] Singh II [illegible] 18 February 1990.

[illegible] introduction by William Crooke. Reprint. [illegible]

Vaudeville, Charlotte. [illegible] pp. 1-48.

Cult and Ideology

The *Gopālakālā* as Reflected in the *Pāṇḍuraṅgamāhātmya* of Pralhāda Mahārāja and the *Abhaṅgas* of Tukārāma

Erik Reenberg Sand

INTRODUCTION

Most of the current research on medieval and modern *bhakti* focusses on its literary, ideological, and mystical aspects. Generally, this is with good reason, so far as we are dealing with the Sant tradition, which is often consciously opposed to ritual behaviour, such as idol-worship, etc. Within several of the more established *sampradāyas*, such as the Rāmānujiyas, the Madhvācāryas, and the Vallabhācāryas such an anti-ritualistic attitude is, however, not found. And, as has already been pointed out by Charlotte Vaudeville, it seems that the Maharashtrian Sant, or Vārakarī, tradition, in some respects (first of all its adherence to the image of Viṭhobā in Pandharpur), differs from the northern Sant tradition.[1]

In the present paper I shall deal with how yet another ritual aspect of the Vārakarī Sampradāya, namely the so-called *kālā* or *gopālakālā*, performed by the Vārakarīs at the end of their pilgrimage to Pandharpur, may be seen reflected in the *Pāṇḍuraṅgamāhātmya* of Pralhāda Mahārāja, and in some of the *abhaṅgas* of Tukārāma.

THE PRESENT DAY *KĀLĀ*

In an earlier paper I tried to indicate that this ritual has been an important element in the Pandharpur pilgrimage ever since the time of Jñāneśvara, for it is mentioned both in the *abhaṅgas* of Nivṛttinātha and Sopānadeva, and is probably also referred to in the oldest Sanskrit *māhātmya* of Pandharpur, the so-called *Pāṇḍuraṅgamāhātmya* attributed to the *Skandapurāṇa*.[2]

In order to give a brief description of the present-day *kālā*, one may say that the different groups of Vārakaris (*diṇḍis*) on the morning of the full-moon day of the month of Āṣāḍha, meet around their *kīrtanakāras* outside the Gopālpūr temple, about a mile south of Pandharpur. After the performance of *kīrtanas*, a pot filled with a mixture of curds (*dahīṃ*) and parched grain (*lāhyā*), hung up in a tree, is broken. After taking part of its contents, or the parched grain otherwise distributed to the pilgrims, they gather inside the temple where they spend some time playing various popular games. After this, they go back to Pandharpur in order to leave during the afternoon.[3]

With regard to the contents of this ritual, we are left in the dark by the previous literature. Nevertheless, it seems pretty obvious that the meaning of what takes place is given by the local myth connected with Gopālpūr and Viṣṇupada, as it is found both in the *Maharashtra State Gazetteer*, and in the small pamphlets sold to pilgrims in Pandharpur. According to these sources, the *kālā* was first instituted by Kṛṣṇa and his cowherd friends after they had reached Pandharpur in their search for Rukmiṇī who, having been offended by Rādhā, had left Dvārakā.[4]

In other words, it seems that the *kālā* is a form of ritual drama or ritual reenactment of the mythical deeds performed here in the old days by Kṛṣṇa and his cowherd companions. This again implies that the mythical descriptions of the *kālā* may carry two levels of meaning, one referring to the mythical *kālā*, performed by Kṛṣṇa and his companions, and the other to the actual *kālā*, as it is performed by the Vārakarīs.

THE *KĀLĀ* DESCRIPTION OF PRALHĀDA MAHĀRĀJA

This is illustrated by the description of the *kālā* found in the *Pāṇḍuraṅgamāhātmya* of Pralhāda Mahārāja,[5] which is a Marathi adaptation of the aforementioned Sanskrit work with the same title. In this text Kṛṣṇa's arrival is not due to Rukmiṇī, but to the sage Puṇḍalīka, as in the original founding myth of Pandharpur,[6] yet the site of the *kālā* performance is likewise the area south of Pandharpur. In vss. 65-81 we get a very lively and detailed version of the *kālā* myth, starting with Kṛṣṇa's departure from the Govardhana mountain:

> Then, after he (i.e., Kṛṣṇa) had taken all the Gopīs, the cowherds, the cattle, and the Govardhana mountain with him, they crossed several countries, inaccessible places, forests and groves. (65)
>
> On the way the cowherds engaged in various kinds of frolics: singing, laughing, and joking, (and) Nārada was walking in front singing about the qualities of Śrīkṛṣṇa.(66)
>
> In this manner they quickly reached the Puṣpāvatī. Nārada said to the lord or Kamalā: "Here we should rest."(67)
>
> Having listened to the words of Nārada, Yadunandana, standing on one and a half feet (and) playing the flute, tended the cattle.(68)
>
> Then the cowherds came running (and) said: "The fire in the stomach has taken proper form, O Kṛṣṇa, (our) hunger has become strong and we cannot bear the hunger any longer." (69)

The All-sustaining one said to them: "The provisions should be brought quickly. O children, you are very hungry, (and) it has become very late today." (70)

Then the playmates hurriedly brought various dishes of food, (and) with extreme fondness (they) fetched bamboos containing curds and milk.(71)

Having sought out a large rock, the party of cowherds (spread) round about. In the middle the one of the colour of a dark cloud (i.e., Kṛṣṇa) was shining, (and) the *gopālakālā* was arranged.(72)

Having untied (their) provisions, they sat on the rock, Hari and the cowherds on one side, the women of Vraja on the other, in such manner that Hari was opposite everyone. (73)

A companion says to the lord of the Yadus: "Let us dine in company." Whatever anyone liked, they offered in the mouth of Kṛṣṇa.(74)

Some were tickling each other. Some were making faces (and) falsely they would say: "The cows have gone astray, suddenly they have gone far away." (75)

Some steal the provisions of each other, while their eyes are turned, and eat (it). Some run away with it and show (their) bare teeth. (76)

Some cowherds take a mouthful of food in the hand (and) eat it while dancing. Some strike the palm of the hand (and) scatter a mouthful of leavings.(77)

At the end of the dinner they drink the remaining curds and milk. Some pour it over each other. Some besprinkle each other (with it). (78)

Having eaten fresh butter, some rub each other's mouths (with it), Some gurgle with buttermilk (and) throw it on each other.(79)

Throughout the sky a row of gods was seated in

(their) chariots looking at the *kālā* (and) showering (down) divine flowers. (80)

They said: "Blessed, blessed (are these) cow-herd people, blessed, blessed the trees (and) stones. Blessed, blessed is the place where the life of the world (i.e. God) plays." (81)[7]

According to this description, the original, mythical *kālā* was a meal which Kṛṣṇa, Nārada, and the cowherds (*govaḷas*) took together after their journey from Vṛndāvana, and the place was in the vicinity of the small river Puṣpāvatī, which joins the Bhīmā near the Viṣṇupada temple.[8] Today also, the most important element in the ritual is the partaking of the *kālā* in the earthen vessel *(dahīhaṃḍī)*, or in the *lāhyā* which is distributed to the pilgrims. Furthermore, the manner in which the cowherds gathered around Kṛṣṇa, the cowherds on one side, the cowherd women on the other, reminds one very much of the way in which today the Vārakarī *diṇḍīs* gather around their *kīrtanakāras*, men and women separate. The fact that Pralhāda Mahārāja lets the *kālā* take place on a great rock, points to the fact that in his day the ritual took place near the present Viṣṇupada temple.[9]

Furthermore, we notice that the entire meal took place in a joyful and joking atmosphere, presumably because it is understood to be the sport of Kṛṣṇa, his *krīḍā* or *krīḍana.*[10] In the present *kālā,* however, the element of play is most marked after the distribution of *lāhyā,* when the participants enter the Gopālpūr temple and play games like the *humbarī* and *phugaḍī.*

In short, the activities described by Pralhāda Mahārāja are all simple acts of cowherd life, like tending cattle, relaxing, playing the flute, and common partaking of the provisions which have been brought from home. With the arrival of Kṛṣṇa and his cowherd friends all these activities are transferred from Gokula to the vicinity of Pandharpur.[11] As far as I am aware, this pastoral idyll has no exact parallel in the Purāṇic accounts of the life of Kṛṣṇa, although passages dealing with Kṛṣṇa's boyhood in the *Viṣṇupurāṇa* and *Bhāgavatapurāṇa* show some similarity.[12] Nevertheless, we here witness a characteristic difference between the Vārakarī Sampradāya and the North Indian *bhakti* traditions. Thus, while both draw their inspiration from Kṛṣṇa's childhood, in the North it is the *rāsakrīḍā* or *rāsalīlā* motif, with its strongly erotic mood, which has inspired ritual, religious drama, and mystical poetry, while in Maharashtra it is the *bālakrīḍā*, the sports of Kṛṣṇa with his playmates, which has become the main theme of ritual and poetry.[13]

THE *KĀLĀ-ABHAṄGAS* OF TUKĀRĀMA

Apart from the mythical descriptions dealt with so far, the *kālā* is likewise used as a motif in *abhaṅgas* of most of the Vārakarī saint-poets, from Nivṛttinātha onwards. In contrast to the more ordinary mythical descriptions, which, as we saw above, may refer both to a purely mythical and to a ritual level, it is evident that many of these hymns, especially since the time of Ekanātha, also refer to a spiritual or mystical level, symbolizing the relationship between man and God. Perhaps this is nowhere clearer than in the case of Tukārāma, under whose name we have several *abhaṅgas* dealing with the *kālā*.

In this connection we are, however, confronted with the initial problem of determining which *abhaṅgas* may be considered *kālā-abhaṅgas*, and which not. Thus, there seems to be no fixed tradition with regard to their classification, which may easily be demonstrated by a comparison of the so-called "Government edition"[14] of Tukārāma's *abhaṅgas* (hereafter GE) and the edition of the *Sakalasantagāthā*[15] by R.C. Dhere.[16]

Although I do not intend to solve this problem of classification here, I will, nevertheless, suggest three reasons for this situation. The most important seems to be the fact that in the actual *kālā* ritual, the *kālā*, or meal proper, and the various types of plays and games are so closely associated that it becomes difficult to distinguish *abhaṅgas* dealing with one theme from those dealing with the other. Another reason is that the basic meaning of the word *kālā* is not the ritual, but rather the special dish which the cowherds eat together, wherefore all hymns dealing with the distribution and eating of food among Kṛṣṇa and the cowherds, a favourite theme of Tukārāma, tend to be classified as *kālā-abhaṅgas*, even though they do not contain the word *kālā*. Finally, the fact that very few of the *abhaṅgas* of Tukārāma which are classified as *kālā-abhaṅgas* contain direct references to the locations of Pandharpur, but, on the contrary, seem to take place in Vṛndāvana,[17] makes them part of the larger *bālakṛīḍā*-theme, with the resulting difficulties in distinguishing one theme from the other.

In short, we are not able to read Tukārāma's *abhaṅgas* in the same way as the local myths, whose aim is primarily to explain the origin and sacrality of Gopālpūr and the area around Viṣṇupada, and of the *kālā* ritual as it is being performed today. Tukārāma's *kālā-abhaṅgas* do not only refer to the *kālā* ritual, but also to Kṛṣṇa's miraculous deeds and activities among men, and, therefore, they become symbolic of the relationship and love which exists between God and his devotee, and of the devotee's mystical career.[18]

Thus, the *kālā-abhaṅgas* may refer both to a mystical and a ritual level. Generally, the hymns containing only mystical references are most frequent. For example, most of the hymns which place the action in Vṛndāvana would seem to belong to this category. However, there are a couple of hymns, most of which are composed using the first person plural, which may refer to both these levels, as they also seem to reflect the actual *kālā* performed by the pilgrims in Pandharpur. The use of the first person is obviously suitable for conveying the idea of identity between the actors of the hymns, the cowherds, and the composer (Tukārāma) and his audience (his fellow Vārakarīs), an identity which may, in fact, refer both to the ritual dramatic situation, and to a mystical interpretation. This identification is clear from the following *abhaṅga*, which obviously may be understood both in the context of the ritual, and mystically:

> We are rustic cowherds, we are not the impudent among people. Let us make a *kālā* of our provisions, let us distribute it among each other. Let us play with each other, our things are with us. Tukā says: Unknowingly we met around Kānhobā.[19] (GE 225)

In one *abhaṅga* we find a quite realistic description of the *kālā*, reminding us of the description of Pralhāda Mahārāja. Here Tukārāma calls upon the women, saying:

> Come, women, let us see Pāṇḍuraṅga on the sandy beach. The *kālā* has been arranged and there is a crowd of cowherds all around. Joyfully, every one is putting a morsel in the mouth of every one else, without distinguishing between small and great. Playing *hamāmā* and *humbarī*, the fife and pipe, they dance around with Hari in the middle. Men and women, as well as all kinds of animals, have been affected with desire and have forgotten their bodily consciousness. There is no doubt in their minds. There is a shower of flowers and crowd of *āratī*s. Having strung together *tulasī*, they will put garlands round their necks. Tukā says, having seen Kānho, the king of the Yādavas, the dear one of the Gopīs, happiness arises in the mind.(GE 211)

Here the fact that the action takes place in Pandharpur is indicated by the use of the name Pāṇḍuraṅga and the reference to the sandy beach (*vālavaṃta*), which is synonymous with the banks of the Bhīmā at Pandharpur. Likewise, the partaking of the *kālā* is depicted as a joyful, common meal in which everyone feeds each other, irrespective of social status, a feature which is in harmony with the social attitude of *bhakti* religion. Furthermore, just as mentioned in the earlier description of the present *kālā*, we hear that the meal is followed by various games and a general merrymaking. However, with regard to the fact that the participants are said to be affected with desire, presumably for Kṛṣṇa, and forget their bodily consciousness (*dehabhāva)* and loose all doubt, this may both be understood as an effect of both the *kālā* ritual and mystical union with Kṛṣṇa.

In another *abhaṅga* Tukārāma compares the *kālā* eaten in Vaikuṇṭha with ordinary food:

> Having been born we go forward. We eat *kālā* (in the form of) curds and rice. In Vaikuṇṭha it is not like this. (There we get only) a small morsel of *kālā*. We put (it) in the mouths of each other (and) happily we do the *humbarī*. Tukā says: Beautiful is the sandy beach. Proper (things) are best. (GE 161)

This may, of course, easily be understood as a comparison between the life of the world and spiritual life. Nevertheless, once we know that, in Vārakarī terminology, both Vaikuṇṭha and the sandy beach are synonyms for Pandharpur, we cannot help seeing in this *abhaṅga* also a possible reference to the actual *kālā*.

A couple of *abhaṅgas* in which Tukārāma makes the cowherds tell Kṛṣṇa that they do not want to go home may also suggest the *kālā* in Pandharpur. In one *abhaṅga* they say:

> We are satiated to our heart's content, no more provisons (*śidorī)* are needed, now let us not lose sight of this one [i.e. Kṛṣṇa] for a moment. Move, move, Kānhobā, let us start a game in the wood. Let us collect the cows and place them in a shady spot. We do not want to go home, if we can avoid the journey. You are our good kinsman, our mother and

> father. Tukā says: The stomach is filled, what sort of complaint can there be now? Look, the road stops behind and before us.(GE 186)

Of course, this may be understood as a purely mystical analogy.[20] However, it is also possible to see herein a reference to the feelings of the Vārakarīs who, during the *kālā* in Pandharpur, in the company of their companions and Kṛṣṇa, are unwilling to start on their journey home.

Leaving aside the allusions to the actual ritual in Tukārāma's *kālā-abhaṅgas*, the comparison between the *kālā* and the food at home, and between the sandy beach of Pandharpur and Vaikuṇṭha, make us realize that, symbolically speaking, the *kālā* which the cowherds partake of is not ordinary, but divine food. It is a symbol of the mutual love between Kṛṣṇa and man, or a symbol or manifestation of *bhakti.* As Tukārāma says in one *abhaṅga:*

> They were united with Hari to their heart's content. Having given them of their own, they would eat what he gave them. Hungry for love, he does not set aside his obligation. He is determined to be united with them for many days. They say: O Kānhobā, eat many mouthfuls. The silly cowherds have great love for God. Tukā says: Now, let us go to our homes. Then we say: O liberal one, in this way we have escaped. (GE 206)

In this way, the *kālā* for Tukārāma seems to be a symbol of almost universal meaning, representing the many individual relationships between God and men, and the many different attitudes of men towards God. Thus, Tukārāma characterizes the behaviour of the different cowherds during the *kālā* with the following words.

> Here is an impatient one; hurriedly he empties out his bag; some will be untying their knots, others are still coming up. One stands still with his load, an idle insincere fellow; some bring up their boiled grain and look pleased as if they were ready; some have halted their cows; some turn them away; there are others whose cows are intractable, they wheel round and scatter themselves. Some cowherds fasten on the broken provisions; they are not intent on real satisfaction. Some say to each other, "Come along", some go on dancing around. Some have sent astray the simple and ignorant children among them; some are sunk in worldly affairs and have left the flowers on their garlands to wither. Some will not open their bundles; they eat what others have brought; they are like pressed men carrying a load, who die under the burden. Some are immersed in family affection; they are deeply engaged; they have nothing of this occasion, for they know nothing of anything. They were doomed to eat what stale food they had; when they had finished it, then their eyes were opened. Some put streaks on their arms and legs; some covered themselves with ashes. Some have shaven their heads clean; some have removed their tuft entirely; some are idlers at heart, but make a pretence of penance with uplifted arms. Those who employed their intellects without any offering to God have all been made miserable. Tukā says, Now let Kānhobā give us each our share; you know we have kept nothing to ourselves. If you leave us, whom shall we go to? The merciful one has shown mercy to us; let us eat our fill.[21] (GE 144)

In this hymn Tukārāma transforms the *kālā* into a miniature of life itself, and, if we take into account that there are similar hymns describing the behaviour of Kṛṣṇa towards the different cowherds, then we may safely say that the *kālā*, as conceived by Tukārāma as symbolic of the play of God with the individual souls, is the Vārakarī counterpart of the *rāsalīlā* that figures so prominently in North Indian *bhakti*-traditions.[22] This, of course, also implies that, instead of cultivating the attitude of the lover for the beloved (*mādhurya bhāva*), the Vārakarī tradition focuses more upon the love a friend feels towards a friend (*sākhya bhāva*).

NOTES

1. Charlotte Vaudeville, "Sant Mat: Santism as the universal path to sanctity" in Karine Schomer and W.H. McLeod (eds.), *The Sants. Studies in a Devotional Tradition of India*, Delhi 1987, pp. 28-29.
2. See my paper entitled "Gopālpūr-kālā. Some Aspects of the History of the Rites and Sacred Places south of Pandharpur", read at the Third International Conference on Maharashtra: Culture and Society in Heidelberg 1988, and to be published in the conference proceedings.
3. For brief descriptions of this ritual, see J. Murray Mitchell in *Indian Antiquary* 11, 1882, pp. 153-54, S.V. Dandekar's *Vārakarī Paṃthācā Itihāsa*, Poona 1966, pp. 79-80, *Maharashtra State Gazetteers, Sholapur District*, Bombay 1977, pp. 936-37 and 940-41, and Erik Reenberg Sand in *Temenos*, 23, 1987, pp. 88-90, and *op. cit.*
4. For more details, see my forthcoming paper.
5. I am here referring to the edition published by V.V. and J.R. Badave, Pandharpur *śake* 1851 (AD 1929).
6. The story of Rukmiṇī's wrath is probably a feature of later, local mythology. For the founding myth of Pandharpur, see Erik Reenberg Sand, "The Legend of Puṇḍarīka: The founder of Pandharpur" in Hans Bakker (ed.), *The History of Sacred Places in India as Reflected in Traditional Literature*, Leiden 1990, pp. 33-61, and "Mātāpitṛbhakti: some aspects of the development of the Puṇḍalīka legend in Marathi literature" in R.S. McGregor (ed.), *Devotional Literature in South Asia. Current research, 1985-1988*, Cambridge 1992, pp.138-47.
7. Translation of passage as given in the Badave edition (see note 5).

8. From the verses following this passage, it is clear that the place of the *kālā* in this text is not Gopālpur, where it is performed today, but the Veṇunāda at the confluence of the Puṣpāvatī and the Bhīmā. For this development, see my forthcoming paper, *op.cit.*
9. See the preceding note.
10. See the final expression of verse 81: *dhanya dhanya teṃ sthāna/jagajjīvana jetha krīḍe.*
11. In accordance with the inner logic of the myth, namely the fact that Kṛṣṇa has not yet incarnated himself in Pandharpur, we note that the description is consequently dealing with Kṛṣṇa, and not with Pāṇḍuraṅga or Viṭṭhala.
12. See, e.g., *Bhāgavatapurāṇa* 10 / 15, and *Viṣṇupurāṇa* 5 / 5 /31-35, and 5 / 9 / 1-8.
13. This does not, however, mean that the *rāsalīlā* motif is totally absent from the Vārakarī tradition. It is quite often found in poetic tradition, but not in ritual contexts. For the anti-erotic attitude of the Vārakarī tradition, See also R.G. Bhandarkar, *Vaiṣṇavism, Śaivism and Minor Religious Systems*, Strassburg 1913, p. 89.
14. *Śrī Tukārāmabāvāṃcyā Abhaṅgāṃcī Gāthā*, ed. by Vishnu Parashuram Shastrī Pandit, repr. by Government Publications, Bombay 1973.
15. Vol. 2, Poona 1983, pp. 552-562.
16. The GE has 111 *abhaṅgas* under the heading *kālā*, out of which 38 are classified according to their association with various popular games, whereas the *Sakalasantagāthā* has separated the *kālā-abhaṅgas* and the *abhaṅgas* classified according to their association with different games, classifying them all under the heading "the sports of the holy Kṛṣṇa" (*srīkṛṣṇalīlā).* This edition has 49 *abhaṅgas* classified as "pure" *kālā-abhaṅgas*, out of which six are not classified as such in the GE, and one is not found at all.
17. Thus, GE 148 is said to take place on the bank of the Yamunā.
18. When first preparing this paper, I was not aware that this theme had already been touched upon by Thomas Dabre in his book *The God-Experience of Tukāram: A Study in Religious Symbolism*, Poona 1987 (I am obliged to Dr. Chr. Shelke, Munich, for this reference). Apart from its obvious Christian bias, Dabre's book has, however, a much broader scope, since he tries to compare the food symbolism in general found in Tukārāma's *abhaṅgas* with the food symbolism found in

the Bible. Although I agree with many of Dabre's interpretations, I nevertheless think that he exaggerates the symbolic element in those *abhaṅgas* which deal with Pandharpur, Viṭṭhala, and the pilgrimage of the Vārakaris, which to him becomes a "symbol of the great pilgrimage that our life is to be" (p.133). No doubt this symbolic level exists, but we also need to pay attention to the "Sitz in Leben" of these hymns, and the fact that many of them might have been composed and sung on the way to Pandharpur, for simple people for whom the pilgrimage and the vision of Viṭṭhala were a most important, living reality.

19. For reasons of space I am not able to quote here the Marathi version of Tukārāma's *abhaṅgas*. All references are, however, to the Government edition.
20. In fact the tending of cows, in Tukārāma's *abhaṅgas*, is one of the most frequent mystical allegories for the devotee's attempt to control the senses, see GE 233, 177, 224, and 241.
21. Translation by J. Nelson Fraser and K.B. Marathe, *The Poems of Tukārāma*, Vol.2, Madras 1913, pp. 14-15.
22. See, e.g., the above quoted *abhaṅga* with the description of the different Gopis during the *rāsalīlā* in *Viṣṇupurāṇa* 5/13/18-22.

Jaina Goddesses in Kannada Literature

Robert J. Zydenbos

1. The oldest mention of the presence of *yakṣis*, female deities, in Jainism is connected with the life stories of Pārśva and Mahāvīra. In the northeastern region of India, where Jainism originated, the last two Tīrthaṅkaras preferred halting at *yakṣasthānas* and avoided brahminical shrines.[1] From these references we may conclude that the *yakṣa-yakṣi* cult was not only of non-brahminical origin, but that there existed a measure of antipathy between these two religious traditions. The presence of *yakṣas* and *yakṣis* is as old as the history of Jainism itself. This does not mean, however, that the *yakṣis* revered by Jainas today are the same deities, or that these deities have not undergone any transformations in the course of their history.

Southern India, particularly the area which is now the state of Karnataka, has always been the region which the Digambara Jainas see as the cultural centre of their religion. Of the nine surviving Digambara *maṭhas*, six are in Karnataka and two in the bilingual part of southernmost Maharashtra. Three of these six *maṭhas* are located in what are considered the main *kṣetras* of the three *yakṣis* who play an immensely important role in Jaina devotionalism, namely Padmāvati (who resides in the *kṣetra* Hombuja), Jvālāmālini (in Simhanagadde) and Kūṣmāṇḍini (in Shravanabelagola). Naturally, this importance also finds its expression in Kannada literature, both written and oral.

2. Some modern scholars have made attempts to trace the origins of the *yakṣis* and their cult, but because of the limited research that has been done on primary sources concerning this subject, most of the theories put forward so far seem not much more than guesses.

According to P.B. Desai, the Jaina teachers of the Kannada land adapted the *yakṣi* cult to local genius and circumstances,[2] selecting only a few *yakṣis* and concentrating their attention on them. It is indeed likely that the particular popularity of certain Tirthaṅkaras and their accompanying *yakṣis* is connected with developments in regional religious history. And indeed it is curious that of the twenty-four *yakṣis* who are each associated with a Tirthaṅkara, only three play a significant role in Jaina devotion in Karnataka. It is also interesting that the *yakṣi* Jvālāmālini is peculiar to the Digambaras, while the Śvetāmbaras have a different goddess in her place.

In passing we may note here that although there are also twenty-four *yakṣas*, they are, with the sole exception of Brahma, not much more than background characters. It seems that we have here a Tantric development, in which the masculine Tirthaṅkaras needed feminine counterparts, as much of the living Jaina ritualistic tradition suggests. But the Tirthaṅkaras being totally liberated from *saṁsāra*, they of course cannot be viewed in a relationship which is expressed in sexual terms, and therefore the *yakṣas* are needed on a different level of religious symbolism.

Other theories are based on the hobby-horses of dogmatic methodologies, usually a reductionism of a Marxist or Advaitic variety, as found, for example, in the numerous statements by various Indian authors that, e.g., Jvālāmālini is the Jaina version of Durgā or that Padmāvati is 'nothing but' a Jaina version of the Buddhist Tārā.[3] In my view, all such 'explanations' suffer from the same shortcomings on the part of their authors: insufficient familiarity with the material, a disregard of the theological context and a desire to take intellectual shortcuts with regard to what is actually a highly intricate and subtle subject.[4]

3. There are several levels of understanding the *yakṣis*, which the theologically more learned Jainas speak about as ranging from 'simple' to 'advanced' and which are characterized by *(a)* the understanding of the relationship between the devotee and the goddesses, and *(b)* the understanding of the relationship between the goddesses and the *pañcaparamēṣṭhis*, the five classes of venerable persons which Jainism recognizes; most particularly the relationship between the goddesses and the Tirthaṅkaras. At the lower end of the spectrum, we find utterances referring to the impossibility of man shaping his own fate, for which one must rely on the grace of the *yakṣis* as guardian mother-deities. Such an utterance is "everything comes from that mother",[5] which we find particularly in oral folk literature. But in many folk stories too, we come across a more 'advanced' understanding of the goddesses, which sees them as souls that are on their way to attaining enlightenment and through their *puṇya* have acquired supernatural powers, which they use to protect and assist Jaina believers[6] and more particularly of the Tirthaṅkaras, the supreme objects of veneration for the Jainas, without whom the Jaina *dharma* would not exist. At the 'most advanced' level of those who have chosen a monastic life, veneration of the *yakṣis* is seen as of limited usefulness for householders, and therefore as worthy of a certain measure of respect, but as an impediment for those who seek *mōkṣa*.[7]

4. Literature in Kannada about the *yakṣis* can be divided into three categories: *(a)* folk stories and songs, *(b)* episodes in the Purāṇas involving the *yakṣis*, and *(c)* written literature in which the *yakṣis* rather than the Tirthaṅkaras are considered to play a major role. In the Purāṇas their role is clearly very subordinate, and often these episodes do not provide us with much information about the *yakṣis*. There is a great deal of folk literature, and in comparison with the folk literature of other communities in Karnataka very little work has been done on it, for obvious communal reasons.

The third category of literature is the most interesting, because of the focus on and elaboration about the *yakṣis*, which tell us more about what these deities are and how the Jaina conception of godliness differs from that of the surrounding Hindus. Although the *yakṣi* cult is ancient, this kind of literature is of quite recent origin. The oldest example is the *Padmāvatīmāhātmya* by Padmanābha, which is also known as the *Jinadattarāyacaritre*. It is considered the main narrative about the goddess Padmāvatī and among other things tells us how she came to Hombuja. The oldest manuscripts of this work are from the middle of the eighteenth century, and the editor supposes that it was written in the late seventeenth century,[8] though it may be considerably older. It is written in verse, in the *sāṅgatya* metre, which suggests that it was intended to be sung as a kind of ballad. Works of this genre are still being produced, although verse has been replaced by a kind of prose that is somewhat emphatically archaic, as an obvious reference to the golden age of Kannada literature in the tenth century, which was a totally Jaina affair. The material is rich, and much work remains to be done on it.

5.1. The date of the *Padmāvatīmāhātmya* is not exactly clear, estimates ranging from the thirteenth to the late seventeenth century. Briefly, the narrative is as follows: The kingdom of Madhure is ruled by king Sakāra, whose only queen Śrīyaḷadvi is from the southern Madhure.[9] On the advice of the Jaina *muni* Siddhāntakīrti they pray to the goddess Padmāvatī for a son, and not long after that Jinadatta is born. Many years later, the king returns from a military expedition and falls in love with the daughter of a savage tribal chieftain. He marries her and returns to Madhure, where the people are so shocked that he must ask and receive the forgiveness of the guru Siddhāntakīrti and decides to abdicate in favour of his son Jinadatta. His first wife leads a very austere life while the former king amuses himself with the second wife and has a son by her. He also cultivates base habits, such as eating meat. The second wife plots to kill Jinadatta, but this plot fails and her own son is killed instead. Jinadatta then flees southwards towards the other Madhure and takes the *mūrti* of the goddess with him, which according to the guru will protect him on the way. When he is halfway south, in the middle of a forest, the goddess tells him that she refuses to go further. A group of tribal hunters accepts him as their king, and on the spot they clear the forest and begin building the capital of their new kingdom. Later Jinadatta's mother and the guru Siddhāntakīrti come to the new city. His mother insists that he marries, and his marriage with his two cousins from the southern Madhure is arranged.

Years later, a fisherman comes to offer Jinadatta two pearls he found in the mouth of a fish. Jinadatta accepts the gift and decides to have two nose ornaments made of them. When the younger of his two wives sees the ornaments, she asks for the larger one, which he gives, and he intends to give the smaller one to the image of the goddess. At night, the goddess appears to him and points out how ungrateful he is. He is overcome by remorse, but she says that in this age such weaknesses are common, and he is only a victim of circumstances. But her magic *mūrti*, which could turn base metals into gold, will disappear, and instead of this image there will be a stone image of her. When he sees his second wife, he notices that the larger ornament has miraculously disappeared from her nose, and the smaller one is there instead. Jinadatta abdicates in favour of his son; he becomes a monk, and both his wives become nuns.

5.2. The book *Śaktiśrī* by the Bangalore authoress Dhāriṇī, published in 1981[10] as a "novel about the Jaina *yakṣi* Jvālāmālini", is actually a 150-page compilation of the main narratives about Jvālāmālini from different sources, both written and oral. The book opens with the story of how Jvālāmālini came into being: There was a prince named Puṇḍarīka, who once was riding his horse through the countryside. The horse grew tired, and he became enraged and began beating it. Just then a few girls leave a nearby temple and one of them, Kāñcanamāle, unmindful of Puṇḍarīka's princely apparel, rebukes him and convinces him of the importance of the cardinal Jaina virtue of *ahiṃse*. Later Kāñcanamāle and her parents are called to the local palace, where the queen asks information about the girl, and finally this leads to a marriage between Kāñcanamāle and Puṇḍarīka. They live happily, but after some time they quarrel about Puṇḍarīka's love of hunting. He says it is a part of Kṣatriya *dharma* to hunt, whereas she sees in it nothing but an unnecessary form of *hiṃse*. He goes on a hunting trip, leaving her behind in a state of depression. In a dream a goddess (*śāsanadēvate*) appears to her and explains that her suffering is due to *karma*. The following day she sees a *kalaśa* in a pond. The *kalaśa* turns into an underwater palace, and she walks down a staircase into the water and into the palace, where she sees the goddess amidst incredible splendour, attended by innumerable other divine beings. She asks the goddess through which *nōmpi*[11] she has acquired all this, and the goddess tells her what to do. She is returned to the surface of the pond together with 1008 lotuses by water spirits and performs a *jinapūje* in the nearby temple. As instructed, she undertakes regular fasts and performs special *pūje*s for the Tīrthaṅkaras and Padmāvati on Fridays. At the end of her life she performs *sallēkhane*, and as a result of her accumulated *puṇya* she is reborn as the *yakṣi* Jvālāmālini.

The book also gives a version of the best known Jvālāmālinī story, connected with the biography of the philosopher-saint Samantabhadra. Prince Śrīvarma hears the stories of the Tīrthaṅkara Candraprabha from his guru, and as a result he becomes a mendicant himself, assuming the new name Samantabhadra. Then he is affected by *bhasmarōga*, a dreadful disease that causes immense hunger. No amount of food he receives from the laity can satisfy him, and he asks his guru for permission for *sallēkhane*. His guru, realizing that Samantabhadra still has important work to do for the cause of Jainism, refuses this permission. He then advises

Samantabhadra to go to Kāñci, where the king brings gigantic daily food offerings to Śiva which remain unused. Samantabhadra goes and tells the priests that he will actually make the huge stone *liṅga* in the temple consume the food. He is left alone in the temple with the food every day and eats it. In time his illness subsides and it becomes impossible for him to continue consuming so much food. King Śivakōṭi becomes suspicious and demands an investigation. Samantabhadra, who is a great devotee of Jvālāmālinī, meditates deeply on her, and when the critical moment comes and the king demands that the temple doors be opened, the goddess sends out a blinding light from the *liṅga* and shows the people the moon in it, which is the *lāñchana*[12] of Candranātha.[13] The king is overwhelmed by this display of divine force, becomes a mendicant himself, Śivakōṭyācārya, and later writes a number of important religious works.

The book contains tales from folklore, examples of how people in difficulty perform austere *tapas* and thereby obtain the assistance of Jvālāmālini. But austerities alone are never enough: they must be accompanied by purity of purpose and may not suffice to overcome an opposed influence of *karma*, such as in the case of a man who performed *tapas* in order to become king: Jvālāmālini told him that his effort was useless, and against her explicit order he turned to look at her in her fierce form, as a result of which he became mad.

When we go through this literature, a number of features seem to set these narratives apart from most known devotional literature cultivated by Kannada-speaking Hindus:

– Although the Jainas consider narratives such as those which I have mentioned above as literature about the *yakṣis*, it is striking that in this literature the presence of the goddesses in narrative time is quite limited. Most attention is given to humans: to their feelings, strivings, actions and motivations, and the goddess intervenes to help, reward or guide. There are no elaborate genealogies of deities, and there is hardly any mention of contacts between various supernatural beings. Individual humans are the focus of attention.

– Most noteworthy is the fact that we have narratives telling us how the goddesses were other living beings in their previous lives: Jvālāmālinī and Kūṣmāṇḍinī were humans, Padmāvatī was a snake. This underlines the Jaina *karma* doctrine, according to which the circumstances of any present life (human, animal, vegetable or divine) are determined by the *karma* of previous lives. Just as these goddesses are not *anādi*, they will not continue forever in their present state either. The only souls that are totally freed are the Siddhas, including the Tīrthaṅkaras.

– Numerous passages in these narratives tell us that the foremost concern of the *yakṣīs* is *dharmapālane* or the protection of *dharma*. This again emphasizes their relatively subordinate role within the religion. '*Dharma*' here is not interpreted as the will of an eternal deity: it is an impersonal conceptual framework, adherence to which is beneficial in view of eternal laws of nature to which all living beings are subject, including deities, but with the one exception of the liberated souls, the *muktas*. Within this framework, the *yakṣīs* have made great progress, whereby they are in a position to intervene supernaturally in the lives of others. But they do not determine what *dharma* is, and an important reason for the reverence they receive is that they protected the Tīrthaṅkaras, the now liberated ones who propounded *dharma*.

– Both in the *Padmāvatīmāhātmya* and in *Śaktiśrī* we read how the *yakṣīs* themselves express their immense reverence of the Tīrthaṅkaras. In the *Padmāvatīmāhātmya* the goddess at first rejects Jinadatta's offer that he build a temple for her in Hombuja, and it is only after he promises that it will be built after the construction of the main shrine, i.e. a temple for Pārśvanātha, that she accepts the offer. In *Śaktiśrī* Jvālāmālinī comes to Samantabhadra's rescue in the Śaiva temple not by manifesting herself — which she is capable of doing, as we read elsewhere in the book — but by showing the people Candranātha's *lāñchana*.

– It is theologically interesting that in Jvālāmālini's short *bhāvāvali* (history of previous lives) the princess Kāñcanamāle is instructed by another goddess to perform a certain *nōmpi* in honour of a third goddess, Padmāvatī, and as a result of this and of her *sallēkhane* the princess becomes Jvālāmālinī immediately after her death. At first sight this could suggest that as a goddess Jvālāmālinī in a certain sense is 'inferior' or at least 'junior' to Padmāvatī; but I have not seen any indication that the Jainas have ever believed so. None of the goddesses is an ultimate object of worship, as is also seen in the differences in temple worship for a *yakṣi* and a Tīrthaṅkara. They have distinct personalities, which appeal to different kinds of devotees, and due to these differences in personality the relationships between these deities and their devotees differ. Thus the *yakṣis* are not really comparable with each other, and they are not compared in this literature — quite unlike in much Hindu literature, where hierarchies of gods are drawn up.

– The *yakṣis* have personalities of their own, and the differences are seen clearly in the narratives. There is something straightforward and direct in the Jvālāmālini stories: difficulties as a rule are overcome by self-discipline, austerities and firm persistence. On the other hand, this is not at all the case in the Padmāvati stories: there is no emphasis on *tapas*, and there is always a mystery that is never completely solved and gives a twist to the course of the story. This also comes out clearly in folk literature, such as the story of Padmāvatī's cave in Shravanabelagola[14] (where until recently annual rituals were performed) or the songs known as *Padmāvatīdēvi baḷe toḍuva hāḍugaḷu*, "the songs of Padmāvati putting on bangles".[15]

To conclude, I wish to express my opinion that the study of this kind of literature is of great value for an increased understanding of several aspects of Indian religiosity. To say that *bhakti* in the Jaina context is a mere importation from Hinduism is in my view a thoroughly unscholarly statement; it is misleading and not much more than the use of a label that is so vague as to be scientifically useless. If we study the phenomenon within the Jaina theological context, from a point of view of phenomenology and psychology of religion, I believe we will learn more about *bhakti* in general. The fact that Jainism is transtheistic and therefore lends itself less to imputation of theistic notions from other traditions, makes such a study all the more valuable.

NOTES AND REFERENCES

1. Asim Kumar Chatterjee. *A Comprehensive History of Jainism [up to 1000 A.D.].* Calcutta: KLM Private. 1981-84; vol.1, pp. 354-55.
2. P.B. Desai. *Jainism in South India and Some Jaina Epigraphs.* Sholapur: Jaina Samskriti Samrakshaka Sangha. 1957, p.171.
3. Or she is a Jaina manifestation of the Hindu goddess Lakṣmī, or of Sarasvatī, etc. Apparently any guess will do, provided that the Jaina deity is reduced to a Hindu one.
4. Most historians assume that *yakṣi* worship is a later development in Jainism. P.B. Desai believes that it originated in Tamil Nadu and spread to Karnataka from there (*ibid.*, pp. 170-71), which seems dubious in view of the oldest references to *yakṣis* and explicit statements such as in the *Padmāvatīmāhātmya* that the goddess came south from Madhure.

   N.N. Bhattacharya (*History of Śākta Religion.* New Delhi: M. Manoharlal. 1974) states that the Tīrthaṅkaras merely expressed the moral values of tribal society in an attempt to flee from a new kind of exploitation and misery that had set in; and Jainism was an atheistic religion that could not resist the popular influence of the Mother Goddess, which "stood for the oppressed peoples, symbolizing all the liberating potentialities in the class-divided, patriarchal and authoritarian social set-up of India", which appears not much more than a vulgarized form of Marxist thought. His analysis also seems somewhat self-contradictory when later he makes the (for Karnataka, in any case) factual error of claiming that the majority of Jainas are well-to-do merchants (p.114). For "Jain counterparts of Manasā and Durga" see p.66.

   The only short modern study to date dealing with the Jaina goddesses in a serious, non-reductionalistic manner which I know of is a fine introductory survey by John Cort, "Medieval Jaina Goddess Traditions," in *Numen* XXXIV, 2, pp. 235-55.

5. *Cf.* Dhāriṇi. *Śaktiśrī.* Gudibande: Vivekodaya Granthamale. 1981, p. 151.
6. *Cf.* e.g. the *Tattvārthasūtrabhāṣya* with *sūtra* IV,12, where it is said about the *yakṣas* and *yakṣis*: *manuṣyān api kecid bhṛtyavad upacaranti* ("some of them also attend people, like servants").
7. Nowadays there is some controversy about the position the *yakṣi* cult ought to have in the Jaina religion, especially among the Jainas who have enjoyed Western-style higher education. The two main causes of opposition to the cult are both of Western origin, viz. *(a)* a new understanding and appreciation of what is termed 'rationalism' in religious matters, and *(b)* an understanding of Jainism in rather antiquarian terms and based on philological studies of Jaina texts, an understanding which was first cultivated by Western Indologists and later spread among the Jaina intelligentsia as well. There is an increasing resistance among the Jainas in Karnataka against what is justly considered by the majority an arrogant, alien and reactionary reformism.
8. Sediyappu Krishna Bhatta on p.iii of his preface in *Śrī Padmāvatīmāhātmya athavā Jinadattarāyana caritre.* Mangalore: Vivekabhyudaya. 1956.
9. The 'northern Madhure' is Mathura, and the 'southern Madhure' is Madurai in Tamil Nadu. Also in a Śvetāmbara canonical commentary we come across a reference to a merchant family of Uttaramahurā that had connections with Dakkhiṇamahurā: *cf.* p. 211 U.P. Shah and E. Bender, "Mathura and Jainism," in D.M. Srinivasan, ed., *Mathura — The Cultural Heritage.* New Delhi: American Institute of Indian Studies. 1989, pp.209-13.
10. *Cf.* n. 5.
11. A *nōmpi* is a vow in which one vows to perform certain rituals, undertakes regular fasts, etc. The Jainas have an elaborate tradition of various such observances.
12. A *lāñchana* is an iconographic symbol for one of the twenty-four Tīrthaṅkaras, whose images otherwise (with the exception of two of them, viz. Supārśva and Pārśva) are hardly distinguishable, because their souls are equally pure.
13. I have heard a folk version, in which the *lāñchana* is not shown, but the *liṅga* is actually split open so that a hidden *mūrti* of Candranātha inside it is revealed.
14. For examples *cf.* S.P. Padma Prasad. *Jaina janapada sāhitya.* Shimoga: Sahana Prakashana. 1987, pp.108-23.
15. *Ibid.*, pp. 386-87

The *Modus Operandi* of the Divine Name as Explained by Jñānadev

S.G. Tulpule

Almost all saints belonging to such different faiths as Hinduism, Islam, Buddhism and Christianity have stressed the value of the Divine Name and its effectiveness in God-realisation. They also tell us almost unanimously that it is the repetitive remembrance of the Divine Name that really matters in enabling one to experience the godhead. But very few attempts have been made to explain the working of the Name. Through repetitive utterance, or rather remembrance of the name of God one attains Him, no doubt; but how? How does the Name work? How is it possible, one may ask, that the simple repetition of a few syllables results in mystical experience of the Reality which is God? The saints never cared to answer this question. They rarely went into any theoretical discussion about the Divine Name and its working. They ate the apple and did not discuss it. But there is a glorious exception, namely Jñānadev, the author of the *Jñāneśvarī* (AD 1290)[1], an exposition par excellence in Marathi of the *Bhagvadgītā*. In the present paper I will try to present the working of the Divine Name as understood by Jñānadev.

Of course, there are others, not saints and mystics, but scholars who came out with their own theories about how a name or *mantra* works. Bhartṛhari, the author of the

Vākyapadīya,[2] for example, provides us with a scholastic approach to this subject. His theory is called *Śabdapūrvayoga*, or "the Yoga of the Word". At the very beginning of his *Vākyapadīya*, he tells us that "Grammar is the door leading to liberation", and at the end of its first chapter he states that the purification of the Word is the means for the attainment of the Supreme Self. According to Bhartṛhari, one who knows the essence of the activity of the Word attains the immortal Brahman. In his Yoga of the Word, the repeated chanting of a *mantra* is an instrument of power. The psychological mechanism involved in this process is described by him as a holding of the *sphoṭa* in place by continued chanting. Repeated chanting of the *mantra*, which is the Name, results in the *sphoṭa* being perceived in all its fullness. It begins at the *vaikharī*, or outer word-level, but the chant becomes more and more internalised on the *madhyamā*, or inner word-level. Eventually all sequenced chanting activity is submerged in the still, steady *mantra-samādhi* of *paśyantī*, conceptual word-level, and the final goal of the *Śabdapūrvayoga* is realised.

Bhartṛhari's approach to the problem of the working of the Word, or *Śabda*, which is the same as *nāma-mantra*, seems to be purely academic and his interpretation scholastic. His understanding of the issue must be correct, but apart from giving the reader some intellectual satisfaction, it does little by way of leading the spiritual seeker in him anywhere.

The so-called mystical explanation of this problem is equally unrealistic. It comes in the form of the vibration theory. Even some knowledgeable persons believe that a *mantra*'s effectiveness depends on the vibrations it arouses, and therefore, on the correct pronunciation of the *mantra*. Aldous Huxley says that "the breathing pattern brought about by the chant and possibly the temporary increase of carbon dioxide in the lungs and blood have a greater effect on the mind than the content, generally unknown, of what is recited."[3] Were that truly so, Blofeld rightly argues: "Sanskrit *mantras* uttered in Chinese, Tibetan or Japanese could scarcely be effective, for the sounds they make are often unrecognisable as Sanskrit (e.g., *Om* becomes *Ing* or *Ong*, etc.) and yet remain marvellously effective when the mental conditions governing the use of mantric syllables are properly observed."[4] Granting that there is some correspondence between the Name, *Śabda*, or *Mantra* on the one hand and sound on the other, vibrations created by repeating a *mantra*, a *nāma-mantra* in the present context, are very different from any physical vibrations; for these are a far cry from the sublime concept of creative power of the *Śabda* or the Name. Still, the Sant-mat as represented by the Rādhāsoāmī cult harps upon the sound aspect of the *Śabda* which is the Divine Name. Fripp, a Rādhāsoāmī follower, tells us that nearly all sounds and lights, such as temple bells, the church organ, altar candles, or icon lights, are all unknowingly made imitations of the divine sounds and lights.[5] In the same strain the Caitanyaites describe the Divine Names as outflows of the power of God and sing them in their *nāma-saṅkīrtanas*. They do so with the faith that they experience thereby the mysterious Presence, the feeling that "God is there". All this is valid on the basis of their definition of the Divine Name as an incarnation of God in the form of syllables: *varṇarūpena avatāraḥ ayam*. But then Hein has a problem, and rightly so. "The difficulty lies", he says, "in appreciating the expansive construction that is placed on these internal experiences".[6] Here Hein is referring to the states of ecstasy experienced by the Name-singers in the Caitanya movement and is asking how the *bhakta*, or the devotee, is able to be confident that these events, i,e, the ecstasies, are revelatory, ultimate in knowledge, saving and the very act of God. The doctrine of non-difference between the *nāma* and the *nāmī*, or the name and the named one, *nāmanāminorabhedaḥ*, is not enough to explain the phenomenon often noticed in the *nāma-saṅkīrtanas* of the Caitanyaites. They have no effective theological explanation to surround their experience.

For a better understanding of the theology and the *modus operandi* of the Divine Name we have to approach Jñānadev who founded his explanation on the basic tenet of the monistic view of life. According to Advaita philosophy, Brahman is the only Reality, and the *jīva*, or the soul, though originally identical with Brahman, has, due to some unknown reason, lost its consciousness of the Self and identified itself with the body. In this process it has been caught up in the never ending cycle of happiness and misery, fulfilment and frustration, birth and death. The only way for the soul to get itself freed from this vicious circle is to regain its identity with Brahman. Here, nothing new has to be achieved. It is not a matter of finding a "way out", but a "way back". It is like the actor enacting some role who regains his original person without any effort when the play is over. As Ramana Maharshi says, "Realisation is nothing new to be acquired. It is already there, but obstructed by a screen of thoughts. When the screen is lifted, the realisation is revealed." To say it in words of Jñānadev, just as awakening is the only remedy for the fear one experiences in a dream, similarly it is spiritual awakening alone which can remove the darkness of ignorance.[7]

The Divine Name and its constant remembrance are the means to this end. But what is the Divine Name? Is it one of the names of God enumerated, for example, in hymns like the *Viṣṇusahasranāma*? Obviously it is not. In fact, we can call the Divine Name 'nameless' as the great mystic, Basava, does. Kabīr calls it *ajara* and *amara*, ageless and deathless. It is revealed in meditation, in *sumiran*, according to him. Jñānadev defines the Divine Name as "a symbol of the response God gives to the ardent call of those who approach him for help in this life of misery." I translate below the relevant passage from the *Jñāneśvarī* which brings out the essentials of the Divine Name.

> "The Supreme Brahman is really nameless;
> but in order that those caught up in the night of
>   ignorance should know it,

the Vedas marked it giving it a name.
Just as a child is not born with a name,
and yet responds to its given name,
so also the Brahman responds to the Name
called out by the afflicted.
It is a *mantra* searched out by the merciful Veda
for the soul so that its estrangement from the
Brahman
should end and the two should meet in union."[8]

According to Jñānadev, this *mantra* is *Oṃ tat sat* as said in the *Bhagvadgītā: Oṃ tatsaditi nirdeśo brahmaṇaḥ trividhaḥ smṛtaḥ* (the Śruti has named the Brahman threefold as *oṃ*, *tat*, and *sat*).[9] Semantically, this *mantra* implies *Oṃ* which is the Reality. Mystically, Jñānadev interprets it as the name of the Brahman which has to be remembered at the beginning, in the process and at the end of every pious act like a sacrifice, or a grant or a penance. Normally these acts, even if they are *sāttvika*, or pious, are supposed to be binding upon the soul. But just as the boat which seems a burden on the earth is a sure means of crossing the waters, so also the acts, though binding by nature, liberate one if done with the consciousness of the Name throughout the work. This is living *in* the Name which is the same as living *in* God because the two, the name and the named one, are really identical. The *nāmanāminorabhedaḥ*, or the identity of the Name and the Nominee, are beautifully brought out by Jñānadev. Just as the sky is the support of the sky, or the rising sun is its own illuminator, so, says Jñānadev, are the *Nāma* and the *Nāmī* one.[10] Therefore, the process of *nāmasmaraṇa*, of meditation on the name, becomes the process of constant identification with the Divine. So long as the consciousness of the Name is there in the mind, we are with God; the moment this consciousness is lost, we are away from God. As Ekanāth puts it: *āṭhava to parabrahma; nāṭhava to bhavabhrama*[11] (Remembrance [of the Name] is Brahman; non-remembrance is illusion). There is no position between the two. One either remembers the Name, or does not, and the change from one position to the other is quite sudden. As the author of the '*Cloud*' says, "In one little time may heaven be won, and lost."[12]

Constant remembrance of the Divine Name changes the structure of the ego and awakens the consciousness of the mind from the worldly to the divine. As J. Krishnamurthy defines it, ego is the product of memory, memory of worldly impressions both pleasant and painful. It is this structure of the ego that has to be changed. Currently the ego is made up of non-self, non-god. Now, meditation on the Name acts doubly as the tape-recorder does. When it records new impressions, it automatically erases the old ones. Similarly, as the mind receives impression of the Divine Name, it automatically gets rid of the worldly impressions it had received in the past. That is exactly what Tukārām did. He tells us that as he filled himself with the name of God, all passions vacated his person: *Tukā mhaṇe deha bharilā Viṭṭhalē/kāmakrodhē kelē ghara ritē.*[13]

The theology of the Divine Name as propounded by Jñānadev finds support in the writings of Plato.[14] His doctrine of reminiscence states that all learning is a kind of remembering of knowledge already present in the soul. Thus, knowledge becomes only a process of recollection. Plato's theory of anamnesis found its best exponent in Bergson for whom memory is not a deliberate act, but re-entrance into the subconscious continuum that is life itself; it is the primal intuition. "Very rare", he says, "are these moments when we re-know ourselves at this point."[15] This fits in well with Marcel's definition of memory as a mode of being: " I am that which I remember in the measure that I re-live it."[16]

This understanding of memory or remembrance from Plato on down has close links with what Jñānadev has to say about *smaraṇa-bhakti*, or devotion to God through remembrance, except that he is speaking not on the physical or mental, but on the spiritual level. For him it is the *ātman*, who possesses the unique faculty of dichotomising himself, that meditates upon his original state which is the Absolute Self. This remembrance on the part of the *ātman* of his primal state is of the recollective type. It is achieved by means of some symbol like *Oṃ*, or the Divine Name which links the *jīva*, or the individual soul, to *Śiva*, the cosmic soul. *Smṛti* or *smaraṇa*, is thus the only channel or way which leads one to the godhead. The *Bhagvadgītā's* inclusion of *smṛti* among the *vibhutis*, or divinities, of God is very meaningful. For it is *smṛti* that enables one to see his own primeval self by remembering it constantly. This happens according to the well-known *nyāya*, or rule, of the imaginary larva which gets itself transformed into a bee just by thinking about being one.

This is done and achieved through the intervention of the Divine Name, which is a symbolic fraction of the object remembered. The Name is a *bindu*, a drop, which enables one to merge with the *sindhu*, the ocean. How this becomes possible is told by Jñānadev in a very novel way. He is the only one who has revealed the secret of *smaraṇa-bhakti* and tried to explain it, but it must be said that even with his very original explanation of the working of the Name, the question still remains elusive. Jñānadev himself says that the earlier *yogīs* were pathfinders and that they had to traverse this misty region in a haphazard manner; and it is the footprints of their experience that left behind a trail which in course of time became the *pantharāj* (the Great Way). It required a genius like Jñānadev to explain this way and provide a rationale for it, but Tukārām, who followed him, was more practical. He left all explanations to God and went on repeating the Name, for he thought that time spent in speculation as to the 'why' of things would be better spent in experiencing that 'what'. Even Jñānadev said the same thing in his *Harīpāṭha* which forms a part of the liturgy of the Vārakarī sect.[17] The refrain of the *Harīpāṭha* is "*Hari mukhē mhaṇā. Hari mukhē mhaṇā*", meaning "Repeat the name Hari, repeat the name of Hari".

REFERENCES

1. *Jñāneśvarī.* Ed. B.A. Bhide. 2nd ed., Bombay 1950.
2. Bhartṛhari's *Vākyapadīya.* Ed. K. Raghavan Pillai. Delhi 1978.
3. Aldous Huxley. *The Doors of Perception.* 1973, pp. 143-45.
4. John Blofeld. *Mantras — Sacred Words of Power.* London 1977, p. 8.
5. Peter Fripp. *The Mystic Philosophy of Sant Mat.* London 1964, pp. 85-87.
6. Norvin J. Hein. "Chaitanya's Ecstasies etc." In Bardwell L. Smith, ed. *Hinduism.* Leiden 1976, p. 26.
7. *Jñāneśvarī,* 15.254.
8. *Jñāneśvarī,* 17.329-31.
9. *Bhagvadgītā,* 17.23.
10. *Jñāneśvarī,* 17.403.
11. *Ekanāth Gāthā.* Ed. N. Sakhre in *Śrīsakalasantagāthā,* vol. 2, Poona 1923, No. 2320.
12. *The Cloud of Unknowing.* Trans. Clifton Wolters. Penguin Classics 1982, pp. 69-70.
13. *Tukārām Gāthā.* Bombay, Government edition, 1950 (being a reprint of vishnu Parashuram Shastri Pandit edition, Bombay: Indu-Prakash Press, 1873) No. 1336.
14. Plato, *Theaetus*: 142a1-210d4, *Philebus*: 11a1-67b13.
15. Henri Bergson. *Matter and Memory.* London 1911, Ch. IV.
16. Gabriel Marcel. *Journal Métaphysique.* Paris 1935, pp. 175 ff.
17. *Cf.* Ch. Vaudeville. *L'invocation: Le Haripath de Dñyāndev.* Paris 1969.

Separation, Connection and Obedience among the Early Mahānubhāvs

Anne Feldhaus

For the Maharashtrian *bhakti* sect the Mahānubhāvs, the *sannidhān*, or presence, of a divine incarnation, an *avatār* of *Parameśvar*, is the most precious thing in the world. Since the last quarter of the thirteenth century, however, with the departure of their founder, Cakradhar, and the death of his guru, Guṇḍam Rāüḷ, the Mahānubhāvs have not had the presence of an *avatār* of *Parameśvar; asannidhān* (absence) or *viraha* (separation) has been the determining condition of their lives.[1]

Smṛtisthaḷ, a text created during the first few generations of the Mahānubhāv sect, provides a narrative account of the group of Cakradhar's followers in the first decades after his departure; it records events of the period of leadership of Cakradhar's appointed deputy, Nāgdev.[2] Dr. S. G. Tulpule and I have recently prepared a translation of *Smṛtisthaḷ*.[3] In the present paper I will briefly sketch some of the responses to Cakradhar's absence recorded in this text, and then discuss in a bit more detail the relationship between some passages of *Smṛtisthaḷ* and commands of Cakradhar recorded in another early Mahānubhāv text, the *Sūtrapāṭh*. Although I do not intend to become too thoroughly enmeshed in the sociological, theological, or perhaps simply semantic question of whether or not what the early Mahānubhāvs did qualifies them to be called a sect, the materials I will discuss are quite important for an understanding of their identity as a group.

Smṛtisthaḷ begins on a note of *viraha*. Cakradhar is gone. Nāgdev's desolation at Cakradhar's absence is so intense that he wanders far off alone, falls unconscious, lies still for a long enough time to allow mushrooms to grow on him, and eats nothing but the drops of fruit juice squeezed into his mouth by some kindly cowherds on a hillside. Meanwhile, his cousin and fellow-disciple Māhādāïseṃ travels hundreds of miles, from the upper Godāvarī valley to Ṛddhipur, in Vidarbha, and back to the Godāvarī valley, searching for him. When she finds him, she must wake him up, brush him off, wrap him up, and carry him away on her back. She feeds him by dipping a twisted end of cloth in some milk and putting it into his mouth (Chapter 2). Telling people along the way, "God's absence has made him go crazy" (Chapter 4), she finally gets him to Ṛddhipur. Here he and she and Cakradhar's other disciples settle down in the presence of Guṇḍam Rāüḷ.

Fourteen years (and one chapter) later, Guṇḍam Rāüḷ dies. The disciples are again desolate. In their grief, Nāgdev and a sizeable group of them go wandering off together, visiting places in the Godāvarī valley where Cakradhar once stayed. This time Nāgdev remains relatively calm. It is another disciple, Bāïdevbās, who is overcome by emotion: he licks so hard at a place where Cakradhar once spat that he scrapes his tongue, and must be told to stop (Chapter 6).

Along with such examples of *viraha*, *Smṛtisthaḷ* also shows various religious techniques the early Mahānubhāvs used to compensate for their deprivation. It shows them practising *smaraṇ*, recollection, of Cakradhar and the other *avatārs*: their names, their looks, their deeds. In trips like the one the group makes after Guṇḍam Rāüḷ's death, *Smṛtisthaḷ* records the beginnings of a practice of pilgrimage to places where the *avatārs* lived or visited. Not only in Bāïdevbās's licking at Cakradhar's long-gone spittle, but also in the jealous care with which the early disciples keep, share, refuse to share, and otherwise discuss objects touched or given by the *avatārs*, *Smṛtisthaḷ* depicts the initial stages of a cult of relics. The text also shows various disciples engaged in lively discussions of the teachings of Cakradhar, and it shows the other disciples accepting Nāgdev's authority, as Cakradhar's appointed deputy, in matters of doctrine and practice. *Smṛtisthaḷ* shows the disciples recording in scriptures the deeds of Cakradhar (in the *Līḷācaritra*[4]) and his utterances (in the *Sūtrapāṭh*[5]). And, finally, *Smṛtisthaḷ* shows the early Mahānubhāvs' attempts to obey the commands of Cakradhar that are compiled in the *Sūtrapāṭh*.

A strikingly large number of *Smṛtisthaḷ* passages quote, echo, refer to, or assume the reader's familiarity with *sūtras* found in the *Sūtrapāṭh*. Some chapters (e.g., 51) consist almost entirely of Nāgdev's comments, or even just glosses, on *sūtras*. In addition, there is a wide variety of other relationships between *sūtras* of the *Sūtrapāṭh* and episodes narrated in *Smṛtisthaḷ*. Here I will concentrate on two *sūtras*.

The first example is the first *sūtra* of the "Ācār" section of the *Sūtrapāṭh*. This *sūtra* reads: *svadesusaṃbaṃdhu tyājyū, svagrāmasaṃbaṃdhu tyājyū, saṃbaṃdhīyāṃcā saṃbaṃdhu* to *visekhatā tyājyū* - "Give up your connection (*sambandhu*) with your land; give up your connection with your village; give up especially your connection with your relatives (*sambandhīyāṃcā sambandhu*)." In *Smṛtisthaḷ*, the most common response to this *sūtra* is one of simple obedience. One of several graphic instances of heroic compliance is that of Kesobās, the man who was later to compile the *Sūtrapāṭh*. The story of Kesobās's renunciation is found in Chapter 13:

> When [Kesobās] gives up his connection with his relatives (*sambandhī-sambandhu*), Bhaṭobās says, "My Keśav is the great Yogī Śuka." [Bhaṭobās is *Smṛtisthaḷ*'s name for Nāgdev.]
>
> Then one day Kesobās's relatives (*sambandhīyeṃ*), hearing [that he had become an ascetic],

> came to take him away. His brother, Gopāḷdev, and his father-in-law came to take him away because they were opposed to what he had done.
>
> They took Kesobās away. They tried to make him give up his initiation; but no matter what they did, he would not give it up.
>
> Then they summoned all the learned men and had them argue with him. But he silenced them in argument. And the learned men washed their hands of him. They said, "We cannot win him over. If he is to be won over now, it is his wife who will do it. Now lock up the two of them in the same room."
>
> So they locked them in. If she lay on the cot, he would sleep on the ground. If she lay on the ground, he would sleep on the cot....
>
> Several days passed this way. Then his wife said, "Let him go now. He has become a Yogī now. It is a sin for me to interfere."
>
> So they all gave Kesobās permission to leave... .

In this passage, the echo of the *Sūtrapāṭh* is seen in the title of the chapter ("*sambandhī-sambandhu*"), and in the text's use of the term "*kesobāsāṃcīṃ sambandhīyeṃ*" for Kesobās's relatives. But neither Kesobās nor any of the other characters in the story refers directly to the *Sūtrapāṭh*'s command. In another story illustrating heroic obedience to this *sūtra*, though, the renunciant himself, Pāṭhak, echoes the *Sūtrapāṭh*'s wording, and refers obliquely to its command (Chapter 151):

> Once Pāṭhak from Seigāv took ascetic initiation from Bhaṭ. Then he went to another area to wander. He went toward the region of Meghaṅkar.
>
> The official of Seigāv heard that Pāṭhak had taken initiation as an ascetic. Still, he would not transfer [Pāṭhak's] hereditary income (*vṛti*) to his son. He said to him, "Go and bring him here. Then I will transfer it."

[Pāṭhak's son] said, "All right," and came to Nimbā. He told Bhaṭobās the whole situation, [and said], "So, Bhaṭ, you should send him."

Bhaṭobās said, "Go to Loṇār. He is doing his religious exercises there."

[The son] came directly to Loṇār. He met [his father] and told him everything, [and said], "So, Pāṭhak, come there."

Pāṭhak replied, "Whether he transfers it to you or not, I cannot go [back to my earlier] connections *(sambandhā yeuṃ naye)*. Go away."

So he went to the village. He told the official everything, [and said,] "He refuses to come."

Then the official said, "He is firm in his resolve. If he had come, I would not have transferred the hereditary income to you. Now I will definitely transfer it."

And he transferred his hereditary income.

Kesobās, Pāṭhak, and several others of the disciples whose stories are told in *Smṛtisthaḷ* [6] provide examples of simple, direct obedience to the command to break one's connection with one's land, one's village, and one's relatives. Others, though, are not as good at obeying this command. Some of these, like Gaurāïseṃ of Vihīṭā (in Chapter 206), are reprimanded by Nāgdev, and must be given further instruction:

Gaurāïseṃ of Vihīṭā took initiation as an ascetic from Bhaṭobās. One day she took leave of Bhaṭobās and went out to wander. In the course of her wanderings, she went to Vihīṭā. She stayed there, in her relatives' village.

Some time later, her companions in wandering came to meet Bhaṭobās. Bhaṭobās said to them, "Where is Gaurāï?"

They said, "She is in her relatives' village."

> Bhaṭobās said, "If you can get *dharma* from the Mahārvāḍā,[7] then the Mahārvāḍā is [where] your relatives [are]. And I, her *dharma*, am here. Why did she go there? Go on. Call her back."
>
> So they went. They brought her back. Then Bhaṭobās instructed her, primarily about relatives (*sambandhāṃce*).

In one chapter of *Smṛtisthaḷ*, we see Nāgdev applying the *sūtra* about *sambandh*[8] to a particular situation. The question arises whether the convert Kāmāïseṃ, the wife of the Yādav king Rāmdev, should be allowed to take initiation as an ascetic renunciant (Chapter 148):

> One day Kāmāïseṃ asked Bhaṭobās, "Bhaṭ, may I take initiation as an ascetic?"
>
> Bhaṭobās said, "You may not take initiation."
>
> "Why is that?"
>
> "The land the Gosāvī told us to stay in belongs to [your husband] the king. And we cannot go to lands which have been forbidden to us. So I cannot let you take initiation."
>
> Kāmāïseṃ kept silent.

In order to understand Nāgdev's reasoning in this passage, we need to know not only the *sūtra* which begins "*svadeśasambandhu tyājyū*," which is assumed here, but two others as well, both referred to more directly: first, "Stay in Maharashtra" (*māhārāṣṭarīṃ āsāveṃ*, "Ācār" 24), the *sūtra* that defines "the land the Gosāvī told us to stay in;" and, secondly, "Do not go to the Kānnaḍa land or the Telugu land" (*kāṇaḍadesā, telaṅgadesā na vacāveṃ*..., "Ācar" 23), the *sūtra* that names the "lands which have been forbidden to us." We may suspect that Nāgdev's somewhat casuistic reasoning in this case may have had some political motivation – Cakradhar's experiences with the Yādav government had not been of the happiest[9]—but Nāgdev's use of *Sūtrapāṭh* *sūtras* to back up his decision is typical of *Smṛtisthaḷ*.

In at least one case, by contrast, Nāgdev allows — in fact, commands — one disciple to disobey the *sūtra* about *sambandh*. The disciple is his own mother, Ābāïseṃ, who is also a fellow ascetic; during a time of political upheaval, Nāgdev tells her to go and stay in the village of his brother, her son, Vaijobā (Chapter 83):

> Once the Sultan of Delhi invaded.[10] The whole region was in turmoil. Bhaṭobās said to Ābāïseṃ, "Ābaï, you stay in Vaijobā's village."
>
> She said, "No, Nāgdev. The Gosāvī has forbidden [us to stay with] our relatives (*sambandhu*)."
>
> Bhaṭobās said, "you have had contact (*sambandha*) with both Gods [Cakradhar and Guṇḍam Rāüḷ], and you have served them in their presence (*sannidhānadāsya*), and you have a son like me. And for whom is [the rule about] relatives? It is for those who are weak."
>
> Addendum (*śodhu*): "And this is an emergency."
>
> So Ābāïseṃ agreed. She stayed in Vaijobā's village....

In this passage, then, Nāgdev convinces his mother to disobey Cakradhar's command. According to the *śodhu* addendum, he uses the concept of *apaddharma*, the idea that the regular rules may be suspended in a time of emergency. But the reasons given before the addendum are of a different type. The rule is for the weak, Nāgdev argues, not for people like his mother. She is special: first, because she has had contact (*sambandha*) with and served in the presence of not just one but two divine incarnations, and, secondly, because she has Nāgdev as a son.

A cynical reading might find in this last reason Nāgdev's underlying motivation. But the cynical reading is not the one the text prefers. Indeed, if the text's authors, compilers, or editors, or the narrators of the oral reminiscences upon which the text is based, had even conceived of the possibility of a cynical reading, they could have omitted the episode, or they might have tried to make excuses for Nāgdev or have shown some other signs of embarrassment. But — except perhaps for the *śodh* editor's addition of the remark about the situation being an emergency–the text makes no such moves.

More generally, *Smṛtisthaḷ* shows no discomfort at all with the fact that not just Nāgdev's mother, but also his sister, his grand-daughter, his maternal cousin, and his maternal cousin's wife are all shown living together with Nāgdev from time to time as ascetics. Neither the text nor any of the characters in the text is taken aback by this, as Ābāïseṃ was initially shocked by the idea that she should stay with her householder son Vaijobā. It is apparently all right for family members to be together, as long as they are all practising asceticism. In Ābāïseṃ's case, her *sambandh* with Cakradhar and Guṇḍam Rāüḷ is strong enough that her *sambandh* with her relatives is no threat to it.

In relation to the *sūtra* about *saṃbandh*, then, we have seen in *Smṛtisthaḷ* simple obedience to the rule in the cases of Kesobās and Pāṭhak; a reprimand for disobedience to the rule in the case of Gaurāïseṃ; assumption of the rule in making (or justifying) a decision in the case of Queen Kāmāïseṃ; sanctioned, short-term disobedience of the rule in the case of Ābāïseṃ; and long-term, unproblematic, apparent disobedience of the rule in the case of a number of relatives who live together after having been initiated as ascetics.

Besides the *sūtra* about *sambandh*, the other example I want to examine here is the short chapter of the *Sūtrapāṭh* entitled "Asatīpari". This chapter, which is considered to be a summary of the *Sūtrapāṭh*'s "Ācār" sections, reads, "*vīkāravīkalpuśunya svabhāomātreṃ nīrāḷaṃbīṃ devatāsmaranēṃ jo janma kṣepī tayāsī parameśvaru puṇarapi āpulā saṃbaṃdha deti,*" "To one who, free from passion and error, not going beyond his nature/with his nature restrained, independent, spends his life in recollection of God, Parameśvara again gives connection with himself." Throughout *Smṛtisthaḷ* we are shown numerous examples of disciples who strive to live independently and simply, to free themselves from passion and error, and to practice continual recollection of God. We sometimes see disciples teaching one another "Asatīparī" by name (Chapters 76 and 195). In one chapter (195), we see a disciple's boastful promise to live by "Asatīparī", and in another (240), we see another disciple's exegesis of the word "*mātrā*" in the compound "*svabhāomātreṃ.*"[11] Finally, in Chapter 40, we see Nāgdev referring to "Asatīparī" with almost bitter irony. For Nāgdev sees other disciples' desire to worship him as jeopardizing his own ability to live up to "Asatīparī's" demands:

> A lay disciple worshipped Bhaṭobās with golden flowers. He offered him a silk shawl. He prepared a seat with a design made of pearls. Then he was about to perform *āratī*[12] with incense.
>
> At that point, Bhaṭobās stopped him. There were tears in [Bhaṭobās's] eyes.
>
> The lay disciple said, "Bhaṭ, why are you sad?"
>
> Bhaṭobās said, "Was 'Asatīparī' prescribed for my father [that is, for someone other than me]?"
>
> And [the lay disciple] kept quiet.

Here Nāgdev's reference to "Asatīparī" silences the lay disciple—and perhaps makes him stop his worship.[13] But on some other occasions reported in *Smṛtisthaḷ*, it is Bhaṭobās who is silenced. Chapter 130 is a good example:[14]

> One day when Bhaṭobās was sitting there, Ākāïseṃ arrived. She bowed to him repeatedly, and then, absent-mindedly, she placed her head on Bhaṭobās's feet and prostrated herself lovingly to him.
>
> Bhaṭobās said, "Ākāï, don't prostrate yourself to

me this way. I have told you over and over again not to do this,[15] but you keep on doing it." And he got angry. He threw her out.

The next day she returned. She bowed to him, and went and sat down near Paṇḍitbās. Softly she said to Paṇḍitbās, "Paṇḍit, religion (*dharma*) means going toward God, but Bhaṭ gets upset when we do homage to him. Though I [try to] do what is right, I end up doing wrong, and that makes me sinful. So ask Bhaṭ, 'May we or may we not do homage to Lord Cakradhar's connection (*sambandhu*) [with him]?'"[16]

So Paṇḍitbās said to Bhaṭobās, "Ākāïseṃ says, 'Religion means going toward God, but Bhaṭ gets upset when we do homage to him.... So may we do homage to Lord Cakradhar's connection [with you]?' This is what she asks."

Then Bhaṭobās said, "You may". So she came and prostrated herself to Bhaṭobās.

Ultimately, then, Nāgdev agrees to accept gestures of reverence or worship. He thus disobeys, however reluctantly, the commands of "Asatīparī." But the argument Ākāïseṃ uses, the argument that eventually convinces Nāgdev to accept her prostrations, is that she is making them to his connection with Cakradhar. The term Ākāïseṃ uses for "connection" is *sambandh*. Nāgdev himself, as we have seen, uses this same term in this same way to convince his mother that she may stay with her householder son during a time of political upheaval: she has had the *sambandh* of both Cakradhar and Guṇḍam Rāüḷ, and has served in their presence. Thus, in both cases, it is the connection, the *sambandh*, of a person with a divine incarnation that is the crucial consideration. This same *sambandh* is also the reward we have seen "Asatīparī" promise to those who live in the way it prescribes.

This *sambandh* is diametrically opposed to the *sambandh* that the first *sūtra* of "Ācār" says to renounce. To become a Mahānubhāv, one must sever one's connection with home and family. But one does this only to forge new ties based on a connection with God. The basis of the Mahānubhāvs' identity as a group, what makes them a sect or something like one, is that they break their *sambandh* with their land, their village and their relatives, and that they form new relationships through their *sambandh* with God.

The fact that *Smṛtisthaḷ* shows no embarrassment when Nāgdev begins to accept other disciples' prostrations, or when he allows his mother to break the rule about staying with relatives, means that the text does not see irony where modern outsiders might be tempted to find it. For *Smṛtisthaḷ* —both for the disciples portrayed in the text and for those who compiled, edited, preserved, and recited it over the generations—in the absence of God, connection with God is the most important thing there is. In the absence of God, connection with a divine incarnation is *even* more important than strict obedience to his commands.

NOTES

1. For works in English that provide an introduction to the Mahānubhāvs, their teachings, and their Old Marathi literature, see I.M.P. Raeside, "The Mahānubhāvas," *Bulletin of the School of Oriental and African Studies, University of London* XXXIX (1976), 585-600; I.M.P. Raeside, "A Bibliographical Index of Mahānubhāva Works in Marāṭhī," *Bulletin of the School of Oriental and African Studies, University of London* XXIII (1960), 464-507; Anne Feldhaus, *The Religious System of the Mahānubhāva Sect: The Mahānubhāva Sūtrapāṭha.* New Delhi: Manohar Book Service, 1983; Anne Feldhaus, "The *devatācakra* of the Mahānubhāvas," *Bulletin of the School of Oriental and African Studies, University of London* XLIII (1980), 101-109; and Anne Feldhaus, "Kṛṣṇa and the Kṛṣṇas: Kṛṣṇa in the Mahānubhāva Pantheon," *Bhakti in Current Research, 1979-1982,* ed. Monika Thiel-Horstmann. Berlin: Dietrich Reimer Verlag, 1983. V.B. Kolte's Marathi studies of Mahānubhāv history, literature, and thought are extremely thorough and reliable. See, for instance, his

Mahānubhāv Tattvajñān. Malkāpūr: Aruṇ Prakāśan, 1945; reprint, 1975; and *MahānubhāvāṃcāĀcārdharma.* Malkāpūr: Aruṇ Prakāśan, 1948; reprint, 1973.

2. The edition used here is that of Vaman Narayan Deshpande. Poona, 1939; third edition, Poona: Venus Prakāśan, 1968. Another edition, intended primarily for university students, was prepared by S.G. Tulpule in 1969 and reprinted with revisions in 1990. Poona: Anamol Prakāśan.
3. Honolulu: University of Hawaii Press. 1992.
4. *Mhāïṃbhaṭ Saṅkalit Śrīcakradhar Līḷā Caritra*, ed.V. B. Kolte. Bombay: Mahārāṣṭra Rājya Sāhitya-Saṃskṛti Maṇḍaḷ, 1978; 2nd ed., 1982.
5. *Śrīcakradharokta Sūtrapāṭh*, ed. H.N. Nene. Nagpur, 1942. A new edition and an English translation are given in Anne Feldhaus, *The Religious System of the Mahānubhāva Sect: The Mahānubhāva Sūtrapāṭha* (See note 1). Citations in this paper are based on the Feldhaus edition.
6. Other stories of heroic renunciation are found in Chapters 53, 97, 134, and 223 of *Smṛtisthaḷ*. Chapter 97, perhaps the most graphic of these, tells the story of Lukhāïseṃ:

Lukhāïseṃ was from Bābuḷgāv. She had received instruction from Bhaṭobās. She withdrew from all pleasures. She was dispassionate. She would eat buttermilk and rice. By vow, she gave up everything but her wedding necklace. She ceased to have sexual relations with her husband. She would go to the river, take a bath, sit for a while, and perform her religious exercises (*anuṣṭhān*). This is how she lived. On her own she went and found a nice young woman for her husband to marry. She got her husband married.

Then one day she came to the river to bathe, and without returning, she went directly to Bhaṭobās at Nimbā.

She met Bhaṭobās. She took initiation as an ascetic. Before initiating her, Bhaṭobās had inquiries made [about her]. She told him about her previous observances and vows.

Then he sent her with Bāïseṃ to Parameśvarpur [that is, Ṛddhipur]. Right afterwards, her people came pursuing her. They said to Bhaṭobās, "Bhaṭ, Lukhāï has come here. Let us see her."

Bhaṭobās said, "She is not here. Take a look." And he convinced them [that she was not there]. And they left. They went to their village.

Lukhāïseṃ went to Ṛddhipur. She bowed to Ṛddhipur. For a year or so she practised intense asceticism. She became emaciated.

Then after a year she came to meet Bhaṭobās. She met him. And one day, realizing her great fortitude, Bhaṭobās said, "Lukhāïseṃ, now you go straight to Bābuḷgāv. Go begging there and come back."

So Lukhāïseṃ went to Bābuḷgāv. When it was time to go begging, she went to that same house [where she had lived]. [Her husband] was sitting at the door. Without recognizing her, he said, "[I] prostrate [myself to you], Mother."

Lukhāïseṃ said, "Do you recognize me?"

And he recognized her and said, "Yes, I recognize you. Now [I] prostrate myself again." And he came forward [to receive her]. He took off his turban. And, with great feeling, he placed his head on her feet. He spread out a cloth for her to sit on. He washed her feet over a plate. He drank the water from washing her feet. He applied it to his forehead.

Then Lukhāïseṃ returned and told Bhaṭobās what had happened. Bhaṭobās was very happy.

7. *Sūtrapāṭh* XII. 149: "Draw out *dharma* from the Mahārvāḍā." The Mahārvāḍā is the part of a village where the Untouchable Mahārs live.
8. In Old Marathi, the nominative/accusative form of masculine nouns like *sambandh* can end either in *-u* or in silent *-a*. In transcribing the original terms occurring in translated passages from Old Marathi texts, I have generally given the word *sambandh* in the form in which it occurs in the passage, but when using it as a word in an English sentence, I write it without the ending.
9. See Günther-Dietz Sontheimer, "God, Dharma and Society in the Yādava Kingdom of Devagirī According to the *Līḷācaritra* of Cakradhar." *Indology and Law: Studies in Honour of Professor J. Duncan M. Derrett*, ed. Günther-Dietz Sontheimer and Parameśvara K. Aithal. Wiesbaden: F. Steiner Verlag, 1982. pp. 329-358.
10. This is generally taken to refer to the invasion of the Deccan by Malik Kāphur, in 1310 A.D.
11. The text of Chapter 240 is as follows:
(Kesobās) justifies word "*mātrā*".

Keśavdev justified the word "*mātrā*" in "Asatīparī" to the paṇḍits by denying that it is any of the three [kinds of] utterance (*yuktitrayeṃ*) rejected by the grammarians and explaining that it is the fourth [kind of] utterance, the word of God (*īśvarokti*) instead. *Sic.*

In translating this passage, Dr. Tulpule and I have relied on the advice of Dr. V.B. Kolte, who suggested (in a letter to

Tulpule dated 16 July 1986) that "*yuktitrayeṃ*" refers to the three kinds of *ukti* — *svokti, śāstrokti, and lokokti* — in *Sūtrapāṭh* XII. 141: "Putting aside what you yourself say (*svokti*), what the scriptures say (*śāstrokti*), and what the world says (*lokokti*), become learned in my learning." The words "*heṃ yathāpratī*" at the end of the chapter mean "It is this way in the manuscript" (that is, literally, *sic*); they indicate that an early scribe or editor of *Smṛtisthaḷ* found the chapter as obscure as we have.

12. A ritual gesture of worship or respect, consisting of waving a tray of small lighted lamps, burning camphor, or, as in this case, incense in front of the person or object to be honored.
13. Other *Smṛtisthaḷ* passages too portray Nāgdev as discouraging his fellow disiples from making gestures of worship to him or treating him with exaggerated reverence. In most of these passages, Nāgdev emphasizes maintaining a clear distinction between himself and God. When Mhāïṃbhaṭ comes to Ṛddhipur to die (Chapter 198), for example, Nāgdev is there and comes out to receive him. Mhāïṃbhaṭ takes Nāgdev's foot in his hands and asks Nāgdev to place it on his forehead. Nāgdev says, "It is the Gosāvī's holy foot which should go on one's forehead. I should put my hand on your forehead." And he does so. In Chapter 129 a stranger asks Nāgdev if he is God (Īśvara); Nāgdev replies clearly, "No. I am a devotee of God." And in Chapter 126 another stranger expresses surprise that Nāgdev's disciples address him as simply "Bhaṭ," rather than "Bhaṭ, Lord" (*hāṃ jī bhaṭo*). To this man Nāgdev explains that he himself has told the disciples to use the simpler form of address: "'Lord, Lord' is only for God (*īśvara*), not for a *jīva*."
14. Another example is found in Chapter 127:

    One day a certain lay disciple washed Bhaṭobās's feet and drank the water. Seeing that, Bhaṭobās said, "You should drink the water from washing only God's feet. And you should eat only God's leftovers as *prasād*."

    The man said, "Yes, Bhaṭ. It is as God's that I am taking it."

    Bhaṭobās remained silent.
15. In Chapter 128, for instance:

    Bhaṭobās did not allow people to make prostrations to him or to place their heads on his feet. Disciples would do this, but he would disapprove and say, "You should prostrate yourself this way to the Gosāvī's holy feet. You should not do this to me."

He would disparage himself this way.

16. Cf. *Sūtrapāṭh* XII. 185: "Parameśvar is to be worshipped; connection (*sambandhu*) with him is to be revered," *parameśvaru bhajya, saṃbaṃdhu vaṃdhyū.*

"Nāmadeva's" *Tīrthāvaḷī* and the Vārakarī Tradition

Sadanand More

At least since the thirteenth century, the Vārakarī Sampradāya has been one of the influential *bhakti* cults in Maharashtra. It is now generally believed by scholars that the Vārakarī cult turned out to be a motivating force, especially through Santa Nāmadeva, for the emergence of the *bhakti* movement in North India.

Although, in so far as the present faithful is concerned, Jñānadeva's *Jñāneśvarī* and the poems of Tukārāma (collectively referred to as the *Gāthā)* are regarded by the Vārakarīs, as major texts, one should bear in mind that: i) Tukārāma is believed to be the incarnation *(avatāra)* of Nāmadeva and the former's poems are the fulfillment of those of the latter; ii) The explanatory—interpretative prose discourses *(pravacanas)* on *Jñāneśvarī* are a new phenomenon in the Vārakarī fold. True, right from its creation, the *Jñāneśvarī* was highly respected and regularly read by the Vārakarīs (to the extent that they do not have lunch unless they have read an *adhyāya* of it), but its *pravacana*s were introduced in the middle of the last century by the sophisticated elites who wanted to imitate the so-called great tradition. The forms officially recognised by the Vārakarī tradition are only two, i.e., *bhajana* (singing of *abhaṅga*s) and *kīrtana* (an explanatory — interpretative discourse on the selected *abhaṅga* by one person who is assisted by chorus when singing). The *bhajana* can take various forms — from one man singing alone to a group of Vārakarīs singing continuously for the whole night *(jāgara)*.

The *Tīrthāvaḷī* is a work which is not only widely sung, partly or fully, in the *bhajana*, but also often cited in *kīrtana*. This itself speaks for the importance of the work in the Vārakarī tradition. The authorship of the *Tīrthāvaḷī* is a controversial issue and a large number of scholars are hesitant to ascribe its authorship to Nāmadeva. The question of authorship is important in itself and few would dare to undermine or disapprove of any sincere and scholarly attempt at either ascribing or denying the authorship of any text to a certain individual. This paper, however, is not concerned with the ascription or otherwise of any precise authorship of the *Tīrthāvaḷī*, to Nāmadeva or any body else. The rationale behind such an attitude is that the problem of authorship is not going to adversely affect the conclusions of this paper.

My main contention is that the belief prevalent in the Vārakarī tradition that Nāmadeva did visit some sacred places *(tīrthayātrā)* is at least pre-Ekanātha, for Ekanātha recorded it.[1] The tradition itself, according to me, forms an authentic source of information and so long as it is not positively disproved there is no harm, theoretically or practically, in believing it, provided it is neither logically inconsistent nor factually impossible. That the tradition regarding the sacred journey of Nāmadeva is further supported by the traditions prevalent in the North, and that it can even be corroborated with geographical locations, strengthens the historicity of the event.[2]

Once the historicity of Nāmadeva's sacred journey is accepted, the problem of the authorship of the *Tīrthāvaḷī* matters little. If one goes through the text of the *Tīrthāvaḷī*, one will realize that it is not simply an account of a journey or a description of places. The journey is relevant only in so far as it provides an occasion for expressing the Vārakarī philosophy of devotion. In other words, even if Nāmadeva is not the author, it does not imply that the event as such is not historical. And more importantly, it does not in any way harm the traditional Vārakarī philosophy it contains.

On the basis of the narrative part of the *Tirthāvaḷī*, the whole event can be divided into three major episodes: i) Jñānadeva's proposal to Nāmadeva that they should proceed on a journey to sacred places; Nāmadeva's initial hesitation and ultimate consent on being requested by Viṭṭhala; ii) The journey as such, and iii) On their return a ritual celebration *(udyāpana)* of the journey managed by the god Viṭṭhala himself in which the Brahmins of Pandharpur are invited and exposed to the teaching of the Vārakarī cult.

A careful reading of the *Tirthāvaḷī* will reveal that there is a fairly consistent thread running through all the episodes: the nature of devotion and the superiority of the devotee. The devices used for developing the thread are events and dialogues. Let me point out the following: 1) In the Vārakarī tradition Pandharpur is the only sacred place and the Vārakarīs do not therefore visit any other *tīrtha*[3] (except for places of the saints such as Alandi, Dehu etc.); 2) Jñānadeva certainly knows this, and although neither Nāmadeva nor Viṭṭhala approve of his proposal, he insists on it because he wants to enjoy the company of Nāmadeva, whom he esteems as a representative of the ideal type of devotee that he himself described in the twelfth chapter of the *Jñāneśvarī*[4]; 3) In spite of their *tīrthayātrā*, the conclusion he reasserts is that it is really futile and unnecessary to undertake such a journey[5]; 4) Apart from the intention of Jñānadeva (whatever it might be), the Vārakarī tradition believes that the real purpose of these pilgrims was to purify the sacred places themselves because it seemed that the places had lost the power to purify sinners. It was, in other words, a kind of revitalisation of them; 5) Further, and perhaps philosophically more important, the Vārakarī tradition also believes that although Jñānadeva asks some questions by way of information and clarification, which Nāmadeva answers to the satisfaction of the former, it is not the case that Jñānadeva was ignorant of the theory or practice of *bhakti* or that he wanted to test Nāmadeva. Quite to the contrary, Jñānadeva indulges in a kind of make-believe for two reasons: (i) He assumes the role of a humble enquirer because he wants to have the pleasure of a dialogue with Nāmadeva, which is itself a kind of experience of *bhaktisukha*; (ii) Jñānadeva is himself a reputed and recognised Yogī and Jñānī too. It is his intention to establish the power and importance of *bhakti* vis-a-vis *yoga* and *jñāna*. However, knowing that Nāmadeva is not known either as a Jñānī or Yogī, he thinks it more appropriate to get *bhakti* established by Nāmadeva. Were he to do it himself, there is every possibility that the power or importance of *bhakti* might be mistaken for that of either *jñāna* or *yoga*. Hence we are told how the thirsty Jñānadeva manages to drink water from a well which is too deep to descend into, by assuming a very small body (or by contracting his own body) by virtue of his Yogic power *(laghimā siddhi)*, whereas Nāmadeva, ignorant of any such power, prays to the god Viṭṭhala who, in response, brings about a miracle, i.e. the well overflows and Nāmadeva quenches his thirst.[6] This episode is also suggestive of yet another dimension of *bhakti* which is lacking in *yoga*. However powerful a Yogī might be, his powers are and remain his personal powers, i.e. they are not useful to society at large, whereas a Bhakta is useful to society. It is interesting to note that public memory has still retained the place (including the well) where this event occurred; 6) The Vārakarī cult is well known for its teaching and practice of equality and a corresponding protest against Brahmanical hierarchy. In the *Tīrthāvaḷī* we read an interesting episode that illustrates this contrast. On Nāmadeva's returning to Pandharpur, Viṭṭhala himself organizes a ritual meal (*udyāpana*) which is a post-requisite of any pilgrimage, on behalf of Nāmadeva. The Brahmins of Pandharpur are invited by a Brahmin named Ananta. However, these Brahmins are astonished and annoyed when they notice that the host Ananta (who is nobody else but Viṭṭhala himself) does not care for the

Brahmanical injunction, and not only dines with Nāmadeva, a non-Brahmin, but enjoys the latter's leftover food (*ucciṣṭa*). It is now for Viṭṭhala (Ananta) to teach these Brahmins the Vārakarī philosophy of equality, which he aptly does.[7] In this way the text establishes the superiority of *bhakti* over *yoga* and *karma* (ritualism in this context).

Additionally and more importantly, the text does not leave the path of *jñāna* (i.e., *advaita brahmajñāna*) untouched and uncontested. Jñānadeva is depicted as presenting a kind of *pūrvapakṣa* from the point of view of *jñāna*, challenging the propriety of *bhakti* as such, and Nāmadeva as ably meeting with the objections. Ultimately even Viṭṭhala is shown to have appreciated and confirmed what Nāmadeva has said.

Lastly and perhaps most importantly, the *Tīrthāvaḷī* also defines some dominant terms of the Vārakarī tradition, such as *bhajana, namana, śravaṇa, manana, nijadhyāsana, bhakti, dhṛti,* and *viśrānti*.[8] Here too it is Nāmadeva who defines them at the request of Jñānadeva. The importance of these definitions is obvious from the point of Vārakarī hermeneutics.

NOTES

1. Tukaramtatya (ed.), 1903, p.425.
2. W.M. Callewaert and M. Lath (eds.), 1989, p.19-20, and p.33.
3. This does not, however, imply any sort of dogmatic envy on part of the Vārakarīs. It is their belief that the other sacred places are based on discrimination and ritualism whereas Pandharpur is free from them. One goes there only for the sake of love.
4. Jñāneśvara, 1987: *Adhyāya* 12th.
5. Babar, Sarojini (ed.), 1970: *abhaṅga* n. 922,923,959.
6. *Ibid*: *abhaṅga* n. 919-21.
7. *Ibid*: *abhaṅga n.* 925-41.
8. *Ibid*: *abhaṅga n.* 917.

BIBLIOGRAPHY

Babar, Sarojini and others (eds.), 1970. *Sri Nāmadeva Gāthā*. Bombay: Government of Maharashtra.

Callewaert, W.M. and M. Lath (eds.), 1989. *the Hindi Padavalī of Nāmdev*. Delhi: Motilal Banarsidass.

Jñāneśvara, 1987. *Jñāneśvarī*, 4th edn. Alandi: Sri Jñāneśvara Mahārāja Sansthāna.

Tukaramtatya (ed.), 1903. *Śrī Ekanātha Mahārājāncyā Abhangāncī Gāthā*. Bombay: Rajarama Tukaram.

The Idea of Sin in the *Dāsabodha*

Christopher Shelke

INTRODUCTION

Santa Rāmadāsa, the author of the *Dāsabodha*, is known in Maharashtra as the Rājaguru, i.e., the teacher of the king. Rāmadāsa had helped Śivājī through the revival of Hinduism to establish the Marāthā-kingdom.[1] In this paper I will examine the idea of sin presented primarily in the *Dāsabodha* and in the other writings of Rāmadāsa such as *Karuṇāṣṭake* and *Manāce śloka*. This concept of sin neither contains the idea of the original nor of the actual sin as in Christianity, however it is comprehensive and sin is considered from the perspectives of man, without much recourse to any God-given revelation. The *Dāsabodha* was completed in the Mārgaśirṣa of *śake* 1603, i.e., in December 1681,[2] just a few months before the death of Rāmadāsa and about a year after the death of Śivājī. *Dāsabodha* is accredited to Rāmadāsa, though his disciple Kalyāṇsvāmī had helped him as a scriptor.[3] The manuscript of Kalyāṇsvāmī and that of Dattātrayasvāmī are similar to each other. The *Dāsabodha* edited by S.S. Dev is based on these two manuscripts.[4] On the other hand, the *Dāsabodha* edited by L.R. Pāngārkar is based on these two manuscripts as well as some early partial manuscripts that were published after 1860.[5] Rāmadāsa wrote this treaty at the fort of Sajjangad[6] near the village of

Cāphala in the district of Sātārā in Maharashtra. The *Dāsabodha* has twenty chapters, each of which has ten *samāsas* (subdivisions). In the *Dāsabodha* Rāmadāsa has depicted his teaching and his mysticism. Besides the *Dāsabodha* he wrote the *Karuṇāṣṭake*, i.e., "Petitions", and *Manāce śloka*, i.e., "Advice to one's own Mind", from which we directly get some idea about his view on sin.

For the term "sin" Rāmadāsa used the Marathi words *pāpa* and *pātaka* which are derived from the original Sanskrit verb *pata* meaning 'to fall dawn'. The literal meaning of these words is either crime, an evil deed or violation of a moral law. In the writings of Rāmadāsa the opposite word to *pāpa* is *puṇya*, which can be translated as 'merit' or 'good behavior' or 'special *dharma*'. Sometimes Rāmadāsa also uses words like *kukarma* and *adhama krutya*, which mean an 'evil deed' or a 'bad action'.

THE *DHARMA*

Hindu society in Maharashtra and in the whole of India was interwoven with the caste system and the caste ethic was in force in all aspects of Hindu life in every village and town. One spoke of *jātidharma*, the duties and obligations of one's own *jāti* (caste). One also spoke of *pitrudharma*, i.e., the duties of a father, or of *putradharma*, i.e., the duties of a son. *Dharma*, which literally means "that which has been incorporated", refers to obligation or duty. In Hinduism there is no particular God-given commandment; however there are many precepts which are traditionally transmitted as a moral teaching in social life, such as *dhramam car* (walk in the path of *dharma)* or *pitru devobhava* (consider your father as God) or *mātru devobhava* (consider your mother as God). All precepts are rooted in the ethical consciousness of man. Man has this consciousness because he has the knowledge of *dharma*, which is incorporated in his own nature as a human being. Therefore it is important to know how the human person comes to know his *dharma*.

THE THREE *DHARMAS* IN THE *DĀSABODHA*

In the writings of Rāmadāsa we find a completely new idea of *dharma* which is nevertheless deeply rooted in traditional thinking. In spite of the concept of *sevā*, before Rāmadāsa no saint had ever spoken about *sevakadharma*. Rāmadāsa wrote a letter to Śivājī in which he explained the *rājadharma*, i.e., the duties of a king. In the same letter Rāmadāsa expounded *kṣātradharma*, i.e., the duties of a fighting force, and *sevakadharma*, i.e., duties of a serving class. It is surprising that he did not explain the duties and obligations of any particular caste but only those of the king, fighters and servants. In this letter he neither explained how these classes are to be defined nor how they should relate to one another. Along with the *sevakadharma* Rāmadāsa introduced the new idea of "*Mahārāṣṭradharma*" in his spiritual doctrine. All three *dharmas*, *rajadharma*, *kṣhātradharma* and *sevakadharma*, are in the service of *Mahārāṣṭradharma*. *Mahārāṣṭradharma* is certainly not an end by itself. It consists in the unity of the people of Maharashtra, the Marathas, for the sake of freedom in practice of worship and prayer. It has a subordinate role to *paramārthadharma*. The achievement of *paramārtha* is the ultimate end of human endeavours, according to Rāmadāsa. In this letter he praises Śivājī for reestablishing *dharma* and offering protection to cows and Brahmins.

> "You are known as a righteous person,
> this I need not tell you.
> You have the fame of establishing the Religion.
> You must keep up this fame of yours".[7]

In the same letter he advises the fighting force to become united for the sake of *Mahārāṣṭradharma*.

> "Those who are unfaithful to God are dogs, they
> must be removed.
> The servants of God will be victorious,
> without doubt, they shall be conquerors.

Hold God firm in your hearts;
the entire region must be filled with revolution;
revolution for the establishment of the Religion."[8]

Further, to the serving class he explains that they should abandon selfishness and be ready to serve the king, who has the power of discernment. When one performs service merely for the sake of money and belly, then through such service only those who seek vainglory profit. Such people are thoughtless. The serving class must not be thoughtless, but must look after the interests of the virtuous one.

"Injustice cannot know Justice,
the thoughtless person cannot know the nature of discernment,
the sinners do not like virtuous ways."[9]

By expounding such an ethic and such norms of behaviour in his letter to Śivājī, Rāmadāsa hoped to achieve the harmony and unity of all people, which is why he refrained from speaking about any particular caste or its specific duties. He aims for the honour and glory of God, which consists in the performance of worship and in the freedom to worship and can be achieved only by establishing the Maratha kingdom. Therefore for Rāmadāsa the Maratha kingdom is merely the means for the glory of God and the service of religion.

THE DIGNITY OF HUMAN LIFE

Rāmadāsa looks at human life[10] in a very positive way. He considers human life as a unique opportunity for eternal life. It is superior to all other lives and births. Other lives are burdens, but human life is a treasure.

"When a life serves the eternal life, then it is considered to be fruitful.
Otherwise the life has been spent in vain.
Through an animal life, there is no salvation,

only through the human life can one obtain the
eternal life". 1.10.21

"Therefore when this life serves to obtain the eternal life,
then this life is considered to be fruitful,
otherwise the human life would be spent in vain;
and on account of various dangers it remains on the
way to death". 1.10.61

According to Rāmadāsa human life has its fulfillment only in God and everyone must realise its importance. Its greatness consists in its being a means to achieve salvation, unity with God.

"Blessed, blessed is the human life,
may it see its own dignity,
may it obtain through every action its highest good.
May it through every action obtain freedom". 1.10.1

"With the support of human life,
with the heaps of various means,
through the discernment of right and wrong
may it obtain liberation". 1.10.18

"Through the human life many have achieved the
highest status;
joyfully leaving self-glory,
they have achieved the real happiness". 1.10.19

Though Rāmadāsa extols the human life, he is aware of the traditional philosophy which says it is constituted of three *guṇas: sattva, rajas* and *tamas*. *Sattva guṇa* is the best of the three *guṇas*. It helps to obtain devotion. Through devotion one achieves the real knowledge of things and through knowledge one achieves unity with the highest person. On the contrary, the *rajas guṇa* creates in man a longing for fame, success and also the consciousness (knowledge) of dualism. This *guṇa* is a hindrance on the way to liberation. Further, the *tamas guṇa* leads to anger and evil deeds. The person who has been conquered by it is led to bondage and condemnation. Rāmadāsa accepted the traditional doctrine of the three *guṇas*, but did not explain how each of them obtains its specific quality.

THE PHENOMENON OF SIN

Rāmadāsa has a very clear idea of values, yet it is most surprising that he speaks very rarely of sin in the *Dāsabodha*. I quote here some of the verses in which he describes the nature of sin:

> "This is not a work that can be achieved indirectly.
> Each one must experience by himself.
> To preach without experience is a sin. 10.10.53
>
> "There is a good deed as truth,
> there is no sin like untruth;
> without experience there is no satisfaction at all". 10.10.54
>
> "Know that the truth means the realization of *svarūpa*.[11]
> Untruth is *māyā*, that is measurement.
> Here I have explained sin and merit along with the *rūpa* (form)". 10.10.55

Sin means for Rāmadāsa the affirmation of self as a different entity from the ultimate reality and the teaching of such a doctrine to others. Therefore the nature of sin is untruthfulness. Sin is to be under the influence of *māyā*, which could be translated as "illusion". It is an illusion to consider that one is by oneself and that one is different from others and the ultimate reality. The human person comes to believe this dualism of self and God because he is under the influence of *dehabuddhi.*[12]

THE UNFORTUNATE ONE

In the *Dāsabodha* Rāmadāsa speaks quite often about unfortunate *karanṭā* people. The term "unfortunate" comes rather close to the term "evil doers". These people are lazy and gluttonous. They hate to work. On account of their laziness they come to such a state that they lack everything—clothes, food, health and friends. This is because they have no discernment and are subject to the evil mind. They even go so far as to consider the evil mind to be virtuous.

On account of sin these unfortunate people suffer misery and poverty; poverty leads them to accumulate more sins. They perform deeds of unrighteousness. Their friends and companions are evil doers and thieves. They enjoy endangering and despising others. These unfortunate ones can be freed from their miserable situation only by their own effort. None can offer them liberation. They must try to obtain it by themselves. Then Rāmadāsa relates how the unfortunate one must arrange his daily programme. At the end he suggests that such an unfortunate one practise *bhakti, vairāgya, jñāna* and *yoga*. Further, Rāmadāsa advises him to hold Rāma firm in his heart. Rāma is the powerful God and through meditating on his deeds, these miserable ones will come to follow the path of freedom. Such a practice will offer them the possibility of freeing themselves from their unfortunate state.

DEHABUDDHI

According to Santa Rāmadāsa, *ahantā* (pride), *mīpaṇā* (self-glory), and *ahankār* (self-pride) are primarily causes of sin. Through these the *dehabuddhi* is actuated and then more and more sins are committed by man. The removal of sin cannot take place by various sacrifices, performance of rituals and through external remedies. Sin is not an external phenomenon, it is deeply internal to human nature. Consequently, the remedy also has to be internal. *Dehabuddhi* causes and increases sin in a person and therefore only through the removal of *dehabuddi* can sin be removed. *Dehabuddhi* cannot be destroyed by fire, weapons or rituals.

Rāmadāsa describes *dehabuddhi* as that which makes man think erroneously that his body is his own self and makes him behave according to this conviction. This attitude causes in the person an increase of pride and a greater longing for sensual pleasures. Such a person cannot walk on the path of Brahman. *Dehabuddhi* can even harm those who have given themselves to the practice of *yoga* and other rituals. Through increase of *dehabuddhi* in oneself one loses personal satisfaction and peace of mind.

Rāmadāsa does not clearly distinguish between *dehabuddhi* and *ajñāna*. On account of *ajñāna* the human person also thinks that his body is important and takes pride in his own self. Through *ajñāna* a man's pride, self-respect, insincerity, anger and harsh speech increase. Such a person fails to realise his own self and is unable to walk on the path of Brahman. *Dehabuddhi* and *ajñāna*, because they increase one's "self glory" (*mīpaṇā*), are the two main reasons why a person cannot follow this path is unable to be united with Brahma.

> "Therefore when the *dehabuddhi* decreases, one achieves the highest good; *dehabuddhi* destroys the unity with Brahman."[13]

Salvation for man consists in freeing himself from the clutches of *dehabuddhi*. Through discernment it is possible for him to be liberated.

> "The one who is bound by the *dehabuddhi*
> can be freed by discernment.
> Such a man transcends the body,
> and attains the heavenly abode."[14]

The real cause of sin is not *dehabuddhi*, but *ajñāna*, non-knowledge. *Ajñāna* is like a cover on the faculty of knowing that binds man and does not allow him to see that God is *nirguṇa*. Further, *ajñāna* makes man blind to the fact that he is more than his own body or more than his own mind. Man suffers from illusion because he does not see that he himself is the *ātman*. This causes in man insincerity, arrogance, pride and anger and makes him use harsh language. Further it makes him forget who he is and what is his real nature.

SVADHARMA

If therefore man has to achieve liberation from sin, then he has to free himself from the bondage of *ajñāna*, which is rooted in his own nature and is experienced in the form of *mīpaṇā*, (pride and self-glory). Therefore the first step in removing sin consists only in freeing oneself from *mīpaṇā*.

> "One who is freed from "self-glory" is truly freed.
> He may be silent or he may proclaim it, but truly he
> is a liberated one."[15]

Liberation therefore consists in being free from *mīpaṇā* and in being one with Brahman. This can be achieved only by the knowledge of Self. The *sādhaka* must make all effort to know *svadharma*, i.e., one's own nature. Today *svadharma* is wrongly understood to be one's own religion, i.e., Hinduism. Many people, like the members of the Śiva Senā[16] and R.S.S.[17] in Maharashtra who take their inspiration from Rāmdāsa and Śivājī, have identified *svadharma* with the Hindu religion. According to Rāmadāsa, *svadharma* is the highest *dharma* and is the main characteristic of the perfect man.

> "Among all *dharmas* the highest is *svadharma*.
> To abide in the *svarūpa* is *svadharma*.
> This is the main characteristic of the *sādhu* (perfect man). 8.9.54

For Rāmadāsa *svadharma* is primarily rooted in the *svarūpa*. The knowledge of *svadharma* presupposes knowledge of *svarūpa*, by which one becomes aware of the obligations and the duties which are rooted in one's own being.

Through *svarūpa* man is united with the highest Brahma, with the infinite being; conversely, on account of *svarūpa*, man is separated and is distinct from the highest Brahma. The *svarūpa* is man's own identity as an infinite being as well as a finite being. Here the two opposites conjoin in unity and form a totally different entity. On one hand, *svadharma* is like an ethical imperative and on the other hand, *svarūpa* is the basis out of which this ethical imperative arises. However these are two different aspects of the same reality. Under one aspect *svadharma* is seen as a dynamic principle that entails actual consciousness of an ethical imperative, and under the second aspect *svarūpa* is seen as a static principle that conjoins the finite with the infinite.

ĀTMAJÑĀNA

In order to be one with God, the human person requires *ātmajñāna*. *Ātmajñāna* is the highest knowledge. It is pure knowledge that consists in knowing one's own self, in seeing oneself united with God, and in continuously knowing what is permanent and impermanent. Through *ātmajñāna* the human person realises that God is *nirguṇa*, without any qualities. Without knowledge of God everything is ignorance. The *ātmajñāna* is the most internal remedy which works in the innermost of the person. Through it all faults, suspicions and illusions disappear. *Ātmajñāna* is more excellent than vows, rituals, alms, pilgrimages or any practice of *yoga*.

> "Hear, the characteristic of knowledge.
> Knowledge means *ātmajñāna*.
> To see through self the self
> is the true knowledge."

To know the highest God,
to realise the true *svarūpa*,
to know the permanent and impermanent
means the true knowledge." 5.6.1-2

The human person who has achieved *ātmajñāna*, or rather the person who continuously possesses it, always lives a meritorious life and is purified of his sins:

"The one who remains in *ātmajñāna* continuously,
his merits have no limitations.
The defilement of wicked sin is removed from him completely." 10.10.65

"In the Vedas and in the Śāstras the true *svarūpa* abides,
such a knowledge itself is the form of *jñānī*,
His merits are innumerous, his good deeds are boundless." 10.10.66

By the search of *ātmajñāna*, the human person realises that his nature is united with the nature of Brahman. This realization is itself a metamorphosis which takes place in the person's nature when, by means of knowledge (*jñāna*), it is united with Brahman. Such a transformed person remains in his body, performs all bodily acts and works like any other person, but performs all actions without desire or without having any purpose. The very greatness of human action is that it is to be performed without aiming at the fruits, the *niṣkāma karma*.

"Though abiding in the body he becomes bodiless,
performing actions he performs none.
These are the characteristics of the liberated person.
They are known by the liberated person alone." 6.9.33

This realization certainly offers man direction and motivation. It is also strength in as far as it changes his nature through unity with the divine. However Rāmadāsa in no way says that this strength completely lies in man and that man by his own effort brings the *ātmajñāna* to its fulfillment.

In the *Karuṇāṣṭake* Rāmadāsa pleads continuously to Rāma, to his personal God, his *iṣṭadevatā*,[18] for liberation from his fallen state, *patita*. He begs Rāma to remove the separation on account of which he is suffering. He tells Rāma that true rest lies only in being with and in Rāma. He begs Rāma to be gracious.[19] adding that it is in his very nature to be gracious, that he fondly helps all and graciously knows the moods and situations of all people. Those who come to the refuge of Rāma are not deserted by him. Only by seeing Rāma does the mind come to rest.[20]

> "O Lord Rāma, visit me graciously,
> on account of separation from you my body pines continuously,
> my desire for honour before men does not cease,
> these painful days do not pass away."
>
> "O God, why have you done so,
> by not relying on you my sins have increased,
> by committing mistakes before my fellow men, I lose honour,
> these painful days do not pass away."
>
> "O poweful one, may you not reject me,
> may you always care for me, your devotee,
> this is my misfortune, that still I am not united with you
> these painful days do not pass away." *(Karuṇāṣṭake*, 17.5-7)

Through these prayers we know that *ātmajñāna* and the strength to perform good deeds do not come merely from the nature of man, but are considered to be the gift of Rāma, the highest and the most powerful God.

SOCIAL CHARACTER OF SIN

In the *Mahārāṣṭradharma*, the unity of all the inhabitants of Maharashtra is of primary importance. This unity is not for the sake of the Maratha-kingdom,[21] but rather for the establishment of *rāmarājya*, the characteristics of which are peace and justice. Unity with others is the result of one's own union with God. The person who is united with God naturally lives in harmony with others. The most evil deeds for Rāmadāsa are harming others and causing them suffering. These deeds spring from the heart that is ruled by pride and by the ignorance that is caused by consciousness of the duality *dvaita* between self and the highest. These people are truly ignorant and unfortunate because they do not know their own *dharma*.

> "By your honourable power, you ought to do good to others,
> however causing others to suffer is a demonic act in itself." 12.10.17

Rāmadāsa says that for the sake of unity we must bear every situation and at every cost harmony must be preserved. Too much argumentation is harmful for unity and harmony. Therefore a virtuous man should always avoid excessive argumentation. In order to foster unity one must praise and accept the good qualities of others and also make these qualities one's own. Rāmadāsa further says that a magnanimous person collects different people in one fold, and by the practice of *bhakti* the true *sādhu* pleases the highest God. For Rāmadāsa the honour and glory of God are the goal of human life. He humourously says that one may die suddenly and be unable to praise God, therefore it is better to lead many more people to praise God before death snatches them away. He further tells that he has made a vow not to ask a gift from his disciples, but desires that after his death they should not cease praising God. The honour and glory of God consist in union with God and in performing acts of charity and doing good to others. By doing good to others one brings them to praise God and fosters in them the desire to be one with the highest.

"Let your body be spent in charity,
may you be helpful to many.
Allow nobody to suffer a want,
no, not even a single person." 12.10.5

"May you share in the sufferings of others.
May the joy of others be satisfaction to you.
May you with your good speech
gather all living beings together." 12.10.7

"You ought to toil yourself,
you ought to bear with others
by spending yourself in various ways,
may you always live in fame." 12.10.8

Meritorious deeds are only for the sake of one's unity with God and are also the result of that union. One cannot be satisfied with one's own union with God but one must also ensure that others attain this union.

"Therefore the human life is excellent,
it is the most excellent among all other lives.
Through it alone will the danger be removed,
the danger of eternal condemnation."

"Your life is in your hands,
hardly is it in the hand of others.
Only by spending it in charity,
may you allow it to last in the form of fame."
1.10.24-25

BALOPĀSANĀ

Rāmadāsa states that on account of sin unfortunate people suffer misery and poverty. Their intellect becomes perverted and they lose the use of reason, thinking that their evil desires are right (18.7.18). They fail to recognize righteous men and their deeds. Poverty means for Rāmadāsa a want of material goods, sickness, lack of health and loss of energy *(balahinatā)*. He condemns every form of laziness and inactivity because through them man begets various evil deeds and increases his heap of sin (19.3.2 and 4). Laziness leads to loss of vigour. Rāmadāsa in his petitions and prayers to Rāma begs that, along with *viveka* (discernment), vigour be fostered in him, and that his desire for effort and activity may increase. Further, in advocating *balopāsanā*, he proposes that his followers worship three deities, Tulajābhavānī, Māruti and Rāma. *Bala* (vigour), *sāmarthya* (power) and *śakti* (energy) are connected with these deities on account of their victories over the evil ones. *Bala, sāmarthya* and *śakti* are advocated in the *Mahārāṣṭradharma: "sāmarthye samartha karuṇi sodavāve"*, i.e., "through power make others powerful" is the motto of Rāmadāsa. Achievement of power and vigour are not here intended for destroying enemies and abolishing opponents. Through the restoration of these qualities, evil is removed and goodness is constituted. Rāmadāsa proposes cultivation of vigour and power because they are embedded in the nature of man, i.e., in *svarūpa*. One who lacks these qualities suffers alienation from the highest because he is estranged from his own nature. He has less participation in the nature of *ātman*, the Self.

The highest Self is *ojas* and *tejas*, power and fullness. Through achievement of the above two qualities man obtains more and more participation with the divine, that is to say a greater unity with the highest Self. He becomes free from vices and governs himself. As *ātmajñāna* gives freedom so also, according to Rāmadāsa, vigour as *tejas* leads to *svatantratā* (freedom, self-mastery or self-government). *Jñāna* and *bala* are constituents of man's nature. The man who realizes his own nature increases vigour and also makes progress in self-knowledge.

"Seeing him, all think him to be virtuous,
none can dare to call him evil.
He abides in everyone,
as if the spirit dwells with fullness in him."

"He is ever ready to help;
whether men be high or low,
with magnanimity in his heart,
he performs acts of charity towards all."

"He is pained by the suffering of others,
he is happy with the happiness of others.
'May all be happy'
this desire he holds firm in his heart."

"A father of a family may have many sons
yet he thinks of them all
in the same way, the righteous man
carries care for all in his heart." (19.3. 22-24)

Only after the removal of sin is man able to do good and meritorious deeds. Such a virtuous man cares for all and establishes unity among all men. Such a life becomes possible for him because he seeks *ātmajñāna* and *bala*, true wisdom and energy. Through them he is united with the highest and achieves greater harmony with all other beings.

In conclusion, sin according to Rāmadāsa is alienation of self, which separates him from all beings, material beings as well as his fellow men, and also from God. Sin is intrinsic to human nature. Rāmadāsa states that it can neither be washed away by bathing in holy rivers, nor be removed by any ritual or sacrament, nor be extinguished by any sacrificial offering. The only way of removing sin is to obtain *ātmajñāna* and *bala* by which man undergoes a kind of metamorphosis that enables him to unite with others and with God.

NOTES

1. In 1645 Śivāji conquered the Toranā fort and later on started ruling in certain regions of Maharashtra from the various forts. He was crowned in 1675.
2. Shelke, C.J. *Don sākṣātkārī.* Pune. 1981, p. 340.
3. Ātmārāmasvāmī. *Dās viśrām.* Dhule. 1923, 121:189.
4. Pāngārkar, L.R. *Śrīsamartha grantha bhāṇḍār.* Bombay. 1978, p. 5.
5. Pāngārkar, p. 5.
6. Literally "the fort a righteous man".
7. Pāngārkar, p. 414.
8. Pāngārkar, p. 415.
9. Pāngārkar, p. 420.
10. Literally *nardeha* means "human person".
11. "One's own form or being".
12. Literally "bodily-intellect".
13. Dev, Ś.Ś. *Satipa dasabodha,* 10th ed. Bombay. 1978, 7.2.39.
14. Dev, 6.2.36.
15. Dev, 7.6.54.
16. A socio-political organization in Maharashtra which was started in Bombay to campaign for the rights of Maharashtrians and for the sake of securing employment for them in the city of Bombay. Recently it has become violent and fundamentalist.
17. Rāshtriya Swayamsevak Sangh.
18. Literally "God that is desired".
19. Literally *anugraha,* "grace".
20. *Mukti.*
21. *Kṣātradharma.*

The Concept of *Māyā* in the *Vacanāmṛtam* of Svāmī Nārāyaṇa

Harald Tambs-Lyche

INTRODUCTION

Weber was convinced that the kind of interrelation he had established between social activity and religious thought, between Protestantism and capitalism, was inapplicable to India, where the other-worldly character of Hinduism precluded similar dynamics (Weber 1930; 1958).

The Svāmīnārāyaṇas of Gujarat, however, may be seen as a significant exception to his generalization, as their sectarian affiliation has coincided with considerable economic enterprise (Williams 1984; Hardiman 1988; Tambs-Lyche 1990 and 1992). But to demonstrate, in Weber's terms, a parallel between Protestantism and the Svāmīnārāyaṇa faith, we must show that the latter differs from the "other-worldly" character of Hinduism as outlined by him. We must further argue that, like Protestantism, the sect lays a particular moral responsibility on the individual so as to motivate him towards an austere, but economically active, life-style.

A fundamental consideration, then, must be the question: Is the world of experience real? If, as stated in several Indian philosophical systems, this world is an illusion, how could one legitimate active involvement in material issues? To clarify this issue involves, therefore, a consideration of the concept of *māyā*.

MĀYĀ AS A FIELD OF DISCOURSE.

"Illusion, deception". This is the primary meaning Dowson ascribes to *māyā*, in his classical dictionary of Hinduism (Dowson 1982; 207).

Turning to the scriptures themselves, we may quote Śaṅkara: "These attributes caused by *māyā* and her effects, are superimposed upon God.... Let a man seek illumination in the knowledge of Brahman, as the scriptures direct. Then those attributes, which our ignorance has superimposed upon Brahman, will disappear..." (quoted in Tuck 1986; 27).

The Vedānta philosopher's views have certainly influenced later commentators, Indian and Western.

In Kinsley's treatment of Hindu Goddesses, the index curtly states: "*Māyā. See* Delusion" (1986; 274). Checking on this reference, we find first an account of Durgā's role in annihilating the demons Madhu and Kaiṭabha. The initial identification of *māyā* is retained: "the entire... episode as told in the *Devī-māhātmya* hinges on Viṣṇu's helplessness as long as he is pervaded by the goddess, whose primary effect on him is to keep him unconscious". Her role in this episode is "exactly the opposite of the normal role of the goddess as a male deity's *śakti*, the power that enables the god to act in the world" (Kinsley 1986; 100). In spite, however, of Durgā's "liminal peripheral nature", she is also a "protectress of the cosmos" when destroying demons (*ibid.;* 101). Here, as elsewhere, the Goddess is identified with three forces or elements: *śakti*, *māyā* and *prakṛti* (*ibid.*). But the distinction between these three forces is not always clear:

"*Māyā*, however, may also be understood as a positive, creative force not unlike *śakti*. *Māyā* may be understood as the power that enables a deity to display or embody himself or herself and therefore as the power that enables a deity to act" (*ibid.;* 104). Thus *māyā* is an ambiguous concept, its unity lying rather in the assertion of the *Devī-māhātmya* that the Goddess *is* the world, she *is* all this" (*ibid.*; 105, citing *Devī-māhātmya* 11.2-3 and 5-6). The dual nature of *māyā* may be seen to stand, then, for the ambiguity inherent in the very fact of existence. "She is life", concludes Kinsley in his treatment of *Mahāmāyā*, and "to the extent that life is cherished and revered, she is cherished and revered" (*ibid.*; 136). While it may be necessary to transcend creation in a spiritual context, "the Devī's identification with existence *per se* is clearly intended to be a positive philosophical assertion" (*ibid.*).

For Biardeau, this dual nature of *māyā* becomes central to her interpretation of Hindu cosmology.

"The term *māyā*, which connotes a magic power creating illusions, becomes, in the classical Sāṃkhya and in the sectarian Vedānta, synonymous with *pradhāna* or *prakṛti*, primordial matter. *Māyā* has a dual power; that of projecting things and beings (that is the cosmic manifestation) and that of veiling them (that is the reabsorption); it is, consequently, the necessary correlative of the dual movement of Yoga" (Biardeau 1981a; 62).

Finally, for Rāmānuja, "*māyā* in no way affects the reality of the external world: one has to see in it only the error that keeps the undelivered soul from reaching that Supreme Person, by whose permission *prakṛti* develops or enfolds within itself..." (Esnoul 1964; 121).

Māyā, then, is an ambiguous concept, capable of a wealth of interpretations. Standing for the ambiguous nature of existence itself, this ambiguity should not surprise us. Clearly, any discourse on man's worldly or spiritual nature, on the conditions for transcending material existence, will in the Indian context have to deal with *māyā*, as S. Radhakrishnan found in his rethinking of Indian philosophy (Tuck 1986).

SVĀMĪ NĀRĀYAṆA: HIS QUEST FOR TRUTH

The child that was to become Svāmī Nārāyaṇa was born of Sarvarīya Brahmin parents in Chappaiya, near Ayodhya, in the year 1781 of the Christian Era. He grew up in a Vaishnavite milieu and even as a child is said to have "shattered" the teachings of the followers of Śaṅkara by his eloquence in defence of the Viśiṣṭadvaita of Rāmānuja (Dave 1967; 8-9; Parekh 1936; 4). While he became the founder of a new sect, the residues of his childhood learning remain important in his discourse.

His mother died when he was eight years old; his father half a year later; and in 1792 the child left home to follow the ascetic path (Parekh 1936; 4). From the many stories concerning his wanderings I will note only a few points here. His main opponents are the representatives of Tantric or Śākta traditions. The Svāmī practised Yogic austerity, and, as Parekh comments, his high degree of Yogic discipline may have influenced the particularly puritanical character of the Svāmīnārāyaṇas when compared to other *bhakti* sects (*ibid.*; 16; Mallison 1974; 449; Tambs-Lyche 1992; 584-86). Following Parekh, we may see the image of the strict Yogī carrying the *Bhagavad-gītā* as a metaphor of the later sectarian formation. As Parekh underlines, the Yogic practices of the Svāmī were not directed at the attainment of magic powers *per se*. Nor was it the goal of merging into the formless Brahman, as taught by Vedāntists, that inspired the young saint; it was all done to attain a perfect *darśan* of Śrī Kṛṣṇa (Parekh 1935; 16).

Wherever he went, he asked, of leading religious personalities, the same five questions:

"What is Jīva? What is Īśwara? What is Māyā? Describe Brahman. Describe Parabrahman" (Dave 1967; 11).

In the course of his wanderings, the young Svāmī came at last to Loj, in Saurashtra, where, at the *āśrama* of one Rāmānanda, he found the answers he sought. Here, in

AD 1801, Ramānanda gave him the two names — Svāmī Sahajānanda and Nārāyaṇa Muni — that later became merged into Svāmī Nārāyaṇa.

THE OPPOSITION: GODDESS CULTS IN SAURASHTRA

Saurashtra, at this time, was still outside direct British influence. The eighteenth century had seen a number of wars and lesser conflicts. When, in 1806-07, the British agent Colonel Walker arranged a system of treaties, the local state formations numbered some two hundred — in an area the size of modern Denmark. They were mostly based on Rajput domination, and the martial culture associated with the caste flourished in the unsettled conditions of the peninsula (Spodek 1976; Tambs-Lyche 1992).

In this cultural complex, the cult of the Goddess had a central place. One of the most important of these Goddesses was (and is) Khoḍiyār, the *iṣṭadevatā* of the royal house of Bhavnagar State, who adopted her in the fifteenth or sixteenth century AD. Her origins, however, go back much further than that (Tambs-Lyche 1992).

Her father, says the myth, was the favourite bard of one of the last kings of the Vallabhī empire, which foundered sometime during the eighth century. The bard, Mamod Gaḍhavī, was childless; for this reason he was deemed inauspicious, and, on the intervention of the Rājpurohit, was expelled from the court. Offering himself in sacrifice to Śiva, he was finally granted seven daughters and a son. The seven sisters, one day, revealed their proper nature; appearing in the terrible form of the Goddess, they killed and ate the neighbour's cattle. The story reaches a climax as they abduct the king's favourite bull, and then kill and devour him, in an act of vengeance against the injustice done to their father. Unmarriageable due to their fierce natures, the daughters are asked to establish themselves away from home. But Khoḍiyār, the youngest of them, does not want to leave. She appeals to the Goddess:

"O Mother! I do not want to look for any other place. My refuge is at your feet. O Parameśvarī, the Śāstras have told us that Jagdambā and Pārvatī are one and the same. Whoever can, for the sake of fun, create this universe in the twinkle of an eye, can also, in the same way, destroy it. And that one is Pārvatī, the wife of Mahādev and the incarnation of Mahāśakti, the essence of Mahādev's *śakti*. Mother, I am the gift of Kailāśpati Mahādev, and therefore I am also your daughter. Please accept me in your refuge". She offers her head in sacrifice to the Great Goddess, but Pārvatī appears before her, blessing her: "I am... giving you part of my own *śakti*, with which you will be able to enlighten the whole Cāraṇ tribe. With the help of the power bestowed upon you, you will be able to perform and complete good deeds. You will be respected and worshipped as a Goddess by the people, and you will be able to bestow blessings upon your devotees".

Khoḍiyār becomes by far the most important Goddess among the seven sisters. Her ties to the *śakti* of the universal Goddess are clearly indicated here. But we may note, too, that she exemplifies the manifestation equally associated with *māyā*. Here, *śakti* and *māyā* are indeed two sides of the same coin. "As time passed", says one of her chroniclers, "it became known to everybody, not only in Saurashtra but throughout Gujarat, that Khoḍiyār had her presence at Gaḷadhara. During the days of Navrātri, she appears in front of her devotees. She blesses the true devotees, male or female, and fulfils their desires. Furthermore, she also helped those minor or major kings who went to her refuge for the defeat of their enemies, and for conquering new lands" (Mehta 1978; 9-23). This, then, gives us a brief idea of the character and the role of one of the most important Goddesses of the area. Born from the Cāraṇ caste, these goddesses did not depend on Brahmin intervention for their cult; their sacred caste origin fulfilled to an extent this intermediary role (Tambs-Lyche 1991). As manifestations of *śakti*, they demanded and got animal sacrifice. As the object of two

Navrātri festivals, they were at the centre of ritual life in the peninsula. Protecting chiefs and kings, they played a role in the political system. Directly accessible to devotees, granting solutions to all kinds of problems, they were — and to this day are — immensely popular.

For most devotees, the epistemological implications of Goddess worship are probably ephemeral. Yet, we should consider what such systematic elaboration of the Śākta view implies: "Śāktism", writes Śrī Jadunāth Sinha, "is a unique type of spiritual monism, which regards Śiva-Śakti as the supreme reality. Śiva is one universal consciousness endowed with Śakti, power of will, power of knowledge, and power of action" (Sinha 1977; 1). "Power is Māyā, which is neither real, nor unreal, nor both, nor neither" (*ibid.*). We are, indeed, far from the concept of *māyā* as illusion (Sinha 1977; 2-3).

While it is true that Sinha's exposition of Śāktism, like Beane's treatise on Goddess worship (Beane 1977), hails from Bengal, his elaboration of the ontological aspects of Goddess worship is hardly very different from what might be found in Gujarat. While the cult has declined on the Gujarat mainland (Pocock 1973) it has remained strong in Saurashtra, where it now seems to be experiencing a revival; its theoretical inspiration, however, is still coming from Bengal.

GOD'S INTERVENTION ON EARTH: A DISCOURSE FROM LOJ

The position of Svāmī Nārāyaṇa with regard to *māyā* may be illustrated by an episode from his stay at Loj:

"One day when the meeting was held, Rāmānanda Svāmī asked his disciples, ... why it was that nowadays God did not come to the rescue of his servants with his weapons as he did when he came in the form of Kṛṣṇa with the discus. Was this because... the contemporary believers were in any way less worthy of such solicitude on the part of God?"

Sahajānanda replied that the believers "were superior to those of olden days and so they did not desire any physical protection from their God; that their one aim was to secure protection from their spiritual enemies such as pride, lust, and anger, and that they were very happy when they found such protection. He added that the discus which God sent forth today was a spiritual one, that it destroyed spiritual darkness and sin, and that God did this because he loved (them)... more and not less, and came to their succour as soon as they desired it and in the way they liked" (Parekh 1936; 41-42).

This is an answer that in a rather fundamental way denies the importance of the two periodic "saviours" in Hinduism — Kṛṣṇa and the Goddess — as immanent, materialized factors in the struggle between virtue and vice. Thus becoming immanent, however, is the very essence of the positive aspect of the concepts centering on *māyā*, as we have seen. But there is another important statement here. Today's believers are seen as superior to those of "olden times" which implies that spiritual progress has been made. This reminds us of an episode in Parekh's biography, where Svāmī Nārāyaṇa meets the four *yugas* in the Himalayas. The Satyayuga, Tretāyuga, and Dvāparayuga, represented, respectively, by the form of a Brahmin, a Kṣatriya and a Vaiśya, pray to the Svāmī that their *dharma* be re-established on earth. Then Kaliyuga, in the shape of a Śūdra, complains that if so happens he will have no place to go. But Svāmī Nārāyaṇa comforts him: "Wherever people would not follow the new faith, he would have room to work his lawlessness" (Parekh 1936; 9-10). This in effect negates the general Hindu idea of decline through the cosmic *yugas*. This decline, incidentally, is often cited by Goddess followers to defend certain practices inherent in their worship as proper to the Kaliyuga, while inappropriate to an earlier age. We must, then, adduce to the Svāmī a concept of progress, of spiritual advance.

This radical reorientation of time — which in the reformed sect has the coming of the Svāmī as its ultimate turning-point — relates intimately to the concept of *māyā*. For, while in outward form the decline of the ages is preserved, the idea of a consequent and opposed spiritual progress implies that the very decline is part of the delusory influence of *māyā*, to be transcended by the knowledgeable. But this transcendence obviates the need for the material intervention, not only of the Goddess in her Purāṇic rout of demons, but equally those made by the local or regional Goddesses, such as Khoḍiyār, in the lives and crises of their devotees. In short, what is maintained here amounts to a denial of *māyā* as power of manifestation, its most positive aspect.

ADDRESSING THE DEVOTEES: THE FIRST DISCOURSE OF THE *VACANĀMṚTAM*.

The earliest of the discourses in the *Vacanāmṛtam* dates from 1820, when Svāmī Nārāyaṇa was established at Gaḍhaḍā in central Saurashtra, under the protection of the minor chief Dādā Khācar, who had become his devotee. His Gaḍhaḍā discourses took place in the *darbār* of this chief, and belong to a period when the Svāmīnārāyaṇa Sampradāya was still at its formative stage.

In this first discourse, Svāmī Nārāyaṇa asks of the audience a seminal question: "Of all the accomplishments, which one is the most difficult to attain?" Nobody answers, and so Svāmī Nārāyaṇa goes on:

"The answer is that the *svarūpa* of Bhagvān has a special significance, and therefore no accomplishment is really too difficult. And the significance is so complete with regard to the mind and soul, that it is not even mentioned in the Śāstras; for the understanding of the *mūrti* of Bhagvān may be compared to the understanding that a man has of his own hands. Such a man has achieved a knowledge of the material object, and so it is with regard to the (understanding of) Bhagvān's *mūrti*; for *jīva*, *īśvara*, *māyā* and *brahman* are seen by him in the *svarūpa*. The desire for (this understanding) is immediately apparent, and Vaikuṇtha, Goloka, Brahmamahol —the abodes of the gods — are all realized directly, for the significance (of the *svarūpa*) rests entirely in the *svarūpa* (itself). Therefore there is really no difficulty of accomplishment and therefore also no great attainment" (*Vacanāmṛtam*, g.p. 1; 27-29).

Thus, the devotee's understanding of the *mūrti*, the *svarūpa* of the God, is a direct, fundamentally simple, experience. The emphasis here is on a *bhakti* interpretation, as opposed to one based on previously attained knowledge. God is not mysterious, he is immediately approachable—but we shall see later that this implies certain conditions, to be specified.

Then Svāmī Nārāyaṇa answers three other questions: one about the *rūp* (form) of *māyā*, one about the place of earnest devotion and one about the importance of gift to the sect.

Thus, the diverse elements of this first discourse provide us with an insight into Svāmī Nārāyaṇa's views, concerning the problems of devotion, of understanding, and of *māyā*. If the latter concept, here, denotes illusion of a worldly nature, this illusion does not result from the world as such. It is up to the devotee to avoid the dangers of delusion that surround him. Thus, *māyā* may be difficult to avoid or transcend, but its avoidance is possible and its transcendance attainable.

The negative nature of *māyā*, as seen by Svāmī Nārāyaṇa, is therefore balanced by his protestation that all that appears to the devotee in this world is not *māyā*.

HOW IS THE *SVARŪPA* TO BE RECOGNIZED?

Truth, then, as well as illusion presents itself to the devotee. But how to distinguish the one from the other? In the twelfth of his early Gaḍhaḍā discourses, also from 1820, Svāmī Nārāyaṇa starts by affirming the points we have already made:

"These are the processes of the world: *puruṣa*, *prakṛti*, *kala*, and the twenty-four *tattvas* of the *māhātattva*. When the *jīva* knows the *svarūpas* of these, to dwell on his own actions becomes *avidyā*, but he obtains release if his actions are like the twenty-four *tattvas*". Muktānanda asked the Svāmī: "O Mahārāj! How are these *svarūpas* to be recognized?" And then Svāmī Nārāyaṇa answers our question: "The *svarūpas* are to be known by their qualities". "The qualities to be mentioned are those that rule *prakṛti* and the different classes pertaining to *prakṛti* : wholeness, eternity, endlessness, truth, that which of itself shines like a star (*svayamjyoti*), the self-illuminating, the dissolution of darkness by the daybreak, the entire form of things mastered and well done, and the really knowledgeable man" (*Vacanāmṛtam*, g.p. 12; 41).

The Svāmī then explains how, just as *prakṛti* or creation is "ruled" by these qualities, so the *jīva*, or individual soul, is "mastered" by the knowledge of the qualities of the *tattvas*, which are the *mahātattvas*, by the *śakti* of Bhagavān, by the properly harmonious balance of the *guṇas* — by all that enters into the making of *māyā* (as creation) — but which is also "ruling" that creation. These are the real powers behind the appearances.

This distinction between appearance and reality is further elaborated:

"Now the qualities of *tattvas* are called *māhātattvas*, that is to say, the true knowledge lies in realizing the identity between the mind and the *mahātattva*, thus understanding the true form of the *mahātattva*, in which rests the whole of *jagat* (the world) and which is in itself immutable and devoid of passion, is of the heavenly mind, is pure, true and peaceful" (*ibid.*; 42).

There follows a lengthy discourse on the relation between matter as appearance and the real qualities of matter, which I shall not go into here. These qualities are also called origins. Wisdom and realization of truth lie in the knowledge of such qualities or origins:

"And of all these (kinds of matter) their origins are known; such is called their origin (or nature), which in their own place rest as they are...." This understanding also applies to the nature of man: "That, in the midst of the unending worthlessness of the universe, (created from) the universe's processes of origin, man (should be created and) should be called *pradhān puruṣa*, the chief and man, (is due to) the initial Puruṣottama such as Kṛṣṇabhagavān from whom the form of man becomes garbed like a chief, be he of the earth. For that chief the origins of *mahātattva* have been offered..." (*Vacanāmṛtam*, g.p. 12; 44). Thus to the nature of man applies the same logic as to *māyā* generally; beyond the appearances, beyond the actions, beyond the manifest thoughts of man there are origins, sources, of a more fundamental, a truer, nature, which are the real causes of that which is manifest. For man to realize his destiny, with regard to the world, is to know these real causes.

In this distinction between the world of appearances and the truth beyond, Svāmīnārāyaṇa follows, I think we may conclude, the lead of Rāmānuja. But, if we compare him to the Śrī Vaiṣṇavas of the North — who are also Rāmānuja's followers — he differs in his conscious popularization of tenets descended from the founder of Viśiṣṭādvaita. With regard to the Vallabhācāryas, his criteria for "truth" are far more severe, leading to a more puritanical attitude.

THE SOUL IN REGARD TO *MĀYĀ* AND *ĪŚVARA*.

The need—an ontological realism, perhaps — to understand the real qualities beyond the world of appearance, necessarily involves a theory of the individual soul, and of its connections to those realities it is to be able to understand, know, or realize.

In the sixth discourse from Gaḍhaḍā, Svāmī Nārāyaṇa sums up his view regarding the different levels of existence:

"In the Śāstras, wherever is treated the spiritual relation between the individual soul and God, there is no agreement, and mistakes are current. So with regard to spiritual conduct reality is, so to speak, what anybody may consider it to be. Gross, subtle and causal, these are the three bodies for which there exists a proper connection to the *jīva*, and from these three bodies, in separation, there arises what is called mastery over oneself. That is, the separate *jīva* consists in the manifest, the deductable and the invisible (and universal) spirit. Along with these three bodily conditions that is called *īśvara* which is properly connected (to them) and so from these three embodiments arise in separation (from them) what is called the *īśvara*'s mastery over himself. *Māyā*, and the effects of *māyā*, are the endlessly worthless universe, with regard to which the whole extension that is called Ākśarabrahman is its connection (or: cause)." (*Vacanāmṛtam*, g. p. 12; 46-47)

Following Rāmānuja, what Svāmī Nārāyaṇa is doing here is to "modify the conception of the Absolute in such a way as to identify the supreme Brahman with the Viṣṇu of Bhakti" (Biardeau 1981b: 124). His system is so close to that of Rāmānuja, that I prefer to leave the specific comparison between the two traditions to further work (*cf.* Mallison 1974).

A MODERN SUMMARY OF SVĀMĪ NĀRĀYAṆA'S VIEWS

It is convenient here to turn away from the *Vacanāmṛtam* to Svāmī Nārāyaṇa's views on *māyā*, *jīva*, and *īśvara* as it appears in H.T. Dave's biography of the saint.

"Māyā", relates Dave, "is prakṛti and the inspirer of Māyā into action is Maheśvar.... She is the generator of evolutionary changes, is of the nature of ignorance (*avidyātmaka*), unborn, holding eight forms and static... she is triguṇātmakā, full of sattva, rajas and tamas guṇas, and is non-sentient" (Dave 1967; 18). Note that the use of Maheśvar here denies the role of the Goddess as *śakti* — the "creator of the universe" as expressed in Khoḍiyār's myth. So far, however, the idea of *māyā* as *prakṛti* is more or less identical with the ideas held by Vedāntists or followers of Sāṃkhya philosophy. "Inasmuch as she holds sentient and non-sentient elements within her womb, she is said to have manifest and unmanifest forms. She is the kṣetra of all the Mahat Tattwas (sic) as well as of jīvas and as Parabrahman's śakti" (Dave 1967; 19). Here, *māyā*'s creation by Maheśvar — which might possibly, but not necessarily, be read as Śiva — is replaced, and implicitly eclipsed, by the identification of *śakti* as emanating from Parabrahman; a step beyond Maheśvar, and, by Svāmī Nārāyaṇa, identified with Puruṣottama.

As for *jīva*, Svāmī Nārāyaṇa stresses its imperceptible, subtle and indestructible nature. But especially, subjectivity is stressed: "(It) is inferred that one who smells, sees and hears, is different from the body and that is the *jīva*" (Dave 1967; 17). We have seen the importance of this subjectivity in establishing the independence of the individual from *māyā*. But the soul remains inextricably bound to *māyā*: "during the pralaya period, the jīvas rest in Māyā and at the time of creation, they take birth according to their Karmans. This metempsychosis of jīvas comes to an end at the time when they are ultimately released from this bondage" (*ibid.*). The latter, of course, relates to the realization of *mokṣa*.

The exposition of the concept of *īśvara* is more complex. "Īśvara's body is composed of Pānca Mahābhūtas out of which the bodies of the jīvas are evolved... (they) are alpa, i.e., insignificant and are not capable of further evolution" (*ibid.*). Thus the body of the high Gods is of the same nature as the bodies of the individual soul, and thus remains firmly bound to *māyā*. This devaluation of the *īśvaras*, however, is far from new. What Svāmī Nārāyaṇa does here parallels Rāmānuja, and may be inspired by the views of Śaṅkara. In Vedānta, *saguṇa* (as opposed to *nirguṇa*, which is relationless) *brahman* is the cause of the world (Tuck 1986; 29). In this role, *saguṇa brahman* becomes *īśvara*. But the world of which *īśvara* is the cause is unreal. It is a mere phantom (*ibid.*; 31). Conceived by the lower levels of knowledge, *īśvara* is ultimately part of *māyā* as its cause, but knowledge of *īśvara*, as *saguṇa brahman*, is imperfect rather than untrue (*ibid.*; 22). The real *brahman* is *nirguṇa* and cannot, ultimately, be described (*ibid.*; 20). It is here that Rāmānuja differs from Śaṅkara, in affirming the reality of the soul (*jīva*) and of the material world (Esnoul 1964; 115). But for him, as for Svāmī Nārāyaṇa, the level of *īśvara* is at best intermediate between humans and God (*cf. ibid.*; 132).

THE LIMITS OF *MĀYĀ*

Svāmī Nārāyaṇa states unambiguously that the *īśvaras* are omniscient (Dave 1967; 17). But how can we explain such omniscience, when they are fundamentally of the nature of *māyā*? "Mahāviṣṇu", it is stated, "rests in the womb of Mūlamāyā known as Hiraṇyamāyā Kośa.... At the time of creation, Parabrahma through Mahāpuruṣa who is Akṣarātmaka, conjoins with Māyā." Thus, the spiritual, "male" element — which is of ultimate reality — combines with *māyā* to produce "Pradhāna and Puruṣa and through them Vairājapuruṣa is born. This Vairājapuruṣa is similar to jīva inasmuch as both are bound by Māyā" (*ibid.*). But, "Vairājapuruṣa at the time of Prakṛta Pralaya, if [he] communes with Mahāpuruṣa, he is freed from Māyā and is released. But as long as he is attached... he remains involved in his activity of creation, sustenance and destruction of the 'jagat' " (Dave 1967; 18). But what is to be said of Puruṣottama himself? Is he not tainted by his union with *māyā*? "Since he disturbs Māyā, he is the cause of Māyā also. But Mahāpuruṣa even though in contact with Māyā, has no desire for the enjoyment of panca viṣayas [the objects of the five senses] as he derives the ānanda [bliss] from the ever blissful form of Paramātmā. He is therefore called a 'mukta', a released soul" (*ibid.*).

CONCLUSION

We now see how the concept of *māyā*, as propounded by Svāmī Nārāyaṇa, does indeed produce an interest in this world of experience, with moral responsibility vested in the individual. This responsibility results from a dual view of the world as experienced by the individual. On the one hand, there are the appearances of this world; in themselves, they are *māyā*, here identified with illusion. But at the same time, the reality behind the appearances is immediately accessible to anybody who cares to look; the qualities making them thus accessible are present in the phenomena themselves and thus clearly discernible. Such discrimination does not depend on mystical or esoteric knowledge; "truth" is a quality ultimately present. There is no excuse, for the individual, if he fails to see it. Sin (*pāp*) — the performance of untruth — is equally recognizable and the responsibility for it devolves squarely upon the individual.

We have seen that much of Svāmī Nārāyaṇa's teaching remains close to the foundations laid by Rāmānuja. For the latter, God is the essence and origin of all beings (Esnoul 1964; 136-38), but the originality of Svāmī Nārāyaṇa seems to lie precisely in his stress on the recognition, by the individual, of such origins or truths within experience itself. Thus an element of knowledge, informing such power of discrimination, is added to the overall recognition or love of God that is central to *bhakti*.

It should be stressed that this world-view, and its moral implications, does not in itself produce the "puritanical" attitude identified, by Weber, with early capitalism. Rather, to understand its effects, we have to consider the devaluation of ritual practices, which Svāmī Nārāyaṇa condemned as outward exhibitionism as well as exemplifying *māyā* in religious terms. Taken together with the emphasis on austerity — resulting from the high evaluation of humility and modesty — and the identification of truth with "useful work", these are the ideological standards produced by the sectarian community rather than by philosophy *per se.* For such moral pressure to carry meaning, however, the affirmation of the reality of truth and truthful activity in this world, with its concomitant need to distinguish truth from *māyā*, would seem to constitute a necessary if not a sufficient condition.

BIBLIOGRAPHY

Beane, W.C. 1977. *Myth, Cult and Symbols in Śākta Hinduism.* Leiden: Brill.

Biardeau, M. 1981a. *Etudes de mythologie hindoue. Vol. I: Cosmogonies purāṇiques.* Paris: Ecole Française d'Extrême-Orient.

——. 1981b. *L'Hindouisme: Anthropologie d'une civilisation.* Paris: Flammarion.

Dave, H.T. 1967. *Life and Philosophy of Shree Swaminarayan (1781-1830).* Bochasan: Shree Akshar Purushottam (Swaminarayan) Sanstha. 1974, 2nd ed. revised. London: George Allen & Unwin.

Dowson, J. 1982. *A Classical Dictionary of Hindu Mythology and Religion.* Calcutta: Rupa.

Esnoul, A-M. 1964. *Ramanuja et la mystique vishnouite.* Paris: Seuil.

Hardiman, D. 1988. "Class Base of Svaminarayan Sect." *Economic and Political Weekly*; 10 September.

Kinsley, D. 1986. *Hindu Goddesses.* Berkeley: University of California Press.

Mallison, F. 1974. "La secte krichnaïte des *Svāmī-Nārāyaṇī* au Gujarāt". *Journal Asiatique*, CCLXII, fasc. 3-4, pp. 435-71.

Mehta, R.R. 1978. *Śrī Khoḍiyārmātā Ākhyān* (in Gujarati). Surat: Śrī Harihara Pustakālāya.

Parekh, M.C. 1936. *Sri Swami Narayana.* Rajkot: Sri Bhagavata-Dharma Mission House.

Pocock, D.F. 1973. *Mind, Body and Wealth.* Oxford: Blackwell.

Renou, L. 1978. *L'Inde fondamentale.* Paris: Hermann.

Sinha, J. 1977. *The Cult of Divine Power.* Calcutta: J. Sinha Foundation.

Spodek, H. 1976. *Urban-Rural Integration in Rural Development: A Case Study of Saurashtra.* Chicago: University of Chicago, Department of Geography, Research Paper No. 171.

Śrī Svāmī Nārāyaṇa. 1968. *Shikshāpatrī.* Bombay: Bharatiya Vidya Bhavan.

——. 1973. *Vacānāmṛtam* (in Gujarati). Ahmedabad: Svaminarayan Temple.

Tambs-Lyche, H. 1990. "Fundamentalism or Secularism? The Case of the Swaminarayanas of Gujarat". Paper presented at the 12th European Conference of South Asian Studies, Amsterdam.

——. 1991. "Le roi et les enfants de la déesse: quelques contes du Saurashtra." *Cahiers de Littérature Orale*, 29, pp. 61-85.

——. 1992. *Power and Devotion: Religion and Society in Saurashtra.* (Dr. Philos. thesis). Bergen: University of Bergen.

Tuck, D.R. 1986. *The Concept of Māyā in Śaṃkara and Radhakrishnan.* New Delhi: Chanakya.

Weber, Max. 1930. *The Protestant Ethic and the Spirit of Capitalism.* London: Allen and Unwin.

——. 1958. *The Religion of India.* New York: Free Press.

Williams, R.B. 1984. *A New Face of Hinduism; The Svaminarayan Religion.* Cambridge: Cambridge University Press.

The Indo-Islamic Expression of *Bhakti*

The Bridegroom Prophet in Medieval Sindhi Poetry[1]

Ali S. Asani

> Beloved, send for this beggar, your little country girl
> For God's sake, O *Muṣṭafā*, my hero, give me courage!
> ...
> Beloved!, put out the fire of *biraha (viraha)* with your own hands. (27)[2]

This verse, addressed to Muḥammad, the Prophet of Islam, was written by a male poet from Sind, the region of the subcontinent that came under Muslim rule as early as AD 711. The composer, ᶜAbd ur-Ra'ūf Bhaṭṭī (d. 1752) or ᶜ*āṣī* "the rebel" as he calls himself, ranks among the first poets to write *maulūds* in his native language Sindhi.[3] Technically intended to be poems describing the Prophet's birth, the Sindhi *maulūds* consist of five to ten verses, patterned after the Sindhi poetic forms of the *wāī* and *kāfi*. *Maulūds* always contain a *thal*, a beginning verse that is repeated as a refrain.[4] As with most Indian poetry, the last verse contains the name of the poet, who usually takes the opportunity to offer a supplication to the Prophet. According to one Sindhi manual, *maulūds* are meant to be recited in a "a sweet and harmonious voice," either by an individual or a chorus, so that the listener's heart is "correctly guided."[5] To this day, the numerous poems composed by ᶜAbd ur-Ra'ūf Bhaṭṭī are recited throughout the villages and towns of Sind, not only at religious assemblies and gatherings but during weddings, general occasions of rejoicing as well as times of mourning.[6]

As the above verse illustrates, ᶜAbd ur-Ra'ūf Bhaṭṭī, though himself Muslim, has adopted into his poetry a symbol central to the Indian literary tradition, namely, the *virahinī*, or a loving and yearning young woman, usually a young bride or bride-to-be, who is tormented by the absence of her husband or lord. Most likely originating in the plaintive songs sung by village women in periods of separation from their husbands, this symbol and the associated concept of *viraha*, "longing in separation," occurs in almost all the vernacular literatures of South Asia. The *virahinī* has enjoyed great popularity in a wide variety of South Asian religious contexts, where she is often identified as a symbol for the human soul. Such usage is in keeping with Indian literary conventions according to which the human soul is always to be represented in the feminine mode, that is as a woman, before a deity who is male.[7] The most renowned use of the *virahinī* in Indian literature occurs, of course, in poetry dedicated to the Hindu god Krishna. In this poetry, the Gopīs (cowmaids), and in particular Rādhā, express their longings for union with their elusive beloved. Jain, Sant and Sikh religious poetry, too, have their *virahinī*s. Within an Islamic context, the *virahinī* appears in many genres of vernacular Sufi poetry ranging from the romantic epics of Awadh to the folk songs of Punjab and Bengal.[8] Interestingly, such poetry equates the concept of *viraha* with the Sufi concept of *ᶜishq*, the burning, consuming longing of the soul for union with God.[9] The woman-soul is also conspicuous in the devotional literature of the subcontinent's Ismaili community where she yearns for the Shii Imam.[10] The use of the *virahinī*, then, in poetry devoted to Muḥammad, the longed-for beloved, is in some ways hardly a surprising development.

Our poet beseeches the Prophet in the voice of a humble

and unsophisticated woman, "a little country girl," who can no longer bear the painful agony of being separated from her beloved, in this case, the Prophet. Not surprisingly, the language and vocabulary he employs are typical of the idiom of Sindhi women, utilizing linguistic forms such as the dimunitive for tender and affectionate address. Only the Prophet, *Muṣṭafā* ("the chosen one"), can put out the fire of longing that consumes this young lady. The yearning, pining woman is a leitmotif that runs through almost all of Bhaṭṭī's poems addressed to the Prophet. Indeed, she is a standard character in much Sindhi mystical poetry, where she is always to be interpreted as symbolizing the human soul in its long quest for God. There, too, the woman-soul endures much pain and suffering as she burns in divine love, and frequently dies from intense longing. By the standards of Islamic religious poetry from the Arabic and Persian speaking Islamic world, this representation of the soul as a woman is definitely unusual. In the Arabo-Persian literary tradition, the woman is generally used as a symbol for something that is negative, such as the seductions of the material world.[11] However, as we saw earlier, the woman-soul, especially in the form of the *virahinī*, is a symbol adopted by many of the subcontinent's Muslim writers as they indigenized their poetry to the literary tastes of their local Indian audiences.

Bhaṭṭī expresses the *virahinī*'s relationship with the Prophet in several different ways. This relationship is one of mutual love, love and mercy being the essence of the Prophet. He is described as "love-intoxicated" (48), "compassionate" (47), "filled with mercy" (3), a "sweet comforting beloved," (65), for whom thousands have sacrificed themselves in yearning like moths (48). Still, this "sweetest of relationships" (1) is painful and soul-consuming for it burns lovers in the fire of *biraha*, a fire which slowly kills:

> Dying from love, those wounded by the prince, weep in yearning. (73)
> All this longing kills me
> O intercessor, yearning for you is killing me. (61)

> Deep passion for the beloved entered my heart, immediately there followed pain
> O compassionate one, save me now; remove the burdens of *biraha*. (65)

Out of intense desire for him, for being in his presence, the Prophet's faithful lover is so anxious to visit his mausoleum at Medina that the very "love for Medina" is difficult to bear. (45)

> Remembering, my eyes yearn; every day lovers come into your presence.
> The pilgrims, who travel to the Arab country, are in love
> There, every day, the travellers recite blessing on the master;
> The Prophet's lovers weep on the roads;
> Journeying on foot, they come with boundless joy. (69)

The journey itself is gruesome and involves traversing difficult, desolate distances, leading the woman-soul to exclaim:

> Would that I would give up my life crawling along the road to Medina! (52)

But as the *virahinī* approaches her destination, she sees the minarets of the Prophet's mausoleum — a sight that acts as a soothing balm for her tired and burning eyes:

> When I saw the minarets of the true master
> The fire in my eyes was soothed
> With longing came the thoughts of the intercessor:
> Muḥammad has met thousands of pilgrims.
> The joys of proximity as I draw near;
> The trembling of emotions (as I think of) Aḥmad (Muḥammad) as my companion. (47)

Love for the Prophet afflicts the *virahinī* like a sickness for which he is the only cure:

> I am love-sick: beloved, you are my health!
> The beloved need only come to my house and
> all pains and afflictions will be cured. (49)

Muḥammad is not only the "medicine of the afflicted" (69) but he is also the physician who can, through his mercy, save a soul dying from love-sickness:

> Revive me so that I may live; otherwise I shall surely die.
> Cure me with the medicines and potions of mercy
> You are the physician and the healer;
> Place your hand on this weak one. (30)

Yet the most dramatic aspect of the *virahinī* symbol in Bhaṭṭī's work recalls the image of the young bride-to-be and her impending marriage with Muḥammad, the bridegroom of Medina. The poet makes condensed references to a host of terms and images pertaining to weddings in Sindhī society. He uses these to allude to the true nature of the woman-soul's devotion to the Prophet in a form that arouses immediate associations and emotions among his listeners.

Like all Indian weddings, this wedding, too, is preceded by a henna *(meṅhdī)* night when the bride's hands and feet are stained with henna; however at this henna party innumerable angels are present (16). As the hour of the wedding approaches, the ladies of the household have climbed on the upper storeys of the house to catch a glimpse of the bridegroom as he arrives (6). Meanwhile the bride anxiously awaits her bridegroom Prophet. In typical Sindhi fashion, he comes wearing a turban of honor, the turban of faith, tied on him by God Himself (16). He arrives riding a horse, a well-harnessed horse (14) with a golden saddle-cloth (10). Or he comes on a camel which the camel-driver makes kneel in front of the bride's house so that the bridegroom Prophet may dismount (6). The waiting bride-soul exclaims:

"O girlfriends! The handsome, beloved bridegroom has come". (8) The procession accompanying the Prophet is comprised of heavenly beings. There are ten million attending angels (9) who distribute musk and perfume to the populace (12). At the same time, they shower Muḥammad with flowers and petals plucked from beautiful rose-gardens (15) as well as precious gems (8). The *houris*, the paradisical virgins, too rejoice and cheer rather noisily (10), making garlands (16), bearing wedding gifts (14), and showering the bridegroom with millions of rubies (11). A fragrant wedding bed, on which the angels have scattered pearls (14) has been prepared for the bridegroom. Finally, he sits on the bed (13), leans against the cushions on which are scattered roses (10). Now the bride-soul knows that her desire to meet the Prophet-bridgroom will be fulfilled:

> The lord sat on the bed, on which lie scattered pearls
> Thanks be to God! The wedding will take place. (13)

By representing the Prophet as a bridegroom, the bridegroom prince of Medina, Bhaṭṭī utilizes a symbol that has become a distinctive feature of many Sindhi panegyrics to the Prophet. Bhaṭṭī employs another literary device, equally fashionable in Sindhi poetry, namely, the use of folk tales and romances as allegories. The culture of Sind is so permeated with folk tales and romances that a scholar of Sindhi literary history considers them to be a pivot around which the bulk of Sindhī literature revolves, regardless of form or theme.[12] In keeping with this tradition, Bhaṭṭī, too, makes allusions to Sindhi romances in his works. He does not narrate them for he assumes his listeners are well aware of the details. He only judiciously refers, by using significant words and phrases, to those tales that feature a *virahinī* and, interestingly, a prospective bridegroom. In this way he continues to preserve a consistency in his symbolism.

A particularly favorite tale of his is the Sassui-Puṅhuṅ romance. It has a simple plot. Sassui, the adopted daughter of a washerman, was the boast and beauty of the town of Bhambhore, a considerable sensation in society. Puṅhuṅ, a handsome Balochi prince, much to the distress of his noble father and brothers, not only falls in love with her but stays with her family as a lowly washerman, until he finally gets to marry her. Outraged by his behavior, Puṅhuṅ's brothers, through force and stratagem, manage to kidnap a very drunk Puṅhuṅ from Sassui as she lay peacefully asleep. On awakening, the deserted bride is heart-broken and desolate. She sets out, alone, in pursuit of her beloved on a fatal two hundred mile march across a dreadful desert and still more dreadful hills.[13]

For Bhaṭṭī, the heroine Sassui is the *virahinī*, separated from her beloved Puṅhuṅ. She represents the soul who longs to meet the beloved Prophet (Puṅhuṅ), ready to undergo all trials and afflictions in the process. Addressing the Prophet as Punhal, an affectionate form of Puṅhuṅ, Bhaṭṭī's Sassui cries:

> Dear sweetheart, I will not forget my beloved, the Prophet
> For you, I spread my hair as a mat, O Punhal, my prince!
> Beloved, more fragrant than musk and ambergris is your sweat;
> On account of your beauty, the moon sacrifices itself.(15)

Bhaṭṭī also alludes to Sassui's arduous journeys in quest of her beloved:

> Remembering, my little heart longs for my Puṅhuṅ:
> Difficult, desolate distances, dear Puṅhuṅ makes me travel!
> O Generous One, show me the tomb of the Prophet. (45)
> I pluck roses along the roadside so that I may welcome Puṅhuṅ when he comes.
> How many tasks shall I undertake for the sake of Puṅhal?
> The journeys are dangerous and difficult, escort me across safely!

May the Generous One show me the mausoleum of
the Prophet. (58)

In another poem, our poet tries to capture Sassui's' agony and pain as she awakens from her sleep to find her friend Puṅhuṅ has disappeared. She is besides herself, there is no meaning in staying any longer in her town of Bhambhore. She is determined to set out in pursuit of him, even if it means being ground by the "fist of death." Though the Puṅhuṅ of folklore was a Balochi, Bhaṭṭī's Puṅhuṅ is, of course, the Prophet. Hence he is addressed as Hāshimī, that is, coming from the Banu Hāshim, the Arabian clan of the Prophet.

O girlfriends! How can I bear this? I, who am walking towards the beloved Puṅhuṅ
While awake, I weep; while sleeping, I have no peace;
Thoughts of the Hāshimite friend overcome me!
Sisters, staying in this Bhambore is poison to me!
The fist of death grinds me along the road;
Seizing me by my roots, love has carried me away!
The grasped hem no longer remains (in my hands);
I live but my life is gone!
The "rebel" ᶜAbd ar-Ra'ūf says, treat me kindly:
I am going to the Prince of Medina and I will return. (71)

How are we to interpret Bhaṭṭī's representation of the Prophet, which some would certainly consider unusual by the standards of Islamic orthodoxy? We may approach this issue from two angles. First, we are clearly dealing here with poetry that emanates from the popular or folk dimension of the Islamic tradition. And like much of the popular poetry written in praise of Muḥammad in other languages of the Islamic world, its conception of the Prophet, influenced by hagiography as well as local culture, will necessarily be different from that espoused by the prophetology of "official"

Islam. But however much this poetry may exalt Muḥammad, it always stops short of expliciting deifying him for even the Prophet's most ardent devotee will admit that ultimately before God, Muḥammad was just a humble *ᶜabd*, a servant, a worshipper.[14] Secondly, we must evaluate Bhaṭṭī's work in light of the two major, often antagonistic, strands that scholars have discerned within South Asian Islam.[15] The first, for the most part associated with those Muslims who interpreted their faith more esoterically or mystically, saw nothing wrong in adapting Islam to the local Indian environment, its mores and traditions, its languages and symbols. Indeed, it is precisely the indigenization of the faith that was instrumental in spreading, so successfully, fundamental Islamic precepts among the local populations. As part of this process, as Bhaṭṭī's poetry reveals, even the figure of the Prophet was "indianized" or "indigenized" and presented in terms that would be familiar and palatable to Indian audiences.

We can also cite here, by way of another example, a rather dramatic case from medieval Bengal where the Prophet became associated with "comparable symbols of the Hindu tradition."[16] From at least the sixteenth century, if not earlier, Bengali Muslim authors of the folk tradition forged an ostensible correspondence between the Islamic concept of prophethood on the one hand and the Hindu concept of the *avatāra* on the other. The personality of Muḥammad was made pertinent to the Bengali religious milieu by being presented as the most powerful *avatār* of the present age or *kali-yuga*, the *kali-avatār*.[17] In their turn, Hindu deities such as Krishna were conceived as prophets who preceded Muḥammad, the final Prophet-*avatār* sent down by God to humankind. Similarly, at the other end of the subcontinent, in Sind, medieval preacher-saints identified the Prophet with the Hindu Brahmā and the Prophet's daughter, Fāṭimah, with Brahmā's daughter Sarasvatī.[18]

At great odds with this assimilative or adaptationist strand was a separatistic and law-bound conservative one.[19]

Conscious of the Muslim community's minority status in a predominantly Hindu milieu, adherents of this second strand were anxious to prevent Islam from being absorbed and overwhelmed by "an environment which could only be described as an anathema to their cherished ideal of monotheism."[20] To preserve and protect Islam from encroachment by "idolatrous" Indian customs and beliefs, the "separatistic" strand cultivated an outlook that has been appropriately termed "prophetic-separatistic" or "Mecca-oriented."[21] It looked to Arabia, the heartland of Islam, for determining the cultural and religious norms for the subcontinent's Muslim community. More significantly, it stressed the Arabian character of Islam by evoking the example of Muḥammad, the Arabian Prophet, as the only reliable quide. The Prophet's Arabian background was highlighted — he was Muḥammad, the Meccan, the Medinan, the Hāshimī, the Quraishī.[22] Indeed, on account of this "Arabian" emphasis, the epithet "Arab" in reference to the Prophet occurs more frequently in Islamic literature from South Asia than any other part of the world. Adherence to the way of the Arabian Prophet to the exclusion of "non-Islamic" Indian elements became so strong in the conservative strand that some of the powerful reformers associated with it identified themselves as following the *ṭarīqah Muḥammadiyyah*, "the Muḥammadan path."[23]

The history of Islam in the Indian subcontinent can quite easily be interpreted within the framework of the dynamic interplay of these two antagonistic strands. However much their philosophies and outlooks differed, it is significant the Prophet occupied a prominent position for both. That is because whether he is perceived through an "Arabia-tinted" or "India-tinted" glass, loyalty to him, as expressed in the second half of the *shahādah* (the Muslim testimony of faith), is a hallmark of Muslim identity. This is why Sir Muḥammad Iqbāl (d. 1938), the Muslim poet-philosopher of Indo-Pakistan, who incidentally wrote mostly under the influence of the Arabia-oriented strand, says in his poem *Rumūz-i bekhudī*: "love for the Prophet runs like blood in the veins of the

Muslim community."[24] Elsewhere (in the *Asrār-i khudī)* he declares in a Persian verse:

dar dil-i muslim maqām-i muṣṭafā ast
abrū-i mā ze nām-i muṣṭafā ast

The Prophet's home is in the heart of the Muslim
The very name of the Prophet is our glory[25]

NOTES

1. This article is substantially based on a broader study that I have undertaken on images of the Prophet Muḥammad in Sindhi and Urdu devotional poetry. That study, along with other essays on Islamic poetry written in praise of the Prophet, appears in a forthcoming publication *Celebrating Muḥammad: Images of the Prophet in popular Muslim poetry*, University of South Carolina Press, in press.
2 The number in parentheses in this and other references throughout this article indicates the poem number in the ᶜAbd ur-Ra'ūf Bhaṭṭī section in Nabibakhsh Baloch, ed. Maulūd. Hyderabad, Sind: Sindhi Adabi Board. 1961, pp. 5-33.
3 Meman ᶜAbd al-Majīd Sindhī, *Sindhī meṅ naᶜtiya shāᶜiri*. Larkana: Sindhī Adabi Academy. 1980. p. 121.
4 *Ibid.*, p. 133.
5 *Ibid.*, pp. 134-135.
6 Nabibakhsh Baloch, *Maulūd*, p. 5.
7 See John Hawley, "Images of Gender in the Poetry of Krishna," *Gender and Religion: On the Complexity of Symbols*, ed. by Caroline W. Bynum, Stevan Harrell and Paula Richman. Boston: Beacon Press. 1986. pp. 231-56.
8 See A. Schimmel, *As Through A Veil: Mystical Poetry in Islam.* New York: Columbia University Press. 1982, pp. 152-154, and A. Asani, "Sufi Poetry in the Folk Tradition of Indo-Pakistan," *Religion and Literature*, 20, I (1988).
9 Charlotte Vaudeville, "La conception de l'amour divin dans la Padmāvat de Muḥammad Jāyasī, *virah* et *ᶜishq*," *Journal Asiatique*, 250 (1962), pp. 351-367.
10 A. Asani, "The Ismāᶜīlī *Ginān* Literature: Its Structure and Love Symbolism," A.B. thesis, Harvard College, 1977.
11 A. Schimmel, *Mystical Dimensions of Islam.* Chapel Hill:

University of North Carolina Press. 1975. Appendix 2: "The Feminine Element in Sufism," pp. 426-435.

12 L. H. Ajwani, *History of Sindhī Literature*. Karachi: Allied Book Co. 1984, p. 40.

13 The summary of the Sassui-Puṅhuṅ remance is closely based on Sir Richard Burton's rather colourful account in *Sind Revisited: with notices of the Anglo-Indian army; railroads; past, present and future*, vol. i. London: R. Bentley and Son. 1877, pp. 129-132.

14 A. Schimmel, *And Muḥammad is His Messenger*. Chapel Hill and London: The University of North Carolina Press. 1985. p. 142-43.

15 See Imtiaz Ahmad, "The Islamic Tradition in India," *Islam and the Modern Age*, XII, no. 1 (1981), pp. 44-62; Annemarie Schimmel, "Reflections on Popular Muslim Piety," *Contributions to Asian Studies*, XVII (1982), pp. 17-26; Yohannan Friedmann, "Islamic Thought in Relation to the Indian Context," *Puruṣārtha*, 9 (1986); Richard Eaton, *Sufis of Bijapur 1300-1700*. Princeton: Princeton University Press. 1978; and S. C. Misra, "Indigenisation and Islamisation in Muslim Society in India," *Indian and Contemporary Islam*. ed. S. T. Lokhandwalla. Simla: Indian Institute for Advanced Study, 1971.

16 Asim Roy, *The Islamic Syncretistic Tradition in Bengal*. Princeton: Princeton University Press. 1983, p. 95.

17 *Ibid.*, p. 98.

18 See Azim Nanji, *The Nizari Ismā'īlī Tradition in the Indo-Pakistan Subcontinent*. Delmar: Caravan Books. 1978; G. Khakee. "The *Dasa Avatāra* of the Satpanth Ismailis and Imam Shahis of Indo-Pakistan," Ph. D. dissertation, Harvard University, 1972; A. Asani, "The Khojahs of Indo-Pakistan: The Quest for an Islamic Identity," *Journal of the Institute of Muslim Minority Affairs*, 8, no. 1 (1987).

19 This separatistic strand was strongly represented among the *ashrāf*, the elite of the South Asian Muslim community, often Turko-Persian in ancestry. See Imtiaz Ahmad, "The *ashrāf*-*ajlāf* dichotomy in Muslim social structure in India," *Indian Economic and Social History Review*, III (1966), pp. 268-278.

20 Yohannan Friedmann, "Islamic Thought," (see n. 15) p. 79.

21 A. Schimmel, "Reflections on Popular Muslim Poetry," (see n. 15), p. 19.

22 A. Schimmel, *As Through A Veil: Mystical Poetry in Islam*. New York: Columbia University Press. 1982, pp. 199-200.

23 A. Schimmel, *And Muḥammad is His Messenger*, pp. 216-238

and "The Golden Chain of 'Sincere Muḥammadans'" in *The Rose and The Rock*, ed. B. Lawrence. Durham: Duke University Program. 1979, pp. 104-134.

24 *Rumūz-i bekhūdī* (Lahore: n.p., 1917), p. 190.

25 *Asrār-i khūdī* (Lahore: n.p., 1915) lines 357-358.

The Devotional Element in the *Nasīhats* of the Bohrā Writings in Gujarat

Balvant Jani

The paper deals with the devotional element in the *Nasīhats* of Shaikh Sādikalī (Ṣādiq'alī) Sāheb, a poet-devotee of the Dā'ūdī Bohrā community of Gujarat.

THE BOHRĀS

The Bohrās form one of the two branches of Ismā^cīlī Shī'a Islam established in Gujarat. The word 'Bohrā' is admittedly derived from the Gujarati verb *vahoravuṃ*: to buy, purchase, collect, store, undertake etc., and alludes to the commercial occupation prevalent among the members of this community. There is no historical information available as to the origins of the Bohrās but according to the traditional legends and miracles recorded in the third volume of *Mausim-i-Bahār* of Muhammad 'Alī, written in 1882 and published in 1884, an authoritative document for the faithful, it was through the preachers sent from Egypt at the fall of the Fatimid rule that Gujarat, and more precisely coastal Saurashtra, witnessed the first conversions to the Ismā^cīlī persuasion. It is a well known fact that before the completion of the Muslim conquest of Gujarat in 1298, peaceful conversions to Islam had occurred in the wake of the first commercial contacts with the Arab merchants who settled in the ports on the coast of Western India'[1] and often brought with them learned scholars and missionaries, all of them indifferent to political power. Yet there remain some uncertainties and incoherencies in the various reports on the first Mustaᶜlī Ismāᶜīlī conversions in Gujarat,[2] yet all seem to agree on the name of the Dāᶜī (envoy) Abdullāh ('Abd Allāh) who arrived from Yemen at Cambay in 1067-68 and was the real founder of the Bohrā community. He is said to have died in 1137 and his tomb in Cambay bears the title of 'Pīr-i-Rāvan' or 'Amar-pīr'.[3] The links between Yemen (where the Mustaᶜlī had taken refuge after their last Imām went into concealment in 1130 and the Fatimid empire had disappeared in 1171) and the mission of Gujarat were very strong, to the extent that in 1539 the head of the movement became and remained an Indian and that soon after, when the Turkish orthodox persecution became unbearable in Yemen, the headquarters were shifted to Gujarat where they are still established. The Hindu rulers were benevolent to the Bohrās, as Muslim rule in Gujarat, during its three phases: the Delhi rule (1298-1403), the Gujarat Sultanate (1403-1573), and the Mughal rule (1573-1757),[4] saw periods of peace alternate with persecution.[5] Under the Sultanate occurred the main schism among the Bohrās headed by Jaᶜfar, a Bohrā from Patan endowed with a charismatic personality (he died in 1441). It led to the secession of the Sunnī Bohrās, who reverted to orthodox Islam.[6] The present Shīᶜā Bohrās are divided into three main branches: the Dā'ūdī Bohrās, the Sulaymānī Bohrās and the Aliyya Bohrās.[7] Shaikh Sādikalī Sāheb belonged to the Dā'ūdī Bohrās.

Certain features are said to be characteristic of the Bohrās: a tender and delicate constitution, graciousness in social intercourse and gentleness, meticulous cleanliness and absence of any addiction or vice. They are fond of communal feasts and frequently arrange mass gatherings of the community. They are better off than their fellow Muslims and the entire administration is systematically carried out under the guidance of the chief Mullāji of the community, known as 'Saiyed'. Their social structure is well planned and literacy is increasing considerably. Being mainly traders they, like the Hindus, worship their account books on the festival of Divālī. Their holidays usually precede those of the Muslims by two days, They maintain their traditional occupations dealing with the trades of glass, hardware, crackers etc. ... Shri Asghar Ali Engineer who provides a precise and elaborate account of the Bohrā community in his book says: "Ethically, and in their value-orientation the Bohrās are, by and large, petty bourgeoisie".[8]

SHAIKH SĀDIKALĪ: LIFE AND WORKS

Sādikalī who lived in the eighteenth-nineteenth century is the only "highly revered Indian poet among the Bohrās".[9] We do not know the date of his birth into the Dā'ūdī Bohrā community of Surat. From childhood he was a *parhejgārī* (adept of abstinence) and a *dīndārī* (inclined towards religion). He learnt Arabic and Gujarati through an expert teacher and had a keen desire to learn Persian as well. For this purpose he found a Maulavī residing at Rander to whom he went every day in spite of difficulties.[10] He had to bear the humiliation and rebukes of the teacher who had a strong aversion for the Dā'ūdī Bohrā community, yet Sādikalī enjoyed increasing to twenty-two the two Persian stanzas taught to him daily,[11] finally becoming an expert. Sādikalī later on lived simply in a hut and spent his time teaching religion to humble and poor people, helping them in their plight.[12] Once he spent the amount of one thousand rupees given to him by the Saiyed, who was anxious to have his dilapidated hut repaired, on helping those who were in need and distressed. His answer to the Saiyed Saifuddīn was: "I am not destined to live longer... It would be much better if I built a house of my own in the vicinity of Allāh—in paradise!".[13] He died in 1818[14] and was buried in the mosque on Haideralī

Kāsamjī street in Surat. The following epitaph appears on his grave:

Shaikh Saiyedī Sādikalī
Mulla Sultanalī
Wafāt Tarikh 22 Jilkād
Hijrī 1233

Shaikh Sādikalī had a son named Shaikh Abdulhussain whose son was Shaikh Abdul Taiyab. He was succeeded by Shaikh Hātimbhāī whose son named Dr Shaikh Sādikalī is alive today. He has deposited all the manuscripts of Shaikh Sādikalī Sāheb in a *Kothār Mubārak* (a storehouse of manuscripts).[15] Shaikh Sādikalī wrote his compositions in Gujarati mixed with Arabic and Urdu. His discourse, thanks to its personal use of a happy combination of Arabic and Gujarati characterized by a lucid and simple diction is powerful and effective. About one hundred and fifty *Nasīhats* have been published, the remaining being still in manuscript form. The script used is always Arabic, with a few exceptions.[16]

THE *NASĪHATS*: FORM AND CHARACTERISTICS

The *Nasīhat* is a metrical composition to be sung or recited on any occasion — joyous or sorrowful — related to the Bohrā community. The form evokes the medieval New Indo-Aryan devotional songs, globally termed *pad-bhajan*. But the *Nasīhats* being comparatively longer (with exceptions), may be identified with narrative metrical compositions such as *pad-mālā*. The *Nasīhats* have a rhythm marked by a tinge of a metre known as *Bhujaṅgī*, but they seem to have a close affinity with the *Nazam-Gazal*, the metre of which is often used. The metres are always adapted to the requirements of the performance, either recitation or group singing. *Nasīhat* means 'precept' or 'admonition'. This points to a didactic genre. Religious admonition, rules of good conduct, with occasional digressions related to popular legends and lives of Islamic saints providing an ideal illustration and model of life, are the themes treated in the *Nasihats*.

A STUDY OF THE *NASĪHATS* OF SHAIKH SĀDIKALĪ[17]

Religious sentiment and didactic injunctions occupy a central position in the *Nasīhats* of Shaikh Sādikalī and in order to provide expression to these two elements, he seems to have used a number of common and essential ingredients of Islam and Hinduism. For instance among the devotional elements stressed in his poems are:

- the repetition of the name of God:

Ai dil tuṃ nām jap hirde khudānā
Na hargīj baith kaim mile havānā.

The name of khudā is to be repeatedly uttered in the heart. Do not sit idle even for a moment.

- the surrender to the omniscient Almighty, and the acknowledgment of His favour and grace, as in:

Ākāś hidāyat-na verse che bharī leje
Hirdānā caman andar hariyālī karī leje.

The kind favours of God are constantly raining in abundance. The same should be caught in your heart, so that it may become full of greenery.

- the consciousness of the priceless value of a human life:

Bākī ā umar tārī bemūl bakiyyo che
Taubāthī sambhālī le ā khairno dariyo che.

> Now what remains of your life is a priceless remnant. It needs to be preserved by penitence.

And as an idea of penitence, Sādikalī proposes:

> *Taubānā khālis pānithī tuṃ mel gunāno dhoje*
> *Kare badī je tārā upar karīne nekī badī khoje.*

> In order to wash away the dirt of your crime with the pure water of penitence, you should exercise kindness even towards those who have caused you pain in their wickedness.

In many *Nasihat*s Shaikh Sādikalī extols the greatness of the Guru or Sadguru (the interior Guru) whose position is, for him, equivalent to that of God:

> *Suni le dilnā kānothī tuṃ hikmatnī kahānīne*
> *Citāri le jigar par Sadgurunī ā jabānīne.*

> The most inspiring words of the Sadguru are to be inscribed on the heart, and to be heard by the ears of thy heart.

Or:

> *Motī Javāhīrothī Gurunā sakhun bhalā che*
> *Khātirnā daftar upar likhkiye to rāh bajā che;*
> *Je jotthī sitārā camke che āsmān par*
> *Guru loknā sakhunmāṃ te jotnī jilā che.*

> The words, statements and counsel of the Guru are invaluable and are compared to pearls and jewels. The profound radiance that illuminates stars in the blue firmament is to be found in the words of Guru as well.

The Sadguru, suggests Sādikalī, will lead us in the right direction provided we listen to His words and keep them in our heart.

The didactic elements in the compositions of Sādikalī emphasize two points: warning against the worthlessness of this transient life and the imminence of death on the one hand and the importance of living a pious, simple and generous life on the other. Concerning the first point he says:

> *Ā āsmān-nā nice jamīn par koī na rahyā*
> *Jo tuṃ baśar gadā che kabarmāṃ be innehā.*
> *Vicāro kahāṃ gayā voh Rao-Rānā*
> *Khalakmāṃ Rājvaṃśī te kahevānā.*

> No one is immortal under this sky nor has remained on this earth. Innumerable people are lying buried deep beneath the earth in their graves. Whither have gone kings and emperors considered as members of a great royal dynasty?— Just think!

Or:

> *Jāt ā jehne saṃvāro cho te māti thāśe,*
> *Gornī khārmāṃ andharmāṃ kidā khāśe.*

> By embellishing your body, you intend to make it look more beautiful and attractive; however the same body will ultimately lie in the pit of the grave, where it will be eaten by worms.

Concerning the model of the life that we should live, Sādikalī proposed examples drawn from the lives of saints as well as from various episodes of popular legends. He tells for instance the story of the poor old 'Alī Valī who had to lock his tin of barley flour for fear that his children would mix sugar and ghee in it and reduce to naught his ascetic habits. As an advocate of an unpretentious life, Sādikalī says:

Nīcā ne ūncā sarvethī karje
Tavā sneh dilnī saphāīthī
Māṃjje ārsī dilnī hardam
Vāhlā dāge riyāīthī.

Forget the differences of high and low, and conduct yourself with discrimination. Keep the mirror of your heart always clean, since the same is smeared with blots of hypocrisy.

And:

Tuṃ na bethīś kai hamiyyatne hindole
Tuṃ hargīj kamsakhun muṃhthī bole.

Do not swing on the swing-board of arrogance, nor speak improper and unpleasant language.

Or:

Mat koi par tuṃ neki karīne kahyā kare.

Do not give wide publicity to your compassion or goodness which you have shown towards someone.

And:

Dhuṃvo caḍhine ābhthī pācho pade che tem
Mat tuṃ caḍhīne āpthi pācho padā kare.

Just as smoke fades after rising upwards and then falls down, likewise refrain from scaling to incredible heights.

The exaltation of an austere life, and the warnings against mundane futility, as well as the advice to invoke in silent repetition the name of God and the acknowledgment of the word of the Sadguru, are reminiscent of the *nirguṇī bhakti* of the Sants of Northern India. Yet not only in content, but also in the mode of expression: the choice of metaphors, the paradoxical examples, the power of diction, we come across a combination of elements of both Hindu and Islamic religion in their respective cultural references. Sādikalī uses rich metaphors; time, for instance, is 'a black cobra'; the process of breathing or respiration, a 'string' so that "the string of our life goes on getting thinner and thinner with each inspiration"; the fear of God is a 'key' indispensable for opening the door of liberation. He says in a *Nasīhat:*

Kāyā che battī ne jīv che dīvo
Jo tuṃ mànmāṃ vamāse.
Tel umarnuṃ ghate che din-din
Ākhar dīvo bujhāśe.

Here the wick of the lamp, which means the human body, dwindles with the passage of time; the oil of the life-span decreases day by day and this will eventually extinguish the lamp of life which is the human soul.

In another *Nasīhat:*

Jisamnā pinjrāmāṃ jīvnā totā upar hardam
Śikāri mautno śakro lāgo che eh jatāvi le.

Here the human soul—a parrot imprisoned in the human body-cage will fall a prey to the falcon of death. A distinct aura of Indian culture emerges from metaphors such as 'black cobra','lamp', 'parrot', 'cage', 'falcon'. In addition, Sādikalī uses another device to make his points: the juxtaposition of two paradoxical ideas or illustrations such as:

Mahelethī utarīne pūrśo kabarnā khādā.

And:

> *Naram talāi kahāṃ ne kahāṃ tame yāro*
> *kabarnī dhūlmāṃ jaī sūśo ek karvat par.*

Or:

> *Umarnī candnī thāśe andharī.*

Juxtaposed and opposed are *mahal* (palace) and *kabar* (grave) or *naram talāi* (soft mattress) and *kabar* again or *cāndnī* (moonlight) and *andhāruṃ* (darkness), manipulated to convey the required emotion. Irony is not far:

> *Dekh kabrastānnī harroj che ābādī.*

concerning the continuous prosperity of the graveyard!

But it seems that the power of the language of Sādikalī stems from his facility in mixing three sorts of vocabularies: Gujarati, such Arabic-Persian as had already been absorbed by Gujarati, and finally Arabic-Persian as yet unknown to Gujarati. Many more examples could be given, such as:

> *Je ghadī cadśe nanāmī par tehne yād kar*
> *Log kahe che ke falānāno janāyo jāy che.*

where the word *nanāmī* and *janājo* (a bier) are used side by side.

Or:

> *Samandarthī je koi gāgarne bharśe*
> *Samandarmāṃ na tethī khot padśe.*

where *samandar* is preferred to *sāgar* but coupled with *gāgar*, an evident choice.

Idiomatic allusions to Hindu culture remain meanwhile the most striking feature, as in the following, almost proverbial, utterance:

> *Śīkhje yā pūchje, pūchethī paṇḍit thavāy.*
>
> One who asks and inquires because of his tireless inquiries will become a *paṇḍit* (learned man).

Or:

> *Je dālī phale bharī che te kāyam namā kare.*
>
> A bough laden with fruit is always leaning towards the earth.

Many images such as the *talāi* (mattress) or the *latkā* (a graceful gesture of the body) are reminiscent in their use of the medieval Saint-Poets of Gujarat like Narasiṃha Mahetā, Niṣkulānand or Dayārām, and the elaborate use of the terminology related to trade and agricultural activity is also identical with that of medieval Gujarati poets.

We may conclude that Hindu culture and religion were for Shaikh Sādikali essential elements in the shaping of his vigorous message to his Dā'ūdī Bohrā community.

NOTES

1. See Nayak, p.126.
2. See the different versions in Master, Jote, Forbes, Campbell, Misra and Daftary.
3. See Master, p.133.
4. See Nayak, p.165.
5. See Master, chapters 1,2,3.
6. *Ibid.*, p. 128 and chapter 63.

7. *Ibid.*, chapters 26, 27. A large number of Shīʿā Bohrās reside in Saurashtra and some in Surat. They bear distinctive surnames of Hindu Brahmins or Banyas such as: Trivedī, Jānī, Joṣī, (*Ibid.*, p. 128).
8. See Engineer,p.150.
9. *Ibid.*, p. 107.
10. 'Nasīhatnā Sāheb', p.9.
11. *Ibid.*, p. 10.
12. *Ibid.*, p. 10. He taught how to read and write to small children as well as to aged persons.
13. *Ibid.*, p. 11.
14. *Ibid.*, p. 9.
15. *Ibid.*, p. 11, and from a letter written by Śrī Hātīm Hamdāni to Śrī Akbaralī Jasdanvālā of Rajkot on the 6-1-1978.
16. The Bohrās are a very secretive community and do not allow outsiders to witness their rituals or avail themselves of their literature. That is why I was obliged to depend upon some of my friends and acquaintances from the Bohrā community in undertaking my research. Their response was very good. The *Nasīhats* are sung or recited, but only the choicest verses, in conformity with the requirements of the sect, are taught to the new generation. I was able to obtain texts in Arabic script and printed form, and from these an audio cassette was prepared. I was introduced to the Arabic script by a Mullājī (a Bohrā preacher) and then, with the help of the cassette, I transliterated some of the best parts from Arabic to Gujarati script. Whatever the language, Gujarati or mixed Arabic-Gujarati, I always consulted my Bohrā friends in order to reach a correct interpretation. I hereby take the opportunity of expressing my deep gratitude to all friends, colleagues and well-wishers including some distinguished personalities such as: Mr Asghar Ali Engineer of Bombay; Mr Akbarali Jasdanwala, who is a renowned poet of Rajkot; Mr S. S. Rabi, another poet of the Bohrā community; Mr Asgharali Jasdanwala; Rahemat-bahen; Miss Sakina and Rubab-bahen, and of course, Honorable Mullā Sāheb.
17. The quotations of the texts are from my personal collection built-up as explained in the previous note (n.16).

BIBLIOGRAPHY

Campbell, James M. ed. *Gazetteer of the Bombay presidency*, vol. IX, part II *Gujarát population: Musalmans and Parsis.*

Bombay: Government Central Press. 1899 (2nd ed. 1990 under the title: *Muslim and parsi Caste and Tribes of Gujarat*, Gurgaon: Vipin Jain).

Daftary, Farhad. *The Ismā[c]ilis: their history and doctrines*. Cambridge: Cambridge University Press, and New Delhi: Munshiram Manoharlal. 1990.

Engineer, Asghar A. *The Bohras*. New Delhi: Vikas publishing House. 1980.

Forbes, Alexander K. *Râs Mâlâ; or, Hindoo Annals of the Province of Goozerat in Western India*. 2 vols. London: Richarson Brothers. 1856.

Jote, Ratnamanirao Bh. *Gūjarātano* (sic) *sāṃskṛtika itihāsa, islāma yuga* 2 vols. Ahmebabad: Gujarat Vidyāsabhā. 3rd repr. 1968 (1st ed. 1945).

Master, Karim M. *Mahāgujarātana musalamāno*. Parts 1 and 2. Baroda: Oriental Institute, M. S. University. 1969. (Śrī Sayājī Sāhityamāḷā, puṣpa 344).

Misra, Satish C. *Muslim Communities in Gujarat*. London: Asia Publishing House. 1964 (2nd ed. 1985, New Delhi : Motilal Banarsidass).

'Nasīhatnā sāheb' in *Anjuman-e-Tāherī*- Hadiyo from Surat.

Nayak, Chotubhai R. *Gujarātī para arabī-phārasīnī asara*. 2 vols. Ahmedabad: Gujarāt Vidyāsabhā. 2nd ed. 1965 (1st ed. 1954).

The Mystical Aspect of Valī Auraṅgābādī's Poetry

Enzo Turbiani

Though Valī was born in the second half of the seventeenth century, a good deal of his poetry represents the *bhakti* trends to be observed both in Hinduism and mystical Islam. It is a well-known fact that Valī was educated at the religious school founded in Ahmedabad by his ancestor Vajīhu'd-Dīn, who started an initiatory brotherhood that recognized *taṣavvuf* as its propulsive force. Valī's up-to-dateness can be seen also in his typical language, which generally approaches colloquial patterns, quite different from the stereotypes employed by his imitators. The elevated level of communication of his language — in which one very often meets with familiar, purely Indian words instead of affected terms and expressions of Persian and Arabic origin, understood only by a learned elite — makes his way of writing poetry universal.

The linguistic code Valī mostly makes use of[1] is easily comprehensible even today, in spite of the diachronical development of Dakanī[2] and Urdu, which in his later poems become practically amalgamated, losing a great part of their distinctive features. The following *ġazal* by Valī shows a standard type of speech which can be considered as a model of good contemporary Urdu:

Āj har gul nūr kī fānūs hai,
koh o ṣaḥrā ṣūrat-i ṭāūs hai.
Gar na nikle sair kõ vo naubahār,
ẓulm hai, faryād hai, afsos hai.
Ae ṣanam, tere dahan ke šauq sõ.
har kalī mẽ nagmȧ-ye nāqūs hai.[3]

"Today every rose is a chandelier of light,
the mountain and the plain are as stately as a peacock.
If that spring-beauty does not come out for a walk,
it is an injustice, it is a wail, it is a pity.
O idol of mine, for the sake of your mouth
the prayer-call bursts from every blossom".

The excerpt of Valī's *ġazal* that has been quoted above is icastic and pregnant: every word is glistening, so to speak, with gaudy colours, which recall the poet's native Deccan. It is quite different from the style of classical poets, such as Nāsix, who identifies the subject with the object, whereas Valī sets the subject (the lover) on a plane distinct from that of the object (the beloved). Valī shapes metaphysical concepts starting from the plasticity and tangibility of the image, as can be seen in the prayer-call bursting from every blossom, thirsty for the mouth of the beloved. It is not difficult to discern here the yearning for mystical reunion with the Friend, the Divine Being of Jalālu'd-Dīn and of other seers and enlightened saints of India and Persia.

Valī's choice of the *ġazal* as a fundamental medium for expressing his inner life and his metaphysical thoughts represents the intention, on the part of the poet, of melting space into time and—conversely—time into space. Sayyid Ẓahīru'd-Dīn Madanī says that Valī chose the *ġazal* because it is a literary genre particularly suited to setting in a single frame the diachronic development — *ek hī naqš mẽ ba yak vaqt*[4]— of his mystical insight. According to Sayyid Ẓahīru'd-Dīn: "Most of his poetical production concerns Sufism, explaining it in such an exquisite garb, with the help of *ġazal*, that it becomes difficult to distinguish between metaphors and reality. Valī has several times made mention of this symbolical character of his poetic diction".[5]

It is just this remark by Ẓahīru'd-Dīn Madanī that will lead us into the spiritual world of the poet from Aurangabad.

In trying to understand what *taṣavvuf* really meant for Valī, it is necessary to recall that his *pīr* (religious master) in Ahmedabad was a saint, a follower of the Suhravardīya school of mysticism: Šāh Nūru'd-Dīn. Secondly, in Delhi Valī met Šāh Gulšan, the *pīr* who introduced him to Persian poetry or, rather, to the so-called Indian style, a "decadentist" literary form which had gained a position of pre-eminence in the Indian subcontinent in Valī's days. We will note that Šāh Gulšan had been a disciple of Šaix Aḥmad Mujaddid Sirhindī, the *Mujaddid i Alf Ṣānī*, "the Renewer of the Second Millenary", who also inspired Muḥammad Iqbāl in the twentieth century. The *Mujaddid* was a native of Sirhind, the homeland of Pīr 'Alī Raẓā, a mystic who had settled in Gujarat, where he had associated with Šaix Yaḥyā Čištī, one of the most shining examples of saintliness of those times. It is well-known that in Gujarat 'Alī Raẓā had brought together a large number of neophytes. It is not improbable that Valī was one of his followers, as he exalts 'Alī Raẓā in the following abstract of a *ġazal*:

> *Bādšah-i Najaf, Valī Ullāh*
> *Pīr-i kāmil 'Alī Raẓā pāyā.*[6]

> "Sovereign of Najaf (i.e. the Caliph 'Alī), Valī Ullāh has found 'Alī Raẓā, the perfect Master".

The parallel drawn between the Caliph of Najaf, a holy place for the Shiites, and Pīr 'Alī Raẓā might even lead us to infer that Valī had a special liking for Shiism. But, as far as we know, the *silsila-e suhravardīya*, "The Suhravardīya school", to which Valī belonged, was a branch of Sunnism. Anyhow, the Caliph ᶜAlī, the son-in-law of the Holy Prophet, is revered both by Shiites and Sunnites, though in Shiism he comes to represent a salvific element for the faithful.

This preliminary statement shows how important Sufism was as far as the development of Valī's personality and philosophical thought is concerned. The poet was initiated into the *silsila-e suhravardīya* by Šāh Nūru'd-Dīn. This mystical school, which was founded by Šihābu'd-Dīn Suhravardī (1155-1191), called also *šaixu'l-šāhid*, "the venerable martyr", considers three great figures of ancient times as its original masters: Hermes, Plato and Zoroaster. Suhravardī's theosophic doctrine — the *hikmatu'l-išrāq*, "the philosophical doctrine of the East" — is strictly esoteric and is based on the following principles: the Absolute, or Godhead, is pure beauty, perfect light, which exists by itself and is eternal; the Godhead is the creator of the universe and He unfolds Himself therein. Every human being feels attracted by the Absolute and is drawn to Him by love; consequently, the 'mystical theory of love' will become one of the paths to tread in order to reach the Godhead. The *ḥikmatu'l-išrāq* is thus very similar, in its substance, to the form of *bhakti* which had spread all over India in the Middle Ages.

Love is transformed into poetry by Valī, who was deeply imbued with the philosophical ideas met with in the Suhravardian school. Love will come to perfection after passing through multifarious stages which can be expressed only by means of figurative language, since they transcend the range of possibilities that common speech offers to man. In Valī's poetical compositions it is possible to recognize the various forms and the different stages of love, from *išq-i ḥaqīqī*, "real love/spiritual love", to *išq-i-majāzī*, "tropical love/mundane love". In Valī we find a complex series of definitions, which have special relevance for understanding the poet's personality and ideology: they possess capital importance from a semantic point of view as well, for they help us to clarify the meaning of many of the images which will be met with in classical Urdu poetry, from Mīr Taqī Mīr to Ġālib and also to such contemporary writers as 'Ābid 'Alī 'Ābid.

With respect to the phenomenological side of love, as distinguished from Absolute love, Valī concisely specifies:

Ḥaqīqat ke na'at kā tarjuma ᶜišq-i majāzī hai,
vo pāe šarah mẽ maṭlab na būjhe jo matan hargiz.[7]

"The rendering of the epithet of the True one is mundane love,
he who never understands the text will find the meaning in the commentary".

Mundane love, *'išq-i majāzī*, is merely a reflection, an illusory appearance, of the Supreme Reality: he who is not spiritually qualified to transcend worldly phenomena, has to content himself with the reflex of Supreme love in the universe. As the poet says:

Ae Valī ᶜišq-i ẓāhirī kā sabab
jalva-e šāhid-i majāzī hai.[8]

"O Valī, the cause of outward love
is the gleaming appearance of an illusory lover".

It is the *vanitas vanitatum* that comes on the scene, with its illusiveness; behind this evanescent display there exists the *maḥbūb-i ḥaqīqī*,"the real Beloved one", that is Absolute beauty, the Godhead. In Valī's opinion, when one has realized the meaning of true love, both *ᶜišq-i majāzī* and *'išq-i ḥaqīqī* have in practice the same significance:

Šuġl-i bihtar hai 'išq bāzī kā,
kyā ḥaqīqī o kyā majāzī kā.[9]

"It is excellent to get engaged in the game of love,
it does not matter whether it is spiritual or mundane".

While reading a few philosophical poems by Valī, we become convinced that Platonism or, better, the Advaita concept of *māyā*, have exerted an influence on his thought. We shall quote an abstract of one of Valī's compositions representing the 'theosophic trend':

Yah hastī-ye mauhūm dise mujkō sarāb,
pānī ke upar naqš hai yah misl-i ḥabāb.
Aise ke upar dil kō na kar hargiz band,
āpas kō na kar xarāb, ie xāna-e xarāb.[10]

"This illusory existence seems a mirage to me,
it is an image on water similar to a bubble.
Do never tie your heart to it,
do not bring yourself to ruin, O disgraceful one".

It is the *sādhu*-dervish that is talking, the eternal voice of India which sees the universe as the faint reflection of the One, absolute and perfect. Even love, with its manifold manifestations, is a game in the infinite phantasmagory of names and forms: only *ᶜišq-i ḥaqīqī* transcends universal illusion. Whoever is aware of the real substance of the world can devote himself to *ᶜišq bāzī*, "the game of love", controlling it thoroughly, without getting involved in it. But why do we meet with so many names of *'ašiqān*, "sweethearts", in Valī's poetry? Does the poet possess a double personality or should we acknowledge a symbolic meaning in the *'āšiqān?*

Valī's Anacreontic poetry has a raison d'être and a peculiar individuality which make it quite different from its Persian counterpart, even if we can frequently recognise a Persian influence as far as the main themes are concerned, and of course, the form of language employed is deeply Persianized when such themes occur. The names of the 'sweethearts' quoted by Valī in many of his poems are of Hindu and Muslim origin: Abu'l-Ma'ālī alternates with Khemdās, Amrit Lāl with Šamsu'd-Dīn, Gobind Lāl with the enigmatic 'Sajjan'. This is certainly an emblematic fact which shows that in Valī's opinion love does not make any distinctions among people of different creeds, but it is the way that leads to the Godhead.

Professor Nūru'l-Ḥasan Hāšimī, an eminent scholar who dealt extensively with Valī's poetical and philosophical work, writes in his introduction to the *Kulliyāt-i Valī*, one of the most important critical studies ever published on the poet of Aurangabad: "Since in the context of Sufism the gaze is directed towards one's inner self, the display of worldly things and objects is observed in the mirror of one's heart as if the whole were concentrated in a particle, the sea in a drop; owing to that, such poetry (i.e., Valī's poetry) is always interiorized. Valī does not feel the urge to observe the outward world, apart from the study of his own heart and from the manifestation of his spiritual experiences. If his look is by chance addressed to the external world, even there he sees only Beauty, whether it is incarnated by Gobind Lāl or Amrit Lāl or Abu'l-Ma'ālī or by the beauties of Gujrat and Surat".[11] Love is consequently something ineffable which only the mystics know, as we can deduce from the following verses:

ᶜĀrifā̃ par hameša raušan hai
ki fann-i 'āšiqī 'ajab fann hai.[12]

"Mystics are always conscious
that the art of dallying is an extraordinary art".

In a *ġazal*, Valī identifies one's being a Muslim with *'išq*, conferring to this appellation a symbolic and esoteric meaning. He says:

Ṭarīqa 'išqbāzā̃ kā 'ajab nādir ṯarīqa hai,
jo kuī 'āšiq nahī is ko musalmān kar nahī̃ ginte.
Valī rāh-i muhạbbat mē̃ vafādārī muqaddam hai,
vafā naī̃ jis mē̃ is kō ahl-i īmān kar nahī̃ ginte.[13]

"The path of lovers is an extraordinary and singular path,
whoever is not a lover, we do not consider him a Muslim.
Valī, on the track of love faithfulness is capital,

> those people having no unshakeable belief are not to be considered faithful".

In the above-mentioned verses it is clearly emphasized that the Muslim — i.e. he who completely surrenders to God — is bound to love: he cannot and must not follow any tracks which limit, even partially, the capacity for loving, which in the language of the Sufis symbolically represents faithful attachment to God. In this way, the lover becomes one with the beloved ; it is an *ascensus mysticus*, a very arduous path that only few initiates can follow, finally dissolving into the Godhead.

The *qaṣīda* bearing the title *Dar na't-i ḥazrat xair bašar salla Allāhu ᶜalaihi wa sallama*, "An eulogy to His Excellency the best of men, that God may bless him and give him his peace", is a philosophical hymn written by Valī in honour of the Holy Prophet. In this *qasīda* we find an unequivocal definition of *'išq-i ḥaqīqī*, "spiritual love", expressed through such words as are met with in the language of the mystics:

> *'Išq mē lāzim hai avval zāt kō fānī kare,*
> *ho fanā fillāhi dāem yād-i yazdānī kare.*[14]
>
> "In love it is indispensable for you to annihilate personality first of all;
> (it is necessary), after merging into the Godhead, to remember the Absolute constantly".

Also for the fifth Sikh *gurū*, Śrī Arjan Dev, the continuous remembrance (*sumiran*) of the Supreme Being represents the point of convergence from which one starts to reach *sahaj*, the state of transcendental equipoise where physical phenomena and the diachrony of events are done away with, and in which one realizes the unity of becoming and being. The fifth *gurū* says:

> *Prabha kai simarani sahaji samānī.*[15]

"By the remembrance of the Lord one gets immersed in the state of *sahaj*".

He adds:

Hari simarani kio sagala akārā,
Hari simarana mahi āpi nirākārā.[16]

"God shaped the whole world of forms for remembrance,
in remembrance God himself appears as formless".

Valī's and *gurū* Arjan's statements as to the inner significance of 'remembering' are equivalent in practice. In the opinion of *gurū* Arjan and of other Sikh *gurūs*, the annihilation of what we might call 'phenomenological personality' corresponds to the extinction of *haumai*, "egotism", whereas Valī considers devout remembrance as the indispensable implement for attaining mystical union with God.

In Valī's poems love in its manifold manifestations is connected to the cult of beauty, which appears under two aspects: the carnal and the spiritual. A few verses will make the implications of the concept of 'beauty' more explicit:

'Ayān hai har ṭaraf 'ālam mẽ ḥusn-i be-ḥijāb uskā,
baġair az dīda-e ḥairān nahī̃ jag mẽ niqāb uskā.[17]

"His beauty without any veils comes into sight everywhere in the world,
outside the range of dim vision there is no veil concealing him in the cosmos".

With these words, Valī implicitly means that he who has eyes apt to see recognizes eternal beauty in each atom existing in the world of phenomena.

In a very interesting *ġazal* to be found in the *Kulliyāt-i Valī* by Nūru'l-Ḥasan Hāšimī we read the following;

Ma'šūq hai baġal mẽ Valī yah sunā hū̃ maĩ;

mat dil ke bāj is kō kahī̃ justujū karo.[18]

'The beloved one is in our arms, Valī, this is what I heard; do not go anywhere in search of him without your soul".

In this abstract of a *ġazal* we have the lexeme *dil*, "heart, insight, intuition", which according to Islamic mysticism represents the centre of supernatural intuition and which Valī Auraṅgābādī deems to be indispensable for knowing the real essence of the Godhead. God is already in us, but we are able to meet him only if we direct our spiritual potentialities towards him. It is a theory to be found in the Suhravardian school, of which Valī was a follower: in Šihābu'd-Dīn Suhravardī's *ṭarīqa* (mystic brotherhood) knowledge in a metaphysical sense is "identical to the very soul, to personal subjectivity, existential (*anâ'îyat*), and which is therefore by its essence light, epiphany, self-conscience (*hayât, nûr, zohûr, sho'ûr bi'-dhâti-hi*)..."[19]

M. Saeed Sheikh, formerly Director of the Institute of Islamic Culture in Lahore, quotes an aphorism by the Holy Prophet whose contents can be considered almost esoteric: "Consult thy heart and thou wilt hear the secret ordinances of God proclaimed by the heart's inward knowledge which is real faith and divinity".[20]

M. Saeed Sheikh's comment on the above-mentioned aphorism is of extraordinary importance for understanding the quintessence of Valī's poetry:

"Such sayings of the Prophet allude to a deep kinship between man's inmost nature and the nature of the Divine Reality. Further they point to a kind of knowledge which comes from the depths of the heart and is different from one that comes from senses and reasoning."[21]

Valī's poems are imbued with sincere spirituality and never display the affected pseudo-mysticism met with in many an imitator of the descendant of Pīr Vajīhu'd-Dīn, whom Valī himself calls *qudvatu'l- 'ārifīn*, "the most excellent of theosophists". In a *tarjī'band* composed in honour of the saint, Valī says:

> *Ae imām-i jamī'-ī ahl-i yaqīn,*
> *qibla-e rāstān Vajīhu'd-Dīn.*[22]

> "O guide of all people who have firm belief,
> point of reference for the righteous, Vajīhu'd-Dīn".

The *qibla-e rāstān* will become the holy inspīrator of Valī in his *ascensus mysticus*. Vajīhu'd-Dīn will be his spīritual guide in the journey towards that point beyond time and space where the illusion of the world of names and forms melts away. Then there will appear only the Supreme Being, *al-Ḥaqq:* Vajīhu'd-Dīn is the *imām* who, with the help of his supernatural grace, grants the *naẓr* or *mušāhada*, "the vision of the Absolute", acting just like a *guru* of the Upanishadic tradition.

* * *

As to the language employed by Valī in his poems, we notice that it is fundamentally the form of Dakanī that bears more resemblance to Northern Rexta, or Dehlavī Hindavī, with some peculiarities which give us philological support when we assert that Valī's original language was Marathi and not Gujarati. I acknowledge that it is necessary to carry out more extensive research in this field, which will also help us to ascertain whether he came from the Marathi — or Gujarati — speaking territory. In point of fact, the linguistic substratum in Valī's poetical work has particular relevance as to pronominal particles, emphatic particles and a few verbal structures.

Let us first consider the elements that are not proper to the morpho-syntactic structure of Dakanī. The possessives *mujh* (*majh*) and *tujh*, meaning respectively "my" and "thy", are very frequent in Valī and are characterized by the aspirate voiced palatal *jh*, which constrasts with the much more common Dakanī deaspirated forms *muj* (*maj*) and *tuj*, to be found for example in Ibn Nišāṭī's *Phul ban*. Mullā Vajhī too sometimes employs *muj* and *tuj* in his *Sab ras*, as in the following short sentence: *Jāū̃ kidhar tuj firāq mẽ*,[23] "Where shall I go, being separated from you?". These possessive forms can consequently be considered as belonging to the classical phase of Dakanī. As we know, both Ibn Nišāṭī and Mullā Vajhī did not live in a Marathi-speaking area, which explains why they did not use the aspirated stop *jh*. In Marathi the possessive adjective "my" appears as *mājhā* (the aspirate *jh* is a rule), whereas the genitive *mujha* of Old Gujarati remains an unproductive form and will be used chiefly as an oblique of the personal pronoun *haũ/hũ*, "I".

It is only Marathi that employs the basic morpho-syntagm *majh* (*cf.* the Sanskrit dative *mahyam* and the Prakrit genitive *majjhaṃ*) with a possessive value. In the words of Jules Bloch:

"In the singular, Marathi has formed an adjective on the oblique; *mājhā*, *tujhā* are, therefore, like the Skr. *māmaka tāvaka*. This creation isolates Marathi from all the related languages."[24]

By way of contrast, it is interesting to read what John Beames wrote about the pronouns related to the first person singular in Gujarati: "Gujarati is very unfixed and irregular in the oblique cases. It takes *maj* alone for the genitive, at least so say the grammars; and, moreover, makes it the oblique stem, to which case-endings are attached, as *maj ne*, "to me", *maj thī*, "from me". The old poets use also *muj*."[25] Nowhere in his *Comparative Grammar* does Beames mention *majh/mujh* with the aspirated palatal *jh*.

Analogously, *tujh*, the possessive adjective meaning "thy" and very frequently employed by Valī, is to be connected to the Marathi *tujhā*: in Old and Middle Gujarati this possessive occurs as *tuj*, without aspirate *jh*. It is true that *maj/maja* and *tuj/tuja* can be found in Old Marathi too, but they are rarely, if ever, used as genitives proper. Alfred Master writes in his classic *Grammar of Old Marathi*: "*Maja, tuja* are not found as clear genitives, their place being taken by *mājhā, tujhā*, the enlarged declined adjective, but they are used in place of the instrumental with *-sīṃ* to form a sociative or with *hūni* to form an ablative."[26] Since Valī makes regular use of *majh/mujh* and *tujh*, which are not common in classical Dakanī literature but are very similar to the Marathi *mājhā* and *tujhā*, we should admit an influence of this speech on his language. Furthermore, the Rexta-Hindavī forms *merā* and *terā* are much more seldom met with in Valī's poetical compositions.

It is consequently a likely supposition that Valī may have followed structural and lexical patterns of his native language, i.e. Marathi, in his *dīvān*, for they sounded more familiar to his ears. Possessive adjectives are frequent linguistic elements which naturally cause conditioned responses also while using another language, especially if this language possesses analogous forms, as is the case with Dakanī unaspirated *muj/maj* and *tuj*. Two examples taken from the *Kulliyāt-i Valī* evidence the possessive use of *mujh* and *tujh* in the poet's compositions:

Mujh dil ke ācaman mẽ kar yak naẓar tamāšā.[27]

"In rinsing my heart, make a spectacle of a glance".

Zād-i rah dil sõ jo bagàl mẽ liyā,
har qadam tujh galī mẽ manzil hai.[28]

"Whoever took in his arms the provisions from the heart,
in your lane finds a caravanserai at every step".

Another trace of Marathi influence on the language of Valī is found in the negative form of the imperative, second person plural: *nako karo*, "do not do", *nako pūcho*, "do not ask", are forms which frequently occur in Valī's poems and recall similar patterns proper to Marathi. Alfred Masters says that *nako* with the supine is "the usual method in modern Marathi of expressing a prohibition".[29] It is interesting to notice that we come across this kind of negative even in the *Jñāneśvarī*, which dates back to the end of the thirteenth century. An abstract from a highly Persianized *ġazal* by Valī confirms the persistence of this peculiar structure even after he had taken up the more fashionable Rexta of Northern India:

> *'Ālam kō teġ-i nāz sō be jā̃ nako karo,*
> *ġamze sō apne ġārat-i īmān nako karo.*[30]
>
> "Do not deprive of life the world with the sword of your blandishments,
> do not destroy the faith with your amorous glances".

Since Gujarati does not have a negative imperative with *nako*, I am even more persuaded that the linguistic substratum which characterizes Valī's Daknī was Marathi, the speech of Aurangabad. Moreover, it is the emphatic particle *c/ca* of Marathi that we very often meet in Valī's poetical compositions. One of the several instances of the use of *ča* (often occurring in the aspirated form *čha*) can be seen in the following abstract from a *ġazal*:

> *Jo haĩ vuh maḥẓ taṣvīrāt-i ixlāṣ*
> *so 'āšiq parvarī ṁẽ vahīčha haĩ xāṣ.*[31]
>
> "If those are merely love images,
> then those very images are excellent for fostering
> the sweetheart".

This emphatic particle is clearly of Marathi origin and occurs with considerable frequency in classical Dakanī, as Professor Šamatov says:"The particle *-č*, borrowed from Marathi *-c*, is fundamentally employed to point out this or that word, to strengthen its semantic significance".[32] He adds that "the particle *-č (-ča)* is often used with a restrictive function".[33]

The supporters of Valī's being of Gujarati origin might object that in Gujarati the emphatical particle is represented by *-j/-ij* and that formerly in Persian and Dakanī the two palatal occlusives were written with the same grapheme. However, a manuscript in Rexta, dated 1103 *hijrī* (i.e. AD 1696) and preserved in the Panjab University Library of Lahore, has distinct graphemes for the three consonant sounds *p, c, z*, which mark a significant improvement as far as the comprehensibility of texts in Perso-Arabic script is concerned. The manuscript we are dealing with is a *Bārah māh* by Sā'īn Maḥmūd, which also contains a poem in Panjabi by Mansā Rām.[34] It was composed about ten years before the oldest manuscript so far known of Valī's *Kulliyāt*, which—following the example of the copyist from Lahore—clearly distinguishes between *c* and *j*. This type of orthography is also the one employed in contemporary Urdu and Panjabi.

NOTES

1. I have employed the syntagmatic unit "linguistic code" in the Saussurian sense of "parole", personal realization of the infinite range of "stylemes" to be found in each language.
2. For an oppositional study of Dakanī, Gujarati and Šimālī Urdu or Doāba, see Ḍākṭar Sayyid Muḥīu'd-Dīn Qādarī Zor, *Hindustānī lisāniyāt*. Lucknow: Nasīm Book Depot. 1978, pp. 105-16.
3. *Intixāb-i Valī* edited by Ḍākṭar Sayyid Ẓahīru'd-Dīn Madanī. Dehli: Maktaba Jāmi'a. 1977, p. 103.
4. See *Intixāb-i Valī* (quoted note 3), p. 7.
5. See *ibidem*, p. 8.
6. See *ibidem*, p. 37.
7. See Ḍākṭar Šārib Radaulavī, "Suxan-i Valī", in *Muṭāla'a-e Valī*. Lucknow: Nuṣrat Publishers. 1972, p. 109.
8. Šārib Radaulavī, *op.cit.*, p. 172.
9. See *Intixāb-i Valī* (quoted note 3), p. 29.
10. See *ibidem*, p. 113.
11. Nūru'l-Ḥasan Hāšimī, *Kulliyāt-i Valī*. Lucknow: Nasīm Book Depot *et alii*. 1982 new edition, p. 14.
12. See *Intixāb-i Valī* (quoted note 3), p. 106.
13. *Cf.* Ḍākṭar Šārib Radaulavī, "Suxan-i Valī", in *op.cit.* note 7, p. 13.
14. See *Intixāb-i Valī* (quoted note 3), p. 117.

15. See Gurū Arjan in "Gauṛī Sukhamanī", *aṣṭapadī* 1, *pad* 7, p. 263 of the canonical edition of *Śrī Gurū Granth Sāhib Jī (damdamī bīṛ)*.
16. See Gurū Arjan in "Gauṛī Sukhamanī", *aṣṭapadī* 1, *pad* 8, p. 263 of *Śrī Gurū Granth Sāhib Jī (damdamī bīṛ)*.
17. See *Intixāb-i Valī* (quoted note 3), p. 26.
18. See Sayyid Nūru'l-Ḥasan Hāšimī, *Kulliyāt-i Valī*, (quoted note 11), p. 443.
19. See Henri Corbin. *Histoire de la philosophie islamique*, vol. I. Paris: Gallimard. 1964, p. 291: "*identique à l'âme même, à la subjectivité personelle, existentielle* (anâ'īyat), *et qui est donc par essence vie, lumière, épiphanie, conscience de soi...*"
20. M. Saeed Sheikh. *Studies in Muslim Philosophy*. Lahore: Sh. Muhammad Ashraf. 1974, 3rd Edition. p. 45.
21. M. Saeed Sheikh, *op. cit.*, p. 45.
22. See *Intixāb-i Valī* (quoted note 3), p. 114 following.
23. See Mullā Vajhī. *Sab ras*. Ed. Šamīn Unhaunavī. Lucknow: Nasīm Book Depot. 1981, p. 171.
24. Cf. Jules Bloch. *The Formation of the Marāṭhī Language* (translated by Dr Dev Raj Chanana). Delhi: Motilal Banarsidass. 1970, pp. 222, par. 210.
25. John Beames. *A Comparative Grammar of the Modern Aryan Languages of India*. New Delhi: Munshiram Manoharlal. 1970 2nd edition, vol. II (1875), p. 306.
26. Alfred Master. *A Grammar of Old Marathi*. Oxford: Oxford University Press. 1964, p. 86.
27. See Nūru'l-Ḥasan Hāšimī, *Kulliyāt-i Valī* (quoted note 11), p. 68.
28. *Idem.*, p. 324.
29. Alfred Master, *op.cit.* note 26, p. 145.
30. See Nūru'l-Ḥasan Hāšimī, *Kulliyāt-i Valī* (quoted note 11), p. 239.
31. *Ibidem*, p. 415.
32. A. N. Šamatov. *Klassičeskij dakhini*. Moscow: "Nauka". 1974, p. 186: *Častica-č, zaimstovannaja jz marathi* -c, *v osnovnom upotrebljaetsja pri vydelenii togo ili inogo slova, usileni ego semantičeskoj stowny.*
33. A.N. Šamatov, *op.cit.*, p. 186: *Častica* -c (-ča) *často upotrebljaetsja kak ogranici tel'naja.*
34. The manuscript (MS. 4899/2) is preserved in the "Šairānī Collection" of the Panjab University Library in Lahore. See Dr Rana M.N. Ehsan Elahie, "Bullhe Shah's Baran Masa", in *Khoj*, Department of Panjabi Language and Literature, Panjab University, Lahore, *Šumāra* 1, *jild* 2, *julāī-disambar* 1979, p. 2.

Nāgnāth and Nasīruddīn: *Pīr*-worship and *Śaiva-bhakti* in the Literature of the Nāgeś Sampradāy*

Hugh van Skyhawk

"...and when the doors of perception are cleansed, we shall percieve that which is truly immortal."
(William Blake, "The Marriage of Heaven and Hell")

Nearly thirty years have passed since Yusuf Muhammed Paṭhāṇ called attention both to the importance and to the regrettable obscurity of the Nāgeś Sampradāy in studies of the religious and cultural history of the Deccan.[1] Though

* In the present paper the following conventions of transliteration have been used: 1) Marathi words have been transliterated according to pronunciation; 2) both the first occurrence of a bibliographical reference to a publication in an Indic language and its entry in the "References" at the end of the paper have been given in full transliteration, that is, with the inherent "a" between syllables and at the end of a word; thereafter, the author's name has been given according to pronunciation, i.e. "Pathāṅ" and not "Pathāṇa", followed by the year of publication and page number of the reference; 3) words of Urdu, Persian, Arabic, or Hindustani origin written in Devanāgarī have been transliterated according to their orthography in Devanāgarī; 4) other words of Urdu, Persian, Arabic, or Hindustani origin have been given according to the transliterations found in Muhmmad Mujeeb's *The Indian Muslims.*

R.C. Ḍhere later provided valuable information concerning the literature of the *Liṅgāyat-bhaktas* of *Vaḍvāḷ-siddha-Nāgnāth*,[2] the question raised by Paṭhāṇ concerning the numerous allusions to the identity of Śekh Nasīruddīn Cirāg-i-Delhī and Nāgnāth in the literature and oral traditions of the Deccan remains unanswered.[3]

Whatever the historical truth of the legend may be, there can be no doubt that the popular belief in the identity of Vaḍvāḷ-siddha-Nāgnāth and Śekh Nasīruddīn Cirāg-i-Delhī and his miraculous journey to the Deccan in order to save his Brāhmaṇ devotee, Hegras-svāmī,[4] from social ostracism has given rise to significant devotional literature both in Old Marathi and in Dakanī.[5] Moreover, the story has occupied the thoughts of numerous followers of the Nāgeś Sampradāy and the Chistī and Biyābānī Sufi-silsilas up to this day.[6]

In the present paper I shall present some examples of the devotional poetry of Ajñānasiddha and Siddhaliṅga-svāmī[7] taken from a little known collection entitled *Ānanda-lahari-vā-sākyā* published by the late Nāgnāth Guṇḍubūvā Kuruḍe and Siddhaliṅga Viśvanāth-svāmī in Mohoḷ *circa* 1950. This small book contains thirty-five devotional poems in Old Marathi, Dakanī, and Sanskrit in the *śikhāriṇī, dohā, ovī*, and *sākī (sākhī)* metres. Up to now I have not been able to gain access to the manuscripts used by Kuruḍe and Viśvanāth-svāmī in editing their collection. However, some remarks on the manner in which I obtained a copy of this nearly inaccessible publication will shed light upon the syncretist milieu in which these poems are still regarded as sacred literature.

The book was given to me by Śekh Abdul Rajhākśāh Biyābānī of Poona, a *shaikh* of the Biyābānī-Qādirī-Sufi-silsila who received it from a devotee of Nāgnāth from Dt. Kolhapur who is also a disciple of Śekh Biyābānī and whose father was both a devotee of Nāgnāth and a disciple of Śekh Biyābānī's *pīr*, Śekh Maḥmūdśāh Biyābānī. In this connection it should be noted that Nāgnāth-Śiva has continued to manifest himself in the form of a fakir to his devotees in the Kolhapur region up to the present time. Similarly, it should be mentioned that *gādīs* (literally: the throne of a potentate) for Maḥmūdśāh Biyābānī (d. 1958), who was regarded as a manifestation of Nāgnāth, are maintained by some devotees in their homes, while at the *samādhi* of Ajñānasiddha at Narendra (Dt.Kolhapur) the *darūd-sharīf* (a well-known hymn praising the Holy Prophet) and the *fāiṭhā* (the opening *sūra* of the *Qur'ān*) are sung before taking *darśan* of the *svarūp* of Ajñānasiddha in an underground vault approximately three metres beneath the floor of the shrine in which *pādukā* of Ajñānasiddha are kept.

Most conspicuous in the poems of Ajñānasiddha and Siddhaliṅga-svāmī is the strong attraction felt by members of a spiritual lineage of *Śaiva-bhaktas* for the great Indian *shaikh*, Nasīruddīn Cirāg-i-Delhī. Even more importantly, this literature bespeaks a milieu of religious syncretism not unlike that of Kabīr-*bhakti*, *haṭha-yoga*, *pīr*-worship – and a world-view characterized by confident strength, openness, and the desire to see the religious and social 'other' as one's spiritual teacher, and thus, as part of oneself.[8]

> Hear the story of the 'first-house' (i.e. the spiritual home) *(ādī gharakī suno bāta)*.
> Hegras-bābā was a brahmin.
> He was the one who brought Nāgnāth (to Mohoḷ)
> (*Hegrasa bābā bamanajāta une lāye Nāganātha*).
> There, where there is no night and no day (i.e. in his heart),
> the great Śekh Nasīruddīn saved (Hegras) straight-away *(jadā nayī* [for *nahī*] *rāta, jadā nayī dīna tabalaga baḍā bacāye Śekha Nasarodīna)*.
> *(sākī* 1)

> Śekh Nasīruddīn is a *walī*,[9] Guru Nāgnāth is Alī
> *(Śekha Nasarodīna vallī guru Nāganātha Allī)*.
> He left Delhi when Bhakta Hegras called him.
> Tell what happened in Candramoḷī (Mohoḷ).
> Tell the story...

Nāgnāth came to Mohoḷ village.
There the *siddha* stopped at *(viman) Ṭekaḍī.*[10]
He took on the *svarūp* of a fakir.
His godly body was magnificient.
On his body he wore the green of a *Qalandar.*[11]
On his neck there was a big cobra.
In his hand there was a *ciphā* (a rattle) and a stick.
Beside him there is a pair of dogs looking fiercely, who are the storehouses of *brahma-bodha* (knowledge of the *brahman*) *(vājū kūtanakā joḍā dekhata nayana deṭhaḍā, brahma bodhakā huṃḍā).*[12]
Speaking profusely, Hegras caught his holy feet:
'You are the *guru*! You are the *guru*!
'You are the *pīr*! You are the *pīr*!
Seeing this sovereign lord of the *yogis*, I am in complete bliss.

(*sākī* 2)

Nāgnāth, o Nāgnāth! How shall we know you?
Behold the universe (in him)!
He knows fifty-six languages, such as *Sinhala, Gauḍa, Baṅgāla,* and *Khurāsanī.*
What kind of brahman he is, no one knows.
(text obscure)...on his feet he wears special leather sandals ... (*caraṇi pāve camāna khāsā*).
On his ankles he wears the anklets of his wonderful victories[13] (*caraṇī toṃḍara* [for *toḍara*] *śobhe brīdāṃcā).*
A great tiger is his vehicle.
He is a *digambara* (naked ascetic). His ornament is a tiger-skin.
In his hand there is a whip of snakes.[14]
His sword has the sharpness of lightning.
A wondrous light shines from his earrings.
His body is (the manifestation) of holy ashes.
On his neck there is a *rudrākṣa.*
On his head there are strange matted locks
from which the *Gaṅgā* emerges.

The *Kāma-dhenu* has taken refuge there.
How shall I describe your characteristics?
Ajñānasiddha says to Nāgeś: 'Give (me) the words of the condition of *mokṣa*'.(*de mokṣapadakī vācā*).
(*sākī* 10)

In the following Dakanī *dohā* of Siddhaliṅga-svāmī the *haṭha-yoga* notion of the *anāhata-śabda* or 'unstruck sound', the *dhvani* that the *yogī* perceives in the *anāhata-cakra*, or 'heart-lotus' of his subtle body,[15] forms the leitmotiv of a poem in which deep devotion for the *guru-pīr* Nasīruddīn Cirāg-i-Delhī is combined with references to well-known techniques of *haṭha-yoga*.[16] Similarly, *guru-sevā* (see verse 8) is combined with the Sufi notion of *fanā fi'sh shaikh* (the absorption of the personality of the disciple in the personality of the spiritual master; see verses 4ff.). Particularly striking are Siddhaliṅga's descriptions of the madness (*unmayī*) of the devotee, who — while immersed in the *guru-pīr* — hears the constant drumming of the 'unstruck sound' (see verses 5 and 18), the sound in which all sound vibrations (*nādas*) are reabsorbed:[17]

Anuhāta-nagārā (*sic*)

('The kettledrum of the unstruck sound')

Beat the kettledrum of the unstruck sound constantly!
The secret light burns in the 'sky-palace'.[18]
There, where there is light without the sun and moon, Siddhaliṅga dwells in perpetual drunkeness (*sadā matavālā*).
(1)

The *guru* gave me the secret drink,
he fed me the sweets as well,[19]
He gave me his hand of beneficence and blessed me

(*diyā dasta paṃjā kiṃyā meherabānī*),
Siddhaliṅga says: 'This is the sign of his feet'.
(2)

The eyes in the eyes saw the Divine.
This same Śekh Nasardīn (sic) is my *guru-pīr*.
The friend of my heart *(dillayārī)* has done a good thing.
The Invisible (*alakh*) is my eyelids.
Siddhaliṅga says: 'These are his divine feet.'
(3)

He is a great *pīr*. Everywhere he stands before me.
I see everything filled with Nāgā![20]
Siddhaliṅga says:'I am mad about this *guru*'.
(4)

I became mad and a *'dildār* ('a dauntless one') took possession of my heart.
I persisted and became immersed (in the *guru)* *(kumārī lage daṃga hokara rahyā)*.[21]
In this state of madness the secret drumming resounds (*gaiba duṃka bajāī*).
Siddhaliṅga says: 'The *guru* is my (only) gain.'
(5)

The *hujur* ('great man') was fixed in my vision.
Jhelatkā! Jamatkā![22] He fed light into my eyes,
The world-*guru* who is (ever) awake is my *pīr*.
Siddhaliṅga says: 'I 'missed' the cycle of births and deaths! (i.e. I am no longer affected by suffering and rebirth)'.
(6)

(Your) precious image is in my eyes.
'Godness' has filled the world completely.[23]
The unseen image of God is fixed in my eye like a diamond.

Siddhaliṅga says: 'Hear me, my *pīr-bhāī.*'

(7)

O friend, hear me! The (the world of) appearances is very mad!
I see (only) a *tamāśā* (folk theatre) in eternal *śūnya* (*sadā sūnya mo dekhataṃ hai tamāsā*).
Become a servant (of God) and ugliness will flee.
Siddhaliṅga says:'You will reach God.'

(8)

Give up your (individual) self and see God in madness (*khudī choḍa de tu khudā dekha divānī*) !
There will be treachery in the future.
the 'doctor' knows (i.e. the spiritual master knows) (*huīsu dagābāda bhiṣāra jāṇe*).
Block the air and the fluid, block it well (*hāvāhī rasa ko baṃda kara khāsa baṃde*)![24]
Siddhaliṅga says: '(Then) this whole business (of suffering and rebirth) will completely disappear.'

(9)

Give up worldly affairs! Have faith, friend!
Give up the body and wealth and the intoxication of youth (*tanna dhanna jovanakī choḍa mastī*)!
If one knows himself and knows what is not the Self,
Siddhaliṅga says:'He will get the Godness of God'.

(10)

Give up your worries! Become a *phakir!* Remember God! (*phikira choḍa phakira ho jikira khudākī ... makara māva?*)
Don't indulge in illusion! The world is momentary! (*makara māvā* [for *māyā*] *duniyā phaṇatila ghaḍikī*).
Take the name of the *pīr*. It's sweeter than sugar (*śakarase mīṭhā pirakā nāma lenā*).
Siddhaliṅga says: 'This is our only gain.'

(11)

Remove your sorrows! Become a derwish in your heart (*darda dura kara dila daraveśa hogā*)!
Have thirst for his feet every moment! Remember his name!
If you have no attachment to the fruits (of your deeds),
you will build the highest throne
(*hāre phala ujita para takyā tuma banāvo*).
Siddhaliṅgā says: 'You must please the *guru*.

(12)

Guru Śekh Nasirudīn Cirāg Delhi is a *pīr* of great miracles
and an immaculate friend of God (*Guru Śekha Nasaradīna cīrā kadhellī karāmata pira yo pāka vallī*).
Lakhs and lakhs of devotees are praising him.
Siddhaliṅga says:'Where is my place among them? (literally:Where should I be among them?) (*kahe lākha baṃde navā jena bīje kahe Siddhaliṃga rahu kahā kahāne*).

(13)

Adam's feet returned to dust. And now that dust has come again in this disguise (*kadama ādama khapa gayā khāka huvā ohī khāka āya bajuda makjuda huvā*).
The *jogī* has come in this *jog* (astrological conjunction), this *jog*, this *jog*.
Siddhaliṅgā says: 'Infidelity has run away.' (*kuphara dura bhāge*).

(14)

Kill Madana (the Indian Cupid) and flay his body!
Suppress the *man* and remove the (sense of) differences.
My heart is constantly fixed on the cave in the sky (*gaganake guṃphame magana dila merā*).[25]

Siddhaliṅga says:'Hear the bringer of the Faith!'
(15)

We should make a patchwork quilt (*godhaḍī*) of the *guru's jñān* (spiritual knowledge).
In a moment the stiches of *parabrahma* are complete.
I have taken the begging-bowl of desirelessness (*nirālaṃbha-jholī*) in my hand.
Siddhaliṅga says:'Iam a low beggar'.
(16)

I am a beggar who begs for the alms of *guru*-worship.
And my master, *pīr-bhujaṅga*, is the alms-giver who cannot be avoided.
He gave me a small gift and I became completely immersed in it.
Siddhaliṅga says: 'It happens naturally' (or: 'It happens in the *sahaj*-condition.').[26]
(17)

Effortlessly (*sahaja mo sahaja*) we get the teachings of the *siddha*.
Once we taste it we remain immersed.
In this madness *(unmayī)* the secret drumming resounds (*gaiba ḍaṃkā bajāī*).
Siddhaliṅga says: 'The *guru* is our (only) gain.'
(18)

While day and night the *naubat* of the Divine Name resounds,
my concentration is only on the feet of the *guru*.
Seeing the Invisible in the invisible (i.e. seeing God) ...(word unclear) ...o friend,
Siddhaliṅga says: 'There is the rememberance.'
(19)

Guru Siddhanāgeś is always my master.
He gave me sipirtual instruction and made me happy.
Siddhaliṅga says:'He gave me the treasure.'

(20)

God has a thousand names. No one can destroy them.
I called to God and just by one call
I got *Pīr-dastagīr.*[27]
Siddhaliṅga says:'This is true, this is true.'

(21)

He explains the *vacanas* of the *Kurān* (sic) and the essence of the *Vedas*.
I got the secret *guru* (*guru-gaiba*) ...the great *pīr*.
Siddhaliṅga says: 'I am neither a begger, a *brahmacārī*, nor a householder.

(22)

I am not begging for alms, or seeking a post, and I don't want any property.
I am only here to uplift the world.
I have no name, no shape, and not a trace of colour'.
Siddhaliṅga says: 'I am the dust on his feet.'

(23)

He is the formless maker of forms, my *maulā*.
This endeavour (to describe him) is completely empty, yet distinctive.
Through the magic of the tongue, see the Unseen.
Siddhaliṅga says: 'Taste the *guru!*[28]

(24)

In great Vaḍvāl[29] he sits on the throne.
There stands the fearless *Nāgeś-pīr*.
The *guru* is eternal. Siddhaliṅga says: In his

gaib bāṇī (secret language) there is a *niśabda-khāṇī* (a mine of unstruck sounds or inaudible, that is, mystical words).

(25)

While the aural experience of the *yogī* in the *unmayī* or *sahaj* condition was the leitmotiv in the previous *dohā*, in the following *dohā*, *"Lāl"*, Siddhaliṅga describes the visual experience of *sahaj*. The poem achieves an extraordinary degree of resonance through the sustained use of the multiple levels of meaning derived from the various senses of the word *"lāl"*. *"Lāl"* is at once the colour red, a ruby, an epithet of the beloved, and by metonymy, a name for the *anāhata-cakra*. As in the previous *dohā* Siddhaliṅga alternates between direct language and *sandhyā-bhāṣā*. In terms of content the poem represents a harmonious fusion of *haṭha-yoga-sādhana* and *guru-bhakti* for "Siddhanāgnāth Cirāg Delhī". Particularly striking is the adoration of Śekh Nasīruddīn Cirāg-i-Delhī as the "perfect man" (verse 1), the "perfect jewel" (verse 6), and the "perfect master" (verse 9). Such descriptions of Nāgnāth-Nasīruddīn point toward the Sufi concept of the *al-insān-al-kāmil* (the perfect man). Similarly, Siddhaliṅga's description of Siddhānageś as "our lamp whose sparkling lamp illuminates the night" (verse 7) alludes to Nasīruddīn's epithet *"cirāg-i-Delhī"* (the Lamp of Delhi), especially so when one considers that at the *dargāḥ* of Nasīruddīn in Delhī a large lamp of ruby-coloured glass hangs over the *mazār* (grave) shedding a sparkling ruby-like light at night:

In my *lāl* red consumed red.[30]
When the red in the red reached the field
(huvā lāla mai lāla maidāna pāyā),
he dissolved the red. He is the complete man, my
great Siddhasāheb (*diyā lāla layā sahī marda sārā
baḍā yo Siddhasāheba merā*).

(1)

The flag of the great *lāl* (beloved) is flying high.
The true Siddhanāgeś stands before (me).
In the flag of blue there is the invisible, the highest beloved *(nilakī niśānī ālakha parama pyārā)*.[31]
A great *lāl* is this Siddhanāgeś.

(2)

My 'heart-sheath' *(dīla-myāne)* is greedy for lots of *lāl*.[32]
Having become immersed, it dwells in madness (*gaye ghuṃga hokara rahe hai divānī*).
The beloved *lāl* placed a diamond in my hand (i.e. spiritual knowledge).
My Siddhasāheb is the great *lāl*.

(3)

The (beloved) *lāl* gave (me) a precious emerald (*diyā lāla pīroja khāsā jīrenā*).
Jhelatkā jhematkā!(onomatopoetic) The earthen pot was empty![33]
Glittering dust filled the sky!
My Siddhasāheb is the great *lāl*.

(4)

The beloved diamond of the five bodies[34] (i.e. the Self, the *ātman)* is shining (*pacyao* [for *pañca*] *tannake lāla hirā jhematkā*).
Understand the heroic beloved (word unclear) ... the *avadhūt (bujo bira lālā baku āradhutā* [for *avadhūta*]).
In breath after breath I see the red star (or the star of the beloved) (*dame kho dame dekhatā lāla tārā*).
My Siddhasāheb is the great *lāl*.

(5)

O *sākhī!* My red 'heart-sheath' is hanging like a pendant from the *lāl* (the beloved).

Know ye, that this *pīr* is Guru Śekh Nasīruddīn!
He is the perfect red jewel of bliss
(*ānandavakī mītkā ratana lala purā*).
My Siddhasāheb is the great *lāl*.

(6)

He is the *sākhī-lāl*, the beloved *lāl*.
He is our lamp. His sparkling lamp illuminates the night.
My *mīpaṇa* ('I-ness') is lost completely.
My Siddhasāheb is the great *lāl*.

(7)

Hear the words of the beloved *lāl:* 'The sheath (i.e. the material body) is empty, just as the sugarcane is known to be hollow inside.'
Hear his voice! The *āriph-dīn* (the master of the esoteric religion) is generous.
My Siddhasāheb is the great *lāl*.

(8)

He is perfect master and the great *pīr-walī* of the world.
Guruśekh (sic) Nasīruddīn is the Lamp of Delhi.
He is the *citta-cirāg* (the illuminator of my mind) in my heart of hearts (*Cirākha Dehalī dīlī dīlame citta cirākha terā).*[35]
My Siddhasāheb is the great *lāl*.

(9)

O *sākhī!* In the desire for the beloved there is madness *(lālase lāla mai tu divānī)*.
The world seems eager, but they are traitors
(*dunīyā bekararāra saddhīse badagumānī*).
The master, the *sadguru* with the perfect heart, is a different (type of) man.
My Siddhasāheb is the great *lāl*.

(10)

O *sākhī*, red has been mixed with red
(*lālase lāla kuṃṭhā milāyā*).
Glass after glass of red has been given to drink[36]
(*lālase lāla pyālā pyālā pilāyā*).
O *sākhī*, the heart of our beloved is willing.
My Siddhasāheb is the great *lāl*.

(11)

O *sākhī*, by angry words one becomes red.
O *sākhī*, through the *lāl* (the beloved) the *citta* enters *dhyān*.[37]
O *sākhī*, I am impatient with desire (for union with the beloved).
My Siddhasāheb is the great beloved.

(12)

The unstruck sound has thundered in the sky!
My wondrous *lāl* is in bliss!
Let the *nagārā* (kettledrum) be beaten constantly:
āghaḍ dhoṃ āghaḍ dhoṃ!
My Siddhasāheb is the great beloved.

(13)

The guru is the hidden *Nāga*, the secret *bhujaṅga*.
Hidden from view the secret light shines unbroken.
He showed me the *siddhāṃta-sārā* (essential teachings) of this *paṃtha*.
My Siddahasāheb is the great *lāl*.

(14)

The *siddha* of Vaḍvāḷ is *Nāganāthā*.
He is neither a name nor a form. He is beyond the six (conditions of the mind).[38]
Siddhaliṅga says: 'He is the one who always ripens the crop.'
My Siddhasāheb is the great *lāl*.

(15)

Acknowledgements

I am grateful to Professors V.D. Kulkarni (Hyderabad) and S.G. Tulpule (Poona) for their help in reconstructing the orthography of the text I used and for their help in translating and elucidating the Dakanī text. I am equally grateful to the South Asia Institute of Heidelberg University for the travel grant that made possible my field research on the Nāgeś Sampradāy.

NOTES

1 Paṭhāṇa, Yū, Ma., *Nāgeśa-saṃpradāya.* Auraṃgābāda: Vahiḥaśāla śikṣaṇa maṃdala: 1963, p. 1.

2 Ḍhere, Rāmacandra Ciṃtāmana, *Prācīna-Marāṭhīcyā-navadhārā.* Kolhāpūra: Moghe-prakaśana. *Śake* 1894 (1972), pp. 115-133.

3 Paṭhāṇ 1963: 9f. Though Paṭhāṇ criticizes Vāsudeva Sītārāma Bendre's categorical rejection of the oral tradition concerning the identity of Nāgnāth and Nasīruddīn Cirāg-i-Delhī as being an "imaginary or ficticious story", he also stresses the importance of many of Bendre's arguments, such as the fact that Nasīruddīn Cirāg-i-Delhī never visited the Deccan (see Bendre, Vā. Sī., *Tukārāmamahārāja-yāṃcī-guruparaṃparā.* Muṃbaī. 1960, pp. 21f. and *passim*). But simply rejecting the story out of hand - Paṭhāṇ observes - neither explains its wide-spread popularity nor its occurrence in such Urdu works as the *Haśyebe-haisiyata* and *Tajakirāte-auliyā.*

4 According to R.C. Ḍhere, Hegras-svāmī was a *"Bhāradvājgotrī brāhmaṇa"* of Mohoḷ (in present day Dt. Sholapur). See Ḍhere 1972: 133.

5 See *Nāgeśalīlāmṛta,* especially the *adhyāyas* 8, 23 and 24. The verses in which Nāgnāth and Nasīruddīn are identified as being one and the same person can be found in the eighth *adhyāya, ovīs* 76f., of the *Nāgeśalīlāmṛta* edited by Śivājīrāva Sadāśivarāva Śeṭe Kolhāpūrkar in Kolhapur in *śake* 1900 (A.D. 1978).

6 See my article "Nasīruddīn and Ādināth, Nizāmuddīn and Kāniphnāth: Hindu-Muslim Religious Syncretism in the Folk Literature of the Deccan" in: Heidrun Brückner, Lothar Lutze,

and Aditya Malik (eds.), *Flags of Fame, Studies in South Asian Folk Culture.* New Delhī: Manohar. 1993, pp. 445-467.

7 The dating of Ajñānasiddha and Siddhaliṅga-svāmī is problematic. The followers of the Nāgeś Sampradāy believe that Hegras-svāmī lived in the late 14th (some even believe in the late 13th), Ajñānasiddha (Hegras's grandson by his daughter Ahalya) in the early 15th, and Siddhaliṅga-svāmī in the late 15th and early 16th centuries. Two important modern scholars of Old Marathi do not attribute such a high antiquity to these early saints of the Nāgeś Sampradāy: S.G. Tulpule dates Ajñānasiddha to the 16th century on the basis of his authorship of the *Pañcakaraṇaprameya* (edited by S.N. Moholkar, Sholapur, 1950; see Tulpule, S.G., *Classical Marathi Literature: From the Beginning to A.D. 1818.* Wiesbaden. 1979, p. 371) and R.C. Ḍhere dates Ajñānasiddha to the 17th century on the basis of a reference to a discussion between Śahā Mutabjī Brahmaṇī ūrph Mṛtyunjaya-svāmī (a prince of the royal family of Bidar who was both a Sufi saint and a *Śaiva-bhakta;* Ḍhere gives 1575 and 1650 as his birth and death dates. See *Musalamāna-Marathi-santa-kavi.* Poona. 1967, pp. 1f.) and Ajñānasiddha that occurs in the eleventh *adhyāya* of the *Avimḍhapamcīkaraṇa* of Mṛtyunjaya-svāmī (a work on Sanskrit and Persian terminology; see Ḍhere 1972:141f. and 153). For a discussion of the legend of Mṛtyunjaya as it is told by the Vaiṣṇava hagiographer Mahīpati see my article "Vaiṣṇava Perceptions of Muslims in 18th-Century Maharashtra" in: Anna Libera Dallapiccola and Stephanie Zingel-Ave Lallemant (eds.), *Islam and Indian Regions*, Vol. 1 Texts. Stuttgart: Franz Steiner Verlag. 1993, pp. 203-215.

8 Of the following three *sākīs* the first two are in Dakanī and the third in Old Marathi.

9 Literally: a friend of God.

10 A small hillock on the northern outskirts of Mohoḷ.

11 The attribute *"Qalandar"* need not mean an initiated follower of La'l Śahbāz Qalandar (d. circa 1266). As Annemarie Schimmel observes, *Qalandar* is a generic term for a roaming derwish with a clean shaven head and chin. Schimmel also refers to the definition of the *Qalandar*s found in the new edition of the *Encylopaedia of Islam*, Vol. IV, p. 471 as a kind of hippy (see Schimmel, Annemarie, *Der Islam III.* Stuttgart Berlin Köln. 1990, pp. 176f. and 200).

12 In the story of Mṛtyunjaya-svāmī (alias Murtaza Qādirī) as told by Mahīpati in the *Bhaktavijaya* (18th century), the two fierce dogs which accompany this *guru-pīr* are called *Vedānta* and

Siddhānta, thus referring to the storehouses of brahmanical and *Liṅgāyat-Śaiva* learning. See my article "Vaiṣṇava Perceptions" mentioned above in note 7.

13 The allusion is to an ancient custom of Dravidian kings who wore anklets on which the names of their vanquished enemies were engraved. I am especially grateful to S.G. Tulpule for making me aware of the precise implication of this metaphor.

14 The same description is given for Cāṅgdev Vāṭeśvar, the 1400 year-old *yogīrāj*, whose pride was broken by Sant Jñānesvar.

15 It is perceived as a red lotus with twelve golden petals, in the middle of which two triangles, one pointed upward and one downward, are arranged so that they encircle a shining *liṅga*. Above the triangles Īśvara and the Rākinī-śakti dwell in sexual union (see Eliade, Mircea, *Yoga: Unsterblichkeit und Freiheit. Zurich*. 1960, p. 251). The notion of the *anāhata-cakra* also forms the basis of the extended metaphor used in the next *dohā* "*Lāl*" ('Red').

16 Such as the blocking of the inward and outward breathing, *recaka* and *khumbaka*, and the *khecarī-mudra* in which the semen (*bindu, meḍhra*) is blocked, that is, prevented from being ejaculated from *yogī's* body (see below, verse 9 and Eliade 1960:256f.).

17 See Vaudeville, Ch., Kabīr. Oxford. 1974,pp. 128f. and note 2.

18 "*gagana mahālameṃ gaiba jotī jagāye*". The 'sky-palace' is an allusion to the *sahasrāra-cakra* which is located on a transcendental plane imagined to be just above the head; it has the form of an inverted lotus with a thousand petals, in the middle of which there is a full moon that contains a triangle. This is the goal of all Tantric *sādhana* and the place of the final union of Śiva and Śakti. This, the condition of ultimate unification, is also called *unmayī* and is described by Siddhaliṅga as a condition of 'madness' (see Eliade 1960:252).

19 Siddhaliṅga alternates between direct language and *sandhyābhāṣā*, or 'intentional language', i.e. the use of words on at least two levels of meaning in his poetry. Though I am not able to explain what exactly the "secret drink" ("*gaibapyālā pilāye*") is, or what the "sweets" ("*mistamevā khilāye*") are, the symbolic associations in this poem are relatively clear. The following *dohā*, "*Lāl*", however, is more complex, containing allusions to at least three levels of meaning.

20 In this connection one is reminded of the verse from the *Divān* of Nī'mat-Ullāh Abdallah of Kirmān(1330-1431) that is inscribed on the southern wall of the *dargāḥ* of Aḥmad Shāh

Walī, the ninth Bahmanī *sulṭān* (1420-1435) and *murīd* of Ni'mat-Ullāh: "I have found Ni'mat-Ullāh in every form of existence, for I have noticed love and infatuation in all. Ni'mat-Ullāh is One in the entire universe; thou shalt not find any one like me, nor one like me can be found (by others)." (Tranlated from the Persian by Gulam Yazdani in his *Bidar: Its History and Monuments*. London. 1947, p. 127.). A similar description of seeing the guru in all things can be found in verses 448 to 456 of the ninth *adhyāya* of the *Śrī-Ekanāthī-bhāgavat* of the 16th century Maharashtrian saint, Śrī Santa Ekanāth (see my *Bhakti und Bhakta: Religionsgeschichtliche Untersuchungen zum Heilsbegriff und zur religiösen Umwelt des Śrī Santa Ekanāth*. Stuttgart: Franz Steiner Verlag. 1990, pp. 75 and 94). The vision of the Sufi-*shaikh* in all things as a stage on the mystical path of extinguishing the individual personality of the disciple in the personality of the *shaikh* (*fanā fi'sh-Shaikh*) is linked to the popular identification of the *shaikh* with the Logos-*quṭb* on which the existence and welfare of the world constantly depends (see Trimingham, J. Spencer, *The Sufi Orders in Islam*. Oxford. 1971, pp. 163ff.).

21 Compare verse 18.

22 Onomatopoeia: "Twinkle, sparkle".

23 See above verse 4 and note 20.

24 The allusion is to the *khumbaka* and the *khecarī-mudrā*, the *haṭha-yoga* technique of breath control and control of the emission of semen in order to keep the *kuṇḍalinī* in the *suṣumṇā* so that it will pass through the six *cakras* (*ṣaṭcakra sādhana*) and reach the seventh or *sahasrāra-cakra*, the ultimate goal of the *yogī*. See above note 16.

25 Perhaps an allusion to the *sahasrāra-cakra*. See above, note 18.

26 The condition of "*sahaj*" ('the natural or innate condition') has been described in various ways: the unlimited, spontaneous condition, the condition in which the *yogī* transcends all dualities, the quintessential condition that forms the basis of all being (see Eliade 1960:277). It is synonymous with *unmayī, unmanā, unmanī* (see Vaudeville 1974:132f.). On the whole, the terminology and metaphors of *haṭha-yoga* have greater power and immediacy for Siddhaliṅga than for Kabīr. In Siddhaliṅga's poetry such terms as *sahaj* or the drum imagery (*nagārā, naubat*) used in connection with the *anāhata-śabda* have not yet become mere jargon on the lips of would-be *sidhas*. In contrast one is reminded of Kabir's *sākhī* "*sahaj*": "They all repeat: Sahaj, sahaj—yet no one knows the

sahaj!". Or the drum imagery in the *sākhī* "Warnings":"Kabīr that *naubat* of yours, but for ten days make it resound. This town, this borough, this lane, never will you see them again!" (verse 3). Or:"*ḍhol, damānā, gaṛgaṛī, śahnāī*, together with *bherī*. The chance to play them has gone and who can bring it back?" (verse 51; see (Vaudeville 1974:pp. 228 and 238).

27 *Pīr-dastagīr* is a famous epithet of Abdu'l Qādir Jīlānī (d.in Baghdad circa 1166 A.D.), the first *shai<u>kh</u>* of the *Qādirī-silsila*.

28 That is, through the magic of language perceive that which escapes sense perception, the Unseen, or God.

29 A village in District Sholapur, situated approximately six kilometers from Mohoḷ and fifty kilometers from Sholapur city.

30 I.e. in my union with the beloved (Nasīruddīn), the subject-object relationship has been dissolved, or, in my *anāhata-cakra* I have perceived the union of *Īśvara* and the *Rākinī-śakti* (who is red).

31 In keeping with the visual leitmotiv of this *dohā* this could be a reference to the *maṇipūra-cakra*, which is conceived to be a blue lotus with ten petals in the middle of which there is a red triangle upon which Mahārudra together with the blue Lākinī-śakti is seen sitting on a bull. This is the *cakra* of vision (see Eliade 1960:251).

32 As the sheath of a sword is conceived to be greedy for blood.

33 I.e. the identification with the material body and the cycle of rebirths and deaths was dissolved completely.

34 The notion of five bodies, or sheaths ('*kośa*') surrounding the Self or *ātman* is as old as the *Bṛhadāraṇyaka-upaniṣad* (4.4.17) and the *Taittirīya-upaniṣad* (1.7.1). In the *Taittirīya-unpaniṣad* (1.7.1.) the five 'bodies' are *annamaya* (consisting of food) *prāṇamaya* (consisting of breath, which is subdivided into *prāṇa* (up breathing), *vyāna* (back-breathing) and *apāna* (down breathing), *manomaya* (consisting of the *manas* or psycho-mental activities) *vijñānamaya* (consisting of understanding, insight), and *ānandamaya* (consisting of bliss). This concept is also discussed in the *Vedānta-sutras* 1.4.11-13 and commented upon by Rāmānuja and Śaṅkara. It should be noted that both Śánkara in the *Brahma-sūtra-bhāṣyā* (1.4.11-13) and Rāmānuja in his *Śrī-bhāṣya* (1.4.11-13) have distinguished his notion from the doctrine of the twenty-five *tattvas* or components of being in the *Sāṃkhya*-system.

35 "*Cirākh Dehlī dīlī dīlme citta cirākh terā*" is a delightful pun derived from the similar sounds of "Delhī", the name of the

city, and *dilī* from *dil* (heart).

36 Possibly an allusion to the well known metaphor in Sufi poetry of the 'wine' of the divine unity on which the mystic becomes 'drunk'.

37 An allusion to the stage of yogic meditation *(dhyān)* in which the *citta* of the *yogī* penetrates and assimilates the object meditated upon *(Yoga-sūtra*, III.2). This verse and the one preceding it are good examples of the harmonious fusion of Yoga, *guru-bhakti*, and the love symbolism of Sufi-poetry in Siddhaliṅga's *dohās and sākīs.*

38 Possibly an allusion to the wide-spread popular notion of the *ṣaḍūrmī:* the six psychomental conditions of the body *(vṛttis):* birth, death, hunger, thirst, grief, delusion.

REFERENCES

Bendre, Vā. Sī., *Tukārāmamahārāja-yāṃcī-guruparaṃparā.* Muṃbaī. 1960.

Ḍhere, Rāmacandra Ciṃtāmaṇa, *Musalamāna-Marāṭhī-santa-kavi.* Puṇe. 1967.

——, *Prācīna-Marāṭhicyā-navadhārā.* Kolhāpūra: Moghe-prakāśana. *Śake* 1894(1972).

Eliade, Mircea, *Yoga: Unsterblichkeit und Freiheit. Zurich.* 1960.

Kolhāpūrkara, Śivājīrāva Sadāśivarāva Śeṭe, *Nāgeśa-līlāmṛta.* Kolhāpūra. *Śake* 1900. (A.D.1978).

Kuruḍe, Nāganātha Guṃḍubūvā and Siddhaliṅga Viśvanāthasvāmī (eds.), *Ānanda-lahari-vā-sākyā.* Mohoḷa (Dt.Sholapur). No date given (circa 1950).

Paṭhāṇa, Yū. Ma., *Nāgeśa-saṃpradāya.* Auraṃgābāda: Vahiḥaśāla śikṣaṇa maṃḍala. 1963.

Schimmel, Annemarie, *Der Islam III.* Stuttgart Berlin Köln. 1990.

Trimingham, J. Spencer, *The Sufi Orders in Islam.* Oxford. 1971.

Tulpule, S.G., *Classical Marathi Literature: From the Beginning to A.D. 1818.* Wiesbaden. 1979.

van Skyhawk, Hugh, *Bhakti und Bhakta: Religionsgeschichtliche Untersuchungen zum Heilsbegriff und zur religiösen Umwelt des Śrī Santa Ekanāth.* Stuttgart:Franz Steiner Verlag. 1990.

Vaudevlle, Ch., *Kabīr.* Oxford. 1974.

Yazdani, Gulam, *Bidar: Its History and Monuments.* London:1947.

Alexander and the Bengali Sufis

Peter Gaeffke

In an article published in the *Journal of the American Oriental Society*[1] I have tried to link the "Indian" *mat͟hnawīs* in Awadhī or Dakanī with the Islamic Alexander story. The evidence was circumstantial because none of the poets in Awadhī or Dakanī has written a poem about Alexander the Great. There are references to his life and deeds in Dakanī *mat͟hnawīs* In Awadhī, however, the evidence is more oblique. This corresponds with the observation that the Northern poets were less educated in *islamica* than the Southerners who knew the Alexander story from Niẓāmī's Persian version. Jāmī's poem on Alexander did not play any role in this process of transmission nor was Amīr K͟husraw's poem on Alexander of any influence though he had lived in Delhi and had exercised a sizable impact on the cultural and religious life of this city.

However, the knowledge of the full Alexander story in Persian was not lost on the more educated circles. The evidence, however, comes from a remote corner of South Asia, i.e., from Arakan[2], the Burmese state on the East coast of the Bay of Bengal.[3] There, about 1670, a Bengali poet, called Alaol,[4] wrote a "translation" of Niẓāmī's *Šarafnāme*, the first part of his *Sikandarnāme*, which forms the fifth section of his famous *K͟hamse*.[5] In the following paper I shall address the question why it happened just in Arakan that the, so far, only Alexander poem in a modern Indian language was composed. To answer this question a number of historical and cultural facts of Arakan in the 16th and 17th centuries have to be remembered before we can deal with the personal circumstances of the poet because they are intertwined thoroughly with the history of this state, Bengal, and India in general.

THE VIEW OF AN OUTSIDE OBSERVER

Apart from Goa, the Portuguese had footholds in Hugly (near what is now Calcutta), and in Dianga (from Bengali Dvi-aṅga "two parts") near Chittagong (Caṭṭagrām), which at this time belonged to the kingdom of Arakan. In 1629 the Augustine friar Sebastian Manrique[6] was sent to administer to the sailor/pirates at Dianga who, with the blessing of the Buddhist Kings of Arakan, looted and pillaged the Bengali countryside and sold its inhabitants as slave workers in Arakan and Burma. In Bengal since 1576 the Mughals, i.e., their Viceroys, were ruling and the Portuguese authorities had pronounced these raids as just because "the Mogors (i.e. Muslims) were the enemies of Christianity" (p. 285). It is, therefore, no surprise that, during his five year sojourn in Mrauk-U (better: Myauk-ru, Arakan's capital), in an attempt to save Dianga from a raid by the furious Thīritudamma (Thirtadharma, king of Arakan (1622-38), who suspected treachery), Manrique collected only few facts but the most vicious rumors about Muslim life in the city. He noticed a community of Muslim merchants at a place not far from the capital (p. 208); he saw the captain of the Arakan cavalry, who was a Muslim (p.360), and the "tabibo," the Muslim doctor of the King, cured him of a fever (p. 165). But he was upset that the king had a Muslim adviser who had told him how to become "invisible and invincible" and in order to ensure his long life, had prescribed burying pregnant women in the foundation of the bathing place for the king's coronation (p. 353) and to prepare a "timiama" from six thousand hearts of his subjects. This description of those cruelties "due to devilish advice" is followed by a long sermon on how a king should choose pious advisers. This, obviously, means that the Portuguese friars would be better counsellors than the Muslims. During his several audiences at the court, the King spoke with him in Hindustani. Manrique did not notice a single Muslim courtier nor does he report the use of Bengali at the court.

ARAKAN-BENGAL RELATIONS

Although the Arakan king were of Burmese stock, from the fifteenth century they had a tradition of excellent relations with Gauṛ, the break-away kingdom from the Delhi Sultanate. In 1400, when the Burmese attacked Arakan, the King even took refuge in Gauṛ, for thirty years and when he returned, he took with him a great number of Bengali Muslims. Moreover, from this time onward all the Arakan kings, besides their Burmese and Pāli names, also took Muslim names down to the time of Manrique.[7] However, with the destruction of the Gauṛ kingdom in 1576, Arakan became a direct neighbour of the Mughal empire and as a result of a strained relationship between both states, the Arakan kings conducted military forays into Bengal for which they enlisted the help of the Portuguese pirates.

MUSLIM PRESENCE

As the Buddhists were obviously not the best military men in the state, the kings of Arakan, and also those of Burma, enlisted mercenaries from "military races", i.e. Muslims, Japanese, and Europeans.[8] Educated Muslims had another well appreciated talent: they were fluent in Persian, the lingua franca of the time, and were trained in the administration of smaller and larger domains. Despite the tension with the Muslims in Bengal, Muslims occupied high positions at the Arakan court and received honors from the king.

They lived under their own law, which was administered by Qāẕīs, had their religious freedom, and their scholarship and poetry were patronized by their own nobles and by the king himself. There existed mosques and Sufi *k͟hānaqās*, whose predominant *mad͟hhab* was the Sunni Islam of the Hanafi School. Alaol, who was born about 1618 in the village of Faṭeḥpūr in Bengal, was the son of a high official and military officer of Šām Šer Quṭub, Nawwāb of Jalālpūr. However, his father was killed fighting the Arakanese and Portuguese pirates. Alaol says that during this raid, in which his father lost his life, he escaped to Arakan. It is more likely that he was taken prisoner and sold in Arakan and that Muslims, recognizing his talents, freed him. In his early works he prides himself in the fact that a son of king became his patron.

MUSLIM EDUCATION

Evidently, in such an environment, traditional Muslim education was thriving. Arabic was taught along with Qur'ānic studies. Persian, the prestigious court language, was studied through the works of its great poets. Alaol himself attests to the high level of learning when he says that to "translate" the *Iskandarnāme* of Niẓāmī, one has to know Arabic, Persian, Christian (Naṣrānī, i.e., Greek), Ihudī (i.e., Hebrew) and Pāhlavī (ch. 13, p. 31). Moreover, the suggestion to translate this work came from the Muslim courtiers who argued with him that to translate such a book would be much more propitious a work than to build a mosque or have a pond dug out (ch. 13, p. 30). So they must have possessed the linguistic tools to read this, for the Arakan Muslims, not so easy work.

SUFI PRESENCE

Wherever Muslims settled, there Sufis established a foothold, often long before Muslim armies occupied a country. There is a long tradition of Sufism in Bengal[9] and consequently Sufis in Arakan continued this tradition. In the sixteenth century Sufis in Northern India had widely adopted the custom of writing poems in Indian languages. When Alaol came to Arakan , this trend was already well established by Qāẕī Daulat (1600-38), who had translated *Saifu'l-Mulūk o Badī'u'l-Jamāl* into Bengali.[10] But since he was sick and weak, Alaol was asked to complete his unfinished poem and to continue his tradition. This made him write his famous Bengali *Padmāvatī*, which squarely established his fame as a poet and Sufi.

EVENTS OF THE SECOND HALF OF THE 17TH CENTURY

In 1639 Šāh Jahān had appointed Šāh Šūjā' as Viceroy of Bengal[11] and when Aurangzeb became Emperor in 1658, Šūjā' rebelled, but was defeated. He fled to Arakan with his bodyguard and his family. In 1660 the Arakan King Sandāthadama (Sanātanadharma?) ordered him and his family to be killed and absorbed Šūjā's soldiers into his army. Alaol, who must have had strong sympathies for the Bengal court, somehow got involved in this affair and after Šūjā's demise, spent ten years in prison. During this time in 1666 Aurangzeb attacked Arakan and occupied Chittagong and the Muslims of Arakan rebelled against the Arakanese ruling class. Since this time there was a continuously growing Muslim influence on Arakan affairs and the former soldiers of Šūjā' became the virtual rulers of the state. That explains why Alaol was released in 1670 and immediately after, Qāẕī Sayyed Mas'ūd Šāh initiated him in the Qādirī order,[12] and he regained his position at the court. It was at this point that his fellow courtiers suggested that he write a *Sikandarnāmā*.

ALEXANDER IN THE MUSLIM PERSPECTIVE

Niẓāmī and Alaol agree that Alexander was a prophet[13] sent by God. This puts him outside Muslim history because for Sunnis there is no prophet besides Muḥammad. But Alexander's propagation and spread of "Isḥāq's religion" makes him relevant for every Muslim, especially for those in the "diaspora." They carried a higher religion and culture into the land of the barbarians or defended the frontiers of Islam against barbaric invaders just as Alexander prevented Gog and Magog from entering the civilized world.[14]

ALEXANDER'S TREATMENT OF THE INDIANS

Alaol follows the story line of Niẓāmī rather closely but the most interesting passages are precisely those where he makes subtle deviations. E.g., after his conquest of Khorāsān, Alexander directed his interest toward Hindustan. Niẓāmī reports two encounters: one with King Kaid (p. 1045) who is impressed by Alexander's forces, offers him his daughter, and asks for peace. The second is with King Fūr (the Poros of Arrian) of Kanaj (i.e., Kanauj) who resists and, therefore, is defeated and destroyed. The representation in Niẓāmī is relatively balanced with an exchange of letters between Fūr and Iskandar (p. 1052f.) and a long description of the beauties of the girl offered by king Kaid (p. 1047f.). Nothing of this is found in Alaol. The defeat of Phur (Beng.) is telescoped into two lines (p. 199) and there is only one line on the girl (p. 195). However the letters and gifts exchanged between Alexander and Kayad (Beng.) are mentioned in full detail (p. 194ff.). The reason is that this story could serve as a lesson for the Arakan king, still struggling with growing Muslim forces, that a submissive king will be treated as a friend and a vassal by the God-fearing Muslims. But it must have been importune at that particular time to go into too much detail about what would happen to an Indian king who wanted to resist the Muslim forces. Furthermore, we can assume the Muslim warriors should not be desirous of the beauty of the Kafir girls so long as the battle was not yet over and so Alaol suppressed the salty details found in Niẓāmī's description of Kaid's daughter.

THE TREATMENT OF THE NON-INDIAN UNBELIEVERS

To give an example from this important section we have to look into Alaol's treatment of Alexander's destruction of the fire cult of Iran. The chapter is called "*Sikāndarer Islām pracār*":

> He brought the nobles who worshipped Ahurmajdā
> to his religion. The great-minded one ordered all the
> Iranians to give up fire worship:
> "There is only one God, witnessed in all places.
> Only he is worthy of worship!
> I am his messenger and you consider this truth and
> follow only the religion of Islam."
> The crowd of Iranian nobles who had an agreeable
> disposition entered the religion of Islam.
> The gurus of the *māgī* who remained in their religion
> he separated and killed.

Niẓāmī's chapter on the end of fire worship in Iran (p. 970ff.), which is the basis of Alaol's foregoing account, has nothing about preaching and execution, but speaks only of Alexander's order to the men of Iran to give up fire worship.

Later on in the same chapter, Alaol describes (p. 127) the custom of *nauroz* (Bengali: *navadin*) in ancient Iran when all the girls came out of their houses, stood in the middle of the roads, laughed and played many games. They knew many magic tricks dangerous to men which captured the minds of the wise and the sages. They wore colorful garments and many ornaments, displayed their breasts and twisted their bodies to overpower the minds of men.

> When Alexander heard of this, he at once forbade
> this custom of shameful behavior of women.
> He let announce to every house: "I shall kill the women
> who do such things!

> Except for their husbands they should not see
> anybody for I shall keep the womenfolk hidden."

Niẓāmī (p. 971) says only that nobody should perform the rites of the fire-worshippers and that beautiful brides should cover their faces and show them only "to the mother or to the husband" (p. 973). The brutality of the above passage is only Alaol's.

CONCLUSION

That this dream of an Islamic society, called today "fundamentalist," is not just the imagination of an Arakan poet, we can witness today in many Islamic countries. However, what could it mean to the Muslims of Arakan? In a time when a victory of Muslim forces seemed likely, it was appropriate to remind them of the actual goal of their efforts: the establishment of a truly Muslim society against Buddhists and Hindus.

Nevertheless the revival of the story of the Muslim prophet Alexander, though it strengthened the self-esteem of the Muslims in the diaspora and reminded them of their cultural mission, was not threatening for the non-Muslim (Buddhists) "whose mind was of a good disposition"[15] but it warned them of the dangers of not respecting the higher culture of the Muslims. For the Muslim individual, the story of Alexander was a powerful model for the struggle for the ultimate worldwide victory of Islam, which was to be gained by great personal sacrifice but with the reward of undying fame. And this is the reason why it was in Arakan that a full-fledged Alexander story was composed.

NOTES

1. *Journal of the American Oriental Society*, 109 (1989), p. 527ff.
2. Arakan, in Bengali Rosāṅg, probably from Mro-houng ("town-

old", i.e., Old Town), also Myong-oo, which was the name of the capital of the Arakan kingdom.

3. The literature on ancient Arakan is very scanty, *cf.* Klaus Fleischmann. *Arakan: Konfliktregion zwischen Birma und Bangladesh.* Mitteilungen des Instituts für Asienkunde Nr. 121, Hamburg. 1981; *Gazetteer of Burma*, compiled by Authority, vol. II. New Delhi. 1983 (First published 1880 under the title "*British Burma Gazetteer*" at Government Press, Rangoon); Yegar, Moshe. *The Muslims of Burma: A Study of a Minority Group.* Schriftenreihe des Südasien-Instituts der Universität Heidelberg, Wiesbaden. 1972 (with further literature).
4. In Bengali Ālā'ul which is the first part of an Arabic nominative+genitive phrase, used in names such as Ālāu'l-Ḥaq, which was probably the full name of this poet. Similar grammatical nonsense forms appeared recently in Western news reports: Mujibur ("Listening to") for Mujību'r-Raḥmān(i) ("Listening to the Merciful One") or Abdul ("Slave of") for 'Abdullah(i) ("Slave of God"). In the following the references are to *Ālāul viracita Sikāndarnāmā sampādanāy Āhmad Śarīf.* Bāṅglā Ekāḍemī, Ḍhākā, 1977.
5. The references are to: *Kulliyāt-i Khamse-yi Ḥakīm Niẓāmī Ganjāwī.* Bāzar Gānī. H. 1341.
6. *Travels of Fray Sebastien Manrique*, 1629-43, a translation of the *Itinerario de las missiones orientales* with introduction and notes by Lt.-Col. C. Eckford Luard, C.I.E., M.A., assisted by Father H. Hosten, S.J., Vol I: Arakan. Oxford (The Hakluyt Society, Series II, vol 59). 1927.
7. During their dependence on the Nawabs of Bengal, the Arakan kings received titles such as: 'Alī Khān, i.e., Min Khari (1434-1459); Kalimasya Šāh (Kalīm "Interlocutor" or Kalīmu'llāh Šāh?) for Basawpyu (1459-1482); Muḥammad Šāh for Dawlya (1482-92) and Baswnyo (1492-94); Nurisya Šāh (Nūrī Šāh) for Yanaung (1494); Jalalasya (Jalāl) Šāh for Minsaw-o (1525); and others.

   Even after their independence the Arakan kings continued this practice: e.g. Zabauk (Dhawwāq "Great Taster") Šāh for Minbin (1531-1533); Sikandar Šāh for Minapalaung (1571-1593); Sālim Šāh for Minyazapyi (1593-1612); Sālim Šāh II for Thirithudama (1622-1638). *Cf.* Yegar (see note 3), p. 19, notes 4,5.
8. *Cf.* Yegar, (see note 3) p. 9f.
9. Girināth Dās, *Bāṅglā Pīr sāhitaya kathā.* n. place. 1976; Saiyid Athar Abbas Rizvi. *A History of Sufism in India.* New Delhi. 1978.

10. An Ashraf Khān asked him to write a poem based on the Lor and Candana story as it appeared in a Rajasthani poem by Sādhan, but he died before completing his work. On Daulat Qāẕī see Sukumar Sen. *History of Bengali Literature.* New Delhi. (2nd ed.) 1971, p. 138ff. More in: Śrīsukumār Sen. *Bāṅglā sāhityer itihās,* 1,2. Kalikaṭā. (3rd ed.) 1975; and Muḥammad Mansūru'd-Dīn. *Bāṅglā sāhitya Muslim sādhanā,* I. Ḍhākā. (3rd ed.) 1981, pp. 229-231.
11. On Šūjā' see Khafī Khān, *Muntakhābu'l-Lubāb,* tr. by Anees Jahan Syed. Bombay, New Delhi. 1977, and Nural Karim, "The Fate of Shah Shuja", *Journal of the Pakistan Historical Society,* I (1953), pp. 392-397.
12. *kṛpa kari dilek kāderī khilāphat* (ch.13, p. 28).
13. In Niẓāmī there are references to the "religion of Abraham," (i.e., the common Islamic term for Judaism) Christianity, and Islam. Why Alaol speaks of "Ishāk nābīr dvīn" in the chapter called "Hindustān Bijay" is difficult to understand other than as a variation in which the name of the son (Isaac, i.e., Isḥāq) is used in place of that of the father (Abraham, i.e., Ibrāhīm).
14. Dhūl-Qarnain is mentioned in Sūra 18 (*Kahf*), 83-98, while for Niẓāmī and the Western Orientalists there was never a doubt that in this passage the Qur'ān refers to Alexander, modern Muslim commentators deny this and offer other possibilities of identification. Abdullah Yusuf Ali. *The Meaning of the Glorious Qur'ān,* Qāharah I, 1938, pp. 760-5, contains a discussion on this issue.
15. *mahanta Irānīgaṇ komal haiyā man.*

Maulānā Dāūd's Teacher Shaikh Zainuddīn

Shyam Manohar Pandey

The author of *Candāyan* Maulānā Dāūd composed his book in AH 781[1] which is equivalent to A.D. 1379. In his work he refers to his contemporary king Firoz Shāh Tughluq[2] his minister Jaunā Shāh[3] and Shaikh Mubārak[4] the Governor of Ḍalmau[5] which is in Rae Bareli district in Uttar Pradesh.

In verse nine of *Candāyan*, the poet refers to his master Shaikh Zainuddīn who was also called Maulānā Zainuddīn or Zainuddīn Alī. In medieval texts numerous references have been made to him. My purpose in this paper is to piece together the information found in the contemporary sources and reconstruct a picture of his personality. I hope this will be useful for those who are interested in the literatures and culture of the medieval period.

Maulānā Dāūd refers to his teacher in *Candāyan* in the following words:

Sekh Jaindī haū pathi Lāvā
dharm panthu jīh pāpu gavāvā
pāp dīnh maī gāng bahāi
dharm nav haū līnh caṛāī
ughare nain hiye ujiyāre
pāyo likhi nau akkhar kāre
puni maī akkhir kī sudhi pāī
turakī likhi likhi hindukī gāī

Jai paie Jāi sekh pasārā
pāp gaye tasīkar mārā
tyahu kā gharu nirmarā jiha citu rahā lubhāi
Sekh Jaindī sevatā pāp nirantaru jāi.[6]

"Shaikh Jaindī (Zainuddīn) put me on the right path. My sins (*pāp*) were destroyed on this virtuous path. They were washed away in the Ganges river. He made me ride on the boat of righteousness, then my eyes and my heart became pure. Afterwards I was able to write new syllables.[7] I learnt the alphabet and composed in *Turkī* to sing the *Hindukī*[8] tale, my master extended his mercy and then my sins were destroyed in the same way as thieves and bandits are killed. He who has affection for Zainuddīn, his house and family will become pure. By serving him continually sins will go away."

Shaikh Muhaddīs Dehlavī[9] who compiled *Akhbārul Akhyār* during the reign of Akbar (AD 1546-1605) mentions Shaikh Zainuddīn and the author of *Candāyan* in the following words: "Shaikh Zainuddīn was a nephew, a successor and the main attendant of Nasīruddīn Chirāgh Dehlavī (d. AD 1356); he was the teacher of Maulānā Dāūd, the author of *Candāyan*. In the beginning of the *Candāyan* he has composed verses in his praise. His tomb is situated in the compound towards the feet of his master Shaikh Nasīruddīn."[10]

Shaikh Zainuddīn, the son of Shaikh Nasīruddīn's elder sister, is mentioned by many authors of the hagiographical works of the Medieval period. There are many references to him in *Khairul Majālis*[11] of Hamīd Qalandar, which was composed in AD 1353. For example: "After the call of the prayer (*azān*) Shaikh Nasīruddīn called Shaikh Zainuddīn who was his sister's son, and asked him to distribute the flowers which were red and white."[12]

"Chirāgh Dehlavī had no attendant at the door. Sometimes his sister's son Shaikh Zainuddīn remained there but sometimes he was absent".[13]

From all Hamīd Qalandar's references it becomes clear that Shaikh Zainuddīn was a nephew of Shaikh Nasīruddīn. Hamīd Qalandar also mentions that Zainuddīn was the son of Buā Abdī, the elder sister of the great Shaikh Nasīruddīn. His other sister was Bībī Lāhirī whose son was Kamāluddīn.

Khaliq Ahmad Nizāmī in his introduction to the Persian text of *Khairul Majālis* says: "Shaikh Nasīruddīn did not sever his relationship with Awadh on being admitted to the discipline of Shaikh Nizāmuddīn Auliyā. His intense love for his mother often drew him to his native town. When she died he felt a void in his life and sought to fill it by long stays with his master. He had two sisters Bībī Buā Abdī and Bībī Lāhirī. The younger one Bībī Lāhirī had died at an early age. Shaikh Nasīruddīn's attachment with Awadh was due to his elder sister, Bibi Bua Abdi and his nephews, when Bībī Buā Abdī died, he brought his two nephews Zainuddīn Alī and the son of Bībī Lāhirī to the *jamāᶜāt khānā* of Shaikh Nizāmuddīn who remarked: "You have done well in bringing your nephews with you". Shaikh Nasīruddīn then decided to stay in Delhi permanently at the feet of his master".[14]

Shaikh Jamālī,[15] a friend of Sikandar Lodi (AD 1489-1517), who lived during the time of Humāyūn (AD 1530-1636) also, says in his *Siyarul ᶜĀrifin* that Chirāgh Dehlavī had only one sister in Ayodhyā and the Shaikh used to go to see her; she had two sons Shaikh Zainuddīn and Shaikh Kamāluddīn.[16]

We have no information about the source of the details Jamālī gives us here. He has copied many things from *Khairul Majālis* and other hagiographical works. His statement that Chirāgh Dehlavī had only one sister contradicts *Khairul Majālis*. We are not in a position to accept Jamālī's view because he is a late author. Hamīd Qalandar, author of *Khairul Majālis* and a contemporary of Chirāgh Dehlavī, clearly mentions two sisters of the Shaikh, Buā Abdī and Bībī Lāhirī. As has already been stated, they were the mothers of Shaikh Zainuddīn and Shaikh Kamāluddīn, respectively.

Shaikh Zainuddīn has been mentioned in *Siyarul Auliyā*[17] (1351-1388) of Amīr Khurd. Amīr Khurd says: "I went to him (Shaikh Nasīruddīn) and sat there. Then I thought of a handkerchief. In the meantime Shaikh called one of his attendants and asked him to bring a handkerchief which Shaikh Zainuddīn had brought. The attendant brought a handkerchief in which fine embroidery work was done. I still keep that handkerchief".[18] *Siyarul ᶜĀrifīn* also refers to Shaikh Zainuddīn as a nephew and the main attendant of Chirāgh Dehlavī. Here it is clear that Jamālī has followed the statement made by Hamīd Qalandar in *Khairul Majālis.* Jamālī says" Hazarat Shaikh Nasīruddīn had no door-keeper. His nephew Shaikh Zainuddīn stayed there sometimes but sometimes Zainuddīn was absent when the Shaikh was in solitary prayer".[19]

Shaikh Nasīruddīn Chirāgh Dehlavī was born in Ayodhyā (Oudh) and before he became one of the principal successors of Khwājā Nizāmuddīn Auliyā in A.D. 1325, he had already taken his sister's sons to his master's *khānqāh.* A precise date cannot be given for Shaikh Zainuddīn's arrival in Delhi, but it must have been shortly before Chirāgh Dehlavī settled there permanently in AD 1324-1325, that is one or two years before the passing away of his master Khwājā Nizāmuddīn Auliyā. It seems that Khwājā had given the certificate of succession to the Shaikh the same year.[20]

Shaikh Zainuddīn is also mentioned in the context of a knife attack on Shaikh Nasīruddīn by a Qalandar named Turābī. Shaikh Zainuddīn, who was in the kitchen at the time, rushed to the Shaikh's aid and discovered a stream of blood flowing there. Hamīd Qalandar gives the following account of the event: "Finding the Shaikh (Chirāgh Dehlavī) alone, Turābī entered his room with a knife and inflicted eleven wounds on him. The Shaikh remained motionless and it was not till his blood flowed out of the water-hole of the room, that his disciples began to suspect something. On entering the room they found the Qalandar stabbing the Shaikh. They would have punished him on the spot but the

Shaikh would permit nothing of the kind. Determined to add generosity to forgiveness, he summoned one of his favourite disciples, Abidul Muqtadir of Thaneshwar along with the physician Shaikh Sadhuddin and his nephew Zainuddīn Alī and asked them to administer an oath to his disciples that they would not seek to harm the Qalandar."[21]

In the "Conversations of Gesūdarāz Khwājā Bandā Newāz",[22] *Jawāmī ul Kalim*,[23] by Saiyyid Husaini Akbar, the following account is given: "He (Chirāgh Dehlavī) put his hand in front of Turābī and Turābī stabbed until all the fingers of the Shaikh had been cut, to the extent that when he wrote he used to keep his fingers unbent and in the ritual of prayer his fingers remained straight. At last the blood passed from the room of the courtyard which was ten *guz* (about thirty feet) broad and flowed out through a conduit to a place near the kitchen where Maulānā Zainuddīn and other *khādims* were sitting. When they saw the stream of blood they ran up. Maulānā Zainuddīn came first. Turābī pursued Maulānā Zainuddīn, ran and struck him with the knife. the latter put on his hand to parry it and he too was somewhat wounded in the hand: the skin was cut. Finally khwājā Bashīr caught him and took the knife from his hand".[24]

Although these two accounts of the stabbing of Chirāgh Dehlavī differ considerably, they throw light upon Shaikh Zainuddīn's activities in the *khānqāh* (monastery) and *jamā*ᶜ*āt khānā* (hospice) of Chirāgh Dehlavī. Shaikh Zainuddīn seems to have been an overall caretaker of the *khānqāh* activities who also rendered personal services to the Shaikh as a principal *khādim*.

There are many other references to Shaikh Zainuddīn in *Jawāmī ul Kalīm*. There is one in which a disciple of Shaikh Zainuddīn was against the *sama*ᶜ' (Singing and hearing of music by Sufis in an assembly) but Gesūdarāz Bandā Newāz, who was also a disciple of Shaikh Nasīruddīn Chirāgh Dehlavī, refutes this. "Gesūdarāz says, one intelligent person who was a disciple of Khwājā Chirāgh Dehlavī and later a successor (*khalifa*) of Shaikh Zainuddīn told me one day that there was nothing significant in *sama*ᶜ. Then I explained to him, he who has no love for *sama*ᶜ does not know what it is. *Samā*ᶜ is a path to reach the beloved one (God), in the same way that prayer, reading the Qur'ān and keeping fasts etc. lead you to God. In fact in *samā*ᶜ there is more concentration of thought which is an asset to a seeker on the path of God".[25] This episode indicates that perhaps Zainuddīn and his disciples, like many other orthodox of his age, did not approve of *sama*ᶜ, although Khwājā Nizāmuddīn Auliyā, Nasīruddīn Chirāgh Dehlavī, Gesūdarāz and many other Chishtī Sufis were very fond of it. To them *sama*ᶜ had the same effect as prayer *(namāz)*, reading the Qur'ān *(tilāvat)* and observing fasts *(rozā)*.

Shaikh Zainuddīn has been especially mentioned in medieval Persian texts as having proposed that Nasīruddīn Chirāgh Dehlavī nominate his successor, but he never suggested the name of Khwājā Bandā Newāz who was very dear to the heart of Chirāgh Dehlavī.

Hamīd Qalandar says: "His nephew Zainuddīn Alī appealed to him to appoint such a successor so that his spiritual line might not come to an end. The Shaikh asked him to draw up a list of the persons whom he considered worthy of the honour. But when Zainuddīn drew up a list in order of merit and placed it before the Shaikh for consideration, the Shaikh simply refused to consider it. "Maulānā Zainuddīn !" he said "they have to bear the burden of their own faith; it is not possible for them to bear the burden of others".[26] "After making this observation", Hamīd continues, "Shaikh Nasīruddīn made the following will: "At the time of my burial, place the *khiraqā* I have received from Shaikh Nizāmuddīn on my chest, lay the staff of my master in my grave by my side; the rosary of my Shaikh is to be wound round my forefinger and his wooden bowl is to be placed by my head instead of the usual clod of earth". The persons present acted according to his will. Sayyid Muhammad Gesūdarāz washed Shaikh Nasīruddīn's body. He then took out the twisted ropes from the cot on which he had washed the body and wound them round his neck. 'This is sufficient *khiraqā* for me,' he declared".[27]

Hamīd Qalandar does not mention in *Khairul Majālis* that Shaikh Zainuddīn ignored the name of Khwājā Bandā Newāz. Jamālī also in *Siyarul ᶜĀrifīn* overlooks this, but one of the disciples of Bandā Newāz, Muhammad Alī Samānī, who wrote Siyar-i-Muhammadī[28] in AD 1428 does mention it: "They made out a list and Maulānā Zainuddīn brought that list to the Shaikh. The name of Sayyid Muhammad was not on the list. When the Shaikh had scanned the list, he said "what a sack of stones and clods of earth you have brought. Tell them to worry about their own faith" He then threw away the list. Maulānā Zainuddīn again made a short list and brought it back with some names omitted. He took it to the Shaikh who said "read it out". He read it out and the Shaikh said "you have not written the name of Sayyid Muhammad". Zainuddīn grew afraid and began to tremble. Immediately he wrote the name of Sayyid Muhammad. The Shaikh took the list and with his pen wrote the letter *sād* (for *sahih* beside the name of Sayyid Muhammad is implied)".[29] There is another reference to Bandā Newāz in *Siyar-i-Muhammadī*, which tells that Shaikh Nasīruddīn had given him a *nihālchā* (quilt).

Simon Digby in one of his articles has described in detail the bitterness of the quarrel regarding the succession between Gesūdarāz and Zainuddīn.[30] What interests us here is that Zainuddīn remained in Delhi for a long time governing the *khānqāh* of Nasīruddīn after his death. His brother Kamāluddīn assisted him. Maulānā Dāūd who composed his *Candāyan* in AD 1379 (AH 781) refers to Zainuddīn as his teacher. This makes us believe that he was already an important figure during that time and was perhaps looking after the *khānqāh* of his master Shaikh Nasīruddīn Chirāgh Dehlavī. Gesūdarāz, perhaps stayed in Delhi for many years isolated and ignored. In 1413 he went to Gulbarga in the South of India where he died in 1422. There he attracted a large following and wrote many books in Arabic, Persian and perhaps in Dakanī.

The ascendancy of Shaikh Nasiruddin's eldest nephew, Maulānā Zainuddīn and the latter's brothers was established at the Shaikh's death. The tomb of Chirāgh Dehlavī itself, the entrance gate and the massive defensive walls date from this period and indicate the patronage of Sultan Firoz Shāh. It was clearly a major *khānqāh* before Timur's invasion in AD 1398.[31] Today it is a neglected place. Shaikh Zainuddīn is almost forgotten. His tomb which is in the right side of Shaikh Kamāluddīn's tomb facing the feet of his master, goes unnoticed. Followers and descendants of Kamāluddīn have erected a fine structure over his tomb.

Whatever scanty information is available about Zainuddīn has been put together here. It does not tell us much about his life, but the following elements emerge explicitly from the above:

(I) Zainuddīn was a son of Shaikh Nasīruddīn's elder sister Buā Abdī. In A.D. 1325, when Khwājā Nizāmuddīn Auliyā died, Shaikh Nasīruddīn succeeded him in Delhi. Zainuddīn and his brother Kamāluddīn, who was the son of Bībī Lāhirī, both seem to have gone to Delhi a few years earlier. The most likely date of their arrival in Delhi is 1323, when Chirāgh Dehlavī was given the certificate of succession by his master Nizāmuddīn Auliyā. By that time Zainuddīn's mother was also dead. Chirāgh Dehlavī used to come to Ayodhyā even after the death of his mother to see his sister Zainuddīn's mother Buā Abdī. Bībī Lāhirī, the mother of Kamāluddīn, had already died.

(2) Shaikh Zainuddīn was a disciple and the principal personal attendant of Shaikh Nasīruddīn Chirāgh Dehlavī.

(3) Because of Shaikh Zainuddīn, Khwājā Bandā Newāz Gesūdarāz could not become the successor of his master Chirāg Dehlavī. This is clear from *Siyar-i-Muhammadī* and *Jawāmī ul Kalīm*. Bandā Newāz was a true spiritual successor.

(5) It seems that Shaikh Zainuddīn was more of a scholar

than a spiritual teacher. Unlike his Chishtī predecessors, he does not seem to have been interested in *sama*[c].

(6) He was buried in the compound of the monastery of Chirāgh Dehlavī. Shaikh Muhaddis Dehlavī speaks about this tomb and about his disciple Maulānā Dāūd the author of *Candāyan*.

REFERENCES

For a detailed study on *Candāyan* see also the following book and articles by Shyam Manohar Pandey:

Lorikāyan and Candāyan in the Hindi Oral Epic Lorikāyan. Allahabad. 1987.

"Love Symbolism in Candāyan", *Bhakti in Current Research*, ed. Monika Thiel-Horstmann. Berlin: Dietrich Reimer Verlag. 1983.

"Maulānā Dāūd and His Contribution to Hindi Literature", *Annali*, Istituto Orientale di Napoli, 38, 1978.

"Some Problems in Studying Candāyan", *Early Hindī Devotional Literature in Current Research*, ed. Winand M. Callewaert. Leuven. 1980.

NOTES

1. *Baras sāt sai hoye ekyāsī*
   tihi yāh kabi saras ubhāsī
   "It was the year seven hundred eighty one when this poet composed this sweet poem" (Above reference to 781 stands for AH which is equivalent to AD 1379). Dāūd, *Candāyan*, ed. Mātā Prasād Gupta. Agra. 1967, verse 17.
2. Firoz Shāh (Tughluq) has been referred to in *Candāyan* as a contemporary king. He reigned from AD 1351 to 1388, in Delhi.
3. Jaunā Shāh: according to Afif, Khān-i-Jahān worked as Wazīr for eighteen years and died in 1368-69 (AH 770), after he had reached the age of eighty. He was succeeded as Wazīr by his son, who had been named Jaunā Shāh by Muhammad Shāh

Tughluq and was also given the title of Khān-i-Jahān by Firoz Shāh. His father Khān-i-Jahān was a converted Hindu from Telangana. The internal administration of the country was in the hands of Khān-i-Jahān. When he died his place was taken by his son Jaunā Shāh who, assumed the same title of Khān-i-Jahān and conducted the Government till the end of the reign of Firoz Shāh Tughluq in 1388. Maulānā Dāūd perhaps refers to this Khān-i-Jahān in *Candāyan* who was called Jaunā Shāh. His tomb is in the village of Nizāmuddīn in Delhi. Kāli or Kalān Masjid in Delhi has an inscription mentioning that it was built in AH 772 (1370-71) by Jūān Shāh Maqbūl entitled Khān-i-Jahān, son of Khān-i-Jahān. This date is not agreed upon by all scholars. For example, Vincent A. Smith gives AD 1370-71 (AH 772) as the year of his death (*The Oxford History of India.* Oxford. 1970. p. 257). Sherwani places Khān-i-Jahān's death in AH 770 (1368-69) (*Comprehensive History of India*, ed. Mohammad Habib and Khaliq Ahmad Nizami, Vol. 5. Delhi: People's Publishing House. 1970, pp. 574-576).

4. Shaikh Mubārak: he was the Governor of Ḍalmau during the period of Firoz Shāh Tughluq. Ḍalmau is a small town on the banks of Gangā river in Rae Bareli district near Lucknow. For details see S.M. Pandey, 1978.

5 Ḍalmau: this town prospered during the reign of Altamsh (Iltutmish) of Delhi about AH 600 (AD 1203). At that time one Makhdūm Badruddīn, a companion of the King, resided there. Thenceforward the town did well till the time of Firoz Shāh Tughluq, who founded a school for the instruction of Muslim lore. Perhaps Maulānā Dāūd, the author of *Candāyan*, was connected with this school. For details see S.M. Pandey, 1978; see also *Gazetteer of the Province of Oudh.* Lucknow, 1877, vol. 1, p. 355.

6. *Candāyan, op. cit.* in note 1, verse 9, p. 8.

7 Perhaps the reference here is to *Kalma* in the Qur'ān.

8 The meaning is not very clear. *Hindukī* seems to mean a Hindu tale, something coming from the Hindus; *Turkī* appears to mean the Arabic alphabet used by Muslims.

9 Shaikh Muhaddīs Dehlavī: the tomb of Shaikh Abdul Haq Muhaddīs (Muhaddīth) is situated on the bank of the Hauz-i-Khās in Delhi. He was one of the famous scholars of the age of Akbar and Jahāngīr. He died in AH 1052 (1642). His life sketch has been inscribed on the wall at the head of the grave. He was a great scholar of Qur'ān and Hadīth and for this reason was called Muhaddīs (Muhaddīth). He went to Mecca

in 1587 and stayed there for two years and studied "Sufism". His book *Akhbārul Akhyār* contains the biographies of 255 saints.

10. Shaikh Muhaddis Delhavī, *Akhbārul Akyār*, published by Muhammad Hashim, Delhi, AH 1280 (AD1863), p. 147. There are two Urdu translations of this work also available to us, one is by Muslim Ahmad Nizami, Delhi (n.d.) and the other is by Subhan Mahmud and Muhammad Fazil, Devband (n.d.).
11. *Khairul Majālis* is a compilation of conversations of Shaikh Nasīruddīn Chirāgh Dehlavī. The compiler of this book, Hamīd Qalandar, was a disciple of Chirāgh Dehlavī. His father, Tājuddīn Bukhārī, was disciple of Khwājā Nizāmuddīn Auliyā (d. 1325). Hamīd Qalandar went to the South in 1326-27 by the order of Muhammad Tughluq when the inhabitants of Delhi were compelled to go to Daulatabad. In the South he came into contact with Maulānā Burahānuddīn Gharīb in Gulbarga, a disciple of Khwājā Nizāmuddīn Auliyā. After the death of Burahānuddīn Gharīb, Hamīd returned to Delhi and in 1354-55 compiled one hundred conversations of Chiragh Dehlavī. Later he added a supplement to it after Chirāgh Dehlavī's death.
12. Hamīd Qalandar, *Khairul-Majālis*, ed. Khaliq Ahmad Nizami. Aligarh, 1958, p. 159.
13. *Ibid.*, pp. 286-287.
14. *Ibid.*, English introduction, p. 45-46.
15. The author of *Siyarul ᶜĀrifīn* Jamālī, whose full name was Hamīd Bin Fazlullah, was called Dervesh Jamālī. His original name is said to have been Jalālī but later his Pīr, Samāuddīn, changed it to Jamālī. He had travelled to Yaman, Rūm, Syria, Iraq etc. It is said that he also met the Persian poet Jāmī in Herat, in 1492 (the year when Jāmī died). Sikandar Lodi (1489-1517) Bābur (1525-1530) and Humāyūn (1530-1556) were all his friends. He died in Gujarat around AH 942 (1536) and was brought to Delhi where his tomb exists at a place one mile south of Kutubminār. Though a Suhrawardīya himself, he also describes fourteen Chishtīya saints in his book *Siyarul ᶜĀrifīn.* His other book *Mehr-o-māh* is a *masnavī.*
16. Jamālī, *Siyarul ᶜĀrifīn*, translated into Urdu by Muhammad Ayub Qadari. Lahore: Marqazī Urdu Board. 1976, p. 127.
17. *Siyarul Auliyā*: the author, Amīr Khurd or Mīr Khurd, was a Chishtī saint. His grandfather Sayyid Muhammad Kirmānī from Kirmān in Persia used to come to Lahore for trade. Farīduddīn Ganj-i-Shakar was his spiritual teacher. Mīr Khurd himself was a disciple of Nizāmuddīn Auliyā while he

was young. Later he became the disciple of Shai<u>kh</u> Nasīruddīn Chirāgh Dehlavī. He died in AH 770 (1368-69). At the age of 50, during the time of Firoz Shāh Tughluq (AD 1351-1388) he composed *Siyarul Auliyā*. He went to the South at the command of Muhammad Tughluq in 1326-27 but later returned to Delhi very disappointed.

18. Amīr Khurd, *Siyarul Auliyā*, translated into Urdu by Ejazul Kudusi. Lahore. 1980, p. 390.
19. *Siyarul Ārifīn, op. cit.*, p. 131.
20. See Mohammad Habib. "Shaikh Nasīruddīn Mahmūd Chirāgh-i-Dehlī as a Great Historical Personality" in *Politics and Society during the Early Medieval Period*, ed. K.A. Nizami. Delhi: People's Publishing House, Vol. I, 1974 (for the Aligarh Muslim University, Department of History, Aligarh), p. 359, n. 6; see also K.A. Nizami, *Khairul Majālis*. Aligarh. 1958, introduction, p. 47.
21. Habib, *Shai<u>kh</u> Nasīruddīn Mahmud Chirāgh-i-Dehli*, p. 389, (see n. 20).
22. Khwājā Bandā Newāz was a great Chishtī saint and a disciple of Shai<u>kh</u> Nasīruddīn Chirāgh Dehlavī. He stayed for many years in Delhi, after the death of his master in A.D. 1356. It is said, that he left Delhi in 1413 and went to Gulbarga where he died in 1422. He had a large following including some Bahmani Kings who had a great regard for him. See Shyam Manohar Pandey, 1980, p. 137. Also, *cf.* Haroon Khan Sherwani's article "Bahmani Kingdom" in *A Comprehensive History of India*, vol. 5 (The Sultanate Period), ed., Mohammad Habib and K.A. Nizami. Delhi: People's Publishing House. 1970, pp. 982-84.
23. *Jawāmī ul Kalīm* was composed by Sayyid Husainī Akbar, the eldest son of Khwājā Bandā Newāz. In this, conversations of Khwājā Bandā Newāz of the year AH 802-803 (AD 1399-1400 AD) have been compiled. Sayyid Husaini died while his father was alive. Gesūdarāz himself made his tomb, which he used to visit. Sayyid Husainī used to write these conversations and get them checked by his father. The work has been translated into Urdu from Persian by Rahīmuddīn Husain, and published by Bandā Newāz Research Institute, Gulbarga, 1972-74.
24. Simon Digby, "Qalandars and Related Groups (Elements of Social Deviance in the Religious Life of the Delhi Sultanate of the Thirteenth and Fourtenth Centuries)", in *Islam in Asia*, ed. Y. Friedman. Jerusalem. 1984, vol. I, p. 95. See also Shyam Manohar Pandey, *Hindī aur Fārasī Sūfi Kāvya*. Allahabad. 1989, p. 25.

25. Shyam Manohar Pandey, *ibid.*, p. 26; *Jawāmi ul Kalīm*, *op. cit.* n. 23 (Urdu translation), p. 253.
26. Habib, *op. cit.*, n. 20, p. 384.
27. Habib, *ibid.*, p. 384.
28. *Siyar-i-Muhammadī* is a biography of the Sufi saint Sayyid Muhammad Gesūdarāz Bandā Newāz, which was completed by his disciple Muhammad Alī Samānī after the sixth year of his master's death in AD 1428. An Urdu translation with Persian text has been published by Bandā Newāz Research Institute, Gulbarga, in 1969; the Urdu translator is Sayyid Shah Nazir Qadari.
29. Simon Digby, "Tabarrukāt and Succession among the Great Chiśtī Shaykhs in Delhi through the Ages", in *Delhi through the Ages: Essays in Urban History and Culture*, ed. R.E. Frykenberg. Delhi: Oxford University Press. 1986, pp. 84-85.
30. *Ibid.*, pp. 80-91.
31. *Ibid.*, pp. 95-96.

Modes of Expression
(Themes, Symbols, Metaphors)

Modes of Expression
(Themes, Symbols, Metaphors)

Metaphors in the *Jñāndev Gāthā*

Catharina Kiehnle

The present study was inspired by Kvaerne's *Caryāgīti* edition and translation, that is, particularly by the images contained in those 'Buddhist Tantric Songs.'[1] The *Caryāgīti* were composed by the Buddhist *siddhācāryas* and date back roughly to the eleventh century. They are based on *kuṇḍalinīyoga* and therefore resemble in many respects the Old Marathi compositions on *yoga* which I have edited and translated during the last few years.[2] 'My' songs ('*abhaṅgas*') belong to the *Jñāndev Gāthā*, a collection attributed to Jñāndev, the author of the Old Marathi commentary on the *Bhagavadgītā ('Jñāneśvarī')*. I have dealt with the authorship question elsewhere, so may it suffice here to say that although some of the songs contained in the *Gāthā* might be by that very Jñāndev, there are indications that many of them were composed by other poets.[3] Consequently, their age is not homogeneous, though some of them may go back to the end of the thirteenth century. As to their contents, most of them reflect a world-view in which folk religion, classical Vaiṣṇavism, Nāth *yoga*, and *advaita* philosophy are harmonized.[4]

In my previous studies some literary aspects remained undiscussed, among them the metaphorical expressions. Although my research into that field is only at its initial stages, I shall present here a survey of various types of metaphors and their explanations in order to invite discussion.

Metaphor, 'transfer,' calling one thing another, is a device well-known in any language. Turbayne holds, for example, that even in science an 'objective' description of the world cannot even be imagined.[5] Such 'transfers' take place in various ways, in nouns, verbs, sentences, etc. Although it would be rewarding to classify the types of metaphor occurring in the *Jñāndev Gāthā* according to Christine Brook-Rose's principles or those of Sanskrit *Alaṅkāraśāstra*, I am not proposing to do so now.[6] First, for lack of time and second, because of the insufficient amount of critically edited material. Third, it seems that the Siddha sects of Northern India participated in a poetical tradition that can be considered in its own right. Whatever the origin of the so-called *sandhyā* or *sandhā bhāṣā*, be it folk or exclusively yogic, their application had developed into a particular poetic form around the eleventh century.[7] It survived in the Sants' compositions of the Middle Ages, and is still extant in the Baul tradition.

In this style, the sense in which many words or expressions are applied can often be understood only with the help of commentaries. In the case of the *Caryāgīti* this source is not always reliable because, for example, *kuṇḍalinīśakti* is a taboo of sorts to the commentator, who takes great pains to interpret the respective passages in Buddhist terms. Nevertheless, he provides information the present-day reader cannot get elsewhere. No commentaries exist for the 'Jñāndev' *abhaṅgas*, so the researcher is often thrown upon similar songs and related literature.

METAPHORS WITH EXPLANATION

There are of course metaphors which in themselves provide the solution, namely *karmadhāraya*-like formations such as *bhavasāgara*, 'ocean of (= which is) existence,' or *āli kāli ghaṇṭā*, 'the bells (which are) vowels and consonants' (CG 11.3). These are *rūpakas* proper in the *Alaṅkāraśāstra*. Jenner holds that they are no metaphors at all because according to Latin and Greek poetics the suggested object should not be mentioned in them.[8] Brook-Rose, however, admits expressions of the 'fire of love'/ *mukhacandra* type in her chapter about 'the genitive link,' and I think they should indeed be dealt with here because they fit the definition of 'calling one thing another.'[9] Examples from the Jñāndev collection occur in L 3.2. *dhāraṇecā hāte[ṃ] jevā dṛṣṭimukhe[ṃ]*, 'with the hand of *dhāraṇā*, eat with the mouth of vision.'[10] Also in allegories (prolonged methaphors) the reader is sometimes given help:

M 32

> *vara muleṃ śeṃḍā khālīṃ dise bāno /*
> *prapaṃcīṃ rāṇorāna vṛkṣa bā re // 1 //*
> *triguṇācyā śākhā upāśākhā bahuta /*
> *nānā yātī yeta pattreṃ jyāsa // 2 //*
> *pakva phala ahaṃ sohaṃ gōḍī tyācī /*
> *sevitāṃ jīvācī āsa pure // 3 //*
> *jñānadeva hmaṇe paripūrṇa jālā /*
> *bīja rūḍhalā jāṇivecā // 4 //*

"(1) The roots above, the top visible underneath, fellows, such a tree is visible in every forest of the world. (2) [Of the tree] to which come the numerous branches and twigs of the three *guṇas*, [and] various classes [of elements] as leaves, (3) the ripe fruit is *aham*, [and] its sweetness *so'ham*. Eating it, the hope of the soul is fulfilled. (4) Jñāndev says, [the tree] has become complete, the seed of knowledge has grown."[11]

With slight abridgements, the eternal *aśvattha* tree of the *Bhagavadgītā* stood sponsor here. In *Jñāneśvarī* 15.89 - 108, and in contemporaneous publications like Satyanand Sarasvati's *Kuṇḍalinītantra*, it serves as a metaphor not only of macrocosm but also of microcosm, which should be cut down with the sword of discrimination.[12] The image occurs in the *Caryāgīti* as well, for example:[13]

CG 45
maṇa taru pāñca indi tasu sāhā /
āsā bahala pāta phala bāhā[14] // 1 //
bara guru baaṇe kuṭhāre chijaa /
Kāṇha bhanaï taru puṇa na uijaa[15] // 2 //
bāṛhaï[16] *so taru subhāsubha pāṇī /*
chebaï bidujana guru parimāṇī // 3 //
jo taru cheba bheu na jāṇaï[17] /
saṛi paṛiā[18] *re mūṛha ṭā bhaba māṇaï* // 4 //
suna tarubara[19] *gaaṇa kuṭhāra /*
chebaha so taru mūla na ḍāla // 5 //

"(1) The mind is a tree (Munidatta, the commentator: as it is the basis of leaves in the form of the psychic-impressions of beginningless existence), the five senses the branches thereof; desire is the abundant foliage, its fruit is distress. (2) With the word of the best of Gurus [as] the axe it is cut; Kāṇha says: the tree does not grow up again. (3) That tree grows (M: on the ground of beginningless *saṃsāra*) due to the water of sin and virtue; [but] the wise man cuts it, [taking] the Guru as his authority. (4) Whoever does not know the secret of cutting (M: rendering free from own-being) the tree, he, having slipped and fallen (M: into the ocean of suffering of *saṃsāra*), O fool, experiences it as existence (M: again grasps existence). (5) The Void (M: the Ignorance-Void) is the tree, the Sky (Clear light) the axe - (M: by the grace of the Guru) cut down that tree (psychic impressions) [so that neither] roots nor branches (M: senses) [remain]!"

Kvaerne observes that the image of the tree is used here in three ways: "A. The *sahaja* or the void; B. the mind; C. the body. At first sight it seems strange that the same image should be employed to express that which is phenomenal and relative (the body) as well as the absolute (*sahaja*, etc.). However, I suggest that it is precisely the paradoxical identity of these two ontological opposites which the songs wish to stress; and while a dogmatic statement of this identity would never be convincing, it may be forcefully expressed by means of a symbol.... Thus if we regard the image of the Tree more closely, it will be seen that CG 45 speaks of one and the same tree throughout; whether it is regarded as the mind (45.1) or the Void (45.5), it is to be cut down, i.e. abandoned as being an *upāya*. The very fact that the Tree is an image of the mind (*manas, citta*) points to its ambiguity; for the mind itself is ambiguous, being simultaneously an aspect of man's empirical nature as well as the absolute ground of his being — thus while CG speaks of *mana taru* (45.1) and of *citta-taru* (M 45.2-4), *Saraha Dohākoṣa* 109 speaks of *addaa-citta taruara*, "the Non-Dual (hence Absolute) mind."[20]

Similary, in the *Jñāndev Gāthā* ignorance as well as knowledge can be called something a seed has grown into - presumably a tree because *paripūrṇa jālā* is masculine. In the light of the *mahākāraṇadeha* and the world, which are declared in the *yoga* songs to be *māyā* as well as *brahman*, or the *guru*, who is *saguṇa* as well as *nirguṇa*, it is perhaps not too far-fetched to suppose that also in the present context the identity of the universal opposites is alluded to.[21]

METAPHORS WITHOUT EXPLANATION: *KŪṬA*

Whereas in the previous examples the authors provided the key to their metaphors, they were not always so considerate, and composed songs listed by the editors of the *Gāthā*s under the name of *kūṭa*, 'riddle.' Twenty-four of them occur in P.N.Joshi's *Jñāndev Gāthā*. The following one is unpublished and belongs to the *yoga* collection:

M 20

ākāśim ho maḷā lāvilā bā eka /
vāṃjhecem bāḷaka śiṃpitase //1 //[22]
agnīkuṃda manem bāḷakeṃ nirmaleṃ /
pratyayāsī dekhileṃ mīyālāgiṃ // 2 //[23]
jñānadeva mhaṇe upharāṭeṃ pahātāṃ /
sarvasaukhyadātā nivṛtti eka // 3 //[24]

"(1) The son of a barren woman is watering one orchard planted in space. (2) The boy created a fire-pit with his mind. I beheld [his] idea for myself. [25](3) Jñāndev speaks, seeing inversely.[26] The giver of all happiness is Nivṛtti alone."

Sākhare and Joshi interpret the song rightly as an illustration of the world's irreality. Taking into account the Nāth context, the son of the barren woman may be the individual Self or *puruṣa* that originates from *māyā/virāṭ*. He is watering — possibly by means of the nectar stream originating below the *brahmarandhra* — the beginning stages of the microcosm in the space *cakra*. The fire-pit might be the *vahnibindu*, one dot of the triangle in the *brahmarandhra* that symbolizes among other things the division of the primordial One into observer, observed, and process of observing.[27]

'May be,' and 'might be' show how insecure the interpretation is when exclusively based on the readers' acquaintance with the *Jñāndev Gāthā* and related texts like those of *haṭhayoga* and of Kashmir Śaivism, and not on any living tradition. Such is also the case with another allegory from the realm of plants that has become famous all over India through the musical interpretation by Lata Mangeshkar:

A 64[28]

> *ivalese*[29] *ropa*[30] *lāvileṃ*[31] *dvārīṃ*[32] /
> *tyācā*[33] *vela*[34] *gelā gaganāvarī* // 1 //
> *mogarā phulalā mogarā phulalā* /
> *phuleṃ*[35] *veṃcītāṃ*[36] *atibāru*[37] *kaḷiyāṃsī*[38] *ālā*[39] /*dhru*//
> *manāc[iye*[40] *guṃtī]*[41] *guṃphilā*[42] *[jh]elā*[43] /
> *bāparakhumādevivarīṃ*[44] *viṭhṭhalīṃ*[45] *arpilā*[46] // 2 //

"(1) I planted a seedling at [my] door: its creeper grew up to the sky. (2) The jasmin bloomed, the jasmin bloomed. When I plucked the flowers, the buds reached their prime. (3) With the (entangled?) threads (?) of my mind I stringed a wristlet [and] offered it to the father, the husband of goddess Rakhumā, Viṭṭhal."

The popularity of the song is partly due to the fact that every member of the Vārkarī sect (the Maharashtrian variety of the Bhāgavata *sampradāya*) recognizes the Vaiṣṇava devotee in the allegory. According to an oral communication by S.G.Tulpule, it cannot mean anything else but the development of faith or *bhakti*. For P.N.Joshi (and for K.V.Belsare, who more or less follows him) the seedling is *ātmavidyā* or *adhyātmavidyā*, which develops flowers in the shape of *bhāvārtha*, 'loving faith' or *bhakti*.[47] Sākhare interprets the seedling in a similar way as the tree was explained above, namely as *kalpit māyecā aṅgīkār*, the acceptance of the imagined *māyā*, which brings us flowers in the form of happiness and sorrow until, with the help of the skill of our mind, we put an end to the whole *saṃsāra*, by offering it to Viṭṭhal. Those acquainted with the Nāth tradition, however, file the composition immediately under *kuṇḍalinīyoga*.[48] In fact, Dādū sings about a similar plant, and I think indeed, that this interpretation is the most satisfactory one.[49] Accordingly, the house is the body, the door *brahmadvāra*, the opening at the lower end of *suṣumnā nāḍī*. There, the awakened *kuṇḍalinī* enters and proceeds upward ('grows,' like a creeper) to the sky of the *yogī*s, the *ākāśacakra* in the region around the *brahmarandhra*. While ascending, she enlivens the *kamala*s (which are small and only faintly glowing in normal individuals) with *prāṇa* so that they unfold into the shining lotus-shaped centres of energy one knows from numerous illustrations.[50] During her ascent she collects all the elements of Sāṃkhya which are distributed over the *cakras*, binds them together with the entanglements of the mind, and leads them back into their origin, pure consciousness, hereby called Viṭṭhal.[51]

THE *RŪPAK*

Even if not all the solutions of the metaphors were handed down, the editors were aware of such figures, and in a particular genre of songs also knew the key to them. I am referring to the *rūpaks*, 'metaphors.' Whether already known by that name or not to the authors, they occur in all the collections from Jñāndev's to Tukārām's, from Nāmdev's to Eknāth's.

One variety of *rūpak* has been mentioned already, the *kūṭa*, which is, it seems, a type of *rūpak* that is harder to crack than the others. Normally, in the *rūpaks* the character of well-known objects, activities, or types of persons (often from folk-religion and low-caste communities) is obvious in itself or from the songs. A *ghoṃgaḍī*, for example, is a dark and rough blanket used particularly by rural people. From the compositions it becomes clear that as a metaphor it can stand for the *guṇas* spread over the Self (F 1036). It should be noted that the relation between *upameya* and *upamāna*, subject and object of (in this case) identification, are not always fixed. The cow (*gāy*), for example, is in one case Hari, in others respectively the *paramātmā*, the *sākṣī*, the *guṇas*, the human being, or, in one *yoga* song, the *amṛtacakra* (see below).

The following is a list of the *rūpaks* that are used in the *Jñāndev Gāthā*:[52]

pāḷaṇā, 'cradle song,' in F 1024 connected with a child without shape, which becomes agitated through the 21 *tattvas*, but is put again to sleep in his Self by god Viṭṭhal.

ṭiparī, a play with sticks, the sound of which is identified with the *anāhata dhvani* in F 1020

hamāmā, a children's play with the musical instrument *ghumrī*, by the sound of which *māyā* is said to disappear in F 1021.

phugaḍī, another play in which children are pooh-poohing each other; in F 1023 just that is done to *saṃsāra*.

gaḷatī, the vessel with a hole in the bottom through which milk streams onto a *śivaliṅga*—a metaphor of the teacher's compassion which is poured on the Self of the pupil in E 957.

ḍaur, the little drum of the *ḍavre gosāvīs*, the *bharāḍīs* (actually a variety of Nāths); its various sounds stand for false *saṃnyāsa*, erudition, *gurus*, *vratopāsakas*, and arrogant *yogī*s in I 1051.

ghoṃgadī, 'blanket,' and *gāy* 'cow,' see above.

pāṃguḷ, 'the lame one,' a traditional beggar who comes at dawn, sits on trees and walls, clad in *laṃgoṭī*, *ghoṃgadī*, turban, with begging bag and a stick with bells, modelled after the lame charioteer of the sun; his caste is something like *marāṭhā-kuṇbī*. In F 1008 the *sadguru* is praised who gives hands and feet to the lame, in F 1009 his call *dharma jāgo* occurs.

āṃdhaḷā, 'blind one' (F1011, 1012), a figure resembling the *pāṃguḷ*, but not mentioned by Ḍhere in his *Marāṭhī saṃskṛtīce upāsak*.

bāḷchaṃd, 'child's joy,' also called *bāḷsaṃtoṣ*, a mendicant wearing children's clothes: *marāṭhā-kuṇbī*; in F 1053 his *chaṃd*, 'joy,' is due to his unity with God.

vāsudev (a designation of Kṛṣṇa or a person belonging to him), appears at dawn, clad in white, with a hat made of peacock feathers, singing and playing flute, cymbals, castanets, accompanied by his ankle bells; *marāṭhā*; the members of the group claim to be descendents of a *brāhmaṇ* and a *kuṇbī* woman. He wakes people up with the call *oṃ namo vāsudevāya*, which is used in F 1005. In F1007 his way of singing and his instruments are referred to.

*goṃdhaḷī*s, musicians, singers and dancers whose main activities take place at *navrātra*. They once held an important position as possession priests. Because they are worshippers of the goddess, they praise Viṭṭhal as a woman friend and mother in F 1060 and 1061.

kāpaḍī, a sort of *yogī*, perhaps Nāth, wearing ascetic's clothes, endowed with stick and flag, and selling rosaries. In F 1058 the *kāpaḍī*s of the *uttarapantha* are at the same time pilgrims to Pandharpur who sing about the state of final emancipation.

mahār, a low caste servant who announces his presence to potential employers by calling out *johār māybāp*. In F 1052 he is Kṛṣṇa's servant waiting at the door. *Johār* is the actual designation of the songs.

pāīk, an armed attendant; in F 1029 the identity of god and his servant is stressed.

In many of the songs pertaining to activities and personalities, the author speaks as if he belonged to the respective group. One is therefore lead to the assumption that '*rūpak*' denotes here 'impersonation, (theatrical) performance' in the sense of the *Nāṭyaśāstra*.[53] The idea of '*imitatio*' is particularly obvious in the case of the *virahiṇī* (the woman separated from her lover/God) and the *gauḷāṇ* (milkmaid/*gopī* of Vṛṇḍāvan). They, too, come under *rūpak* in the *Gāthā* edition of Sākhare, who most probably would have shared the opinion of the author of the *Rāmakṛṣṇakathāmṛta*. The latter remarks with respect to Śrī Caitanya, that "in his ecstatic music Chaitanya assumed the role of Rādhā and manifested the longing to be united with Kṛṣṇa."[54] Similarly, Rāmakṛṣṇa "continued to sing, assuming the attitude of a woman devotee infatuated with love for Gauraṅga... assuming the mood of Rādhā, he sang in a voice laden with sorrow... Thus singing, he completely lost himself in Rādhā and could not continue the song..." etc.[55]

Another type of woman is the *saurī*, or *sairī*, a sister of the *abhisārikā* of Sanskrit poetry, with a cousin also in the Vīraśaiva *vacanas*.[56] She is the independent woman who frees herself from family ties, or, in the songs called *aṃbulā* and *dādula* ('husband'), a woman who seeks for happiness with the *parapuruṣa* ('the other man' and 'the highest being'), irrespective of reproaches:

F 320

> *hoya saurī ātāṃ ughaḍā ghālī māthā /*
> *parapuruṣiṃ ramalyā bāī tyācī pativratā // 1 //*

"I have become now an independent woman, [and] make my

head bare. Woman, only those who enjoy in the other man/ the highest being are faithful wives."

F 313.1a

varhāḍa na hotāṃ hotoṃ kheḷemeḷe /

"Although there was no marriage, we were living in fun and merriment."

F 303

aṃbulā māherīṃ bhogi ghaṇīvarī /
maga tayā śrīhari sāṃgo gūja // 1 //
mājheṃ sukha mīca bhogīna /
kṣemeṃsī nigena aṃgoaṃgīṃ // 2 //
sāṃdunī kulācāra jālīye nirlajja /
tumhī kāya maja śikavāla // 3 //

"(1) In the house of my mother I enjoy my husband to my heart's content, then I tell to this Śrīhari (my) secret. (2) I shall enjoy my own happiness, I shall go for an embrace body to body. (3) Abandoning the family rules I became shameless — what will you (people) teach me?"

Whereas in the *bhakti* songs of the *Jñāndev Gāthā* the devotee is female, and God or *paramātmā* male, the *Caryāgīti* have it the other way round. The *sādhaka* is male, and the entity aimed at, *nairātmā* (*sahajasundarī* in CG 28.2), female. Both are called by various names, so that the *ḍombi, meherī, śabarī, mataṅgī, baṅgālī, caṇḍālī* may amuse herself with the *kāpālī, cora, śabara, baṅgāla,* or *caṇḍāla:*

CG 10

ālo[57] *ḍombi toe sama karibe ma sāṅga /*
nighiṇa Kāṇha kāpāli joi lāga // 2 //

"Ho Ḍombi! I shall associate with you, (I,) Kāṇha, a *kāpāli*-yogin, shameless (M: free from the fault of shame, etc.) *and naked.*"

Munidatta explains 'naked' as 'thus obtaining perfection, the Great Seal consisting of the union of Wisdom and Means.'

I think, however, with the Nāth songs in mind, one can explain 'naked' in a more comfortable way: the moment Kāṇha reaches the point where the two opposites unite, all the *tattvas* and the three *guṇas* disappear and leave whatever has remained as an observer without the cover of the relative. Moreover, one should note that in the background of the Jñāndev *yoga* songs, the female entity of the Buddhists might also be *suṣumnā* (Buddhist *avadhūtikā*) or *kuṇḍalinī*. In the *abhaṅgas*, she is just *nārī*, 'woman,' without the sexual frills of the *bhakti* compositions or the *Caryāgīti*:

M 67

ādhārāpāsūnī sahasradaḷāvarī /
niḥśabda niraṃtarī nārī eka //
jñānadeva mhaṇe anubhava jetha /
toci jīvanmukta saṃta yogī // 2 //[58]

"(2) From *ādhāra[cakra]* up to the thousand-petalled [lotus reaches] the one woman, soundless, uninterrupted.[59] (3) Jñāndev says, in whom [there is such an] experience, he alone is one liberated while living, a *santa*, a *yogī*."

The constituents of the relative are the relatives (particularly the in-laws) who are done away with. The Buddhists and the Maharashtrian poet-saints tackle the matter with equal relish:

F 309

saguṇa aṃbulā nirguṇa paiṃ jālā /
gharācāra samasta buḍavilā // 1 //
āśā he sāsu asatāṃ buḍavilī /
śānti māūlī bheṭoṃ ālī // 2 //

"(1) The husband with properties has been left without, [I] drowned the whole household. [2] I drowned hope, she being the mother-in-law, [and] mother peace came to visit [me]."

F 315

aṃbulā vikunī pavitra jhālī /
poṭīṃcīṃ bāleṃ kautukīṃ mārilīṃ // 1 //

"I sold my husband (or: I sold myself to the husband) [and] became pure; out of love I killed the children in my womb."

CG 11

māria[60] *śāsu*[61] *naṇanda ghare śālī*[62]
māa māria[63] *Kāṇha bhaïla*[64] *kabālī* // 5 //

"(5) Killing (M: rendering free from own-being) the mother-in-law (M: vital-breath), the aunt (M: the senses), and sister-in-law in the house,[65] killing the mother (M: *māyā*), Kāṇha became a Kāpālika (able to retain great Bliss)."

This type of allegory is also found among the Vīraśaiva *vacanas*.[66] It was still in vogue at the time of Eknāth (sixteenth century) whose *sairī* promises to offer goddess Bhavānī a *roḍgā* (a baked dough) if she wipes out the family — except for the sister-in-law who should be widowed, and her child who should have itch all over.[67]

TECHNICAL TERMS

The vast majority of metaphors in the *Jñāndev Gāthā* is less spectacular, but nevertheless important for a general classification. For example, the *cakras*, 'wheels,' or *kamalas*, 'lotuses,' which are designations of the energy centres along the spine are ex-metaphors (like the 'neck' of a bottle), because they are generally accepted vocables.[68] Other technical terms, like *candra*, 'moon,' (the origin of the *amṛta* liquid the *yogīs* experience in their bodies) have remained within the limits of *yoga* jargon. Such expressions can be called 'metaphor' only with reservation because they do not stand for anything else but fill gaps in the language. The subject of *yoga* makes it occasionally rather difficult to find out what they actually designate, especially since many of them belong to the network of Tantric philosophy.[69] Particularly knotty examples are *trikūṭa*, *golhāṭa*, and *śrīhāṭa* (places near the *brahmarandhra*) or *haṃsa*, 'goose' (denoting the Self which is connected with the body); *auṭhapīṭha*, 'seat of three and a half' (the space between forehead and *brahmarandhra*, filled by the three and a half elements of the *praṇava*); *sattrāvī kalā*, 'the seventeenth digit' (the origin of the *moon* near the *brahmarandhra* from which the *amṛta* flows), etc. The technical terms gave rise to 'real' metaphors sometimes, such as *gāy*, 'cow,' for the moon just mentioned. This cow was taken literally by later teachers of the *cakra* system, who considered it as a mythical animal and provided a painting of it.[70]

A resurrection not in iconography but in apparent surrealism happened to the *haṃsa*:[71]

M 42.0.1

motīyāce ḍohī buḍālā caṃdramā /
to hmaṇe vihaṃgamā kāḍ[h]ī maja // 1 //[72]
vih[aṃ]gama jhepāvalā jaḷacare grāsīlā /
ca[ṃ]dre māvaḷalā muṃgīmukhī // 2 //[73]
volhāvaleṃ cāṃdane prakāśe nirālamba /
teṃ bija svayaṃbha sattrāvīce // 3 //[74]
jñānadeva hmaṇe anubhavī jāṇe /
saṃta yeṇe khuṇe saṃtoṣītī // 4 //[75]

"(1) The moon drowned in the depth of the pearl. He (the moon) says to the bird: 'pull me out!' (2) The bird jumped forward [and] was swallowed by the one [walking] in the water (or: by the aquatic animal). The moon set in the mouth of the ant. (3) The moonlight has cooled down, the supportless one shines forth: that is the self-existing seed of the seventeenth. (4) Jñāndev says, the one endowed with experience knows. The *santas* become content by that sign."

The meaning is that during the last steps of *kuṇḍalinī*'s ascent, in the course of the dissolution of everything existing, the moon in the *sahasradala* seems to disappear in the blue pearl (the most subtle body, the *mahākāraṇadeha*, also called the 'eye of an ant'). The *haṃsa*-bird is the incorporated Self in the triangle inside the moon.[76] It still exists at the beginning of the experience but cannot help getting swallowed as well by 'the one walking in the water,' which is either the moon, or *caitanya* inside the blue pearl. The latter possibility is more probable because 'water,' may also mean 'lustre' in connection with pearls, and lustre is in fact an important element of the most subtle fields of consciousness.[77] 'Getting swallowed' means that the trinity of seer, seen, and the process of seeing (or the trinity of the three *guṇas*, considered to be a triangle in the moon) breaks down at that time.

To conclude, many songs of the *Jñāndev* and other *Gāthās* by the Maharashtrian poet saints are not isolated from the rest of Indian literature but belong to the Siddha tradition. Not only the compositions on *yoga* resemble the *Caryāgīti* with respect to the usage of metaphors, but also in *bhakti* songs one finds similarities. Trees, creepers, lotuses, geese, cows, milk-oozing moons, blue pearls, temple walls, golden neck ornaments, sparkling eyes, fire wheels, etc. make up a universe of beauty deserving the attention not only of *bhaktas* but of lovers of poetry. To uncover the treasures, research in several directions is necessary. The basic requirements, of course, are editions as critical as possible. Only then, can one think of preparing

— a dictionary of technical terms and metaphors

— a 'Grammar of Metaphors,' similar to the one by C. Brook-Rose, also taking into account the poetical tradition in Sanskrit

— translations and explanations of the *kūṭa* and *rūpaks* on the background of folk traditions and poetical conventions of the Siddhas

— comparative studies of the metaphors in the *abhaṅgas* and those of *Anubhavāmṛt* and *Jñāneśvarī*

— a 'map' of metaphors, showing their distribution over various regions of India

— etc.

BIBLIOGRAPHY

Aklujkar, Vidjut. 'In Search of the Unholy Cow.' *Religious Traditions*, in print.

Baḍthvāl, Pītāmbardatt (ed., comm.). 1979 (1943). *Gorakh-Bānī*. 4th edn, Prayāg. Hindī Sāhitya Sammelan.

Belsare, K.V. 1988. *Saṃtāṃce ātmacaritra*. Mumbaī: Tridal (?) Prākāśan.

Bhagavadgītā: Sastry, Alladi Mahadeva (transl.). 1977 (1897). Madras: Samata Books.

Bhattacharya, Biswanāth. 1982. *A History of Rūpaka in the Alaṅkāra-śāstra*. Vārāṇasī/Delhi: Chaukhambha Oriental Research Studies 23.

Broido, Michael M. 1985. 'Intention and Suggestion in the Abhidharmakośa: Sandhābhāṣā revisited.' *Journal of Indian Philosophy*, 13, pp. 327-81.

Brooke-Rose, Christine. 1958. *A Grammar of Metaphor*. London: Secker & Warburg.

Ḍhere, R.C. n.d. *Marāṭhī lokasaṃskṛtīce upāsak*. Puṇeṃ?: Jñānarāj Prakāśan.

Eknāth Gāthā in: Jośī, Kāśīnāth Anaṃt (ed.). 1967 (1923). *Śrīsakalasaṃtagāthā*, pt. II. 2nd edn. Puṇeṃ: Śrīsaṃtavāṇmāyā Prākāśan Maṃdir.

Gerow, Edwin. 1971. *A Glossary of Indian Figures of Speech*. The Hague/Paris: Mouton.

Jenner, Gero. 1968. *Die poetischen Figuren der Inder von Bhāmaha bis Mammaṭa*. Schriften des Europa-Kollegs Hamburg Bd. 5. Hamburg: Ludwig Appel Verlag.

Jñāndev. *Śrījñāneśvarī*. 1977 (ed.) Mahārāṣṭra Rājya Śikṣaṇ Vibhāg, Sacivālaya, Muṃbaī.

——, Gokhle, V.D. (ed.). 1967, 1968. *Anubhavāmṛt* by Jñāndev. 2 vols., Puṇeṃ: Nīlkaṃṭh Prākāśan.

——, *Abhaṅga Gāthās*:

A Goṃdhḷekar, Rāvjī Śrīdhar; Goḍbole, Raghunāth Bhāskar (ed.). 1891. *Śrī Jñāndevācā Gāthā*. 2nd edn. Puṇeṃ: Jagaddhitecchu Press.

A1 Pāṃgaḷ, Tātyā Nemināth (ed.). 1927. *Śrī Jñāneśvar Mahārājaṃcī Gāthā*. Puṇeṃ: Sarasavāṇgmaya Prasārak Maṃḍalī.

B Dātār, Goviṃd Nārāyaṇ Śāstrī (ed.). 1906. *Śrī Jñāneśvarmahārājācyā Abhaṃgāṃcī Gāthā*. Muṃbaī and Vaḍoḍeṃ: Dāmodar Sāṃvlārām āṇī maṃḍalī.

C Jog, Viṣṇu Narasiṃha (ed.). 1907. *Jñāndevācī Gāthā*.

Puṇeṃ: Iṃdirā Press.

C1 Jośī, Kāśīnāth Anaṃt (ed.). 1967 (1923). *Śrīsakalasaṃtagāthā* pt. 1. Puṇeṃ: Śrīsaṃtavāṅmāyā Prākāśan Maṃdir.

D Avṭe, Tryambak Hari (ed.). 1923. *Śrījñāndevmahārāj yāṃcyā Abhaṃgāṃcī Gāthā.* Puṇeṃ: Iṃdirā Press.

E Sākhare, V. N. (ed.) 1934. *Śrījñāneśvarmahārāj yāṃcī Sārtha Gāthā.* Āḷaṃdī: Sādhakāśram.

E1 Paṃḍit, B.J. (ed.). Śake 1899. *Śrī Jñāneśvar Mahārāj viracit Amṛtānubhav, Cāṃgdevpāsaṣṭī, Haripāṭh, Abhaṃgagāthā.* Āḷaṃdī devācī: Śrījñāneśvarmahārāj Saṃsthān.

F Jośī, Pralhād Narahara (ed.). 1969. *Sārtha Śrī Jñāndev Abhaṃga Gāthā.* Puṇe: Suvicār Prākāśan Maṃḍal.

—— *Haripāṭh*, see C.Vaudeville, L'Invocation.

Kiehnle, Catharina. (1994).1. *The Sealed Letter, Texts and Teachings of the Mahārāṣṭrian Nāth Yogīs.*

—— (1994).2. *A Garland of Songs on Yoga.*

—— (1994).3. *The Conservative Vaiṣṇava.*

—— 1992. 'Authorship and Redactorship of the Jñāndev *Gāthā.*' In McGregor (ed.) *Devotional Literature in South Asia.* Cambridge: Cambridge University Press, pp. 126-137.

Kuḷkarṇī, S.R., (ed.). 1958. *Jñāndevviracit kapilagītokta Pañcamudrā.* Muṃbaī: *Marāṭhī Saṃśodhan Patrikā* varṣa 5, aṃka 4.

Kvaerne, Per. 1977. *An Anthology of Buddhist Tantric Songs, A Study of the Caryāgīti.* Det Norske Videnskaps-Akademi, II. Hist.-Filos. Klasse, Skrifter, Ny Serie No. 14. Oslo: Universitetsforlaget. 2nd edn. Bangkok: White Orchid Press, 1986.

Leadbeater, C.W. 1984. *Die Chakras. Eine Monographie über die Kraftzentren im menschlichen Aetherkoerper.* 5. Auflage, Freiburg i.Br.: Verlag Hermann Bauer.

Master, Alfred. 1964. *A Grammar of Old Marāṭhī.* Oxford: Clarendon Press.

Michaël, Tara. 1979. *Corps Subtil et Corps Causal: 'La description des six Cakra' et quelques textes sanscrits sur le Kuṇḍalinī Yoga.* Paris: Le Courrier du Livre.

Molesworth, J.T. 1975. *Marāṭhī-English Dictionary.* Corrected reprint, Poona: Śubhadhā Sārasvat.

Musaeus, Johann August. 1920. *Volksmaerchen der Deutschen,* mit einer Einleitung, einem Woerterverzeichnis und Anmerkungen herausgegeben von I.E.Poritzky, erster Band. Berlin: Propylaeen-Verlag.

Nieraad, Juergen. 1977. *"Bildgesegnet und bildverflucht,"*

Forschungen zur sprachlichen Metaphorik. Erträge der Forschung, Bd. 63. Darmstadt: Wissenschaftliche Buchgesellschaft.

Nikhilananda, Swami (transl.). 1974 (1944). *The Gospel of Śrī Ramakrishna* (by 'M,' Mahendranāth Gupta). 6th edn. Madras: Śrī Ramakrishna Math.

Ok, Vāman Dājī. 1894. *Anek kavikṛta padeṃ, kaṭāv, lāvṇyā vagaire padasaṃgraha*. Kāvyasaṃgraha 13 pt. 1. Muṃbaī: Nirṇayasāgar Press.

Panse, M.G. 1953. *Linguistic Peculiarities of the Jñāneśvarī*. Repr. from *Bulletin of the Deccan College Research Insitute* X, Poona, (contains an index verborum of the *Jñāneśvarī*).

Ramanujan, A.K. 1979 (1973). *Speaking of Śiva*. Harmondsworth: Penguin Books.

Ruegg, D. Seiffort. 1985. 'Purport, Implication and Presupposition: Sanskrit *abhiprāya* and Tibetan *dgoṅs pa / dgoṅs gži* as Hermeneutical Concepts.' *Journal of Indian Philosophy 13*, pp. 309-25. Dordrecht/Boston: D.Reidel Publishing Company.

Šāligrām, B.T. 1979. *Śrī Jñāneśvarāṃcā Paṃtharāj: bhaktimārgādhiṣṭhit kuṃḍalinī yogāvarīl saṃśodhan*. Puṇe: Svādhyāy Mahāvidyālay Prākāśan.

Satyananda Sarasvati. 1984. *Kundalinī Tantra*. Munger: Bihar School of Yoga.

Shahidullah, M. (ed., transl.). 1928. *Les Chant Mystiques de Kāṇha et de Saraha, Les Doha-Koṣa (en apabhraṃśa, avec les versions tibétaines) et les Caryā (en vieux-Bengalī), avec introduction, vocabulaires et notes, édités et traduits*. Textes pour l'étude du Bouddhisme tardif. Paris: Adrien-Maisonneuve.

Thiel-Horstmann (transl.), M. 1991. *Dādū, Lieder*. Beiträge zur Südasienforschung Bd. 138, Südeasien-Institut Heidelberg, Stuttgart: Franz Steiner.

Thieme, Paul. 1966. 'Das Indische Theater.' In H.Kindermann (ed.) *Fernöstliches Theater*, Stuttgart: Alfred Kroener, pp. 22- 120.

Tulpule, S.G. 1979. *Classical Marāṭhī Literature, From the Beginning to A.D. 1818*. A History of Indian Literature, Vol. IX, fasc. 4, Wiesbaden: Otto Harrassowitz.

Turbayne, C.M. 1962. *The Myth of Metaphor*. Revised edn. 1970. New Haven.

Vaudeville, Charlotte. 1969. *L'Invocation, Le Haripāṭh de Dñyāndev*. Paris, Publications de l'École Française d'Extrême-Orient vol. LXXIII. Adrien-Maisonneuve.

——, 1987. 'The Shaivite Background of Santism in Maharashtra.' In Milton Israel and N.R. Wagle (eds.) *Religion and Society in*

Maharashtra. South Asian Studies Paper 1, Centre for South Asian Studies. Toronto: University of Toronto.

NOTES

1. Kvaerne 1977. - Note on the transliteration in the following: Sanskrit is transcribed according to the established rules, except for a few Marathi *tatsamas*. In Old Marathi the (later) inherent *-a-* is pronounced and therefore written. In modern Marāṭhī, the actual pronunciation is the guideline.
2. Kiehnle, (1994).1,2.
3. Kiehnle (1994). 1,2 (introduction), 3, and Vaudeville, 1969: 1-18.
4. Vaudeville 1987: 5-8, Kiehnle (1994).1: ch. VI E.
5. Turbayne 1962: 5, quoted after Nieraad 1977: 108.
6. Brook-Rose 1958: 195; for *rūpaka* in the *Alaṅkāraśāstra* see e.g. Bhattacarya 1982; Gerow 1971, especially 131-39 (*utprekṣā* and *rūpaka*), 239-259 (*rūpaka*); Jenner 1968: 64 - 71, 179-88.
7. Kvaerne 1977: 5 - 7; for a rediscussion of origin and meaning of *sandh(y)ābhāṣā* see Broido and Seiffort Ruegg 1985.
8. Jenner 1968: 68.
9. Brooke-Rose 1958: 148.
10. CG stands for *Caryāgīti* in the following, L for the collection of 8 songs on *yoga* (*Lākhoṭā*) which are dealt with in Kiehnle (1994).1, M (*Mālā*) for the 138 *yoga* songs in Kiehnle (1994).2. For the remaining abbreviations see the bibliography under 'Jñāndev.' Those which are not explained concern the ms readings.
11. Kiehnle (1994).1: ch. VI D 1 a. 1ab) S1,2 inverse *śeṃḍā khālīṃ*; b) S1 *bāīno*, S2 *bāīyāno*. 2c) S1 *yāt*, S2 *yāta* 'in it,' for *yeta*, which is also possible. *Yeta* is *yeti*, changed for the sake of rhyme with *bahuta*. d) S1 *mātra* for *pattreṃ*; S1 *tyāsī* for *jyāsa*, S2 *sāce*; 3a) S1 *prakṛta* for *pakva*; b) S2 *yāci* for *tyācī*. 4b) mss and editions add *vṛkṣa* at the beginning of the *caraṇ*. It is lacking (and rightly so) in S2 because it is merely explanatory and spoils the metre.
12. BhG 15.1 *ūrdhvamūlam adhaḥśākham aśvatthaṃ prāhur avyayam / chandāṃsi yasya parṇāni yas taṃ veda sa vedavit*; 2 *adhaś cordhvaṃ prasṛtās tasya śākhā guṇapravṛddhā viṣayapravālāh / adhaś ca mūlāny anusantatāni / karmānubandhīni manuṣyaloke.*

13. Here and elsewhere in this study, texts and translations of the *Caryāgīti* are taken from Kvaerne 1977.
14. S *pātaha bāhā.*
15. AS *-aü.*
16. S, M *bāṭ-.*
17. S *bhebaü na jāiṇa.*
18. AS-*ã.*
19. S *sunataru M suna tarubara.*
20. Kvaerne 1977: 42.
21. For the identity of opposites see Kiehnle (1994).1: ch. VI C 8 c, VI D 1 a, and VI D 3.
22. a) with S 1,2; rest no *ho*; b) S1 *lāviyelā*, S1 no *bā*, C1 *vā.*
23. a) S1 *āgnikuṃḍā*, S2 *manā*; b) S1 *bālaka*, S2 *nirmili*; c) S2 *dekhīlī.*
24. d) *nivṛtīrāja*, S2 *nivṛtila.*
25. *Dekhileṃ* (c) is apparently used with an indirect object (*pratyayāsī*) as in modern Marathi.
26. Kiehnle (1994).1: ch. VI B.
27. Kiehnle (1994).1: ch. VI D 1 a.
28. The basic version is taken from the earliest *Gāthā* edition by Rāvjī Śrīdhar Goṃdhḷekar (A, 1891), the rest from the later *Gāthās* (see the bibliography), a poetry collection by Vāman Dājī Ok, a manuscript made available by V.C.Ḍhere (Ḍh), and Latā Maṅgeśkar's record (LM). Square brackets in the song indicate readings from versions other than A.
29. B,C,C1,D *ivaleṃseṃ*, E, E1,F *ivaleseṃ*, Ḍh *ivalesa.*
30. Ok for *ivalese ropa: kaivalyasvarūpa.*
31. B *lāviyeleṃ*, Ḍh *lāvīle*, Ok *lāvīyeleṃ*, LM *lāviyale*(*ṃ*?).
32. Ḍh *dārī*, which might be the original reading (Sanskrit forms being often a sign of modernization). It is, however, also possible that *varī* of the next line made the poet choose the form with *v.*
33. LM *tayācā.*
34. F, LM *velu:* unsupported by the mss; the ending may have been supplied by educated editors who expected the ancient nominative ending.
35. Ḍh *phule.*
36. B *veṃcitāṃ vecitāṃ*, C,C1 *vecitā*, Ḍh *vecītā.*
37. Ḍh *ātībharu*; LM *baharu* does away with *ati*, which is slightly misplaced in connection with a Persian word. The *Gāthā* editors (C,C1,D,E,E1,F), too, felt uncomfortable with the *duṣṭasamās*, and substituted *(ati)bhāru*, 'great weight/burden,' for *baharu*, 'the season or state of greatest abundance' (Molesworth); B note on *bāru: bahāra.*

38. B,E,E1,F *kaḷiyāṃsī*, D *kaḷiyāsī*, Dh *kaḷīyāsī*.
39. Ok for the whole line: *phuleṃ veṃcī tāta bā! rūkaḷī yāsī ālā*, a fine example for a wrong division of words.
40. with C,C1,D,E,E1,F; Ok *manāciye*; A,A1,B,Ḍh,LM *maṇāce*.
41. with C,C1,D,E,E1,F; LM *guṃteṃ*, which is actually singular, but explained on the record by 'by the threads.' A,A1,B *yugutīṃ*; Ḍh *vīgutī*; Ok *maṇīṃ*. Neither of the readings is satisfactory. Prof. S.G.Tulpule suggests *guṃphā(ṃ)*, 'in the recesses (of my mind),' which is an ingenious conjecture, but unsupported by the readings, and not within the image of the song where something like strings can be expected. I think, either *guṃthaṇeṃ* 'to string,' lies behind *guṃtīṃ* (with the aspirate having been lost during transmission), or *guṃtaṇeṃ*, 'to tangle, to be occupied,' of which exists according to Panse *guṃtī*, 'obstacle, difficulty.' The latter would point to the sufficiently known entanglements of the mind, which disappear the moment *kuṇḍalinī* reaches her destination.
42. A1,C,C1,D,E,E1,F,Ok,LM *guṃphiyelā*; Ḍh *guṃphilā*.
43. With Ok; editions, LM *śela*; Ḍh *selā*, or a faint possibility of *jhelā*. So *śelā*, 'a sort of scarf,' is supported by the mss and editions. Nevertheless it is wrong (S.G.Tulpule, oral). In Ḍhere's ms it is obvious how the reading came into existence: *jhe* is almost indistinguishable from *se* in handwriting.
44. A1 *-devīṃ-*; B *-devī-*, C,C1 *-vara-*, D,E,E1,F *-varu-*; Ḍh *bāparakumādevīvarī*, Ok *baparakhumadevīvaru*. The locative *-varīṃ* indicates the care with which the flowers are put there (note the difference between *mahādevālā phuleṃ ghātaleṃ* and *mahādevāvarīm phuleṃ ghātaleṃ*).
45. Ḍh *vīṭalī*, Ok *vīṭhṭhalā*, LM *viṭṭhalem*?
46. Ḍh *ārpilā*.
47. Belsare 1988: 45.
48. As Mukund Lath assured me during the Bhakti conference in Paris, this is so with North Indian listeners (who are apparently more accustomed to the Nāth elements in Sant literature than the Maharashtrians).
49. Thiel-Horstmann 1991: 172-73 (song 8.36), 263 (20.21).
50. Leadbeater 1984: 4.
51. The Buddhist and the Vaiṣṇava Sahajiyās, and the Nāths, called the same entity by the name they had for the highest principle in their respective traditions.
52. The descriptions of *pāṃguḷ*, *bāḷchaṃd*, *vāsudev*, *bharāḍī*, and *goṃdhaḷī* are taken from V.C. Ḍhere's *Marāṭhī lokasaṃskṛtīce upāsak*.
53. Thieme 1966: 29.

54. Nikhilananda 1974: 398. I am referring to the translation because I could not get hold of the Bengali original so far.
55. Nikhilananda 1974: 246, 398.
56. Ramanujan 1973: 49-52, 135, 141.
57. M *alo.*
58. Kiehnle (1992).1: ch. VI A 2. (2cd) S1 *niśadī yekalīca nārī niraṃtara*, S2 *nīśadava* (?) *nīraṃtarī yekalīca;* 3b editions and S1 *anubhava aisā jetheṃ*, S2 *ānubhavī jāṇe; aisā* is an explanatory addition, see the last list of Kiehnle, 1992.1 (1992): ch. III D 2; S2 *hmaṇe yogirāja.*
59. For the play on *nārī-nāḍī* in Tantric texts see *Jñāndev Gāthā* F 762.1, 804.1, perhaps 249, 1070, M 71.5,8, etc., and B.T.Śāligrām 1979: 351-56.
60. M *mārī.*
61. AS *sāsu.*
62. AS *s-.*
63. AS *āa mārī.*
64. Ś *bhaïa.*
65. After 'house,' 'Lotus of Great Bliss' is added in brackets, which must be a mistake because whatever is killed belongs to the created world within the body.
66. Ramanujan 1973: 49.
67. *Eknāth Gāthā* no. 3920, Tulpule 1979: 357.
68. See Nieraad 1977: 2ff for the usage of metaphors.
69. The following terms are dealt with in Kiehnle (1994).1: ch. VI A 1 - 3, C 7, D 1 a.
70. Kiehnle (1994).1: ch. VI C 7, Michaël 1979: 217; V. Aklujkar deals with a song from the *Gorakhbānī* but interprets the cow as *kuṇḍalinī* by mistake.
71. The song is also dealt with in Kiehnle (1992).1: ch. VI D 1 c.
72. a) S6 *motiyāṃce*; c) editions drop *hmaṇe.*
73. a) *vih[aṃ]gama* with orthographical variations in all the mss. b) *jaḷacare* with S2b, S4; S3 *jaḷacex*(?); S2a,7,8 *jaḷacarī[ṃ]* ('in the one walking in the water/the aquatic animal,' which is also possible). S7 *ceṃdra;* S2b,S3 *voḷalā*, S8 *nimālā;* 2d) S7 *muṃgīsukhī;*
74. a) *volhāvaleṃ* with S8; S2a *vikāśale*, S3 *vikāśele*, S2b *vikāśe*, S4 *voḷale*, S7 *voḷaleṃ*, S6 *vixx;* b) *prakāśe* with S2b, S7 *prakāśa*, rest *prakāśale* (which increases the number of syllables unduly); *nirālamba* with S8 (*nirālaba*); S2a *nirāveva*, S2b,3 *nīreva*, S7 *niḷārambha*, S4 *biṃba;* c) with S7,8; S2a *tevī jaḷa svayaṃbha*, S2b *te jaḷa svayameva*, S3 *te jaḷa svayaṃbha*, S4 *teci sohaṃbija*, S6 *ye bijaxxx;* in S8 another stanza is

added here: *lopalyā caṃdrakaḷā dṛṣṭī māvaḷalī / sekhi pāhu ālā caṃdrabi[ṃ]bā.* The rhyme in b,c is defective, but cannot be mended for lack of other versions. Translation: 'The digits of the moon disappeared, vision vanished, in the end the disk of the moon came into sight.' The last part of the sentence does not make sense in the context of the song: the whole *abhaṅga* and the beginning of the sentence ask for the disappearance of the moon.

75. b) with the majority of mss; S7 *saṃtācī he khūṇa*; S8 *hecī voḷakhaṇeṃ*; cd) S7 *ajñāna āpaṇa jāṇatī nā*; c) with S2a,b, S3,4; S8 *bhakta hecī khuṇa*; d) with 2b; S2a *saṃtoṣale*; S4 *pusatila.*

76. The *brahmarandhra* is called *sthāna vihaṃgamāce* in *Pañcamudrā* 14. The *Pañcamudrā* is a small work attributed to the *Jñāneśvarī* Jñāndev (Kuḷkarṇī 1958).

77. Kiehnle (1994).1, ch. VI D 2b. It is interesting to note that Musaeus 1920: 55, also describes pearls 'von dem reinsten Wasser,' 'of the purest water.'

Images and Expressions of Beauty in the Works of Tulsīdās

Teiji Sakata

I

Tulsīdās, the leading *bhakti* poet of the sixteenth century, created many religious literary works by drawing materials from various sources. He is widely esteemed for having established Hindu Rām *bhakti* literature and for inculcating moral precepts among his contemporaries. Tulsīdās wrote about the life of the hero Rām in the epic *Rāmcaritmānas* in Awadhi and in the rather compact *Gītāvalī* in Braj-bhāṣa. Such a poet, who enjoyed rich religious literary traditions and was adept in the two main Hindi literary dialects of his day, is naturally expected to have created suitable images and expressions for each situation in the life of Rām. In this paper, the expressions that depict "beauty" will first be illustrated, then examined according to the contexts and situations in which they are employed, and lastly brief comments will be made about particular expressions that seem to have been of special importance to the poet in creating and expressing his images.

The examples will be drawn basically from the first half of the so-called *Bāl kāṇḍ* of *Gītāvalī* and *Rāmcaritmānas*. Some will also be taken from an interpolated portion of the *Rāmcaritmānas*, viz. *Lav-Kuś kāṇḍ*, in order to compare images and expressions created by Tulsīdās with those added or interpolated by later people. The numbers given in parentheses after the examples refer to the song number and line of *Gītāvalī* and the *dohā/caupāī* number of *Rāmcaritmānas*. The texts relied upon are: *Gītāvalī*, ed. Kamlapati Tripathi, et al. (*Tulsī granthāvalī*, vol. 2), Varanasi, *saṃvat* 2031; *Rāmcaritmānas*, edited and annotated by Hanumānprasād Poddār, Gorakhpur, *saṃvat* 2018; and the *Lav-Kuś kāṇḍ* of *Gosvamī Tulsīdāsjī kṛt Rāmayaṇ*, edited and annotated by Jvālaprasād Miśra, Bombay, *saṃvat* 2027.

II

The concept of "beauty" may differ from person to person and from language to language. Semantically, "beauty" can be explained as that which delights the sight or other senses or mind of the person who experiences it. The range of the sensory experience will include at least what can be observed by the eyes and what can be heard by the ears. More complex and abstract phenomena may also be accepted as "beauty".

We have ample material to illustrate which words are traditionally understood to represent "beauty" or that which is "beautiful". A small glossary compiled by Sudhākar Śukla to provide synonyms of important notions or concepts useful in Hindi poetry, entitled *Śabd sudhākar* (Tikamgarh, 1952), gives forty *nām* ("names", pp.167-68) related to <*sundara*> ("beautiful"). Transcribed below are the words or phrases as given in the glossary, with conjunctions in parentheses:

rucira cāru rucikara sarasa sundara vara abhirāma,
mañju manojña kala kalita (ca) lalita lalāma.
sughaṭa sughara śobhita subhaga
        saumya (ca) suṣṭhu sudeśa,

madhura manorama, sughara[1] *suṭhi*
śobhādāma suveṣa.
svākṛti śobhana suhavana kāmya kānta kamanīya,
suṣuṭhi bhavya śuci hṛdaya (aru)
ramya rāma ramanīya.

Looking through all these words, we appreciate the rich variety of the related expressions with their various connotations. Among them, some are used often and others less so in our sources of study.

III

In the texts of Tulsīdās examined for this paper we observe that some expressions appear very often, and it seems that they give one substantial grounds for suggesting what kinds of image the poet had in mind. Some typical expressions frequently employed are given below, using a dash (—) to represent the word related to "beauty" given in angled brackets. Expressions are first quoted from *Gītāvalī*, then, after the sign | |, from *Rāmcaritmānas*.

a. <*cāru*> "agreeable, beautiful"

locana — (7.1) = "eyes —"; *carana kamala* — (10.3) = "feet lotus —"; — *bhaiyā* (8.1) = "— brothers"; — *carita* (18) = " — deed" | | *bilocana* — (230.2) = "eyes —"; *mukutā mani* — (11.5) = "pearls jewels —"; — *bājāru* (213.1) = "a market —"; — *bhāī* (13) = "— brothers".

b. <*chabi*> "beauty, grace"

dvija (dantiyā̃) — (22) = "two [teeth] —"; *mukha* — (19.6) = "the

1 The word *sughara* is given twice.

face — "; *bāla* —(24.1) = "the child —"; *cāla* — (10.3) = "movement —"; *rāmacandra* — (31.6) = "Rām—" | | *phūla* — (219.4) = "flowers —"; *mukutā* — (11.1) = "pearls —"; *madana* — (194.4) = "the God of Love —"; *raghupati* — (232.3) = "The Raghu's prince —".

c. <*rucira*> "bright, beautiful, pleasing"

— *bhūṣaṇa* (23.3) = "— ornaments"; — *tilaka* (10.1) = "— auspicious mark"; —*bhojana* (37) = "— food"; — *purī* (1.6) = "— town"; *rajanī* — (5.3) = "night —"; —*rāma-sisu* (7.1) = "— the child Rām" | | — *mālā* (219.3) = "— garland"; — *cautanī* (219) = "— caps"; *bedikā* — (226.1) "the altar —"; — *rajanī* (226.1) = "— night".

d. <*sundara*> "handsome, beautiful, pleasing, excellent"

sravana adhara — (22 = "ears lips —"; *nakha-sikha* — (19.4) = "from top to toe —"; — *tanu* (31.1) = "— body"; — *ajira* (35) = "— courtyard" | | — *śravana* (194.5) = "— ears"; *cauhaṭa* — (213.2) = "the crossroad —"; — *sadana* (213) = "— palace"; — *bhāī* (209.2) = "— brothers"; — *suta* (195.1) = "— sons".

e. <*sobhā*> "beauty, splendour"

mukha — (30.2) = "face —"; — *aṅga* (22) = "— body"; — *dīpaṭi* (10.3) = "— lamp stand"; — *purī* (4.9) = "— town"; — *sāgar* (19.6) = "— ocean" | | *mukha* — (207.3) = "face —"; — *sindhu* (192.1) = "— ocean"; *bhuvana* — (213.4) = "the world —"; *sīya* — (230.3) = "Sītā's —"; *bālaka bṛnda* — (219.1) = "group of children —".

IV

A brief survey of the above quoted expressions in itself

reveals various facts and peculiarities. The most important fact to be noticed is that all of the expressions have something to do with bodies and ornaments of the central characters. This is also the case with other expressions frequently employed to indicate "beauty" in the works used for this study.

Also worth noticing is the relationship of the components of the illustrated expressions. These expressions consist of two elements, one of which describes or modifies, and another which is described or modified. Hereafter the element which describes or modifies will be referred to as a "describer" and the element which is described or modified as the "described". One describer is applied to various items and situations, and one described is also accompanied by various describers. In this way, the describer and the described have a wide range of application in the works under consideration. For example *rāma* is described with *<chabi> (rāmacandra chabi)*, *<rucira> (rucira rāma-sisu)*, and *<sundara> (sundara sutu); mukutā* is described by *<cāru> (mukutā mani cāru)*, and *<chabi> (mukutā chabi); purī* is described by *<rucira> (rucira purī) and <sobhā> (sobhā purī)*. Thus, that which is described is often related to various descriptive expressions and a describer is often related to various things being described. *<rucira>* can describe a wide range of nouns, from *bhūṣaṇa* ("an ornament") to *bhojana* ("food") to *rāma-sisu* ("the child Rām"). This shows that the relationship of the describer to the described is not tightly bound.

A more detailed analysis reveals another phase of the relationship. Let us consider the case of the prince Rām. As mentioned above, he is described by three different describers in the quoted expressions. The first expression *rāmacandra chabi* (*Gītāvalī*, 31.6) is employed in the context of Sītā noticing Rām's *<chabi>* when she casts a glance at him through a curtain before she proceeds to the wedding altar. In this scene Rām is already completely prepared for the wedding ceremony. He is of course beautiful here, but it would be more appropriate to describe him as graceful or brilliant when he is observed by Sītā because the connotation of <*chabi*> suggests these qualities.

The second expression *rucira rāma sisu* (*Gītāvalī*, 7.1) is employed in the scene in which Rām's mother Kausalyā looks at him while she embraces him. In the eyes of the mother the son looks both beautiful and pleasing. The third expression *sundara suta* (*Mānas*, 195.1) appears when the people of Awadh celebrate the anticipated and auspicious births of the princes. People can see the princes from a certain distance and as a result the expression suggests the quality of distance and formal "handsomeness".

Thus it is quite clear that although the various describing expressions have something in common relating to images of beauty, every expression has a particular connotation according to the situation or the scene of the epic. The same Rām is graceful and brilliant in the eyes of the bride-to-be, pleasing and cute in the eyes of the mother, handsome and splendid in the imagination of the people. Situations and scenes may be explained according to: (1) who is the observer of the so-called beauty, (2) the position from which one observes, and (3) the relationship of observer and the observed.

A few comments will be made here on the expressions of the interpolated *Lav-Kuś kāṇḍ* of *Rāmcaritmānas*. Here also, abundant expressions are employed to describe beauty, but it is quite obvious that the epigone who tried to supplement the portion that was "expected but left incomplete" had little poetic genius. Only two words <*sundara*> and <*suhāvanā*> are employed there in overwhelming frequency, the former when the image is perceived by the eyes and the latter when it is sensed by feelings or sentiments.

V

The relationship of the describer and described is significantly different in *Gītāvalī* and *Rāmcaritmānas.* As already mentioned in the previous section, all the expressions representing beauty have something to do with the bodies and ornaments of the central characters in the epic. Closer scrutiny of the expressions will reveal that the ones appearing in *Gītāvalī* are more body-oriented or static, while those in *Rāmcaritmānas* are more action-oriented or dynamic. The examples of <*sundara*> given above in III.d can explain the difference very eloquently. In *Gītāvalī*, <*sundara*> is employed to describe "ears [and] lips", "from top to toe", "body", and "courtyard", viz., all the described here are parts of the body, except for the inanimate "courtyard". On the other hand, the same adjective in *Rāmcaritmānas* is employed to describe "ears", "the crossroad", "palace", "brothers", and "sons", apparel, inanimate objects, and the characters of the epic. This tendency pervades all the expressions given in III. Static descriptions in *Gītāvalī* remind us of miniature paintings, while the descriptions in *Rāmcaritmānas* remind us of a drama or *rāmlīlā* itself.

This also shows that the same describer is employed in a wider range of contexts and situations in *Rāmcaritmānas*, and as a result similar situations may be described by different describers. Thus, the complexity of the relationship between describer and described varies greatly in the interpolated portions of *Rāmcaritmānas*, *Gītāvalī*, and the original *Rāmcaritmānas.*

VI

The two describers <*chabi*> and <*sobhā*> function in two manners. They are employed to describe specific objects or matter as given in III, viz., *mukha chabi, raghupati chabi*; *sobhā aṅga, sīya sobhā.* Moreover, they are also employed to describe a broader range of situations and are not restricted to particular descriptive expressions. Let us first consider the use of <*chabi*> ("beauty, grace"). Among many examples, only one from each of the two works will be cited. Take the following line from *Gītāvalī* (19.4):

> *ko kavi jo chabi kahi sakai*
> Which poet of which beauty can describe?
>
> *nakha-sikha sundar saba aṅga*
> From top to toe beautiful the whole body.

In this line, "the whole body from top to toe" is described as <*sundara*>, and <*chabi*> in the first half of the line describes the situation given in the latter half, which is introduced by the relative pronoun *jo*. It may be said that <*chabi*> here concerns the situation already described by another describer, thus the situation describer is on a higher or abstract level.

In *Rāmcaritmānas* we find a line (198.3) where <*chabi*> has a similar function:

> *syāma gaura sundara doū jorī,*
> *nirakhi chabi jananī̃...*
> the dark, fair, beautiful two brothers,
> watching the beauty the mother...

Here also, <*chabi*> describes the whole situation already described by another describer <*sundara*>.

As to this kind of function performed by <*sobhā*> ("beauty, splendour"), we find in *Gītāvalī* (8.2):

> *...manohara aṅga...,* *sobhā nirakhi...*
> ...charming body..., grace watching...

and in *Rāmcaritmānas* (213):

...sundara sadana, *sobhā kimi kahi jāti*
...beautiful palace, grace how can be described?

In both cases, one can easily observe that both occurrences of <*sobhā*> describe situations which are already described by other describers.

Such kinds of higher-level or abstract function are performed, in the works examined, only by two words, <*chabi*> and <*sobhā*>, and by no others. These two peculiar words may refer to the most important images the poet had in mind. Thorough and elaborate examination of these expressions are intended.

VII

By examining the expressions employed in *Gītāvalī*, *Rāmcaritmānas*, and the interpolated *Lav-Kuś kāṇḍ*, some significant facts and phases have been revealed which may be of great importance in appreciating the works of the poet. The sources that generated these rich expressions have not been examined at all in this paper. More detailed and minute examination may shed light on the images the poet created while narrating the story of the life of Rām.

Bhakti and/or Irony in Vidyāpati's *Puruṣaparīkṣā*

S.D. Serebriany

Vidyāpati is a well-known name in the history of literature in New Indo-Aryan languages. This paper, however, will focus not on Vidyāpati as a vernacular poet of devotion (*bhakti*), but on Vidyāpati as a prose writer in Sanskrit, whose attitude towards *bhakti* seems to be rather ambiguous or at least problematic. The analysis of Vidyāpati's *Puruṣaparīkṣā*, a book of stories in Sanskrit, may shed some light on the nature of his lyrics in Maithili (*Maithilī*) and, accordingly, on the genesis of the vernacular poetry of Vaiṣṇava *bhakti* associated with the name of Vidyāpati.

Like many other famous names in the history of pre-modern Indian literatures, the name "Vidyāpati" is associated with many different texts which evidently have not been composed by *one* person, during *one* life-time. The case of Vidyāpati is especially, though by no means exceptionally, complicated. The original Vidyāpati, the ādi-Vidyāpati so to say, lived in Mithila (*Mithilā*) at the end of the fourteenth and through the first half of the fifteenth century (Jha 1972; McGregor 1984: 29-33; Serebriany 1973: 92-96; Serebriany 1980: 130-31). He must have composed lyrics in Maithili, the New Indo-Aryan language of Mithila. Maithili was one of the first New Indo-Aryan languages to become a medium of poetic creation, and Vidyāpati must have been one of the first poets to use this medium (Mishra 1976)[1]. In some of Vidyāpati's Maithili lyrics there appear the names of Kṛṣṇa and Rādhā (or themes that could have been linked with these names). Some of such poems reached Bengal, impressed Caitanya and other Vaiṣṇavas there, and were later included in the collections of Bengali Vaiṣṇava *pods* (sometimes with certain linguistic and/or semantic changes). These Maithili lyrics inspired Vaiṣṇava poets in Bengal, who composed their own *pods* in Bengali or in the so-called Braja-buli (a kind of artificial poetic language, half-Bengali half-Maithili; *v.* Sen 1935), sometimes signing those *pods* with the name (pen-name?) "Vidyāpati". Thus "Vidyāpati" in the Bengali Vaiṣṇava tradition is a composite figure, something like Sūrdās in Braj-bhāṣā (Soûr Dâs 1971; Hawley 1984), though, of course, on a lesser scale. It is this composite Bengali "Vidyāpati" that seems to be more known to the world at large (Vidyāpati 1915). But the original Vidyāpati of Mithila deserves at least as much interest of scholars, of those who study Indian literature and culture.

At this point it may be noted that dividing the history of Indian literature into separate parts or streams, like Sanskrit literature, Apabhraṃśa literature or literature in New Indo-Aryan languages, is a convenient but sometimes misleading device. Thus Vidyāpati (and from now on by Vidyāpati is meant only the original Vidyāpati of Mithila) composed his works in at least three languages: Maithili, a late Apabhraṃśa and Sanskrit (Serebriany 1973: 88-92; Serebriany 1980: 132-47). In order to understand Vidyāpati as an integral literary (cultural) personality, moreover, to understand the trends of the development of North Indian literature and culture of that time, we must consider all the works of Vidyāpati, in all the languages, as a whole. Next, venturing into the sphere of comparative studies, it would be interesting to compare Vidyāpati with such European authors as Dante, Petrarca or Boccaccio who also wrote both in the classical language and in a vernacular.

Of course, such comparison would immediately highlight

the differences between Indian and European traditions (cultures). Vidyāpati's Maithili lyrics have been preserved mainly by oral traditions of Mithila; there are very few manuscripts, all of uncertain dates and uncertain reliability, so that we can hardly be sure that this or that particular poem belongs to Vidyāpati, but can only reconstruct some most general features of the poetry that Vidyāpati might have actually composed (Serebriany 1980: 148ff). In fact, in Mithila too (like in Bengal, though in a different way) "Vidyāpati" as a vernacular poet is a composite figure: many later poems, composed by others, stuck, as it were, to the famous name in the course of centuries (somewhat like a rolling snowball). In other words, the name "Vidyāpati" has become a kind of label which was attached to particular types of poems in Maithili.[2]

Nevertheless we *can* reconstruct with certain plausibility some of the features that must have been there in the Maithili poetry of Vidyāpati. This poetry evidently followed the tradition of "court-poetry" in Sanskrit which mostly depicted love situations. The heroes of Vidyāpati's poems were sometimes anonymous (as in most of Sanskrit love poetry), but were sometimes called Rādhā and/or Kṛṣṇa (Jayadeva's *Gitagovinda* may be cited as a probable model). As for the pragmatics of Vidyāpati's lyrics in Maithili, it might have been also court poetry, meant to entertain and praise the poet's patron (McGregor 1974: 31). In the poems ascribed to Vidyāpati in Mithila most often the name of Rājā Śivasiṃha is mentioned, who is praised as a connoisseur of poetry and women and is sometimes compared to Kṛṣṇa.

As we can only *reconstruct* the form and meaning of the original Maithili poetry of Vidyāpati, we can hardly do more than *imagine* the actual human personality that created that poetry. This is, again, quite a common situation for students of pre-modern Indian literatures. But in case of Vidyāpati we do have at our disposal a certain amount of specific historical information which permits us to base our speculations on more or less solid ground.

Among other things, we know that Vidyāpati lived in a rather complex milieu of cultural and political pluralism. During his life-time Mithila, though ruled by Hindu Rājās (Vidyāpati's patrons), was subordinate to a powerful Muslim state, the Sultanate of Jaunpur, an important centre of Indo-Muslim culture.[3] In this respect the situation in Mithila anticipated, as it were, the situation of later Hindu principalities drawn into the orbit of the Mughal Empire. Vidyāpati, as a poet in Maithili, may be considered, on the one hand, one of the most important precursors of devotional literature in New Indo-Aryan languages; on the other hand, he also anticipated, as it were, the more "secular" court poetry in Braj-bhāṣā of later centuries. I may note in this connection that as in case of Vidyāpati's Maithili lyrics, so in case of many a later Braj-bhāṣā poet (belonging to the so-called *rīti-kāl*), it is quite often difficult to draw a distinction between the "devotional" and the "secular" ("non-devotional"?).

Now we can turn to the *Puruṣaparīkṣā*, a book of stories written by Vidyāpati in Sanskrit. This book deserves more attention from scholars than it has so far received, both as a piece of narrative art and as a document of Indian culture. Among other things, as has been already said, the *Puruṣaparīkṣā* may be used as a kind of commentary on Vidyāpati's Maithili poetry, because this book (as it is stated in the text itself, see below) was written by the order of the same Rājā Śivasiṃha who is evoked in many Maithili *padas* of Vidyāpati. But in case of the *Puruṣaparīkṣā* we need not *reconstruct* the text; it is given to us in a number of more or less reliable manuscripts (and the variations do not seem to be too great). Usual methods of text interpretations may be used, and we may even hope to obtain some more tangible information about the person who created this text (as well as, presumably, the lyrics in Maithili).

But so far the *Puruṣaparīkṣā* has not been studied adequately; it has not yet been even published (edited) critically.[4] The only translation into a European language (English) published so far, that by Sir G.A. Grierson (*Vidyāpati*

Ṭhakkura 1935) is not compete and rather far from being adequate.[5] The *Puruṣaparīkṣā* is mentioned in the standard histories of Sanskrit literature (though is not always described accurately), and is usually listed together with such famous books of stories as the *Pañcatantra*, the *Hitôpadeśa*, the "Twenty-five stories of Vetāla" and so on (*v.*, e.g., Keith 1973: 293). But here an important distinction must be made. The various *versions* of the *Pañcatantra* and of the other collections of stories just mentioned were exactly *versions* of traditional patterns and structures. But the *Puruṣaparīkṣā* is a more individual work of art, though it also contains a lot of traditional elements.

Of course, the *Puruṣaparīkṣā* would not stand comparison with the famous *Decamerone* of Boccaccio, but, I suppose, it can well be compared with such earlier European books of stories as the *Disciplina clericalis* of Petrus Alfonsi or *El Conde Lucanor* of Juan Manuel. The important difference is that the latter two books proved to be the precursors of the later glorious growth of European narrative prose, whereas the *Puruṣaparīkṣā*, in this respect, looks like a precursor of what never came to be, a brilliant beginning of an abortive development.

Like the *Pañcatantra* and like other books of stories, Indian and European, the *Puruṣaparīkṣā* has a "frame-story", though rather a meagre one. A Rājā wants to find a husband for his daughter and asks an old wise man whom to choose. The wise man says:"You must marry her to a man *(puruṣa)*."[6] The Rājā is rather perplexed and retorts that in any case only a man can become a husband of a woman. But the wise man explains that not all those who look like men are real men. Some are only men in appearance *(puruṣâkārāḥ)*. Real men are of three types: "heroes" *(vīrāḥ)*, "wise ones" *(sudhiyaḥ)* and "experts in certain branches of knowledge or in certain skills" *(savidyāḥ)*. And only such real men reach the four aims of human existence. Then the wise man goes on to narrate stories about various kinds of real men and the four aims of human existence. There are forty-four such stories arranged in four parts. These stories contain various kinds of plots and motifs, and it is evident that most of these plots and motifs, if not all, have been taken by Vidyāpati from *tradition*, not *invented* by himself. But it is no less evident that the specific realizations of traditional plots and motifs bear the stamp of Vidyāpati's individual ideas and attitudes.

As we have just seen, devotion *(bhakti)* is not mentioned among the necessary qualities of a "real man". But the idea of devotion and the very word *bhakti* are not altogether absent in the book. In the very first introductory stanza the author bows to *Śakti* (*...tām ādi-Śaktiṃ śirasā prapadye*). Then, in the colophons, the concluding formulas of the four parts of the book, it is said repeatedly that the book was written by the order of the *mahārājâdhirāja Śrīmac-Śivasiṃha-deva* who, among other things, is *Bhava-bhakti-parāyaṇa*, "intent on devotion to Śiva".

But in the book itself, in its stories, no devotion to any god occupies any important place. It is worth noting that the names of Kṛṣṇa and Rādhā are nowhere mentioned in the book. In one stanza, near the end of the third part, Śivasiṃha is compared to Kṛṣṇa or rather to Viṣṇu himself (called Nārāyaṇa), and this is one of the few, though very important, specific links between the *Puruṣaparīkṣā* and the Maithili lyrics of Vidyāpati: in the *bhaṇitās*, the endings of some of the Maithili *padas* ascribed to Vidyāpati, Śivasiṃha is also compared to Kṛṣṇa.

The *Puruṣaparīkṣā* as a whole, in its pragmatics, is a kind of panegyric to Rājā Śivasiṃha. Not only again and again is he mentioned as the patron of the author, but at the very beginning of the book he is praised as having all the qualities of a "real man", is then compared to Viṣṇu (see above) and Śiva, and at one place to Rājā Vikramâditya, as a connoisseur of poetry and women. This pragmatical meaning of the *Puruṣaparīkṣā* may be taken as a kind of comment on the pragmatical meaning of Vidyāpati's Maithili lyrics (see above)

We may say that the *Puruṣaparīkṣā* is rather a "secular" work (though I am aware that one must be extremely cautious applying such European terms to Indian culture). The theme of religion and, in particular, of the relations between gods and humans does appear quite often in the work, but the treatment of it is sometimes rather peculiar. Thus, in the very first and the very last stories encounters are described between human beings and gods, and in both cases, incidentally, do the words *bhakti* or *bhakta* appear, but let us see what kinds of *bhakti* and *bhaktas* are there.

In the first story it is related how Rājā Vikramâditya interfered in the transactions between another Rājā and the Devī. Vikramâditya found out that the other Rājā let himself be devoured every night by the Devī, who then regularly revived him and granted a boon: a house of gold, distributed by the Rājā among his subjects. Vikramâditya was very much impressed by the self-sacrifice of the Rājā, but wondered why the Devī should devour him again and again instead of granting the boon once and for all. So one night Vikramâditya went to the place earlier than usual and by some kind of trick made the Devī devour him several times in succession. After some time the Devī recognized Vikramâditya and said that actually she was not at all anxious to eat human flesh but just pretended to be so in order to test the Rājā's valour. She then offered a boon to Vikramâditya. The latter addressed her with the following words:

> *Devī! Bhakta-vatsalâsi, jagan-mātā...*
> ("Goddess! You tenderly love your *bhaktas*, you, the mother of the world...") —

and then asked her to stop devouring the other Rājā again and again and to grant him once for all the desired boon. The Devī easily agreed to do this. Do we not see a kind of irony in this story about the Devī and her *bhaktas*?

In the last story of the book, Rājā Bhartṛhari, the elder brother of Rājā Vikramâditya, renounces the kingdom, withdraws to a forest and enters into the state of *samādhi*. Once he comes back to his senses and sees that his clothes need some repairing. Nārāyaṇa, using this opportunity, approaches Bhartṛhari and, addressing him as his *bhakta*, offers a boon:

> *Re Bhartṛhare! Tvaṃ mama bhakto'si. Tvayy ahaṃ prasanno'smi. Tarhi varaṃ vṛṇu!*
> ("O Bhartṛhari! You are my *bhakta*. I am satisfied with you. So choose a boon!").

The hermit answers (with a beautiful stanza) that he has no desires and that the Lord should approach those who have desires. The Lord Nārāyaṇa says:

> *Vatsa Bhartṛhare! Tvaṃ niṣkāma evâsi. Tathāpi mayi trailokya-nāthe vāñchita-dātari mama dāna-rabhāsā-rakṣârthaṃ kim api yācanīyam bhavati bhavatā*
> ("My dear Bhartṛhari! You have no desires, that's all right. But you must ask me for something to keep up my passion for giving, for granting boons, as I am the Lord of the three worlds and the giver of boons").

Bhartṛhari takes it as an order which cannot be ignored and asks to make the thread pass quickly into the needle's eye. Nārāyaṇa is so impressed by this request, that he immediately grants *mukti* to Bhartṛhari (without any specific request from the hermit's part). Again, I wonder whether or not this story should be taken quite seriously or as an exercise in irony.

Here is one more story from the *Puruṣaparīkṣā*. It is titled *Anūśayī-kathā*, or, in G.A.Grierson's translation, "The Story of a Contrite Prince". Indeed, it is a story of sin and repentance. A young prince inherits a kingdom from his father, but proves to be a very bad king himself. Worst of all, he proves to be a *nâstika*. When some old wise people try to remind him of *dharma*, of the Vedas and the Parameśvara whom they describe as the creator *(praṇetā)* of the Vedas, the young king retorts:

> *Parameśvara eva nâsti, kutas tat-praṇītā vedāḥ? Yadi bhavati, tadôpalabhyate, mayā dṛśyate ca. Nôpalabhyate cet, tadā nâsty eva*
>
> ("There is no Parameśvara, how can there be the Vedas created by him? If he had been there, he would have been perceived, he would have been seen by me. But as he is not perceived, it means he does not exist").

After some time this *nâstika* Rājā had to give up the throne and to go into exile, to a forest, accompanied only by a hetaera. They lived in the forest and had only one blanket for both of them. Once the former Rājā went to a neighbouring town in order to steal another blanket. But it so happened that he failed to steal another blanket and lost the one he had got. This outcome made him rethink his ideas about the world and God. He said to himself: "I wanted things to be one way, but they happened another way. There must be somebody according to whose will things happen in this world. And this somebody must be the Lord *(īśvara)* about whom the wise men told me"[7]. And so the contrite prince decides to be a devotee of the Parmeśvara, whom he identifies with Siva. It is not clear what exactly he was going to do, but at least he brought the hetaera from the forest back to the city and parted with her.

More stories from the *Purusaparīksā* could be retold. But, I suppose, the above is already sufficient to make clear the point of the paper. The point or rather the question is: whether the effect of irony appears only in *our* (or in *my*) reading of the fifteenth-century Indian text, or something like this was really *meant* by the author himself? Are there ways to give a definite answer to such a question? Next, if

Vidyāpati did have in mind a kind of irony, by what Sanskrit word would he describe this attitude of his? Could we say that this "something like irony" (if it was really there) was an organic, natural (perhaps even traditional) part of Vidyāpati's religious outlook, or might it be taken as a sign of a critical attitude towards traditional religion, a sign of the process that is well known in modern European history, but was and still is so slow to develop fully in India? Vidyāpati was a pioneer, a pathfinder in the sphere of literary expression: one of the earliest poets in a North Indian vernacular, an original prose writer in Sanskrit.... Could he not be as bold in the sphere of speculative thought? Most probably, such questions cannot possibly be answered, but one can hardly help asking them.

NOTES

1 The history of Maithili as a literary language may be compared with the history of the "langue d'oc" or "occitan" language in Europe. Both languages were among the first vernaculars in their cultural areas to reach the status of a literary language, but both were later overwhelmed by neighbouring "relatives": by French and Italian in the European case, by Bengali, Hindi and Urdu in the Indian case. To continue the comparison, we may say that Vidyāpati as a poet in Maithili may be compared with the "troubadours" of the "langue d'oc".

2 Let me repeat that "Vidyāpati"'s case is by no means exceptional, but rather represents a common phenomenon in the history of Indian literatures. More or less the same can be said about such names as Kabīr, Sūrdās, Mīrābāī, Raidās and many others (*v.* other contributions in this volume). This phenomenon must be studied in the general context of the history of Indian culture (Serebriany 1979).

3 The confrontation of Hindu Mithila and Muslim Jaunpur is most vividly presented by Vidyāpati himself in his poem *Kīrtilatā* written in a late Apabhraṃśa. This poem has been edited in India several times with translations in modern Indian languages (Bengali and Hindi), but so far no study by a Western scholar has appeared, nor a translation in any European language.

4 The nearest approximation to a critical edition is that by Ramanath Jha (Vidyāpati Ṭhākur 1990). My quotations below are from this edition.

5 My translation of the *Puruṣaparīkṣā* in Russian (with an afterword and notes) is in the press.

6 Incidentally, exactly the same question and answer are found in one of the stories in *El Conde Lucanor.* The count of Provence asks Saladin "to kindly advise him as to whom she (the count's daughter) should marry". Saladin answers: "... My advice is this, that you marry your daughter to a man" (Juan Manuel 1977: 105).

7 This "proof of the existence of God" does not look like any such proof in the Christian tradition. Perhaps, some parallels may be found in Muslim theology. In this connection it may be noted that Muslims appear in several stories of the *Puruṣaparīkṣā* and are mostly portrayed rather appreciatively.

BIBLIOGRAPHY

Hawley, J.S., *Sūr Dās, Poet, Singer, Saint.* Seattle and London: University of Washington Press, 1984.

Jha, Ramanath, *Vidyāpati.* New Delhi: Sahitya Akademi, 1972.

Juan Manuel, tr. Keller, J.E., and L.C. Keating, *The Book of Count Lucanor and Patronio. A Translation of Don Juan Manuel's El Conde Lucanor.* Lexington: The University Press of Kentucky, 1977.

Keith, A.B., *A History of Sanskrit Literature.* Delhi: Oxford University Press, 1973.

McGregor, R.S., *Hindi Literature from its Beginnings to the Nineteenth Century (A History of Indian Literature* ed. by J. Gonda; Vol.8, Fasc. 6). Wiesbaden: Harrassowitz, 1984.

Mishra, J., *History of Maithili Literature.* New Delhi: Sahitya Akademi, 1976.

Sen, Sukumar, *A History of Brajabuli Literature, Being a Study of the Vaiṣṇava Lyric Poetry and Poets of Bengal.* Calcutta: University of Calcutta, 1935.

Serebriany, S.D., "On some aspects of the concepts 'author' and 'authorship' as applied to the history of Indian literatures", *Literatura i kul' tura drevnei i srednevekovoi Indii* (Literature and culture of ancient and medieval India).Moscow: Nauka, 1979 [In Russian].

——, "Materials for studying the work of Vidyāpati Ṭhākur", *Literatury Indii* (Literatures of India). Moscow: Nauka, 1973 [In Russian].

——, *Vidyāpati*. Moscow: Nauka, 1980 [In Russian].

Soûr-Dâs, *Pastorales*, Traduction de la langue braj avec introduction, notes et glossaire de Charlotte Vaudeville. Paris: Gallimard, 1971.

Vidyāpati, *Bangīya Padābali*, tr. by A.Coomaraswamy and A.Sen. London: Old Bourne Press, 1915.

Vidyāpati Ṭhakkura, *The Test of a Man: being the Purusha-parîkshâ of Vidyâpati Ṭhakkura*, tr. into English by Sir G.A.Grierson. London: The Royal Asiatic Society, 1935.

Vidyāpati Ṭhākur, *Puruṣaparīkṣā*, ed. by Ramanath Jha. Darbhanga, 1960 (Darbhanga Series, N 1).

The God Dharma, Human Sacrifice and *Bhakti* in the *Dharma Maṅgal*

France Bhattacharya

This paper consists of two parts. In the first, I attempt a presentation of the god Dharma as he is shown in medieval Bengali literature : an all-encompassing god, ideally identified with Viṣṇu-Nārāyaṇa, but one who has many common points with Yama-Dharmarāja, and also with Sūrya and Rudra-Śiva. In the second part of this paper, I try to show how sacrifice, *yajña*, which includes the offering of victims, is transformed both in the *Dharma maṅgal* and in the main ritual concerning this god, the *Gājana*, into self-sacrifice, *ātmā-tyāga*, and how the sufferings endured by the devotee, a recurrent theme and a component of the cult of "terrible deities", is remodelled by the *bhakti* value-code and given a metaphorical meaning.

The god called Dharma is the centre of the Bengali narrative poems of the medieval period called *Dharma maṅgal*. He is also mentioned in most cosmologies of the *Manasā maṅgal*, in at least one of the *Caṇḍī* and in the Bengali stories of the Nātha Gurus.[1]

It is very difficult, if not altogether impossible, to determine the origin of this god, a problem which has been much written about. Specialists differ: some insist on his non-Aryan features, others see in him a survival of Buddhism, though this theory has hardly any more propounders to-day, and others try to bring him close to well established deities of the Hindu pantheon and to understand him in the context of the theogony as a whole.[2] The authors of the various versions of the *Dharma maṅgal*, probably influenced by the post-Caitanyan *vaiṣṇava* devotion, insist on saying that Dharma is no other than the supreme God Viṣṇu-Nārāyaṇa, residing in Vaikuṇṭha. One of them, Rūparām (Rūprām), gives him the title of *Arjuna sārathī*, the charioteer of Arjuna, a name of Kṛṣṇa. This author, probably one of the earliest, if not the first in the long line of *Dharma maṅgal* poets, as well as some others, including Mānikrām, place at the beginning of his work an invocation to Caitanya.[3]

In the cosmologies, the first narrative part of the *maṅgal*, Dharma, called most often *Nirañjana*, "the stainless one", *Ādyadeva*, "the god of the beginning", and *Anādi* "the one without a beginning", appears even before the start of the creation process. He is then the Supreme *Puruṣa* who takes support on the void. By means of a sigh, he emits the bird *Ulūka* and sits on its back. Later, Dharma spits ambrosia and thus brings into existence the mass of waters. The god's feminine counterpart, called *Nārāyaṇī* by Rūparām and *Ādyadevī* by the other poets, comes into existence. The presence of the primeval couple permits the coming into being of the three gods of the *Trimūrti*: Brahmā, Visnu and Śiva, who respectively take charge of creation, preservation and destruction. However, it must be said that a few *maṅgal* poets prefer to distinguish Dharma, a superior form of the Creator, comparable to the classical *Hiraṇyagarbha*, from Nirañjana, whom they equate with the eternal, formless and stainless *Brahman*.[4] In this case, Nirañjana is not very different from the *nirguṇa* god of the medieval mystics, though the first reference of the poets is more likely to be the *brahman* of classical philosophy.

In all cases, Dharma is presented as the initiator of the cosmic evolution process which he regulates and holds. He is shown as the supporter of the manifestation (*DHṚ* > *dharma*).

Epic and Purāṇa literatures do no more than take the first

step towards the personification of Dharma while they keep its importance as a concept. The *Mahābhārata*, for example, gives Dharma as a father to Nārāyaṇa without indicating whether this filiation should be taken in a literal or figurative sense.[5] In fact, it is Yama, under the name of Dharmarāja, who figures in most Epic and Purāṇa narratives.

The Dharma of the *maṅgal* cosmologies is the god who initiates the cosmic process of evolution and, as such, is aptly represented in many of his sanctuaries as a tortoise. This animal has been a cosmogonical symbol since the Vedic period. *Kūrma* was made to derive from the root *KṚ* "to make", "to do", and a living tortoise was placed under the layers of bricks in the sacrificial altar.[6] One should remember also the tortoise as the second incarnation of Viṣṇu. Like the first, the fish, it is meant to organize the triple world. Viṣṇu, in the shape of a tortoise, forms the base on which rests the churning stick during the churning of the cosmic ocean that produced ambrosia for the gods and consigned the Asuras to the lower world.

Cosmic structuration entails destructuration, evolution calls for involution. The *Viṣṇu* and the *Kūrmapurāṇa* compare the earth, ablaze during the cosmic resorption, to a tortoise-shell. At the individual level, the *yogī* who has isolated his senses from the sense-objects is metaphorically likened to a tortoise whose head and limbs have been retracted into its shell (*Bhagavadgītā*, adh. 1, v. 58). But for men, the most obvious experience of resorption is death. The tortoise is also the symbol of the Yamunā, river of rebirth and transmigration, identified with Yamī, Yama's twin sister and the primeval woman.[7] We have not deviated much from the *maṅgal* literature according to which Dharma is the first ever to die. He opens the way to death, says the poet.[8] This is precisely what is also said of Yama. Both Yama and Dharma share the same direction: the South.[9]

To summarize, Dharma is present both at the beginning and at the end of a cosmic cycle, as also at the birth and at the death of individuals. Nothing, nobody is outside the pale of Dharma, both as a god and as a concept.

The *mangal* poet, in the portrait he draws od the god, emphasizes his whiteness. Dharma has a white complexion, his clothes, his seat and his abode are white, as are the *campaka* flowers around his neck and the banners on his chariot.[10] On his enemies he inflicts leucoderma, *śvetī*, the white disease.[11] This emphasis on white may be symbolic of the *sattvik* quality of the "Stainless one". It is also an excess of *sattva* that awakens the creator from his yogic sleep and brings to an end the period of cosmic dissolution. This is further indication that Dharma might be linked with the Brahmā-Nārāyaṇa of the Purāṇa cosmologies,[12] but it cannot be excluded that the whiteness may also call to memory the ashes of the funeral pyre and the pallor of dead bodies.

Dharma is a king, as is Yama-Dharmarāja. Both of them carry a *daṇḍa*, a rod of justice. At the beginning of the *Gājana*, Dharma's festival, in a village of Burdwan district, in West Bengal, the god is said to appear in the form of a stick, found sticking up in a pond, on the fourteenth day of *Vaiśākha*. The priest removes it from the water and it is venerated by the devotees. Later, on the full moon day, the stick is left in another pond from where it mysteriously disappears three days later.[13] The poet mentions also an umbrella which is held above the god's head, as is customary for a King.[14] Dharma moves about in a chariot, a *ratha*, and, during the celebrations of the *Gājana*, his sandals are placed in a shed built in the shape of a chariot, according to Rūparām.[15]

When Dharma shows himself to men, however, he takes on the appearance of a Śaiva renouncer, a *sannyāsī* : his clothes are red; he wears a *rudrākṣa mālā*. The colour of blood, mentioned for his dress, seems to evoke his dangerous *(ugra)* aspect. A *sannyāsī* and a *brahmacārī*, he is also a member of the brahmanical class. He wears the skin of a black antelope around his waist. A ring of *kuśa* grass adorns his finger and he recites the Vedas.[16] These details evoke a *ṛtvij*, a performer of sacrifice. In the course of such a *yajña*, it was customary to offer the gods animal victims. The red colour of Dharma's dress may symbolize the blood of the dead animals. When Dharma appears on earth, presenting himself as he has been described, he comes to receive the offerings of his devotees. These play the part of the *yajamāna*, the sacrificer in the classical sacrifice. Like him, they have prepared themselves for the god's descent by observing strict rules of conduct. The *yajamāna's* physical suffering is an integral part of the sacrificial act.[17] Furthermore, the animal victim is only a substitute, the real victim being the *yajamāna* himself.

Similarly, in the *maṅgal* the god demands from his devotee a self-renunciation which can entail the taking of his own life in the ritual act. Dharma seems unable, or unwilling, to respond to his devotee's call unless he has shed his blood to arouse him.[18] This practice may be seen as a characteristic of the cult of inferior gods or "demons", and the *Dharma maṅgal* may hence appear as an effort on the part of brahmanism to integrate this god and his ritual into brahmanical Hinduism. This viewpoint finds partial confirmation in the social composition of most of Dharma's devotees, priests and *deyāśī*, who generally belong to the lower strata of the population.[19] We do not know if it has always been the case since one counts an important number of brahmins, *kāyastha* and middle-ranking castes among the authors of *Dharma maṅgal* as well as among the first mythical devotees.[20]

Yet the part played by *ḍoma*, *bāitī*, *caṇḍāla* and other very low castes in the *Dharma* story is very important, compared to the *Caṇḍī* and even the *Manasā*. The *bhakti* religion, giving to all the possibility of obtaining salvation, is certainly responsible for the place held by these so-called "untouchables". "There is no distinction of *varṇa* in the abode of Dharma", says the poet.[21] But speaking of the *ḍoma*, it should be noted that this caste, at least a section of it, is linked with the disposal of corpses and the treatment of death. Yama-Dharmarāja is never very far from our Bengali Dharma.

The connection between Dharma and Sūrya has often been underlined. Both move about in a chariot. The poet calls Dharma *"diner divakāra"*, a name of the sun. The *Dharma maṅgal* recitation lasts twelve days, analogous, perhaps, to the twelve solar months.[22] The final trial of the *maṅgal* hero is to obtain from Dharma the rising of the sun in the West. Yet if the relation between them is close, the two gods are different, as the story itself shows. Sūrya comes to bear witness to the greatness of Dharma: the Purāṇas call the Sun "Eye of the world" and "Witness of the acts".[23] The *Ṛgveda* (X, 14) credits to the Sun Vivasvat the paternity of Yama and Yamī. At another level of analysis, the relationship between Sūrya and Dharmarāja is linked to the role played by the Sun as an agent of destruction. As Kālāgni, he is the form taken by the supreme god to put an end to the world. At the individual level, he is equated to the fire of the funeral pyre, and, as such, related to Yama.

We cannot analyze in detail the relationship between Rudra-Śiva and Dharma. Only a few points can be raised. At the time of the "death" of Dharma, Śiva alone recognizes his "father" at the sight of his corpse, and so Dharma gives his daughter-wife Ādyā to him, and not to Viṣṇu or Brahmā.[24] Rudra-Śiva, like Dharmarāja, is involved in the destructive process. Both are an aspect of Kāla, Time, and, as such, they are related to one another. It is interesting to note that, at the village level, their main celebrations, called in both cases the *Gājana*, have so much in common that the *Gājana* of Śiva is in the process of replacing that of Dharma.[25] These two gods require from their devotees of whatever caste a great deal of ascetic practice. During the celebrations, both grant them a divine lineage *(deva gotra)* that obliterates all differences of status. In the case of both Śiva and Dharma, the worshippers try to satisfy a demanding god whose "terrible" face is to be feared and whose benevolence knows no bound.

Such is the personality of Dharma in the *maṅgal*. We have

to study now the way in which he demands from his *bhakta* a complete self-sacrifice. Both ritual suicide and the killing of the devotee's nearest kin, i.e. his son, are characteristic of the Dharma story. Yet *bhakti* modifies to a great extent their import. Three episodes from the *Dharma maṅgal* will illustrate this.

The first is a secondary narrative, told as a tale within a tale. Queen Rañjāvatī asks her husband permission to celebrate the *Gājana* of Dharma in the hope of getting the favour of a son. The King replies that he does not know this god. His wife then tells him the story of king Hariścandra on whom Dharma bestowed an heir. Far from being a simple digression, this tale shows how a myth can be transformed to take into account both the "dangerous" aspect of a deity, demanding a sacrificial victim, and the affectionate relationship existing between a god and his devotee according to the ideology of *bhakti.* The origin of the story goes back to the *Aitareyabrāhmaṇa,* VII, 13-18. Hariścandra, a king of the Ikṣvāku lineage, has no son. Nārada advises him to pray to god Varuṇa for one. Varuṇa accepts to give him an heir provided the king sacrifices the child later to him. After the birth of Rohita, Hariscandra's child, the king delays the sacrifice. The god waits patiently, but when the young prince runs away into the forest to escape being killed, Varuṇa, angry, inflicts hydropsy on the king. Later, the prince finds himself a substitute named Śunaḥśepha, son of a poor brahmin named Ajīgarta. The prince buys the boy, with the intention of killing him, but when he is tied to the sacrificial post and begins to offer his prayers to the gods, his bonds fall apart, and he is set free. Hariścandra is cured and can keep his son and heir. Śunaḥśepha is adopted by Viśvāmitra. Such is the story in the Brāhmaṇa.

Interestingly, the Varuṇa of this tale has much in common with Dharma. He is a god and a king "who maintains natural and moral laws *(ṛta)* under its ethical aspect of order" and he ties with his noose those who are guilty of not keeping their promises. During the late Vedic period, Varuṇa is said to "act as a dark character, somewhat assimilated to the god of Death".[26]

Valmīki *Rāmāyaṇa (bālākāṇḍa* 17-19) tells the same story with different names but puts the emphasis on the rivalry between Vaśiṣṭha and Viśvāmitra. The *Mahābhārata* (II, chap. 11) introduces the idea of the exceptional generosity of Hariścandra, a quality which is acknowledged by several Purāṇas as well as by the Bengali tradition. In the *Mārkaṇḍeyapurāṇa* (chap.7,8) the king is made to offer the gift of his kingdom and his family to Viśvāmitra. His queen and their son are sold as slaves. The king himself is bought by a Caṇḍāla, keeper of the cremation-ground, who is no other than the god Dharma. In spite of his social and physical degradation, the king remains faithful to the code of kingly conduct. His son's death shows how perfect is the *tyāga* of Hariścandra. At the end, Dharma gives him back his life.[27] The Bengali *Rāmāyaṇa* of Kṛttivāsa *(ādi kāṇḍa* p. 8-13) borrows the Purāṇa story and emphasizes the king's social degradation making him the slave of a *hāḍi*, a scavenger. Again, Dharma comes to the rescue of Hariścandra.

The *Dharma maṅgal* story takes its inspiration from the Brāhmaṇa, but changes the name of the god from Varuṇa to Dharma.[28] The king has no son in spite of many offerings made to Viṣṇu and Kṛṣṇa. His wife learns how to celebrate the *Gājana* of Dharma. Satisfied, the god grants them a son provided the child is offered to him in sacrifice. After the birth, Dharma does not claim his due till the day when the child hurts the bird *Ulūka* with his catapult. Dharma, dressed as a *sannyāsī*, comes into the palace of king Hariścandra to ask for food as he is hungry. He wants to eat meat, but not of the usual type. He requires *mahāmāṃsa*: human flesh. It can be interpreted as a demand for sacrificial offerings which the fire of his digestion, acting as the sacrificial fire, will devour. The *sannyāsī* orders the king to kill his son and tells the queen to cook his flesh for him. The couple is condemned to lose their most beloved son and is compelled to act in a way contrary to the householder's *dharma* which prohibits murder and the handling of corpses. In vain the king and the queen offer their own flesh in exchange for the life of their son. When Dharma threatens to destroy the kingdom if he is not obeyed, the helpless king performs his usual *pūjā*. Later, he bathes the child, dresses him in a red garment and passes gold bracelets around his wrists.[29] The prince accepts his fate, placing his confidence in Kṛṣṇa. The king cuts off his son's head and the queen cooks his flesh, ready to serve Dharma various dishes. The god wants a sweet and sour dish made with the head of the child. He insists that the couple share his meal, refusing to eat alone. Conscious of the duty of hospitality, the king lifts a morsel to his mouth. At that moment of supreme shame and horror, the *sannyāsī*-god stops him. Praising Hariścandra's unsurpassed generosity, he gives to the queen the favour of her son's life.[30] In the poet's words, all this gruesome scene is but an effect of the *māyā* of the *māyādhara*.[31]

Dharma who wants the total surrender of his devotee, who compels a pious king to put aside the householder's usual code of conduct inflicting on him the condition of a *caṇḍāla* or a *kāpālika*, can still be addressed by the prince, his victim, as "an ocean of compassion". In fact, the god has no other intention but to test the generosity of the king, as in the *Mārkaṇḍeya* story. The Hariścandra episode builds thus a bridge between (1) the cult of inferior deities who are offered meat and alcohol by low caste devotees, (2) the classical tradition of sacrifice with animal victims, and perhaps even human ones, and (3) the religion of *bhakti* which favours above all a relation of love uniting men and gods.[32]

The story of Hariścandra is not the only incident in the *maṅgal* where the god is shown to deal with his devotees in the same ambivalent way. The next example is called "*Śāle bhara*", or "the weight on the iron nailed plank".[33] Queen Rañjāvatī wants a son but her husband is old. She performs the *Gājana* of Dharma in the hope that the god will grant her the favour of a son. The priest warns her that Dharma is an exacting deity who takes delight in the physical suffering of his devotees. The celebration of the *Gājana* is potentially dangerous, says he, and one must be prepared to die to obtain divine grace. Dharma is brought down to earth by asceticism.[34] Ready to sacrifice her all in order to have a son, the queen is initiated to the ten-syllable *mantra* of Dharma and joins the devotees who have taken *sannyāsa* for the duration of the ritual. The blacksmith makes for her an iron-nailed plank on which she is to lie down. Waiting for its completion, she burns herself with incense, pierces her tongue with an arrow, breaks another one on her chest, walks on fire and puts fetters on her feet. She dances, carrying around her neck a smaller version of the iron nailed plank.[35] When the big piece of wood is ready, the queen performs worship then throws herself on the plank. The spikes pierce her body through and through. Rivers of blood flow. Before dying, she once more requests Dharma to give her a son.

The suicide of this pious woman is tantamount to murder, and Dharma is moved. Appearing as a *brahmacārī*, the god lifts the body of the queen, bathes it and, with the help of a *mantra*, gives Rañjāvatī a new body. The queen who has recovered her life, but is still childless, threatens to cut her own neck again. Dharma has to show himself to her in his four-armed form of Viṣṇu-Nārāyaṇa. He tells the queen that she will find two coconuts in the river. She should offer the first one to the Sun and eat the second one, as in it will be enclosed the "life of her future son.[36] As says the poet: it is a life against a life[37] by offering her life, the queen has obtained a son.

The third, and last, sacrificial death is that of Lāusena, the son of queen Rañjāvatī. He is the hero of the *maṅgal* story, and the cult of Dharma is spread thanks to his efforts. A partial incarnation of the god, in heaven, he is said to be the son of Kaśyapa. This indication serves as a reminder of the cosmic tortoise, emblem of Dharma. Lāusena's birth on earth is the result of a curse. His name alludes to the emptied and dry gourd used as the *kuṣmaṇḍa* often offered in sacrifice in place of an animal victim.[38] Asceticism and renunciation are important characteristics of his. The poet, who calls him *Dharmer tapasvī* and *Tapodhana*, attributes to him a fondness for chastity that makes him accept only reluctantly the wives befitting his princely status. To the prostitute who offers him hospitality Lāusena declares that he keeps a strict fast on Saturdays, Dharma's consecrated day. As a servant of the god, he does not look for pleasures: he does not take oil-bath nor does he chew betel nut. He never sleeps outside his own home, and when he travels he chooses to lie down under a tree.[39] Such a rigorous way of life is quite unusual for a king.

Lāusena thus shares with Dharma the combined character of a king and of an ascetic. In the case of Dharma, the author of the *maṅgal* does not mention his consort, whose usual name is Kāminyā. The god appears as a celibate, a *brahmacārī*.[40] Yet during the *Gājana*, Dharma seems to have, apart from Kāminyā represented by a pot full of water, another wife, called Mukti, whose symbol is some grains of rice in a pot.[41] These two names bring to memory the two dimensions of Dharma as the supreme deity: Kāminyā, his relationship with the transmigrating world, and Mukti, his salvific role.

Lāusena, by his austere penances, must obtain from Dharma the rising of the sun in the West, an event which is meant to bear witness to the greatness of the god. The young man fasts and offers worship daily to the Sun, in company of the twelve *Gājana bhaktas*.[42] As he does not obtain the favour he wants, he cuts off chunks of his own flesh till he is reduced to a mere skeleton. Later, he chops off his own head. All the *bhakta*s die along with him and a dog remains alive to look after the *pūjā* offerings.[43] At last, Dharma, dressed as a *brahmacārī*, comes down on earth, sorts out Lāusena's bones, washes them and brings his devotee back to life with an aspersion using Kuśa grass. Because his request that the sun rises in the West has not been complied with, Lāusena threatens to kill himself again. Dharma stops him, makes himself known as *Nirañjana* and *Anāther Nātha.* He orders the sun to rise in the West for a short while. This whole episode, the dramatic culmination of the *maṅgal,* is called *Hākaṇḍa.*[44] It bears witness to the greatness of Dharma in the eyes of men. The sun is Dharma's witness, and Dharma, as the supreme deity, is also the sun.

The *maṅgal* seems to point out the necessity of human sacrifice (*naramedha*) to move the god Dharma to action, but it gives it a twist which makes it acceptable within the framework of the *bhakti* religion. This *naramedha* is nothing but ascetic practice (*tapas*) carried to the extreme point of self-sacrifice. It is identified with total surrender to the divine will (*sarvatyāga*) and in *bhakti* terminology is called *saraṇāpanna.*

As a counter-example, the poet proposes the sacrifice which Lāusena's maternal uncle, the main opponent of Dharma and his cult, plans to offer to the Goddess: he wants to sacrifice to her his nephew, whom he hates. This would be a sinful act as the chosen victim must never be the sacrificer's enemy; on the contrary, it must be the person who is the dearest to him, that is to say himself or his nearest kin.[45] This is in accordance with the classical notion which presents the victim as the substitute of the worshipper.[46] The *Dharma maṅgal* takes literally this requirement and conciliates in so doing the cult of "terrible" deities who feed themselves on the blood of their devotee and the faith in a benevolent and loving god who demands from his *bhakta* a total surrender, but not his physical death. The bloody sacrifice appears then as the metaphor of the call expressed by Kṛṣṇa in the *Bhagavadgītā* (*adh.* XVIII, v.66): "Leave aside all the rules and come to me as your only refuge; I shall make you free from all, do not worry".

NOTES

1 The three main authors of *Dharma maṅgal* are Rūparām

Cakravartī, Ghanarām Cakravartī and Mānikrām Gaṅgulī. The first wrote in the middle of the 17th century, the second in the beginning of the 18th and the last at the end. The edition of Rūparām published by Sukumār Sen and Pañcānan Maṇḍal, Barddhamān Sāhitya Sabhā, 1351 B.S. (1942) does not include the whole text as the second volume has never come out. In 1986, Akṣay Kumār Kayāl edited and published a complete edition of Rūparām's text. Ghanarām has been published by Calcutta University and edited by Pīyūś Kānti Mahāpātra in 1962, and Mānikrām's version was edited by Bijitkumār Datta and Sunandā Datta, and published by Calcutta University in 1960.

2 Bhaṭṭācārya, Āśutoṣ 1958:617-663, 670-776, Dasgupta, S.B. 1946: 259-310; Sen, S. 1960: 54-60, 136-140, and the introduction to his edition of Rūparām. See also Bhattacharya, N.N. 1978: 327-340. The thesis of Sandra P. Robinson *The Dharmapūjā: A Study of Rites and Symbols Associated with the Bengal Deity Dharmarāj*, defended in 1980 at the University of Chicago, is not yet published. In her very interesting study, she does not go into the question of the origin of Dharma and considers him as the Supreme deity, according to the views expressed by her informants, vol. I, p.52-58, and p. 65.

3 *Caitanya vandanā*, Rūparām, ed. Sen-Maṇḍal p.8-9, and Kayāl p.3-4; *Gauraṅga vandanā*, Mānikrām, p.5-7.

4 See, as examples, Nārāyaṇ Dev's *Padmā purāṇa* and Viṣṇu Pāl's *Manasā maṅgal* as well as Mānik Datta's *Caṇḍī maṅgal*.

5 *Mahābhārata* XII, 334 8-9, quoted by M. Biardeau in *Dictionnaire des Mythologies*, vol.2, p. 153. Nārāyaṇa, son of Dharma, has taken a quadruple form: Nara, Nārāyaṇa, Hari and Kṛṣṇa. Vālmiki's *Rāmāyaṇa, āraṇya kaṇḍa* 4 12, mentions the god Dharma amongst the gods assembled at the *āśram* of Agastya *muni*. In the *Brahmavaivartapurāṇa, Brahmakhaṇḍa*, 3 41-47, Dharma springs out from Kṛṣṇa's chest after the Trimūrti gods, and from his left side comes out his consort Mūrtī.

6 Biardeau, M. and Malamoud, Ch. 1976: 18, quoting the *Śatapathabrāhmaṇa*, VI 1, 1 12, VII 5, 1,5.

7 Biardeau, M. 1971:69, quoting *Viṣṇupurāṇa* VI 3 23 and *Kūrmapurāṇa*, 45 23. M. Biardeau calls the Yamunā "the river of the origins" while Gaṅgā is "the river of Salvation", *Dictionnaire des Mythologies*, vol. I, p. 442.

See *Ṛgveda*, X 10, translated into French by L. Renou 1956: 55-57.

8 For the narration of the "death" of Dharma in the *maṅgal* and the *Śūnya purāṇa*, as well as a commentary on this myth, see my thesis *Etude comparée des Maṅgalkāvya bengalis: Manasā et Caṇḍī*. Université de Paris III, 1990, vol. 1.

9 The temporary structure raised for the celebration of the *Gājana* must be facing the South, Mitra, Aśok ed. 1969: vol. IV, p. 234.
Rūparām mentions also that the Dharma *pūjā* is facing South, p. 78. The relation between the South and Yama-Dharmarāj is mentioned in the *Bṛhadāraṇyaka upaniṣad* III 9, 21.

10 On the whiteness of the god, see *vandanā* by Rūparām, ed. Sen-Maṇḍal, p. 3-4.

11 On leucoderma and leprosy which are inflicted on Dharma's enemies, see *Mayūrbhaṭṭa Dharmamaṅgal*, ed. Kayāl, intr. p. 14.

12 Biardeau, M. 1969:61, quoting the *Vāyupurāṇa*. Sandra Robinson notes that the flowers Dharma is said to prefer are the lotus, very much a cosmogonical symbol, vol. I, p. 122-123 and p. 168.

13 The putting back into the water of the *daṇḍa* is the *visarjana* of the divine image, Basu, T.K. 1963: 168-169. Robinson's description varies in as much as it is a carved plank of wood, in the form of an arrow with nails and spikes sticking out, called *Choṭa Bāṇeśvara*, that is put into the water, vol. I, p. 79 et 304-305.

14 Rūparām, ed. Sen-Maṇḍal, p. 78.
Robinson also insists on the obvious signs of the royalty of Dharma, vol. I p. 206.

15 Rūparām, *id.* p. 72.

16 *Id.*, p. 78.

17 Biardeau, M. et Malamoud, Ch. 1976: 19 and 161.

18 S. Robinson, whose thesis I had not read when I made the first draft of this paper and presented it at the July 1991 Conference, mentions also as a characteristic of Dharma the necessity for the *bhakta* to attract him (*ākarśaṇa*) to the *pūjā* site, *op. cit.* n. 2, vol. I, p. 29. She establishes also a direct link between self-sacrifice and the arousing of Dharma and his coming down to accept the cult of his devotees, *id.* p. 35 and p. 103.

19 According to Basu, T.K. 1963:166, in 1959 there was not a single *sannyāsī* coming from the higher castes (brahmins, *kāyastha*, *vaidya*) but there were a few from the middle-ranking castes, the *navaśākha*. In the village he studied the chief *sannyāsī* is always a *sadgopa*, and his priest a *bāgdi*.

For the *Gājana* of Śiva, the same year, out of 59 *sannyāsī*, there were 4 brahmins, 4 *navaśākha* and the rest coming from 9 different low castes, p. 156. Robinson states that "the initiates all belong to communities ranked as untouchable" *op. cit.* vol. I p. 82.

20 Amongst the composers, the three most important ones are brahmins as well as Mayurbhaṭṭa, held to be the first ever but by whom no complete manuscript has been found. There are also a wine-distiller and seller *(śūdi)* and a *kaivarta*, both very low castes. Rūparām gives the names of the first worshippers: King Bhoja, Yudhiṣṭhira, Āśoyā *caṇḍāla*, Dhūṣadatta *vaṇika* and King Hariścandra, ed. Sen-Maṇḍal, p. 27-28. The mention of Yudhiṣṭhira is interesting as he is called the son of Dharmarāja in the *Mahābhārata*.

21 Rūparām, ed. Kayāl, p. 354.

22 Both the Sun and Dharma are said to inflict and cure leprosy and leucoderma.

23 Dowson, J. 1973: 310-311.

24 See Bhattacharya, F. vol. I, p. 71-72 for Jagatjīvan Ghoṣāl's *Manasā maṅgal* in which Dharma, after his "death" enters into Śiva.

25 Śiva's *Gājana* is held at the end of the month of *Caitra* (middle of April) and that of Dharma at the full moon of *Vaiśākha* (April-May). In a village of Burdwan district, Buḍorāja is worshipped as a Śiva who has taken Dharma within his own self, *ātmasāt.* The object of the cult is a *liṅga*, but the *Gājana* takes place on *Vaiśākha pūrṇimā*. He-goats are sacrificed to the *śakti* of Śiva, the god not accepting animal sacrifices, and in a secluded place "untouchables" kill a pig, maybe to Dharma or his wife, Ghoṣ, B. 1976-1978 vol. 1: 142-146.

26 Renou, L. 1947 vol. I: 317-318.

27 The *Yātra*, Bengal's traditional theatre, got inspiration from the Purāṇa version; many plays exist on this theme that are available in popular editions.

28 a) The passage from Varuṇa to Dharma is made easy by the fact that Varuṇa also is considered as the guardian of Order. The *Śatapathabrāhmāṇa* calls him Dharmapati, V. 3 3 1.
b) In the *maṅgal*, the son of Hariścandra is called Lui, name which can be a corrupted form of Rohita. During the *Gājana*, a kid, called Loue, or Luye, is sacrificed to Dharma after it has been allowed to roam at will during a year, Robinson, vol. II, p. 241-242.

29 The blood red colour is worn by Dharma when he appears as a *sannyāsī*. It certainly has a terrible (*ugra*) connotation. The

priests of goddess Kālī wear red clothes and the flowers offered to her are red.

30 "There is no donator equal to you on the earth" says Dharma to king Hariścandra, Rūparām, ed. Sen-Maṇḍal, p. 86.

31 The *maṅgalkāvya* calls *māyā* the faculty the gods possess to change forms and create illusion. Robinson also notes this particularity of Dharma, calling him "the god of transformation", vol. II, p. 415.

32 Alcohol, rice cakes and raw sugar are usual offerings to Dharma. The stone representing the god is sometime washed in alcohol. Robinson mentions the ritual, called *bhā̃ḍāl jāgāno*, the awakening of the jug in which alcohol has been prepared. The *bhakta* bring this jug in procession to the temple of Dharma, vol. I, p. 121. This jug is a symbolic representation of Dharmarāj, not just an offering. With lotuses on top, it evokes the creative and energizing power of the god.

33 The queen's action is called *Śāle bhara:* to put one's weight on a spike, Sen, S. 1971 vol. II: 701.

34 Rūparām, ed. Sen-Maṇḍal, p. 85.

35 This plank, called *pāṭa*, is a small piece of wood on which are fixed "a peculiarly shaped iron hook and a spike (called *kājjalī* and *mānak* respectively) and some smaller ones (*śalya* > *śāla*) on which in course of penance the main devotee of Dharma has to lie for some time."Sen, S. 1971 vol. II: 545.

36 Dry coconut is the symbol of the sacrificial human victim because it bears some resemblance to a skull.

37 Rūparām, ed. Sen-Maṇḍal, p. 96.

38 *Lāu*, from the Sanskrit *Alābu*, gourd, a shell of gourd, Sen S. 1971 vol. II: 816.
The last part of Lāusena's name, *Sena*, common with his father, might be an attempt to give them Kṣatriya status.

39 See *Jāmati pālā and Golāhāṭa pālā*, Rūparām, ed. Kayāl, p. 148 and p. 171.

40 Mitra, A. 1972: 73-80, and Ghoṣ, B. 1976-78 vol. II: 98 and 119.

41 In Mitra Aśok, ed. 1969 vol. IV: 228-241, a complete description of the *Gājana* is given. Mukti is materialized by five ser of *ātap* rice in a pot. A temporary shed (*cālā*) is built for her on the eastern side of the main structure, where only the *paṇḍita*, Dharma's *deyāśī*, can enter.
Robinson does not mention this rite. In her field work, she witnessed the marriage of Dharma with Muktā (sic), presented as a pitcher, vol. II, p. 331.

42 The number twelve is again noticeable.

43 Reminder of the dog accompanying Yudhiṣṭhira to heaven who was Dharma, the Pāṇḍava's father. In the religion of *bhakti*, the dog, as a low status animal, has a place.

44 The river on the bank of which this ritual takes place is called Hākaṇḍa. The whole episode of Lāusena's sacrificial death bears the same name. Sen S. 1971 gives the spelling as *hākanda* and links it to *hākanda*, "piteous cry", vol. II: 915.

45 When the victim is unwilling to be sacrificed, the sacrifice is perverted. Its destinator is, most generally, a terrible form of the Goddess, such as the famous Ḍākāte Kālī, the Kālī of the robbers.

46 Biardeau, M. and Malamoud Ch. 1976:19.

BIBLIOGRAPHY

Basu, Tara Krishna 1963. *The Bengal Peasant from time to time.* Calcutta, Indian Statistical Institute: Asia Publishing House.

Bhaṭṭācārya, Āśutoṣ 1958. *Maṅgalkāvyer Itihās. 3rd ed.*, Calcutta: A. Mukherji & Co.

Bhattacharya, France 1990. *Etude comparée des Maṅgalkāvya bengalis: Manasā et Caṇḍī.* Thesis. Paris: University Paris III - Sorbonne Nouvelle.

Bhattacharya, N.N. 1978. "The Cult and Rituals of Dharma Ṭhākur", *History and Society: Essays in honour of Professor Nihar Ranjan Ray.* Ed. Debiprasad Chattopadhyay. Calcutta: K.P. Bagchi.

Biardeau, Madeleine 1969. "Etudes de mythologie hindoue II, Cosmogonies purāṇiques", *Bulletin de l'École française d'Extrême-Orient*, LV, and in *Etudes de mythologie hindoue*, tome 1 *Cosmogonies purāṇiques*. Paris: Publications de l'Ecole française d'Extrême-Orient, 1981.

Biardeau, Madeleine 1971. "Etudes de mythologie hindoue III", *Bulletin de l'Ecole française d'Extrême-Orient*, LVIII.

Biardeau, Madeleine and Malamoud, Charles 1976. *Le sacrifice dans l'Inde ancienne.* Paris:Presses universitaires de France.

Biardeau, Madeleine 1981. Entries in *Dictionnaire des mythologies.* 2 vol. Paris: Flammarion.

Cakravartī, Ghanarām 1962. *Dharma maṅgal.* Ed. Piyūṣkānti Mahāpātra. Calcutta: Kalikātā viśvavidyālaya.

Dasgupta, S.B. 1946. *Obscure Religious Cults.* 3rd ed. 1969. Calcutta: Firma K.L. Mukhopadhyay.

Datta, Mānik 1384 B.S. (1977). *Mānikdatter Caṇḍīmaṅgal.* Ed. S.K. Ojhā. Uttarabaṅga Viśvavidyālaya.

Dev, Nārāyaṇ, 1947. *Padmāpurāṇa* 2nd ed. Tamonāścandra Dāsgupta. Kalikātā viśvavidyālaya.

Dev, Nārāyaṇ *Padmāpurāṇa*. Ed. Sādhanā Majumdār. Calcutta: University of Calcutta. In press.

Dowson, J. 1973 repr. *A Classical Dictionary of Hindu Mythology*. New Delhi: Oriental Books Reprint.

Gaṅgopādhyāy, Mānikarām 1960. *Dharmamaṅgal*. Ed. Bijitakumār Datta & Sunandā Datta. Calcutta: Kalikātā viśvavidyālaya.

Ghoṣ, Binay 1976-78. *Paścimavaṅger saṃskṛti* 3 vol. Calcutta: prakāśa bhavana.

Kṛttivās 1364 B.S. (1957). *Rāmāyaṇa*. Ed. Harekṛṣṇa Mukhopādhyāy. Calcutta: Sāhitya saṃsad.

Mahābhārata 1974. Transl. Bengali of Kālīprasanna Siṃha, 6 vol. Calcutta: Sākṣaratā prakāśan, Paścimavaṅga Nirakṣaratā Dūrīkaraṇa samiti.

Mārkaṇḍeyapurāṇa 1390 B.S. (1983). Transl. Pañcānan Tarkaratna & Śrījīva Nyāyatīrtha. Calcutta: Navabhārata Pābliśārs.

Mayūrbhaṭṭa Dharmamaṅgal 1381 B.S. (1974). Ed. A.K.Kayāl & Citrā Dev. Calcutta: G.Bharadvāj & Cie.

Mitra, Amalendu 1972. *Rāḍher saṃskṛti*. Calcutta: Phārma K.L.Mukhopādhyāy.

Mitra, Aśok ed. 1969. *Paścimavaṅger pūjā-pārvaṇao melā*. 4 vol., Nutan Dilli, Census of India.

Pāl, Viṣṇu 1968. Manasāmaṅgal. Ed. Sukumār Sena, Bibliotheca Indica. Calcutta: The Asiatic Society

Renou, Louis & Filliozat, Jean 1947. *L'Inde classique: Manuel des études indiennes*, vol.1. Paris:Payot.

Renou, Louis 1956. Transl. *Hymnes spéculatifs du Veda*. Paris: "Connaissance de l'Orient" Gallimard.

Robinson, Sandra P. 1980. *The Dharmapūjā: A Study of Rites and Symbols Associated with the Bengali Deity Dharmarāj*. 2 vol. Thesis. University of Chicago.

Rūparāma 1351 B.S. (1975). *Dharmamaṅgal*. Ed. Sukumār Sena & Pañcānan Maṇḍal, Ist part. Barddhamān Sāhitya-sabhā.

Rūparāma 1986. *Dharmamaṅgal*. Ed. A.K. Kayāl. Calcutta: Bhāravī.

Sen, Sukumar 1960. *History of Bengali Literature*, New Delhi: Sahitya Akademi.

Sen, Sukumar 1971. *An Etymological Dictionary of Bengali. c. AD 1000-1800*, 2 Vol. Calcutta: Eastern Publishers.

Vālmīki *Rāmāyaṇa* 1927. Transl. Makhan Lal Sen, 3 vol., Calcutta: Oriental Publishing Company.

The Saint and the Bandit

W.L.Smith

Both the saint in the ashram and the bandit in the wilds seek, in their very different ways, to escape the constraints of Indian society; since their goals and methods are antithetical, it is not surprising that an encounter between the two is a familiar hagiographical motif. Perhaps the earliest of such accounts is the well-known story of Buddha and Aṅgulimāla. Their meeting is said to have taken place in 508 B.C.[1] Buddha, we are told, left Sāvatthi where he had spent the rainy season, and, despite repeated warnings, proceeded to walk alone into the bandit's forest stronghold. When Aṅgulimāl saw a lone monk passing by, he rushed out, sword in hand, and commanded him to stop. Buddha replied that he had indeed stopped and that it was Aṅgulimāla who had not. This puzzled the dacoit, and once the apparent riddle had been explained, the terrible Aṅgulimāla had renounced his crimes and taken refuge in Buddha to become, eventually, an exemplary monk.

Much later, in medieval hagiography, quite similar stories often appear. We are told that Gurū Nānak transformed a village of *ṭhag*s into devout Sikhs,[2] that Caitanya converted several notorious South Indian bandits,[3] that a dacoit chief became the disciple of Hit Harivaṁś,[4] and that the singer Vaṁśīdās reformed the bandit Kenārām.[5] One of the most wide-spread versions of the motif, one in which the role of the bandit is played by the poet Vālmīki, can be found in the

Adhyātmarāmāyaṇa, various vernacular versions of the Rāma story which drew upon it, and the oral tradition as well.[6] In this apocryphal tale, the saint is collectively represented by the Seven Sages. When the sages enter Vālmīki's forest lair, he holds them up and demands their clothing. The sages suggest that he ask his wife and children whether they are willing to share the burden of guilt he has acquired. Vālmīki agrees, asks and is informed that while they are quite willing to share the fruits of his crime, the sin he has incurred is another matter altogether. Their refusal causes him to change his ways.[7] The same story appears in a *Janam-Sākhī*, where Gurū Nānak plays the role of the Seven Sages and the bandit is named Bhola;[8] in an oral version, the bandit is again Vālmīki whom Parameśvar sends Nānak to save.[9] In a Muslim variant, the saint is Nizāmuddīn Auliyā and the bandit Nizām Dacoit.

Vālmīki and Bhola, like Aṅgulimāla, are brought to realize the Karmic consequences of their deeds and, most likely, to fear punishment in an appropriate hell, though this is not specifically mentioned. Gurū Nānak, however, most certainly exploits the latter fear when he finds himself surrounded by a gang of *ṭhags* during his wanderings. As the bandits prepare to kill him, Nānak points to the smoke of a nearby fire and asks that they kill him there instead. The robbers oblige and take him to the source of the smoke which turns out to be a funeral pyre. There they see the minions of Rāma and Yama fighting over the possession of the soul of the deceased. Yama's underlings want to deliver it the hell of pots, *kumbhī narak*, for punishment. The sight terrifies the bandits who fall at Nānak's feet, confess their crimes and ask to be attached to the Name.[10]

Terrifying a sinner into repentence, a procedure many a Christian revivalist preacher would approve of, does not, however, seem to be the rule in such stories. Very often a song or verse suffices. This is the case in a story about Hit Harivaṁś. Hit Harivaṁś settled in Vrindaban when it was still a wilderness. When the local bandit chieftain learned of his arrival, he sent some of his men to expel him. The bandits, however, were impressed by his luminous appearance and returned without molesting him. Then the bandit leader himself went to the saint. As he arrived, Harivaṁś was reading verses from his *Caurāsī Pad.* As soon as he heard these, the bandit captain burst into tears and asked Harivaṁś to be his guru. We are told that in the course of time the bandit became a saint himself.[11] In still another incident, Gurū Nānak is invited to stay overnight at the home of one Shekh Sajan, or Sajjaṇ, a pious dissembler who invites travellers into his home, then murders them in their sleep and steals their possessions. When Sajan urges Nānak and his companion to retire for the night, Nānak tells him that he would like to sing a *śabad* first; and at the sound of the verses, Sajan falls at Nānak's feet and admits his crimes.[12]

In a somewhat deviant variant in one of the East Bengali ballads, the role of the saint is played by the rather unlikely figure of Vaṁśīdās. Vaṁśīdās was a professional singer and author of a *Manasā Bhāsan*, a poem celebrating the deeds of the Bengali snake goddess Manasā. Here, in order to make him conform to the prototypes, Vaṁśīdās is described as garbed as a Vaiṣṇava with long locks and appropriate *tilak*, in a constant state of devotional ecstasy (*bhāvete bibhor*), and accompanied by a train of pupils. In the Forest of Reeds the bandit Kenārām abruptly appears before the group. Vaṁśīdās tries several different approaches. He points out to Kenārām that his wife and children will refuse to share his burden of guilt, but Kenārām replies that this makes no difference as he has neither wife nor children. He tells him that he is destined for hell; he urges him to turn to Hari, Manasā and Kālī, but nothing has any effect. Vaṁśī then asks permission to sing Manasā's song a final time before he is killed, and, sword in hand, the bandit sits to listen. Vaṁśī's singing can cause stones to melt and it is his song that finally succeeds in softening the heart of the bandit; and it is not at all the religious content of the song, rather its pathos, the heart-rending description of how Behulā is widowed on her wedding night, which has its effect. *Karuṇa rasa* succeeds where all else fails. Kenārām bursts into tears and renounces his evil ways. After his capitulation, Kenārām becomes, of course, a singer of Manasā songs.[13]

Conversions can even take place without the saint uttering a word or moving a muscle as can be seen in a purported incident from the life of Debendranāth Tagore who was known under the title of Maharshi because of his leadership of the Brahmo Samāj. In the 1860's Debendranāth often visited Shantiniketan, then a desolate waste tract, in order to meditate. It was also a haunt of bandits and one day a band of them surrounded him as he sat beneath a *saptaparṇa* tree, so deep in meditation that he was completely unaware of their presence. The bandit leader, profoundly impressed, waited for Debendranāth to open his eyes, and when he did so, asked his pardon and vowed to serve him for the rest of his life.[14] Here Debendranāth displays one of the hallmarks of the Bengali saint—*jaḍa*, the ability to be so lost in meditation that one resembles a corpse or a stone statue, and this the bandit instantly recognizes.[15]

Finally we can look at a case where the bandit is converted without the saint even being physically present. The saint of the story is the 16th-century Bengali Śrīnibās and the bandit one Bīrhambīr, a local *rājā*, or, to be more precise, robber baron. Once, when Śrīnibās had sent a cartload of books to Bengal from Vrindāban, Bīrhambīr got wind of the shipment and, presuming the cart to be loaded with treasure, ordered his men to hijack it. Opening the crates, he found sacred manuscripts, and at the mere sight of them (*granthadṛṣṭimātrete*) his mind became pure (*śuddha*). He realized then that his evil deeds had born fruit and vowed that if he ever met the *sādhu* whom he had injured, he would ask his forgiveness. When Śrīnibās eventually came in search of the stolen manuscripts, Bīrhambīr burst into tears and begged him to save him from the consequences of his sins.[16] Later Bīrhambīr became a zealous supporter of Śrīnibās's missionary activities and went so far as to order his subjects to repeat the name of Kṛṣṇa a stipulated number of times each day.[17]

Saints' lives are intended to edify and inspire, and the motifs employed in them are selected or devised in order to illustrate the teachings the saint embodies. The point in this motif seems obvious. The saint and the bandit are moral opposites. The saint is totally indifferent to or scornful of wealth; the bandit readily kills to gain it. There is obvious irony in the fact that the bandit selects a saint as a victim. Kenārām goes through Vaṁśīdās's cloth bag and finds it empty; puzzled, he asks what the point of being a wandering singer of songs is, if one doesn't earn a single cowry doing it. Bīrhambīr expects gold and finds the *Bhāgavatapurāṇa*. Vālmīki and Bhola, having presumably learned from experience, take one look at their prospective victims and demand their clothes. These, at least, they have.

There is another point as well. It should be kept in mind that the Indian bandit inspired as much terror as does the modern urban mugger. Aṅgulimāla, Finger-Garland, was given his ominous name because of the grisly habit of cutting off the right-hand fingers of his victims and stringing them about his neck as trophies. Kenārām was so frightening that at the very mention of his name people shook with fear and trees shed their leaves. The dacoit is death personified. Vālmīki is the very image of death (*jīvānāmantakopama)*. Kenārām appears as Yamarāj; and the name of the bandit converted by Hit Harivaṁś is, quite appropriately, Narvāhan, another epithet of the God of Death. Where lesser mortals quake in terror or faint from fear, the saint is unmoved or, more often, amused. The prospect of death no more sways him than does material desire. Facing Vālmīki, the Seven Sages are unfazed (*avyagrāḥ*). When Gurū Nānak tells the *ṭhag*s they can kill him as long as they do so by yonder fire, they say, "We have killed many men, but laughing none has said 'kill me'".[18] When Kenārām appears before Vaṁśīdās and his pupils, the pupils weep in terror while Vaṁśīdās stands calmly with a smile on his lips. "There is no-one on this earth who does not fear me," the astonished bandit says, "the dewāns and the kāzis shake in fear. Armies flee when they hear my name. Who are you, Sir, who are not afraid of me?"[19]

The bandit can also be seen as the arch-sinner, one who will shun no crime in order to gratify his material desires. But, as these stories demonstrate, even the hardest of hearts yields to the saint. The bandit's conversion is sudden and complete and the saint's almost effortless accomplishment provides very impressive evidence of his powers. Perhaps the saint might even see the bandit as a challenge. Such has been the case in modern times. In the summer of 1960, for example, Vinoba Bhave sought out the gang of the notorious Man Singh and induced eighteen of its members to surrender.[20]

It seems also significant that when biographical details about the bandit are provided, these are always presented with understanding and even sympathy. None of our dacoits is described as taking up a career of crime out of simple perversity. They are, rather, the victims of circumstance. All are Brahmans led astray. Aṅgulimāla's troubles were forecast by his birth under a malignant star. As a youth he was honest but during the course of his studies in Taxila, jealous fellow-students poisoned his teacher's mind against him, and when the course of studies ended, the teacher demanded as his stipend a necklace of one thousand human fingers and in this way he launched Aṅgulimāla on his sanguinary career.

Environmental and economic forces conspire to turn Vālmīki into a bandit. Though born a Brahman, Vālmīki was raised among the Kirātas, one of whose usual occupations, according to classical literature, was highway robbery. Having grown up amongst the Kirātas, Vālmīki adopted Kirāta ways. In the *Daśakumāracarita* of Daṇḍin we find a rough parallel in the story of Mataṅga, who explains that he is one of many renegade Brahmaṇs who dwelt in the wilds amongst the Kirātas. Mataṅga redeems himself by sacrificing his own life to save that of a Brahman traveller whom his Kirāta companions want to kill.[21] Not only had Vālmīki been raised in the wrong environment, he had also fathered numerous children on a *śūdra* woman; his family was large and he felt forced to rob in order to feed it.[22]

Kenārām, like his two predecessors, was also born a Brahman, but his tale is far more tragic. His mother died when he was very young, his father then handed him over to a maternal uncle who cared for him until famine struck the land. Faced with starvation, the uncle sold him for some sacks of grain. Kenārām was purchased by a householder who practiced banditry on the side and it was there he learned the trade. The final blow fell when his purchaser betrayed him to the local dewān for a reward of five hundred rupees.

Deceived or betrayed by the world, the bandit repudiates it. The saint repudiates the world as well and when the bandit capitulates to him, we are shown which path of rejection is the superior.

NOTES

1. The story can be found in the *Majjhima Nikāya*, 86, and its commentary, the *Papañcasūdanī*. A somewhat different version appears in the *Paramatthadīpanī*. The date is after Hans Wolfgang Schumann, *Der Historische Buddha. Köln:* Eugen Diederichs Verlag. 1982, p. 148.
2. The *Ādi Granth*, trans. Ernest Trumpp. London. 1877, p.xviiiff.
3. A.N.Chatterjee, *Śrīkṛṣṇa Caitanya: A Historical Study on Gauḍiya Vaiṣṇavism*. New Delhi: Associated Publishing Company. 1983, p.11.
4. Charles S.J. White, *The Caurāsī Pad of Śrī Hit Harivaṁś*. Hawaii: The University Press of Hawaii. 1977, p.27.
5. Kṣitiś Candra Maulik, ed., *Prācīn Pūrbabaṅga Gītikāl*. Calcutta: Firma K.L. Mukhopadhyay. 1970, p.249ff.
6. Kāmil Bulke, *Rām Kathā, Utpatti aur Vikās*. Prayāg: Hindī Pariṣad Prakāśan. 1962, p.39ff.
7. *Adhyātmarāmāyaṇa*. Gorakhpur: Gita Press. *Saṃvat* 2001, 2.6.65ff.

8. W.H. McCleod, ed. and trans., *The B-40 Janam-Sākhī*. Amritsar. 1979, p.42ff.
9. Bulke, *op. cit.* p.44.
10. Trumpp, *op. cit.*, p.xix; the version in the *B-40 Janam-Sākhī* (p.201), differs in details.
11. Charles S.J. White, *op.cit.*
12. Trumpp, *op.cit*, p.xiv; according to W.H.McCleod, *Early Sikh Tradition; A Study of the Janam-Sākhīs*. Oxford: Clarendon Press. 1980, p.122; the verse cited served to prompt this narrative anecdote.
13. Maulik, *op. cit.*
14. Sisirkumar Mitra, *Resurgent India*. Bombay: Allied Publishers. 1963, p.89-91.
15. June McDaniel, *The Madness of Saints: Ecstatic Religion in Bengal*. Chicago: University of Chicago. 1989, p.9.
16. Narahari Cakrabartī, *Bhaktiratnākar*. Calcutta: Gauṛiya Miśan. 3rd ed. 1987,p.341ff.
17. A.N. Chatterjee, *op. cit.* p.57.
18. Trumpp, *op.cit.* p.xviii.
19. *āmāre ye nā ḍarāẏ eman nāi ta bhubane* | |
deśera deoẏāna kāji bhaẏe kampabanā
phauja paścān jhaṛiẏā palāẏ śuniyā āmāra nāma |
bhaẏa nāi ye kara tumi ke hao ṭhākura |
Maulik, *op.cit.* p.267.
20. Kalyan Mukherjee & Brij Ray Singh, *Malkhan: the Story of a Bandit King*. New Delhi: Lancer International. 1985, pp. 153 & 158.
21. *Daśakumāracarita*, 1,2.
22. *putradārādayaḥ santi bahavo me bubhukṣitāḥ*; 2.6. 70.

Genres

'*Barvai*' Metre in Tulsīdās and Rahīm

Rupert Snell

Indian literature abounds with couplet metres well suited to concise gnomic expression and punchy aphorisms, and in the Hindi part of this realm it is the well-known *dohā* that wears the crown: but compared with the less well-known *barvai* couplet, the *dohā* seems longwinded and diffuse. Indeed the *barvai* epitomises Brian Stone's comment (1987:180) that 'in all the arts, tight formal requirements of organic beauty have proved the best moulds for such qualities as intensity of expression, economy, and purity and power of focus'. What follows is an analysis of the *barvai* metre firstly in terms of its formal characteristics, and secondly in terms of the stylistic devices through which poets have achieved the qualities that Stone describes.

The *barvai* couplet belongs to the large group of Hindi metres defined quantitatively according to the number of *mātrās* or metrical 'instants' to the line. Such metres comprise a set sequence of feet, defined in terms of their overall *mātrik* length, their internal arrangement of long and short syllables being variable. The *barvai* has a line of 19 *mātrās*, with a caesura after the twelfth *mātrā* (m). In its overall shape and cadence, with trochaic end-rhyme (¯˘), the *barvai* resembles the *dohā*. But the *barvai* appears only quite rarely, taking at best a cameo role alongside the regular stars of Hindi prosody such as the *dohā, caupāī, chappay, kavitt* and so forth. The opening couplet of Tulsī's *Barvai Rāmāyaṇ* stands as an example of the metre:

केस मुकुत सखि मरकत मनिमय होत ।
हाथ लेत पुनि मुकुता करत उदोत ।।[1]

Jagannāth Prasād (1935:83) defines the *barvai* simply in terms of 12+7m construction, adding that the line ends most attractively with a *jagaṇ* (˘¯˘) while a *tagaṇ* (¯¯˘) is also encountered. Prasād records the alternative names *kuraṅga* and (rather confusingly) *dhruv* for this metre; he also describes an extended variant, called *atibarvai*, of 12+9m. G.A. Grierson (1893:201) defines the *barvai* line as comprising 6+4+2+4+2+1m.

Maheshwari Sinha Mahesh (1964:125) cites the Apabhraṃśā metre *Bhramarāvalĭ* as a precedent; the one-line example of this metre appearing in Rājaśekhara's *Chandaḥśekhara*, an eleventh-century Sanskrit version of the *Svayambhūchanda*,[2] does indeed show a 12+7 *mātrik* pattern (with the name *Bhramarāvalĭ* itself constituting the 7m *pāda*).[3] The text of the *Svayambhūchanda* itself yields a *catuṣpadī* example with the name *Bhramararin̄cholī*.[4] These *lakṣaṇa* stanzas show a 7m *pāda* in (˘̄ ˘̄ ¯ ˘ ¯), with no sign of the *barvai's* internal construction or trochaic cadence, which may therefore derive from the *dohā* model rather than from the *Bhramarāvalĭ* specifically.[5] Metrical characteristics apart, there is clearly a problem in deriving the name *barvai* (बरवै, बरवे, बरवा) from *Bhramarāvalĭ* (if that is what Mahesh implies), not least in the loss of aspiration from the first consonant.[6]

The name *barvā* is applied also to a *rāga* in Kāfi *ṭhāṭ* (Govind Rām Gupta 1970:18). Śatrughna Śukla (1983:58) quotes the *Rāg darpaṇ*, Faqīrullāh's 1665 Persian translation of Man Singh's Brajbhāṣā musicological treatise *Mānkutūhal*, as reporting that 'the song [Persian *nagma*] called '*barwa*' [transcribed in Devanagri as बरवः] is nowadays called *barvā* in ordinary speech, and some people call the same thing *ṭhumrī*'. In his discussion of this reference, Peter Manuel (1989:37) notes that *barvā* was one of various 'distinctive modal types used by courtesans in the Doab for interpretative Braj songs' and that these forms constituted a kind of proto-*ṭhumrī*. But it is unclear what connexion, if any, exists between the musical genre and the metre.

OCCURRENCES OF *BARVAI* METRE

Barvai is not a very common metre, but is found scattered here and there in early Hindi poetry, most examples being characterized by some eastern (Avadhī) elements. The metre is notably absent from the (Brajbhāṣā) *Chandamālā* of Keśavdās, one of the first Hindi poets to write on prosody, though Keśav was himself active at the time from which the earliest extant *barvai* examples seem to date; it is also absent from S.H. Kellogg (1938), whose lengthy list of metres presumably draws on a range of Hindi prosodic works (but is silent as to its sources). But the absence of *barvai* from these lists may simply reflect the fact that the taxonomies of pandits like Keśav and the Reverend Kellogg are a poor guide to actual poetic practice.

As a vehicle for autonomous sequences of verses, *barvai* metre is primarily known from three short compilations: the brief *Barvai Rāmāyaṇ* by Tulsīdās (c. 1532-1623), and two texts attributed to his younger contemporary Abdurrahīm '<u>Kh</u>ān<u>kh</u>ānā' (1556-1627) of the Mughal court, known in Hindi literature by his *bhanitā* 'Rahīm'.[7]

THE *BARVAI RĀMĀYAṆ* OF TULSĪDĀS

Tulsī's *Barvai Rāmāyaṇ*[8], in common with his other minor works, is largely neglected by Tulsī scholars: it is difficult to find any analysis of the text beyond the most general genuflexions towards its poetic quality. This is partly explained by uncertainty about the state of the text, a rather inchoate collection of couplets perhaps from diverse sources. Yet the quality and interest of some of these couplets, and the intriguing use of the rare *barvai* metre, rewards a close reading of the text despite its uncertain status.

The *Barvai Rāmāyaṇ* (RĀM) comprises 69 *barvai* couplets, thus a total of 138 lines. Wide discrepancies of reading are reported amongst the manuscripts[9]; attribution to Tulsīdās is itself far from proven, and it is likely that the text represents at best a posthumous anthology, or perhaps a late compilation based on a core of original verses attributable to Tulsī. Whatever the case, no discussion of RĀM can assume that the received text was known in this form to the poet himself.

The language of the text seems inclined more towards Avadhī than to Braj — though the majority of the morphology is in any case shared, especially in Sanskritic contexts. Amongst the Avadhī forms are: the possessive pronoun *rāura*, the genitive postposition *ka*, *-ba* as future tense termination *(kahiba)* and as verbal noun *(sikhaba)*, verb stem as present imperfect tense *(kaha)*, perfective participles in *-eu (dekheu, jāneu, sokheu)* and perhaps the locative postposition *mahā̃*. The perfective participles *kīna, līna, dīna* (all rhyme-forms) are on the other hand more common in Braj.

While nominally divided into seven 'books' *(kāṇḍ)* of the standard *Rāmāyaṇ* format, the distribution of verses is very uneven in the published text. *Bāl kāṇḍ* opens with the praise of Sītā (vv. 1-6); it then describes Rāma, touching briefly on *svayamvar* and *śṛṅgār* themes (7-18), and ending out of sequence with a couplet describing the infant Rāma progressing from a toy bow to a real one (19); *Ayodhyā kāṇḍ* describes the forest exile, the splendour of Rāma and Lakṣmaṇ, and the ferryboat incident which seems particularly to have appealed to Tulsī (20-27); *Araṇya kāṇḍ* outlines the Sūrpaṇakhā episode, and depicts Rāma's grief at losing

Sītā (28-33); *Kiṣkindhā kāṇḍ* refers to Sugrīva's encounter with Rāma and Lakṣmaṇ (34-35); *Sundar kāṇḍ* describes Sītā's *virah* in captivity (36-41); *Laṅkā kāṇḍ* praises Rāma's victorious army in a single couplet (42); *Uttar kāṇḍ*, like its equivalent in Tulsī's *Kavitāvalī*, abandons the linear narrative for a eulogy of *bhakti* and of the efficacy of repeating the divine Name (43-69). Many of these 'episodes' are nothing more than the briefest of allusive sketches, and can only be identified by reference to their fuller equivalents in the *Rāmcaritmānas*. In a translation by K.P. Bahadur (1980:3-21) the *Bāl kāṇḍ* is re-ordered to give sequential descriptions of Rāma, Sītā, the *svayamvara* and marriage[10], but the manuscript evidence for this change is not cited. The Bahadur order, while to some extent tidying up the narrative, is not without its own problems: it makes Rāma (and not Sītā) the subject of our couplet 4, whose reference to 'large hips' is surely not intended to describe a child, especially not a male one[11]:

> बड़े नयन कटि भ्रुकुटी भाल बिसाल ।
> तुलसी मोहत मनहिं मनोहर बाल ।।

RAHĪM'S *BARVAI NĀYIKĀ-BHED* AND *BARVAI*

The *Barvai nāyikā-bhed* (NBH) consists of an initial *dohā* followed by 119 *barvai* couplets: thus the *barvai* lines number 238. Its language has a much more markedly Avadhī flavour than either RĀM or Rahīm's *Barvai* (BV). In particular it features very common occurrences of eastern diminutive and definite suffixes, of which more below. Among other Avadhī forms are: 3rd sg. past participles in *-eu* and *-esi* (*lakheu, bhayesi* etc. — many examples of these), in *-ā (gā)*, and in *-ila* or *-ala (bhaïla, bharala* — a form described by Lakshmi Dhar (1949:246) as being borrowed from Bihārī); 1st sg. past participles in *-eũ (paṭheũ)*, etc. The absolutive *hvai (hvaïkai, hvaikai)* seems however to be primarily a Braj form. Another important counter-example is in the opening *dohā* the sole location in this text of the Braj perfective participle in *-(y)o (kahyo, vicaryo)*: given the introductory content of this *dohā*, it seems that the author intended a deliberate distinction of dialect between this couplet and the poem proper.

कबित कह्यो दोहा कह्यो, तुलै न छप्पय छंद ।
विरच्यो यहै विचार कै, यह बरबै रस कंद ।।१।।

The contents of NBH are the conventional categories of heroine, presented in a tone which accentuates the *śṛṅgār* element of the descriptions (though the overall effect is often saucy rather than erotic). The opening *dohā* quoted here may indicate that the use of *barvai* for this text is something of a novelty, perhaps implying that NBH predates BV[12].

Rahīm's poem entitled simply *Barvai* (BV) is a loosely arranged anthology of mainly Kṛṣṇaite material.[13] The text comprises 109 *barvai* couplets, hence 218 lines. The Avadhī features noted for NBH are almost entirely lacking here, save a few stray examples *(leu, bhaïla, chitaba)*; instead, Braj participles in *-(y)o/-(y)au* are commonplace, and the characteristic Braj 1st sg. personal pronoun *haū̃* also appears.

The first six couplets of the poem are invocatory, addressed to Gaṇeś, Kṛṣṇa, Sūrya, Śiva, Hanumān and the *guru* respectively; the remainder of the text takes up a conventional *gop*īs' lament, falling sporadically into a kind of *bārah-māsā* pattern, and including at random a number of didactic verses stressing the importance of devotion and so forth. A peculiarity of the poem, reflecting its author's polyglot background, is its inclusion of four Persian couplets[14].

OTHER TEXTS

Some poems making use of *barvai* metre cited by R.S. McGregor (1984:191, 195n, 153, 197 respectively) are perhaps to be seen as belonging to the same tradition as Rahīm: a composition on poetics by Jagatsiṃh of Bhigna (c. 1805) and a *Khaṭ-ṛtu* attributed to one 'Sabal', both coincide in genre with Rahīm's works; Nūr Muhammad's Avadhī *Anurāg bāsurī* (1764) and the *Iśq-nāmā* of Bodhā (c. 1760), on the other hand, apparently use the *barvai* as an asymmetrical foil to the foursquare rhythms of *caupāī* and *savaiyā* quatrains respectively — a role taken elsewhere by *dohā* and/ or *sorṭhā*. While the language of such texts is uncertain, there is a clear tendency for *barvai* to be associated with works in which eastern forms predominate. This does not quite imply that the language of these various texts is automatically to be regarded as Avadhī, since in some examples the eastern forms seem to amount to little more than a formulaic inclusion of features such as the suffixes so characteristic of Rahīm's NBH. In many cases, to make a clearcut distinction between Braj and Avadhī is no easy matter, as already mentioned; a case in point is the little sequence of three *barvai* verses in Kṛpārām's *Hit-taraṅginī* vv. 166-168 (1541?; certainly pre-dating Rahīm), supposedly the earliest Brajbhāṣā *nāyikā-bhed* work: here the only specifically Avadhī forms are the definite suffixes in *banaravā* and *larikavā*, and the participle *sunala*:[15]

आजु मोहि दधि बेचत, हुइ गइ सांझ ।
गए सुवन बिच दौरति कंटक मांझ ।।

पठवत बालम मोहि जमुन के तीर ।
सखि उत सुनल बनरवा फारत चीर ।।

बालम हँसिहिं लरिकवा देवरहि देखि ।
निसि दिन चोंथत मो तन सखि अवरेखि ।।

Similar forms appear in a *Barvai nāyikābhed* attributed to Yaśodānandana; this unpublished text is described by Rāmcandra Śukla as comprising nine couplets in Sanskrit and fifty-three in *'ṭheṭh Avadhī'*. Śukla (1974:210) cites the following examples:

यदि च भवति बुधमिलनं किं, त्रिदिवेन ।
यदि च भवति शठमिलनं किं नियरेण ।।

अहिरिनि मन कै गहिरिनि उतरु न देई ।
नैना करै मथनिया, मन मथि लेई ।।

तुरकिनि जाति हुरुकिनी अति इतराइ ।
छुवन न देइ इजरवा मुरि मुरि जाइ ।।

पीतम तुम कचलोइया, हम गजबेलि ।
सारस के असि जोरिया फिरौं अकेलि ।।

The origin of the connexion between *barvai* metre and eastern forms is perhaps lost to us; but the connexion itself seems a pervasive one. J.B. Chaudhuri (1954:8) goes so far as to claim that 'Barve cannot be composed in Vraja Bhāṣā'. The *dohā* quoted above, in which Rahīm seems to claim some originality for his use of *barvai*, has to be seen in the context of (at least) Kṛpārām's earlier *barvai* sequence. In one of the commonplace but ahistorical traditions of Hindi literary history, Tulsī's use of *barvai* is said to imitate Rahīm's; this allegation derives from a statement in the hagiography *Mūl-gusāī̃-carit*, that (in VS 1760) Rahīm composed some *barvai* verses and sent them to Tulsīdās, who was then inspired to try his own hand in this metre (Mātāprasād Gupta 1965:53):

कवि रहीम बरवै रचै पठए मुनिवर पास ।
लखि तेहि सुंदर छंद में रचना कियो प्रकास ।।

METRICAL ANALYSIS

(a) Tulsī's *Barvai Rāmāyaṇ*

A 12+7m metrical pattern, with a distinct caesura, applies in all but eight lines of the text. The eight exceptions all readable as 11+8m:

37b	जगत जरत अस लागु, मोहिं बिनु राम[16]
42b	जलधि सरिस को कहै, राम भगवंत
50a	माय बाप गुरु स्वामि, राम कर नाम
50b	तुलसी जेहि न सोहाइ, ताहि बिधि बाम
51b	लोक सकल कल्यान, नीक परलोक
52a	तप तीरथ मख दान, नेम उपवास
62a	कामधेनु हरिनाम, कामतरु राम
63b	बड़े भाग अनुराग, राम सन होय

It appears that this 11+8m pattern exists as a 'regular' variant to the predominant 12+7m pattern, in a general manner found commonly in, for example, Apabhraṃśa prosody, but found only rather rarely in Hindi (it is not easy to find a transgressed caesura in Tulsī's *dohās*, for example, although semantic transgressions are of course common enough). Three of the eight examples have the word *rāma* immediately following the caesura, and several of the lines (e.g. 62a) show internal alliteration: this suggests the variant pattern to be formulaic, or perhaps to intend a deliberate catalexis-like effect. As Nilratan Sen says (1973:15) in the context of the Bengali *caryāpada*, 'The dichotomy of sense-pause and rhythmic pause often creates a sense of happy variation, and bring some tonal relief in the monotonous duet of the songs'.

Amongst the 130 lines counted above as 12+7m , 13 have a caesura which dissects a word.[17] In each instance the caesura falls after an initial *laghu*, e.g. —

	∪∪∪ –∪/∪∪ –/∪ ∪//∪∪ ∪∪/–∪
25b	चढहु नाव पग धोइ क-रहु जनि बाद
	∪∪–/∪∪ ∪∪ ∪∪/∪ ∪//∪∪ ∪∪/–∪
65b	तुलसी अब नहिं जपत स-मुझि परिनाम

Such lines can be read syntactically and semantically as 11+8m, and so could be classified with the eight lines already referred to (bringing this group to a total of 21, or 15% of the total)[18]; but the general preponderance of the 12+7m pattern suggests that these too are best seen as belonging to the 12+7m type.

(b) Rahīm's *Barvai nāyikā-bhed* and *Barvai*

In both Rahīm texts the 12+7m pattern is followed without exception; Tulsī's variant pattern with a caesura after the 11th *mātrā* is apparently not an option for Rahīm. NBH and BV both feature the use of noun terminations in *-iyā*, (often with a diminutive sense) and a common use of the characteristically eastern definite suffix *-vā;* both suffixes may be nasalized. Such forms occur in just 18 lines (8%) of BV; but in NBH they become a thoroughly formulaic feature, appearing at the end of the first *pāda* in 209 lines (88%).[19] The usage of diminutive and other *-iyā* words includes not only well-established vocabulary items such as *kanhaiyā* (NBH 17a), but also a wide range of base forms including tatsamas, semi-tatsamas, tadbhavas, and non-IA words:

15a	*muraliyā*	<	*muralī*	(tatsama)
63a	*abhisariyā*	<	*abhisāra*	(tatsama)
111a	*aparadhavā*	<	*aparādha*	(tatsama)
90a	*bidesiyā*	<	*bidesī*	(Skt. *videśī*)
64a	*sĩgaravā*	<	*sĩgāra*	(Skt. *śṛṅgāra*)
108b	*parabinavā̃*	<	*parabīna*	(Skt. *pravīṇā*)
3a	*bā̃suriyā*	<	*bā̃surī*	(Skt. *vaṃśī*)
82a	*ādhiyariyā*	<	*ādhiyār-*	(Skt. **andhīkāra*)
94a	*tiriyavā*	<	*tiriyā*	(Skt. *strī*)
85a	*jaratariyā*	<	*jaratārī*	(Pers. *zartārī*)
95a	*khabariyā*	<	*khabar-*	(Ar. *<u>kh</u>abar*)
116a	*juluphiyā*	<	*julaphī* (etc.)	(Pers. *zulfī*)

In NBH the *-iyā* and *-vā* prefixes very frequently cause a metrical shortening of a long initial or medial syllable. Most examples are of *e* or *o* (26b *naveliyā*, 8b *urojavā*)[20]; *ā* is sometimes graphically shortened to *a* (18a *gulabavā* < *gulāba*, 42b *arasiyā* < *ārasī*, 75a *javakavā* < *jāvaka*).[21] Occurrences are not limited to the final position in the first *pāda* of the line: 89a *bagiani* (< *bāga*) occurs at the beginning of a second *pāda*.

While this particular process of syllable shortening is clearly determined by suffixation, the conventional licence which allows *e* and *o* vowels to be read as short in unstressed syllables is also exploited quite generally in NBH: short *e* in 31a *bhayesi*, short (unstressed) *o* in 19b *coṭāra*, and even short (stressed) *e* in 23a *kheta*. The text gives also some final *ī* vowels which must be read as metrically short, e.g. 48a *nicavaī*.[22] This is another example of a contrast between NBH and BV, for in BV the extremely restricted exploitation of metrical licence (reading *e* or *o* as short) is almost invariably associated with the process of suffixation discussed above, itself only a limited feature of the BV text. BV consequently gives an impression of a much tighter metrical construction throughout, showing perhaps a greater proficiency in (or familiarity with ?) the *barvai* form. This conclusion would be consistent with the hypothesis that NBH may have been the earlier of Rahīm's two *barvai* texts.

In terms of content, *-iyā* and*-vā* words in NBH very frequently constitute the descriptive labels of the *nāyikā* being described; in terms of the composition, the very high frequency of these forms in final position within the first *pāda* contributes a strong sense of *pāda* closure, emphasising the couplet construction as being of four discrete 'quarters', often with assonance or weak rhymes between the 'odd' *pādas*.

Another aspect of this tendency in the NBH *barvai* line to follow a set formula is in the composition of the second *pāda*, where in 168 lines (71%) the trochaic rhyme cadence (¯˘) constitutes a single word[23]: this statistic contrasts rather strongly with 104 lines (48%) in BV and 64 lines (46%) in RAM.[24] While doubtless largely the product of chance, this characteristic does contribute to an overall impression that the NBH line construction follows a conventional stereotype rather more narrowly than is the case in the other two poems. NBH 92 stands as an example of this stereotyped pattern:

बहुत दिवस पै पियवा आएहु आज ।
पुलकित नवल दुलहिया कर गृह काज ।।

A peculiarity of BV not found in NBH (or in RĀM) is the transgression of a *gaṇa* boundary by the long vowel *e* (four times), or *o* (once).[25] Whether this reflects some echo of the historical status of these vowels as diphthongs, or is a simple exploitation of metrical licence, is not certain, though the latter seems much more likely. The fact that all the examples fall between the first and second *gaṇa*s suggests perhaps that this particular *gaṇa* boundary is not a fully defined feature of the line in this poet's usage.

⏑⏑- ⏑⏑/⏑ ⏑⏑⏑/- //⏑⏑ ⏑⏑/-/⏑
19a उलहे नये अँकुरवा, बिन बलबीर

⏑⏑⏑ ⏑ ⏑⏑/⏑ ⏑⏑⏑/ -// ⏑- ⏑/-/⏑
37b गनत न चढे अटन पै सने सनेह

⏑⏑- ⏑⏑/⏑ ⏑⏑⏑/ -// ⏑- ⏑/-/⏑
77a जिहिके लिये जगत में, बजै निसान

⏑⏑ - ⏑⏑/⏑ ⏑-/⏑⏑ //--⏑ ⏑/-/⏑
77b तिहिं ते करे अबोलन, कौन सयान

-- ⏑⏑/⏑ ⏑⏑⏑/- // --⏑ ⏑/-/⏑
102b पैया परो ननदिया, फेरि कहाव

Alliteration, assonance or patterns of metrical equivalence across the caesura occurs several times in BV[26] (in a manner hardly to be maintained in NBH, where *pāda*s so often end with suffixes):

सुगमहि गातहि गारन, जारन देह ।
अगह महा अति पारन, सुघर सनेह ।। २० ।।

जब तें बिछुरे मितवा, कहु कस चैन ।
रहत भरचौ हिय साँसन, आँसुन नैन ।। ५८ ।।

Although it has been shown above that Tulsī favours a more flexible interpretation of the caesura (as being primarily a rhythmic feature) he too makes similar use of alliteration between the two *pāda*s of the line. Here, though, it is found in the context of a more integrated use of alliteration, typical of Tulsī's subtly modulated verse construction in which alliterative patterns are an intrinsic part of the fabric of the verse, rather than an embroidered pattern on top of it (RĀM 3):

सियमुख सरद कमल जिमि, किमि कहि जाइ ।
निसि मलीन वह निसिदिन यह बिगसाइ ।।

GAṆA COMPOSITION IN THE *BARVAI* LINE

The prosodic prescription of a *mātrik* metre does not fully determine an appropriate rhythm *(gati)*, without which a stanza which is metrically 'correct' can still contain impediments to natural flow *(gatibhaṅg)*.[27] The ephemeral quality of rhythm is rather the product of a separate (and perhaps unconscious) set of constraints which may overlay the line and regulate the disposition of stressed syllables.

This concept of stress-based rhythm, though rather alien to traditional *chandaḥśāstra*, is implicit in the actual functioning of some NIA metres. This has been recognised in poetic works of much earlier date than the Hindi *barvai* poems, most notably in Nilratan Sen's (1973) analysis of Bengali *caryā* songs.[28] Varieties of Hindi verse such as the *bānī* of the Sant poets, presumed to have been composed orally within an 'aliterate' tradition, often offend against the exact prescriptions of metrical construction while nevertheless achieving the appropriate rhythmic shape which is the hallmark of such standard metres as the *dohā* and the *caupāī*. While the standard *mātrā*-counting conventions give precise and objective analysis of a line of verse, rhythm is a subjective and therefore far more problematic thing — especially when the reader is programmed to expect the relatively strongly stressed rhythms of English verse.

Connie Fairbanks' work on stress in Hindi metrics (1981) shows how a 4m *gaṇa*, with an ictus on the first *mātrā*, persists not only in metres of the symmetrical *caupāī* type but also in asymmetrical metres such as the *dohā*. Fairbanks finds that the *dohā* can be seen as having a line of 4 + 3 'beats', and her small sample of *dohā*s from the *Rāmcaritmānas* shows a high correlation between rhythmic ictus and natural word stress. The main exception to this in the *dohā* is in the final syllable of the first *pāda*, which always bears an ictus despite being unstressed. The rhythmic arrangement thus divides the line into seven *gaṇa*s with a *mātrik* composition of 4+4+4+1, 4+4+3. Her example is the well-known opening of the *Ayodhyā kāṇḍ*:

–́ ⏑⏑ ⏑́⏑⏑ ⏑–́⏑ ⏑–́ ⏑́⏑ ⏑⏑ ⏑́⏑⏑ ⏑–́⏑
श्री गुरु चरन सरोज रज, निज मन मुकुरु सुधारि[29]

Fairbanks notes that 'Regardless of the fact that modern reciters of Tulsī's *dohā*s consistently divide the metrical line in the above irregular pattern, it might be argued that they are merely imposing this rhythm on the *dohā*, with no historical grounds for doing so. However, a study of the correlation between natural word stress in modern spoken Hindi and the drum beat (or ictus) in recitation of the *dohā*...shows that there can be no doubt that Tulsī composed the *dohā* to the...4 *mātrā gaṇa* rhythm.' Applied to *barvai* metre, this principle yields a five-*gaṇa* line with a composition of 4+4+4, 4+3 *mātrās*:

–́◡ ◡◡́◡ ◡◡ –́◡◡ ◡́◡◡ ◡–́◡
सात दिवस भए साजत, सकल बनाउ ।
–́ –◡́◡ ◡◡ –́◡◡ ◡́◡◡ ◡–́◡
का पूछहु सुठि राउर सरल सुभाउ ।। (RĀM 20)

–́◡◡ ◡́◡◡ ◡◡́◡– –́◡◡ –́◡
पोछहु अधर कजरवा, जावक माल ।
◡́◡◡◡ –́◡◡ ◡́◡– ◡́◡ ◡◡ –́◡
उपजेउ पीतम छतिया बिन गुन माल ।। (NBH 50)

–́– ◡́◡◡ ◡–́◡◡ ◡́◡ ◡◡ –́◡
बंदौ विघन बिनासन त्रधि सिधि ईस ।
–́◡◡ –́◡ ◡–́◡◡ ◡́◡ ◡◡ –́◡
निर्मल बुद्धि प्रकासन, सिसु ससि सीस ।। (BV 1)

This arrangement is necessar:ly impossible whenever the fourth and fifth *mātrās* togethe form a *guru*. Such occurrences can be read from a tabulation of the 6m *gana* (the statistics here necessarily simplify the reality, since they gloss over metrical irregularitie:s):

First *gaṇa* (6m) in first *pāda*

	RĀM (138 lines)	NBH (238 lines)	BV (218 lines)
1 /¯ ˘ ¯ ˘/	23 (17%)	3 (1%)	10 (5%)
2 /¯ ˘ ˘ ˘ ˘/	22 (16%)	38 (16%)	21 (10%)
3 /˘ ˘ ˘ ¯ ˘/	15 (11%)	6 (2%)	8 (4%)
4 /˘ ˘ ˘ ˘ ˘ ˘/	16 (12%)	30 (13%)	27 12%)
5 /˘ ˘ ˘ ˘ ¯/	18 (13%)	67 (28%)	34 (16%)
6 /˘ ˘ ¯ ˘ ˘/	15 (11%)	11 (5%)	30 (14%)
7 /¯ ˘ ˘ ¯/	11 (8%)	44 (18%)	30 (14%)
8 /˘ ˘ ¯ ¯/	9 (6%)	18 (8%)	15 (7%)
9 /˘ ¯ ˘ ˘ ˘/	3 (2%)	1	5 (2%)
10 /¯ ¯ ˘ ˘/	3 (2%)	5 (2%)	15 (7%)
11 /¯ ¯ ¯/	1	6 (2%)	12 (5%)
12 /˘ ¯ ˘ ¯/	1	1	6 (3%)
13 /˘ ¯ ¯ ˘/	1	8 (3%)	5 (2%)

In RĀM, *gaṇas* whose fourth and fifth *mātrās* together constitute a *guru* (i.e. types 1, 3 and 13) appear in 39 lines, nearly a third of the total; all but one occurrence have the trochaic rhythm /˘̄ ˘̄ ˘ – ˘/[30]. In NBH a *guru* in this position appears in only some 17 lines (7%)[31], and in BV the number is 23 (11%). Within such lines, both the Rahīm texts favour the *gaṇa* /˘– –˘/, whose palindromic structure has the effect of containing and neutralizing the variant rhythm. By broadly defining trochaic rhythm as a *gana* showing /˘̄˘̄˘˘̄˘̄˘/ (groups 1-3), we find such rhythms occurring in 60 lines (44%) of RAM, as against 47 (19%) of NBH and 38 (17%) of BV. Only three times in the entire corpus of three texts[32] does this pattern occur in both lines of a single couplet. Furthermore, the high proportion of second (4m) *gaṇas* beginning ˘ ˘ (see groups 1 and 2 in the table below) ensures a certain 'recovery' from any element of trochaic rhythm in this first *pāda*.

The inference of these comparisons is that while Tulsī is happy to accommodate trochaic rhythm as a variant against a generalized tetramoric pattern, Rahīm is more conservative (or perhaps more formula-bound ?) in preferring the clearer stresses of a foursquare rhythm.

Second *gaṇa* (4m) in first *pāda*

		RĀM (138 lines)	NBH (238 lines)	BV (218 lines)
1	/˘ ˘ ˘ ˘/	55 (40%)	206 (87%)	75 (34%)
2	/˘ ˘ –/	52 (38%)	14 (6%)	79 (57%)
3	/– ˘ ˘/	10 (7%)	18 (8%)	38 (27%)
4	/– –/	6 (4%)	0	26 (19%)
5	/˘ – ˘/	15 (11%)	0	0

In this second *gaṇa*, RĀM shows 15 occurrences of amphibrachs (˘–˘) (precluding, incidentally, a reading of the *pāda* as comprising three 4m *gaṇas*). By contrast, neither NBH nor BV have a single amphibrachic second *gana*. NBH strongly prefers four *laghus* here (and the incidence rises significantly if diphthongs are reckoned as two *laghus*), perhaps as a rhythmically neutral foil after the variations of the previous *gana*; RĀM and BV show a more even distribution of the various possibilities. There is a marked contrast between the two Rahīm texts in the occurrence of spondees: sequences of long vowels seem a common feature of BV.[33]

First *gaṇa* (4m) in second *pāda*

		RĀM (138 lines)	NBH (238 lines)	BV (218 lines)
1	/˘ ˘ ˘ ˘/	73 (53%)	119 (50%)	109 (50%)
2	/¯ ˘ ˘/	44 (39%)	73 (31%)	65 (30%)
3	/˘ ˘ ¯/	9 (6%)	34 (14%)	21 (10%)
4	/¯ ¯/	1 (1%)	9 (4%)	8 (4%)
5	/˘ ¯ ˘/	3 (2%)	3 (1%)	15 (7%)

This table reveals a surprising consistency in the composition of this *pāda* throughout the three texts. RĀM shows the smallest amount of rhythmic variation here, especially given the fact that five of its nine anapests comprise the word *tulasī*. The striking prominence in all three texts of the rhythmically neutral *gaṇa* /˘˘˘˘/ offers minimal interference to the obligatory rhyme cadence in /¯˘/ which follows immediately after; the next most common *gaṇa*, /¯˘˘/, anticipates and reinforces the rhythm of that cadence. The only significant divergence among the texts is in the appearance of amphibrachs; the long syllable in RĀM and NBH occurrences of this foot is usually a diphthong, and may thus be read as two short syllables. This reading makes the BV statistic of 15 occurrences stand out in even sharper contrast.

As in any prosody depending wholly or partially on stress, the question arises of the extent to which the ictus coincides with the natural stress pattern of the individual word. While Fairbanks finds a high correlation here, the *barvai* sample shows there to be a fair degree of variation in this respect. If the following examples are read in the five-stress fashion suggested above, for example, then the ictus falls variously on different syllables within the same word:

बड़े नयन कटि भ्रुकुटी भाल बिसाल (RĀM 4a)

कस प्रभु नयन कमल अस, कहूं बखानि (RĀM 10b)

अवधि अवधि लौं दुस्तर, परत लखाइ । (BV 60b)

करत घुमड़ि घन धुरवा, मुरवा सोर (BV 7a)

घन घुमड़े चहुँ ओरन, चमकत बीज (BV 11a)

उमड़ि उमड़ि घन घुमड़े दिसि बिदिसान (BV 7a)

Are such precisely measured distinctions really of any significance, or is this a case of metrical analysis gone mad? Though stress in Indian languages is clearly less marked than in English, a reasonable answer to this question lies in William Beare's comment on English versification (1957:40): 'The reader will choose from among the permitted variations of stress that which brings out the metrical base; he will *not* stress unimportant monosyllables so as to convey a wrong meaning, nor will he shift the normal accent within a word from one syllable to another'. From the point of view of the versifier, composition is no doubt a largely instinctive process, depending on an innate sense of rhythm rather than a pedantic mechanical computation of *mātrās* and syllables.

Even when certain metrical configurations seem to infringe the (necessarily artificial) conventions, there is nothing in the resulting rhythms which would seem alien in the context of Indian musical rhythm, in which the defining *ṭhekā* or basic pattern of drum-beat syllables is not a set theme but rather a basis for variations within the *tāla* structure.[34] In the *barvai* examples, trochaic rhythm stands as an important alternative to the '4m *gaṇa* with initial ictus' which emerges from Fairbanks' hypothesis, but with greater frequency in Tulsī than in the two Rahīm texts (which are statistically similar in this respect). In the second *pāda*, the two stressed beats are more clearly regular, since here they fall on the first syllable of the *pāda* and the long syllable of the rhyme cadence respectively (and the end of the line is always likely to be its most regular part).

SYNTACTIC AND RHETORICAL CONSTRUCTION OF THE *BARVAI* LINE

Though resembling the *dohā* so closely in overall shape and cadence, the *barvai* is quite distinct from it both in line length and in the relative proportions of the line's two *pādas*. In comparison with the nearly-symmetrical *mātrā* ratio 13:11 in the *dohā*, the *barvai* ratio of 12:7m is markedly asymmetrical; and its brief second *pāda* is very much more restricted in terms of potential syntactic combinations. What then are the effects of this compactness on the composition of the *barvai*? As a basis for comparison, the following Tulsīdās *dohā* (*Dohāvalī* 48, Rāmcandra Śukla 1974:90) shows a typical *dohā* construction in having a semantic and syntactic balance across the four quarters of the couplet:

> तुलसी रामहिं आपु तें सेवक की रुचि मीठि ।
> सीतापति से साहिबहिं कैसे दीजै पीठि ।।

In this example, the two 11m *pādas* have room for respectively (a) noun phrase + predicate, (b) adverb + verb phrase. Although very much a random example, this may be compared with a *barvai* couplet such as RĀM 46:

काल कराल बिलोकहु होइ सचेत ।
रामनाम जपु तुलसी प्रीति समेत ।।

Here, the 7m *pādas* comprise respectively (a) substantive verb + predicate, (b) noun + postposition. Such narrowly restricted patterns are typical of *barvai* construction and show a marked difference in sentence balance when compared to the prevalent *dohā* type; the construction and compression of the *barvai*'s second *pāda* is ideally suited for giving a variety of rhetorical and sententious effects to the line, especially in the closing quarter of the couplet. It is often the laconic nature of this *pāda* which lends the couplet its poetic quality; and this is particularly apparent in Tulsī's skilful use of the metre.

A speciality of NBH is the use of a 'foregrounding' technique, in which the final quarter of the line stands out against the remainder. The focus of NBH 68's depiction of the *parakīyā utkaṇṭhitā nāyikā* rests on the final two words *sūnī khāṭa*, further emphasized by their long vowels:

उठ उठ जात खिरिकिया जोहत बाट ।
कत वह आइहि मितवा सूनी खाट ।।[35]

A switch from a material to an abstract context foregrounds the final *pāda* in NBH 91, describing the *gaṇikā pravatsyatpreyasī nāyikā:*

पीतम इक सुमिरिनियाँ, मोंहि देइ जाहु ।
जेहि जपि तोर बिरहवा, करौं निबाहु ।।[36]

A description of the *premagarvitā nāyikā* in NBH 28 has a similar change from literal to metaphorical language in the final *pāda:*

आपुहि देत कजरवा, गूँदत हार ।
चुनि पहिराव चुनरिया, प्रान अधार ।।[37]

An equal but opposite effect is achieved in NBH 92, where the change of context describing the *mugdhā āgatapatikā nāyikā* is from the sublime to the domestic:

बहुत दिवस पै पियवा आएहु आज ।
पुलकित नवल दुलहिया कर गृह काज ।।[38]

In NBH 118 the final *pāda* is reserved for a narrative dénouement which defines the quality of the poem's subject, the *vacana catura nāyaka*, whose (elliptical!) musical prowess outdoes the cuckoo:

सघन कुंज अमरैया सीतल छाँहि ।
झगरन आइ कोइलिया फिर उड़ि जाँहि ।।[39]

Similarly in NBH 73, the first three *pādas* set the narrative context, while the fourth describes the consequence (for a *parakīyā vāsaka sajjā nāyikā*). The verse structure is emphasized by the placement of a verb participle at the beginning of each quarter:

सोवत सब गुरु लोगवा जानेउ बाल ।
दीन्हेसि खोलि खिरकिया, उठिकै हाल ।।[40]

In a related context, the final *pāda* of NBH 105 leaves the besotted heroine suspended in a time-warp, mechanically telling her rosary while remembering her beloved:

पिय मूरति चितसरिया देखत बाल ।
बितवत औध बरसवा जपि जपि माल ।।[41]

Similar constructions can be found in BV; the subject of stanza 67, Kṛṣṇa, is foregrounded by making an epithet occupy the whole *pāda:*

उझकि उझकि चित दिन दिन हेरत द्वार ।
जब ते बिछुरे सजनी, नन्दकुमार ।।[42]

In general, though, BV tends to show a more straightforward line construction in which the function of the caesura is rather more prosaic, BV 79 being a typical example:

बिरहिन को सब भाखत, अब जनि रोय ।
पीर पराई जानै, तब कहु कोय ।।[43]

Amongst the rhetorical schemes favoured by Tulsī in particular is the inversion of two sentence components vis-à-vis a neutral word order — a universal technique, equally beloved of English verse with its 'Oft did the harvest to their sickle yield' and so on. Thus noun + adjective (4a *bhāla bisāla*), noun + cardinal number (22b *manasija dou*), intransitive verb + subject noun (8b *lasata kapola*), transitive verb + direct object (28a *khaṇḍi akāsa*), complement + subject pronoun (22a *harihara kou*), etc. An extension of this device is found in 38a, where the rhetorical weight of the sentence is thrown into the second *pāda*, being held off until that late part of the line by the interposing of both the main verb and a vocative parenthesis: *aba jīvana kai hai kapi āsa na koi* (Sītā's words to Hanumān: 'now of life remains, O monkey, no hope at all'). Though such inversion may equally well be found in other metres, the fact that rhetorically significant or loaded phrases are here isolated as discrete *pāda*s adds to their poetic impact. The tendency for the semantic content of the second *pāda* to bear the main burden of the sentence becomes quite a general feature in Tulsī's unobtrusively skilful versification. RĀM 45, while quite unremarkable in terms of its formal composition, well exemplifies the beguilingly easy fluency which is so characteristic of Tulsī's poetic style:

स्वारथ परमारथ हित एक उपाय ।
सीयराम पद तुलसी प्रेम बढ़ाय ।।

A more ambitious and perhaps self-consciously literary effect is obtained in the zeugma or *dīpaka* trope (said by Vladimir Miltner[44] to be 'very rare' in Tulsīdās). In the two RĀM examples, verse construction both parallels and emphasises the trope structure:

कोउ कह नर नारायन, हरिहर कोउ	RĀM 22a
एहि ते अधिक न एहि सम जीवनलाहु	RĀM 57b

In the first example, *harihara kou* is a second referent of *kaha;* in the second, *jīvanalāhu* is the subject of the two comparative phrases which precede it. Two examples of zeugma in BV have the verb *rah-* as common element:

रहत भरयो हिय साँसन, आँसुन नैन	BV 58b
रहे प्रान परि पलकनि, दृग मन माहिं	BV 66a

Further examples of zeugma in Rahīm also exploit the integrity of the second *pāda:*

पोछहु अधर कजरवा, जावक भाल	NBH 50a
बन घन फूलहि टेसुआ, बगिअनि बेलि	NBH 50a
करत घुमड़ि घन धुरवा, मुरवा सोर	BV 7b

In a similar way, the brief closing *pāda* of the *barvai* acts very effectively as the key to unlock metaphors which depend on the non-equivalence of the *upameya* and *upamāna* (respectively subject or 'tenor' of comparison and object or 'vehicle' of comparison). The point of the metaphor in RĀM

5, for example, is that the brightness of Sītā's complexion cannot be matched by her champak garland; the garland's inevitable 'fading' is alluded to only in the closing phrase *jaba kūbhilāi*, which at the last minute supplies the frame of reference for the whole couplet:

चंपक हरवा अँग मिलि अधिक सोहाइ ।
जानि परै सिय हियरे जब कुँभिलाइ ।।

Comparable effects are found in 2b, 3b, 6b, 12b, 18b, 27b, 41b, etc. The autonomy of the second *pāda* is often further strengthened by alliteration, as in 10a *tulasī baṃka bilokani, mṛdu musukāni*, 57a *rāmanāma para tulasī neha nibāhu*, and 61a *sumirahu nāma rāma kara, sevahu sādha*; a similar effect is that of epizeuxis (immediate repetition), as in 59b *rāma japata bhae tulasī tulasīdāsā* and in the punning BV 81a, *lakhi mohana kī baṃsī, baṃsī jāna*).

Features of parallelism and contrast typical of *dohā* construction are of course found in the *barvai* also. Examples are the two contrastive statements, with distinctive pronominal subjects, in 3b *nisi malīna vaha nisi dina, yaha bigasāi* (another example of the metaphor-key motif discussed above); and again 63a *tulasī kahata sunata saba, samujhata koya*, in which the contrast between the busy wordiness of the first *pāda* (with its paired participles) and the laconic brevity of the second *pāda* perfectly echoes the semantic point of the line. The caesura's function as a break between clauses is commonly exemplified. The second *pāda* virtually never comprises a single word — unsurprisingly perhaps, because the average word-length is considerably less than seven *mātrās* (the exception is *tulasīdāsa*, which occurs four times); but more notable is the rarity of noun compounds occupying this *pāda*, the few examples[45] being mostly restricted to the latter part of the text, whose theological context generates a number of formulaic compounds such as *joga-samādhi* (48a) and *nāma-prabhāu* (54a) etc.

SOME CONCLUSIONS

The *barvai* couplet is rather more than just a little brother of the *dohā*: its construction is ideally suited to a range of literary effects, especially of the kind associated with *muktaka* verse. The historical development of this metre is not readily traceable, manuscripts of its presumed Apabhraṃśa antecedents having long since succumbed to the indifference of their owners and the hunger of white ants, but it is likely that its overall shape and rhythm owes much to the *dohā*, and indeed those few poets who have composed *barvai* verses seem all to be established *dohā*-poets also. *Barvai* is perhaps too specialized a metre to have found a broader following; its asymmetrical shape and obtrusive cadence make it unsuitable as a vehicle for extended composition or serial narrative, when eventually its lilt would seem a limp.

The three texts examined here are distinct one from another in various ways. In terms of the formal construction of the metre and (if a more subjective assessment is allowed) of poetic quality, Tulsī's verses stand apart from Rahīm's, raising doubts about the authenticity of the allegation that Tulsī was imitating Rahīm in his use of the *barvai*. As elsewhere in his poetry, Tulsī shows himself to be the master and not the slave of his adopted conventions. By contrast, analysis of the metrical data confirms an initial impression that Rahīm, despite having an eye for metaphor, tends towards the formulaic in his verse composition. BV seems a more even work than NBH in terms of metrical regularity, but at the same time appears less ambitious than NBH in its exploitation of the *barvai's* rhetorical possibilities; in short, it is perhaps more limited by conventions inherited from *dohā* composition.

This paper has not gone beyond the published texts of the three poems, and perhaps begs many questions which the manuscripts alone could resolve. The metrical analysis itself provides more problems than solutions. Do NBH and BV really derive from the same author? Is the latter part of RĀM

— roughly coextensive with *Uttarkāṇḍ* — distinct from the earlier part in origin or period, or are its (rather dimly perceived) differences of style simply a function of its thematic distinctness from the narrative part of the text? Given some general similarities of metrical licence between Rahīm (in NBH) on the one hand and his near contemporary Raskhān on the other, are there grounds for suggesting that Muslim poets may have been more drawn to stress-based rhythms in their composition? There are also some quite general questions relating to Hindi prosody: how are structural features of the verse line exploited for syntactic and rhetoric effects? What are the parameters for the exploitation of metrical licence, and do these differ substantially between poets? Are long vowels more susceptible to shortening *metri causa* than syllables which are long by position? What is the status of diphthongs in Hindi metrics? And finally: was it really necessary to write such a long paper about such a short metre?

NOTES

1. The pearls in her hair, friend, are as emerald gems;
   when she takes them in her hand they glow again.
2. Rājaśekhara's text was in turn one of the sources followed by Hemacandra (H.C. Bhayani 1953:37).
3. अस्य चरणव्यत्यये । भ्रमरावली ।।४६।। (H.D. Velaṇkar 1962:132).
4. बारह पढुमतइअए । सत्तावरे ।।
   होइ भमररिंछोली । किर एरिसी ।।
   [द्वादश प्रथमतृतीययो: । सप्तापरयो: ।
   भवति भ्रमरपङ्क्ति: । किल ईदृशी ।।११।।] *Ibid.* p. 64

5. There is also a *varṇa* metre having the name *Bhramarāvalī̆*. Nilratan Sen (1973:24) cites a 'tetrarhythmic, twenty moric form' with the 'rigid short-long syllabic arrangement' of five *sa-gaṇa* (/˘ ˘ ¯/, wrongly illustrated by Sen as /˘ ¯/). H.D. Velaṇkar (n.d.:136) cites this same 'five x *sa-gaṇa*' metre in

Prākṛtapaiṅgalam 2.154; further examples are *Vṛttajātisamuccaya* 4.61 (H.D. Velaṇkar 1929:66) and *Saṃdeśarāsaka* 3.173 (Jina Vijaya Muni and Harivallabh Bhayani 1945:70).

6. If this is indeed the etymology, then the form *barvā* would presumably be a back-formation based on a supposition that the *-ai* / *-e* forms represented a plural.
7. Abdurrahīm '*Khānkhānā*' was evidently an important channel of court patronage for Hindu devotional institutions. The seventeenth-century Rādhāvallabhī hagiology *Rasik-ananya-māl* (Lalitāprasād Purohit n.d.: 44-48) relates how a *kāyasth* named Sundardās Bhaṭnāgar, a *dīvān* of Abdurrahīm, undertook the building of a temple to Rādhāvallabha in Vrindaban. When enemies of Sundardās reported to Abdurrahīm that Sundardās was misappropriating funds for this project, Abdurrahīm chastised him, told him to ask for funds openly, and himself provided ornaments and funding *(bhūṣana paṭa aru kharaca)* for the deity. (In building the temple, Sundardās accepted the (accurate) prediction that whoever undertook this task would die a year after its completion; previous would-be builders who were put off by this prediction included Raja Man Singh, who 'went elsewhere' *(aura ṭhā̃ gayau)* — presumably a reference to his building of the great Gauḍīya temple of Govind Dev.)
8. Following the convention of Hindi scholarship, for which Sanskritic 'purity' still represents an irresistable norm, this title adopts a spelling with retroflex *ṇ* which is alien to the phonology of the text itself.
9. Dhīrendra Varmā (1959:317) reports that a manuscript dated VS 1797 (AD 1740) lacks the first 22 and the last 11 couplets of the published text, while it includes an additional 25 couplets not found in the published text. Mātāprasād Gupta (1965:230) also points to the unsatisfactory nature of the text and the need for a critical edition.
10. Bahadur's Stanza numbers (in bold) relate to our text as follows: **1**:4, **2**:8, **3-4**:9-10, **5**:12, **6**:11, **7**:8, **8**:19, **9-11**:1-3, **12-13**:5-6, **14-19**:13-18.
11. The noun *bāla* is of course ambiguous as to gender, but is here best read as feminine and referring to Sītā. Mātāprasād Gupta (1965:260) finds a difficulty in reading *kaṭi* as qualified by *baṛe*, firstly because of gender and secondly because the *kaṭi* should be small, not large: but *baṛe* is masculine because it qualifies also adjacent *nayana;* and *kaṭi* must surely be read in its (Sanskrit) sense 'hips' rather than its (Hindi) sense 'waist'.

12. R.S. McGregor 1984:122.
13. Text and translation of 35 selected couplets is given in Rupert Snell 1991b:122-127.
14. Stanzas 86 and 94-6: the metrical patterns of these stanzas do not seem to owe any debt to Persian metrics. The first of these serves as an example:

    मीगुज़रद ई दिलरा, बे दिलदार ।
    इक इक साअत हमचूँ, साल हज़ार ।।

    (The Rahīm texts are taken from Samar Bahādur Siṃha 1961:360-94).
15. This sequence (Sudhākar Pāṇḍey 1964:40) describes respectively *nāyikās* of the *bhūt surat gopanā, bhaviṣya surat gopanā* and *bhūt bhaviṣya surat gopanā* categories, and is from the third *taraṅga* of the text.
16. An irregular construction of 11+7m (with *o* in *mohī* being read as short) may alternatively apply.
17. The full list is: 4b *ma-nohara*, 7b *ka-hā*, 11b *pa-rai*, 13a *u-daya*, 18b *u-nīde*, 19a *sa-kuci*, 24b *na-cāihi*, 25b *ka-rahu*, 28b *la-ṣana*, 44a *pa-rihariya*, 56a *su-labha*, 60a *ka-kahata*, 65b *sa-mujhi*.
18. Throughout this paper, all percentages are rounded to the nearest whole number.
19. These instances are nearly equally divided by *-vā* forms (103 lines, 43% of the text) and *-iyā* forms (106 lines, 45%).
20. A single counter-example is the first syllable in 23b *chohariyā*, which remains long.
21. *Cf. haravā (<hāra)* in RĀM 5a.
22. *Cf.* the *deī/leī* rhyme in the second couplet of Yaśodānandana quoted above.
23. The initial *dohā*, NBH 1, also conforms to this pattern. A 'single word' is here defined — admittedly rather naively — as a word printed separately in the published texts; a rather higher count is achieved in all three texts if members of compounds such as *tulsīdāsa, gunanātha* or *manimāla* are counted separately.
24. Though word-boundaries are largely to be ignored in line scansion, Nilratan Señ's analysis of old Bengali prosody (1973:10, 33 etc.) shows their relevance in some NIA versification. *Cf.* also Kenneth Bryant's analysis of *gaṇa* construction in *Sūrsāgar* verses (1992:214), wherein for example he notes that almost 80% of lines beginning with a three-*mātrā* word continue with a second three-*mātrā* word.

25. A reading of *au* as two *laghus*, e.g. in 39a *bhalau*, is of course more commonplace than that of *e; cf.* also the spellings *raini* verses *raĩni* in identical positions in lines NBH 82a and 83b respectively. The vowels *ai* and *au* may both appear as the *guru* in the trochaic cadence of a *dohā* line, but rather less frequently than other long vowels: in the three *barvai* texts under consideration here, trochees with *ai* or *au* long syllables appear in only a total of six rhyme cadences (of which NBH 87 and 88 share the same rhyme, and NBH 104 has the imperfect rhyme *ṭhaura/cakora*). For a discussion of *-ai* participles scanned as two *laghus* see R. Snell 1991a.
26. Some further examples are: 7a, 26b, 27a, 36b, 56a, 58b, 73a, 81a, 103b.
27. It is not too difficult to contrive a verse of doggerel which, though metrically 'correct' in terms of 6+4+3, 6+4+1m construction, is quite unacceptable in terms of the expected *gati* of a *dohā:*

    अनुकूल मन जनकसुता, सदाई दया हीय ।

    उदार सुकुमार सुभाय, सुसीला सखी सीय ।।
28. The role of stress-accent has also been commented on by George Grierson (1920) in his study of the Kashmiri *Lallā-vākyāni* (he notes that 'it is evident that the rude village compositions which developed into the verses of Lallā were originally intended to be based on some standard metre, but that in the mouths of the rustics stress became substituted for quantity'): by S.K. Chatterji (1970) in Bengali verse; by Christopher Shackle (1972) in his study of the Siraiki *dohṛā;* by Constance Fairbanks (1981) in the *Rāmcaritmānas* and the *Ālhā Khaṇḍ;* and by Kenneth Bryant (1992) in his analysis of the *Sūrsāgar.*
29. This principle of scansion raises several points not taken up here — not least, the allocation of stress to the final syllable of the first *pāda* versus the possibility of reading a silent stress at the caesura. (The quoted line is here re-transcribed into Nāgarī from Fairbanks' roman text).
30. The exception is /˘ ¯ ¯ ˘/ in 63b *baṛe bhāga.*
31. Four of these — 82a, 84b, 85b and 86b — all begin *calī,* suggesting formulaic composition.
32. RĀM 26a /*kamala kaṃṭa*/, 26b /*nisi malīna*/; RĀM 41a /*sarada cãda*/, 41b /*bidhuhi jori*/; BV 84a/*kahā kānha*/, 84b /*kauna hota*/.
33. The first *pādas* of two lines — 23a and 39b — consist entirely of *guru* syllables.

34. It is in *pada* metres such as 16+12m *sāra* (discussed by Bryant 1992 and Snell 1983) that the similarities between word rhythms and *ṭhekā* variations are most closely felt. Consecutive 16m *pādas*, if read with an ear for their inherent rhythm rather than their linguistic or semantic content, seem to echo very closely the modulations of a drum performance in *tāla*. This parallel can perhaps be taken a little further by pointing to the features of the drum mnemonics or *bol*, which themselves approximate to IA phonology. *Bols* are differentiated on a phonological model, a soft dental sound such as *ta* (produced on the rim of the drumhead) being distinguished from a hard retroflex sound such as *ṭa* (produced on the hard black disc or *syāhī* in the drumhead's centre). A second level of differentiation is that between the two constituent drums of the tabla pair: the left-hand drum *(bāyā)* may add voice and/or aspiration to *bols* produced by the right-hand drum *(dāyā* or *tablā)*, so that the *dāyā* sound *tā*, for example, when played simultaneously with the *bāyā* sound *ghe*, gives the composite sound *dhā*. A parallel for the metrical lengthening 'by position' of a short vowel before a consonant cluster is found in a *bol* such as *kat-tā* (2+2 *tāla mātrās*) James Kippen (1988:xvi-xxii, 145-55 etc.) gives a detailed analysis of tabla sounds and mnemonics; Anoop Chandola (1988, *passim*) takes the speech-*tāla* connexion considerably further.
35. Constantly she goes to the window, watching the road;
'When will he come — my beloved — to my empty bed?'
36. Give me a rosary of memories before you leave
To tell, my love, when I'm lovesick, and find reprieve.
37. She puts on her own collyrium; weaves her garland;
Picks and wears a dappled mantle — my soul's foundation.
38. 'After so many days my beloved comes home today!'
Our young bride thrills at the thought, as she works away.
39. In the dense mango-grove's cool shade
The cuckoo comes with a challenge, but flies away.
40. The elders at last are sleeping: she knows it well!
She opens wide the window, in passion's spell.
41. The maid spies her lover's face in the gallery;
A year goes by as she tells her rosary.
42. With leaping heart she ever looks toward the door
Since he has gone away, my dear, this Nandkumār.
43. Everyone advises the lovesick, 'From tears refrain';
Let her so speak who can perceive another's pain.
44. Miltner (1967:40) cites a single example from *Vinay-patrikā*: *loka kahai rāma ko gulāma haũ kahāvaũ*. (*Vinay-patrikā* 72.5;

Rāmacandra Sukla 1974:415) 'where *rāma ko gulāma* functions on the one hand as an object of *kahai* and on the other as a nominal predicate, with a copulative verb *kahāvaū*, of *haū*.' (Transliteration adjusted for this paper.) It should be pointed out that Miltner's reference to 'zeugma' here is in a primarily grammatical rather than rhetorical context.

45. 9a/12b (an identical *pāda*), 11a, 31a, 42b, 43a, 47a, 48a, 54a, 55a, 57b, 69b.

REFERENCES

Bahadur, K.P. (trans.), 1980. *Complete Works of Goswami Tulsīdās: VI, Minor Works*. Varanasi: Prachya Prakashan.

Beare, William, 1957. *Latin Verse and European Song: A Study in Accent and Rhythm*. London: Methuen.

Bhayani, H.C. (ed.), 1953. *Paümacariu of Kavirāja Svayambhūdeva*, I. Bombay: Bharatiya Vidya Bhavan.

Bryant, K.E., 1992. "Three-three-two versus four-by-four: metrical frames for the *padas* of Sūrdās". In R.S. McGregor (ed.). *Devotional literature in South Asia, Current research, 1985-88*. Cambridge: Cambridge University Press, pp. 209-224.

Chandola, Anoop, 1988. *Music as Speech: An Ethnomusicological Study of India*. New Delhi: Navrang.

Chatterji, Suniti Kumar, 1970. *The Origin and Development of the Bengali Language*. London: George Allen and Unwin.

Chaudhurī, J.B., 1954. *Khān Khānān Abdur Rahīm...and Contemporary Sanskrit Learning*. Calcutta: Prācyavidyā Mandir.

Dhar, Lakshmi, 1949. *Padumāvatī: A Linguistic Study of the 16th Century Hindi (Avadhi)*. London: Luzac.

Fairbanks, Constance Elizabeth, 1981. "The Development of Hindi Oral Narrative Metre" (PhD thesis, University of Wisconsin-Madison).

Grierson, G.A., 1893. 'Notes on Tulsi Das'. *The Indian Antiquary* (August 1893), pp.197-201.

Grierson, G.A., and L.D. Barnett, 1920. *Lallāvākyāni, or the Wise Sayings of Lāl Dēd*. London. Asiatic Society.

Gupta, Govind Rām, 'Vasant', 1970. *Rāg koṣ*. 2nd edn. Hathras: Saṅgīt Kāryālay.

Gupta, Mātāprasād, 1965. *Tulsīdās: ek samālocanātmak adhyayan*. Allahabad: Allahabad University.

Kellogg, S.H., 1938. *A Grammar of the Hindi Language*. 3rd edn. London: Routledge & Kegan Paul.

Kippen, James, 1988. *The Tabla of Lucknow: A Cultural Analysis of a Musical Tradition.* Cambridge: Cambridge University Press.

Mahesh, Maheshwari Sinha, 1964. *The Historical Development of Mediaeval Hindi Prosody (Rāmānanda-Keśava, 1400-1600 A.D.)* Bhagalpur: Bhagalpur University.

Manuel, Peter, 1989. *Ṭhumrī in Historical and Stylistic Perspectives.* Delhi: Motilal Banarsidass.

Mc Gregor, Ronald Stuart, 1984. *Hindi Literature from Its Beginnings to the Nineteenth Century.* (*A History of Indian Literature*, Vol. VIII, Fasc. 6). Wiesbaden: Otto Harrassowitz.

Miltner, Vladimir, 1967. *The Hindi Sentence Structure in the Works of Tulsīdās.* Delhi: Munshiram Manoharlal.

Muni, Jina Vijaya, and Harivallabh Bhayani, 1945. *The Saṁdeśa Rāsaka of Abdul Rahaman.* Bombay: Bharatiya Vidya Bhavan.

Paṇḍey, Sudhākar (ed.), 1969. *Kṛpārām aur uska sāhitya.* Varanasi: Nāgarī Pracāriṇī Sabhā.

Prasād, Jagannāth, 'Bhānu Kavi', 1935. *Chandaḥprabhākar.* 8th edn. Bilaspur: The Author.

Purohit, Lalitāprasād (ed.), n.d. *Rasik-ananya-māl* (of Bhagavat Mudita). Vrindaban: Veṇu Prakāśan.

Sen, Nilratan, 1973. *Early Eastern New Indo-Aryan Versification: A Prosodical Study of Caryāgītikoṣa.* Simla: Indian Institute of Advanced Study.

Shackle, Christopher, 1972. 'Sirāikī and Sirāikī Literature, c. 1750-1900, in Upper Sind and South-West Panjab' (PhD thesis, University of London).

Siṃha, Samar Bahādur, VS 2018 (AD 1961). *Abdurrahīm Khānkhāna.* Chirgaon: Sāhitya Sadan.

Snell, Rupert, 1983. "Metrical Forms in Braj Bhāṣā Verse: The *Caurāsī pāda* in Performance". In Monika Thiel-Horstmann (ed.). *Bhakti in Current Research, 1979-1982.* Berlin: Dietrich Reimer Verlag, pp. 353-383.

— 1991a. *The Eighty-four Hymns of Hita Harivaṃśa: An Edition of the Caurāsī Pada.* Delhi: Motilal Banarsidass.

— 1991b. *The Hindi Classical Tradition: A Braj Bhāṣā Reader.* London: School of Oriental and African Studies.

Stone, Brian, 1987. 'False Friends and Strange Metres'. In William Radice and Barbara Reynolds (eds.). *The Translator's Art: Essays in Honour of Betty Radice.* Harmondsworth: Penguin, pp. 175-186.

Śukla, Rāmcandra, et.al.(ed.), 1974 (VS 2031). *Tulsī granthāvalī,* Vol. II. Varanasi: Nāgarī Pracāriṇī Sabhā.

Śukla, Śatrughna, 1983. *Ṭhumrī ki utpatti, vikās aur śailiyā̃.* Delhi: Delhi University.

Varmā, Dhīrendra (ed.), 1959. *Hindī sāhitya*, II. Allahabad: Bhāratīy Hindī Pariṣad.

Velaṇkar, H.D. (ed.), 1962. *Svayambhūchanda*. Jodhpur: Rājasthān Prācyavidyā Pratiṣṭhān.

— 1929. 'Vṛttajātisamuccaya of Virahāṅka'. *Journal of the Bombay Branch of the Royal Asiatic Society* (New Series), V, pp. 34-94.

— n.d. *Jayadāman*. Bombay: Haritosha Samiti.

The Thematic Range of *Dhrupad* Songs Attributed to Tānsen, Foremost Court-Musician of the Mughal Emperor Akbar

Françoise 'Nalini' Delvoye

> "...a form (of singing) liked by the common man and favoured by the elite.... It deals with the magic of love and the wondrous affairs of the heart."[1]
>
> Abū'l Faẓl on Dhrupad in the *Ā'īn-i Akbarī* (1595-1596).

INTRODUCTION

Dhrupad songs are one of the main forms of lyric (*gey pad*) in Braj-bhāṣā, meant to be sung in the Dhrupad genre of Indian art-music since the 16th century.[2] Created by poet-composers (*vāggeyakāra*), usually singers patronised by Hindu and Muslim rulers, they have been transmitted by means of oral tradition and occasionally compiled in lyric anthologies and court-musicians' repertoires that are extant even today.

The name of some of the poet-musicians who were known as Dhrupad experts appear as a "signature" (*bhaṇitā* or *chāp*) in many compositions noted down from the oral tradition and still available in manuscript, lithographic or printed form in Western and Northern India and also in Bengal. Among them, Tānsen is well-known as the most famous singer of medieval Northern India.

Foremost court-musician of the Mughal emperor Akbar (r. 1556-1605), Tānsen is both an historical figure and a legendary character. His fabulous personality overshadows his poetical genius, though this is apparent in the *dhrupad* songs attributed to him, found in both the written and the oral repertoires.[3]

I. *DHRUPAD* SONGS IN LYRIC ANTHOLOGIES

Dhrupad songs constitute a vast corpus which developed parallel to the Vaishnava *bhakta-kavi* or "Saint-poet" tradition. From a musicological point of view, they belong to the category of musical compositions called *prabandha*, which are classified in numerous varieties according to their melodic elements (called *dhātus*) and other specific components (called *aṅgas*) relating to their tonal structure, their text and their rhythm.[4]

Dhrupad songs were generally composed in *madhyadeśiya bhāṣā*, the language of the "Middle Country", or *gvāliarī*, the language of Gwalior, which came to be known as Braj-bhāṣā in the 18th century.[5] This vernacular language was simply called *bhākhā*, "the spoken language," by Persian writers on music such as, for instance, Navāb Saïf Khān 'Faqīrullāh' in his *Rāg Darpan* ("The Mirror of Rāgas"), completed in 1666,[6] and Mīrzā Khān in his *Tuḥfat al-Hind* ("The Gift of India"), written in 1675.[7] The language of *dhrupad* songs may be described as a kind of *darbārī* Braj-bhāṣā, which has many regional and stylistic varieties, and borrows some of its vocabulary from Persian. To my knowledge, no *dhrupad* texts in Sanskrit have been found so far, despite the mention of their existence in the well-known Sanskrit *lakṣaṇas* of *dhruvapada* by Bhāvabhaṭṭa, a court-musician and theoretician of music whose treatises were commissioned by Anūp

Singh, Rājā of Bikaner, in the late 17th century, and who was one of the governors sent by Aurangzeb to the Deccan.[8]

Until recently, for different reasons, *dhrupad* songs were not well-researched. For long they were not "appealing" to scholars of literature, for whom they belonged to the "field of music" and were not valued as poetry, perhaps because most of them are not metrical. The textual corruption of *dhrupad* songs found in later manuscript collections inclines us to think that, in recent times, vocalists did not really care much for the texts they sang, and this is truer than ever today. In the 1940s, scholars of music were not much interested in song-texts because most of them were given without notation and were therefore considered as of "no use for the study of music". This has been contradicted by recent studies from a more literary perspective.[9]

Among more than seventy written sources collected by the present author while seeking *dhrupads* ascribed to Tānsen, the earliest manuscript documents are *padāvalīs* or *pad-saṅgrahs*, collections of lyrical texts, in which the classification of *padas* was made according to the melodic type (*rāg*), independently of the literary thought-content, the thematic range or the musical genre in which they were composed or sung at the time of their compilation. Very few *dhrupad* songs are found scattered in these anthologies, which comprise mostly metrical poems composed by Vaishnava poet-devotees, without any apparent order of authors or subjects.

Among the early collections of *dhrupads*, the *Kitāb-i Nauras* ("The Book of the Nine Flavours or Sentiments") is a remarkable example of a *rāg*-wise anthology. It contains fifty-nine songs akin to *dhrupad* and seventeen couplets (*dohrā*) composed in the Dakanī language and revealing several other vernacular features. They were composed by Ibrāhīm Ādil Shāh II, who was Sulṭān of Bijapur from 1580 to 1627 and a great patron of the arts of poetry, music, painting and calligraphy. Most of the ten manuscripts of the *Kitāb-i Nauras* preserved in various libraries in India were used for the critical edition published by Nazir Ahmad in 1956, with an English rendering.[10]

The first example of a collection solely of *dhrupad* texts made under royal patronage, seems to be the *Hazār Dhurpad* ("The Thousand *Dhrupads*") or *Sahasras* ("The Thousand Delights"), a *rāg*-wise compilation of one thousand and four *dhrupad* texts ascribed to Nāyak Ba<u>kh</u>śū, poet-musician at the court of Rājā Mān Singh Tomar, who was king of Gwalior from 1486 to 1516 and is known as the first great patron of *Dhrupad*. It appears that Shāh Jahān developed a great liking for the *dhrupads* of Nayāk Ba<u>kh</u>śū and ordered a compilation to be made from court-musicians of all compositions ascribed to him, with an obvious care for their authenticity, which is expressed in the anonymous Persian preface to the *Sahasras*. This extremely valuable work, which has been critically edited from two manuscripts in Persian script and rendered into Devanāgarī by Prem Lata Sharma, deserves further research, in view of its relevance for the history of medieval Indian music and dance.[11]

In the late 17th century, some *dhrupad* collections were compiled from the oral tradition of court-musicians to illustrate Sanskrit theoretical treatises on music, such as the *Anūpa Saṁgīta Ratnākara* and the *Anūpa Saṁgīta Vilāsa* of Bhāvabhaṭṭa, whom I have already mentioned. A few manuscripts are preserved in the Anup Sanskrit Library in Bikaner and the City Palace Library in Jaipur. They offer a wide variety of lyrics, which are mostly *dhrupads* attributed to many poet-composers and often include the names of royal patrons, such as Akbar, Shāh Jahān and even Aurangzeb.[12]

Later on, in the 19th and early 20th centuries, manuscript, lithographic and printed anthologies of *dhrupad* songs noted down from the court-musicians' repertoires – such as the *Rāmpur Rāg-mālā*, the *Saṁgit Rāg-Kalpadrum*, and a number of court-repertoires – were compiled in Bengal, Gujarat and other princely states.[13] Modern writers on the textual aspect of *dhrupad* songs have used some of the compositions from early anthologies, but without any critical approach.[14]

Besides their linguistic and literary value, the manuscript anthologies of lyrics including *dhrupad* songs are valuable sources for the history of Indian music. The later collections represent an equally interesting body with which to study the textual transmission of *dhrupad* compositions in various cultural contexts. They also serve as a rich corpus for analyzing the subjects which were favoured by different patrons at different times.

II. THE THEMATIC RANGE OF *DHRUPAD* SONGS

Modern writings on Dhrupad insist on its ancient– often purportedly Vedic– origin, its exclusively religious inspiration and the severe character of its musical expression. It is a fact that the mediocre lyrics performed today in the Dhrupad genre of Indian vocal music do not reveal the poetical qualities which were noticed by the scholars who studied lyrical repertoires of the 19th and the 20th centuries. However, their observations about the literary value of Dhrupad confirmed the information supplied by a number of Indo-Persian documents on Indian art-music. Moreover, the 17th– and 18th–century manuscript anthologies of song-texts composed by court-musicians provide a fair illustration of the wide range of subjects that inspired *dhrupad* songs.

1. *Indo-Persian sources on Dhrupad: their stress on the textual aspect and the verbal content.*

Indo-Persian writings on music provide documents of the highest importance on the art-music of India, in its theoretical and practical aspects. This is particularly true in the case of Dhrupad, whether considered as a musical genre or as a poetical form.[15]

Persian writers on Indian music often set out the various song-forms composed in different vernacular languages, which they mostly describe from the textual point of view, with a few remarks on their language, their thought-content and the region and context in which they were sung.

In the case of Dhrupad, these comments are worth noticing as they indicate the familiarity of the Persian writers with the texts of the *dhrupad* songs performed in the Mughal court, which implies a fairly good knowledge of the vernacular language in which they were composed. It also indicates a good appreciation of Indian literary traditions and particularly of the Hindu background underlying most of the lyrical poetry.

From the 16th century, a number of Indo-Persian texts mention Dhrupad as the favourite poetico-musical form patronised by Hindu and Muslim rulers. Following the famous chronicles of Abū'l Faẓl (end of the 16th century) about twenty Indo-Persian texts have described Dhrupad (in its musical and mostly textual aspects), its most famous poet-composers and exponents, such as Nāyak Ba<u>kh</u>śū and Tānsen, and its aristocratic patrons, beginning with Rājā Mān Singh Tomar of Gwalior.[16]

A few representative examples of Persian documents stressing the poetical content of Dhrupad, its vernacular language (*bhākhā*), the variety of its topics and its innovativeness, have been given elsewhere.[17]

2. *The thematic content of* dhrupad *songs*

The content of most *dhrupad* texts scattered in the earliest manuscript sources is devotional and was inspired specifically by the *Kṛṣṇa-līlā*. Some of the compositions found in these ancient lyric-anthologies are still used as hymnologies for some rituals in the Vallabha Sampradāy and the Rādhā-Vallabha temples in the region of Mathura, in Rajasthan, and in Gujarat. Today they are said to be sung in the Dhrupad "style", by the musicians themselves and by some theoreticians of music, which appears to be a rather controversial statement from the musicological point of view.[18]

We have noticed that most recent accounts of Dhrupad do mention its "exclusive" concern with religious subjects or praise to kings and patrons, or with other "serious" topics.[19] However, a close examination of the oldest written collections of *dhrupads* leads one to reconsider the importance of the religious motifs, so far as the *dhrupads* attributed to Nāyak Bakhśū collected in the *Hazār Dhurpad* or *Sahasras*, the *Kitāb-i Nauras* of Sulṭān Ibrāhīm Ādil Shāh II, or the *dhrupads* attributed to Tānsen and other poet-composers of the Mughal time, such as Bāz Bahādur, are concerned.[20] The various historical and cultural contexts in which those songs were composed account for the variety of the themes dealt with in the *dhrupads* compiled in the main collections or recensions known to date.

Besides religious and eulogistic subjects, *dhrupad* songs deal with a wide range of other topics such as *nāyak-nāyikā bhed* (dealing with particular kinds of love and types of lovers in different circumstances), the description of nature and seasons, and philosophical or more personal views of life and similar topics, which are roughly the same as those treated by Braj-bhāṣā court-poets of the same period.[21]

Music and dance are also dealt with in *dhrupad* compositions, being more specific to the lyrical texts of this type. All the collections consulted so far present a wide choice of compositions dealing with musical topics, which deserve a thorough study by historians and scholars of music. They cover all aspects of music from the philosophical point of view, with references to the concept of Nāda Brahma and other abstract concepts of sound (*nāda*), and with images like *nāda-nagara* (the city of sound), *nāda-mandira* (the temple of sound), *nāda-gaṛha* (the fort of sound), *nāda-samudra* (the ocean of sound), *nāda-agādha* (the infinite sound), etc.

The *Kitāb-i Nauras* and the *Hazār Dhurpad* or *Sahasras*, provide a great number of compositions inspired by music, sometimes in its most theoretical aspects.[22]

Since a number of poet-composers refer to the well-known theoretical treatise of Śārṁgadeva, *Saṁgīta Ratnākara*, and use some terms concerning musical techniques, it shows their familiarity with the contents of such theoretical texts, as well as with both vocal and instrumental practices. Such references also indicate that the patrons of the court-musicians were equally familiar with those texts on the theory of Indian art-music, which is an interesting fact for the history of artistic patronage in medieval India. Musical terms from early recensions that are provided by *dhrupad* songs and also by Indo-Persian writers on music (who often give equivalents in Sanskrit, Persian and vernacular languages, borrowed from the written tradition as well as from the musicians' oral tradition) could constitute the basis of multilingual glossaries which would be useful for reconstructing the history of Indian music.

One of the most controversial aspects of the thought-content of *dhrupad* songs and song-texts in general, is their appreciation from either a religious or a secular point of view, which is also true for all medieval court-poetry composed in Braj-bhāṣā.[23] The understanding of the religious or secular significance of *dhrupad* songs, as well as the appreciation of their poetical value, is finally left to the audience, according to its religious and cultural background.[24]

III. TĀNSEN

Tānsen is celebrated for the magical effects allegedly produced by his singing, on account of which he is still famous even among people who are not particularly fond of art-music. He is hardly remembered as a poet-composer, in spite of the fact that many lyrics bearing his name as a "signature" (*chāp*) – hence attributed to him – are still known and occasionally sung by musicians today.

Though Tānsen is the most famous figure of North Indian music in the medieval period, any attempt to reconstruct a relatively authentic biography has so far been disappointing.[25] A number of documents in Sanskrit, Persian and vernacular languages, as well as some iconographical evidence, provide no more than fragmentary information about his life, his music and his personality.[26] However, they highlight his importance as the foremost court-musician of the Mughal emperor Akbar and as the founder of one of the most illustrious musical lineages (*gharānā*) to which belong not only some specialists of Dhrupad – in which Tānsen excelled – but also other eminent musicians, mostly instrumentalists.

1. Sources on Tānsen as a poet

Among the Indo-Persian sources on Dhrupad, some texts deal with the poetical aspect of Dhrupad and Tānsen in particular. The best example remains the comments the Mughal emperor Jahāngīr made about Tānsen as a poet, in his Memoirs, *Tūzuk-i Jahāngīrī.*[27] In March 1617, during a halt by the side of a pond in Sahrā, Jahāngīr noticed the differences between two varieties of lotus flowers in the following words:[28]

"The flower of the *kaṇwal* is larger than the kumudini. Its flower is red. I have seen in Kashmir many kanwal with a hundred leaves (petals). It is certain that it opens during the day and becomes a bud at night. The kumudini, on the contrary, is a bud during the day and opens at night. The black bee, which the people of India call *bhauṇrā*, always sits on these flowers, and goes inside them to drink the juice that is in both of them. It often happens that the kanwal flower closes and the bee remains in it the whole night. In the same manner it remains in the kumudini flower. When the flower opens it comes out and flies away. As the black bee is a constant attendant on these flowers, the poets of India look on it as a lover of the flower, like the nightingale, and have put into verse sublime descriptions of it. Of these poets the chief was Tān Sen Kalāwant, who was without a rival in my father's services (in fact, there has been no singer like him in any time or age). In one of his compositions he has likened the face of a young man to the sun and the opening of his eyes to the expanding of the kanwal and the exit of the bee. In another place he has compared the side-glance of the beloved one to the motion of the kanwal when the bee alights on it."

The word *dhrupad* does not occur in Jahāngīr's mention of Tānsen's lyrics, though it occurs elsewhere as *durpat* with reference to the music taught to the Sulṭān of Bijapur, Ibrāhīm Ādil Shāh II, by Ba<u>kh</u>tār <u>Kh</u>ān Kalāvant, who visited the Mughal emperor in Ajmer in 1614.[29] Even so, Jahāngīr obviously refers to *dhrupad* songs composed and sung by Tānsen. His remarks about their poetical value reveal his thorough knowledge of the literary Braj language and his familiarity with the Indian imagery which they employ.

2. *Lyric collections containing* dhrupad *songs attributed to Tānsen*

The *dhrupad* compositions ascribed to Tānsen belong to various collections of lyrics from the court and the temple traditions.[30] The exploitation of such sources raises a number of interesting problems, such as the identification of *dhrupad* songs, establishing the authenticity of their authorship (based on the "signature" or *chāp* that a poet-composer often inserts in the last verse, which is called *ābhog* in *dhrupad* songs) and their musical rendering, *i.e.* their mode, rhythm and musical expression in the past.

The oral transmission and the textual corruption which it provokes, make the critical edition of songs rather difficult but render even more interesting the study of the different linguistic, musical and other cultural or historical factors involved in such distortions. Obviously the problems raised while compiling and studying more than one thousand eight hundred compositions attributed to Tānsen cannot be presented here. The complexity of editing *dhrupad* songs and art-music lyrics in general has been discussed already in some publications.[31]

3. *The thematic range of the* dhrupad *songs attributed to Tānsen: some illustrations*

The *dhrupads* attributed to Tānsen seem representative of the genre and provide a fairly good sample for literary studies. Their thematic range reveals the variety of subjects treated in Dhrupad, a fact which – as I mentioned earlier – was noticed by Indo-Persian writers but which is ignored by most modern scholars of music, and often even Dhrupad performers.

A few examples from 17th-century and later anthologies may be used to illustrate some of the favourite themes inspiring *dhrupad* songs, such as the praise of God and Puranic stories, the eulogy of a royal patron, the Kṛṣṇa legend, *nāyak-nāyikā bhed*, music, the description of nature and *dhrupads* of a more personal inspiration.

– *The praise of God and Puranic themes*

Laudatory *dhrupads* in praise of God are very similar to the lyrics composed by medieval *bhakti* poets. They are addressed to Ganeś, Sarasvatī, Sūrya, Viṣṇu, Nārāyaṇ, and more rarely to Śiv in the earliest collections, in which devotional *dhrupads* predominate. We consider *dhrupad* songs about Kṛṣṇa under his many epithets to constitute a separate category close to the *nāyak-nāyikā bhed* one. We also find *dhrupad* songs with the "signature" of Tānsen in praise of Allāh and with references to some Sufi saints. Puranic and Islamic references are also found in many *dhrupads* attributed to Tānsen and addressed to Akbar, which were sung until recent times, as attested to by court-musicians' repertoires compiled in Bengal, Northern India and Gujarat in the 19th and early 20th centuries.

In a composition attributed to Tānsen and conserved in various court-musicians' repertoires, the poet eulogises the Goddess Sarasvatī, addressing her with the epithets of other goddesses like Durgā and Pārvatī:[32]

Te re sarasuti ghaṭa ghaṭa pūri rahī nāṁu dharāyo bākabānī...

"O Sarasvatī You fill each and every body and You hold the name of Vākavāṇī "the Speech Incarnate".

In the ocean and on earth, You are famed as Jālapā and Bhavānī, hence You are named Sarvānī.

You have myriads of voices, O Mṛḍānī and You extend over the Seven Islands (of the Earth), O You who are the Queen of Nagarkoṭ !

Bestow Your favour on Tānsen, O Bhavānī, Compassionate and Learned, O You who sustain song in his throat !"

– The eulogy of Akbar as a connoisseur of music

Among the *dhrupad* compositions attributed to Tānsen, the eulogistic texts addressed to various patrons are the most mediocre, from the literary point of view. Their vocabulary is generally poor and the subjects inspiring them are rarely original and often repetitive. However, a number of *dhrupads* "signed" with the name of Tānsen constitute an exception to this rule. Addressed to the emperor Akbar by name, they highlight his qualities as a connoisseur of music.[33] The curiosity of the emperor, and possibly his real musical skills, might have struck Tānsen enough to have led him to compose a few poems on musical themes, occasionally of a very technical character, with the hope of arousing the interest and provoking the generosity of his patron.

Tānsen is addressing the *gunīs* or accomplished artists, in a *dhrupad* conserved in both the anthologies of Bhāvabhaṭṭa:[34]

Gāyana gunī gana gaṁdrapā sādhi calo mili apa apanī vidhi sāhi baiṭhyau sabhā maṁḍala...

"O singers, accomplished artists and skilful musicians, go playing in your own fashion before the Emperor who sits in the audience hall.

Play the seven notes on the *vīṇā* to the accompaniment of the pleasure-giving *mṛdaṅga*. Take the *rabāb*, *kinnara* and other melodic instruments with you to the music pavilion.

Just as Brahmā circumambulates, while keeping the whole Gaṅgā in a small ascetic's pot, concentrate while playing the *pañca-śabda* for he, whose body, mind and face are full of excellence.

The humble Tānsen makes this prayer, O Lord, may these skilful ones captivate the Emperor Akbar, while combining knowledge and pleasure, as if to hold the whole Universe in their power !"

– The Krishnaite theme

The *Kṛṣṇa-līlā* inspired a number of *dhrupads* composed both in the style of the Saint-poets and of the poets and poet-composers of the royal courts. Kṛṣṇa is variously named Hari, Govind, Mādhau, Mohan, Śyām, Kanhā, Gopāl, Nand Dulāre, etc. Some *dhrupads* describe his beauty, his divine play with Rādhā, or the magic effect of his glance or of his flute or depict the love tainted with resentment of the *gopīs*, deceived by Kṛṣṇa's sweet charming words.

In the following *dhrupad*, the poet wonders about the effects of Kṛṣṇa on the inhabitants of Braj:[35]

Ghara ghara gheru mathanu suniyatu he rī māī kauna maṁtru paḍhi ḍāyauṁ kanhāī...

"O my friend, in every house, the churning of restless minds is heard. What a magic spell Kṛṣṇa cast on everyone !

Whoever sees his face, withers like a flower ! Are they enchanted by his *tilak* made of musk, or by the curve of his eyebrows ?

Or is it the line of his eyes or his gentle enchanting smile ? Or is it the beauty of his body that makes them forget their body and mind ?

Who can tell this untellable story ? On my life all this is the wonder of the *tāns* of the Lord of Tānsen !"

An unusual composition deals with the blanket of Kṛṣṇa, a later motif which does not appear in the *Bhāgavata Purāṇa*:[36]

Dhani dhani kāmarī rī mohana śyāma kī...

"Blessed, blessed the blanket of the Charming Dark Lord, O my friend !

The one which he wears in the forest, the one from which he makes his couch, the same one that shelters him from the raindrops and which gives him shade in the sun.

Blessed be the blanket that covers him well and protects him from the cold ! Or again which, spread on the floor, ravishes the modesty of myriads of women !

It is that [blanket] which has attacked social divisions and conventions *(jāti-pāṁti-paripāṭī)*. The humble Tānsen too, weary of his burdens, would like its comfort."

– The nāyak-nāyikā bhed theme

Close to the Krishnaite theme, the *nāyak-nāyikā bhed* theme inspires many *dhrupad* songs found in court-musicians' repertoires. Some of them are "felt" to be Krishnaite, though neither Kṛṣṇa nor Rādhā, nor the *gopī*s, nor the Yamunā, nor the flute are referred to in these compositions.

As an illustration, a composition found both in a late 17th-century and an early 19th-century court-musicians' repertoire is presented, in which a *sakhī* is consoling the "innocent" (*mugdhā*) heroine:[37]

Ūṁce [ci] tai rī nīceṁ kata citavati tūṁ hārati lājani sotini jitavati...

"O my friend, look up, why are you looking down ? You always feel defeated because of your modesty and your rivals are victorious !

Your eyes were cooled by a vision of him, the Lord of your life, who is the God of Love ! Without bodily union, without approaching him, and without even attachment to him, O my friend, how can your body find contentment while you pass your days ?

As long as you do not accept your beloved in your mind, in the same way, my dear friend, you will not find love growing in your heart !

Fools and wise men both agree, if you accept the ways of the Lord of Tānsen, why should you waste your youth like this ?"

– Musical terminology and metaphors

As we have already noted, music constitutes an important subject widely dealt with in *dhrupad* songs, which provide a rich corpus for the history of medieval art-music. In particular, they contain technical terms belonging to the oral tradition (*sampradāy*), which is not documented in Sanskrit theoretical texts. The English rendering of such compositions – even when music is referred to in a quite metaphorical manner – requires an apparatus of explanatory foot-notes for technical terms which can rarely be translated accurately. Hence, besides the illustration of this particular theme, already provided by a *dhrupad* song describing the musicians of the Emperor Akbar, we will present a composition in which music is treated in a metaphorical way, with relatively little technical terminology. Music is also featured in a depictive way in another song given as an illustration of the treatment of nature and seasons in *dhrupad* compositions.

The following example from an early 19th-century court-musicians' repertoire offers a description of "Sound" (*nāda*) as a beautiful and powerful fortress, hard to conquer because of the intricacy of its elements:[38]

Nāda gaḍha sughara gaḍha vākau kīnoṁ sapta sura koṭi kagūrā vikaṭa gaḍha ṣāī...

"The fortress of Sound is a well-built fortress ! The seven notes make the ramparts and all the intricacies make the moats of the fortress !

The ascending scale (*ārohī*) and the descending scale (*avarohī*), the twenty-one modal scales (*mūrcchanā*) make the four towers, the four armouries, and the cannons pointed in the four directions.

The Creator has made this fortress in such a way that the range of *tāns* make excellent and sharp [weapons].

Mīāṁ Tānsen says : listen, elegant young man, you cannot capture it with the force of your arm alone !"

– The description of nature

The description of nature and seasons with their emotional connotations – such as the arrival of the rains and their strong effect on love-sick heroines (*nāyikā*) – inspires a number of *dhrupad* compositions with rich metaphors and similes.

One such song provides an illustration of the reference to music magnifying the effects created by the coming of spring on young women who adorn themselves and gather to celebrate the cheerful occasion. Many songs describing seasons implicitly refer to the *Kṛṣṇa-līlā*, and the Braj country is likely to have been the setting, though no mention is made of Kṛṣṇa in this composition:[39]

Sava mili karau anega raṁga kauṁ ava āi ho ritu vasaṁta...

"Let us play together in different ways, now the spring season has come !

Among the young women, O my friend, one is laughing while beating time, another is playing the lute *(kinara)*, a third sports a diadem [of flowers].

A woman is singing, another plays the drum *(mṛdaṅga)*, a third one applies perfume on her body.

All together with their *sakhīs*, all exhilarated, they surrender to the Lord of Tānsen."

– Dhrupads *of personal inspiration*

Some *dhrupads* with the *chāp* of Tānsen of a more personal inspiration are also found in the 17th-century anthologies, especially in the *Anūpa Saṁgīta Ratnākara* of Bhāvabhaṭṭa which includes seven compositions of this type, some of which are found later in other court-musicians' repertoires.

Here Tānsen, to whom the following composition is attributed, addresses his mind:[40]

Dhīrem̐ dhīrem̐ re mana dhīrem̐ saba kachu hoī...

"Slowly, slowly, O my mind, everything takes its time !

You are very clever and impatient, but Knowledge and Illumination cannot be obtained by mere repetition, as deceit cannot be washed away, like dirt from a cloth !

You must reflect on yourself, but instead you pass the day agitated and the night asleep !

If you equal the Lord of Tānsen, you will "eat your cake and have it too" [lit. you will have a buttered *roṭi* and two as bonus]!".

CONCLUSION

At the intersection of the devotional lyrics of the Saint-poets (*bhakta-kavi*), and the amorous verses of the court-poets (*darbārī-kavi*), *dhrupad* songs provide a rich sample of a little-known tradition of Braj lyrical poetry. They are worthy of study for their linguistic and their literary value as well as for their documentary contribution to the history of music and of the artistic patronage to vernacular poetry in medieval India.

Among the *dhrupad* compositions compiled from the oral tradition of court-musicians, those attributed to Tānsen, which are scattered in a number of lyric anthologies written in various scripts from the 16th century to the recent past, and from Gujarat to Bengal, provide a fairly representative example of the genre and offer a vast corpus for further literary studies. Their thematic variety, which is also to be found in vernacular court-poetry, their musical references and expression, all contribute to their originality and illustrate the artistic awareness of royal patrons who seemed to have enjoyed their performance as well as their poetic and aesthetic content.

NOTES

NB. I am grateful to Sanjay Subrahmanyam for revising my English.

1. See Abū'l Fazl 1877: II, 138. My translation.
2. See Bṛhaspati 1976 and Srivastava 1980. For bibliographical references on Dhrupad, see Delvoye 1986, 1987a, 1988a, 1989, 1990a, 1991a, 1992a and 1991c : 140-141, 180-185.
3. See Delvoye 1990c and 1992b.
4. See Śārṅgdeva 1989 : 209-324. For the structure of *dhrupad* songs, see Srivastava 1980 : 10-19; Lāṭh 1987 : 28-32; Delvoye 1990c : 26-27.
5. See Siṁh 1964; Varma 1935 and 1954; Dvivedī 1955.
6. See 'Faqīrullāh' 1981 : 35; Sarmadee Forthcoming 2; Delvoye 1991c : 152-155 and note (47) : 152 for bibliographical references.
7. See Mīrzā K͟hān 1976 : 351; Ziauddin 1935; Delvoye 1991c : 154-155 and note (51) : 154 for bibliographical references.
8. See Upādhyāya 1986; Delvoye 1987b : 36-37 and 1990c : 22-25.
9. See Caudharī 1986 : 20-35; Delvoye 1987b : 33-60 and 1991c: 140-141.
10. See Ibrāhim Ādil Shāh II 1956; Delvoye : 1991b and 1993b.
11. See Śarmā (ed.). 1972 and 1972-1974; Delvoye : 1990b and 1991c : 170-174.
12. See *supra* note 8 and Delvoye 1990c : 22-23, 82-83, 326-331, *passim* and 1991b : 168-169. See *infra* notes 32 and 35 for references to the manuscripts used.
13. See the original manuscript of the *Rāmpur Rāg-mālā* in the library of the Uttar Pradesh Sangit Natak Akademi, Lucknow and Bṛhaspati 1976 : 322-395. See also lithographic copies of the *Saṁgīt Rāg-Kalpadrum* in the Bhārat Kalā Bhavan, Varanasi and other libraries in India, and its printed editions, 1914-1916. For a discussion see Delvoye 1990c : 83-86, 332-352.
14. See *supra* note 8 and Delvoye 1990c : 86-87, 352-359.
15. See Ahmad 1984; Sarmadee Forthcoming 1 (for a systematic descriptive catalogue of Sanskrit, Indo-Persian and vernacu-

lar sources on Indian music); Delvoye 1986 : 103-106, 1987b: 34-35 and 1991d.

16. See Delvoye 1990c: 34-68 and 1991c: 149-155.
17. *Idem.*
18. See Delvoye 1991c : 141-146.
19. However, see Srivastava 1980 : 27-46 for a representative selection of *dhrupad* songs from secondary sources.
20. See for instance Ahmad 1956; Śarmā 1972: [125]-[132] and 1972-1974: 47-48; Bṛhaspati 1976: 252-274; Delvoye 1991c: 166-168.
21. See for instance Agravāl 1950.
22. See Ahmad 1956: 46-55, 61-63, 68-73; Śarmā 1988; Delvoye 1990c : 418-424 and 1993b.
23. See McGregor 1984 : 118-129; 173-203. Agravāl 1950; Naik 1966.
24. See Willard 1965 : 103-105; Delvoye Forthcoming 1.
25. See Mītal 1960; Brahaspati 1979; Dvivedī 1986; Dhar 1989.
26. See Delvoye 1990c : 149-310.
27. See Jahāngīr 1978 : 1st Part, 412-413; Delvoye 1990c : 167-169.
28. *Idem.*
29. See Jahāngīr 1978 : 1st Part, 271-272.
30. See Delvoye 1990c : 320-352.
31. See Delvoye 1987b, 1988b : 161-165, 1990c : 92-95; Śarmā 1987.
32. See the Ms. No 3367 of the *Anūpa Saṁgīta Vilāsa* (*ASV*) of Bhāvabhaṭṭa, conserved in the Anup Sanskrit Library (ASL), Bikaner : f. 72b in *rāg Khabhāvatī Belavalī*; see also the Ms. of the *Rāmpur Rāg-mālā* (*RRM*) : f. 53a in *rāg Asāvarī* and *tāl cautāl*, published in Bṛhaspati 1976, No. 23 : 370 and the *Saṁgīt Rāg Kalpadrum* (*SRKD*), litho. : 54 and printed edn. Vol. I : 107 in *rāg Ṭoḍī*. See the text in Braj and the French translation in Delvoye 1990c: 370. I am grateful to Prem Lata Sharma for clarifying the meaning of the *dhrupads* found in these collections.
33. See some other examples of a similar inspiration given with the text in Braj and the translation into French, in Delvoye 1991c: 176-179.
34. See *ASV* (ASL 3367): ff. 60a-b and the Ms. No. 7339 of the same text, conserved at the City Palace Library, Jaipur: ff.

71a-b. This *dhrupad* in *rāg Deśākhya* appears also with some reading-variants in *ASR* (ASL 3356) : ff. 124a-b.

35. See the Ms. No. 3356 of the *Anūpa Saṁgīta Ratnākara* (*ASR*) of Bhāvabhaṭṭa, conserved in the Anup Sanskrit Library (ASL), Bikaner: f. 94b, in *rāg Kalyān* and in a Ms. dated 1748, No. 221 of Āgarcand Nāḥtā's private collection (Bikaner), in *rāg Iman-kalyān* published in "Dhrupad-Dhamār-Aṅk" 1964: 193. See Śārṅgdeva 1978 : Chapt. I, Sect. 4, for the technical term *tān* : vv. 27-90 and the English translation : 179-228.
36. See *ASR* (ASL 3356) : f. 129a, in *rāg Bailāvalī*.
37. See *ASR* (ASL 3356) : f. 127b, in *rāg Bailāvalī* and *RRM* : f. 38a in *rāg Imānī Virāuri* and *tāl cautāl*, published in Bṛhaspati 1976: No. 48 : 374.
38. See *RRM* : f. 84a in *rāginī Mālasirī* and *tāl Sūrphāktā*, published in Bṛhaspati 1976, No. 68 : 377. See Śārṅgadeva 1978: Chapt. I, Sect. 4, for technical terms such as *mūrcchanā*: vv. 9-26b and the English translation: 167-179 and *tān*: vv. 27-90 and the English translation: 179-228.
39. See *RRM* : f. 250b in *rāg Hiṇḍol* and *tāl cautāl*, published in Bṛhaspati 1976, No. 73 : 378.
40. See *ASR* (ASL 3356) : f. 137a, in *rāg Suhavī*. See also the *SRKD*, litho. : 54, printed edn., Vol. I : 107 and the *Nād Binod Graṁth*, Gosvāmi 1896 : 427 in *rāg Ṭoḍī* and *tāl cautāl*.

BIBLIOGRAPHICAL REFERENCES

Abbreviations : *DA 86* to *DA 93* for *Dhrupad Annual 1986* to *Dhrupad Annual 1993*.

Abū'l Fazl. 1877. *Ā'īn-ī Akbarī* (1595-1596). Persian edn., Blochmann, H., 2 vols., Calcutta: Asiatic Society of Bengal.

Agravāl, Sarayūprasād. 1950. *Akbarī darbār ke hindī kavi*. Lucknow: Lakhnaū Viśvavidyālaya.

Ahmad, Najma Perveen. 1984. *Hindustani Music. A Study of its Development in 17th and 18th centuries*. New-Delhi: Manohar Publications.

Ahmad, Nazir (ed.). 1956. *Kitab-i-Nauras by Ibrahim Adil Shah II*. New-Delhi: Bharatiya Kala Kendra.

Bhāvabhaṭṭa. nd. *Anūpa Saṁgīta Ratnakāra, Rāgādhyāya*. Manuscript No. 3356, Anup Sanskrit Library, Bikaner.

—. nd. *Anūpa Saṁgīta Vilāsa, Rāgādhyāya.* Manuscript N° 3367, Anup Sanskrit Library, Bikaner; Ms. No. 7339 (dated 1695), "Khasmohor Collection", City Palace Library, Jaipur.

Bṛhaspati (Ācārya), Kailaś Candra. 1976. *Dhruvapada aur uskā vikās.* Patna: Bihār Raṣṭrabhāṣā Pariṣad.

Brahaspati, K.C.D. 1979. "Tānsen", *Composers.* (ed.) Raghavan, V. New-Delhi: Publications Division, pp. 75-88.

Callewaert, W.M. and Lath, M. 1989. *The Hindi Padavalī of Nāmdev, A critical edition of Nāmdev's Hindi songs with translation and annotation.* Delhi: Motilal Banarsidass.

Caudharī, Subhadrā. 1986. "Dhrupad ke "pad"-pakṣa kā adyatan adhyayan: cune hue kāryoṁ kī samīkṣā", *DA 86*, pp. 20-33; English Summary, "Contemporary Studies in the Textual Aspect of Dhrupad Songs: A Summary of Selected Works", pp. 34-35.

Costanzo, Maria Maurizia. 1989. "Dhrupad and Caryagiti: Some Considerations on the Rituality of Dhrupad", *DA 89*, pp. 71-74.

Delvoye, Françoise 'Nalini'. 1986. "Bibliography on Dhrupad", *DA 86*, pp. 95-115.

—. 1987a. "Bibliography on Dhrupad - II", *DA 87*, pp. 119-121.

—. 1987b. "Sources of Material for Critical Studies in Dhrupad Song-Texts", *DA 87*, pp. 33-60.

—. 1988a. "Bibliography on Dhrupad - III", *DA 88*, pp. 98-102.

—. 1988b. "Problems & Prospects of Critical Studies of Lyrical Texts", *Saṁgīt meṁ anusandhān kī samasyāeṁ aur kṣetra - Problems & Areas of Research in Music.* (ed.) Chaudhary, S., Ajmer: Krishna Brothers, 1988, pp. 149-194.

—. 1989. "Bibliography on Dhrupad - IV", *DA 89*, pp. 105-107.

—. 1990a. Bibliography on Dhrupad - V", *DA 90*, pp. 117-120.

—. 1990b. "The Verbal Content of Dhrupad Songs from the Earliest Collections: I. The *Hazār Dhurpad* or *Sahasras*, a collection of 1004 *dhrupads* attributed to Nāyak Ba<u>kh</u>śū", *DA 90*, pp. 93-109.

—. 1990c. *Tānsen et la tradition des chants dhrupad en langue braj, du XVIe siècle ā nos jours*, D.Litt. Thesis, Paris, Sorbonne Nouvelle University. (Unpublished)

—. 1991a. "Bibliography on Dhrupad - VI", *DA 91*, pp. 30-33.

—. 1991b., "The Verbal Content of Dhrupad Songs from the Earliest Collections, II. The *Kitāb-i Nauras* of Ibrāhīm Ādil

Shāh II, Sulṯān of Bijapur (r. 1580-1627) and its Persian Preface by Mullā Nūr al-Dīn Muḥammad 'Ẓuhūrī'–Part I, *DA 91*, pp. 38-54.

—. 1991c. "Les chants *dhrupad* en langue braj des poètes-musiciens de l'Inde Moghole", *Littératures médiévales de l'Inde du Nord, Contributions de Charlotte Vaudeville et de ses élèves.* (ed.) Mallison, F. Paris: École Francaise d'Extrême-Orient, pp. 139-185.

—. 1991d. *A Descriptive Inventory of the Indo-Persian Sources on Music in India*, Paris, IFRI and New Delhi, CSH. (Unpublished)

—. 1992a. "Bibliography on Dhrupad - VII", *DA 92*, pp. 112-115.

—. 1993a. "Tānsen and the Tradition of *Dhrupad* Songs in the Braj Language, from the 16th century to the Present Day", *DA 93*, pp. 37-44 (Abstract of D.Litt. Thesis, see Delvoye 1990c)

—. 1993b. "The *Kitāb-i Nauras* of Ibrāhīm Ādil Shāh II, Sulṯān of Bijapur (r. 1580-1627) and its Persian Preface by Mullā Nūr al-Dīn Muḥammad 'Ẓuhūrī'—Part II", *DA 93*, pp. 1-23.

—. Forthcoming 1. "Revitalisation of Dhrupad in the second half of the 20th century; musicological literature and patronage", *Cultural Reorientation in Modern India* (provisional title). (ed.) Grewal, J.S. Shimla: Indian Institute of Advanced Study.

Dhar, Sunita. 1989. *Senia Gharana - Its Contribution to Indian Classical Music.* New Delhi: Reliance Publishing House.

Dhrupad Annual. 1986– *Vol. I–*, Varanasi: All India Kashi Raj Trust, on behalf of the Maharaja Benares Vidya Mandir Trust.

"Dhrupad-dhamar-aṁk". 1964. *Saṁgīt.* (ed.) Garg, L.N., Vol. 30, 1-2.

Dvivedī, Hariharnivās. 1956. *Madhyadeśīya-bhāṣā (gvāliyarī)* (1955). Repr. Gwalior (Murār): Vidyā Mandir Prakāśan.

—. 1986. *Tānsen, jīvanī, vyaktitva tathā kṛtitva.* Gwalior: Vidyā Mandir Prakāśan.

'Faqīrullāh', Navāb Saif Khān. 1981. *Rāg Darpan* (1666), "Rāga Darpana", with the "Ṣaut al-Nāqaus" of Muḥammad ᶜOsmān Qais. (ed.) Anṣārī, N.H. and Shukla, Sh., Delhi: *Persian Research Journal Special Number.*

Gosvāmī, Pannalāl. 1896. *Nād Binod Graṁth.* Delhi: Nārāyaṇdās Jaṅgalīmal.

Gupta, Rakesh. 1967. *Studies in Nāyaka-nāyikā-bheda.* Aligarh: Granthayan.

Ibrāhīm Ādil Shāh II. 1956. *Kitāb-i Nauras.* (ed.) Ahmad, N., New Delhi: Bharatiya Kala Kendra.

Jahāngīr. 1978. *Tūzuk-i Jahāngīri or Memoirs of Jahāngīr* (1605-1624). English transl., Rogers, A.; rev. annotated edn, Beveridge, H. Repr., New Delhi: Munshiram Manoharlal.

Lāṭh, Mukund. 1987. "Dhrupad kā itihās, ek naī dṛṣṭi kā āgrah", *DA 87*, pp. 16-27; English summary: "The History of Dhrupad: Plea for a New Approach", pp. 28-32.

McGregor, Ronald Stuart. 1984. *Hindi Literature from its Beginning to the Nineteenth Century*. Wiesbaden: Otto Harrassowitz.

Mīrzā Khān. 1976. *Tuḥfat al-Hind* (1675). (ed.) Anṣārī, N.H., Teheran: Intishārāt-i Bunyād Farang-i Irān.

Mītal, Prabhudayāl. 1960. *Saṁgīt-samrāṭ Tānsen, jīvanī aur racnāeṁ*. Mathura: Sāhitya Bhavan.

Naik, Chhotubhai Ranchhodji. 1966. *ᶜAbdu'r Raḥīm Khān-i-khānān and his Literary Circle*. Ahmedabad: Gujarat University.

Rāmpur Rāg-mālā. nd. Original manuscript kept in the library of the Uttar Pradesh Sangit Natak Akademi, Lucknow. Handwritten copy of this Ms. with indexes in the library of the Department of Musicology, Banaras Hindu University, Varanasi.

Saṁgīt Rāg-Kalpadrum of Kṛṣṇānand Vyās 'Rāg-sāgar'. 1842. Lithographic copy in the library of the Bhārat Kalā Bhavan, Varanasi and other libraries in India.

Saṁgit Rāg-Kalpadrum of Kṛṣṇānand Vyās 'Rāg-sāgar'. 1914-1916. (ed.) Vasu, Nagendra Nath, 3 Vols. Calcutta: Bangiya Sahitya Parishad.

Śarmā, Premlatā (ed.). 1972. *Sahasarasa, Nāyak Bakhśū ke dhrupadoṁ kā saṅgrah*. New Delhi: Saṁgīt Nāṭak Akāḍemī.

Śarmā, Premlatā. 1987. "Dhrupad ke padoṁ meṁ "chāp" aur us-se udbhūt samasyāeṁ", *DA 87*, pp. 84-98 and the English Summary, "Signature in Dhrupad Song-Texts and the Problems Arising Therefrom", pp. 99-101.

—. 1988. "Dhrupad ke padoṁ meṁ saṁgīt kī pāribhāṣik śabdāvalī", *DA 88*, pp. 15-47 and the English Summary, "Musical Terms in Dhrupad Texts", pp. 48-51.

Sarmadee, Shahab. Forthcoming 1. *Nūr-Ratnākar*. 2 Vols., Calcutta: Sangeet Research Academy.

—. Forthcoming 2. Critical edn and English Transl. of the *Rāg Darpan* of Navāb Saīf Khān 'Faqīrullāh'. New Delhi: IGNCA.

Śārṅgadeva. 1978. *Saṅgīta Ratnākara of Śārṅgadeva*. Sanskrit Text and English Translation, Vol. I (Treatment of Svara), (eds.) Shringy, R.K. and Sharma P.L., Varanasi: Motilal Banarsidass.

Śārṅgadeva. 1989. *Saṅgīta Ratnakāra of Śārṅgadeva.* Sanskrit Text and English Translation, Vol. II (Chapters II-IV) (eds.) Shringy, R.K. and Sharma, P.L., New Delhi: Munshiram Manoharlal.

Sharma, Prem Lata. 1972-1974. "Sahasarasa (a compilation of Dhrupad texts ascribed to Bakshoo), Synopsis of a Treatise", *Indian Music Journal*, 8-9-10, 15-20, pp. 41-48.

Siṁh, Śiv Prasād. 1964. *Sūr-pūrva braj-bhāṣā aur uskā sāhitya* (1958). 2nd edn, Varanasi: Hindī Pracārak Pustakālay.

Srivastava, Indurama. 1980. *Dhrupada, A Study of its Origin, Historical Development, Structure and Present State.* Delhi: Motilal Banarsidass.

Upādhyāya, Ādināth. 1986. "Bhāvabhaṭṭa ke granth aur un-meṁ dhruvapada", *DA 86*, pp. 69-92 and the English Summary, "The Works of Bhāvabhaṭṭa and the Treatment of Dhrupad Therein", *DA 86*, pp. 93-94.

Varma, Dhirendra. 1935. *La langue braj (Dialecte de Mathurā).* Paris: Adrien-Maisonneuve.

Varmā, Dhīrendra. 1954. *Braj bhāṣā.* Allahabad: Hindustānī Academy.

Willard (Captain) A.A. 1965. "Treatise on the Music of Hindoostan" (1834), *Hindu Music from Various Authors* (1875), (ed.), Tagore, S.M., 2nd rev. edn, Varanasi: Chowkhamba Sanskrit Series, pp. 1-122.

Ziauddin, M. 1935. *Mirza Khan's Grammar of the Braj Bhakha.* Calcutta: Visva-Bharati Book-Shop.

Bhakti and *Viraha* Songs from Early Films and Their Relation to Traditional *Bhakti* and *Viraha* Songs

Maya Burger

INTRODUCTION

As soon as the the first talkie was released in 1931 in Bombay, songs became an essential component of Indian cinema.

After a brief historical survey of the formative period of the early songs and their development during the forties (I), I shall concentrate on how film songs can be defined (II) and proceed with an analysis of *bhakti* songs and the concept of *viraha* in the context of films (III).[1]

I IMPORTANT HISTORICAL ELEMENTS

Silent movies had musical accompaniments, mostly piano, clarinet, harmonium, singing, tabla and violin, more or less westernized in their styles. Sometimes bands also played, depending on the facilities offered by the cinema hall. When the first talkie, *Ālām Ārā*, was shot, the producer, Ardeshir M. Irani, created all the songs and they were sung by the actors themselves. The first hit, "De de khudā ke nām par pyāre, tāqat hai gar dene ki", sung by W. M. Khan, was a tremendous success. Though we have no recordings or films of the first years of the talkies, newspaper clippings serve as a testimony of the Indian audience's incomparable fascination with songs. With the introduction of records (78), the song acquired its definite structure and has remained a must ever since.[2] Yet, during this creative period of the songs, two types must be distinguished: a) the early songs; b) the film song as a developed autonomous phenomenon.

a) Cinema in India was born out of the theatre. The first films were often just filmed stage acting. It is important to acknowledge this source, as it has had a lasting impact on the conception of film and songs.[3] Theatre has a very long and old tradition in India. Besides the Sanskrit drama, there are innumerable local and regional traditions, some of which contributed greatly to the shaping of the cinema. The places where the cinema was growing were also flourishing centres for dramatic art: Calcutta, Bombay and Pune, for example. Singing and musical accompaniment were an integral part of the dramatic art and were woven into the narrative plot. By the beginning of the century, this increased to such an extent that a lot of popular dramas were just "... a string of songs, a musical soirée. No plots, no actors, only songs and singers".[4]

M. Lath has shown in an article that it is possible to link film songs with the aesthetic theories and devices of Sanskrit dramaturgy.[5] I shall not explore the subject further here, but will instead underline the importance of local and regional theatres, such as *yātrā*, *tamāśā*, Parsi theatre, *rāsa līlā*, *khyāl*, *nauṭankī*,[6] themselves influenced by Sanskrit drama, which have contributed to making songs an essential medium for conveying feelings, emotions and thoughts.[7] For instance *tamāśā*, a kind of dance drama especially popular in Maharashtra, came into prominence in the 18th century. It was indebted to Marathi literature as well as local dramatic traditions.[8] In its revival phase, after the 18th century, *tamāśā* replaced the mood of devotion of the popular dramas with an atmosphere of everyday love, earthy matters, teasing and tantalizing, and often boisterous humour, though without excluding religious feelings. *Tamāśā* still uses dance and music, simultaneously incorporating *rāga*-based music and folk melodies, being an entertainment of the *lokadharmī* style with elements from the Sanskrit tradition. It was a ready-made form from which early film makers could draw inspiration. Similarly the Parsi theatre also yielded many of its stars to the new cinema. Besides the artists, other aspects of the repertoire of the Parsi theatre also found their way into the early films. Mythology, Persian/Arabic/Indian legends, and increasingly romantic elements became more prominent features in cinema. *Ālām Ārā*, for instance, was a production of the Parsi theatre, another example is the Urdu drama *Indrasabhā*.

The impetus of the dramatical source is also important from a linguistic point of view. In order to attract a wide audience, theatres would stage Hindi (Khaṛī boli) and Urdu plays that were popular.[9] The film was to pick up the same trend in order to secure the largest possible audience.

Due to their theatrical background, the early film songs were more like sung speech than proper songs, like verses set to tunes. Early songs were based on classical music, more precisely the North Indian Hindustānī style, that would be familiar to a wider audience than regional and folk music. The song producers of that time were, themselves, often trained classical musicians, and they made use of the *rāga/tāla* system and the theory of musical moods (*rasa*) to create desired effects and moods. The songs of movies like *Amarjyotī* (1936), *Gopāl Kṛṣṇa* (1938, for the Hindi version), to name only two, were based on *rāgas*, and sung in a traditional style.

b) After this initial phase of the song, play-back singing became popular, and songs turned into a flourishing business. Along with the play-back stars, the music director and the lyric-writer came into existence. Whereas, in the beginning, the song was totally dependent on and woven into the narrative, it slowly outgrew these early conditions and became appreciated outside of the film context as pure song, though it was, and still is, an essential part of the film story. Ranade draws our attention to the fact that cinema, especially during the first decades, was very much based on literature.[10] When the films started to stage rural settings, viewed in an idealized manner by urban society, it also meant a change for the film song. Stylized rural people were made to sing folk songs, a fact that allowed a broadening of the repertoire of the music employed so far. Slowly, songs became detached from the classical model and increasingly used the heterogenous elements that form the typical film song till today. The number of songs was limited to six songs per film, whereas the first films had up to seventy songs, and most frequently around fifteen. From the forties onwards we may say that the popular film song took shape, ever ready to incorporate the challenge of new fashions.

II DEFINITION OF FILM SONGS

Movie songs belong to the realm of enjoyment; music and dance contribute to make it a very much appreciated form of entertainment. More than that, the songs are also an essential means of communication. During the movie, whenever a thought, a feeling or a precise emotion, a particular atmosphere has to be rendered, then this is done by singing. A song may also simply take place to lessen the dramatic tension.

Among the songs that I've collected, by far the most frequent songs are the love song and the song of separation.[11] According to traditional classification love and love in separation actually belong to the same category, but I've preferred to place the *viraha* song separately because of its overall importance.[12]

Three elements are considered here: 1) artistic and meaningful devices to construct the songs; 2) the lyrics; 3) the music.

1. *Artistic and meaningful devices to make a song*

I shall illustrate this by referring to a love scene. *Śṛṇgāra rasa* is the king *rasa* and has been omnipresent in all artistic expressions, human or divine, through the centuries. The determinant elements or conditions of love (*vibhāva*)[13] occur as precise signs in the film. These signs are very much like the ones found in traditional art forms such as miniature painting, where the conditions proper to the emotional state of *rati* (love) are painted accurately and in minute detail. In a manner similar to a painting, the song director will construct the atmosphere to be expressed. Beautiful surroundings, flowers, spring, flute (music), bumblebees (as a symbol of love), rain, clouds, and two beings filled with the feeling of love, freshness, water, mountains, and "hill stations". The consequences of these conditions are also codified (*anubhāva*) and express much of the behaviour of lovers, such as the moving of the eyebrows, the lowering of eyelashes, longing looks, dance, games of hide and seek, frolicsome expressions; choirs of friends or people may join in the dance and the song. Innumerable examples could be cited here; from a historical point of view, the love songs in the film *Street Singers* (1937) are a prototype of a very pure style.[14]

The film song has a very particular structure. As soon as it starts, we leave the plane of ordinary reality and merge into a world that is comparable to the world of dreams. The protagonists of the songs may all of a sudden be in an entirely new surrounding, dressed up in a way appropriate to the emotions exposed. In this song-world, the ordinary limitations of life do not exist. Freed from space, time and causality boundaries, we are taken far above the ordinary world.

In the realm of religious films, songs are the direct access to the world of the gods; in the secular realm, they are the gateway to the inner world of dreams, fantasies and emotions.

Movies, in a general sense, may be qualified as vision. Though the film is the medium best suited to the rendering of daily and ordinary reality, in the sense that the spectator perceives the screen activity as real, films are symbolic in their main character and the filmic image, polysemic. In spite of its realistic aspect, the film belongs to an imaginary world into which it draws the spectator, though he may always sense the duality of the projected image: so real, yet so unreal.[15] To push this phenomenology of perception further, we may try to consider, for our present purpose, films in relation to myth. In this sense, a film could be seen as having the function of a myth which by definition, exposes and explores in a symbolic manner our relation with other human beings, as well as with the Ultimate.[16] Indian cinema in particular may be considered mythical in that sense, since it displays in a repetitive manner the main structures of Indian cultural life.[17] Myths have the capcacity, by their reference to an "archetype", to guide human actions. "Just as dreams are according to the Jungian doctrine, the expression of resurgence of archaic symbols and the indefinite prolongation of the radiance of archetypes, the cinematograph, be it used consciously or unconsciously, can give us a privileged aspect of this resurgence and this prolongation".[18] If we take this statement seriously, and I would invite us to do so, we find important means to read the Indian film, in the light of a long tradition and its present day outcome.

Songs, more than any other filmic element, belong to the world of dreams. Myth and dream share the same structure of a double meaning; they are symbols. Movies are at the same time mythical and oneiric and songs in particular translate deep-rooted archetypes, as I shall illustrate in part III.

2. *The lyrics*

The poetry of the songs uses a simple language (Hindi, Kharī bolī). Vocabulary might differ according to the subject dealt with. Devotional songs use more Braj bhāṣā; love, and especially *viraha*, songs have a lot of Urdu words. Vocabulary of regional dialects can also be used.

The texts of all songs follow the same structure imposed by the recording system, which lasts three and a half minutes. They are often introduced by a *pāda* or Urdu *śer*, followed by the music and then three stanzas (often of four lines, regular in their *mātrā*) that have a catchy line (*mukhṛā*) musically interwoven and repeated. Over the years this structure has had a far wider impact than the film, so much so in fact that many folk songs and *bhajan* follow the same pattern today.[19]

Lyrics are sustained by the music, the two elements being inseparable. Yet, the words always remain clear, for they should also be understood in the meaning of the film plot. If we again take the example of a love song, it is perhaps the only moment in the film when the lovers will express their feelings for each other. The music director and the lyric-writer play an important part in the film industry. The quality of the songs (lyrics and music), depending on their authors' merit, may range from subtle and elaborate songs to poor poetry and shallow music.

3. *The music*

From the forties onwards, the film song's most relevant characteristic has been its orchestration. Ever since it came into vogue, it has not ceased to change and incorporate new musical elements from almost everywhere in the world: there have been Spanish, Arabic, jazz, disco, rock, cha cha cha and African influences. Songs are often still based (though sometimes vaguely) on one or more classical *rāgas* at a time, incorporating *ṭhumrī* and folkstyles. The hybridity of the musical orchestration is a unique phenomenon that has known over the years an incomparable impact and attraction, as well as, tremendous skill.

Play-back singing introduced the "star-system" of singers. These singing heroes may be as important as the acting heroes. Often their voices correspond to the feelings expressed, a star can cover the full range of emotions, such as Lata Mangeshkar, or be a specialist of a certain feeling, such as Talat Mehmood for *viraha* and sad songs.

III BHAKTI AND VIRAHA SONGS

In the last part of this paper, I shall attempt to show how Hindi film songs can be seen as a direct continuation of a long-attested tradition and be the vectors of the popular and dominant culture of today's India. I see early films as important aesthetic and human documents that allow us to enter the dominant cultural trend of the first decades of the cinema. The song in particular seems to translate many features of that time. In order to build a hermeneutics of the songs, it is essential to analyze them in their cultural context. Songs belong to a codified cinematographic language that has its roots in deep-seated tradition and they tend to play a paradigmatic role for the entire palette of emotions they express.

1. *Bhakti songs*

Since the beginning of the talkies, different types of *bhakti* song have been sung very regularly in films, be it more so in films with mythological and religious themes, or in romantic films, where a hero or a heroine may implore the love or assistance of a god. They are very much patterned on traditional songs. Initially they consisted simply of lines from the most famous *bhakta*-poets of the medieval period.[20] Their language was Braj bhāṣā in the beginning, with more and more Hindi later on. It is only after the forties that a new kind of *bhakti* song emerged proper to the world of film and defines a new genre of devotional song. In *Baijū Bāwra*, we find, for instance, a type of *bhakti* song in a romantic setting that has, in spite of the fact that it is based on a classical *rāga*, a typical filmic character ("ao duniyā ke rakhevāle", based on *rāga* Darbārī). According to my research, the *bhakti* songs of the sad type (*dukhānt bhakti gīt*) in which the hero and the heroine question god about the meaning of their suffering, are the most frequent and of a filmic type. In fact, these songs are very close to the *viraha* songs of the more secular or romantic type. Among many others, examples of such songs would be "barī der bhayī","duniyā na bāye mohe ab to bulā le", in *Basant Bahar*, that are film *bhakti* songs. Let me quote a few lines from *Baijū Bāwra* mentioned above, based on *rāga* Darbārī:

> Lord
> O Keeper of the World, listen to my song of sorrow.
> You have decorated the world with the two colours of hope and dispair.
> (Together) with the boat (you) made the storm,with the meeting (you made) separation.
> God, I have seen your injustice,
> my world of love has been robbed,
> now, is it enough to make you weep!
> The rains of *śrāvan* became fire,
> The flowers became burning coals,
> The sweet night became the female snake,
> The stars became stones.
> All my shelters are broken, take back the life you gave me, Giver of Life.
> The foolish sun is chasing the moon, evening searches for the morning.
> I'm also searching for that beloved who could not be mine.
> O God, I wish you well (I hope you are happy).
> Luck is broken, still hope is not.
> I've got blisters on my feet.
> O Keeper of the World,
> The palace is sad and the streets are empty.
> The walls are silent.
> When the heart is deserted, the whole world is deserted.
> All the green seasons are angry.
> How will we spend the life?
> A broken temple can be built again,
> (but) who will take care of a broken heart,
> O Keeper of the World.

Some of the later *bhakti* hit-songs have found their way

into the temples, which shows that the film song should be considered as a significant element of a changing society.

Before dealing with *viraha* songs, I would like to mention here another film that is extremely important for the understanding of *bhakti* during the early film period. A brief evaluation of the film *Vidyāpati* will introduce our analysis of *viraha* songs, as both types of songs, *viraha* and *bhakti*, are intermingled and strongly represented in this film. *Vidyāpati* was produced at New Theatre, Calcutta, in 1937 by Debaki Bose, with the music of R.C. Boral and the lyrics by Kedar Sharma. The main theme of the film is love, more precisely, it explores the two dimensions of love, the divine, or/and the secular. It is the story of *Vidyāpati*, the famous *vaiṣṇava* poet and the different kinds of love that revolve around his personality. In a word, he becomes a friend of the king's of Mithila and settles at his court. By doing so, he leaves his village as well as a silent devotee of his, Anurādhā. She follows him and expresses her feeling of *viraha* in a beautiful song entitled "Gokul se gaye giradhārī, huī sūnī nagarī sarī", in which she compares her love to that of the Gopīs when Kṛṣṇa departed from Gokul. In the court, the king's beloved wife Lakṣmī, falls totally in love with the poet. Her love is so strong that it becomes obvious to everyone. At first the poet condemns her love, which he qualifies as sinful. Anurādhā, however, makes him understand that such a pure and total love, as displayed by queen Lakṣmī, is equal to the love of god. The latter kills herself at the altar of Lord Viṣṇu, where her love is shown in all its purity. It knew no boundaries or social restrictions, it was a total love and as such, only a real devotee would have been capable of it.

The different arguments exposed in the film regarding love are very interesting in light of *vaiṣṇava bhakti*. The king suffers, says Anurādhā, because he desires in return the love of Lakṣmī, whereas Lakṣmī simply loves, without making any demands. The king says of himself, that he is no *bhakta*, for he loves the queen in a worldly manner. Anurādhā tells him however, that his dedication to the queen is typical of the devotion of a *bhakta*. In the end, the king will die, simply out of love, together with the queen. Vidyāpati himself, recovering from all the tension he was exposed to, explains that in due time such devoted, singleminded love, as shown by the queen, will turn into the love of god. And Anurādhā helps the queen by explaining to her that such true love leads to *mukti* and is the true way to god. Human love can be divine, and the king and the queen have given proof of it: their love ends at the feet of the god. Human love stands as a metaphor for divine love: true love, be it divine or secular, leads to the union with god. The film ends on the marvellous song, sung by K.C. Dey, that underlines the transitory character of worldly love in the light of *vaiṣṇava bhakti* where true love leads to the union with god. It is the song "kāhe der" of which I shall simply quote two lines: "āj jo apne pās hai sajanī, uskī bheṃt carhāna hai, ..., tū tū na rahe maiṃ maiṃ na rahūṃ kuch aise ham dhūl mil jāye". Very often in this film, and we should underline this in the analysis of the role of the songs in Indian films, the dialogue is far less important than the songs. They truly give the key meanings of the film, as much from the point of view of the lyrics as from the underlying musical effect.

2. *Viraha Songs*

If our hypothesis that film songs belong to the realm of "dream and myth" is accurate, (the dream understood in the sense defined above, as a receptacle of the human cultural treasure and a prolongation of the archaic, and the myth as the bridge between the world of the known and the unknown), then this will now become more evident by the study of the *viraha* songs and the concept of *viraha*.

The *bhakti* period (that spread over India from the eleventh century onward), has emphasized the emotional character of the religious behaviour of the *bhaktas*. This trend is so important that we have accepted the definition of this *bhakti* as emotional. More so, when it is *Kṛṣṇa bhakti*, with which we are mainly concerned here. This emotional *bhakti* has been studied in its evolution in the brilliant work of F. Hardy, who goes as far as to equate emotional *Kṛṣṇa bhakti* with *viraha bhakti*[21]. In this sense, the latter concept encompasses experiences far beyond the theological or religious boundaries and imparts strong influences on all levels of society[22]. *Viraha* songs of a more secular type draw however much inspiration from devotional songs that deal with the feeling of separation; we may consider them as belonging to an analogous quest.

It is in the mythology of emotional *bhakti* that we shall find the sources for the emotional patterns displayed by the film songs. Kṛṣṇa of Vṛndāvan is the prototype of a lover, divine or human. He plays music (flute), a sign that will always be associated with love and feelings. He arouses various emotions according to the type of love that is bestowed on him. He is the source of the craving for a perfect union, which may be expressed romantically by Rādhā and the Gopīs, or more spiritually by the songs of Mīrābāī. Through the separation from the Gopīs, the Kṛṣṇa legend builds up the elements for the study of religious and psychological implications of separation. However the Gopīs are not the only ones to express the deep sorrow and pathetic pain engendered by the separation from god. Theologically speaking, *viraha* is a key element of emotional *bhakti*. We find numerous interpretations and descriptions of the suffering of devotees separated from their object of love. Kabīr says, "don't call *viraha viraha*, *viraha* is the king. In whose body *viraha* doesn't move, that body is always a cremation ground"[23]. The pathetic suffering of separation is also deeply rooted in the folk literature[24], and many examples could be quoted here.

In order to understand *viraha* in the context of film songs, we first have to look at the way love is represented. The early Indian cinema depicts a highly idealistic type of love. Far into the late fifties, we find a strong belief in a pure and true love. K. Valicha states that the Rādhā-Kṛṣṇa type of love has a very deep signification in the Indian and especially film context, "...the cult symbolizes the Indian conventions of romantic love—a love that is pure and transcendental, and a yearning for the perfect mate realizable only in a mythical world"[25]. There is a quest for the perfect union. In *Barsāt*, Reśamā, who has been inevitably drawn to Prāṇ by the sound of his violin, states in a difficult moment of her life that true love can never die, whatsoever may happen in appearance. The love depicted in the first films is an etheral kind, and may be qualified as belonging to a higher quest than its social outcome. This romantic love is always of an absolute kind, even if it lasts only for a short period. It is not expressed verbally, but rather tends to be silent, just as suffering is not spoken about out loud, both feelings are, however, expressed in song. It is precisely the song in the film that allows us to ascend to an "archetypal" level of existence, in a extra-ordinary world, a dreamlike scenery, sustained by music and often dance. Hence, the lovers experience a moment of eternal love and bliss. Yet this kind of love is impossible, for various reasons[26].

Not only is love impossible, it is also risky. Love has inevitably, it seems, its other side, for, to quote the opening line of an old song, "you risk your life in love, the same way the mustard seed does in the grinder". Once the love period and the love song is over, there follows the sorrow that is engendered by this intense love and culminates in the *viraha* song that translates the pain endured by the hero or the heroine separated from the beloved. As an example, I shall quote a song from *Madan Mohan*, set to *rāga* Ahīr Bhairav: "Merī vīṇā tum bin roye". The theme of the song underlines how much music is the perfect agent for translating emotional states of being.

> Without you my *vīṇā* cries
> Beloved, ...
> My lover, where ever you are living,
> I don't know that village.
> I don't know when this sinful evening of separation will pass.

O when will we have a sweet meeting again?
Without you my songs are incomplete,
They are shy on my lips.
I pick up my *viṇā*
(but) the strings are not tight (they can't be tuned)
They are suffering,
No one knows my pain.
Beloved...

The film *Devdās* , of 1935, is the prototype of the impossible union[27]. This impossibility is lived with an extreme vehemence, and often turns into a tragedy. True love exists, but it is not meant to last; it has no social outcome, but rather remains in the sphere of the impossible (or at least for a certain time)[28]. Just as love is pure and intense when it happens, so the suffering that follows carries an intensity almost above the capacity of human beings and their emotions[29]. In the case of *Devdās*, where the beloved obeys the orders of her father, the former finds no other solutions than to die. In other films, such as those of Rāj Kapūr, love starts out in a very simple manner and then turns into utter agony. To quote from *Barsāt* once more, Nīlā ends up committing suicide after having awaited the return of Gopāl for months in the state of *viraha*. In *Vidyāpati* all the characters bring love to its highest level, where it culminates in union with God and is not exposed to any limitation of the norms established by ordinary life. The queen's love is finally approved because it is a complete surrender.

The actual experience of separation is not the mere pain of having lost a husband or a lover, but is the apotheosis of the quest for union, divine or secular. It puts the notion of *viraha*, of separation, in the realm of a dominant cultural aspiration. The quest for the perfect union continues in all the early films, it is a search for the truth; I may say a desperate search to ally transcience with permanence.[30] *Viraha* is the other side of the perfect union, and may be another way of exploring or living this union, this time in separation. *Viraha* film songs, albeit in a more secular manner (though not only so), participate in the long-lasting search that the concept of *viraha* has generated in Indian society, and more so in the literature of emotional *bhakti*. The concept of *viraha* constitutes a recurrent and deeply-rooted myth, and songs are an appropriate way of communicating it.

NOTES

1. In this paper I shall be concentrating on Hindi songs and Hindi films only.
2. In 1937, Wadias tried a movie without songs, which did not have any success; hence, the idea was quickly dropped.
3. I do not wish to exclude other sources and influences, such as western films and Hollywood productions, but they can't be dealt with here. This information will be treated in a forthcoming publication on film songs.
4. "Indian Film Song", Bhaskar Chandavarkar, in *70 years of Indian Cinema*, Bombay: Cinema India-International Publication, 1985, p. 246.
5. "Bhārata Munī and Hindi Films", Mukund Lath, in *Jijnasa, A Journal of the History of Ideas and Culture*, Department of History and Indian Culture, University of Rajasthan, Jaipur, 2, April 1975, pp. 84-106.
6. *Khyāl*, for instance, are rhymed dramas in which singing is prominent, dealing with mythological and legendary material of Indian and Islamic origin.
7. It is important to consider that local and regional dramatic expressions have been influenced and structured by Sanskrit theatre; the latter too has picked up elements of the so-called "little"tradition. Over the centuries there was a constant interaction between the "great"and the "little"tradition. On this important issue see *Traditional Indian Theatre, Multiple Streams*, Kapila Vatsyayan, New Delhi: National Book Trust, 1980.
8. Sources were, among others: *Gondhal*, a kind of religious discourse with recitation and singing and *Lāvṇī*, a more secular and romantic singing tradition. Both use a dialogue form of singing with music.
9. On dramas and their evolution, see for instance *Hindi Literature of the 19th and early 20th Century*, R.S.McGregor,

Wiesbaden: Otto Harrassowitz, 1974, especially pp. 91-98.
10. *On Music and Musicians of Hindoostan*, A.D. Ranade, New Delhi: Promilla & Co Publishers, 1984.
11. Over 200 collected songs have been classified into the following categories (in order of frequency): *premgīt; viraha gīt; yathārthavādī gīt; bhakti gīt; mile jule gāne* (that includes, among others, such songs as *rāṣṭrīya* and *lorī gīt*); *prākṛtik saundaryā gīt; intazār gīt; mastī gīt.*
12. See for instance, *Rasa Theory and Allied Problems*, G. K. Bhat, Baroda: The M. S. University of Baroda, 1984.
13. *Op.cit.* (12), particularly p. 47- 48. See also chapters 6 and 7 of the *Nāṭya śāstra of Bhārata muni* (translation by a board of scholars, Sri Sat Guru Publication, series no 2, Delhi, no date, pp. 70-113).
14. "Sāṃvariā prem kī bāṃsī";"prītam se prīt nibhāūṃgī", for example.
15. On this topic, see for instance, *Le cinéma ou l'homme imaginaire*, Edgar Morin, Paris: Les Editions de minuit, 1956.
16. *Images et symboles*, Mircea Eliade, Paris: Gallimard, 1952.
17. S. Kakar in a similar way, though through a psychoanalytical framework, expresses the opinion that the Hindi film functions very much like a fairy tale, where unconscious desires find their outlet in a similar way. See "Psychanalyse du film," S. Kakar, in *Les cinemas indiens*, Cinèmaction, Paris: Cerf. 1984.
18. *Métaphysique du cinéma*, Henri Agel, Paris: Petite bibliothèque Payot, 1976, p. 197.
19. See "La musique, la dance et le film populaire", S. Prakash, in, *Les cinémas indiens*, Cinèmaction, Paris: Cerf, 1984, pp. 194-201.
20. Most of these songs have been registered in the film song collection of Hāthras, *Saṅgīt, filmī śāstrīya gīt aṅk.* This collection has written out the music of most of the songs that are based on learned music (*śāstriya saṅgīt*)
21. *Viraha Bhakti*, F. Hardy, Oxford: Oxford University Press, 1983.
22. "The cultivation of *viraha bhakti* has been not only a cult, but in fact the foundation or stimulus for a major component of Indian culture over a period of more than a millenium". F. Hardy, op. cit. (21), p. 582.
23. Kabīr, quoted from Kabīr Granthāvalī, Sākhī 2.16, *Kabīr-vāṇī: Western Recension*, ed. C. Vaudeville, Pondichéry: Institut Français d'Indologie, 1982, p. 56.
24. See for instance, *Bārahmāsā in Indian Literatures*, Charlotte

Vaudeville, Delhi: Motilal Banarasidas, 1986, specifically, pp. 14-36.

25. *The moving image*, Kishore Valicha, Bombay: Orient Longman, 1988, p. 48.
26. These reasons should be analyzed carefully in the light of a changing society.
27. The part of Devdās is played by no other than the famous K. Saigal, whose style of singing and voice got for long time identified with the feeling of pain created through love.
28. There can be a reunion, for final *viraha* is difficult to accept, but more often than not, not in the confines of the social model.
29. For further details, see K. Valicha's analysis of love in Indian films, especially the prototype developed by Devdās, op. cit. (25) pp. 43-60.
30. This period seems, however, to be over. In the sixties films translate very different problematics that carry with them the very fast changes occurring in the Indian society.

Textual Transmission
(Manuscripts and Anthologies)

The *Sarvāṅgī* of the Dādūpanthī Gopāldās

Winand M. Callewaert

In this paper I would like to introduce a unique work, of which I discovered and copied the only existing manuscript in 1973, in Jaipur. As far as I know, even that manuscript is now no longer available. This book is not only a fascinating product of a 17th-century memory, or a marvellous synthesis of *bhakti* literature; it is a wonderful experience to sing it or have it sung in long sessions. When we did so, the good songs immediately stood out, even before we saw the *bhaṇitā:* Sūrdās, Kabīr, Dādū.

When I first discovered this huge manuscript I was baffled by the neatness of its handwriting, the immense variety of the *bhaktas* quoted in it and its size—1.6 Mbyte, or more than half of the size of the *Ādi Granth*.[1] Only when the input of the text in the computer was completed, could I grasp the importance of this document. It contains 1,669 *padas* and 6,568 *sākhīs* of 138 identified *bhaktas* and ca. 640 *ślokas*. Of Kabīr alone the compiler Gopāldās quotes (in AD 1627) 358 *padas* and 609 *sākhīs* while of Dādū he gives 401 *padas* and 1,452 *sākhīs*.[2]

The variety of songs makes one wonder how a person could be acquainted with so many repertoires. Some 13,900 lines of the approximately 26,800 in the complete work contain *padas* of 138 identified *bhaktas*. There are a further

4,413 lines with literature by (so far) unidentified poets (of which some *sākhīs* are no doubt of Dādū and Kabīr, but without a *bhaṇitā*).

It has taken me years to discard the notion that Gopāldās compiled his anthology from existing manuscripts lying on the floor in front of him. It was so hard to imagine that without manuscripts a person could produce such a wonderful selection of songs and couplets and classify then according to theme. But slowly, as I made progress in the wonderful world of performers rising before me from the manuscripts, I started to imagine a *bhakta* of the Dādūpanth with a fabulous memory. He must have spent many days over several months listening to travelling singers and storing in his memory whatever he heard. In the colophon of his *Sarvāṅgī*, Gopāldās states that he was thirty seven years of age when he completed the collection and wrote it down on paper (in AD 1627). He must have been fourteen when Dādū died in 1603, and he declares himself to be a disciple of Santadās, one of Dādū's disciples. Since he does not call himself a disciple of Dādū, we may presume that Gopāldās was initiated into the Dādūpanth after 1603. Nārāyaṇdās (1979)[3] suggests that Gopāldās may have been "of the family" of his Guru Santadās. There is otherwise no information available about Gopāldās.

It is not only amazing that Gopāldās could store such an amount of literature in his memory. How could he make a selection based on 126 different themes? It is clear that he received his material from the singers' single repertoires: with only two exceptions, the *rāga* in which a *pada* was to be sung is indicated. We have shown in our studies of Nāmdev and of Raidās[4] that the *rāga*-tag was an essential part of the 'text' of a *pada*, and that variation in the *rāga* takes the researcher back to the period of oral transmission. In the singer's repertoires, *padas* appear to have been classified in *rāga*-clusters: in Gopāldās's *Sarvāṅgī* too, the *rāga*-tag is preserved, but the *padas* do not appear in clusters of identical *rāgas*. On the contrary, we often find in one chapter as many *rāgas* as there are *bhaktas* quoted. Only towards the end of the work does Gopāldās seem to copy more directly from one singer's repertoire: more songs of a particular *bhakta* are given under the same *rāga*. It is also amazing how the compiler remembered, according to the content, songs which in existing repertoires must have been classified under a different *rāga*. In chapter 61 for example, Gopāldās quotes eight *padas* of Sūrdās and each of them has a different *rāga*. each of which must originally have belonged to a different *rāga*-cluster. It is further to the credit of Gopāldās's memory that, as far as I could see, not a single line is given twice!

There seems to be a regular pattern in the way Gopāldās arranged the material available to him. The basic frame is a selection of *padas*, interspersed in most chapters with *sākhīs*. However, there are also chapters with only *sākhīs*. Not all the chapters are equally long. Chapter 12 has only 44 lines and Chapter 82 has 18 lines, while chapter 17, *Sādh mahimā* has 33 *padas* and 83 *sākhīs* or *ślokas*. Similarly chapter 35 is very small but chapter 36 is huge. Chapters 62-64 are again huge and chapter 78 has 94 *padas* of 15 *bhaktas*. Often Gopāldās gives first a *pada* of Kabīr, followed by one of Dādū. If he was a Dādūpanthī, this would confirm how high the esteem for Kabīr was in the early Panth.

There is also the relatively high number (1,300 or 4.8%) of lines in Sanskrit or pseudo-Sanskrit, often at the end of a chapter. No doubt the presence of Sanskrit quotations (mainly from the *Bhagavadgītā* and the *Bhāgavata*) was meant to enhance the status of an anthology in the vernacular. But it raises questions. Who created the numerous lines by Hybrid Sanskrit? Should we expect in the early Panth (around 1627, i.e., one generation after Dādū) such traces of brahmanization as are seen in the enlarged versions of the biography of Dādū? In the manuscripts of the *Dādū janma līlā* (dated AD 1654, 1739 etc.) I noted additions and changes in the text that are not found in the earlier manuscripts (1653, 1658, 1666). These changes and interpolations were clearly meant to underline the non-Muslim origin and occupation of Dādū.[5] From that account it appears that Dādū was often at loggerheads with the Brahmans. Would Gopāl's generation have tried to soften the rough edges by giving the Dādūpanthī literature a firm footing in Sanskrit? Was that a local trend meant to please the Brahmans, or is it a part of a more general phenomenon of looking for authority by adding Sanskrit?

Very frequently one can discover a kind of mnemonic device in the fact that a similar keyword occurs in consecutive *padas* or *sākhīs* of different poets. Without these obvious devices, one keeps wondering how Gopāldās could link one *pada* to another. It would appear also that at times the *rāga* is the mnemonic device, especially when the *rāga* is otherwise not frequently found.

In not a few chapters, Gopāldās gives subtitles. This is clearly the result of scribal editing, since singers would not have used subtitles during their performances.

During the same period of search for manuscripts in 1973, I managed to copy four manuscripts with the *Sarvāṅgī* of Rajab, a disciple of Dādū.[6] In this work, Rajab has grouped thematically, in 144 *aṅgas*, *sākhīs* and *padas* in Hindi, Persian and Sanskrit from his own *vāṇī* and those of 88 identified *bhaktas*.[7] About 102 titles are identical with titles of chapters in the *vānī* of Rajab.[8] In the colophon the work is said to contain 8,000 verses.[9] This compilation has recently been edited by Iraqi (1985) but this edition is not a faithful or accurate reprint of the manuscripts consulted. It should be noted that the editor also gives *candra-bindus*, which are totally missing in the manuscripts. Unfortunately, there is no detailed index or table of contents.

A comparison of the two *Sarvāṅgīs* confirms the notion that early in the 17th century the Dādūpanth was an important nucleus of literary activity in northern India. The results of that activity were rivalled only by the endeavours of Gurū Arjun in Panjab, but both traditions have equal relevance for later generations. In the *Sarvāṅgīs* we find a treasure-trove of largely unpublished material. For the material that was already published, I found the recension of both *Sarvāṅgī*s to be very accurate and well preserved.[10]

If we accept that a copying tradition may undergo fewer intentional changes in a work of compilation than in a sectarian text of just one poet, it becomes evident that the *Sarvāṅgī*s are important for a text-critic wishing to study a *bhakta* of the period. It is a well-known fact that for modern editions of *bhakti* literature, often only a few and not the oldest manuscripts have been consulted. In these anthologies we have (in an 18th-century manuscript) a text reflecting a particular set of singers' repertoires written down early in the 17th century.

When we look at the structure of the two *Sarvāṅgī*s, we note that both works are independent products of compilation, differing both in the amount and the choice of the material and in the way it has been arranged. It is clear that the *Sarvāṅgī* of Gopāldās is based on sources which are very different from those underlying the *Sarvāṅgī* compiled by Rajab.

NOTES

1. The results of the first analysis of this manuscript were published in Callewaert 1974. The complete work is now published: Callewaert 1993.
   Only two manuscripts of this work came to my notice. One was (Nov. 1973) with Svāmī Mangaldās, then in Kucaman City, Rajasthan, dated VS 1785 AD 1728, with 385 folios. Apparently, this is the manuscript consulted by Svāmī Nārāyaṇdās, as he refers to it in his *Śrī dādūpanth paricay*, vol. 2, p. 400. The *lipikartā* is Sahajrām, disciple of Śivdāsjī. It was written in Sultānpuri, Haryana. I made three (difficult) journeys to the ashram in the Kucaman City, but never managed to see the document. It may well be (still) there, if ever it was.
   The second manuscript which was copied was (in 1973) in the Dādū Mahāvidyālaya, Jaipur. It is dated VS 1781 AD 1724. with 364 folios, of ca. 15x27 cms. Each page has about 32

lines, of ca. 12 cms long. The scribe is Khānezād Gulām, disciple of Mohan Bābā Kisandār, disciple of Jaitarām.

2. The standard edition by Tivari of the *Kabīr-granthāvalī* gives 200 *padas* of 737 *sākhīs*. The standard edition of the *Dādūdayāl granthāvalī* by P. Caturvedi gives 443 *padas* of Dādū and 2,453 *Sākhīs*. See Callewaert-Op de Beeck 1991.
3. Vol. 2, p. 399.
4. Callewaert & Lath 1989 and Callewaert & Friedlander 1992.
5. For more details see Callewaert 1988, pp. 18ff.
6. See Callewaert 1978.
7. Not '66' as is said in Tivari 1961, p. 143.
8. Varma 1963.
9. For more details about the date of composition and for the Table of contents, see Callewaert 1978, pp. 73, 402-438.
10. See Callewaert & Lath 1989, p. 125.

BIBLIOGRAPHY

Callewaert, W.M. 1974. 'A 17th c. Anthology of Hindī Poetry'. *Orientalia Lovaniensia Periodica.* Leuven, 5, pp. 187-196.

Callewaert, W.M. 1978. *The Sarvāṅgī of the Dādūpanthī Rajab.* Orientalia Lovaniensia Analecta, 4, Leuven, 446 p.

Callewaert, W.M. 1988. *The Hindī Biography of Dādū Dayāl.* Delhi: Motilal Banarasidass.

Callewaert, W.M. & Mukund Lath. 1989. *The Hindī Songs of Nāmdev.* Orientalia Lovaniensia Analecta, 29, Leuven, 432 p.

Callewaert, W.M. & B. Op. de Beeck. 1991. *Devotional Hindī Literature: Nirgun-Bhakti-Sāgar.* Heidelberg: South Asia Institute, New Delhi: Manohar, 1175 p.

Callewaert, W.M. & P. Friedlander. 1992. *The Life and Works of Raidās.* Delhi: Manohar.

Callewaert, W.M. 1993. *The Sarvāṅgī of Gopāldās.* Delhi: Manohar, 520 p.

Caturvedi, P. 1966. *Dādū Dayāl Granthāvalī.* Benares.

Iraqi, S. 1985. *The Sarbangi of Rajjabdas.* Aligarh, 632 p.

Nārāyaṇdās Svāmī. 1979. *Śrī dādū panth paricay,* 3 vols., Śrī Dādū Mahāsabhā, Jaipur, Pushkar.

Tivari, P.N. 1961. *Kabīr-granthāvalī.* Allahabad.

Varmā, V. 1963. *Rajjab-Bānī.* Kanpur.

Vaudville, C. 1974. *Kabīr.* Oxford: Clarendon Press.

The Core of the *Vāṇī* of Raidās

Peter G. Friedlander

Raidās is one of the great saints of Northern India, and he is regarded by a large section of the untouchable community as their spiritual leader. This paper outlines the development of the study of Raidās and presents some of the findings from my dissertation on the life and works of Raidās. In particular it shows that there is a group of seventeen *pads* which are likely to be derived from the repertoire of songs which were current in the early Raidāsī oral tradition.

I. NINETEENTH-CENTURY STUDIES

The earliest Western reference to Raidās was in H.H. Wilson's *Sketch of the Religious Sects of the Hindus* published in 1862 which was based upon articles he published in the journal *Asiatick Researches* in 1828-9.[1] His account of Raidās's life was mainly based upon the information found in the *Bhaktamāl* of Nābhādās and Priyādās's *Bhaktirasabodhinī* commentary. This describes seven episodes relating to Raidās: his past life as a Brahman, his birth as a Chamar and initiation by Rāmānand, his childhood devotion to God, the test of the philosopher's stone, the miracle of the gold coins and the vision of God in a dream telling him to build a temple and his consequent test before the king with the Brahmans of Banaras, the initiation of Queen Jhālī, the feast at Chittorgarh and the revelation of a golden sacred thread within his breast. He also supplemented this account with a translation of a *pad* similar to *pad* number eight in my thesis. He also mentioned that some of Raidās's compositions were included in the *Ādi Granth* and that they also formed part of the collection of hymns and prayers used by the Sikhs in Banaras.

The second reference to Raidās was in the *Histoire de la littérature hindouie et hindoustanie* by Garcin de Tassy which was first published in 1839.[2] This work included a section on Raidās which was substantially the same as Wilson's article, augmenting it only by including a translation of the stanza by Nābhādās on Raidās.

The importance of these two articles was not just that they were the earliest Western references to Raidās, but also that their reliance upon Nābhādās and Priyādās set the tone and contents for what was to become the standard orthodox view on Raidās.

A very different account of Raidās was given in the vernacular census of Marwar for 1891. According to this account Raidās was a Chamar who lived at Mandu. It tells how once when Raidās was sitting in the bazaar at Mandu some water from his bowl splashed onto the king's clothes as he was passing by. One of the king's servants then tried to wash off this water, but it would not come off by rubbing and so he licked it to try and get the stain out; however, the stain tasted sweet and the servant attained enlightenment. This miracle persuaded the king to become a follower of Raidās.

Another story it tells describes how Raidās was a great devotee of the goddess of the Ganges and how, when Raidās's daughter was to be married, Gaṅgā herself came to Raidās's house. The beauty of Raidās's daughter was such that news of it reached the ears of the king of Chittorgarh, who sent his soldiers to carry her off by force, but when his soldiers got to Raidās's house Gaṅgā manifested herself as a flood flowing out of Raidās's well and washed the soldiers away.

It says that the people of the Chambal valley claim that the Chambal river issues from Raidās's water bowl, but comments that this is an error because it is only four hundred years since Raidās lived and the Chambal river is far older.

It also remarks on the fact that Raidās's statue and his water bowl are still to be found at Mandu and that the water from his bowl is a cure for several dreadful diseases. It also says that Raidās had two wives, the offspring of one wife being the Chamars and the children of the other Raigars. The Raigar community, it says, are *Vaiṣṇavites* who worship *śālagrāms*, are devotees of the Gaṅgā, and wear cotton sacred threads.

The significance of this account of the life of Raidās is that it demonstrates that there was in existence at least one set of oral traditions about Raidās which was in no way compatible with the orthodox view set out by Wilson and others.[3]

The next work which includes references to Raidās was *Tribes and Castes of the North-western Provinces and Oudh*, by W. Crooke, published in 1896. This work also contains some extraordinary details regarding Raidās. In its section describing the Chamars it conflates Raidās and the sect it calls the 'Srinarayani' or 'Siunarayani' which it says was founded by Raidās or Ravidās, who was a disciple of Rāmānand, and retells the incidents described in Priyādās's *Bhaktirasabodhinī*. However, it also adds a reference to a legend from the 'Dakkhin' according to which 'Rohidās' was born at 'Chambhargonda now Ahmadnagar', and was a contemporary of Kabīr in the twelfth or thirteenth century.[4]

A further brief reference to Raidās is found in the report of *The Census of India* for 1901. In a note on 'Rai Dasis' it says that Raidās was a disciple of Rāmānand and refers to Priyādās's account. However, it also adds that 'local tradition says he was born in Mandu near Dhar in 1591'.[5] This was to be the last note on the connection between Raidās and Mandu until 1941.

II. EARLY TWENTIETH-CENTURY STUDIES

In 1908 the first major printed collection of the *vāṇī* of Raidās was published by the Belvedere Press as a part of its *Sant vāṇī* series. This work contained some eighty or so *pads* and six *sākhīs*. Although no sources were given for the texts, they closely resemble the recensions of the *vāṇī* found in Rajasthani manuscripts. This work became highly influential because it remained the only widely available text for the *vāṇī* of Raidās, apart from the recension in the *Ādi Granth*, until 1956.[6]

The book also included a short account of the life of Raidās, which largely followed Priyādās's account. It expands on Priyādās in that it gave the names of Raidās's father, Ragghu, and mother, Ghurabiniyā, and suggested that there was a connection between the Queen from Chittorgarh and Mīrābāī. It also mentioned the tradition that Raidās lived to an age of 120.

It also contained a previously unpublished story about Raidās. Once a rich man came to Raidās's *satsaṅg* and in rejecting Raidās's *caraṇāmṛt* managed to spill it on his scarf. Then, when he got home he gave away the cloth to his washerman, who gained good health, and despite taking numerous ritual baths himself, fell ill with leprosy. In the end, unable to cure his leprosy with medicines, he had to beg Raidās's forgiveness and ask to be cured of his affliction. It also contains a version of a story about Raidās's gift to the Gaṅgā and her gift of a bracelet. It says that this version was given as a part of the Sanskrit examination at Kasi Government Sanskrit College in 1907.[7]

Another milestone in the study of Raidās was reached in 1909 when Macauliffe published his monumental work *The Sikh Religion*. This included an account of Raidās's life, based entirely on Priyādās, and translations of the forty *pads* and one *sākhī* by Ravidās in the *Ādi Granth*. These translations of the *pads* of Ravidās came to be accepted as effectively the standard English version of the *Ādi Granth vāṇī* of

Raidās.[8]

Turning once more to ethnographic works, in 1911 Ibbetson published a work called *A Glossary of the Tribes and Castes of the Punjab and North-West Frontier Province.* This included a rather unusual account of Raidās which contained distinctive variations upon Priyādās's account:

> Rāmdās was a descendent of Chanu. His mother, Khalsia, was childless, but one day a faqir came to her and she gave him flour, in return for which he promised her a son. On his return his gurū cross-questioned him, as he was unable to pronounce the name 'Parameshwar' and learning of his promise declared that, as no son had been bestowed on Khalsia in her destiny, the faqir himself must be born to her. So he was reborn as Rāmdās, who is called Raidās in Bāwal. As his mother was a Chamāri he refused her breasts, until his gurū bade him suck. One day when placed by his mother at a spot where Rāma Nand used to pass, he was touched by that teacher's sandals, and when he cried out was told by him to be silent and repeat 'Rām Rām'. Thus was supernatural power bestowed upon him. Contrary to the Chamār's customs Rāmdās wore a *janeo*, sounded a conch, and worshipped idols. The Brahmans appealed to the magistrate, whereupon Rāmdās cast the idols into a tank, but they returned to him, whereas the Brahmans failed in a similar test. Again, cutting his neck Rāmdās exhibited 4 *janeo*, of gold, silver, copper and thread, typical of the 4 *yugas*. Thenceforth he was known as a famous *bhagat*.[9]

A further ethnographic work, *The Tribes and Castes of the Central Provinces of India* by Russell published in 1916, also included notes on Raidās and mentions 'Lona Chamarin' as the mother or grandmother of Raidās the disciple of Rāmānand.[10]

In 1918 and 1920 entries under the headings 'Rai Dasis' and 'Sadhs' by G.A. Grierson were included in *The Encyclopedia of Religion and Ethics*. The account of the life of Raidās that they give was again largely based upon Priyādās. However, they also include the earliest printed references to a tradition that Raidās was the guru of Uddhavadās the founder of the sect called the Sadhs.[11]

English translations of *pads* by Raidās also appeared in Ahmad Shah's *Hindī Religious Poetry* published in 1925.[12] In his note on Raidās he says that he was a Chamar from Banaras who lived in the fifteenth century, died at the age of 120, and was a disciple of Rāmānand and the guru of Mīrābāī. He also translated seven *pads* by Raidās and gave their texts, but no indication of their source.

The next major development in the study of Raidās was marked by his inclusion in the pioneering *Hindī sāhitya kā itihās* of Rāmacandra Śukla published in 1926.[13] The brief entry for Raidās recorded that he was a Chamar from Banaras who became a disciple of Rāmānand. It points out that Raidās mentioned Kabīr and Sain in his works, and was himself mentioned in the works of Mīrābāī and Dhannā. It also included a reference to the tradition that Uddhavadās was a disciple of Raidās, and gives a few examples of Raidās's work.

This set the pattern for subsequent sections on Raidās in Hindi histories of Hindi literature. The entries in Rām Kumār Varmā's *Hindī sāhitya kā ālocanātmak itihās* (1938)[14] and Hazārīprasād Dvivedī's *Hindī sāhitya* (1955)[15] both repeat substantially the same facts as given by Rāmacandra Śukla.

The striking thing about all the references to Raidās in these works is how much, like Wilson over a hundred years before, they rely on Nābhādās and Priyādās, and how little they add to information already available on Raidās.

III. MODERN STUDIES

In contrast to this a major work which first appeared in 1941 was *Bhagavān Ravidās kī satya kathā* by Rāmacaraṇ Kurīl.[16] This book contains on the one hand a mine of stories and episodes concerning Raidās written from the viewpoint of a devout member of the Ravidāsī community and on the other a certain amount of factual information relating to sites sacred to Raidās. In particular it contains full details of the sites at Mandu referred to in the *Maraduśumārī Rāja Māravāḍ* 1891 and Eckford-Luard 1902 mentioned above. Moreover, it attempts to synthesise all of the elements in the hagiography of Raidās into a coherent whole and to present Raidās's teachings through expositions on the meaning of his *pads*.

Another milestone in the study of Raidās was reached in 1956 when Rāmānand Śāstrī and Vīrendra Pāṇḍe published *Saṃt Ravidās aur unkā kāvyā*. This work was the first attempt at a serious academic study of Raidās and included a study of his life and an edition of his works. It was the first new edition drawn from manuscripts since the Belvedere Press edition of 1908, and the first attempt to accurately edit a text on the basis of manuscript sources.[17]

Paraśurām Caturvedī's colossal study of the Sant traditions of Northern India, *Uttarī Bhārat kī Saṃt paraṃparā*, first published in 1952, also contained an extensive section on Raidās and his followers.[18] This gave a critical and extensive summary of what was known about Raidās at that time, examining for the first time with a critical eye issues such as whether he really was a disciple of Rāmānand and Mīrābāī his disciple.

There was renewed interest in Raidās during the nineteen-seventies and a steady flow of works on him began to be published in India. In 1972 a critical appreciation of Raidās was published by Yogīndra Singh accompanied by a new version of the text of his works drawn from manuscript sources. The systematic approach in this work led to arrangement of the *pads* by alphabetical order and the addition of footnotes giving some variant readings, but not as yet their sources.[19]

In 1973 A.P. Singh published a work called *Ravidās*

darśan, which contained the text of some two hundred sayings attributed to Raidās along with translations into Hindi verse. However, their source was reported as a manuscript lost in the partition of the Panjab and no longer available for inspection and so there is no way to determine the authenticity of this unique collection of the works of Raidās.[20]

The year of 1976 was, according to the view put forward by A.P. Singh, the six hundredth anniversary of the birth of Raidās and a number of works appeared around that time to coincide with the celebrations, notably a study by Padam Guracaran Singh[21] and the first complete book in English on Raidās, by Darshan Singh.[22]

In 1978 B.P. Śarmā published what claimed to be a true critical edition of the works of Raidās.[23] From manuscripts in the libraries and monasteries of Rajasthan he assembled a collection of one hundred and eighty *pads*. However, he did not discriminate between different manuscripts in the final work and it is hard to tell where any of the *pads* come from or how old the manuscript was from which it was copied.

IV. RECENT STUDIES

The nineteen-eighties saw continued interest in Raidās. In 1981 Darshan Singh published *A Study of Bhakta Ravidāsa*, the first really critical appreciation in English of his life and works.[24] This was followed by a work by K.N. Upādhyāya which examined the life of Raidās from the viewpoint of a follower of the Rādhāsoāmī movement and gave translations, in a style reminiscent of Macauliffe's, of *pads* selected from the *Ādi Granth*, the Belvedere Press edition, A.P. Singh's book and Śarmā's edition of the works of Raidās.[25]

A very different approach to Raidās and his followers was apparent in Juergensmeyer's study *Religion as Social Vision* published in 1982. In this he traced how the politics of the uplift of the untouchables in the Panjab and the various untouchable religious movements, particularly the Ravidāsīs, had become intertwined.[26]

An invaluable work on Raidās was published in 1986 by J.S. Sābar. This collected nearly all of the source material on Raidās into one volume and transliterated all of the Devanagari sources into Gurmukhi.[27]

A further development in literary interest in Raidās also became evident when Hawley published an article in 1988 in which he used the example of Raidās to show how there was frequent conflation of what was by Raidās, and what was about Raidās and discussed the impact of the *chāp* of Raidās in his verses.[28]

Hawley's interest in Raidās also led to his inclusion in his book *Songs of the Saints of India* published in 1988. In this he gave some details on the contemporary Ravidāsīs in Banaras and translations of some of the works of Raidās included in the *Ādi Granth.*[29]

V. EARLY MANUSCRIPTS CONTAINING THE SONGS OF RAIDĀS

The text of the critical edition of the *vāṇī* of Raidās presented in my thesis was based upon twelve manuscript sources which dated from AD 1582 to AD 1698. The manuscripts came from four traditions. First, a non-sectarian tradition represented by the Fatehpur manuscript of AD 1582. Second, the Dādūpanthī tradition, represented by eight manuscripts of AD 1636 to AD 1698 (manuscripts DVAHIMPU). Third, a Rajasthani Nāth Siddha tradition represented by two manuscripts of AD 1660 and AD 1681 (manuscripts CJ), and fourth, the Panjabi tradition as represented by the *Ādi Granth* of AD 1603-4.

FM-Fatehpur manuscript CPJ	5 *pads*	AD 1582
D-DMVJ, no. 12	71 *pads*	AD 1636
V-VBJ, no. 34	70 *pads* 2 *sākhīs*	AD 1658
A-Amritsar, GNDU, no. 875	65 *pads* 6 *sākhīs*	AD 1675
H-Naraina, private copy	65 *pads*	AD 1653
I-VRI, no. 9693	81 *pads* 4 *sākhīs*	AD 1643
M-DMVJ, no. 2	68 *pads* 6 *sākhīs*	AD 1676
P-Patiala, no. 2706	68 *pads*	AD 1698
U-VBJ, no. 12	62 *pads*	AD 1686
C-CPJ, no. 3322	65 *pads* 6 *sākhīs*	AD 1660-69
J-CPJ, no. 1853	65 *pads*	AD 1681
AG-The *Ādi Granth*	41 *pads* 1 *sākhī*	AD 1603-4

VI. URTEXT OR ORAL TRADITION?

My thesis set out to establish a critical text of the works of Raidās as they were found in manuscripts dating from before AD 1700 and to examine the relationship between the oral traditions in which these works were created and the early written forms of the works.

The term 'oral tradition' refers to the traditions in which songs were performed at social and religious gatherings. The songs were transmitted either directly from teacher to disciple or through hearing songs performed at communal gatherings.

The aim was not simply to identify what was, or was not, composed by Raidās, but rather to identify the processes by which the early core of the works of Raidās came to be augmented during their oral transmission. It was argued that improvisation upon the basic text of a song formed an integral part of the performance of a song within these oral traditions. The improvisation itself apparently mostly took the form of adding commentatorial material to the songs. These commentaries themselves later became embedded within the songs and in addition to this at the same time entirely new songs were added to previously existent collections which commented upon the works already included.

I believe it was important to adopt an approach which took into account oral traditions, because it allowed me to identify both the early common core to the Raidās tradition and the nature of the earliest influences which came to bear upon it. Moreover, the fact that Raidās was himself a member of an oral tradition could not be ignored, for this meant that the processes which influenced his works during their later oral transmission must also have influenced his own initial creation of his songs. And I argue that an approach based on the search for a written Urtext of Raidās's works cannot be valid in this context for here we are dealing with material which was created as a part of an ongoing process in an oral tradition.

Instead the focus was placed on the processes which may have been active within the oral traditions that transmitted the works of Raidās. And it was argued that it is only in this way that there could be any explanation of the relationship between the core of the works of Raidās and the countless variations in the texts found in even the earliest extant written recensions of his work.

VII. THE EARLIEST *VĀṆĪ* OF RAIDĀS

Is it possible to envisage the earliest forms of the songs of Raidās as they were performed at *satsaṅg*s in Raidās's own home? There is a strong possibility that song 73 describes just such a *satsaṅg*. It describes how the beloved of God have come to Raidās's home and how they sing of the glory of God and tell tales about Him and expound upon their meanings:

pad 73

refrain On this day I offer myself to You, for to my home have come the beloved of Rām.

1. Courtyard, compound and home have become sanctified, as Hari's servants sit and sing of Hari's glory.

2. I prostrate myself before them and wash their feet, and offer my body, mind and fortune to the devotees.
3. They tell the tales and consider their meaning, they liberate themselves and cause others to attain liberation.
4. Raidās says, through meeting with the servants of God, the bonds of birth after birth are cut.[30]

However, there is the question of whether such a song as this accurately records how a Raidāsī sang this song, or whether it is a sectarian emulation of how a Raidāsī song should be performed. I would propose that it is most likely that the songs of Raidās preserved in the Dādūpanthī manuscripts, and other manuscripts, were probably the ones performed by Raidāsīs at the various *satsaṅgs* they attended. In this regard it is of note that in the *Bhaktamāl* of Cain there is a reference to how the descendants of Raidās were uplifted by Dādū Dayāl.[31] This suggests that Raidāsīs were accepted into the Dādūpanthī *satsaṅgs*. I think that it may well have been Raidāsīs themselves who would have sung the songs of their teacher at early Dādūpanthī *satsaṅgs*. And although there is no direct evidence that Raidāsis were also welcomed into Nāth Siddha and Sikh *satsaṅgs*, I would also propose that it is likely that wherever Raidāsī songs are found in later manuscript traditions it indicates that Raidāsīs were originally members of early *satsaṅgs*.

VIII. THE ORGANISATION OF THE MANUSCRIPTS

A further question which needs to be addressed is how were the songs performed at the *satsaṅgs*? I will not here address the question of how exactly they were sung but will consider rather, what may be learnt from how the manuscripts are structured. The manuscript sources for the songs follow four different patterns.

The first pattern in found in the Fatehpur manuscript. In

this the works of numerous different Sants and Bhaktas are given in no particular order of either composer or *rāg*.

The second pattern is exemplified by the *pañcavāṇī* manuscripts and the Nāth Siddha manuscripts. In these the repertoire of each Sant is given as an unbroken sequence, and each Sant's repertoire is classified according to a series of *rāg*s, and this is the pattern followed for each Sant and Nāth Siddha in the manuscript.

The third pattern is that found in the *sarvāṅgī* manuscripts of the Dādūpanthīs in which the arrangement was by theme rather than composer or *rāg*. Thus within each thematic section (*aṅg*) works by diverse Sants and Nāth Siddhas were given and no particular sequence of *rāg*s was followed.

The fourth pattern is that of the *Ādi Granth*. In this the primary structure is a sequence of *rāg* and then within each *rāg* the works of the Sikh Gurūs and the Bhagats are given according to a predetermined sequence.

Now, if these patterns of organisation in the manuscript reflect anything more than simply how the manuscript were organised, then surely they may reflect something of the patterns of performance at the *satsaṅg*s the manuscript derives from. With regard to the pattern found in the *pañcavāṇī* manuscripts it is also of note that the order of the *rāg*s follows more or less a progression starting around dawn and continuing through the day and into the deep of the night.[32] Is it possible that this reflects the traces of a form of *satsaṅg* at which the songs of one particular Sant alone were performed throughout a whole day? Can we imagine a five-day festival for five Saints, Dādū, Kabīr, Nāmdev, Raidās and Hardās, as the origin of the *pañcavāṇī* manuscript tradition?

IX. RAIDĀS AS A SINGER

Turning now to a point about Raidās that has great importance, in all of the early stories about Raidās much stress is laid on not only his greatness as a devotee but on the fact that he was an outstanding singer. One of the stories about Raidās which lies close to the core of his hagiography tells of his victory in a singing contest over the Brahmans of Banaras. When challenged over his right to worship a *śālagrām* by the Brahmans, it was fixed that whosoever could make an image of the Lord come to their side would be the victor. The Brahmans sang their Vedic chants to no avail, for the statue remained immobile. But when Raidās sang and sang, for hours on end, it finally so moved God that he caused His image to move to Raidās's side.[33] As far as I know there are no tales of how Kabīr, Dādū, Nāmdev, nor any of the Sants apart from Raidās demonstrated their faith through the power of their singing. This surely suggests that there must have been something truly remarkable about Raidās's singing. So whatever else we may say about Raidās we must bear in mind that above all the impression left in the minds of those who met him was of a great devotee and a remarkable singer.

According to Priyādās, the song by which Raidās won this contest included the line 'Manifest Yourself today, O You whose name is the uplifter of the fallen'.[34] This song, or one very like it, is found in all of the early Dādūpanthī and Nāth Siddha manuscripts and is a fairly short lyric in *rāg rāmakalī*. However, Anantadās's description of this contest also dwells on how the whole day passed while Raidās sang his song before his eyes filled with tears so that God was finally moved.[35] This suggests that one aspect of the songs which the manuscripts fail to adequately convey is that individual songs might form the basis for hours of improvisation. So when one spends a few moments reading the text of this *pad* perhaps we should bear in mind that its performance may have gone on for hours:

refrain I have come, I have come, O God, into Your refuge,
know me to be Your servant and be merciful to me.

1. I dwell in diverse births in dreadful fear of death,
   Wandering, I have roamed around without praising You,
   drunk on the wine of selfishness, pride, and sensuality,
   amidst these pleasures I never crossed the uncrossable.
2. Believing in Your Name I have abandoned hope in any other,
   let my mind be not fixed in worldly affairs;
   accept the service of the servant Raidās, O God of Gods,
   manifest Your Name 'the uplifter of the fallen!'.[36]

X. THE CORE OF THE *VĀṆĪ* OF RAIDĀS

Finally, I would like to suggest that although we may never be able to experience what it felt like to hear Raidās's singing, and though we may never known whether any of the texts attributed to him are really accurate recordings of the texts of the songs he sang, we can still get closer to the early Raidāsī tradition than at first appears likely.

This is because there are seventeen *pads* with the *chāp* of Raidās/Ravidās which are common to the Panjabi, Dādūpanthī, and Nāth Siddha traditions, and of these *pads* there are two that are also found in the non-sectarian tradition.[37]

I would like to suggest that the occurrence of these *pads* in three of, or all of, the early traditions, indicates that they must have been the most popular of all the *pads* of Raidās, and that they represent a common core which underlies the larger recensions of the *vāṇī*. Furthermore, that these *pads* were known in such distinctly differentiated traditions indicates that they are the most likely of the *pads* to be derived from the original oral Raidāsī tradition and that therefore there is a high probability that they were originally composed by Raidās.

Moreover, I would argue that this common core contains in itself all of the fundamental teachings in the *vāṇī* of Raidās, and that the contents of this common core could have provided the basis for the larger recensions of the *vāṇī*.

In these *pads* Raidās clearly spoke of himself as a Chamar[38] and he described the poverty and difficult circumstances under which he lived.

My company is low,
  and I worry night and day,
my labours are hard,
  and my birth is ill-favoured.[39]

My caste is low, my lineage is low,
  and my birth is low;
I have not served king Rām,
  Says Ravidās the Chamar![40]

That he shared the common Sant view on the illusory nature of the world can also be seen in a *cetāvaṇī pad* in the common *pads*.

Why are you sleeping? O fool wake up,
Did you think that life in this world was real?

The days which come will pass away again,
we must depart, there is no abiding for ever;
our companions are going and we must go too,
we must travel far and death hangs over our heads.[41]

He also spoke of his lack of belief in conventional exterior worship and stressed the fact that he did not even known how he could perform formalised outward worship of God.

How can I offer worship to Rām?
I cannot find any perfect fruits or flowers.
I do not know how to adore or worship You Rām,
Raidās says, what is to be my fate?[42]

He also rejected the authority of the Vedas and Purāṇas and said that they could not remove men's doubts.

You may ponder over *karma* and *akarma*,
due to doubt, you may listen to the Vedas and Purāṇas,
but when doubt constantly dwells in your heart,
then apart from Rām who can conquer your pride?[43]

For Raidās it was through devotion that the lowly could be uplifted and he quoted the example of Vālmīki, another untouchable saint like Raidās himself, in order to illustrate how the lowly might be exalted through devotion.

O mind awake! Awake! Why are you unaware?
Look at Vālmīki!
None has ever reached such a state through caste,
but only through special devotion to Rām.[44]

He asserted that he had escaped from the bondage of life in the phenomenal world by fixing his mind upon Rām.

Your lotus feet are home for my mind,
drinking Your nectar I found the treasure of Rām.
Veils of fortune and misfortune, *māyā* and wealth,
Your servant is not engrossed in them.[45]

Raidās declares that he has caste aside worldly matters and become a trader in Spontaneity (*sahaj*).

O load up the caravan of Hari!
I am a trader in Rām:
I have found the fortune of the Name of Rām,
through that I trade in Spontaneity (*sahaj*).[46]

For Raidās it was the spontaneous realisation of the immanence of God which was the experience which liberated the individual and conquered duality.

refrain Whoever has abided in the mystical experience of Ram,

has been touched by the philosopher's stone, and
has no sense of duality.
Raidās says, this is the supreme renunciation,
O lucky one, why do you not chant the Name of Rām?
The wise churn the curds for the sake of the ghee,
the liberated while living are in perpetual nirvana.[47]

Above all then, Raidās says it is the name of Rām which enables the individual to meet with Rām, and through this encounter the individual is uplifted and united in a loving union with the supreme spirit.

The fervour of Raidās's devotion is also testified to in these verses. He speaks of 'loving devotion'[48] and in a key verse describes how he has given even his soul to God in exchange for his love.

1 I remember You in mind, I see [You] with my eyes,
I fill my ears with your utterances and praises;
I make my mind a bee, and hold Your feet in my heart,
I relish with my tongue the nectar of Your Name Rām.
refrain Let my love for Govinda not decrease!
I have paid a high price,
giving my soul in exchange.
2 Without the company of the pure love does not arise,
and without love there can be no devotion to You;
Ravidās asks this one petition of You, Hari,
keep your promise to me, O my King Rām.[49]

Finally, there is one *pad* which is found in every one of the manuscripts used in this study. This must have been the most famous of all the *pads* in the *vāṇī* of Raidās, and it is surely this *pad* which above all others is likely to be based upon an original Raidās *pad*. Moreover, its refrain and first *antarā* are substantially the same in all versions and it is surely these four lines from the *vāṇī* of Raidās which are the most likely of all to accurately record the core text of one of his original *pads*.

> How can there be any difference,
> between You and I, I and You?
> between gold and bracelet, water and wave?
> **refrain** If I did not sin, O infinite one!
> how could Your Name be the uplifter of the fallen.[50]

These then must be teachings that lie at the heart of the *vāṇī* of Raidās. Above all, Raidās was renowned for his teaching that the individual self is but a manifestation of the ultimate reality, and that the Name of God can uplift those who have fallen into duality and lead to a union of the finite self and the infinite supreme self.

XI. CONCLUSION

If one considers the basic aims which have motivated the study of Raidās, it is clear that there have been several phases in which different questions have been addressed. In the first phase the basic question posed was simply concerned with how Raidās could be identified. Wilson and his followers sought to answer this question by relying on the information found in Nābhādās's *Bhaktamāl* and Priyādās's commentary upon it, while the ethnographic school sought the answers mostly in oral traditions which they had access to. In the second phase the basic issue addressed was the creation of an anthology of the *vāṇī* of Raidās. This phase was initiated by the Belvedere Press edition and Macauliffe, and continues to this day to be an active concern, notably of such authors as Śarmā and in the forthcoming edition of the *vāṇī* of Raidās by Shukdev Singh. Coupled with this has been a desire in many author's minds to create a 'Ravidās Granth' which contains the complete *vāṇī* of Raidās and an historical account of his life. However, the most recent phase in the study of Raidās has seen a shift away from these earlier interests towards an examination of the role that

Raidās plays in contemporary society, as in Juergensmeyer 1982, and the relationship between composer and work as studied in Hawley 1988.

In my thesis I set out to take a fresh look at the first two issues by examining the early hagiographic sources dating from before c. AD 1700 and editing a text of his *vāṇī* based on early manuscripts only. In addition to this I studied what could be deduced from the early manuscripts about the relationship between the oral traditions in which the works of Raidās originated and the versions of his *vāṇī* found in the earliest manuscripts.

In this paper I have shown something of the contents of the songs of Raidās which are found in all the early traditions and have suggested that they are likely to be derived from the earliest level in the Raidāsī oral tradition. This is of interest not just because it tells us about what may have been the earliest form of the *vāṇī* of Raidās, but also because it sets a standard by which one may examine the songs found in only one or other tradition to see what they tell about the nature of the early influences upon the Raidāsī tradition. It was apparent in my study that each sectarian recension of the *vāṇī* of Raidās contains a mixture of Raidāsī and sectarian material. I would argue that non-sectarians, Nāth Siddhas, Dādūpanthīs and Sikhs all sang versions of the *vāṇī* of Raidās as seen from the viewpoint of their own belief systems, and their written versions of the *vāṇī* of Raidās contain both a common core of Raidāsī material and sectarian comments upon the earlier text.

Finally I would like to suggest that an analysis of the *vāṇī* of Kabīr undertaken from this angle might yield very interesting results. In the case of Kabīr it would be possible to compare the recensions of his work in the *Bījak*, the *Ādi Granth*, the Dādūpanthī tradition and the Nāth Siddha tradition. This might make it possible to identify what aspects of Kabīr's *vāṇī* derive from its earliest oral traditions and the nature of the early sectarian influence upon his *vāṇī*.

In the end I suggest that one must remember that the

works of Sants such as Raidās and Kabīr were created as part of an ongoing process within oral traditions. Due to this it will only be possible to understand how the recensions of their works in early manuscripts came into being if we can gain a better understanding of the relationship between the oral traditions in which they were created and the written traditions in which they were preserved.

ABBREVIATIONS

CPJ City Palace, Jaipur
DMVJ Dādū Mahāvidhyālaya, Jaipur
GNDU Guru Nanak Dev University, Amritsar
VBJ Vidyā Bhūṣaṇ Collection, Jaipur
VRI Vrindaban Research Institute, Vrindaban.

NOTES

1. Wilson, H.H. 1904, pp. 57-9.
2. Garcin de Tassy 1870. Vol. II, pp. 527-31.
3. *Maradusumārī Rāj Māravāḍ.* 1891, Vol. II, p. 540-2.
4. Crooke, W. 1896. Vol. II, pp. 185-7.
5. Eckford-Luard 1902. Vol. XIX part 1, p. 82.
6. *Raidās jī kī bānī aur jivan caritra*, Allahabad: Belvedere Press. 1908 (2nd ed. 1918).
7. For the Panjabi version of this story see Friedlander 1991, pp. 51-2.
8. Macauliffe, 1909, Vol.VI, pp. 316-42.
9. See Ibbetson 1911, Vol. II, pp. 147-151.
10. See Russell 1916, Vol. II, pp. 403-424.
11. See Grierson 1918 *The Encyclopedia of Religion and Ethics* Vol. X pp. 360-1, and Grierson 1920 *The Encyclopedia of Religion and Ethics* Vol. XI, pp. 46-7.
12. Shah, Ahmad and Ormerod, E.W. 1925, pp. 39-42.
13. Śukla 1926, pp. 81-2.
14. Varmā 1954, pp. 224-6.
15. Dvivedī 1955, pp. 136-9.
16. Kurīl 1950, pp. 173-177.

17. Śāstrī and Pāṇḍe 1955.
18. Caturvedī 1972, pp. 239-52.
19. Singh, Yogīndra. 1972.
20. Singh, A.P. 1973.
21. Singh, P.G. 1977.
22. Singh, Darshan. 1977.
23. Śarmā 1978.
24. Singh, Darshan. 1981.
25. Upādhyāya, K.N. 1982.
26. Juergensmeyer 1982.
27. Sābar 1984.
28. Hawley J.S. 1988. "Author and Authenticity in the Bhakti Poetry of North India". *The Journal of Asian Studies*, 47:2, pp. 269-90.
29. Hawley and Juergensmeyer 1988, pp. 9-32.
30. *āji nāṃ dyausā nā lyau balihārā,*
mere graha āyā rājā rāṃmajī kā pyārā | | *ṭeka* | |
Friedlander 1991, *pad* 73, p. 304.
31. Nāhāṭa, A. 1965. p. 282: *raidāsa vaṃśī dayāla sudhāre.*
32. The following *rāg* order for the *vāṇī* of Raidās is found in the majority of the *pañcavāṇī* manuscripts: *rāṃmagarī* (after sunrise); *gauṛī (evening)*; *āsāvarī* (*early morning)*; *soraṭhī* (evening) *bhairau* (after sunrise); *bilāvalā* (early morning); *toḍī* (early morning); *gauṇḍ* (noon, late morning); *sāraṃg* (midday); *kanaḍ* (deep night); *kedār* (early night); *jaitaśrī* (??); [*āratī*] *dhanāśrī*. Source for times for performance: Daniélou 1968. However, Mukund Lath (personal communication 1991) points out that the relationship between modern and medieval theories about the times for the performance of *rāg*s is unclear.
33. This story is told in many places. For an original of the story see Rāghavadās' account in Nāhatā, A. 1965 pp. 55-6, and for a paraphrase of (Priyādās's version of) the story see Wilson 1904, pp. 58-9.
34. "*Patita pāvana nāma kījiye prakaṭa āju:*" *Bhaktirasabodhinī, chappay* 266, Rūpakalā, S. Bh. ed. *Bhaktamāl.* 5th edn., Luknow : Tejkumār Book Depot. p. 478.
35. See Anantadās, *Raidāsajī kī paracai viśrāma* 6, stanzas 25-6, India Office Library Hindī manuscript A 12/1 (f); ff 35a-47a.
36. *āyau ho āyau deva tumha saranāṃ, jaṃnīṃ kripā kījai āpanauṃ janāṃ* | | *ṭeka* | |
Friedlander 1991, *pad* 8, p. 179.
37. The *pads* common to the *Ādi Granth*, Dādū Panthī and Nāth MSS:

no.	D	A	V	I	M	P	H	U	C	J	AG	FM
1	1	1	1	1	1	1	1	1	10	10	36	
13	13	13	13	13	13	13	13	13	22	22	32	
24	23	22	24	23	22	22	22	20	32	32	2	
32	24	24	26	25	-	-	-	51	1	1	6	
34	27	25	31	28	30	25	25	52	4	4	1	*f*
39	32	37	33	33	35	30	30	30	38	38	13	
40	33	38	34	34	36	31	31	31	39	39	10	
43	36	41	37	37	-	34	-	33	41	41	9	
44	37	42	38	38	39	35	34	34	42	42	7	
53	45	34	46	47	47	43	42	42	47	47	35	
55	47	36	48	49	49	45	44	44	49	49	18	
57	50	-	-	52	51	51	47	46	52	52	14	
64	58	44	58	55	52	48	47	21	55	55	26	
78	71	64	70	70	68	60	59	60	8	8	4	
86	57	61	57	73	72	62	61	-	59	60	22	*f*
87	53	56	53	74	73	63	62	-	62	63	40	
88	55	59	56	77	74	65	63	-	61	62	24	

38. *kahu ravidāsa camāra.* See Friedlander 1991, *pad* 78, AG 4.4, p. 320; *kahi ravidāsa camārā, ibid.*, *pad* 43, AG 9.3, p. 242.

39. *merī saṃgati poca, soca dinu rātī* | |
merā karamu kuṭilatā, janamu kubhāṃtī | | 1 | |
Ibid., *pad* 24, AG 2.1, p. 206.

40. *jātī ochā pātī ochā, ochā janām hamārā* | |
rājā rāma kī seva na kīnī, kahi ravidāsa camārā | | 3 | |
Ibid., *pad* 43, AG 9.3, pp. 252-3.

41. *kiā tū soiā jāgu iānā* | |
tai jīvanu jagi sacu kari jānā | | *rahāu* | |
Ibid., *pad* 64, AG 26.0-1, pp. 294-7.

42. *rāṃmahiṃ pūjā kahā caḍāṃūṃ,*
phala aru phūla anūpa na paṃūṃ | | *ṭeka* | |
Ibid., *pad* 39.0 and 39.4 p. 235.

43. *akaraṃma karaṃa bicāriye,*
suni saṃkyā beda purāṃna |
saṃsau sadā hiradai rahai,
rāma bina kauṃna harai abhimāṃna | | 2 | |
Ibid., *pad* 32.2, pp. 218.

44. *re cita ceti ceti aceta kāhe, bālaṃmīka kau deṣa* |
jātī thaiṃ koī padi na pahuṃcyā rāṃma bhagati baseṣa | | *ṭeka* | | *Ibid.*, *pad* 53.0, p. 265.

45. *tujhahi carana arabiṃda bhavana manu* | |
pāna karata pāio rāmīā dhanu | | *rahāu* | |
Ibid., *pad* 40, AG 10.0-1, p. 236.

46. *hari kau ṭāṃḍau lādeṃ jāī re,*

maiṃ baṇijārā rāṃma kā |
rāṃma nāṃa dhana pāiyau,
tāthaiṃ sahaji karauṃ byaupāra re ||ṭeka||
Ibid., pad 78.0, p. 312.

47. *paracai rāṃma ramaiṃ je koī!*
pārasa parasem dubidha na hoī ||ṭeka||
Ibid., pad 1, p. 166.

48. *prema bhagati nahīṃ upajai,*
tāthaiṃ jana raidāsa udāsa ||7||
Ibid., pad 32.7. pp. 218.

49. *merī prīti gobiṃdu siu jini ghaṭai ||*
mai tau moli mahaṃgī laī jīa saṭai ||rahāu||
Ibid., pad 86, AG 22, p. 326.

50. *jaupai hama na pāpa karaṃtā, ahe anantā||*
patita pāvana nāmu kaise huṃta ||rahāu||
Ibid., pad 34, p. 225.

Bibliography

Caturvedī, P. 1964 (orig. ed. 1952). *Uttarī bhārat kī saṃt paramparā.* Allahabad: Bhāratī Bhaṇḍār.

Crooke, W. 1896. *The Tribes and Castes of the North-Western Provinces and Oudh.* Calcutta: Office of the Superintendent of Government Printing.

Daniélou, Alain. 1968. *The Rāga-s of Northern Indian Music.* London: Barrie and Rockliff.

Eckford-Luard, C. 1902. Report. *Census of India, 1901*, Vol. XIX. Lucknow.

Friedlander, P.G. 1991. *The Life and Works of Sant Raidās.* Doctoral dissertation for the School of Oriental and African Studies, University of London.

Garcin de Tassy. 1870 (orig. ed. 1839). *Histoire de la littérature hindouie et hindoustanie.* Paris: Adolphe Labitte.

Grierson, G.A. 1918. 'Rai Dāsīs'. Vol. X, pp. 360-1. *In The Encyclopedia of Religion and Ethics.* Ed. James Hastings. Edinburgh: T.&T. Clark.

Grierson, G.A. 1920. 'Sādhs'. Vol. XI, pp. 46-7. In *The Encyclopedia of Religion and Ethics.* Ed. James Hastings. Edinburgh: T. & T. Clark.

Hawley, J.S. and Juergensmeyer, M. 1988. *Songs of the Saints of India.* New York, Oxford: Oxford University Press.

Ibbetson, D. 1911. *A Glossary of the Tribes and Castes of the Punjab and North-West Frontier Province.* Lahore: Samuel T. Weston.

Juergensmeyer, M. 1982. *Religion as Social Vision.* Berkeley: University of California Press.

Kuril, Rāmacarana. 1950. *Bhagavān Ravidās kī satyakathā.* Ed. Madhukar Miśra. Kanpur: Kṛṣṇa Press.

Macauliffe, M.A. 1909. *The Sikh Religion.* Vol. VI, Oxford: Oxford University Press.

Maraduśumārī Rāj Māravāḍ. 1891. Jodhpur: Jodhpur State.

Nāhaṭā A. ed. 1965. *Rāghavadās kṛt bhaktamāl.* With commentary by Caturdās. Rājasthān Purātan Granthamālā no. 78. Jodhpur: ROFI.

Russell, R.V. 1916. *The Tribes and Castes of the Central Provinces of India.* London: Macmillan and Co.

Sabar, J.S. 1984. *Bhagata Ravidāsa srodha pustaka.* Amritsar: Guru Nanak Dev University Press.

Shah, Ahmad, and Ormerod, E.W. 1925. *Hindī Religious Poetry.* Cawnpore.

Śāstrī, Rāmānand, and Pāṇḍe, Virendra. 1955. *Saṃt Ravidās aur unkā kāvya.* Lucknow: Navabhārat Press.

Śarma, B.P. 1978. *Saṃt Guru Ravidās vāṇī.* Delhi: Surya Prakāśan.

Sherring, M.A. 1972. *Hindu Tribes and Castes as Represented in Benares.* London: Trubner and Co.

Singh, Āzād Prithvī. 1973. *Ravidās darśan.* Chandigarh: Śrī Gurū Ravidās Sansthān.

Singh, Darshan. 1977. *Sant Ravidās and His Times.* Ludhiana: Kalyani Publishers.

Singh, Darshan. 1981. *A Study of Bhakta Ravidāsa.* Patiala: Punjabi University.

Singh, Padam Gurucaraṇ. 1977. *Saṃt Ravidās - vicārak aur kavi.* Jalandhar: Navacintan Prakāśan.

Singh, Yogīndra. 1972. *Samt Raidās.* Delhi: Akṣar Prakāśan.

Śukla, Rāmacandra. 1926. *Hindī sāhitya kā itihās.* Varanasi: Nāgarī Pracāriṇī Sabhā.

Upādhyāya, K.N. 1982. *Guru Ravidās: Life and Teachings.* Radha Soami Satsang, Beas.

Varmā, R.K. 1954 (orig.ed. 1938). *Hindī sāhitya kā ālocanātmak itihās.* Allahabad: Rāmanārāyaṇ Lāl.

Wilson, H.H. 1904. *Religious Sects of the Hindus.* Revised edition, London and Madras: Christian Literature Society for India. Originally published in 1828-9 as 'A sketch of the Religious Sects of the Hindus'. *Asiatick Researches.* XVI p. 79f. Reprinted in one volume in 1861 as *Religious Sects of the Hindus.*

The Bhārat Kalā Bhavan *Sūrsāgar*[1]

John Stratton Hawley

The *Sūrsāgar*, attributed to the sixteenth-century poet Sūrdās, is one of the great collections of Hindi poetry. It is an anthology. Almost all the poems, or *pads*, it contains are independent compositions, but most of them are united by a common subject: Krishna. In the version that is currently standard, the edition prepared under the auspices of the Kāśī Nāgarīpracāriṇī Sabhā (hereafter NPS), the *Sūrsāgar* is a massive reality— truly the "ocean" that its title implies. It contains upwards of 5000 *pads*. And one nineteenth-century manuscript contains almost twice that number.[2]

This, however, is only the tip of the iceberg—or perhaps I should say the bottom. For only if one inverts that block of ice in one's mind, standing the pyramid on its head, does one see the reality of the *Sūrsāgar* as it developed over time. It began small, with a tip that only contained several hundred poems—241 in the oldest available manuscript, which dates to AD 1582 (VS 1639).[3] Then, as a succession of dated manuscripts shows, it typically doubled its size every fifty years or so until it gained its current mass.

Some *Sūrsāgars*, though by no means the majority, have been illustrated. Of these, the best known examples come from Mewar, the region responsible for having produced by far the richest collection. The earliest among them is a justly famous series that can be dated to about 1650-1655 and is largely dispersed in private collections.[4] Andrew Topsfield, who has studied the illustrated Mewar *Sūrsāgars* in some detail, reports that at least six or seven additional sets of paintings were produced at Udaipur between the 1670s and 1740s. They are "of varying length (some probably quite short) and differing format," both vertical and horizontal (Topsfield 1992). Some contain illustrations large enough that sophisticated use can be made of the technique of continuous narration; others are smaller and simpler. While the majority of these paintings can be seen in the Government Museum at Udaipur, which contains the palace collection, others are now to be found elsewhere in India and abroad. Individual pages exist, for example, in the collection of George P. Bickford, in Cleveland; in the Sackler collection; in the collection of Gunter Heil, in Berlin; in the collection of Vinod K. Kanoria, in Patna; in the Baroda Museum; in the Los Angeles County Museum of Art; in the National Gallery of Victoria; in the National Gallery, Ottawa; and in the San Diego Museum of Art.[5]

Although the illustrated *Sūrsāgars* from Mewar form much the largest and most celebrated group and constitute a tradition all their own, they are not alone. In this essay we will focus on a distant cousin that is housed at Bhārat Kalā Bhavan, Benares, and has the unusual distinction of being preserved intact. Unfortunately, this does not mean it contains a colophon. Like the *Sūrsāgars* from Udaipur, it is undated, and it lacks any information as to its provenance. On stylistic grounds museum authorities in Benares think of it as having come from the region of Jaipur. Andrew Topsfield, however, feels the connection with Jaipur court painting is too weak to justify such a conclusion. At least on the basis of black-and-white reproductions, he sees it as displaying "a North Indian provincial style" that might perhaps be associated with "the Mathura region or even further east, from somewhere in Uttar Pradesh" (Topsfield 1992). As for date, Bhārat Kalā Bhavan authorities locate the manuscript at some point in the eighteenth century. Topsfield agrees, proposing a date of about 1750, or perhaps somewhat earlier.

A study of other manuscripts of the *Sūrsāgar*—unillustrated ones—would seem to confirm this judgment. Because the *Sūrsāgar* was not strictly a written tradition but an oral one as well, it tended to grow in a fluid but more or less regular way over the years. Various new "Sūrs" would add their poems to the collection that already existed, and it apparently did not take too long for many of those poems to become known across the rest of Sūr's world, in a process that from a text-critical point of view is known as "contamination": direct lineages of manuscripts copied from one another are the exception rather than the rule. What one has instead, if one looks from a certain distance, is a sort of stratigraphic pattern. Within a certain range of error, eighteenth-century manuscripts of the *Sūrsāgar* can be distinguished from seventeenth-century ones on the basis of the poems they contain. Manuscripts in a given generation, even if they belong to identifiable recension families,[6] often bear quite strong resemblances to each other in the poems they include.

Judging by the poems it contains—that is, judging by a comparison between those poems and poems contained in other, dated manuscripts—it seems fair to say the Kalā Bhavan *Sūrsāgar* probably did not come into existence before the second quarter of the eighteenth century. Perhaps, as Topsfield suggests, a midcentury date would be the most accurate guess, for its selection of poems is particularly close to what one finds in the relevant sections of a large *Sūrsāgar* written in Vrindaban in AD 1756.[7] The major difference between the two manuscripts is that the Kalā Bhavan *Sūrsāgar* has a much more restricted scope, perhaps by design but perhaps because it is incomplete.

It is the purpose of this essay to acquaint readers in a preliminary way with the general contours of this as yet unpublished manuscript. Simply on account of its lavishness and beauty, it deserves to be better known. Yet my description of the Kalā Bhavan *Sūrsāgar* will not be systematic and complete in the way one would expect if I were actually "publishing" it here. Authorities at Bhārat Kalā Bhavan are hopeful of doing that, and it is appropriate that I leave the task to them. Rather, my interest will be thematic. I will direct particular attention to questions that concern the relation between text and illustration: Which came first, both literally and in the mind of the illustrator? When there are disparities, how can we account for them? And how is one to view the process of selection that moved the illustrator to transfer certain aspects of the text into a pictorial mode, while allowing others to remain, from a visual point of view, mute?

Before addressing these thematic concerns, nonetheless, we need to consider at least a few of the basics. First, the manuscript lacks an internal title; "Sūrsāgar" is merely a convenient generic designation. Second, it lacks a date, since there is no colophon of any kind. As for size, the manuscript consists of 98 hand-made folios, each measuring 31.4 cm. in height and 22 cm. in width. Of these, 195 consecutive sides bear text or pictures or both. The present binding is not original.

The individual pages of the manuscript seem to have been prepared in more than one way. On some, the text was evidently inscribed first—by either of two scribes, to judge by the handwriting. On the page that shows the newborn Krishna being carried across the Jumna by Vasudev (4396), for example, the billowing clouds of a rainy night have been drawn in such a way as to take advantage of the precise space left by the last line of text. Where subscript vowel markings are absent, the clouds fill in the space. On other pages, however, the first stage in preparing the manuscript must have involved roughing in the area that would be devoted to the paintings by applying the background colour. And in some instances, at least, several of the more basic colouristic elements in the drawing were also introduced at this point. Then one of the scribes inserted the text, sometimes failing to estimate the space correctly and having to write the last words in the area where colour had been applied. Finally, the details of the painting were added in, as we know from the fact that they, in turn, sometimes were drawn over portions of certain letters that had strayed into the area designed for the painting. This sequence can be inferred quite clearly, for example, from layers of paint and ink that are visible at the upper left-hand corner of the illustration shown in figure 7, a page that shows how gods and Brahmins celebrated the birth of Krishna (4405).[8]

We might mention one more preliminary matter, and that concerns the preliminary page of the manuscript itself. Considering that the text of this *Sūrsāgar* has an exclusively Krishnaite theme, it is arresting to see that its frontispiece, an elaborate full-page painting, is dedicated to Rām (figure 1: 4376). Perhaps this was mandated by a patron who was a *rām bhakta*, though we have no evidence as to who he may have been. In any case, this miniature focuses on the action of a Brahmin, probably Vaśiṣṭha, Rām's family priest, who places a *tilak* on the forehead of the god-king in a gesture that qualifies as a sort of visual *maṅgalācaraṇ*. Rām sits with Sītā on an elaborately carved *caukī*-type throne, and they are attended by a group of scholar- saints, some with meditation beads, others with books, and by three musicians. Others in the royal entourage include Lakṣmaṇ, Bharat, Śatrughna, and three monkeys—presumably Hanumān, Aṅgad, and Sugrīv—all of whom stand behind the officiating Brahmin and receive the auspicious gaze of Sītā and Rām.

On the next page the Krishna story commences. The manuscript begins with a fairly typical subject for a *Sūrsāgar* of its generation, the birth of Krishna, and in a fairly typical style, with a long narrative poem. What was typical then, however, is hardly typical now. Modern editions of the *Sūrsāgar* rarely begin with the birth of Krishna. Instead they start where the *Bhāgavatapurāṇa* does: with Viṣṇu—Viṣṇu before he descends into any of his *avatārs*. Clearly the person responsible for the design of the Bhārat Kalā Bhavan manuscript is unaware that a proper *Sūrsāgar* ought to look like a transcreation of the *Bhāgavata* in this way.[10] Yet he seems to be trying to accomplish the same purpose by another means. He starts with a poem that begins by referring to Parīkṣit (figure 2: 4377), the king whose question to Śukdev gets the *Bhāgavata* under way. Then the artist (who may also be the compiler and/or one of the two scribes) takes this a step further. He has Śukdev respond by actually reading Parīkṣit the text, as if it had already been composed.

This hints at the way in which the artist may conceive the work he is illustrating. Apparently he understands it as something in the nature of a connected narrative—a *purāṇa* like the *Bhāgavata*—and the first poem helps him present it as such:

vāla vinoda bhavati līlā / ati punīta muni bhākhī
sādhu sādhu tuma sunahu parīchit /
sakala deva muni sākhī

The alluring play of his childhood games,
which sages call so pure—
Listen Parīkṣit, it's perfect! perfect!
So all the gods and sages swear.

(NPS 622:1-2)

So it is notable that this *Sūrsāgar* opens with Parīkṣit. A second important feature of the poem in question (622 in the NPS edition) is that it itself resembles a little *purāṇa*: it is long and strictly narrative in format. Most poems in the *Sūrsāgar* last for only six or eight verses, but this one goes on for another eighty lines or so. It is a very different sort of poem from the short, episodic lyrics that almost exclusively made up the *Sūrsāgar* in its earliest phases. Earlier poems assumed the narrative in the minds of their hearers, they did not declare it. Often, in fact, as Kenneth Bryant has shown on the basis of a sampling from both the older and more recent reaches of the *Sūrsāgar*, these poems attempted to conceal or pervert the narrative so as to surprise the audience into seeing old things in a new light (Bryant 1978: 43-

71). But the poem at hand is an entirely different beast. Its aim is to retell the old story completely and straightforwardly; there is no question of deception or surprise or beginning *in medias res*.

The oldest Sūr collections known to us contain only a few poems of this type and length. Interestingly, in a manuscript dated VS 1697 (AD 1640), one of these poems, *braj bhayo mahar ke pūt* (NPS 642), was used to do precisely what the poem at hand is intended to accomplish. A scribe put it at the beginning of his manuscript as a nice, thick bookend to hold up the collection of brief child Krishna poems that would follow. With this act he anchored a series of oral poems and made them look like a book. That was in an unillustrated *Sūrsāgar* prepared at Ghanora (near Banswara), as his colophon reports.[11] Not far away—probably in Udaipur and almost certainly somewhere within the Mewar domain—the pattern may have been repeated in visual form. In a *Sūrsāgar* page now in the Heil collection we can see an elaborate and multifaceted painting associated with the same poem.[12] It is intriguing that the illustration is given after only four verses of the poem: additional paintings for the same poem may have followed. The painting we have, which is given in a large vertical format, takes up almost the entire page and is filled with dense detail, including a picture of the poet himself, as in several manuscript pages from Mewar to which reference has already been made.

In Mathura, which was undoubtedly a good bit closer to the eye of the Sūr hurricane, the same sort of bookending was also taking place. There, however, the *Sūrsāgar*'s prestige apparently suggested that it could only be understood as a form of *the* book—the *Bhāgavata*, or at least its tenth canto. So in a Mathura manuscript of 1641[13] we find the first mention—perhaps the invention—of the very poem that begins the Kalā Bhavan manuscript. Its first words state the subject quite clearly: *vāla vinoda bhāvatī līlā*, "the alluring play of [Krishna's] childhood games...."

It is fascinating to see what our artist does with this long poem. Rather than rationing his efforts so that he will have plenty of space for other compositions, he jumps right in and begins illustrating this one with elaborate care. Evidently its straightforward and poetically uninteresting narrative suits his needs admirably. He devotes almost an entire page to the couplet that tells how Kaṃs betrothed Devakī to Vasudev—only the couplet itself competes for space—and follows on the next page by presenting the marriage itself, this time occupying the full page indeed. The next page (figure 3: 4380) is devoted to the nuptial procession, in which Kaṃs serves as Devakī's coachman. Soon afterward, however, Kaṃs has a premonition that her progeny will be his downfall. In the next moment the artist chooses to represent, therefore, the mood is radically different as Kaṃs grabs Devakī by the hair, ready to kill. At this, Vasudev intercedes with Kaṃs, proposing to bring Devakī's offspring to Kaṃs for him to dispose of as soon as they are born. The result is that Kaṃs and Devakī are temporarily reconciled, and the artist capitalizes on the moment by showing their conversation against the background of a perfectly symmetrical Mughal garden (figure 4: 4382).

The story continues in text and icon, page by illustrated page. Vasudev does indeed bring Devakī's children to Kaṃs. The artist shows us one of those sons being delivered to Kaṃs, then carried away, presumably into captivity. As Vasudev brings another, however (4385, top), Nārad reminds Kaṃs of the gravity of the situation (4386, bottom), with the result that Kaṃs sets about to kill them all. On the next two pages, therefore, we are shown how Kaṃs receives Vasudev, takes the child in his hands despite Vasudev's entreaties, and has a servant dash it to death as if it were laundry being beaten on the steps of a streamside *ghāṭ* (figure 5: 4387).

The story proceeds with the same dense illustration. The artist accords full- or almost full-page paintings to the scenes in which Devakī takes counsel with Vasudev (4388) and then appeals to Viṣṇu, who is identified in the poem as the husband of Śrī dwelling in the Milk-Ocean (*śrīpati*, NPS

Figure 1. Frontispiece (4376). Vasiṣṭha honors Rām with a *tilak*.

Note : All illustrations come from the Bhārat Kalā Bhavan *Sūrsāgar*, whose individual pages are cited by accession number. Photographs are courtesy of Bhārat Kalā Bhavan, Banaras.

Figure 2. Parīkṣit's question to Śukdev (4377).

Figure 3. Nupital procession of Devakī and Vasudev (4380).

Figure 4. Reconciliation of Kaṃs and Devakī (4382).

Figure 5. Kaṃs receives a child of Devakī from Vasudev, then has it killed (4387).

Figure 6. Birth of Krishna (4394R).

Figure 7. Celebration in Gokul—by gods, Brahmins and others—of the birth of Krishna (4405).

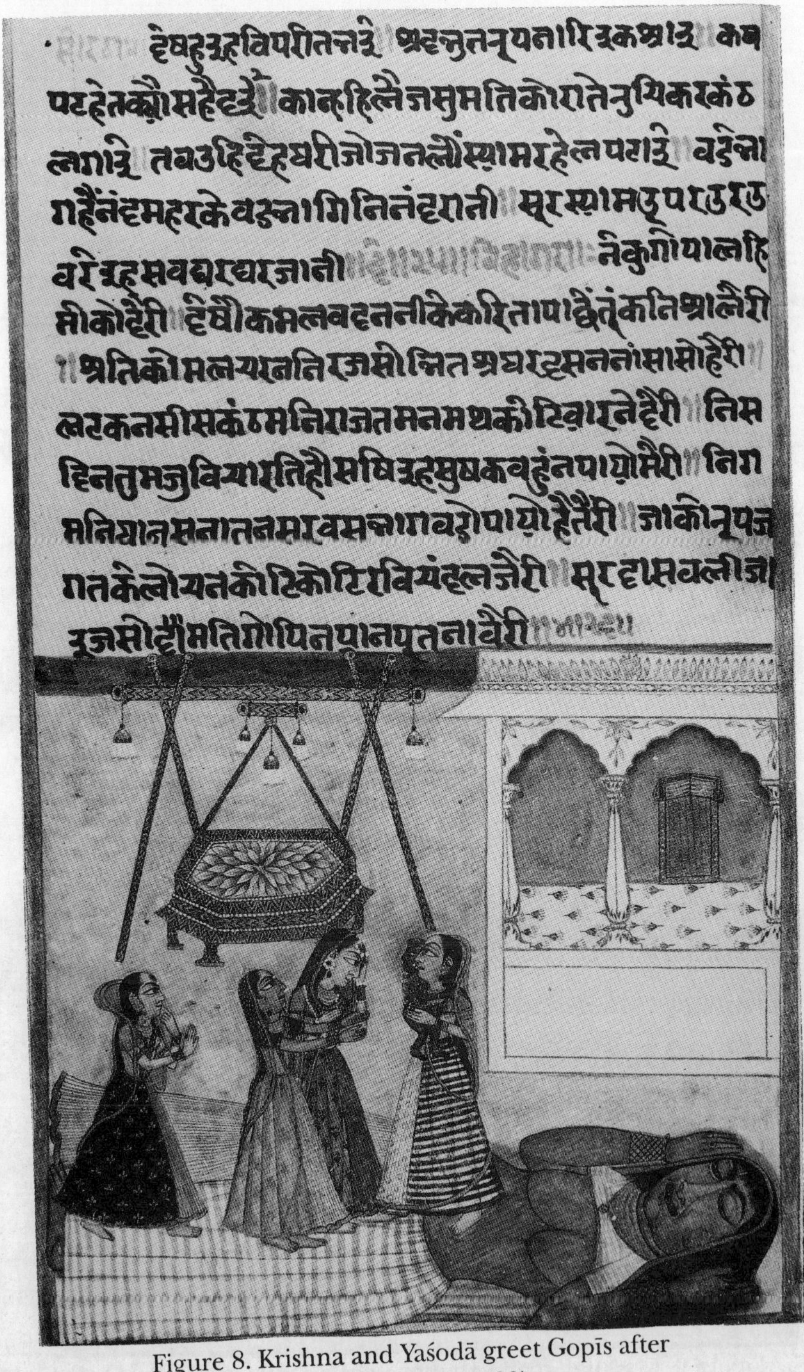

Figure 8. Krishna and Yaśodā greet Gopīs after he kills Pūtanā (4420).

Figure 9. Krishna, stealing butter, sees his reflection in a shiny pillar (4540).

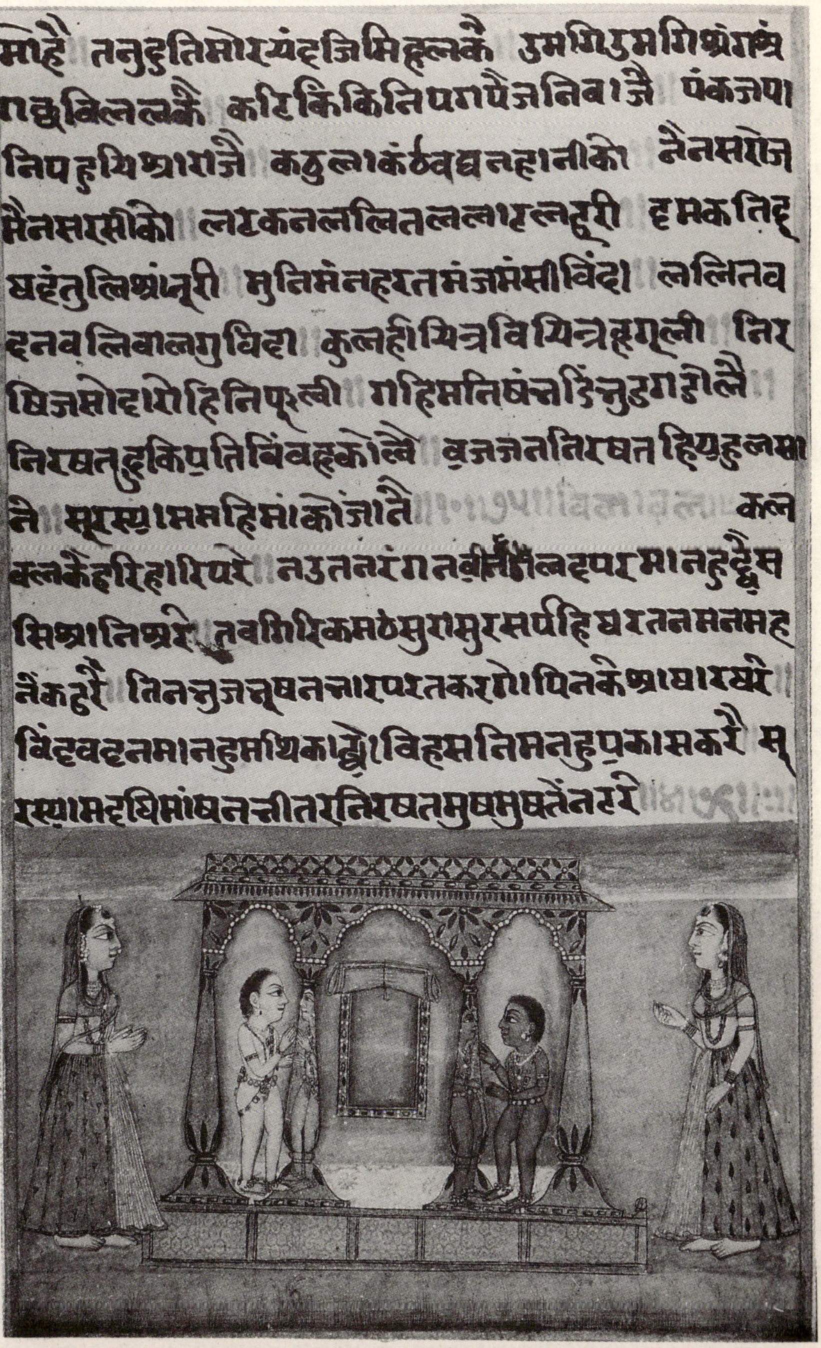

Figure 10. Balarām and Krishna see their reflections in pillars as Rukmiṇī and Yaśodā look on (4453).

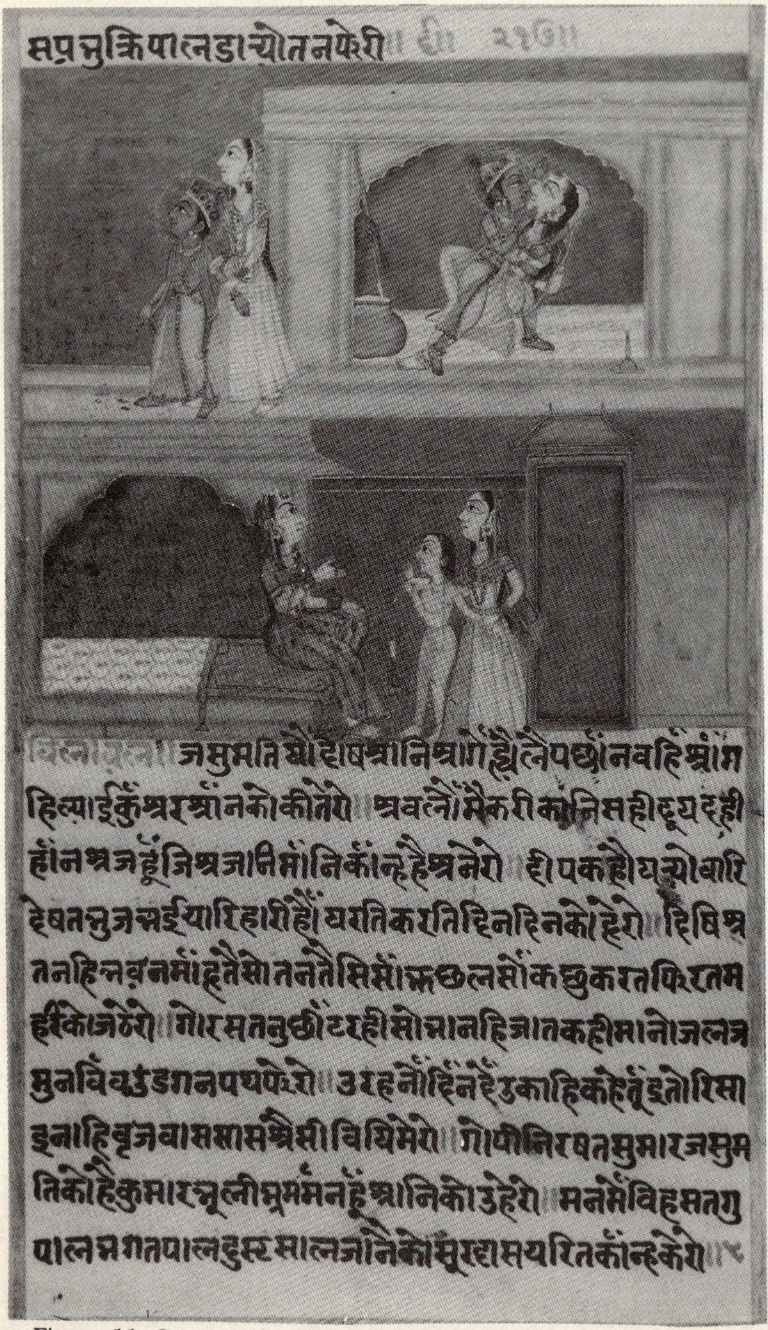

Figure 11. Gopī catches Krishna stealing butter. They embrace, and she leads him off to Yaśodā to complain (4553).

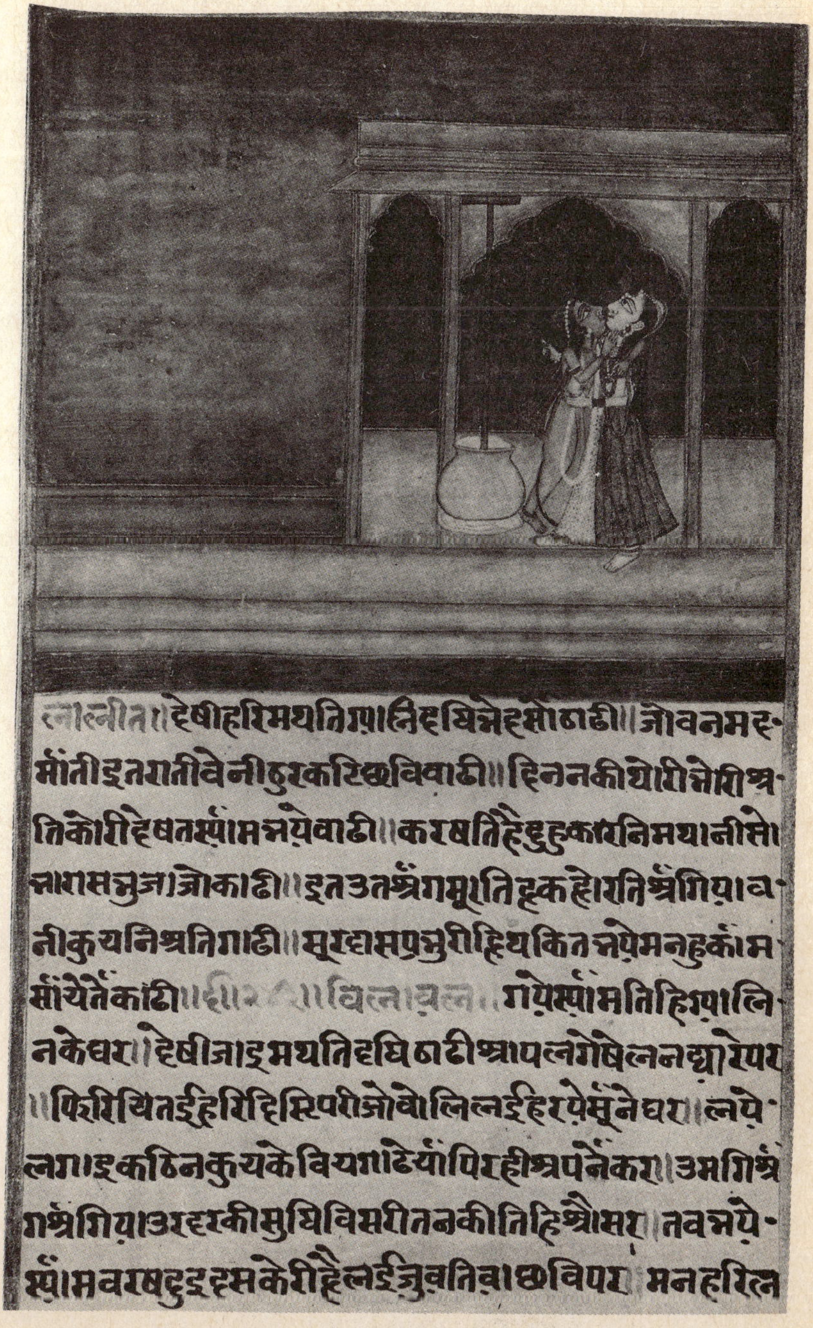

Figure 12. Krishna and Gopī embrace near a butter churn (4562R).

622:26; *chīr samudra māh̃, cf.* NPS 622:29). Sure enough, our artist confirms this identification by showing Viṣṇu recumbant at sea on the serpent Śeṣ, as Śrī massages his knee and fans him (4389). In a beautiful painting that follows on the next page, all the gods—not just Śiva and Brahmā, as the text says (NPS 622:27)—are shown assisting Devakī with her prayer. Viṣṇu pledges that he himself will descend, and from that moment Devakī's face "begins to glow" (*badana ujāro lāgyo,* NPS 622:35). It glows to the point that Kaṃs himself, on an inspection tour, notices. And well he might: for the first time, the artist shows Devakī with a halo (4391).

At that point Kaṃs lays on a stiff guard (4392), but at the critical moment the guards sleep the sleep of *māyā.* Only sages and gods (*sīv sanakādī āhi brahmādik,* NPS 622: 53) and parents are in wakeful attendance as Krishna is born. The artist shows this scene to us on facing pages. He devotes the verso side largely to the text, but saves space for a panel that shows ascetics (i.e., *sīv sanakādī?*) against a wilderness background, joining their hands in prayerful praise (4393). On the opposite page we see what they are saluting: the birth itself. Gods such as Śiva and Brahmā watch from thrones that float in the sky, while below both parents salute a four-armed Krishna, who is flanked by his winged vehicle Garuḍ (figure 6: 4394R).

This takes us through fifty-four lines of text, but there is still much more to come: the deliverance of the child to the other side of the river (4395-96), the exchange of infants (4397-99), and Kaṃs's effort to kill the child he takes to be Devakī's eighth (4400-01). Seeing the dead child rise to heaven and take its true form as a goddess, Kaṃs is penitent. He lowers his head before Devakī and Vāsudev, remembering how he has killed their other children, and remarks that what fate has ordained cannot be erased (4402). And with that he calls his astrologers to find out where Krishna is—he fears the child is still abroad—and sends out men who act like demons in slaughtering any infants who could possibly be he (4403).

At this point the poem shifts its attention to Gokul, the cowherd settlement on the other side of the Jumna, and quickly reaches its triumphant conclusion (NPS 622:75-82). Our artist's mood shifts just as quickly. It takes only a quarter of a page to record these happy, final verses, and he devotes the rest of the page to showing how the gods rain flowers and Brahmins do sacrifices while Yaśodā gazes on the newborn son she thinks is her own (figure 7, 4405, NPS 622:76, 78). Then in an admirable double-page spread that is entirely free of text and serves as the visual culmination of this poem, our painter contrasts the celebrations that occur in the women's quarters with those that occupy the men. The text strikes a fair balance between actions specific to the sexes (NPS 622:77, 81) and those that group them together (NPS 622:79), but the illustrator keeps the sexes quite separate. On the verso page (4406) he shows how the women bring potfuls of milk products, caress the head of the newborn child, embrace one another, feed the cows, lift *ārati* plates. Just opposite, on the recto side (4407), we see the men embracing, dancing to the music of drums, and receiving blessings and a *tilak* from the hands of Nanda. Some of these details are given in the text, but many others are added by the artist; and some that the text does supply—the women's insult songs, for example (NPS 662:80)—are not carried over into the painting. Yet text and image do agree on the mood: it is utterly exuberant.

Thus we have what anyone would have to call an amply illustrated poem. There are thirty-one miniature paintings in all, and many of them occupy all or most of a page. The ratio between illustrations and verses—not poems, but verses!—is better than 1:3. And then what? As on the Sabbath, our artist rests. Remarkably, he lets the next five poems go by without the slightest stroke of a brush (4407, 4408).

Simple fatigue? I think not. The poems he passes over are of the *Sūrsāgar*'s original type. They are short divertimentos, and here is the point: if they had been illustrated they would have confused the single narrative line the artist has been so at pains to establish. As independent compositions, there was no reason they should take up just where the first poem left off, so indeed they deal with such themes as Devakī's despondency and Vasudev's reassurances to her—moments that from a visual point of view have already passed. At one point the artist did leave himself some room—perhaps a third of a page (4408)—to illustrate *bhādō kī andhyārī rāt* (NPS 630), a particularly lovely poem about the dark night on which Krishna was born and one whose pedigree goes back to the earliest Sūr collections. In the end, however, the artist left the space blank. Perhaps he found he had set himself too difficult a task, for to have illustrated this poem would have been backtracking. It would have complicated the visual narrative he had established so clearly in connection with *vāla vinoda bhāvatī līlā*.

The logic, then, seems tolerably clear. Our artist is building a visual canon—something that makes sense in its own terms, apart from the text. He takes his cue from the poetry he has before him, often recording specific details, but he is not bound by his text. He may add something that it omits, as in the case of several motifs included in the celebratory scene we have just discussed. And he may omit something that, from his visual point of view, the text repeats. It is understandable that a series of originally independent poems could be inspired by a single moment in the story of Krishna, but when this happens our artist invariably finds a way not to carry this "repetition" into what he paints.

This same logic manifests itself at many points in the manuscript, though sometimes in different ways from what we have so far seen. Take for example the artist's rendering of the Pūtanā episode, in which he provides striking illustrations for four of the five poems the manuscript devotes to Krishna's infant encounter with that poisonous messenger from Kaṃs (4417-20). Figure 8 shows the last in the series (4420), which directly follows and is evidently an illustration for the poem *neku gopālahi mokõ de rī* (NPS 673). This composition—in its NPS version, which differs very minimally from what we are given in the Kalā Bhavan *Sūrsāgar*—has been translated by Kenneth Bryant (1978:48) as follows:

1 "Just give me Gopāl for a second, my friend!
2 Let me have a good look at his face,
  then I'll give him right back, my friend!
3 So soft his flower-like hands and feet,
  I just love those lips, those teeth, that
    nose, my friend!
4 His dangling locks, the jewels at his throat—
  he's the beauty of a million Kāmas, my friend!
5 I think about him night and day;
  I've never known such fortune, my friend!
6 Treasure of the Vedas, and of the sages all;
  you're just so lucky to have him, my friend!
7 He whose form, in the eyes of the world,
  shames a million suns and moons, my friend!"
8 Yaśodā, Sūr dotes on your son,
  the Gopīs' darling—and Pūtanā's foe.[14]

Bryant introduces this poem by saying that this "remarkable *pada* restricts itself to the flattery of Yaśodā, the prelude to Pūtanā's treachery" (Bryant 1978: 48). But our artist, in conformity with the position given the poem in his manuscript—that is, at the end of the Pūtanā section—apparently interprets it in quite a different way. Judging by the painting he produces, he reads it as recording not "the prelude to Pūtanā's treachery" but the completion of Krishna's victory over her. His visual interpretation takes the quotation out of Pūtanā's mouth—she had already addressed Yaśodā in the preceding illustration (4419, NPS 668)—and gives it, effectively, to several of Yaśodā's friends, whom the artist introduces into the scene for the first time here. With Pūtanā dead at their feet, the demoness can hardly be Yaśodā's interlocutor; they make far better candidates. The artist may well understand, in fact, that the quotation continues through the last verse, as it does in many other poems in the *Sūrsāgar*. In poems such as these Sūr speaks the whole poem—but for his own signature—from within the narrative confines of Krishna's world. On this pattern, the final verse would therefore read:

8 Yaśodā," says Sūr, "I dote on your son,
the Gopīs' darling and Pūtanā's foe."

This reading of the poem deadens the drama and irony that Bryant so rightly discovers in it, but from a visual point of view it accomplishes another objective. It enables the artist to provide a painting that concludes the Pūtanā episode. Here the demoness is truly and fully dead. Not only has she fallen to the ground in a faint, as in the preceding illustration, where the child sucks the lifeblood out of her, but she lies there alone while Krishna returns to his mother's arms. And the Gopīs who are Yaśodā's friends serve as witnesses to the scene, conveying the sense of wonderment that the artist evidently hopes everyone who sees this page will feel.

Here again, then, as with the first poem in the Kalā Bhavan *Sūrsāgar*, we see a triumph of narrative line, and here even more than before it is achieved by establishing a visual sequence that is not quite present in the verbal text. In fact, the situation with the Pūtanā poems is somewhat more typical for this manuscript than what we met with regard to *vāla vinoda bhāvatī līlā*, in that the raw material upon which the artist draws is a collection of short poems rather than a single, extended one. Such poems form the great bulk of this or any *Sūrsāgar*. Yet the artist's desire to depict these poems as a narrative progression not unlike that established by *vāla vinoda bhāvatī līlā* is clear. We cannot know for sure whether he was aware of sometimes doing violence to the words of the text in producing his visual canon. But given that he was probably working with a sequence of poems that had already been established in other manuscripts, and given that *Sūrsāgar* editors of this period took a growing interest in filling in the narrative holes that independent poems inevitably bequeathed to them, the answer is probably no. Nonetheless the effect is plain. There is a stark contrast between what was undoubtedly the original intention of the poem in question—the Bryant reading—and the interpretation given to it here.

Since space is limited, we must now skip forward to the end of the manuscript, to see how the story comes out. When we do so, we discover that it comes out, well, nowhere. The manuscript stops in the middle of a verse (35a) in the middle of a poem (*bhojan bhayo bhāvate mohan*, NPS 1831) that describes Krishna in the middle of a meal. Had this poem been completed, it would have been, by the scribe's count, poem no. 272. Despite the fact that it sets out an appetizing list of delicacies—just the sort of thing our artist was happy to paint elsewhere—the poem (or at least its first 35 verses) is left without any space that would have permitted an illustration. Instead, the last picture to appear in the manuscript belongs to the preceding poem (*uṭhe nandalāla sunata jananī vā̃ṇī*, NPS 1059), in which Yaśodā offers Krishna and his cowherd friends a little snack as they go out to herd the cows. And on the poems before that one, mostly poems of Krishna's *levée*, the artist was even harder at work, creating two illustrations to a page. How startling, then, when only a few pages later the music suddenly stops. Like Bach's "Art of the Fugue," our manuscript trails off to nothing in the midst of a substantial and unresolved counterpoint.

What happened? Certainly the manuscript was not intended to end here, but how far the initially projected scope would have taken it is impossible to say. If we take other *Sūrsāgar*s as our guide, we may guess that it would not have stopped with Krishna's childhood. It would have gone on to describe the thousand ins and outs of adolescent love, the Gopīs' debates with Ūdho, and Krishna's later adventures in Dvārakā and Magadha. There would also have been poems about Rām, the Ganges, the *Mahābhārata*, and the poet's own plaintive dealings with his god.

If such a projection is right—if we have been cut off in the early stages of what would have been a much longer work—then we have to ask whether the artist's own fascination with Krishna's childhood may have been his undoing. Did he lavish so much attention there that his patron's money or his own life gave out before he could finish? And if that was the case, was his own enthusiasm for the early moments in Krishna's life something idiosyncratic, or was it symptomatic of a general trend that reshaped the *Sūrsāgar* and the worship of Krishna in the eighteenth century?

Again, there is no real way to say. It is true that in this period the *Sūrsāgar* was apparently coming to be perceived as the place one went for a detailed treatment of childhood episodes in Krishna's life. By its nature the *Bhāgavata* was a more or less fixed text, while the *Sūrsāgar* could be expanded with newly composed childhood poems that would add to the corpus in this increasingly beloved area. Perhaps that is why this artist or his patron—or both—chose to illustrate the *Sūrsāgar* in the first place. And perhaps that is why they lost their interest once the bulk of the childhood material had been presented to the eye. We will never know.

Suffice it to say that this artist's depictions of some of the scenes from Krishna's infancy are among the most vivid we have. We have already looked at an example of how he treats the Pūtanā scene, and his rendering of the incident involving Tṛṇāvart is scarcely less memorable (4433).[15] These two vignettes bear the full authority of the Sanskrit pedigree provided by the *Bhāgavatapurāṇa*, where they are described, and can be seen in numerous illustrations of that text. But other moments from Krishna's infancy are also recorded in the *Sūrsāgar*, and our artist delights in giving these visual form as well. The time when little Krishna demands the moon for a plaything is one such scene: this incident was well known to Tamil speakers many centuries before Sūr but apparently never achieved Sanskrit status.[16]

And the rather mysterious episode involving a crow-demon (*kāgāsur-badh*, as the NPS editors call it), which is also absent from the *Bhāgavata*, is similarly well illustrated.[17]

Among the scenes that are not contained in the *Bhāgavata-purāṇa* and other Sanskrit sources, is a vignette that affords the opportunity to see Krishna twice and must therefore have been particularly attractive to a visual artist. This is the moment in which Krishna looks at his own reflection in a highly polished pillar (*maṇikhambh*), thus providing the onlooker with a chance for two *darśans* at once. In the *rās līlā* plays of modern Brindavan much is made of this episode, and it is understood to form a part of the general narrative in which Krishna steals butter from the houses of various Gopīs. The little thief takes his reflection as another little boy who is watching him; he fears that he has been caught in the act.

This scene is duly portrayed by the artist of the Kalā Bhavan *Sūrsāgar* when he encounters a sequence of poems (NPS 882- 883) that describe this *līlā* (figure 9, 4540). What is especially interesting, however, is that he also gives us a similar scene elsewhere, at quite a different point in the manuscript. The poem *ā̃gan khele nand ke nand* ("Nanda's Joy plays in the courtyard," NPS 735), which occurs much earlier in the collection (as poem no. 75), provides him with another chance for a *maṇikhambh* miniature, and he seizes upon the opportunity with an eagerness that is perhaps best explained by the intrinsic visual fascination of this motif. The poem in question touches on a variety of themes and could have been illustrated in a number of ways, but our artist focuses on the passage that describes how Krishna and Balarām used the pillars in their courtyard to pull themselves from a crawl to a standing position, then practised their half-shaped childhood vocables in the mirrors the pillars so conveniently provided (figure 10, 4453). Interestingly, the artist had to double back to include this moment among his miniatures. The space that had been left blank for a painting actually comes after the next poem in the sequence (*kala bala ke hari hāri pare*, NPS 759). The artist had to leave that poem unillustrated so that he could present the *maṇikhambh* moment instead.

Clearly he loved his visions of Krishna as a little child. One is tempted to suggest that he was the sort of devotee who preferred the language of *vātsalya bhāva*, the parental emotion, to that of *mādhurya*, the erotic mood. Sūr himself was increasingly cast in this role, and Vallabhācārya, his supposed teacher, along with him. But let us not jump to this conclusion ourselves before considering another aspect of the series of paintings that depict Krishna as a thief of butter.

Certainly the butter thief presented a fine childhood subject, and our artist accords him a fair amount of attention. For instance, he gives full play to a poem (*gvālini ghara gae jāni sā̃jh kī ādherī*, NPS 893) in which we learn how much each of the Gopīs secretly wished Krishna would come steal butter from her. Then he goes on to show how they marched him off to Yaśodā to complain of his exploits when he did (figure 11, 4553; *jasumati dhō dekhi āni*, NPS 894). We see the culprit being led away in the upper frame. Yet what we also see in the upper frame is that there is something not entirely childish about all this, and this amorous note is one that the artist is inserting on his own. There is no textual warrant in the poem.

That does come in time, with a pair of compositions (NPS 907, 916) that he chooses to illustrate several pages later. Both are poems that appear in the *Sūrsāgar* only at about this point in the history of its growth, and both are poems that could have been illustrated by drawing attention to a number of different details. But our artist, apparently riding the wave of his age, depicted both with a version of the scene we see in figure 12 (4562R; *mathati gvāli hari dekhī jāt*, NPS 916). Here Krishna's aggressive search for butter is paired up with his equally aggressive search for love, that is, for a kiss from the Gopī who appears on the scene to remonstrate. Or so it seems, for both scenes of embrace seem to imply that if Krishna got something he wanted, the Gopīs got something they wanted too. And this tends to exculpate Krishna of any wrongdoing, a point that is increasingly and plainly made in poems added to the *Sūrsāgar* in this period.[18]

There may be yet another reason why our artist was so eager to display this simultaneous thief of butter and hearts: once again, it may have suited his narrative needs. In a much earlier sequence concerning rituals of infancy (4412-14) he had selected details that would allow him first to prepare his visual space with auspicious *aśok* leaves (4412), then fill it with musicians (4413), then welcome the astrologer Garga as a musician himself (4414).[19] Here in the same way, even some pages before the manuscript breaks off, he may have been setting the stage for the amorous poetry that would soon have filled many more of its lovely pages if...but we do not really know if what.

NOTES

1. I wish to acknowledge the great courtesy and generosity of Bhārat Kalā Bhavan, which have made the writing of this essay possible. I am particularly indebted to Mr. O. P. Tandan, the administrative officer in charge; to Dr. T. K. Biswas, the museum's director; and to Drs. Sarla Chopra and Prakash Rao, who discussed various points concerning the manuscript in question. Others to whom I owe a debt of gratitude are Daniel Ehnbom and Andrew Topsfield, whose expertise in the field far exceeds my own, and who have been kind enough to comment on drafts of this essay. I am also grateful to Edwin Bryant, who kindly facilitated communication with Bhārat Kalā Bhavan at a time when I could not travel myself, and to Joachim Bautze for information about the Heil collection. The plates presented here were provided through the courtesy of Bhārat Kalā Bhavan. I am grateful for permission to reproduce them.
2. This manuscript is no. 951 in the collection of the erstwhile Datia State Library, now housed at the Government Degree College, Datia. It consists of 1028 folios and credits itself with 10,038 *pads*. Owing to misnumberings, however, 219 should be subtracted from that total, and very occasionally the compositions of other poems than those attributed to Sūrdās are included in the sum.

3. A facsimile of this manuscript, written at Fatehpur, is found in Bahura 1982.
4. I adopt the dating of Andrew Topsfield (1992), arrived at in conversation with Robert Skelton, and am grateful to Topsfield for directing me to printed sources where a number of examples of these paintings may be seen: Welch 1985, cat. no. 231; Chandra 1981, pl. 2; Archer 1957a, pl. 6; Archer 1957b, pl. 29; Archer 1957c, cat. nos. 26-29; Rawson 1961, p. 125.
5. One of the Bickford pages, in which the kiss of Krishna as a child is compared to his kiss as a man, is reproduced in Hawley 1984: 34. The same page also appears in Czuma 1975: fig. 62. A detail from a page of a *Sūrsāgar* in the Nasli and Alice Heeramaneck Collection of the Los Angeles County Museum of Art appears in Hawley 1984: 162. This detail shows the poet observing the *līlā* of Rādhā and Krishna in their bower. The page from which it is drawn, a "twin" to the one reproduced in Spink 1971: fig. 104, whose whereabouts I do not now know, shows a whole series of encounters between Krishna and Rādhā. I am grateful to Joachim Bautze (in a letter dated March 27, 1992) for making me aware of the page in the Heil collection, which is an illustration for the well known poem *braj bhayo mahar ke pūt*, about which we will soon have more to say. Other published *Sūrsāgar* illustrations have been drawn to my attention by Andrew Topsfield (1992), as follows: Gangoly 1961, pl. 40a; Spink 1971, fig. 26 (now in the San Diego Museum of Art); Pal 1978, cat. no. 28; Topsfield 1980, nos. 62, 96, 97, cf. 110; Heeramaneck 1984, pl. 44; Lee and Montgomery 1960, no. 18 (now in the National Gallery, Ottawa).
6. For two early descriptions of how those families might look in the case of the *Sūrsāgar*, see Bryant 1980: 5-12 and Bryant's essay, "The Manuscript Tradition of the Sūrsāgar: The Fatehpur Manuscript," in Bahura 1982: xiv-xvi. Bryant has expanded and refined these insights over the years, and will present his results in his critical edition of the early poems of Sūrdās (Bryant forthcoming).
7. VS 1813. Vrindaban Research Institute microform 1201, from the collection of Harishamkar Das, Vrindaban.
8. For purposes of identification here and throughout the essay, I adopt the system of enumeration used by Bhārat Kalā Bhavan, which proceeds by accession number. In quoting the *Sūrsāgar*, the text at hand, rather than any printed edition, is used. That text, however, is identified by means of the

number assigned to the corresponding verse or poem in the standard two-volume Nāgarīpracāriṇī Sabhā edition of 1972/1976. The cumulative NPS number, not the *skandha* number, is cited.

9. Particular thanks are due to Sarla Chopra for help in identifying the figures depicted in this painting. As a solution to the discontinuity between Rām and Krishna, she suggests that the frontispiece may have been painted at a later date than the remainder of the manuscript.
10. The person who determined the manuscript's design may be the artist or may be someone independent of him. The artist, in turn, may or may not be the same person as one of the scribes. For simplicity's sake, nonetheless, let us here speak as if the artist were the agent.
11. The manuscript is U1, now in the collection of the Rajasthan Oriental Research Institute, Udaipur. For details, see Hawley 1984: 54-55.
12. I am grateful to Joachim Bautze (1992) for supplying me with a photocopy of this illustrated *braj bhayo mahar ke pūt*.
13. B4, now in the Anup Sanskrit Library, Bikaner. See Hawley 1984: 45-47.
14. Bryant, *Poems to the Child-God*, p. 48.
15. This is published as figure 22 in Hawley 1987: 160.
16. See Hawley 1983: 248-251 and figure 39, which reproduces illustration 4489 of the Kalā Bhavan manuscript. The illustration accompanies NPS 808 (*āche mere lālana aisī ārī na kījai*).
17. 'Ratnakar,' Vajapeyi, et al. 1972: 281; Hawley 1987: figures 24 (4421-22) and 25 (4423-24).
18. As against earlier poems, in which studied care is taken not to justify Krishna's actions on the basis of the Gopis' desires (see Hawley 1983: 122-134).
19. This painting, an illustration for NPS 703 (*mahara bhavana riṣirāja gae*), is reproduced in colour on the cover of *Songs of the Saints of India* (Hawley and Juergensmeyer 1988).

BIBLIOGRAPHY OF THE WORKS CITED

Archer, W.G. 1957a. *Indian Painting: Fifteen Colour Plates*. New York: Oxford University Press.

——, 1957b. *The Loves of Krishna*. London: George Allen & Unwin.

——, 1957c. *Indian Paintings from Rajasthan: Catalogue of an Exhibition of Works from the Collection of Sri Gopi Krishna Kanoria of Calcutta*. London: Council of Great Britain.

Bahura, Gopal Narayan (ed.). 1982 (actually published 1984). *Pad Sūrdāsjī kā/The Padas of Surdas.* With an introductory essay by Kenneth E. Bryant. Jaipur: Maharaja Sawai Man Singh II Museum.

Bautze, Joachim K. 1992. Personal communication, June 24.

Bryant, Kenneth E. 1978. *Poems to the Child-God: Structures and Strategies in the Poetry of Sūrdās.* Berkeley: University of California Press.

——, 1980. "Toward a Critical Edition of the *Sūrsāgar.*" In W.M. Callewaert, ed. *Early Hindi Devotional Literature in Current Research.* Leuven: Departement Orientalistiek, Katholieke Universiteit.

——, Forthcoming. *The Poems of Sūrdās*, volume 1. (Volume 2, containing translations and annotations, is by J.S. Hawley)

Chandra, Moti. 1981. *Mewar Painting.* New Delhi: Lalit Kala Akademi.

Czuma, Stanislaw. 1975. *Indian Art from the George P. Bickford Collection.* Cleveland: Cleveland Museum of Art.

Gangoly, O.C. 1961. *Critical Catalogue of Miniature Paintings in the Baroda Museum.* Baroda: Government Press.

Hawley, John Stratton. 1983. *Krishna, the Butter Thief.* Princeton: Princeton University Press.

——, 1984. *Sur Das: Poet, Singer, Saint.* Seatttle: University of Washington Press, and Delhi: Oxford University Press.

——, 1987. (actually published 1989). "Krishna and the Birds." *Arts Orientalis* 17, pp. 139-161.

Hawley, John Stratton and Mark Juergensmeyer. 1988. *Songs of the Saints of India.* New York: Oxford University Press.

Heeramaneck, Alice. 1984. *Masterpieces of Indian Painting from the Former Collections of Nasli M. Heeramaneck.* New York: Advent Books.

Lee, Sherman E., and George Montgomery. 1960. *Rajput Painting.* New York: Asia House.

Pal, Pratapaditya. 1978. *The Classical Tradition in Rajput Painting: From the Paul F. Walter Collection.* New York: Pierpont Morgan Library and Gallery Association of New York State.

'Ratnākar' (Jagganāth Dās), Nandadulāre Vājapeyī, et. al. 1972 (vol. 1), 1976 (vol. 2). *Sūr Sāgar.* 2nd edn., Vārāṇasī: Kāśī Nāgarīpracāriṇī Sabhā.

Rawson, Philip. 1961. *Indian Painting.* Paris: P. Tisne and New York: Universe Books.

Spink, Walter. 1971. *Krishnamandala, a Devotional Theme in Indian Art.* Ann Arbor: Centre for South and South East Asian Studies.

Topsfield, Andrew. 1980. *Paintings from Rajasthan in the National Gallery of Victoria.* Melbourne: National Gallery of Victoria.

——, 1992. Personal communication, July 2.

Welch, Stuart Cary. 1985. *India: Art and Culture 1300-1900.* New York: Metropolitan Museum of Art

An Early Nineteenth-Century Collection of Hindi Devotional Poems

R.S.McGregor

W. Price's anthology entitled *Hindee and Hindoostanee Selections* (Calcutta, 1830) contains a lithographed collection of some 200 poems (pp.223-50) entitled *sādhāran hindī gān.* Eighty of the poems are named as *padas*, 10 others as *viṣṇupadas* or *dhurpadas*; many of the *padas* are ascribed to Sūrdās, and a few to other authors. About 40 poems are classed by theme, under titles such as *hōli, badhāvā/ mubārakbād*, etc. A few poems are given under *malār rāg, ṭhumrī* and *khiyāl.* The rest arc popular *ṭappā* songs.

It may be assumed in default of evidence to the contrary that Price (1780-1830), who was a teacher at Fort William College, was not responsible in the first instance for the selection of the poems. The poems are, in that case, all the more useful evidence for the content and character of early nineteenth-century popular poetry in the form of songs.[1] This paper will begin an examination of the themes found in the poems and of their treatment, concentrating on the songs of devotional type, with the aim of throwing light on the later evolution of devotional attitudes in north India and on their forms of expression.

1. STRUCTURE OF THE COLLECTION

The 80 *padas* with four *viṣṇupadas* and six *dhrupadas* *(dhurpada)* make *padas* the best represented song type in the collection. About half of the *padas*, with most of the *viṣṇupadas* and *dhurpadas*, are placed within the first quarter of the text (41 out of the first 49 verses). A further quarter (20) of the *padas* occur in an unbroken sequence at the end. The remaining *padas* are placed in four small groups (of from eight down to two verses) between the groups of other song types that make up the rest of the collection: *hōli/horī* (18, with one *hiṇḍol*); *badhāvā/mubārakbād* (5/1); *malār* (2); *khiyāl, kaharvā* and *ḍomra* (9, 2, 1); *ṭappā* and *ṭhumrī* (68, 6). *Asthāī* lines and *antarā* sections are designated for each song, throughout the text.

The above arrangement, being more than casual, suggests that the compiler of the collection was familiar with the major song types and their subject matter, and was concerned to give prominence to the *padas*: songs of predominantly religious character. The respective numbers of the different song types would seem to bear this out, as does the positioning of the *ṭappā* songs (songs of essentially secular character, and the only group to rival that of the *padas* in size) so far towards the end (yet not *at* the end) of the collection. Noting these features of arrangement of the collection we will be justified, when examining the *padas* to assess the devotional attitudes which they reflect, in paying particular attention to the concluding group of verses.

2. LANGUAGE OF THE *PADAS*

The language of the *padas* is essentially a Sanskritised Brajbhāṣā of a rather mixed, and late type reflecting an appreciable grammatical impact of Khaṛī bolī. Thus the postpositions *ne* and *ko* (oblique case marker) occur occasionally in the text (7, 8,[2] 28; 14, 196); masculine perfectives in *-ā* (*lagāyā, 9; khāyā, 109*); masculine nouns in *-ā* (*khilaunā, 18*); the pronouns *koī*, 49 &c., *tumhaiṁ*, 189; the future in *-go* (21); and the emphatic form *hai gī*, 43.

There is a small amount of regional variation having an eastern tendency (diminutives in *-vā*, 88, 90;? the pronouns *morī, torī*, 6 &c.; the possessive postposition *kerā*, 190), and an occasional Panjabi element (the participles *pīndā, khāndā*, 61; the postposition *nūṃ*, 39;? the oblique plural in *-ā(m)*, 190).

A more significant component of this mixed language is its Arabic and Persian vocabulary, rather greater in extent than what is typically found in the Brajbhāṣā texts of the 16th and 17th centuries. Some examples are: *nāhak*, 45, 10; *mard*, 58, 185; *naubat*, 3, and the hybrid compound *non-harāmī*, 19. Use of masculine plural concord with a feminine subject pronoun (*ham bhaye*, 12) similarly seems to illustrate the impact of Khaṛī bolī-based Urdu.

The following passages illustrate grammatical and lexical mixing of the above kinds in the language of the text:

> *tero ahisān rī piyā ko milā de* 11(Brbh., Khb., Arabic) 'by your kindness unite (me) with my beloved';
> *pahruvā tū jāg re...torī nagrī meṁ āyā cor* 88 (?E. Brbh., Khb.) 'watchman, awake!... a thief has come to your town';
> *hama nāhaka jaihaiṁ pakre* 45 (Brbh., Arabic) 'I would be wrong to (hope to) catch it'.

The Sanskritic component of the text shows a rather high proportion of *tatsama* spellings as opposed to semi-*tatsamas*, e.g. *vyākula*, 2; *aṣṭagāndha, puṣpa*, 6; *vṛthā*, 14; *mukhārvinda*, 23. &c.; *krodha, tṛṣṇā-*, 109; *kṛpā*, 190; *kaṣṭa*, 192. Conversely, the text of v.16 avoids the old *tadbhāva* form *loi* 'people' found in earlier versions of this verse.[3] The tendency to increased Sanskritisation seems to reflect a reaction among Hindi speakers, especially in urban areas, to new conditions of the mid- to late 18th century in which they were encountering increased numbers of Persian and Arabic words and expressions as Urdu developed.[4]

The mixed language of the songs illustrates what might be expected in a late development of Brajbhāṣā as a vehicle for popular poetry, emancipated to some extent from the stylistic norms of earlier Kṛṣṇa poetry and competing to reflect contemporary attitudes with the new Urdu of the 18th century in urban as well as country contexts.

3. THE *PADAS* ASSIGNED TO AUTHORS, AND THEIR TEXT

Twenty-eight verses are ascribed by *bhaṇitā* to known poets: sixteen to Sūrdās, five to Kabīr, two to Keśavdās and Tulsīdās and one each to Mīrābāī, Parmānanddās and Haridas Svāmī. The identity of 'Viṣṇudās' (vv.6 and 8) is uncertain.

Of the 'Sūrdās' verses, as few as four correspond to *padas* listed in the standard edition (SS) of *Sūrsāgar*;[5] but of these four, three prove to be recorded in old (pre-AD 1700) manuscripts.[6] A comparison of the readings of the latter three *padas* with the *Sūrsāgar* text and with accessible information about the early manuscripts readings illustrates that not only details of wording but also ideas, transmitted via changed wording, could be passed down reasonably intact from the early Sūrdās *pada* tradition to the 19th century.[7] On the other hand, the number of otherwise unrecorded verses or versions of verses in our material illustrates the great extent to which innovation continued within the Sūrdās inventory, and suggests that new elements arising within the evolving tradition were at risk of being transmitted in increasingly corrupt form.[8]

Of the five verses ascribed to Kabīr, none corresponds to *padas* listed in Tivārī's edition of Kabīr. For all Kabīr's fame, an accurate tradition of his verses was clearly not accessible to the compiler of the collection. Of the two 'Keśavdās' verses, v.40 from *Rasik-priyā* is transmitted fairly accurately, though without full understanding,[9] v.46 amounts to not much more than a list of categories of heroines: *khaṇḍitā, adhīnapaṭikā, kalahāntaritā, &c.* Keśavdās verses, though evidently accessible, were perhaps not of much general interest and may have been represented in this popular collection for form's sake only.

Tulsīdās, though less well represented by *bhaṇitā* even than Kabīr and Keśavdās, probably had a greater influence than either on the authors of the songs. Apart from the general influence of *Rām-carit-mānas* in inculcating the religion of Rām, which may be assumed, one of the verses ascribed here to Tulsīdās contains a clear echo of a *Rām-carit-mānas* passage[10], and one other verse (see 4,1 below) contains a pointed quotation from *Rām-carit-mānas*.

4. SUBJECT MATTER OF THE *PADAS*

Some ten separate themes can be distinguished. All except the two minor items 7. and 8. are introduced within the first 20 verses of the collection.

1. *Devotion to Rām.* The first verse of the collection deals with the Name of Rām, *rāma japu rāma japu rāma japu bāvare* (other verses taking up this theme are 43, 62, 190). V. 62 on the devotee's absorption in Rām, *mere mana rāma rāma aura nāhiṁ koī,* throws light on the modern status of the teaching of the Name: *aba to bāta phaila gaī jāne sabai koī.* Consorting with the good is felt here to be of no significance and to be even harmful compared to devotion to Rām, (*santana ḍhiga baiṭha baiṭha loka lāja khoī);* but a different view is given in v. 190. V. 44 attributes devotion to the Name of Rām to Sūrdās, *rāma sumira kyau na leta;* the older tradition of Sūrdās' *bhakti* extending to Rām is accurately preserved here. In v.202 Sītā is presented as source of Sūrdās' well-being, with a similar implication.[11] V. 43 on the topic of Rāma and the boatman Guha confirm that both this context, and the *Rām-carit-mānas* text describing it, were familiar.[12] V. 35

echoes another well-known *Rām-carit-mānas* context (see section 3 above). V. 59, a *savaiyā* on the waking of the child Kṛṣṇa, *jāgiye kṛpā nidhāna, jāna rāya rāmacandra* shows the Kṛṣṇa emphasis found already in Tulsīdās' handling of this theme.

2. Virah, *and the* Bhramargīt *theme.* More verses deal with *virah* than with any other topic (at least 12[13]; over 20, if verses on *Bhramargīt* subject matter are counted). V. 2 introduces the *Bhramargīt* theme of the abandoned *gopīs* (others, 10, 42, 54). In vv.54 and 193 the Kṛṣṇa aspect of the theme is widened with references of *Smārta* type to sacrifice, and to self-immolation of the devotee at Banaras, (*kāsī jāya karavaṭa līnoṁ*); and more pessimistically, to the inability of observances to bring freedom from sin. The *Bhāgavata purāṇa* is by an error revealing of a modern perspective called *Bhāgavata gītā purāṇa* (193). Uddhav is mentioned specifically in one verse (5), and alluded to in others (141,201) as the bringer of Kṛṣṇa's message about knowledge of the unqualified and qualified.

3. *Mythological references.*

(a) Śiva. Vv 58 and 185, which must descend from a common source, deal with the fearsome aspect of Śiva. The distinctive Persian vocabulary of the opening phrase of both, *eka marda tana garda*...and the occurrence of an identical half-line in both, *prāta samaiṁ guna gāyā (gāyau) rī*, make the relationship between the verses clear. V. 185 gives the more detailed description of Śiva and stresses Śiva's prestige, *sadāśiva sura nara muni bhāyau*, as well as bringing out an element of opposition between Śiva and Braj-oriented worship, *bikaṭa rūpa...dekhi braja logana śora macāyau.*

(b) Gaṇeś. V. 55 presenting Gaṇeś as the patron of beginnings associates him with both Rām and Kṛṣṇa, (*thaṇḍhī rāmu sukha bhagata rahana do kisanacanda se hauṁ caranāyaka*).

(c) Ganges. The stream is blessed and (by word-play on

meanings of the word *dhār*) 'a saw allowing sin to be cut away', *dhane dhana gaṅgājī kī dhārā pāpa kaṭana kau ārā*, v.60; as well as a symbol of *mokṣa*, fourth of the four fruits of life.

(d) Sītā. V. 203 (the second of two consecutive verses on Sītā) seems to illustrate transmission of the story of her abduction via *Rām-carit-mānas*, and with some corruption: for Mārīca did not assume a deer's body as an 'armour', *kavaca mṛga mārīca dhāryau bapu*, but as a deception *(kapaṭa mṛga bhaeu)*.[14]

(e) Dvārakā. A fine picture is presented of the splendour of Dvārakā as seen by Sudāmā, *nagarī kī sobhā dekhata duja kī sudha bisarāī* (v.8, attributed to Viṣṇudās).

4. Nīti, *or* cetāvanī. Several verses counsel religious or moral enlightenment, or simple prudence. Vv. 13 and 44 urge reform of life while time remains, and mindfulness of Hari[15] or Rām, and the vanity of the world. V. 36 (corrupt text) is pessimistic about the prospect of rebirth. In v.37 the soul personified as feminine searches for the city of mercy (*dayāpurī*) where the citizens (*sādh[u] sant)* are ruled by knowledge (*jñān*), while corrupt officials of the city symbolise human vices. V.38 attributed to Kabīr uses a simple *ulaṭbāṁsī* symbolism, that of a backgammon game played in a spirit of *vairāg* with the Beloved[16], who inspires the renunciant to closure of the senses' doors, (*pī ke mana te nija mana ko juga bāṁdhyau dasau duvārai*). Vv.88 and 92 are secular in character.

5. *Hari.* The unqualified and qualified aspects of Hari (Bhagvān), and a connection between them, are clearly recognised. V.14 shows Hari's mind (*khyāl*) as unknowable by the intelligence, *buddhi pahuṁcegī nāṁhīṁ*, and Gopāl as source of prospective joy (*sukha sapane*); hence 'be mindful of the Lord', *mana te sumira bhagavāna ko.* Vv. 197 and 200 contrast Hari's nature and his supreme status with

the concepts of *śruti* and *smṛti*, and the status of Śiva and Brahmā: *śruti and smṛti* may be accepted (it is implied) but why forget Hari's name, and his might as made known to Pūtanā and to Kaṁsa? (200), *śiva brahmā jāko dhyāna dharata hai beda sumṛti hai bānī: so tū kyauṁ hari nāma bisārata* (197). V. 200 takes as its starting-point the phrase *abigat[i] gati* used by 'Sūrdās' (later manuscripts, v.1) in defining Kṛṣṇa's unqualified aspect, and moves to emphasising the qualified aspect on broadly similar lines to v.197.

6. *The child Kṛṣṇa.* Aspects represented are: Kṛṣṇa's waking (16, 27); learning to walk (24); asking for the moon to play with (45); eating curds (23, 61); Kṛṣṇa's physical beauty (22, 25, 189 and passim); the *dadhi-līlā* (15, 53, 106); Kṛṣṇa and Balrām quarreling (187); and Kṛṣṇa's departure with Balrām for Mathura (194). In the *padas* featuring Yaśodā and Nand *vātsalya bhāva* is prominent. V. 194 (on the perils facing Kṛṣṇa and Balrām in Mathura) is a highly effective dramatic monologue. This verse is to be connected with *Bhāgavata purāṇa* X. 39 and the theme of the *gopīs*' lament before Kṛṣṇa's departure. V.106 (*dadhi-līlā*) is similarly dramatic.

7. *Rādhā-Kṛṣṇa, and the sakhīs*. This topic receives perhaps less attention than that of the child Kṛṣṇa. V. 17 is a simple description of Rādhā's beauty and the *bhāva* of her dance with Kṛṣṇa (Lālan). V. 21 shows '*catur chabīlī*' Rādhā with the *sakhīs*, preparing an assignation with Kṛṣṇa. Haridās Svāmī's *pada* (v.39) evokes the 'deadly beauty' (*nain kaṭārī-sī*) of Candrāvalī (Candrasakhī) in the *abhisāra* context in a way reminiscent of Sufi metaphor. The same *sakhī*'s passion of *virah* is the subject of v.198. V.33 deals with the *sakhīs*' (or Rādhā's) devotion for Gopīnāth/Kanhāī. Other verses on the *sakhīs* include vv. 18 and 22. V. 28 attributed to Mīrābāī describes the *sakhīs* weighing Kṛṣṇa on the scale of their love, *hamane apane kāṁṭe prema ke liyā dhāri tola rī govindā.* V. 48 evokes the mood of spring, and Holī dance of *sakhīs* and *sahelīs*.

8. *Sectarian awareness.* V.191 ascribed to the Vallabhan Parmānanddās contains an appropriate Vallabhan emphasis in its reference to residence in Vṛndāvan.

9. *Secular love.* Any clear distinction between religious and secular love remains as difficult to draw in most of the poetry of this collection as in earlier *bhakti* poetry. Some verses are undoubtedly secular, however, e.g. vv. 29, 49, 90, 91. A few verses show some influence from poetic theory, e.g. 90 and 91 (*abhisāra*); 185 (*hāva, bhāva*) and the verses attributed to Keśavdās (see above, section 3).

10. *Parameśvar.* The verses where the Supreme Being is seen as 'Lord' (*sāhib*) show affinities with the *nirguṇī* and Sant approaches in assigning qualities of *jñān* (192) or *sāṁcā* (19, 204) to the Supreme Being; this Being is seen as all-pervasive, *ghaṭa ghaṭa raha samāī* 109, *ghaṭa ghaṭa basai nirantara* 204; as '*guru*' in v. 109; and in v.204, the last of the collection, as *parameśvar. Parameśvar* here subsumes explicitly the roles of Śiva, Brahmā and the avatārs of Viṣṇu. Elsewhere, however, the *saccā* and *jñānī sāhib* stands closer to Viṣṇu in mercy, benevolence and in receiving the love of devotees conscious of their unworthiness, *tumharī mihira sahāya hamārī; sāhiba dhanī pyāro tumahīṁ kaṣṭa haryau mere sāhiba saba adṛṣṭa nibāre* (192; also 19). In v. 188 the *nāyak* and *sāhib* who maintains Vedas and Purāṇas, *veda purānana hota nibere,* acts and causes, *saba hota kiye saba terai,* and supports the destitute, *bin[a] ṭhākura ko sahāyaka cere* is seen finally as approachable only with the grace of Hari, *śri rasaraṅga dayā hari ke binu koū nikaṭa na āvai terai.*

V.196 attributed to Kabīr is unique in the collection in its expression of spiritual uncertainty and despair at the end of life. The soul is personified as both feminine and masculine. Service, and submissive worship (*sevā, pūjā, bandagī*) are at an end and no confidence is now placed in serving a guru or in the fellowship of the good (*sādhu kī saṅgati*); one's loved parents have died, *māta pitā ko apnā samujhe koī, doū hari-dhāma gaye* and one relies on husband's relatives or on wife and son(s) largely in vain. Is it not too late to repent? Unless one is wedded to the Lord (the verse concludes) there is no true happiness, *suno santau vina sāṁīṁ koī sohāga na hoī.*

CONCLUSION

The collection ilustrates that *pada* traditions, especially those of Kṛṣṇa *padas*, continued to evolve freely down to the 19th century, yet that contact was kept with their older forms. There had been a more direct transmission of Tulsīdās's reworking of the Rām tradition, in which north Indian Sant teachings and Smārta attitudes had been largely subsumed. There was a consciousness of the relative newness of this modern religion of Rām that had, by now, become firmly established; and, it seems, a sense of its vitality. On the other hand, the approximation between aspects of Kṛṣṇa and Rām religion seen in Tulsīdās' poetry evidently continued. With a waning of the *bhakti* impulse, Smārta elements appear to take a somewhat larger place alongside Kṛṣṇa and, especially, Rām elements, than had been the case in earlier devotional poetry more specifically oriented towards Kṛṣṇa and Rām. The small, but distinct place given to Śiva is notable in this material. Yet finally a Vaiṣṇava emphasis remains dominant in it.

NOTES

1. For French translations from this collection by Garcin de Tassy, see Sayida Surriya Husain, *Garcin de Tassy, Biographie et étude critique de ses oeuvres*, Pondichéry, 1962, p. 85.
2. In v.8. perhaps a scribe's or other late alteration of a text originally without *ne*, following on a pronunciation change in a loanword: *bis[?v] akarmā <ne>āpa banāī.*
3. Cf. *Sūr-sāgar* [SS], ed. Nanddulāre Vājpeyī et al., 4th ed., Banaras, 1965, v.828.

4. *Cf.* R.S.McGregor, 'Some material bearing on the early history of Sanskritised prose style in Hindi dialects', *Indian Linguistics*, XXX, 1969, p. 69.
5. See n. 3.
6. John Stratton Hawley, 'The early *Sūr Sāgar* and the growth of the Sūr tradition', Journal of the American Oriental Society, 99.1 1979, p. 64ff.; details of *padas* in MSS predating VS 1763 communicated by Professor Hawley.
7. E.g. v.187, *cf.* SS v.783.
8. A good example in v. 186, *cf.* SS v.830.
9. *Cf. Rasik-priyā*, ed. Viśvanāthprasād Miśra, *Keśavgranthāvalī*, I, Allahabad, 1954, p. 8.
10. V. 35; cf. *Rām-carit-mānas* [RCM], ed. Śambhunārāyaṇ Caube, Banaras, 1948, II. p. 4.
11. Our verse, with its *bhaṇitā* line *ceta cita sūra sītā hita mero*, goes beyond SS v.506 (an old verse) in its suggestion of Rāmaite devotion.
12. *Cf.* RCM II. 100. Tulsīdās' half-line *tariniuṁ muni gharinī hoi jāī* is reproduced entire in this verse. Our verse like that of Tulsīdās makes no direct reference to the Ahalyā motif (which Tulsīdās' source, the *Adhyātmarāmāyaṇa*, had introduced at a corresponding point in the story). Ch. Vaudeville, *Étude sur les sources et la composition du Rāmāyaṇa de Tulsī-dās*, Paris, 1955, p. 139f.
13. Viz. 6, 11, 12, 31, 34, 49, 86, 87, 105, 108, 193, 198.
14. RCM III. 21.
15. As in verses ascribed to the poet Nanddās, e.g. vv.22, 48 in the *padāvalī* section of Vrajratnadās, ed., *Nanddās granthāvalī*, Banaras, 1949.
16. *piyā* and *piya*.

General Information

Soviet Studies of Pre-modern Devotional Literature in New Indo-Aryan Languages

S.D.Serebriany

In 1980, in the "Proceedings of the International Middle Hindī Bhakti Conference" (*Early Hindī Devotional Literature in Current Research*, ed. by Winand M.Callewaert), there were published the notes of Professor G.A. Zograph on "Recent Soviet Publications", supplemented by the "Notes of the editor" (Zograph 1980). This paper of mine was originally conceived as a continuation of Professor G.A. Zograph's notes.[1] But while actually working on my paper, I had to broaden the terms of reference both in respect of subject matter and time limits.

First, as the "International Middle Hindī Bhakti Conference" developed into "International Conferences on Devotional Literature in New Indo-Aryan Languages", I had accordingly to encompass a broader field of research and, therefore, to include, as far as the time limits are concerned, also the 1970s, covered by Professor G.A. Zograph in his notes.

Second, in 1991 the so-called "Soviet" period of the history of my country, which began in 1917, at long last came to an (inglorious) end. I therefore thought it worthwhile to look also before the 1970s and to attempt a general review of the work done during the whole of the "Soviet" era in the field of devotional literature in New Indo-Aryan languages.

The history of Soviet studies in Indian devotional *bhakti* literature[2] is part — a small, but exemplary fragment — of Soviet history as a whole. The stages of the former reflect, in a peculiar way, the stages of the latter. What is more important, the research work and the publications of Soviet scholars, even on such an exotic subject as Indian devotional literature, bear, one way or another, the imprint of the various ideological pressures which may be collectively called the "Soviet ideology"[3]. This raises the problems of evaluation, of value judgments. It is rather clear that some of the works mentioned further in this paper (and included in the attached bibliography) are not so much contributions to Indology as source materials for studies in the "Soviet ideology" and its baneful effects on scholarship. But probably it is still too early to try and consistently separate the grain from the chaff. Besides, it would be hardly possible for *me* to do it *sine ira et studio*. So I have chosen to try and make this review as inclusive and comprehensive as possible.[4] As for value judgments, I have tried to keep to the golden mean and express my opinions only on the most evident points.

Before 1917 Russian Indologists paid rather little attention to New Indo-Aryan (as well as Dravidian) languages and their literatures (Zograph 1972,260). The greatest achievements of Indology in Russia were in the field of Sanskrit and Buddhist studies. It is sufficient, in this connection, to recall, on the one hand, the "Petersburg Dictionary" compiled by O.Boehtlingk and R.Roth in the second half of the nineteenth century and, on the other hand, the names of S.F.Oldenburg (1863-1934), the founder of the series "Bibliotheca Buddhica", and F.I.Shcherbatsky (1866-1942), the author of the *Buddhist Logic* and other well known books.[5]

It is only after 1917 that in St. Petersburg (which in 1914-1924 was called Petrograd and in 1924-1991 Leningrad), the main centre of Russian Indology, scholars began to study in earnest New Indo-Aryan languages and literatures. It seems that this kind of study was encouraged by the new regime, probably in some connection with the hopes of bringing the "world revolution" to the "oppressed masses of the East".

The story of Russian and Soviet[6] work in the field of pre-modern devotional literature in New Indo-Aryan languages may begin with the name of M.I. Tubiansky. Born in 1893, he was a pupil of F.I.Shcherbatsky. A scholar of New Indo-Aryan languages (as well as of Sanskrit, Tibetan and Mongolian), M.I.Tubiansky was the first to translate the works of Rabindranath Tagore straight from Bengali into Russian. In connection with his studies of Tagore he published, in 1925, some translations of poems ascribed to Caṇḍīdās and Vidyāpati (Tubiansky 1925; see also LEMA, 426-29). A paper of his on the mythology of Devī may also be mentioned in the present context (Tubiansky 1927). But from the late 1920s M.I.Tubiansky concentrated on Buddhist studies. For several years he lived and worked in Mongolia. Soon after his return to Leningrad, in 1937, he was arrested and perished.[7]

Ironically, the same year, 1937, was marked by the first major contribution in Russian to the study of Indian *bhakti* literature. It was a Russian translation of the well known work by Lallū jī Lāl, *Prem-sāgar*, with a long and learned introduction by the translator, A.P.Barannikov (Barannikov 1937). The book was announced as "Legends about Krishna. Vol. 1", but no other volumes ever appeared. This translation of the famous Hindi text has not proved to be a major contribution to Russian literature, but the work as a whole was, no doubt, a remarkable scholarly achievement.

Aleksei Petrovich Barannikov (1890-1952), who graduated from the University of Kiev in 1914, managed to adjust himself very successfully to the post-1917 circumstances. A versatile scholar, teacher and administrator, he is often acclaimed as the founding father of Soviet studies in New Indo-Aryan languages and literatures. From 1922 till the end of his life, A.P.Barannikov taught at the University of Petrograd /Leningrad. In 1938-1940 he was the director of the Institute of Oriental Studies (then in Leningrad). In 1939 he was elected the full member of the USSR Academy of Sciences, the highest possible distinction for a scholar in the academic hierarchy. But his scholarly achievements as such now look rather controversial. Much of his writing is dated because he tried hard to adopt what was considered "Marxism" in the 1930s and 1940s.[8]

Anyhow, A.P.Barannikov was for many years the most prominent (and almost only) figure in the field of *bhakti* studies in the Soviet Union. His *magnum opus* is a translation of Tulsīdās's *Rām-carit-mānas* accompanied by a long introduction and detailed notes (Barannikov 1948). The bulk of the work was done during World War II, in Kazakhstan, where A.P.Barannikov lived in "evacuation". It must have been indeed a work of great devotion: A.P. Barannikov tried to reproduce in Russian the poetical form of the *Rām-carit-mānas*. But the scholar was not a poet, and the result was a dismal failure: the translation is a hopeless doggerel. Nevertheless, in the 1940s and later this work of A.P. Barranikov was an important source of knowledge about Indian culture for many people in our country. Some of the scholar's contributions to the study of Indian *bhakti* literature may also be found in a posthumously published book (Barannikov 1959).

Roughly from the middle of the 1950s, after Stalin's death, there began a new epoch of Soviet history, sometimes called the "Thaw". There came a considerable liberalization of political and cultural life. Stalin had been rather hostile to independent India, but Khrushchev made friends with J.Nehru. All this created a better atmosphere for Indian studies, but the main emphasis was on modern India and on current political, economical, social and literary issues. Nevertheless, at least some work on traditional India, along more academic lines, was also done.

From the late 1950s Moscow started to rival Leningrad as a centre of Indian studies, but Leningrad scholars tried their best to preserve and develop the traditions of Russian Indology. The Department of Indian Philology at the University of Leningrad was for many years headed by Professor Viktor Iosifovich Balin (1925-1991), a specialist in Hindi language and literature. He taught courses in "medieval Hindi poetry" and even prepared a kind of reading-book for his students. Unfortunately, he published rather little (see Balin 1961, 1962, 1967, 1975). Professor (Mrs.) Vera Aleksandrovna Novikova (1918-1972) taught Bengali language and literature. Her main interests were in the literature of the nineteenth century and R. Tagore, but she also got published a book on old Bengali literature (Novikova). Another teacher of Bengali language and literature in Leningrad/ St.Petersburg is Dr. (Mrs.) E.K.Brosalina. She offers courses in the *caryā-gītis*, *maṅgal-kāvyas* and *Caitanya-caritâmṛta*. In 1974 the University of Leningrad published a slim textbook called *A Short History of the Literatures of India* (SHLI).

In the 1950s a new Institute of Oriental Studies was founded in Moscow. What remained in Leningrad was called the "Leningrad branch of the Institute of Oriental Studies". For many years the Department of South and South-East Asia at this "branch" was headed by Professor Georgy Alexandrovich Zograph (1928-1993), one of our leading specialists in Indian (South Asian) languages. Unfortunately, he did not publish much in the field of devotional literature, but here at least two publications of his must be mentioned (Zograph 1960, 1974), apart from his historiographical works referred to earlier.[9]

In Moscow, from the late 1950s, there was a lot of activity in the field of Indian (South Asian) literary studies. Among other works there appeared a whole series of "brief outlines" of major literatures of South Asia: Panjabi (Serebriakov 1963, 1968), Nepali (Aganina), Bengali (Tovstykh 1965), Urdu (Glebov-Slukhochev), Telugu (Gurov-Petrunicheva), Hindi (Chelyshev 1968), Marathi (Lamshukov 1970), Sinhalese (Vykhukholev). Quite a lot of research work was done for the "Concise Literary Encyclopedia", published in nine volumes in 1962-1978 (CLE). The main editor of the Indian (South Asian) materials was Dr. I.S.Rabinovich, who himself contributed the entry on "Indian literature" (Rabinovich 1966). Later he got published a thick book, a kind of general survey of Indian literature (Rabinovich 1969), which is an interesting, though rather idiosyncratic work.

Two joint Soviet-Indian projects (collections of papers) that must also be mentioned were prepared in the late 1960s to commemorate the 500th anniversary of Gurū Nānak's birth (Gurū Nānak)[10] and the 100th anniversary of Mirzā Ghālib's death (Ghālib 1972).

On the whole, however, in the 1960s there were rather few Soviet publications specifically on devotional literatures in New Indo-Aryan languages. It remains to mention a paper on Shaikh Farīd (Ashrafian-Tolstaya) and the earlier paper of Dr.Yu.V.Tsvetkov on Sūrdās (Tsvetkov 1969).

By the end of the 1960s Soviet studies of Indian literature came to be affected by the peculiar fad which was called "the theory of the Renaissance in the East". This "theory" was put forward by Nikolai Iosifovich Konrad (1891-1970), a noted specialist in Japanese and Chinese literatures, and then applied to other literatures of Asia. In a nutshell, the "theory" claimed that in the major civilizations of Asia there was also a "Renaissance period", comparable to the one in Europe. The main exponent of this "theory" in Indian studies was Professor E.P.Chelyshev (see, e.g., Chelyshev 1969, 1974; the latter paper was summarized by W.M.Callewaert in Zograph 1980, 209-10; see also Rabinovich 1972). This "theory" affected to a large extent the textbook on the *Literatures of the East in the Middle Ages* (LEMA), published by the University of Moscow in 1970 (the chapter on India was written mostly by Professor [Mrs.] E.V.Payevskaya). Later, in the 1970s, the "theory of the Renaissance in the East" went out of fashion. Among Indologists, it seems, only Professor E.V.Payevskaya remained interested in this "problématique" (Payevskaya 1979, 1979b, 1985).

Coming back to the 1960s, I would like to mention two books published in the series "The Treasury of Lyrical Poetry". One was called "Kabīr: Lyrical Poetry. Translation from Hindi by S.Lipkin" (Kabir-Lipkin), the other "Mirzā Ghālib: Lyrical Poetry. Translation from Urdu by Vera Potapova" (Ghalib-Potapova). Both S. Lipkin and V. Potapova are noted poets. Of course, neither S. Lipkin knows "Hindi", nor does V.Potapova know Urdu. In both cases they wrote their poetical versions using literal ("word by word") translations prepared for them by specialists (I.S. Rabinovich and I.D.Serebriakov in case of Kabīr, L.Vasilyeva in case of Ghālib). In both cases the resulting Russian poems may often be rather far from Kabīr's or Ghālib's originals, but they do stand as *Russian poems* and, in any case, are so far practically the only available Russian *poetical* translations of Kabīr and Ghālib.

In the 1960s and early 1970s a conspicuous and influential figure in our Indology was A.M. Piatigorsky, a versatile scholar and a picturesque personality. His books on Tamil literature, with a lot of translations, (Piatigorsky 1962, 1963) were an important contribution to Soviet *bhakti* studies, but in 1974 he emigrated to England. The same wave of emigration (the so-called "third wave") carried away I.S. Rabinovich (in 1975, to the USA), as well as many other scholars.[11]

Nevertheless, in spite of heavy losses, the 1970s as a whole proved to be rather rich in Soviet publications on Indian devotional literature. In the first place, I may refer to two collections of papers which were both called "Literatures of India" (LI 1973, LI 1979) and both contained several contributions on devotional literature in New Indo-Aryan Languages.[12] Most of the scholars, now active in the fields, were represented in those books.

Dr. Yu.V. Tsvetkov went on with his studies on Sūrdās and the *Sūr-sāgar* (Tsvetkov 1973, 1979, 1979a). In 1987 he published a book on Tulsīdās (Tsvetkov 1987).

From the early 1970s, Professor (Mrs). N.M.Sazanova has been publishing her works on Sūrdās and *bhakti* literature in Braj-bhāṣā in general (Sazanova 1973, 1973a, 1974, 1978, 1978a, 1979, 1979a, 1983, 1985, 1991, 1992) and Dr. (Mrs.)

N.B.Gafurova her studies on, as well as translations of, Kabīr (Gafurova 1972, 1973, 1976, 1979; Kabir-Gafurova).

Professor (Mrs.) A.A.Suvorova published her earlier studies on Shāh 'Abdul Latīf under her maiden name Dekhtiar (Dekhtiar 1973, 1979). In 1992 appeared her book on Indian Sufi poems (Suvorova).

Professor V.A.Chernyshev is a linguist who specializes in Hindi and its "dialects". Here one should mention his paper in which he compares the so-called "*rīti* poetry" in Hindi with some works of *bhakti* poets (Chernyshev 1973), as well as his entries on Braj-bhāṣā and Mālvī literatures in the CLE (Chernyshev 1978, 1978a).

Dr. V.V.Kuzin has done some research on the Maithilī poetry of Vidyāpati (Kuzin 1974, 1989).

Dr. (Mrs.) I.A.Tovstykh has been concentrating on Bengali *maṅgal-kāvyas* (see Tovstykh 1979). She produced a Russian translation of the first part of Mukundarām's *Caṇḍī-maṅgal* (Tovstykh 1980) and hopes to get published sometime a translation of the second part too. She also published her Russian translations of Shaikh Faizullah's *Gorakṣa-vijay* (Tovstykh 1988) and of Vijay Gupta's *Padma-purāṇa* (Tovstykh 1992)

Professor I.D.Serebriakov, a well known scholar of Sanskrit and Panjabi literatures, published his translation into Russian of a rather enigmatic Braj-bhāṣā text called *Sunesār* (Serebriakov 1976; the book contains a facsimile of the only manuscript of the text). Professor I.D.Serebriakov continues his work on a book about the "Literary process in India in the thirteenth-eighteenth centuries." (see Zograph 1980, 209). Some of the ideas and materials for this work have been included into a book already published (Serebriakov 1985). Professor I.D.Serebriakov is also working on a second edition of his book on Panjabi literature (Serebriakov 1963, 1968).

Here I may also refer to some of my publications. My research work on Vidyāpati (on his Maithilī poetry, as well as on his other works) is represented in two papers (Serebriany

1973, 1974) and in a book (Serebriany 1980). I have also prepared a Russian translation of Vidyāpati's book of stories in Sanskrit called *Puruṣa-parīkṣā* (Serebriany in press). In another paper I analyzed some features of the poetical technique of Tulsīdās in his *Rām-carit-mānas* (Serebriany 1978). In yet another paper some problems of the concept of "authorship" as applied to pre-modern Indian literature (including literature of devotion) are discussed (Serebriany 1979). In my paper on Jayadeva's *Gītagovinda* I have discussed, among other matters, the influence of this poem on later devotional literature in the vernaculars (Serebriany 1985). I have also tried to do some research on the *caryā-gītis* (Serebriany 1985a).

In the late 1970s I edited two collections of Indian poetry (mostly pre-modern) in Russian translations (CPI, 7-190; "The Heaven of Love"). The first collection included, among other texts, the first part of Jayadeva's *Gītagovinda*, some *caryā-gītis*, some poems of Lāl-ded, some of Vidyāpati, Caṇḍīdās, Sūrdās, Mīrābāī, Tukārām, Rāmprasād and Mīr Taqī Mīr, as well as an episode from Tulsīdās's *Rām-carit-mānas*. The poetical translations, more or less successful, were done by various poets: the literal ("word by word") translations, by myself, I.P.Glushkova (for Tukārām) and V.L.Korovin (for Rāmprasād). Till now I am rather proud of that work, as it is the most representative collection of pre-modern Indian poetry in Russian translation. The other book ("The Heaven of Love") contains translations of poems by Vidyāpati, Sūrdās, Mīrābāī and Dādū, an episode from Jāyasī's *Padmāvat*, an episode from Tulsīdās's *Rām-carit-mānas* and my lengthy introduction.

This brings me to the 1980s which were not too rich in publications on Indian devotional literature. In addition to what has been already referred to, I can mention only an excellent edition of Ghālib's poetry: texts in Persian and Urdu with parallel literal (and literary!) translations (Ghālib 1980); and another book *about* Ghālib, by Dr. (Mrs.) N.I.Prigarina (Prigarina).[13] By the end of the 1980s, Dr. I.P.Glushkova began publishing the results of her work on Tukārām and the Vārkarī tradition (Glushkova 1988).

Now, for better or for worse, a new period in the history of our country has begun. The 1990s look rather promising for Russian research work in the field of Indian devotional literature. Some of the established scholars go on with their research. There have appeared also some new names and new trends.

Dr.I.P.Glushkova has published more papers on the Maharashtrian *bhakti* (see Glushkova 1991, 1991a, 1992) and goes on with her work on Tukārām.[14] Dr. B.I.Kuznetsov, who works in St. Petersburg, has prepared a complete Russian translation of *Jñāneśvarī* which now awaits publication. Now B.I. Kuznetsov works at a new Russian translation and interpretation of the *Bhagavadgītā* in the light of *Jñāneśvarī.* Dr. (Mrs.) I.V.Zotova has already sent to the press her translation and study of 'Ibn Nishātī's *Phūlban*, a Sufi poem in Dakanī (Zotova). Now she is working on her translation of another Sufi poem in Dakanī, Nusratī's *Gulshan-i-ᶜIshq.* Dr (Mrs.) O.M.Solntseva is an earnest scholar of Sinhalese literature (see Solntseva). Dr.(Mrs.) G.V.Strelkova has done interesting research work on Nāmdev (see Strelkova).

As for new trends, Dr. A.M.Dubiansky, a scholar of ancient Tamil literature (see Dubiansky 1989), seems now to pay more attention to *bhakti* poetry in Tamil (Dubiansky 1991). What is more striking, our historians and philosophers seem to have taken more interest in Indian *bhakti* too (see Kliuyev-Litman;[15] Vanina; see also Korabelnik).

By way of conclusion, I may express the hope that in our country the study of Indian devotional literature, as well as the study of Indian culture in general, will continue and develop, and that our scholars will actively participate in international scholarly endeavours.

NOTES

1 While this paper was under preparation, Professor G.A.Zograph died in St. Petersburg, in the night 24-25 April, 1993.

2 In the context of this paper the long expression "Soviet studies of the devotional literature in New Indo-Aryan Languages" may be shortened to "Soviet studies in Indian devotional literature", because very little has been done in the field of non-Indo-Aryan devotional literature. Apart from the general surveys of various Dravidian literatures in textbooks (LEMA; SHLI), in the *Concise Literary Encyclopedia* (CLE) and in the volumes of the *History of World Literature* (HWL) and apart from two books on the histories of Dravidian literatures, Telugu (Gurov-Petrunicheva) and Tamil (Bychikhina-Dubiansky), one can refer only to the works of A.M. Piatigorsky (Piatigorsky 1962, 1963; Somasundaram-Piatigorsky) and to a recent paper of A.M. Dubiansky (Dubiansky 1991).

3 Here I use the word "ideology" in the sense in which it was used by K.Marx and F.Engels in their book *The German Ideology*: a set of false ideas (preconceptions) that hinders the adequate understanding of reality.

4 Besides Zograph 1980, see also Zograph 1960a, 1967, 1970, 1972; Sazanova 1974a; BI 1965, 1976, 1982; Miliband (a new, revised and enlarged edition of this very informative reference work is in the press).

5 See, e.g., *Asiatic Museum*, 235-59; Bongard-Levin and Vigasin; Roerich. The paper of G.N.Roerich is informative, but very dated and contains a number of factual mistakes. The book of G.M.Bongard-Levin and A.A.Vigasin was published in 1984 and is a typical product of the Soviet "double-think"; it conceals at least as much as it reveals and combines solid scholarship with cheap propagandistic tricks. The *Asiatic Museum*, written in the aftermath of Khrushchev's "thaw", is most telling and reads like a martyrologue.

6 In this case "Soviet studies" is almost a synonym of "Russian studies", because in the Soviet Union almost all the work in the field of Indian devotional literature (with very few exceptions) was done in Russia proper and in the Russian language.

7 The official date of M.I.Tubiansky's death is 1943, but most probably he was shot soon after his arrest. About M.I.Tubiansky and his work see, e.g., *Asiatic Museum*, 162-65; Miliband (q.v.); BI 1965, 1976 (by index). Ethnically, Mikhail Izrailevich Tubiansky was a Russian Jew. It may be

noted that among Soviet scholars of Indian culture the percentage of Jews was always rather high (which was one of the reasons why our Indology was heavily decimated in the 1970s through the emigration to —or via — Israel).

8 About A.P.Barannikov see Zograph 1960a; Zograph 1972, 261-65; CLE, vol. 1, 442.

9 Mrs. I.A.Svetovidova (1930-1968), a scholar of Bengali, who also lived and worked in Leningrad, started a Russian translation of *Śrī-Kṛṣṇa-Kīrtan*. Later this translation was completed by Dr. (Mrs.). E.M.Bykova, in Moscow. But the translation has not been published.

10 The contributions by I.D.Serebriakov (Serebriakov 1972) and N.B.Gafurova (Gafurova 1972) have been listed by G.A.Zograph (Zograph 1980, 206). But one must also recall the contribution of I.S.Rabinovich (Rabinovich 1972) in this book.

11 Here I should mention at least two more scholars: Dr.Yu.Ya.Glazov (emigrated to Canada) and Professor A.Ya.Syrkin (emigrated to Israel). The former was a scholar of Tamil (see Glazov 1963, 1966), the latter is a scholar of Sanskrit. A.Ya.Syrkin translated into Russian Jayadeva's *Gītagovinda*, but did not manage to get it published before leaving Russia. Had this translation (with a long introduction and notes) appeared in print, it would have considerably influenced our *bhakti* studies.

12 All in all there are four collections of papers called "Literatures of India". The earliest one (LI 1958) contained almost nothing on devotional literature. The latest one (LI 1989), again, contains very little: a paper by V.V.Kuzin on the Maithilī poetry of Vidyāpati (actually, non-devotional) (Kuzin 1989) and a paper of V.K.Lamshukov in which, among other matters, he discusses some *bhakti* poets and their work (Lamshukov 1989).

13 In the 1960s, 1970s, and probably later, some work on Ghālib was also done by Uzbek and Tajik scholars in their native languages (see BI 1976, 409; BI 1982, 94-95).

14 In May 1995 Dr. Glushkova plans to convene in Moscow the VIth International Conference "Maharashtra: Culture and Society". The venue of the Conference is to be the Centre of Indian Studies (the Institute of Oriental Studies, Moscow).

15 Professor Alexei: Davidovich Litman (27.12. 1923-21.08 1992) was an expert on Modern Indian Philosophy which he interpreted in the Soviet 'marxist' ways.

BIBLIOGRAPHY

Aganina: Aganina L.A., *Nepal'skaia literatura. Kratkii ocherk*, Moskva, "Nauka", 1964. (Aganina L.A., *Nepali Literature. A brief outline*, Moscow, 1964).

Ashrafian-Tolstaya: Ashrafian K.Z., Tolstaia N.I., "Sheikh Farid", *Poeziia narodov Indii. Sbornik statei*, Moskva, Izdatel'stvo vostochnoi literatury, 1962, p. 149-61. (Ashrafian K.Z., Tolstaya N.I., Shaikh Farīd).

Asiatic Museum: *Aziatskii Muzei-Leningradskoe otdelenie Instituta vostokovedeniia AN SSSR*, Moskva, "Nauka", 1972. (*The Asiatic Museum - The Leningrad branch of the Institute of Oriental Studies, the USSR Academy of Sciences*, Moscow, 1972).

Balin 1961: Balin V.I., "Stikhi Kabira v perevodakh Rabindranata Tagora", *Uchenye zapiski Leningradskogo universiteta*, 1961, N294, Seriia vostokovednykh nauk, vypusk 12, pp. 189-98. (Balin V.I., The poems of Kabīr in R.Tagore's translations).

Balin 1962: Balin V.I., "Lirika Vid'iapati (k kharakteristike geroev)", *Uchenye zapiski Leningradskogo universiteta*, 1962, N306, Seriia vostokovednykh nauk, vypusk 16, pp. 112-26 (Balin V.I., The lyrics of Vidyāpati).

Balin 1967: Balin V.I., "Poeticheskie aforizmy Rahima", *Vestnik Leningradskogo universiteta*, 1967, N2, pp. 64-70. (Balin V.I., The poetic aphorisms of Rahīm).

Balin 1975: Balin V.I., "Hindi literatura", *Kratkaia literaturnaia entsiklopediia*, tom 8, Moskva, "Sovetskaia entsiklopediia", 1975, pp. 282-90. (Balin V.I., Hindi literature).

Barannikov 1937: Lallu dzhi Lal, *Prem Sagar*, Perevod s hindi, vstupitel'naia stat'ia i primechaniia A.P.Barannikova, Moskva-Leningrad, Izdatel'stvo AN SSSR, 1937. (Lallū jī lāl, *Prem Sāgar*, Translation from Hindi, introduction and notes by A.P.Barannikov, Moscow-Leningrad, 1937).

Barannikov 1948: Tulsi Das, *Ramaiana ili Ramacharitamanasa. More podvigov Ramy*, Perevod s indiiskogo (hindi), kommentarii i vstupitel'naia stat'ia akademika A.P.Barannikova, Moskva-Leningrad, Izdatel'stvo AN SSSR, 1948. (Tulsī Dās, *Rāmāyaṇa or Rām-carit-mānas. The Sea of the Deeds of Rāma*, Translation from Indian [Hindi], notes and introduction by academician A.P.Barannikov, Moscow-Leningrad, 1948).

Barannikov 1959: Barannikov A.P., *Indiiskaia filologiia. Literaturovedenie*, Moskva, Izdatel'stvo vostochnoi literatury, 1959. (Barannikov A.P., *Indian Philology. Literary Studies*, Moscow, 1959).

BI 1965: *Bibliografiia Indii. Dorevoliutsionnaia i sovetskaia literatura na russkom iazyke i iazykakh narodov SSSR, original'naia i perevodnaia*, Moskva, "Nauka", 1965. (*Bibliography of India. Prerevolutionary and Soviet literature in Russian language and the languages of the USSR, origional and translated*, Moscow, 1965).

BI 1976: *Bibliografiia Indii. Dorevoliutsionnaia i sovetskaia literatura na russkom iazyke i iazykakh narodov SSSR, original'naia i perevodnaia*, Moskva, "Nauka", 1976. (*Bibliography of India. Prerevolutionary and Soviet literature in Russian language and the languages of the USSR. origional and translated*, Moscow, 1976).

BI 1982: *Bibliografiia Indii 1968-1975. Sovetskaia i perevodnaia literatura*, Moskva, "Nauka", 1982. (*Bibliography of India 1968-1975. Soviet and translated literature*, Moscow, 1982).

Bongard-Levin and Vigasin: Bongard-Levin G., Vigasin A., *The Image of India. The Study of Ancient Indian Civilisation in the USSR*, Moscow, Progress Publishers, 1984.

Bychikhina-Dubiansky: Bychikhina L.V., Dubianskii A.M., *Tamil'skaia literatura. Kratkii ocherk*. Moskva, "Nauka", 1987. (Bychikhina L.V., Dubiansky A.M., *Tamil Literature. A brief outline*, Moscow, 1987).

Chelyshev 1968: Chelyshev E.P., *Literatura hindi. Kratkii ocherk*, Moskva, "Nauka", 1968. (Chelyshev E.P., *Hindī Literature. A brief outline*, Moscow, 1968).

Chelyshev 1969: Chelyshev E.P., "K voprosu ob epokhe Vozrozhdeniia v indiiskoi kul'ture", *Teoreticheskie problemy vostochnykh literatur*, Moskva, "Nauka", 1969, pp.202-09. (Chelyshev E.P., Towards the problem of the Renaissance epoch in Indian culture).

Chelyshev 1974: Chelishev E.P., "Renaissance in India", *Problems of modern India*, Calcutta, Indian Statistical Institute, 1974, pp.77-105.

Chernyshev 1973: Chernyshev V.A., "K voprosu ob otsenke perioda riti v istorii literatury hindi", *Literatury Indii. Stat'i i soobshcheniia*, Moskva, "Nauka", 1973, pp. 126-36. (Chernyshev V.A., Towards the problem of evaluating the period of *rīti* in the history of Hindi literature).

Chernyshev 1978: Chernyshev V.A., "Bradzh literatura", *Kratkaia literaturnaia entsiklopediia*, tom 9, Moskva, "Sovetskaia entsiklopediia", 1978, pp.144-45. (Chernyshev V.A., The literature of Braj-bhāṣā).

Chernyshev 1978a: Chernyshev V.A.. "Mal'viiskaia literatura", *Kratkaia literaturnaia entsiklopediia*, tom 9, Moskva,

"Sovetskaia entsiklopediia", 1978, pp. 144-45. (Chernyshev V.A., Mālvī literature).

CLE: *Kratkaia literaturnaia entsiklopediia*, toma 1-9, Moskva, "Sovetskaia entsiklopediia", 1962-1978. (*Concise literary encyclopedia*, Vols. 1-9, Moscow, 1962-1978).

CPI: *Klassicheskaia poeziia Indii, Kitaia, Korei, V'etnama, Iaponii* (Biblioteka vsemirnoi literatury), Moskva, "Khudozhestvennaia literatura", 1977. (*The classical poetry of India, China, Korea, Vietnam, Japan* [The library of world literature], Moscow, 1977).

Dekhtiar 1973: Dekhtiar' A.A., "O kompozitsii pamiatnika sindhskoi literatury 'Poslanie Shakhā'", *Literatura i vremia*, Moskva, "Nauka", 1973, pp. 26-34. (Dekhtiar A.A., On the composition of the monument of Sindhi literature "The Message of Shāh").

Dekhtiar 1979: Dekhtiar' A.A., "Shakh Abdul Latif - klassik sindhskoi literatury (Nekotorye aspekty zhizni i tvorchestva)", *Literatury Indii. Stati'i i soobshcheniia*, Moskva, "Nauka", 1973, pp. 94-102. (Dekhtiar A.A., Shāh 'Abdul Latif, a classical author of Sindhi literature [Some aspects of his life and work]). *See also further under Suvorova A.A.*

Dubiansky 1989: Dubianskii A.M., *Ritual'no-mifologicheskie istoki drevnetamili'skoi liriki*, Moskva, "Nauka", 1989. (Dubiansky A.M., *The ritual-mythological origins of ancient Tamil lyrical poetry*, Moscow, 1989).

Dubiansky 1991: Dubianskii A.M., "Sviashchennyi idol - drevnii obriad i srednevekovaia poema". *Sad odnogo tsvetka. Stat'i i esse*, Moskva, "Nauka", 1991, pp. 263-76. (Dubiansky A.M., The sacred idol: an ancient rite and a medieval poem).

Gafurova 1972: Gafurova N.B, "Proizvedeniia Kabira v "Adi-Granth" (Perevod s bradzha i primechaniia)", *Guru Nanak. K 500-letiiu so dnia rozhdeniia poeta i gumanista Indii*, Moskva, "Nauka", 1972, pp. 122-64. (Gafurova N.B., The works of Kabīr in "Ādi-Granth" [Translation from Braj-bhāṣā and notes]; corresponds to pp.55-96 of Gafurova 1976).

Gafurova 1973: Gafurova N.B., "Problemy tvorcheskogo nalediia Kabira," *Literatury Indii. Stat'i i soobshcheniia*, Moskva, "Nauka", 1973, pp. 66-76. (Gafurova N.B., The problem of Kabīr's poetic legacy).

Gafurova 1976: Gafurova N.B., *Kabir i ego nasledie*, Moskva, "Nauka", 1976. (Gafurova N.B., *Kabīr and his legacy*, Moscow, 1976).

Gafurova 1979: Gafurova N.B., "Nekotorye printsipy stroeniia aforizmov Kabira", *Literatury Indii. Stat'i i soobshchenia*, Moskva, "Nauka", 1979, pp. 72-78. (Gafurova N.B., Some principles of the structure of Kabīr's aphorisms).

Ghālib-Potapova: Mirza Galib, *Lirika*, Perevod s urdu V.Potapovoi. Sostavlenie i kommentarii L.Vasil'evoi. (Seriia "Sokrovishcha liricheskoi poezii"), Moskva, "Khudozhestvennaia literatura", 1969. (Mirzā Ghālib, *Lyrical poetry*, Translated from Urdu by V.Potapova. Compiled and commented by L.Vasilyeva, Moscow, 1969).

Ghālib 1972: *Mirza Galib - velikii poet Vostoka. Sbornik statei*, Moskva, "Nauka", 1972. (*Mirzā Ghālib, a great poet of the East. A collection of articles*, Moscow, 1972).

Ghālib 1980: Mirza Galib, *Izbrannoe*, Sostavitel' Zoe Ansari. Perevod s farsi G. Iu. Alieva i N.I.Prigarinoi. Perevod s urdu N.V.Glebova. Predislovie N.I.Prigarinoi, Moskva, "Nauka", 1980. (Mirzā Ghālib, *Selected Works*, Compiled by Zoe Ansari. Translations from Persian by G.Y.Aliev and N.I.Prigarina. Translations from Urdu by N.V.Glebov. Preface by N.I.Prigarina, Moscow, 1980).

Glazov 1963: *Tirukural. Kniga o dobrodeteli, o politike i o liubvi*. Perevod s tamil'skogo Iu. Glazova i A.Krishnamurti. Predislovie i kommentarii Iu. Glazova, Moskva, Izdatel'stvo vostochnoi literatury, 1963. (*Tirukkural*. Translated from Tamil by Yu.Glazov and A.Krishnamurti. Preface and notes by Yu.Glazov, Moscow, 1963).

Glazov 1966: *Povest' o braslete. Shilappadikaram*. Perevod s tamil'skogo, predislovie i primechaniia Iu.Ia.Glazova, Moskva, "Nauka", 1966. (*The Lay of the Anklet*. Translation from Tamil, preface and notes by Yu.Ya.Glazov, Moscow, 1966).

Glebov-Sukhochev: Glebov N.V., Sukhochev A.S., *Literatura urdu. Kratikii ocherk*, Moskva, "Nauka", 1967. (Glebov N.V., Sukhochev A.S., *Urdu literature. A brief outline*, Moscow, 1967).

Glushkova 1988: Glushkova I.P,. "Pandharpur, Vithoba i varkari", "*Aziia i Afrika segodnia*", (Moscow) 1988, N9, pp. 55-57. (Glushkova I.P., Pāṇḍharpur, Viṭhobā and Vārkarīs).

Glushkova 1991: Glushkova I.P,. "Semisotletie Dnianeshvari", "*Aziia i Afrika segodnia*", 1991, N3, pp. 45-46. (Glushkova I.P., The 700th anniversary of the Jñāneśvarī).

Glushkova 1991a: Glushkova I.P, "Obraz Tukarama v marathskoi literature poslednikh desiatiletii". "*Diapazon*" (Moscow), 1991, N2, pp. 51-55. (Glushkova I.P., The image of Tukārām in Marathi literature of the recent decades).

Glushkova 1992: Glushkova I.P., "Zapiski palomnitsy", "*Aziia i Afrika segodnia*", 1992, NN1-6 (a series of essays). (Glushkova I.P., Notes of a woman-pilgrim).

Gurov Petrunicheva: Gurov N.V., Petrunicheva Z.N., *Literatura telugu. Kratkii ocherk*, Moskva, "Nauka", 1967. (Gurov N.V., Petrunicheva Z.N., *Telugu literature. A brief outline*, Moscow, 1967).

Gurū Nānak: *Guru Nanak. K 500-letiiu so dnia rozhdeniia poeta i gumanista Indii.* Moskva, "Nauka", 1972. (*Gurū Nānak. For the 500th anniversary of the birth of the poet and humanist of India*, Moscow, 1972).

The Heaven of Love: *Nebo liubvi. Iz srednevekovoi indiiskoi poezii.* Perevod G.Ashkinadze. Sostavlenie i podstrochnyi perevod Iu. V.Tsvetkova. Predislovie i kommentarii S.D.Serebrianogo, Moskva, "Nauka", 1980. (*The Heaven of Love. From medieval Indian poetry*, Moscow, 1980).

HWL 2: *Istoriia vsemirnoi literatury*, Tom vtoroi, Moskva, "Nauka", 1984. (*History of world literature*, Vol.2, Moscow, 1984).

HWL 3: *Istoriia vsemirnoi literatury*, Tom tretii, Moskva, "Nauka", 1985. (*History of world literature*, Vol.3, Moscow, 1985).

Kabīr-Gafurova: *Kabir. Granthavali (Sobranie)*, Perevod s bradzha i kommentarii N.B.Gafurovoi. Vvedenie N.B.Gafurovoi i N.M.Sazanovoi.(Pamiatniki pis'mennosti Vostoka XCV), Moskva, "Nauka", 1992. (*Kabīr Granthāvalī*, Translation from Braj-bhāṣā and commentaries by N.B.Gafurova. Introduction by N.B.Gafurova and N.M.Sazanova, Moscow, 1992).

Kabīr-Lipkin: Kabir, *Lirika*, Perevod s hindi S.Lipkina. Vstupitel'naia stat'ia S.Lipkina i I.Rabinovicha. Sostavlenie i primechaniia I.Rabinovicha. Podstrochnye perevody I.Rabinovicha i I.Serebriakova. (Seriia "Sokrovishcha liricheskoi poezii"), Moskva, "Khudozhestvennaia literatura", 1965. (Kabīr, *Lyrical Poetry*, Translated from Hindi by S.Lipkin, Moscow, 1965).

Kliuyev-Litman: Kliuev B.I., Litman A.D., "Bhakti - fenomen obshchestvennoi mysli Indii (postanovka voprosa)", *Indiia: religiia v politike i obshchestvennom soznanii. Sbornik statei*, Moskva, "Nauka", 1991, pp. 172-79. (Kliuyev B.I., Litman A.D., *Bhakti*, a phenomenon in the social life of India).

Korabelnik: Korabel'nik N.M., *Sotsial'nye i religiozno-filosofskie vozzreniia srednevekovogo indiiskogo myslitelia Chaitan'i (1486-1533) (po "Chaitan'iacharitamrite")*, Avtoreferat dissertatsii na soiskanie uchenoi stepeni kandidata istoricheskikh nauk. AN SSSR. Institut vostokovedeniia, Moskva, 1984 (16p.). (Korabelnik N.M., *Social and religious-philosophical views of the medieval Indian thinker Caitanya [1486-1533] (according to the Caitanya-caritāmṛta)*, Summary of thesis..., Moscow, 1984 [16 pp.]).

Kuzin 1974: Kuzin V.V., "Obrazy Radhi i Krishny v stikhakh

Vid'iapati Thakura", *Voprosy indiiskoi filologii*, Pod redaktsiei A.T.Aksenova i N.M.Sazanovoi, Moskva, Izdatel'stvo Moskovskogo universiteta, 1974, pp. 108-18. (Kuzin V.V., The images of Rādhā and Kṛṣṇa in the poems of Vidyāpati Ṭhākur).

Kuzin 1989: Kuzin V.V., "Istoricheskii faktor v khudozhestvennoi traditsii (na primere maithil'skikh stikhov Vid'iapati)", *Literatury Indii. Sbornik statei*, Moskva, "Nauka", 1989, pp. 61-72. (Kuzin V.V., The historical factor in a poetic tradition [as exemplified by the Maithilī poetry of Vidyāpati]).

Lamshukov 1970: Lamshukov V.K., *Marathskaia literatura. Kratkii ocherk*, Moskva, "Nauka", 1970. (Lamshukov V.K., *Marathi Literature. A brief outline*, Moscow, 1970).

Lamshukov 1989: Lamshukov V.K., "Printsip 'podvizhnoi perspektivy'", *Literatury Indii. Sbornik statei*, Moskva, "Nauka", 1989, pp. 230-49. (Lamshukov V.K., The principle of "moving perspective").

LEMA: *Literatura Vostoka v srednie veka*, Chast' I, Moskva, Izdatel'stvo Moskovskogo universiteta, 1970. *(The literature of the East in the Middle Ages*, Part I, Moscow, 1970).

LI 1958: *Literatury Indii. Sbornik statei*, Otvetstvennye redaktory I.S.Rabinovich i E.P.Chelyshev, Moskva, Izdatel'stvo vostochnoi literatury, 1958. (*Literatures of India. A collection of articles*, Moscow, 1958).

LI 1973: *Literatury Indii. Stat'i i soobshcheniia*, Otvetstvennyi redaktor I.S.Rabinovich, Moskva, "Nauka", 1973. (*Literatures of India. Articles and reports*, Moscow, 1973).

LI 1979: *Literatury Indii. Stat'i i soobshcheniia*, Otvetstvennyi redaktor N.I.Prigarina, Moskva, "Nauka", 1979. (*Literatures of India. Articles and reports*, Moscow, 1979).

LI 1989: *Literatury Indii. Sbornik statei*, Otvetstvennye redaktory N.I.Prigarina i A.S.Sukhochev, Moskva, "Nauka", 1989. (*Literatures of India. A collection of articles*, Moscow, 1989).

Miliband: Miliband S.D., *Biobibliograficheskii slovar' sovetskikh vostokovedov*, Moskva, "Nauka", 1975 (1977). (Miliband S.D., *Biobibliographical dictionary of Soviet orientalists*, Moscow, 1975 [1977]).

Novikova: Novikova V.A., *Ocherki istorii bengal'skoi literatury X-XVIII vekov*, Leningrad, Izdatel'stvo Leningradskogo universiteta, 1965. (Novikova V.A., *Essays on the history of Bengali literature of the 10th-18th centuries*, Leningrad, 1965).

Payevskaya: Paevskaia E.V., *Razvitie bengal'skoi literatury XII-XIX vv. (Etapy stanovleniia natsional'noi literatury)*, Moskva, Izdatel'stvo Moskovskogo universiteta, 1979. (Payevskaya

E.V., *The development of Bengali literature in the 12th-19th cc. [The stages of the formation of a national literature]*, Moscow, 1979).

Payevskaya 1979a: Paevskaia E.V., "K voprosu ob istochnikakh zhanrovoi formy mongol-kabbo v bengal'skoi literature", *Problemy vostochnoi filologii*, Moskva, Izdatel'stvo Moskovskogo universiteta, 1979, pp. 108-14. (Payevskaya E.V., On the problem of the origins of the genre "maṅgal-kāvya" in Bengali literature).

Payevskaya 1979b: Paevskaia E.V., "Tema liubvi v tvorchestve Chondidasha", *Literatury Indii. Stati'i i soobshcheniia*, Moskva, "Nauka", 1979, pp. 49-57. (Payevskaya E.V., The theme of love in the work of Caṇḍidās).

Payevskaya 1985: /Glava/ "Indiiskie Literatury", *Istoriia vsemirnoi Literatury*, Tom tretii, Moskva, "Nauka", 1985, pp. 595-607. (Payevskaya E.V., [A chapter on] Indian literatures).

Piatigorsky 1962: Piatigorskii A.M., *Materialy po istorii indiiskoi filosofii*. Moskva, Izdatel'stvo vostochnoi literatury, 1962. (Piatigorsky A.M., *Materials for the history of Indian philosophy*, Moscow, 1962).

Piatigorsky 1963: *Povest' o zakoldovannykh shakalakh. Drevnie tamil'skie legendy*, Perevod, predislovie i primechaniia A.M.Piatigorskogo, Moskva, Izdatel'stvo vostochnoi literatury, 1963. *(A Tale about Charmed Jackals. Ancient Tamil Legends*, Translation, preface and notes by A.M.Piatigorsky, Moscow, 1963).

Prigarina: Prigarina N.I., *Mirza Galib*, Moskva, "Nauka", 1986. (Prigarina N.I., *Mirzā Ghālib*, Moscow, 1986).

Rabinovich 1966: Rabinovich I.S., "Indiiskaia literatura", *Kratkaia literaturnaia entsiklopediia*, tom 3, Moskva, "Sovetskaia entsiklopediia", 1966, pp. 130-37. (Rabinovich I.S., Indian literature).

Rabinovich 1969: Rabinovich I.S., *Sorok vekov indiiskoi literatury*, Moskva, "Nauka", 1969. (Rabinovich I.S., *The forty centuries of Indian literature*, Moscow, 1969).

Rabinovich 1972: Rabinovich I.S., "'Iznachal'naia kniga' i 'Kniga desiatogo guru' - pamiatniki indiiskogo Vozrozhdeniia", *Guru Nanak. K 500-letiiu so dnia rozhdeniia poeta i gumanista Indii*, Moskva, "Nauka", 1972, pp. 82-121. (Rabinovich I.S., "Ādi-Granth" and "Daśama-Granth", the monuments of the Indian Renaissance).

Roerich: Roerich G.N., "Indology in Russia", *The Journal of the Greater India Society*, Calcutta, XII, 1945, N2, pp. 69-98.

Sazanova 1973: Sazanova N.M., *"Okean poezii" Sur Dasa*, Moskva,

Izdatel'stvo Moskovskogo universiteta, 1973. (Sazanova N.M., *The "Ocean of Poetry" of Sūr Dās*, Moscow, 1973).

Sazanova 1973a: Sazanova N.M., "Ob osnovnykh zhanrakh literatury bkakti", *Literatury Indii. Stat'i i soobshcheniia*, Moskva, "Nauka", 1973, pp. 60-65. (Sazanova N.M., On the principal genres of *bhakti* literature).

Sazanova 1974: Sazanova N.M., "'Zhitiia poetov' (sbornik 'Zhitia vos'midesiati chetyrekh vishnuitov')," *Voprosy indiiskoi filologii*, Pod redaktsiei A.T. Aksenova i N.M. Sazanovoi, Moskva, Izdatel'stvo Moskovskogo universiteta, 1974, pp. 149-64. (Sazanova N.M., The "Vitae of poets" [The collection "Vitae of eighty-four Vaiṣṇavas"]).

Sazanova 1974a: Sāzānovā N.M., "Soviyet saṅgh meṃ bhakti sāhitya kā adhyayan", "*Śastra aur śāstra*" (Dillī), 1974, jūn, pp.18-21 (in Hindī). (Sazanova N.M., The study of *bhakti* literature in the Soviet Union).

Sazanova 1978: Surdas, *Krishnayana*, Leipzig und Weimar, Gustav Kiepenheuer Verlag, *Band 1*. Das hohe Lied des Gottes Krishna. Eine Auswahl aus dem zehnten Buch des Sursagar. Herausgegeben und aus dem Braj (Alt-Hindī) übertragen von N.M.Sazanova. Deutsche Textfassung der Lieder und Zusammenstellung der Krishna-Legende von Roland Beer. *Band 2*. Kommentare. Russische und Englische Textfassung (Sazanova N.M.Die Volkskultur von Braj und das poetiche Schaffen des Dichters Sūrdās. Idem. Surdas' Humanism and the Folk Culture of Braj).

Sazanova 1978a: Sazanova N.M., "Sūr Dās's Humanism and the Folk Culture of Braj", *Sūr Dās - Poetry and Personality*, Agra, Khandelval Prakashan, 1978, pp. 38-45.

Sazanova 1979: Sazanova N.M., "Nekotorye osobennosti poezii bhakti XVI veka na iazyke bradzh (K voprosu o stanovlenii krishnaitskogo bhakti na bradzhe", *Literatury Indii. Stat'i i soobshcheniia*, Moskva, "Nauka", 1979, pp. 65-71. (Sazanova N.M., Some specific features of the 16th-century *bhakti* poetry in Braj-bhāṣā [Towards the problem of the formation of Kṛṣṇa-*bhakti* in Braj-bhāṣā]).

Sazanova 1979a: Sazanova N.M., "Poeziia rasikov XVI veka na bradzhe", *Problemy vostochnoi filologii*, Moskva, Izdatel'stvo Moskovskogo universiteta, 1979, pp. 114-21. (Sazanova N.M., The poetry of the 16th-century *rasikas* in Braj bhāṣā).

Sazanova 1983: Sazanova N.M., "The *bhakti* Poetry and the Enlightenment [in] Hindī Literature. Sūr Dās and Bhāratendu", *Proceedings of the Fourth International Conference on the Theoretical Problems of Asian and African Literatures*,

Bratislava, Literary Institute of the Slovak Academy of Sciences, 1983.

Sazanova 1985: Sazanova N.M, " 'Okean poezii' Surdasa i ego rol' v obshchestvennoi zhizni Indii", *Klassicheskie pamiatniki literatur Vostoka (v istoriko-funktsional'nom osveshchenii)*, Moskva, "Nauka", 1985, pp. 49-68. (Sazanova N.M., The "Ocean of Poetry" of Sūrdās and its role in India's social life).

Sazanova 1991: Sazanova N.M., "Indiiskie varta i drevnerusskie zhitiia (Opyt tipologicheskogo izucheniia)", *Vestnik MGU*, Seriia 13,Vostokovedenie, 1991, N3, pp. 35-41. (Sazanova N.M., The Indian *vārtās* and the old Russian hagiographies [An essay in typological study]).

Sazanova 1992: Sazanova N.M., *Net zhizni bez Krishny (Iz srednevekovoi indiiskoi poezii)*, Moskva, Izdatel'stvo Moskovskogo universiteta, 1992. (Sazanova N.M., *No life without Kṛṣṇa* [*From medieval Indian poetry*], Moscow, 1992).

Serebriakov 1963: Serebriakov I.D., *Pendzhabskaia literatura. Kratkii ocherk*, Moskva, Izdatel'stvo vostochnoi literatury, 1963. (Serebriakov I.D., *Panjabi literature. A brief outline*, Moscow, 1963).

Serebriakov 1968: Serebryakov I.D., *Punjabi Literature. A Brief Outline.* Tr. by T.A. Zalite, Moscow, "Nauka", 1968.

Serebriakov 1972: Serebriakov I.D., "O literaturnom nasledii Nanaka (Opyt kharakteristiki)", *Guru Nanak. K 500-letiiu so dnia rozhdeniia poeta i gumanista Indii*, Moskva, "Nauka", 1972, pp. 57-81. (Serebriakov I.D., On Nānak's literary legacy).

Serebriakov 1976: Bakhtavar, *Sunesar*, Perevod s bradzha, vstupitel'naia stat'ia i kommentarii I.D.Serebriakova, Moskva, "Nauka", 1976. (Bakhtāvar, *Sunesār*, Translation from Brajbhāṣā, introduction and notes by I.D.Serebriakov, Moscow, 1976).

Serebriakov 1985: Serebriakov I.D., *Literatury narodov Indii*, Moskva, "Vysshaia shkola", 1985. (Serebriakov I.D., *The literatures of the peoples of India*. Moscow, 1985).

Serebriany 1973: Serebrianyi S.D., "Materialy dlia izucheniia tvorchestva Vid'iapati Thakura", *Literatury Indii. Stat'i i soobshcheniia*, Moskva, "Nauka", 1973, pp. 86-110. (Serebriany S.D., Materials for the study of Vidyāpati Ṭhākur's work).

Serebriany 1974: Serebrianyi S.D., "Istoki bengal'skoi vishnuitskoi poezii XVI-XVII vv. i razvitie liriki trubadurov XII-XIII vv. (Opyt istoriko-tipologicheskogo sravneniia)", *Tipologiia i vzaimosviazi srednevekovykh literatur Vostoka i Zapada*, Moskva, "Nauka", 1974, pp. 441-76. (Serebriany S.D., The sources of the

Bengali Vaiṣṇava poetry of the 16th-17th cc. and the development of the lyrical poetry of troubadours in the 12th-13th cc. [an essay in comparison]).

Serebriany 1978: Serebrianyi S.D., "Formuly i povtory v "Ramaiane" Tulsidasa (k postanovke problemy)", *Pamiatniki knizhnogo eposa. Stil' i tipologicheskie osobennosti*, Moskva, "Nauka", 1978, pp. 106-40. (Serebriany S.D., Formulas and repetitions in Tulsīdās's *Rāmāyaṇa*).

Serebriany 1979: Serebrianyi S.D., "O nekotorykh aspektakh poniatii "avtor" i "avtorstvo" v istorii indiiskikh literatur", *Literatura i kul'tura drevnei i srednevekovoi Indii. Moskva*, "Nauka", pp. 150-82. (Serebriany S.D., On some aspects of the notions "author" and "authorship" in the history of Indian literatures).

Serebriany 1980: Serebrianyi S.D., *Vid'iapati*, Moskva, "Nauka", 1980. (Serebriany S.D., *Vidyāpati*, Moscow, 1980).

Serebriany 1985: Serebrianyi S.D., "'Gitagovinda' Dzhaiadevy v Indii i na Zapade", *Klassicheskie pamiatniki Literatur Vostoka (v istorkio-funktsional'nom osveshchenii)*, Moskva, "Nauka", 1985, pp. 69-107. (Serebriany S.D., *Jayadeva's* Gītagovinda *in India and the West*).

Serebriany 1985a: Serebrianyi S.D., "Char'ia-giti - poeticheskii zhanr v literaturakh Indii i Tsentral'noi Azii", *Spetsifika zhanrov v literaturakh Tsentral'noi i Vostochnoi Azii*. Moskva, "Nauka", 1985, pp. 145-56. (Serebriany S.D., The *Caryāgīti*, a poetical genre in the literatures of India and Eastern Asia).

Serebriany in press: Vid'iapati, *Ispytanie cheloveka ("Purusha-pariksha")*. Perevod s sanskrita, posleslovie i kommentarii S.D.Serebrianogo, Moskva, "Nauka" (v pechati). (Vidyāpati, The Test of a Man [*Puruṣa-parīkṣā*], Translation from Sanskrit, afterword and notes by S.D.Serebriany, Moscow [in press]).

SHLI: *Kratkaia istoriia literatur Indii. Kurs lektsii*, Leningrad, izdatel'stvo :eningradskogo universiteta, 1974. (*A short history of the literatures of India.* Leningrad, 1974).

Solntseva: Solntseva O.M., *Zhanr poemy-poslaniia v singal'skoi literature (XIV-XV vv.)* Avtoreferat dissertatsii na soiskanie uchenoi stepeni kandidata filologicheskikh nauk, Moskva, MGU, 1990. (Solntseva O.M., *The genre of the message-poem in Sinhalese literature [the 14th-15th cc]*, Summary of a thesis...,Moscow, 1990).

Somasundaram-Piatigorsky: Somasundaram P., Piatigorskii A.M., "Svami Ramalinga - tamil'skii religioznyi reformator", *Ideologicheskie techeniia sovremennoi Indii*. Moskva, "Nauka",

1965, pp. 161-73. (Somasundaram P., Piatigorsky A.M., Svāmī Rāmaliṅga, a Tamil religious reformer).

Strelkova: Strelkova G.V., *Gimny Namdeva v "Adi Granth"*, Avtoreferat dissertatsii na soiskanie uchenoi stepeni kandidata filologicheskikh nauk, Moskva, MGU, 1990. (Strelkova G.V.,*The hymns of Nāmdev in "Ādi-Granth"*, Summary of a thesis..., Moscow, 1990).

Suvorova: Suvorova A.A., *Indiiskaia liubovnaia poema (masnavi)*, Moskva, "Nauka", 1992. (Suvorova A.A.,*The Indian love poem [the* mathnavī*]*, Moscow, 1992).

Tovstykh 1965: Tovstykh I.A., *Bengal'skaia literatura. Kratkii ocherk*, Moskva, "Nauka", 1965. (Tovstykh I.A., *Bengali literature. A brief outline*, Moscow, 1965).

Tovstykh 1979: Tovstykh I.A., "Stilisticheskie osobennosti bengal'skikh srednevekovykh poem–mongolkabbo (Kharakteristika sravnenii)", *Literatury Indii. Stat'i i soobshcheniia*, Moskva, "Nauka", 1979, pp. 58-64. (Tovstykh I.A., Some stylistic peculiarities of the Bengali medieval poems "maṅgal-kāvya" [A characterization of similes]).

Tovstykh 1980: Mukundoram Chokroborti Kobikonkon, *Pesn' o blagodarenii Chandi (Chondimongol). Skazanie ob okhotnike (Akkhiti-upokkhan)*, Perevod s bengal'skogo, vstupiteli'naia stat'ia, kommentarii i ukazateli I.A.Tovstykh (Seriia "Pamiatniki pis'mennosti Vostoka" LX), Moskva "Nauka", 1980. (Mukundarām Cakrabarti Kavikaṅkan, *A Song in Praise of Caṇḍī (Caṇḍī-maṅgal)*, Translation from Bengali, introduction, notes and indexes by I.A.Tovstykh, Moscow, 1980).

Tovstykh 1988: Shekkh Pkhoidzhulla, *Pobeda Gorokkho. Gorokkhobidzhoi.* Perevod s bengal'skogo, vstupitel'naia stat'ia, kommentarii I.A.Tovstykh, Moskva, "Nauka", 1988. (Shaikh Faizullah, *The Victory of Gorakh. Gorakh-vijay*, Translation from Bengali, introduction and commentary by I.A.Tovstykh, Moscow, 1988).

Tovstykh 1992: Bidzhoi Gupto, Skazanie o Padme (Podmapuran), Perevod s bengal'skogo, predislovie, kommentarii i prilozhenie I.A.Tovstykh (Seriia "Pamiatniki pis'mennosti Vostoka" C), Moskva, "Nauka", 1992. (Vijay Gupta, *The Story of Padma* [Padma-purāṇa], Translation from Bengali, preface, commentary and an appendix by I.A.Tovstykh, Moscow, 1992).

Tsvetkov 1969: Tsvetkov Iu.V., "O kompozitsii i zhanre "Sursagara" (indiiskogo poeta XVI v. Surdasa)", *Teoreticheskie problemy vostochnykh literatur*, Moskva, "Nauka", 1969, pp. 218-24. (Tsvetkov Yu.V., On the composition and genre of the "Sūr-sāgar" [by the 16th century Indian poet Sūrdās]).

Tsvetkov 1973: Tsvetkov Iu.V., "K kharakteristike okruzheniia Surdasa", *Literatury Indii. Stat'i i soobshcheniia*, Moskva, "Nauka", 1973, pp. 77-85. (Tsvetkov Yu. V., Towards a characterization of the milieu of Sūrdās).

Tsvetkov 1979: Tsvetkov Iu.V., *Surdas i ego poeziia*, Moskva, "Nauka", 1979. (Tsvetkov Yu. V., *Sūrdās and his poetry*, Moscow, 1979).

Tsvetkov 1979a: Tsvetkov Iu.V., "Poeziia hindī XV-XVI vv. (Osnovnye napravleniia)", *Literatury Indii. Stat'i i soobshcheniia*, Moskva, "Nauka", 1979, pp. 79-87. (Tsvetkov Yu.V., Hindi poetry of the 15th-16th cc. [The main trends]).

Tsvetkov 1987: Tsvetkov Iu.V., *Tulsidas*, Moskva, "Nauka", 1987. (Tsvetkov Yu.V., *Tulsīdās*, Moscow, 1987).

Tubiansky 1925: Tagor R., "Iz 'Gitandzhali'. Predislovie, primechaniia i perevod s bengal'skogo M.Tubianskogo", "*Vostok*", kniga 5, Moskva-Leningrad, 1925, pp. 47-57. (Tagore R., From the *Gītāñjali*, Preface, notes and translation from Bengali by M.Tubiansky).

Tubiansky 1927, Tubianskii M.I., "K istolkovaniiu mifa o Mahiṣa-mardanī", "*Vostochnye zapiski*" tom 1, Leningrad, 1927, pp. 60-70. (Tubiansky M.I., Towards the interpretation of the myth of Mahiṣa-mardanī).

Vanina: Vanina E. Iu, "*Bhakti*: istoki, tipologiia, perspektivy evolutsii", *Indiia: religiia v politike i obshchestvennom soznanii. Sbornik statei*, Moskva, "Nauka", 1991, pp. 180-96. (Vanina Ye.Yu., *Bhakti:* the origins, the typology and the perspectives of evolution).

Vykhukholev: Vykhukholev V.V., *Singal'skaia literatura. Kratkii ocherk*, Moskva, "Nauka", 1970. (Vykhukholev V.V., *Sinhalese literature. A brief outline*, Moscow, 1970).

Zograph 1960: Zograf G.A., *Opisanie rukopisei hindi i pandazhabi Instituta vostokovedeniia*, Moskva, Izdatel'stvo vostochnoi literatury, 1960. (Zograph G.A., *A description of the manuscripts in Hindī and Punjabi at the Institute of Oriental Studies*, Moscow, 1960).

Zograph 1960a: Zograf G.A., "Stanovlenie novoindiiskoi filologii v Leningrade", *Uchenye zapiski Instituta vostokovedeniia*, tom 25, 1960, pp. 162-76. (Zograph G.A., The formation of the New Indo-Aryan philology in Leningrad).

Zograph 1967: Zograf G.A., *Indian philology*. (Fifty years of Soviet Oriental studies. Brief reviews), Moscow, "Nauka", 1967.

Zograph 1970: Zograf G.A., "Indian philology", *Soviet Oriental Studies*, Calcutta, 1970, pp.38-55.

Zograph 1972: Zograf G.A., "Novoindiiskaia filologiia", *Aziatskii*

Muzei - Leningradskoe otdelenie Instituta vostokovedeniia AN SSSR. Moskva, "Nauka", 1972, pp. 260-69. (Zograph G.A., New Indo-Aryan philology).

Zograph 1974: Zograf G.A., "Glagol'naia sistema v "shlokakh" Kabira", *Problemy istorii iazykov i kul'tury narodov Indii. Sbornik stateipamiati V.S. Vorob'ieva-Desiatovskogo*, Moskva, "Nauka", 1974, pp. 192-210. (Zograph G.A., The verbal system in Kabīr's *salokas*).

Zograph 1980: Zograph G.A., "Recent Soviet publications", *Early Hindī devotional literature in current research*, Ed. by Winand M.Callewaert. Leuven, 1980, pp. 206-10.

Zotova: Ibn Nishati, *Phul'ban*, Perevod, predislovie i kommentarii I.V.Zotovoi, Moskva, "Nauka" (v pechati). ('Ibn Nishātī, *Phūlban*, Translation, preface and commentary by I.V.Zotova, Moscow [in press]).

List of Contributors

Dr Ali S. Asani is currently Professor of the Practice of Indo-Muslim Languages and Culture at Harvard University. His main research interests include Islamic literatures in the regional languages of South Asia, Islamic devotional poetry, Sufi and Shii movements in the Indian subcontinent. He is the author of several articles on these subjects and two books: *The Bujh Niranjan: An Ismaili Mystical Poem* (1991) and *The Harvard Collection of Ismaili Literature in Indic Languages: A Descriptive Catalog and Finding Aid* (1992).

Dr France Bhattacharya is Professor of Bengali Language and Literature at the Institut National des Langues et Civilizations Orientales, Paris. Her main research interests are the religious and intellectual history of medieval Bengal through textual analysis, Bengali fiction, and literary translation. Her PhD thesis (1990) is entitled "Étude comparée des Maṅgalkāvya bengalis: Manasā et Caṇḍī"; her publications include *La Complainte du sentier* (translation of Bibhuti Bhushan Banerji's novel *Pather Pāñcālī*), *Le Monastère de la félicité* (translation of Bankim Chandra Chatterji's *Ānandmaṭh*), and (co-authored with P. Dasgupta) *Manuel de Bengali*, vol. 1.

Dr Maya Burger is privat-docent at the Section des Langues et Civilizations Orientales and Coordinator of the Department of History and Science of Religion at Lausanne University, where she has taught Indian religions and Hindi since 1988. She is also Director of the Study Centre Sri Rampura,

Jaipur. She has published and researched on *bhakti* traditions (Kabīr, Mīrā, social system) and artistic traditions (early Indian films and music). Her publications include articles on the Hindu social system, *viraha* in medieval *bhakti* poetry, and Kabīr and the recitation of the name of Rām.

Dr Winand M. Callewaert, D. Lit., is Research Director of Indian Studies at the Department of Oriental Studies, Leuven. With the collaboration of scholars and devotees in India he has made an outstanding microfilm collection of the oldest manuscripts of Sant literature. His publications include *The Sarvāṅgī of the Dādūpanthī Rajab, Bhagavadgītānuvāda: A Study in Transcultural Translation* (with S. Hemraj), *The Hindī Biography of Dādū Dayāl, The Hindī Songs of Nāmdev* (with Mukund Lath), *Nirgun-Bhakti-Sāgar: Devotional Hindī Literature* (with Bart Op de Beeck), *The Life and Works of Raidās* (with P. Friedlander), and *The Sarvāṅgī of Gopāldās.*

Dr Catherine Champion (Centre National de la Recherche Scientifique, Paris) works on oral traditions in North-eastern India, particularly on Bhojpuri narrative songs. She initiated the Research Team on Oral Literature in India, Pakistan, and Nepal, at the Centre of Indian and South Asian Studies (CEIAS), Paris. In 1989 she published (with R. Garcia) *Littérature orale villagoise de l'Inde du Nord.*

Dr Vasudha Dalmia teaches in the Department of Indology and Religious Studies, University of Tübingen. She has published articles in various scholarly journals. Her book *Poetics, Plays and Performance: Modern Hindi Theatre and Brecht* is due to appear soon. She has co-edited *Hinduism: The Construction of Religious Traditions and National Identity* (Delhi, 1994). At present she is working on a book on Bhāratendu Hariścandra.

Dr Françoise 'Nalini' Delvoye is an independent scholar attached to the Centre d'Études de l'Inde et de l'Asie du Sud, Paris. For her PhD she produced a critical edition and French translation of the *Bhaṃvar gīt* of Nanddās, and she was awarded a D.Litt. degree for her dissertation (in French) on "The Tradition of Dhrupad Songs in Braj, from the Sixteenth Century to the Present Day", an English version of which is in press. She has published a bibliography and articles on *dhrupad* and is currently continuing her research on aristocratic patronage of music as documented in Indo-Persian and vernacular songs, along with the compilation and editing of court-musicians repertoires from manuscript sources.

Dr Anne Feldhaus is Professor of Religious Studies at Arizona State University. She is the author of several works on the Mahānubhāvs and their literature, including *The Deeds of God in Ṛddhipur* (1984) and, with S. G. Tulpule, *In the Absence of God: The Early Years of an Indian Sect* (1992). Her other studies in the religious history and geography of Maharashtra include *Water and Womanhood: Religious Meanings of Rivers in Maharashtra* (in press).

Dr Peter Friedlander is a research fellow at the Wellcome Institute for the History of Medicine, London. He is at present working on a descriptive catalogue of the extensive collection of Hindi manuscripts in the library of the institute. His publications include *The Life and Works of Raidās* (Callewaert and Friedlander, 1992) and "The Struggle for Salvation in the Hagiography of Raidās" (in J. Leslie, ed., *Myth and Mythmaking*). His research interests include the early history of Hindi literature, the development of medical, astrological, and divinatory literature in Hindi, and the history of Jain Hindi literature.

Dr Peter Gaeffke is Professor of Modern Indian Literature at the University of Pennsylvania. He studied at Mainz University, where he took an MA in Classics and German and a Ph.D. in Indo-European comparative linguistics. He works in Hindi, Bengali, Urdu, and Dakanī Urdu and has published books on Hindi Syntax, Hindi novels, Jayshankar Prasad, Hindi literature, and a translation of Tulsīdās. Topics he has worked on recently are the rediscovery of Buddhism in India, the press in India, and comparative rhetoric of Muslims and Hindus.

Dr Friedhelm Hardy is a Lecturer in the Department of the History and Philosophy of Religion, King's College, London. In addition to a number of articles dealing with various aspects of Hinduism, he has published *Viraha-Bhakti: The early history of Kṛṣṇa devotion in South India* (1983) and has edited *The Religions of Asia* (1988) in a series entitled *The World's Religions.*

Dr John S. Hawley is a Professor in the Department of Religion at Barnard College, Columbia University, New York. He has published numerous articles on devotional literature and various aspects of Hinduism and several books, including *At Play With Krishna: Pilgrimage Dramas from Brindavan* (1981), *Krishna, The Butter Thief* (1983), and *Sūr Dās: Poet, Singer, Saint* (1984). He is currently working on a translation of the oldest poems of the *Sūr-sāgar.*

Dr Monika Horstmann (pen-name; formerly Thiel-Horstmann), is Professor of Modern Indian Studies, University of Bamberg. Her current research interests are the literature and history of North Indian *bhakti*, archival sources on the economics of religion, and narrative literature from Rajasthan. Her major publications are *Sadani-Lieder: Studien zu einer nordindischen Volksliedliteratur* (1978), *Crossing the Ocean of Existence: Braj Bhāṣā Religious Poetry from Rajasthan. A Reader* (1983), and *Dādū: Lieder* (1991).

Dr Balvant Jani is Professor and Head of the Department of Gujarati Language and Literature at Saurashtra University, Rajkot. His main research interests are late Apabhramsa and Old Gujarati literatures, the bardic, folk, and oral literatures of Saurashtra, the Islamic literature of the converted communities of Saurashtra, the religious traditions of the Harijans, and medieval *bhakti* literature in Gujarat. Among his latest publications are *Cāraṇī Sudāmācaritra: Cāraṇa kaviśrī Māvaḷa Varasaḍā kṛta vipra voḷāvaḷa* (with Ratudan Rohadiya, (1992), *Mahāmātya Vastupāla: jīvana kāvya ane rāsakṛtio* (1992), and *Bhāṇiyā tathā sūī Haradāsakṛta Rāmāvaḷā* (1993).

Dr Catharina Kiehnle is "Hochschuldozent" at the Institute of Indology and Central Asian Studies, University of Leipzig, where she teaches Sanskrit, Marathi, and Hindi. Her research primarily concerns Indian religions and Sant literature, especially in Maharashtra. Her main publications are *Vedisch ukṣ/vakṣ: Wortgeschichtliche und exegetische Untersuchungen* (1979), and three volumes (in press) of Jñāndev Studies entitled *The Sealed Letter: Text and Teachings of the Mahārāṣṭrian Nāth Yogīs*, *A Garland of Songs on Yoga*, and *The Conservative Vaiṣṇava*.

Dr Françoise Mallison (École Française d'Extrême-Orient, and École Pratique des Hautes Études, Paris) researches on *bhakti* literature (hymnology and hagiography) in Western India and specializes in pre-modern Gujarati religious literature and traditions (Vaishnavism, Ismaili Islam). She has published, *Au point du jour: les Prabhātiyāṃ de Narsiṃha Mahetā* (1986), and "Les chants Garabī de Pīr Shams" in *Littératures médiévales de l'Inde du Nord*, which she edited in 1991. She heads a research team at the École Pratique des Hautes Études on textual studies on medieval and modern India, working at present in the field of hagiography.

Dr R. Stuart McGregor is Lecturer in Hindi at the University of Cambridge. His main research interests are Hindi language and literature and lexicography. His main publications are *Outline of Hiṇdi Grammar* (1972), *The Round Dance of Krishna and Uddhav's Message* (1973), *Hindi Literature of the Nineteenth and Early Twentieth Centuries* (1974), *Hindi Literature From its Beginnings to the Nineteenth Century* (1984), and he was editor of the *Oxford Hindi-English Dictionary* (1993).

Dr Sadananda More holds the post of Reader in the Department of Philosophy of the University of Poona. He took M.A. degrees in Philosophy and Ancient Indian History and wrote his doctoral thesis on the philosophy of the *Bhagavadgītā*. His research interests focus on the Maharashtrian Sant Tradition and he has published *The Gita: A Theory of Human Action* (1990) and *Manthan*, a collection of research articles on devotional literature and philosophy.

Dr Shyam Manohar Pandey is a member of the Department of Asian Studies, Istituto Universitario Orientale, Naples. After receiving his PhD from Allahabad University he taught for some years at the University of Chicago and the School of Oriental and African Studies, London. His publications include *Madhyayugīn premākhyān*, *Sūfī kāvya vimarś*, *Sūfī Mansūr Hallāj kī bānī*, *Hindī aur fārasī sūfī kāvya*, and a series of volumes presenting versions of the oral epic of Lorikī and Canainī.

Dr Heidi Pauwels is about to take up a post as Lecturer in Hindi at the School of Oriental and African Studies, London. Her research interests are early and modern Hindi literature and Hinduism. She has just completed her PhD dissertation at the University of Washington, Seattle, which is entitled "Harirām Vyās's *Rās-pañcādhyāyī and Mān kī śṛṅkhalā: A Critical Interpretation*".

Dr Teiji Sakata is Professor of Hindi at Takushoku University, Tokyo. He is interested in folk tales and medieval devotional literature of the Hindi area and is responsible for an extended project of translating medieval and modern literature of Northern India into Japanese. His publications include *Indo no Bungaku* (History of Indian Literature, 1977), *Kita-Indo no Mukashi-gatari* (Story telling in Northern India, 1981).

Dr Eric Reenberg Sand is Associate Professor at the Institute of the History of Religions, University of Copenhagen. His main research interests are Indian religions, Sanskrit studies, and eighteenth-century Danish ideas of religion and culture. His publications in English include articles on Pandharpur and the legend of Puṇḍarīka.

Dr Sergei Dmitriyevich Serebriany has been a research fellow for more than twenty years at the Gorky Institute of World Literature in Moscow. At present he is a member of the Institute of Advanced Studies in the Humanities, Russian State University for the Humanities. His research interests have been mainly in South Asian and comparative literature. He has also tried his hand at translations into Russian from Sanskrit, Hindi, Bengali, and (Indian) English. His publications are listed in one of his contributions to this volume.

Dr Christopher Shelke is presently a guest-lecturer in LM Universität München and Jnana Deepa Vidyapeetha, Pune. He worked for several years on ecumenical Bible translation in Marathi and his special interest is in comparative mysticism and dialogue between Hinduism and Christianity. He has published articles on mysticism and books in Marathi entitled *Don Sākṣātkāri*, *Prabhudarśan*, and *Śrādha āni salokhā*, as well as *Cokhāmelā: Lobpreis des göttlichen Namens*.

Dr William L. Smith has been on the staff of the Department of Indology, University of Stockholm, since 1985. His research has chiefly dealt with popular Hinduism, *Rāmāyaṇa* studies, and Medieval Maithili.

Dr Rupert Snell is Reader in Hindi at the School of Oriental and African Studies, London. His PhD thesis was published as *The Eighty-four Hymns of Hita Harivaṃśa: An Edition of the* Caurāsī Pada (1991). His other publications include articles on Braj Bhāṣā literature, *The Hindi Classical Tradition: A Braj Bhāṣā Reader* (1991), *Hindi and Urdu since 1800: a Common Reader* (with C. Shackle, 1990), and *Teach Yourself Hindi* (with S. Weightman, 1989).

Dr Harald Tambs-Lyche is Associate Professor in social anthropology at the University of Trondheim. His main fields of research are the migrant Indian communities in Norway and the United Kingdom, especially Gujaratis in the U.K., and the religious traditions, castes, and society of Saurashtra. In addition to many articles, he has published *London Patidars: A Case Study in Urban Ethnicity* (1980). His D. Litt. thesis on "Power and Devotion: A Study of Hinduism in Saurashtra" is in press.

Dr Shankar Gopal Tulpule was Head of the Department of Marathi in the University of Poona until his retirement in 1968. Since then he has entered the field of comparative religion and has been a Visiting Professor at the University of Heidelberg. His numerous publications include *Classical Marathi Literature* (1979), *Mysticism in Medieval India* (1984), and *The Divine Name in the Indian Tradition* (1991), as well as several books in Marathi, one of which will shortly appear in English translation as *The Great Poet-saints of Maharashtra*.

Dr Enzo Turbiani graduated in Modern Philology in 1966 and then joined the editorial staff of one of the most important publishing houses in Italy. Subsequently he was a high-school English teacher and has been a college principal since 1983. His interest in Indology and Islamic mysticism began when he was still a university student. He is affiliated with the Institute of Central and West Asian Studies, University of Karachi. His principal works are *La* Vairāgya-Sandīpanī *di Gosvāmī Tulsīdās* (1977), *Il Sikhismo: la religione dei divini Maestri* (1987), and articles on early Hindi, Panjabi, and Urdu language and literature.

Dr Hugh van Skyhawk is Assistant Professor in the Department of Indology, South Asia Institute, Heidelberg University. His main research interests are the hagiographies of Hindu and Muslim medieval saints of the Deccan, in Old Marathi and Dakanī, and the oral traditions of the Central Asian epic of Gesar in Burushaski. He has published *Bhakti und Bhakta: Religionsgeschichtliche Untersuchungen zum Heilsbegriff und zur religiösen Umwelt des Śrī Sant Ekanāth* (1990), edited "Minorities on Themselves" (South Asian Digest of Regional Writing, vol.11, 1986), and published many articles.

Dr Robert J. Zydenbos studied Sanskrit, Indian philosophy and religion, and modern Dravidian and Indo-Aryan languages at the University of Utrecht. He has held teaching and research posts at the universities of Heidelberg, Madras, Utrecht, and Toronto and is at present affiliated with the Institut francais d'indologie at Pondicherry. His main research interests, on which he has published articles, are Jainism, Madhva Vaisnavism, and Kannada literature. His doctoral thesis on post-Independence Kannada fiction is in press and he is at present writing a history of Kannada literature.

INDEX